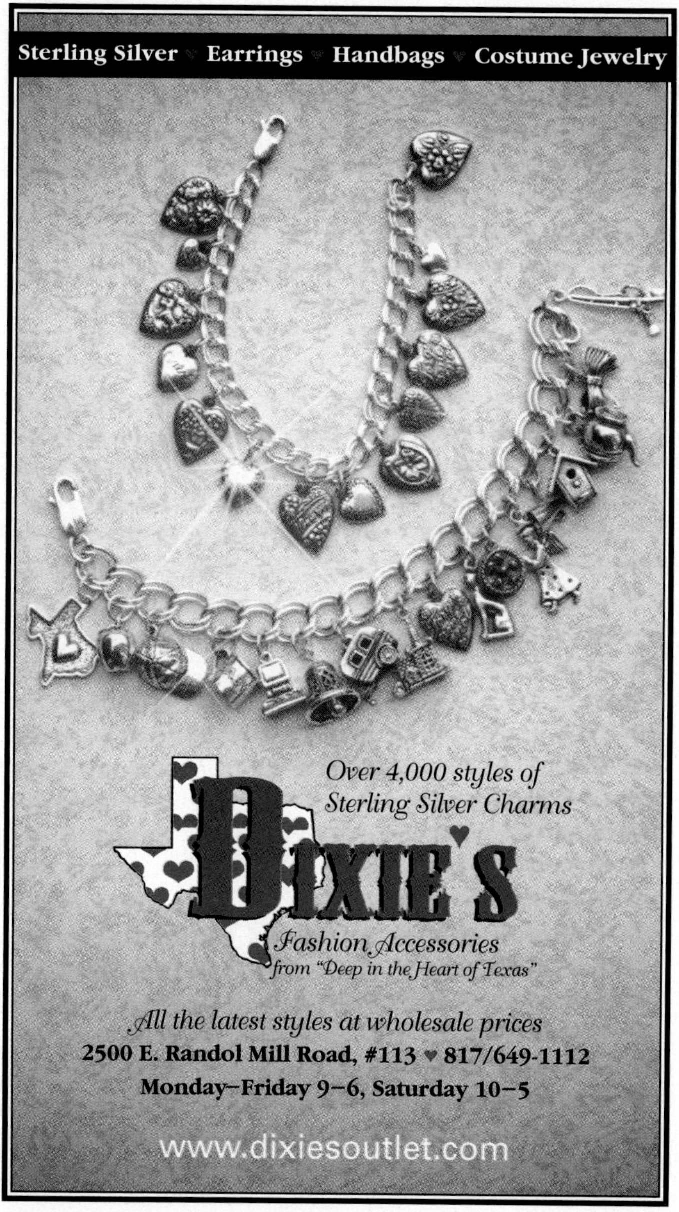

Dallas/Fort Worth

By Sue Goldstein

Other books by Sue Goldstein

Great Buys for People Over 50 **Viking**

Great Buys For Kids **Viking**

Great Buys By Mail (And Phone!) **Viking**

The Factory Outlet Guide **Viking**

Great Buys From The Underground Shopper, Houston/Galveston Edition **Taylor**

Secrets From The Underground Shopper **Taylor**

The Underground Shopper's Guide to Off-Price Shopping **Warner Books**

The Underground Shopper's Guide to Fitness & Health **Ballantine**

The Underground Shopper's Guide to Mail Order Shopping **Andrews/McMeel**

The Home Shopper **McGraw-Hill**

The Underground Shopper's Bargains by Mail **Talk Productions**

Other Underground Shopper Editions:

Houston

Central Texas (San Antonio/Austin)

Boston

New York City

Detroit

Minneapolis/St. Paul

Chicago

St. Louis

Tulsa

Phoenix

Atlanta

Southeast Florida

UNDERGROUND SHOPPER®

the consumer's best friend

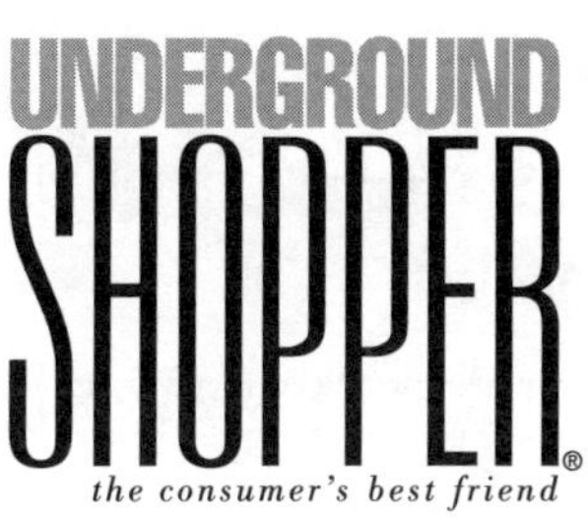

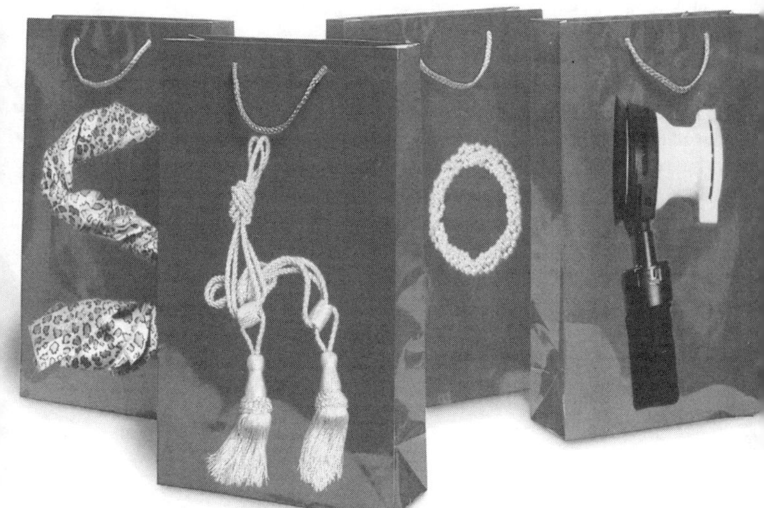

Dallas/Fort Worth

By Sue Goldstein

www.undergroundshopper.com

Published by:

Talk Publications
Talk Productions
2002 Academy Drive, Suite 200
Dallas, TX 75234

The entries appearing in this book were selected based on a number of criteria including their appearance of being "less than retail," of representing an extraordinary value to the consumer or the personal value judgment of the author and her staff and the team of shoppers who shopped the listed merchants. The *Underground Shopper* is the culmination of years of experience in shopping the Dallas/Fort Worth metropolitan area and additional research from national shopping directories from the author.

Printed in the United States of America

10 9 8 7 6 5 4 3 2 1

ISBN 1-879524-15-5

Special thanks to the following for providing items for cover photography:
Billie B's, Dixie's Fashion Accessories Outlet, Fabracadabra
Cover design by Betsy L. Semple
Photography by Tres Smith; illustration by JR Mounger
Production by Reneé Higgins, Bridget Barrios, Robin Carter, Ray Green,
Robin Highers, Sara Miller, James Strese, Matt Washington
Printing by Hart Graphics, Austin, TX
Distributed by Hervey's Book Link

Table of Contents

Table of Contents

To Josh and Bob,
my family at last.

Disclaimer

All advertisements in the book appear in special sections or the inside covers only to help defray part of our production costs.

We shop the stores and write about them based on standards we established and tweaked since 1972. There is nothing scientific or ominously covert about the way we shop a store, except that we are anonymous. As soon as we leave the store (so we don't forget), we write down labels, prices, the experience we had, the layout of the store, things that are indisputable. Then we attempt to compare that experience and those prices to stores that are known as full price stores (like most department stores) and other discounters in the same category. We further verify each and every listing by phone prior to publication.

We look at five major criteria when shopping a store:

- Quality and selection of merchandise
- Prices/percentage of savings
- Personnel (service, personality, greeting)
- Atmosphere (ambiance, convenience, credit availability, dressing rooms)
- Something special – that added touch

Nothing magical about it; but it's often subjective. The shoppers call it like they see it and the write-ups are based on those experiences. Hopefully, through the visit and our years of experience, we capture the essence of each merchant reviewed.

Ratings have no relation to whether or not a merchant advertises with us, either in the book, magazines, radio or online. Many of our four-and five-star merchants have never advertised with us and probably never will. You will find that most of our advertisers are four-or five-star rated, however. Is this because they advertise with us? The answer is an emphatic NO! The fact is, we do not accept advertising from just any merchant that wants to give us money. To protect the reputation of The Underground Shopper, a merchant must offer a true VALUE to consumers before we will even allow their advertising to appear in our publications because, even though their ad does not imply our endorsement of their product or service, many of our readers perceive that it does. We all agree, if they don't measure up, let them go to another publication to spend their ad dollars.

We had more listings in our database than ever before so as the saying goes, some had to bite the dust — although some had been listed for years. We tried to include as many new finds as possible, particularly if they also had a presence online. With only so much space, we have tried to include a representative sampling of what's out there in each category. For the latest and the greatest, be sure to pick up a copy of our monthly magazine at your favorite value merchant, bookstore, local grocery stores and Blockbusters, to name a few. Tune in to my local radio show on the all new talk FM station, KYNG 105.3, from 2-5 P.M. Saturdays. Then, watch the bargains fly on the many newscasts and talk shows that both Judd Anstey, our Online Reporter and I do for local television stations.

And lastly, log on to our web site, *www.undergroundshopper.com*, where everything you've always wanted to know about bargains is available online and more.

We think we've put together the most accurate, up-to-the-minute and comprehensive guide to where to shop in the Dallas/Fort. Worth area. We welcome your comments, questions and suggestions. Know of a merchant that we should know about? Find a mistake? Need to know where to find something that is not listed in this edition? Just call us at 972/245-1144.

To contact *Underground Shopper*:

Mail:

2002 Academy Drive, Suite 200
Dallas, TX 75234

Phone:

214/420-0050

Fax:

972/245-1155

Email: *editor@undergroundshopper.com*

Editorial comments and suggestions: *editor@undergroundshopper.com*

Sales: *sales@undergroundshopper.com*

Sue Goldstein: *askthediva@undergroundshopper.com*

Acknowledgements

Attention Shoppers. We are now entering our 29th year, and there's a whole lot of shopping going on. Talk about a growth spurt! At this end, it's been an avalanche. From 10 employees to over 100, from one building to looking for the third, from being the boss, to being the bossy ... well, they never said it was going to be easy.

Then again, growing can be the best of all worlds. I still get to do what I do best ... my favorite four-letter words (S.H.O.P) and (T.A.L.K) and now, with a mighty crew behind Sue, I can spread the word as we build our mini-conglomerate as "the consumers' best friend!"

With radio syndication, coast-to-coast, local TV segments, national vignettes, appearances on national TV, the serious development of our web site (now receiving almost 1 million hits a month), I can now say, I came. I saw. And I'm doing a lot of shopping.

With "gorilla-like" warfare as our methodology, we can now address the battle of the budget and win the skirmishes single handedly. Whether it's with a click of the mouse, a toll-free call, a visit to a nearby "to die for" shop or your neighborhood money-saving find, going underground just got bigger ... and better.

Behind every advance lies a bank of talented team members and lots of burgeoning stars in every department.

Thanks to a huge IT department, enter our ever-changing, substantial, real time database with real shoppers shopping with you in mind.

After all, who doesn't love a bargain?

But that's just for starters.

Behind every successful woman, there's a man. Well, not exactly one man or one woman, either. But really an extraordinary gathering of talent that has contributed to the solid foundation for building my dreamscape.

There are so many wonderful contributors to this year's expansion that for the first time in 29 years, I won't have enough space to name them all. Hopefully, their work and their dedication speak for themselves. Nevertheless, even without singling out each and every one of their contributions, I will simply say, "Thank You" to them all.

Jerry Schraeder, the man who used to be known as the King of Closeouts, is now the King of the World ... oops, the Company. He now rules the kingdom as the COO. If it weren't for his devotion and diligence, I would not be where I'm at today. (A cliché, but truer words were never spoken.)

Behind the mike is a mighty powerful voice of reason, my first radio producer, and now my radio co-host, Judd Anstey, the Online Reporter. He's young. He's handsome. And he's smart. That's why I can pick on him. He's also cheap. Well, maybe just frugal, but nonetheless a dedicated online shopper who's winning the war on high prices with one click of the mouse. He performs admirably as my battered half on the radio and stands alone, head and shoulders above the rest.

There are many other impressive talents who claim fancy titles and contribute immensely to their respective areas because ... quite frankly, they are the best. Bean counter, Brian Bullock our CFO; Rah-Rah Rich Bedford, VP Sales & Marketing; Head Techie Randy Russell, VP IT Department; Dialing for Deals Shari Wilson-DelMazo, VP Radio; did I leave any VPs out? Maybe Al Gore will be joining the line-up soon, too.

But what's a Veep without their value add ons? My engineers and producers can never be ignored since my great words of wisdom need a voice that can be heard over the airwaves. Special thanks to the entire radio crew: Mark Groves, Carlos Moreno, Susan Bates et al.

Special thanks to Steve Walker and Mike Simeone who've booted me up when I've wanted to boot them out. Somehow I've become somewhat dependent upon two guys who hold the key(s) to my future. Give them a round of applause, too, for the greatest little full-equipped and functioning radio studio.

Head honcho in the Magazine Department is a former editor of newspapers and magazines, Kit King, now Editor-In-Chief of *Underground Shopper* magazine. A wonderful woman of independent means who can also keep Shop Talk, feature stories, my columns and which Above Ground column goes to which city in order.

Newcomer Irma Lazos-Kennedy came to us from a five-year stint as a producer at "20/20" and as the senior producer of "Canal de Noticias NBC", a 24-hour Spanish-language cable news network to Latin America and Spain. Now, I've got her eating bagels and traveling with me to the far reaches of the world. Handling the press, booking media appearances, taking care of my appearances on national TV, well, who better than someone who has worked with Barbara Walters to tend to the Diva?

Without my visuals, life on TV would be a drag. Thanks to head prop lady, Mara Davis and assistant producer Sadie Abtahi, we are a sight to behold. Sending 17 boxes to the "Ainsley Harriott Show" is nothing to these two workhorses. Without whining, they get me to a first place position every time.

Melinda Surbaugh used to be my right hand. Now she's both hands. As the Director of Research, an awesome and crucial position that is the crux of our entire editorial strength, her department of killer researchers helps me find the best buys everywhere and continues, with great aplomb (or a plum), in making sure I am always in the know. Melinda also contributes to TV and radio segments, features for the magazine and is a valued addition to our multi-media convergence as *the* best buy shopping consortium.

What's research without a graphics platform to it show off? Enter Betsy Semple, Art Director, and Reneé Higgins, Production Director, and their graphic arts studio cast and crew. Being creative is one of their strong suits. Being responsive to the readers is another. Paying attention to detail and artistically inclined, of course, also helps. Taking the challenge of producing an award-winning magazine is right before our eyes. Congratulations!

Our Dallas sales team of senior associates Cynthia McDaniel and Lori Harvey are one-of-a-kinds. If they could only clone themselves, we could make a pattern and conquer the world. As sales persons, they just don't get any better. As shoppers, they can keep up with me. What a combination.

Another serious contender for the most thankless job award goes to GW Flinn. And he thought being the father to four boys was tough. Now, he's daddy to all of the employees as the head of our Human Resources Department. Once he opened his door and we discovered he was a great listener, the floodgates were released. If someone is not at lunch or in the rest room, they're probably working through an "issue" with GW. That's his job and I'm so glad he's our man.

To juggle all the rolls (no I mean roles) I put on my plate, I turned to Lois Kinman, a former TV anchor woman and reporter who's also had a stint in the public relations department at a huge phone company. By comparison, this job is a piece of cake. Besides her creative juices and maniacal work ethic, she's a dog lover. A serious dog lover. Need I say more?

There are others who answer phones, book radio stations, handle client relations, sales managers, advertising personnel in the field, check writers, prop carriers, office managers, database creators, writers of checks, investor relations dynamos, magazine hander-outers, web site designers ... gee, there are so many people to thank, I'll need to write another book, just to give credit where credit is due.

But there's also a personal thank you, if you'll indulge me just a little more. Bob Blair, Director of Media Relation. Though that's his job, he also plays a role in my after-hours' life ... as my confidant, best friend, significant other and the father to our three dogs and three cats. He's also the rock I lean on when I'm too tired to cry, too wound up to sleep, too cranky to be civil. A man who's there when I need him and there when I don't. And the first man in my son's life who is also there for him. It doesn't get much better than that. At long last, I can finally say I'm lucky in love and lucky in business.

What a wonderful time I'm having because of it all.

Ratings and Codes

About the Five-Star Merchants

The five star rating helps separate the great from the greatest. When you see the five star rating next to a merchant's name, it means our shopping team felt that the store stood apart from the rest. The ultimate. The best of the best. It does not mean that the four or fewer star merchants are unworthy of your consideration. Unless otherwise stated, all deserve a look-see. It is all in the stars, according to how our shoppers see it. Consider our star-studded system your road map to the stars, and enjoy your celestial journey into the Underground. And though some merchants use the ratings to their advantage in their signage or *Yellow Pages'* advertising, make sure they correspond with the current year's information. Some times merchants fall off the wagon, lose their stars, but still try to capitalize on their past reviews.

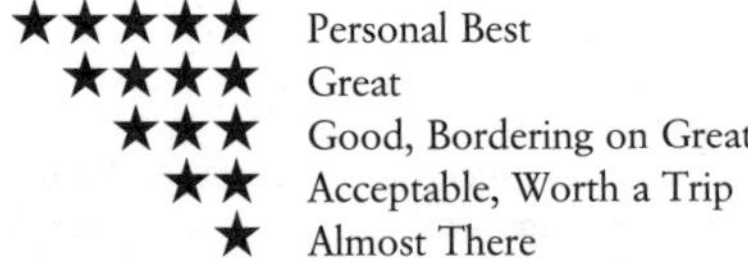

★★★★★ Personal Best
★★★★ Great
★★★ Good, Bordering on Great
★★ Acceptable, Worth a Trip
★ Almost There

Since space was at a premium, we still had to eliminate some merchants from last year's edition to bring you as many new finds as possible. Hopefully, the ones we dropped either won't be missed or you already know about them. Yes, even our paperback book has its limits and we have reached ours.

We had to cut corners (without sacrificing quality of your shopping and money-saving experience) so we also eliminated those who were marginal.

Just because we leave out a popular, well-know merchant doesn't mean they don't qualify. It means you already know them and we don't want to appear redundant. Anybody out there that doesn't know the nearest Wal-Mart, K-mart, Target – get the message?

Five Heart (♥♥♥♥♥) means it's a **Fabulous Find** and holds a special place in our heart. One-of-a-kind, little-known, out-of-the-way, maybe a bit pricey but still affordable, extraordinary service and merchandise, special and unique.

If there is no rating listed, it means the store was never visited. Either the store was not open when the shopper knocked or we heard about it after our deadline and it was rumored to be a goodie.

A **Check Mark** (✔) means **Periodic Sale**. Occasionally, a full-price retailer or manufacturer will open their warehouse doors to a sale that's worth noting. Like the Dallas Sample Sale, the annual wholesale sale to the public for samples from showrooms of the World Trade Center, Apparel Mart and Trade Mart. Too bad it's not an everyday thing. Still, watch your newspaper and our magazine, tune in to our radio and TV shows 'cause we're always talking about where to get it wholesale.

What's better for **Entertainment** than a **Smiley Face** (☺) to show enjoyment opportunities worth a mention in a book known for its pleasures and delights? It's not everyone that can shop all day. So for those that cannot survive on shopping alone – these listings are for the fun of it.

Services are included with a **Diamond** (✧) rating, rather than a star rating since price was not the dominant consideration. Those included, however, did meet our criteria of quality of workmanship, value, dependability, guarantees and customer satisfaction–just like the surveys tell us consumers demand nowadays. They are graded based on the degree of value, years of service, quality of workmanship and guarantees or warranties offered as well as price.

Credit Codes used include **CK** (checks accepted), **MC** (MasterCard), **V** (Visa), **AE** (American Express), **D** (Discover), **DC** (Diners Club), **CB** (Carte Blanche). Some stores accept **SEARS** other store charge cards and these are listed as well. All accept cash, money orders and traveler's checks. **C** marks the few merchants that hold firmly to a cash-only policy. **MOC** means mail order catalog available, while **MO** means the merchant has mail or phone order and/or shipping capabilities. **PQ** means price quote is available.

Addresses:
We list only one address in the header of each listing. If a store has two other locations, we try to list those in their write-up. In an effort to save space, if they have three or more locations, we ask that you check the phone directory for the location nearest you.

Phone Numbers:

We list area codes for all entries. In some cases, "long distance" numbers listed are metro numbers, meaning that you don't have to dial a "1" to reach the number. Don't forget, you must dial "1" when dialing a toll free (800, 877 or 888) number. There are additional area codes but I can't keep up with them. If we've gotten any of our 214s, 940s, 972s, 817s and others mixed up, we hope you'll understand. Remember, today's the day of the 10-digit dialing so get that speed dial up to snuff.

Prices Listed:

When prices are printed for an item in this book, they are for *illustrative purposes* only and were in effect at the time the store was shopped. Do not necessarily expect to pay that price, or even to find that particular item in stock. Many prices will be higher, and some, especially in the computer section, will be lower!

Blanket Apology:

As we wrap up this 29th edition, we realize that once again, we are not perfect. Although every effort was made to ensure accuracy in phone numbers, addresses and other data, there will always be a few typos, snafus and remarks you may totally disagree with. So, with one short note, "We're sorry!"

FOREWORD

Welcome to the 29th year of The Underground Shopper. If you are new to saving money, this is the book for you – putting values galore at your fingertips.

Though some of the merchants listed have been a part of my life since 1972, many are only a few years old. Some even babies.

Until merchants realize that consumers have the power to sculpt a retail environment that fits their perception of value, there will still be department stores and full price retailers struggling to survive. After all, somebody's got to pay retail!

There are stores that have been precariously hanging (Montgomery Ward and Service Merchandise to name a few). Look at them again. Yes, they've really gotten better.

Shoppers always love to know who's in, who's out, who's good and who's not?

Bargains are in—at whatever price level you want. From custom area rugs for the price of a ready-made to a less-expensive surface than granite or marble, consumers want the best. But even alternatives will do the trick.

Ask me where I got my 4-Carat, 14Karat ring without having to buy an extra rider on my homeowners insurance.

Underground Shopping is fun. And besides it pays off in great dividends. Enjoy the savings. And think of me from now on as "your new best friend."

Hello to Rave Waves KYNG, 105.3 FM.
You might have already tuned in to my new radio home away from home every Saturday from 2-5 P.M.

After years elsewhere, we decided we wanted to put our money where are mouths were and chart our own radio course.

Through our Talk Productions Network, Inc. (TPN) that syndicates the radio show nationally, along with several other diverse content shows, you can hear thoughts on a lot of different subjects every Saturday and Sunday on KYNG.

Weekend programming for stations has never been a priority with traditional radio mindsets. It is with us. Digital Information & Virtual Access, Inc., our parent company, negotiated a strategic alliance with Infinity Broadcasting's local Dallas station, KYNG. This collaboration and the creation of a weekend business model for the new 105.3 FM Talk station gives us additional opportunities for cross media programming locally in preparation for a rollout nationally.

So, tune in and shop smart.

Antiques & Auctions

★★★★ 156 Speedway Auction — 940/464-3164

9535 Industrial Blvd. — *Fri 5-10*
Justin, TX 76247

Be sure to wave the checkered flag as you head into the parking lot of this auction house located near the Texas Motor Speedway. Starting at 7 every Friday evening, bid on new and used merchandise up for auction. Merchandise varies, but expect CRAFTSMAN, DEWALT and other American-made tools, shop equipment, tool boxes, chests and air compressors, as well as saddles/tack, lawn and garden ornaments, pressure washers, ZEBCO rods and reels, ceiling fans, pots/pans, cleaning, laundry and deodorizing supplies, furniture, light fixtures, knives, vacuums, watches, health and beauty aids, baby items, toys and many more miscellaneous products that vary from week to week. See vehicles, bikes, sporting goods, TVs, VCRs, electronics, pet supplies, gift items, seasonal decorations and more head to the auction block. Previewing of items begins at 5 each Friday evening. Food is available from their concession stand, and there's no buyer's fee at the door. Take the Highway 114 exit from I-35 W to Highway 156. Call for information regarding placing items for auction. *CK, MC, V*

★★★★★ Accent Antiques — 972/226-9830

616 Hwy. 80 — *Mon-Sat 10-5; Sun 11:30-5*
Sunnyvale, TX 75182

"Je ne fais que regarder" means "I'm just browsing" in French. Try it out and see if they speak the language–which is a distinct possibility. This 14,000-square-foot showplace specializes in French and Italian antiques, but you don't have to travel to Paris to pay less. Yes, even the French are frugal. All items are hand-picked by Ron Robinson, so don't expect his opulence to come cheap, even in this gigantic warehouse. Choose from French to country French, Continental, majolica, lots of bombé secretaries and chests, Louis XV and XVI armoires, rush chairs, gilt armchairs and treasures, all pricey but discounted dramatically. Beautiful French and Italian carved walnut bedrooms, plus consoles. You'll also find rococo entry pieces, Normandy armoires, Galt mirrors, French clocks and Bengal chairs, as well as wardrobes to convert to entertainment centers or to hang your latest silks from the resale shops. Much of the inventory is sold to dealers, so wouldn't you rather shop direct and save paying the commission? Just take the Eastfork exit, 5 miles east of I-635. Almost exactly halfway between 635 and the Forney antique shops, you'll find Accent next to Eastfork Restaurant. *CK, MC, V*

★★★★ Affordable Antiques — 214/741-2121

1201 N. Industrial Blvd. — *Mon, Wed, Fri-Sat 10-5; Sun Noon-5*
Dallas, TX 75207

You'll go ape for this huge antique warehouse. Without monkeying around all day shopping elsewhere, consider making a banana stop here and peeling off a few bucks. You can't miss them. There's a 6-foot gorilla to greet you at the front of the cream building with red tile around the door. If you still can't find it, look for the screaming-red "Affordable Antiques" signs that seem to be everywhere. One of the best on the strip for dining room and bedroom sets, which are their specialty. Open to the public (though dealers are welcome), these Affordable Antiques include the typical as well as the unusual in armoires, chests, beds and dining suites in mahogany, art deco, oak and pine sitting majestically side-by-side with primitives, secretaries, parlor sets, CHIPPENDALE and DUNCAN PHYFE. Exit Oak Lawn from I-35 and go west to Irving Boulevard/Industrial. Turn left and Affordable Antiques is at Howell and Industrial. *CK, MC, V, D, Layaway*

★★★★ Antique Co. Mall — 972/548-2929

213 E. Virginia St. — *Mon-Sat 10-5:30; Sun 11-5*
McKinney, TX 75069

What was once the outlet capital of North Texas is now looking so old they might be referred to as the antique capital of North Texas. Shopping in McKinney is definitely a throwback to the good old days, and right smack in the heart of the historic downtown district is an antique mall owned by Bill and Diane Haight. They offer a full range of antique possibilities–from furniture to collectibles, including glassware, toys, autographed items, coins, pottery, jewelry and quilts. To complement the antiques, other items are mixed in, including as custom floral arrangements and a portrait studio that has joined the downstairs merchants. More than 200 dealers are housed in this 22,000-square-foot mall, the largest in McKinney. *CK, MC, V, AE, D*

Antique Imports Unlimited

504/892-0014

PO Box 2978
Covington, LA 70434
Mon-Sat 10-8

This company's made some intercontinental moves in their day, beginning in Ireland and crossing the Atlantic ultimately to land in Louisiana. What you lose by forgoing a browse through an antique shop is about 60-70 percent off retail prices. If you know your stuff, period, you'll love to order from their ample lists in a variety of categories. Others include Antique & Collectible Jewelry. All items are one-of-a-kind. An early Victorian 10-Karat yellow gold and miniature painting on porcelain brooch/pendant was $310. A Victorian/Early 20th century measuring cup was $30. The items listed are for collectors and those who love antiques. Shipping charges apply. All items are sent via registered USPS, except heavier items, which are sent via UPS. Full refunds (less postage) if returned within two days of receipt. *CK, MC, V, C ($3)*

★★★★★ Antique Sampler Mall & Tearoom

817/461-3030

1715 E. Lamar
Arlington, TX 76006
Mon-Sat 10-7; Sun Noon-6
www.antiquesampler.com

Arlington is home to the Rangers, Six Flags, WBAP Radio and the Antique Sampler Mall & Tearoom. Which one is a bargain-hunter's paradise? Antique Sampler Mall is our choice for collectible bargaining. Antiques spread across 50,000 square feet await a new home for the true-blue bargain shopper. Hundreds of antiques and collectibles (about 120 vendors line the aisleways) with everything from Battenburg lace to antique lace lingerie. Ooh! Just picture it! Tons of goodies from the past...perfect for the pickin'. After you've finished taking in the lamps, furniture, quilts, movie memorabilia, porcelain dolls, collectible plates and Depression glass, check out some of their new stuff. Yes, there is something for everyone here. Be sure to stop by The Tea Garden for a scrumptious lunch, dessert or a spot of tea. Just don't forget to pick up the kids from Six Flags when you've finished shopping. You'll find their second location at 2985 Hwy. 360 South, 972/647-4338. We frequently have problems getting through on their website, almost to the point where it's useless, but we'll keep listing it in case they get this problem worked out. *CK, MC, V, AE, D*

★★★★★ Antiqueland

972/509-7878

1300 Custer Rd.
Custer at 15th
Plano, TX 75075

Mon-Wed 10-6; Thu-Sat 10-8; Sun 11-6
www.antiquelandusa.com

Gather ye antiques while ye may and put them inside this 85,000-square-foot former Wal-Mart store. Hire some of the best chefs in town to run the Palm Court Restaurant and the tea garden, and it spells S-P-E-C-I-A-L. Manager Jean Allred is a leading proponent of making you feel special, especially if you want to book a shower, wedding party, club meeting or anything else that requires someone's undivided attention. The mall has a split personality, with half devoted to approximately 80 percent antiques/20 percent reproductions and the other half housing antiques and designer furnishings. If you think it's not crucial to take a break these days, think again, drop-ins are welcome from 11-2:30 for lunch and afternoon tea. In Plano, Antiqueland has put a roof over the heads of 350 dealers of American, French, English and Primitive furniture and collectibles with nary a young one in sight. There are also 125 design-related spaces, a TV lounge for couch buy-standers and a meeting/classroom. For once, if someone says to you, "You're not getting any younger," you certainly can shrug it off and say, "Thank goodness!" Also associated with the Rufe Snow Antique Mall, 820 North at Rufe Snow Drive in North Richland Hills, 817/498-0733, where there are 200 dealer spaces and a tearoom and bakery open Mon-Thu 10-6, Fri-Sat 10-8, Sun Noon-6; Unlimited, Ltd. at 15201 Midway Rd., 972/490-4085; Forestwood Mall at 5333 Forest Lane, 972/661-0001, and others in Florida, Indiana and Kansas. *CK, MC, V, AE, D*

★★★★★ Antiques & Moore

817/543-1060

3708 W. Pioneer Parkway
(Pioneer Parkway at Park Springs)
Arlington, TX 76013

Mon-Sat 10-6; Sun Noon-6

Sue Moore is past president of the Tarrant County Antique Dealers Association, so you can bet your sweet bippy she knows a thing or two about antiques. One of our favorites, with more than 50,000 square feet packed with 150 dealers, this monster is her brainchild. The delivery is simple: hard labor seven days a week. If you're into collecting glass, china, antiques and more, this is the first place to visit. Crystal, Dresden, furniture, pianos (including spinets), porcelain dolls, birdhouses extraordinare, lamps, armoires, tables, chairs, desks, bookcases, Western memorabilia, bedroom suites, photographs and a million-and-one other treasures are nestled into the specialty boutique booths. Just don't expect to walk down the aisle in one of their antique dresses, though they were all in mint condition. My, how times have changed! Then, off to the hatboxes, stacked underneath the potpourri, around to the men's gifts, beside the candles and in between all the other niceties you must go. Just when you think you've exhausted every inch of possibilities, you discover the Tea Room and their specialty tea in the Rose Garden. Add to all of that an upscale Southwest clothing boutique featuring many well-known brands, (including Texas-made styles). For example, DIAN MALOUF, DOUBLE D RANCHWEAR from Yoakum; GERARD, HAUSTON ROBERSON and ROPA and jewelry. After a scrumptious lunch, get your second wind and hit the aisles again! *CK, MC, V, AE, D*

★★ Antiques Etc. Mall — 972/436-5904

201 S. Mill St., Suite 180 — *Mon-Sat 10:30-5:30; Sun 1-5*
Lewisville, TX 75057 — *www.antiquesetcmall.com*

A chip off the Old Town Lewisville block is a fun detour from Main Street with good old-fashioned, down-home hospitality. This buried treasure is finally coming into its own, as the shopping center continues to add more and more antique shops to its roster. Nothing fancy, mind you, just lots of collectible glass, pottery/ceramics, some antiques, furniture, what looked like African crafts, glassware, stained glass, vintage furniture, old magazines/comics, estate-type jewelry, framed pictures, dolls, toys, interesting conversation pieces and collectibles from A to Z. Looking for old farm tools or pottery to add that decorator touch to a rustic decor? Pick up something here. Brand names in Depression glass and collectible pottery, including MCCOY, OLD ROSEVILLE and SHAWNEE, should get the collector's juices churning. *CK, MC, V*

★★ Artifacts Antique Gallery — 972/723-1411

210 W. Avenue F — *Thu-Sat 10-6*
Midlothian, TX 76065

Meander through the countryside 'til you find this charming artifact of the antiquing kind. Furniture nestled in every nook and cranny ready to be relocated to your nooks and crannies. Furniture from the good ole days set the stage for a bounty of accessories. Specialty of this house is old English pieces from the 1940s and 1950s, plus American antiques by DUNCAN, et al. They are only open Thursday through Saturday, but you can schedule an appointment for the rest of the week. *CK*

★★★★★ Atrium Antique Mall, The — 972/243-2406

3404 Belt Line Rd. — *Mon-Sat 9-7; Sun 11-6*
Farmers Branch, TX 75234 — *www.atriumantiques.com*

Location, location, location is first and foremost on most shoppers' lists. The Atrium is no exception, hovering on a major boulevard of dreams. More than 70,000 square feet of new and old objects of your affection is housed here. Home to only 30 dealers (and some of those related to the owner, Eddie Parker), it's possible to wheel and deal throughout this expansive showroom. As we were preparing to go to press, they had closed the Upper Crust restaurant, and were in the process of renovating the area in order to open a new spot to grab a bite to eat while you shop. Look for the "porte-cochere" and park nearby. The diversity is stupefying. From massive and ornate antiques to the delicacy of a beveled glass window, pottery to jewelry, you're apt to find something to admire. There are monthly $2 million auctions and daily mall-wide discounts from 20 - 75 percent. By the time you see everything, you may be an antique yourself, just browsing through 150 glass showcases alone. But be sure to stop by Parker Antiques & Auctions. With a prominent front-row space on the east side of the mall, it will be hard to miss. You'll save up to 50 percent off furniture, lamps, oil paintings, statues, silver, glass, crystal, chandeliers, ceramics, china, books, iron, copper, brass, marble, rugs, alabaster, bronze, clocks and tapestry. Auctions are every four - six weeks from in-store inventory. *CK, MC, V, AE, D*

★★ Bargain House — 972/288-9151

1839 N. Galloway — *Mon-Fri 10-5; Sat 11-5*
Mesquite, TX 75149

A bargain is a bargain...especially in this 7,000-square-foot shop full of antique and flea market booths. It won't be difficult to furnish your entire household from the Bargain House. Marie McBride's more than 20 years of hands-on experience collecting others' castoffs culminates in this thrifty abode. The success can't be denied as they recently relocated to the other end of the shopping center from their previous 4,000-square-foot location. Sofas, loveseats, dining room tables, bedroom suites, dinettes, chest of drawers, book shelves and lots of knickknacks are all bargains waiting to be embraced. Looking for flowers? Do they have flowers? Both silk and dry. Then, there's the other side of the coin–dirt cheap garage sale items, housewares (but no small appliances), china, glassware, vases and figurines. So off to Grandma's house you must go if you're looking for some goodies to fill up your basket. *CK*

Antiques & Auctions

★★★★ Cabbage Patch Antiques 972/272-8928

901 S. Jupiter Rd. *Tue-Sat 10-6*
Garland, TX 75042

Uncle Wiggly and Peter Rabbit would love this Cabbage Patch! Bargain hunters think it's worth its weight in carrots, too. They carry authentic antiques as well as beautiful reproductions, great floral arrangements, candles, potpourri and home décor items. Don't look for sales, per se; however, they mark items down weekly. For additional savings, look into buying a club card for $30. With it, you'll receive discounts on all purchases. Add the option of layaway for items $300, or more, with interest-free financing and this is nearly a fairy tale shopping experience! Located on Jupiter Road near the Forest Lane intersection, it is just a hippity-hop away. *CK, MC, V*

★★★★ Choices on Park Hill 817/927-1854

2978 Park Hill *Tue-Fri 10-6; Sat 10-5*
(University at Park Hill)
Fort Worth, TX 76109

As everyone knows, it's a woman's prerogative to change her mind, and at Choices on Park Hill, she's given the opportunity to change her mind...often. This upscale consignment store features items from the 1940s to the present, offered either by the main storeowner of this three-story emporium or different dealers specializing in a variety of furnishings, accessories and jewelry. Near TCU and the entrance to the zoo, this antique/consignment shop has been home the past five years to the fine things of many a TCU-area resident who've decided to downsize and relocate their collections to Choices. Take a tour of well-preserved furniture and accessories in room settings from previous estates and Tarrant County homes. Shop often, as items change frequently. If you are living right, you might be there on a day when they get in some of their more eye-catching items. Scandinavian wooden carved angels had three holds on them the second day in the store and eventually sold for $12,000. Or you might find LALIQUE crystal. A pair of swans sold for $5,000. They also carry paintings by Fort Worth's own HENRIETTA MILAN. One was appraised at $4,000, but is listed here for $1,800. One dealer travels the world for antique jewelry and another showcases vintage costume jewelry alongside women's vintage clothing from the '30s and '40s. They also have new and specialty jewelry, including sterling, gold, amber and costume jewelry, as well as hand-woven fine Persian rugs and an extensive FLOW BLUE and majolica collections. The third floor houses PATTY STROUD, who specializes in faux painting, trompe l'oeil, slip covers and window treatments. Looking for a variety of vintage stained glass? Prices range from less than a dollar to several thousand dollars. Art and ambiance can go hand in hand. *CK, MC, V, D*

★★ Clements Antiques of Texas — 972/564-1520

Hwy. 80 @ FM 740 — *Mon-Sat 9-5*
Forney, TX 75126

If you've ever driven to Shreveport or to East Texas, you've likely wondered about the many antique warehouses waiting for you on Highway 80, 25 miles east of downtown Dallas. A highway bargain strip awaits antique hounds or simply curious shoppers. This is one of the better bargain stops and easy to find. Coming from Dallas, they are the first shop on the left, with a front filled with statuary. Wander through more than 60,000 square feet of antique shopping bliss, but not always a bargain. If you see a nick or a ding, they have the ability to do the restoration. However, the restoration is for in-house projects only. You can't beat the selection, and as for the prices, well, they go hand-in-hand with the quality. Some pieces even appeared to be museum-quality and were priced accordingly. During their auctions and estate sales, which they run periodically, you're apt to see the complete contents of an antique shop or a Highland Park estate go buy-buy on the shopping block. Novices are in luck because Clements is run by friendly folks who are used to answering questions from the antiquely-challenged. *CK, MC, V, D*

★★ Cobwebs Antiques Mall — 972/423-8697

1400 Ave. J — *Mon-Sat 10-5; Sun 1-5*
Plano, TX 75074

A web of more than 30 dealers selling everything from estate jewelry to vintage clothing populates this mall. Furniture from the Victorian, American Primitive and Early American milieu make this little spider weave in for a stop or two. Add to that an assortment of bric-a-brac and Depression glass, and enjoy the refreshing tearoom Mon-Sat 11-2:30. Experience one of the oldest antique malls in the Metroplex, and sweep out with something from Cobwebs. Small enough to walk through, large enough to spend the day. Clear the cobwebs from your mind and spin around amongst the smaller items, such as HAVILAND china, sterling silver and nostalgic memorabilia. Located in historic downtown Plano, right off 15th St., pull into their parking lot for a shopping experience like the good old days. *CK, MC, V, D*

Antiques & Auctions

★★★★★ Divine Designs

972/248-7149

18101-B Preston Rd., Suite 201
Mon-Sat 10-6
Dallas, TX 75252

Bette Midler might be the Divine Miss M, but being the Diva, Divine Designs is my kind of buy. At the northwest corner of Preston and Frankfort, Bette-r not plan much else the day you visit them because this 4,000-square-foot store will keep you singing a happy tune. Not your typical "discount" arrangement, but they do pride themselves on being affordable; much of what you'll see is a collage of antiques, home furnishings, accessories, furniture, custom silk floral arrangements, candles, crystal, lamps and more. They are particularly proud of their silk trees, and their new furniture is as appealing as the antiques. Imagine New York's Henri Bendel specialty boutique without the pomp and circumstance. At Divine Designs, at least you won't get burned. Small floral arrangements began around $15 (if you bring your own container) and go up to the kind you'd see at the Mansion for $400-$500. Tons of objets d' conversation mixed in to keep you talking for many moons. Just arrived this spring was a complete line of custom-designed iron furniture, with the king of the collection, an iron cathedral king-size bed. If you buy the scrolled iron bench for the entryway, for example, you will also find a pad to accentuate the beautiful ironworks alongside a picture to hang on the wall above. *CK, MC, V, AE, D*

★★★★★ Dusty Attic, The

972/613-5093

3330 N. Galloway, #225
Mon-Sat 10-6; Thu 10-8; Sun 1-5
Mesquite, TX 75150
www.thedustyattic.com

Why do antique and collectible stores sometimes sound so sneezy? Because they often carry what you might find in a dusty attic ... minus the dust. Just down the street from Town East Mall, you'll find a mall of a different sort, but every bit as amusing. Some 500 vendors are housed in more than 30,000 square feet of shopping pleasure–crafts, Southwest items and antiques abound. However, there are two sides to the story: one side is devoted to crafts, the other to antiques, and never the twains shall meet. On the crafts side, you'll find all kinds of florals, clothes, candles, ceramics, yard art, stained glass, birdhouses and more. In antiques, you'll find FENTON, MAGSTICAL, MCCOY HULL, ROSEVILLE GLASSWARE and RS PRUSSIAN; deco, chrome primitive and traditional furniture; costume jewelry, watches, rings, Victorian hats, FIESTAWARE dishes, books, sports equipment, guns, coins, HUMMEL and PRECIOUS MOMENTS. Don't forget to check out the sports cards, autographs, Beanie Babies, Pokemon, comics and other collectibles. A general store and a light lunch (soups, salads and sandwiches) make this stop a delightful tourist attraction, especially for visitors who complain there's nothing to do in Dallas but Six Flags and the Sixth-Floor Museum. You'll get a hoot out of specialty stores such as Charolett's Country Kitchen, The Old West Store, Soda Fountain of Memories (with a huge selection of authorized Coca Cola memorabilia), Shop In The Woods and The Victorian Garden. *CK, MC, V, AE, D*

★★★★★ Englishman's Antiques 972/980-0107

15304 Midway Rd. *Tue-Sat 10-5:30*
Addison, TX 75001 *www.englishmans.com*

Put an accent on this side of the Atlantic and it sounds sweeter than wine. Get a taste of the English countryside in North Dallas and see how those of us not born with a silver spoon in our mouths can still have a home that smacks of royalty. Between their accent pieces and their accent, you can see why this 15,000-square-foot warehouse is as good as Yorkshire pudding. It's stocked to the gills by an English couple who regularly cross the Atlantic toting a bevy of beautiful antique furniture from England and France. Bargain hunters will wax ecstatic over replicas of English Welsh dressers, WAKE dining room tables and WINDSOR chairs made from antique wood and more. If you wish for a dish of FLOW BLUE china along with original or reproduction STAFFORDSHIRE porcelain, look no further than the ones displayed in their numerous china hutches. Who's going to know the difference? Remember, older might be better, but then you might never want to eat off it or sit on it! You'll also find leather furniture, leather-inset desks with fine gold embossing, clocks and many more fine collectibles, from watches to ink wells. But this couple is not content with just one location on Midway, they've built another from scratch. Down the street at 14655 Midway (972/386-5996, Mon-Fri 10-5:30; Sat 10-6:30; Sun 11-6) you'll find the new 30,000-square-foot showroom resembling the Greek Parthenon, stocked mainly with reproductions. So, relax in either world–the look of yesteryear with the comfort of this year, whether it's with a Greek accent or English. Either way, you'll be getting a plum. *CK, MC, V, AE*

★★ Finishing Touch Antique Mall 972/446-3038

1109 Broadway *Mon-Fri 10-5; Sat 10-5:30; Sun 1-5*
Carrollton, TX 75006

If you want to put the finishing touches on your room's decor, consider adding an antique or collectible. If you want to sell antiques or collectibles, why not take a booth here? (That's if you have good taste, sell at least 80 percent antiques and collectibles, and have no craft items 'cause that is a major "no-no!") You can get away with a few new things, like candles, but this mini-mall means business when it comes to antiques. A favorite shopping stop if you're in historic downtown Carrollton on the Square, there are several nice tea room-type places to lunch while you are visiting. About 30 vendor spaces brimming with antiques, kitchenware, primitives, linens, pictures, clocks, dolls, glassware, jewelry, handcrafted items and more, all priced accordingly. Merchandise arranged attractively with old-fashioned, courteous personnel on hand. *CK, MC, V*

★★★★★ Forestwood Antique Mall — 972/661-0001

5333 Forest Lane
(Forest and the Tollway)
Dallas, TX 75244
Mon-Sat 10-7; Sun Noon-6
www.antiquelandusa.com

There's a triad of jointly owned antique malls that should be at the top of anybody's list. Let Joyce be your guide through the 200-300 dealers that do everything but collect dust on their wares. On one side, you'll see serious stuff, such as expensive French armoires, English antiques, china, pottery and collector books such as an original "Uncle Tom's Cabin" published in 1891; the other side contains less pricey and more down-to-earth items, such as French beds, armoires, bookcases, costume and Victorian jewelry and more. Add books, paintings, rugs, American, English and French furniture, primitives, silver, Depression and cut glass, vintage linens, costume and estate jewelry and majolica (an Italian tin-glazed pottery) and what do you get? A week's worth of shopping at Forestwood Antique Mall. Dine in the Garden Tea Room, Mon-Sat from 11-3, and savor any of their casseroles or other specialties of the house. Or enjoy a light lunch of a fruit plate and finger sandwiches, fabulous soups and a cobb salad, and spend the day in North Dallas comfort. Visit sister malls: Antique Land Antique Mall and Designer Center, 1300 Custer at 15th in West Plano, 972/509-7878, and the Rufe Snow Antique Mall, Rufe Snow at Loop 820W, N. Richland Hills, metro 817/498-0733. Owner Steve Schaeffer has a stronghold with probably the only chain of antique malls in the Metroplex, and he still keeps one operating in St. Louis as well. *CK, MC, V, AE, D*

★★★★★ Gallery Batavia — 214/288-4523

1047 E. Highway 121, Suite D3
Bay Tree Storage Complex
Lewisville, TX 75067
Tue, Wed, Sat 10-3; Also By Appt.

After living in Indonesia for several years, the ladies who own Gallery Batavia decided to come home and share their imported antique finds with the Metroplex. They carry both old, authentic pieces and reproductions of the best that was. Bronze accessories, hand-woven textiles, batiks, collectibles, tables, cabinets, chairs, benches, all with the flavor of life found in the Far East. A turn of the century cabinet with inset glass sold for $698, and an antique, solid teak bench sold for $659, with some large (6 feet and longer) benches offered at prices up to $900. Travel off the beaten path and say "sayonara" to the ordinary. *CK*

♥♥♥♥♥ Gathering, The — 214/741-4888

1515 Turtle Creek Blvd. — *Mon-Sat 10-6*
Dallas, TX 75207

Not far from where Turtle Creek Boulevard and Oak Lawn meet is The Gathering, a design showroom with 30 dealers of antiques, art and accessories. One specialty is original paintings in mediums of impressionism to traditional, all beautifully framed. Another not-to-miss dealer offers rugs from Iran and Turkey, as well as pillows and other accessories. Many of the furniture and glass antiques are 18th or 19th century from France, Austria, England, Germany and other Continental countries. True finds in chandeliers and clocks, but absolutely no ifs, ands or art deco. Shop a large selection of furniture, glassware, paintings, silver, antique lighting, tapestries, bronzes and more. If you're hungry, the café is open from 11-3 Mon-Fri. The personnel are helpful and you'll come away with a history lesson in art and antiques. *CK, MC, V, AE, DC*

✔ General Services Administration — 817/978-2352

Fort Worth, TX — *Periodic Sales*

To get on their mailing list, you have to be a CIA operative. No doubt about it. We talked to a dozen different phone extensions, including the Federal Witness Protection agency. If you're the type who will not be happy until you've made the connection, keep trying. Then, check out the catalog for their next sale. For real property (real estate) sales the number to call is 817/978-4275. With the typical government gridlock, their surplus auction sales are almost impossible to check out unless you have a subpoena or a divining rod. For personal property sales, call 817/978-2352 and punch in "1" when cued by the recorded message. Surplus from government seizures comes from all walks of life (except from the Post Office and the Department of Defense) and runs the gamut of vehicles, office furniture, computers, equipment and just about everything that can be sold at auction from the government (and all sold "as is"). If this write-up doesn't deter you, you are one of the thousands of GSA diehard shoppers. They accept cashier's checks, money orders and personal checks (with bank guarantee). For real estate, they accept sealed bids but charge a $2 fee for the federal sales listings via their toll-free number above. *CK with bank guarantee, Cashier's CK, MO*

★★★★★ Harris Antiques & Classic Design — 817/246-8400

7600 Scott St. — *Mon-Sat 8:30-5:30*
Fort Worth, TX 76108

One of the oldest and most respected names in the Tarrant County antique business is the Harris family, and their legend keeps getting stronger and more impressive as time goes by–just like their collectibles (which are valued at more than the reproductions and are congregated to one side of the store.) Lots of retail gift stores buy here, so why shouldn't you? You know the minute it goes on the retail showroom floor, the price doubles. You couldn't ask for a better selection–hundreds of chairs, armoires, tables, headboards, hand-carved desks, china cabinets, leaded-glass lamps and even CHIPPENDALE items. We made a clean sweep of a marble-topped washstand when it called out, "Take me home!" This 445,000-square-foot showroom and warehouse almost defies description, and the Diva is rarely at a loss for words. It's jammed with antique furniture, decorative items, lamps, marble items, bronzes and more. Pack your bags and expect to stay a while if you're trying to take it all in, in one day. *CK, MC, V, AE, D*

✧✧✧✧ Help Me Ronda — 214/526-3542

Dallas, TX 75205 — *By Appt. Only*

The Dallas Business Journal calls Ronda Hooks the "Queen of the Estate Sale." She handles about two sales a month. Not bad, especially when you add it to her philosophy of garnering "the largest amount of cash possible for clients liquidating their investments." I'd say give her a try when you need to sell, sell, sell. Selling your personal belongings can be a trying experience in the best of times, so why not get a professional to lighten the load, then save that money for the mother lode.

★★★ Jayroe's Premier Antiques — 972/960-8516

5333 Forest Lane — *Mon-Sat 10-7; Sun Noon-6*
(Forestwood Antique Mall, Between Inwood and Tollway)
Dallas, TX 75244

Don't be like the old man that bumped his head and didn't wake up in the morning. Jayroe's offers the unique service of converting an odd-size antique bed to a standard double, a modern queen-size and sometimes even one for a king. For only $100 (if you buy your bed here, $150 if you bring in a bed) the conversion won't detract from the value of the antique nor will it do any damage to the bed, and it's completely reversible. Bring them your footboard first, they'll convert it at their shop and deliver it to your house; then they'll convert the headboard and set it all up. I personally know some basketball players who could use this service. They also have a complete line of restored French-import antiques. Plus, don't keep it a secret because they have one of the largest selections of true French antique armoires in DFW. Or take advantage of their full line of antique furniture from mirrors and clocks to tables. Service prices on the bed adjustments are for Dallas and Plano only; areas outside of these designated cities will cost more based on distance and time. *CK, MC, V, AE, D*

K's Victorian Galleries — 972/780-8120

511-A E. Camp Wisdom Rd. — *Mon-Sat 10-5*
Duncanville, TX 75116

One mile west of Redbird Mall, (I-20 to Cockrell Hill exit), K's is A-OK for good-ole fashioned luxury. If your ancestors date to Napoleon, then you'll feel right at home with these French reproductions–without having to pay for antiquity. These look-alikes are every bit as glamorous as, and definitely less pricey than, the originals. Italian marble and hand-carved mahogany are crafted into reproductions just as in the originals (so don't expect a cheap imitation!). Rather a living room sofa and two matching chairs may settee you back $2,000 (a small price to pay for the look and the quality). Italian dining room suites were priced from $6,000-$13,000. French, Italian and Victorian reproductions are nestled between accessories such as lamps, pillows, tapestries and mirrors. Wandering through the 4,500-square-foot showroom helps you step back in time without fast-forwarding into future earnings. Join the old rich and newly famous by hanging a framed picture from their vast collection of posters and gallery prints straight from their factory in Alabama and killer-priced at least 50 percent off. *CK, MC, V, AE, D, Financing*

★★★★★ Linda's Treasures & Antiques — 214/824-7915

1929 Greenville — *Mon-Sat 11-7; Sun 1-6*
Dallas, TX 75206

Part of the treasures at this shop includes awards and accolades. Named *Best Used Furniture Store* for '96, '97, '98 and '99, and the *Reader's Choice* for '98 and '99 by the *Dallas Observer,* expect to find the best and you probably won't be disappointed. Look for the Arcadia Theater in the hubbub of Lower Greenville and begin your search for the elusive best buy. Located three blocks south of Belmont in an old brick building with other shops on Summit and Greenville. If you want to arm yourself with armoires, you might consider bringing a semi, because there were tons. Armoires make the perfect entertainment center, computer workstation, even bar–and can be easily converted per your specifications. In fact, that is their specialty. Start the ball rolling ...collectibles, art deco, old-American pieces, some old, some newish, some antiques and some–like the Victorian lamp shades–well, who knows. *CK, MC, V, AE, D*

★★★★★ Little Red's Antiques — 972/564-2200

10274 W. Hwy. 80 — *Mon-Tue, Thu-Sat 9-5; Sun 1-5*
Forney, TX 75126

Talk about rising from the ashes! After a 1995 fire, they have come back smaller but stronger. They must have a cast-iron stomach. Speaking of cast-iron, that's one of their specialties. Exit 212/217, cross over the overpass on Hwy. 80; they're the first antique shop on the right. Expect to explore the zillions of imports from Mexico such as urns and patio sets that every yard and pool requires. Since we've known them for years, we would never cast aspersions on their quality or prices. Everything for the amateur decorator to the serious collector is priced to sell at this family-owned business operated by the son of Red. (Down the street is the original Red's Antiques.) Choose from china, curio cabinets and armoires to complete bedroom suites. English and Austrian imported antiques are still some of their featured treasures, but it's their reproductions, such as Tiffany lamps, aluminum-cast Mexican imports and especially their five-globe cast-iron aluminum street lights, urns, mirrors, stained glass (small to large), outdoor lamps for $250 (wired and ready to be lit), that cast a glow on our most recent trip. Everything for the amateur decorator to the serious collector is priced to sell. Enjoy a weekend wandering inside and out every nook and cranny. Add interest to your home and garden and turn over an affordable old or new (table) leaf. *CK, MC, V, AE, D*

★★★ Love Field Antique Mall — 214/357-6500

6500 Cedar Springs — *Mon-Sat 10-7; Sun 11-6*
(Cedar Springs at Mockingbird) — *www.wavex.com/dallasmall/lovefield*
Dallas, TX 75235

Don't let the bickering between DFW Airport and Love Field keep you grounded. At this antique showroom, love is still a many splendored thing. If you know how to get to Love Field, you know how to land at this 13-year-old antique mall. More than 250 dealers in 70,000 square feet of selling space congregate their collections and wait for you to contribute to the plate. Scan their showcase gallery and their unlimited selection of unusual gifts. For a meeting, shower or luncheon, consider booking their private dining room, Café Avion (214/351-9989). It's available for groups up to 20 or for individuals and is open Mon-Sat 11-2:30. Then, after the gathering, scatter and shop. At the corner of Cedar Springs and Mockingbird Lane, this mall also plays host to a classic antique car collection (for display or purchase) which has included a World War II Sherman Tank, a Model A, a Maserati, a '57 Chevy and a Rolls Royce. *CK, MC, V*

★★★★★ Miller's Antiques and Pine Furniture Warehouse 214/741-9020

1225 N. Industrial *Mon-Sat 10-5; Sun Noon-5*
Dallas, TX 75207

If you're wondering how the West was won, the answer may be inside this building. Look for the building with the wagon wheels out front, then expect a bang-up collection of antiques inside. Wholesale pricing on one of the largest selections anywhere. Containers full of items are brought in direct from England, France, Italy, Belgium, Holland and other European countries. An exciting shipment from England is coming to help jump start the millennium, so be sure to stop by and check it out. And if you are a fan of pine furnishings, you'll be pining over these–priced factory direct. European, Southwestern and cowboy designs sit side-by-side with sideboards, dining room suites, armoires, individual pieces and collections–without a fight in this 10,000-square-foot expanse. Custom orders available. Take I-35 to the Market Center exit and head west to Industrial. *CK, MC, V, AE, D*

★★★ Montgomery Street Antique Mall 817/735-9685

2601 Montgomery at I-30 *Mon-Sat 10-6; Sun Noon-6*
Fort Worth, TX 76107 *www.300-antiques-4sale.com*

One-stop antique shopping has never been so good, unless you are a web surfer that is. Online shopping is still a touch and no-show experience. Links on their site were either empty or not loaded correctly. So, if it ain't fixed, forget shopping online until further notice. Instead, head on foot to Fort Worth's largest antique mall under one roof. There are more than 270 dealers in the Showcase Gallery who look high and low for antique treasures to display here seven days a week. On the corner of Montgomery and I-30 and down the street from the Amon Carter and Kimball Museums, this 61,000-square-foot facility used to be Ben Hogan's golf ball factory. It still offers a wealth of opportunities to sink a deal-in-one. Though catering to serious antique buffs, there is one little corner that carries reproductions and gifts such as Beanie Babies, Department 56, assorted dishes and odds and ends. Antique lovers will find metals, glass, pottery, porcelain, books, housewares, toys, sports items, jewelry, advertising and lots more. They have delivery starting at $45 and layaway if your appetite exceeds your bill of fare. Children's strollers and wheelchairs available upon request. Also savor the flavor at The Secret Garden Tea Room, open 'til 4 every afternoon. *CK, MC, V, AE, D*

Net Auctions — 817/579-0400

2321 Solona St. — *24 Hours Online*
Fort Worth, TX 76117 — *www.net-auctions.com*

As the caterpillar turns into a butterfly, this auction house has moved away from just computer auctions to include almost anything. Go online or in person and bid around the clock on computers, dolls, toys, recreation vehicles, jewelry, and more. Anyone can reserve an auction site and put merchandise up for sale. Net Auctions takes 5 percent of the selling bid as a flat fee. Watch their furniture arena with the sale of closeout furniture showrooms from North Carolina. What will they shoot off the auction block next? Live auctions once a month; preview the day before. Check the website for the next live auction date. *MC, V, D, AE*

★★★ Nicole's Antiques and Tobacco Shop — 214/821-3740

3611- A Lower Greenville Ave. — *Mon-Thu 10-7; Fri-Sat 11-8; Sun Noon-6*
Dallas, TX 75206 — *www.citysearch.com*

Puff is no magic dragon here. In fact, if you're not careful, you might go up in smoke. Never mind, cigars are in. Even Hollywood has gone up in smoke. Witness the cigars that are now gracing the mouths of these brutes: Arnie, Sty and Bruce. In fact, they're even investing in their own cigar factory so as to get a jump on the cigar-making craze. So, sit back and puff to your heart's content on leather couches. Enjoy a cup of espresso, turn on the TV and relax. How '60s. And if you want to buy the cigars, since 1993 Nicole's has consistently had one of the best selections, more than 80 brands with prices that won't put your budget aflame, so don't be stogie and try a stogie. There's only one way to go and that's up, up, and up...in a cloud of smoke. Then, of course, whoever figures out how to get the smell out of your clothes, hair and draperies will be the smoke ring of the year. One suggestion is to check out the candle selection. You'll also find gift items including humidors, sterling silver jewelry, picture frames and much more. There's also art deco furniture from which to choose: dining room tables, pop-up bars, vanities, wardrobes as well as antique clocks and lamps, even '30s to '60s martini sets. No smokescreen surrounds the MULHOLLAND BROTHERS fine leather goods and wearable art. What a menagerie of merchandising. To enter their website, first go to www.citysearch.com, click on the Dallas area and enter "Nicoles Antiques" or "cigar." Lights out! *CK, MC, V, AE, D, Gift Certificates*

★★★ Norma Baker Antiques — 817/335-1152

3311 W. 7th St. — *Mon-Sat 10-5*
Fort Worth, TX 76107

Norma Baker specializes in putting families together–newly married couples and long lost flatware families, that is. Generously discounted sterling silver flatware, cut glass and a general line of antiques makes for a family shopping trip. Have Norma put out an all-points bulletin for missing pieces for many sterling silver patterns, for a fee. Update Granny's silver with new pieces as your family grows. Also, any name-brand sterling pattern can be ordered, at your service, for substantially less than retail. Furniture, lamps, American cut glass and more. The smattering of everything old (but in relatively good shape) combines with free wedding gift wrap and free bridal registry for good family value. *CK, MC, V*

★★★★★ Oak Lawn Antiques & Consignments — 214/219-1982

1311 Inwood — *Mon-Sat 10-6; Sun Noon-5*
Dallas, TX 75247 — *www.oaklawnantiques.com*

When business is booming, you gotta keep moving, and that's exactly what Oak Lawn Antiques has done. Now located in the Inwood Trade Center along with the Crate and Barrel Outlet, they've still got one of the most amazing selections of furniture and accessories around. For more than five years, owners Carl Lowery and Damon Powell spent every free moment scouring the countryside to find unique pieces that would have the Metroplex begging for more. And so be it...as the story goes. They also take in consignments of fine furniture, accessories and antiques and that adds up to an unmatched selection and down-to-earth prices. From a carousel horse to a Victorian rocking chair for $170, you will find affordability at every turn. Fainting couches to dressing tables, dining room suites to accent chairs, there is so much to choose, so little time. They have a mix of mid-19th century antiques and modern art, home furnishings, rugs, chandeliers, bronze, crystal, florals and other accessories. Shoppers continue to rave about their low prices and high-quality pieces. It's a decorator's haven for home furnishings at about half what you'd expect to pay elsewhere. They are very open to taking quality furniture of any style if in excellent condition and attractive, regardless of age. *CK, MC, V, AE, D*

★★★ Old Town Village Antique — 972/938-9515

307 S. Rodgers — *Mon-Sat 10-5; Sun 1-5*
Waxahachie, TX 75165

This three-story approach to shopping for antiques comes complete with balconies and history. Take Business Exit 287 and continue on past the courthouse for two blocks to finally land at this former JCPenney store (circa 1936). It's a Waxahachie landmark, offering lots of time-honored historic shopping opportunities. Return to the days when shopping was not just an activity, but an experience. Generate warm feelings of yesteryear, when wandering the square wasn't just a place to Roam for the Home but also a history lesson. They have glassware and collectibles everywhere, and furniture is nestled side by side. For a dining respite, visit the nationally famous, reportedly haunted, Catfish Plantation Restaurant, which is housed in an 1895 Victorian cottage at 814 Waters Street (that is, if you'd like to dine in a restaurant that was featured on TV's "A Current Affair"). For a change of pace, visit the Waxahachie Antique and Craft Mall down the street. Reminisce through the floors of antiquity and relish the days when BELLECK porcelain and Battenburg lace were the rigueur of the day. Some things are always on someone's wish list, so you might as well partake in pleasure while shopping for treasures. *CK, MC, V, AE, D*

★★★ On Consignment — 214/827-3600

2927 N. Henderson — *Mon-Sat 10-5:30*
Dallas, TX 75206

Keep your eyes on this spot nestled in what is now considered Antique Row. Many antique shops line both sides of Henderson, but On Consignment is a what-comes-in is what-goes-out kind of place. When it comes to home furnishings and decorative accents, there's always a nice mix of traditional and antiques. We bought a great little curio art deco bar with top lift, as is, for $75, (what a great place to hide the hooch). Everything in this repository appears to have been hand-picked and displayed with style. Arranged around the fireplace, you'll find chandeliers, armoires, iron beds and other eclectic accent pieces that make a house a home, along with desks, chairs, tables, sofas and more. It's located near plenty of expensive antique shops, so don't get confused. "Too much of a good thing may not be such a good thing, after all," Confucius once said. But then, he never shopped at On Consignment, did he? *CK, MC, V*

★★★ Park Cities Antiques 214/350-5983

4908 W. Lovers Lane *Mon-Sat 10-6; Sun Noon-6*
Dallas, TX 75209 *www.parkcitiesantiques.com*

Park your car at the Park Cities Antique Mall and take a walk down Memory Lane. Just past the Inwood Theatre, watch miracles materialize even on the Miracle Mile. Well, miracles never cease to amaze us–especially with owners Caryl Smarr and David Lee at the helm. From mediocrity to "mahvelous, dahling," collectibles to 18th century English and French furniture, estate jewelry to fine linens–oomph pa pa's! More than 90 unique shops in one location, superior quality at quasi-affordable prices and all specialists in their respective fields–African, English, French, Primitives even Orientalia, architectural and garden antiques, majolica, silver, Staffordshire and more. They even hold parties at the mall for Park Cities clubs and events. Three blocks west of Inwood, near the Shelton School, this stand-alone building is strictly the real McCoy for the hoi-polloi. It's also the repository for The Wrecking Bar's architectural Remains of the Day. *CK, MC, V, AE, D*

★★ Pease-Cobb 817/763-5108

3923 Camp Bowie Blvd. *Daily 10-5:30*
Fort Worth, TX 76107

Don't pass up this consignment showroom featuring antique collections of estate and decorative items, lamps, chandeliers, rugs, sofas and chairs. The inventory was attractively arranged in vignette settings, and you can often rub elbows with professional decorators here. It is hard to determine the retail value of many items, but they seemed in the ballpark of good values. Do you have antiques wasting away in the cellar? Dust them off and see if Pease-Cobb can help you make some hay while the sun shines with their 60/40 percent split. Estate sales on location also can be arranged. *CK, MC, V*

★★★★★ Philbeck's Antiques & Reproductions 972/564-9842

119 E. Hwy. 80 *Mon-Fri 9-5; Sat 9-5:30*
Forney, TX 75126

As born-to-forage shoppers, we had to go off to Forney and visit Philbeck's 32,000-square-foot store. Don't miss the custom-built furniture with the look and charm of an antique from pine specialists, Randy and Gayle Philbeck. Specializing in things that used to be, they have everything from antiques and reproductions, stained glass, iron and horn chandeliers and wicker prams hanging in mid-air. Wander in and out of the many rooms and into the wondrous warehouse in the rear. The armoires, buffets, desks, dressers, candlesticks and chests run the gamut from the intricate and the elaborate, from the authentic to reproductions. You will be duly impressed by direct imports from Germany, England, the Czech Republic and Indonesia–countries that have yet to exhaust their splendor–as well as domestic antiques. Don't expect to see the usual and customary found in antique stores throughout the Metroplex. They have rather a most unusual gathering. *CK, MC, V, AE, D, Layaway*

★★★★ A Place In Time 817/329-0622

210 N. Main *Mon 10-4; Tue-Sat 10-6; Sun Noon-5*
Grapevine, TX 76051

With a new name and new approach, the new owner is making changes to this 11,000-square-foot shop probably as you are reading this. Just east of Elliotts Hardware, what was once Julia's Antiques is now A Place in Time. You can still find great antique items here, but now the selection is almost entirely furniture. The accessories and collections are being discontinued or phased out gently. Also the new requirement for the 60 or so vendors here is that they must offer at least 80 percent antiques among their wares. You'll find armoires, beds, cabinets, tables, desks and more in styles from primitive to renaissance. This is the perfect respite for the mall-frustrated shopper. Everything's at your fingertips–they leave you alone to browse, and then they help you load it in the car. When it's time for some R&R, relax in their new Café 210, open Mon-Sat 11-2:10. *CK, MC, V, AE, D*

★★★★★ Select Collections 972/492-2491

3733 N. Josey Lane, Suite 100 *Mon-Sat 10-6*
(Rosemeade at Josey) *www.angelfire.com/biz/antiqueman*
Carrollton, TX 75007

Paul Harvey may have his "Select Comfort," but the Diva has "Select Collections" for heavenly deals on bedroom suites, dining rooms, living room furniture, accent pieces, armoires, chests and more. If you want something old, something that was borrowed (before), something blue-tiful and something new–three out of four ain't bad! It's the off-the-wall, one-of-a-kind things that are their forte. Better described as upscale furniture and refined consignments, soothingly priced. Customers rave about their prices and we do, too. In fact, they could almost rest on their laurels, but luckily they don't. They continue to strive to offer impeccable taste and display areas not like crop rows or piled on top of one another. Their attention to one-of-a-kind items, pricing things right and emphasizing antiques makes Select Collections different from other consignment stores. What do they do differently that keeps their old customers coming back for more while the list of new customers keeps growing and growing and growing. Inventory changes weekly and with prices like these, it's no wonder the turnover's so fast. Look for a second location at the northwest corner of Coit and Campbell, 972/248-7021. *CK, MC, V*

★★ Silver Eagle — 214/741-2390

1933 Levee St. — *Mon-Fri 10-5:30, Auctions on Sat*
Dallas, TX 75207-6701 — *www.silvereagleantiques.com*

This Silver Eagle has expanded their auctions and that's good news. Their stationary store was not like uncovering the golden goose. Supposed warehouse prices were greeted with sticker shock. Our experience shopping fine European antiques in their 13,000-square-foot warehouse left us with eyes wide shut. One massive black leather kingsize headboard was the only drama amidst the clutter of dining room, bedroom and living room furniture, chairs, tables, lighting, china, crystal and more. Some didn't appear antiques in the truest sense of the word (100 years old or older), though many appeared carved from mahogany, oak, walnut or pine. Receiving containers directly from Europe provides a quick turnover through their twice-monthly auctions. Call for times and a listing of items or check out their website. They will feature furniture, antiques, art, collectibles, accessories, primitives, books, etc. from an entire estate or collections consigned from individuals or dealers. Located at Levee and Express, exit Motor then head west to Irving Boulevard/Industrial, south to Express, then back west to dead-end into Levee. Call for times and a listing of items or check out on the Internet. *CK, MC, V, AE*

★★★★★ Smith Antiques — 817/265-7048

3650 Garner Blvd. — *Mon-Fri 7:30-4*
Arlington, TX 76013

This store used to sell antiques long ago but now they limit themselves to antique restoration. And in this case especially, specialization is a good thing. If you have an antique piece that needs a little more care than a simple spit and polish shine, then the people at Smith Antiques are here for you. Return your tattered antique piece to the masterpiece it once was. Expert scratch removal, refinishing and simple reconstructions to add to the value of your furniture are their forte. Pick up and delivery is available for a charge; and quick turnaround of two to three weeks is the norm. *CK, MC, V, AE, D*

★★ Sutton Place Antiques — 972/578-1282

1030 E. 15th St. — *Mon-Sat 9:30-5*
Plano, TX 75074

Specializing in authentic oak antiques might be enough to make this antique shop a mighty contender, but Sutton Place also can be said to cater to the carriage trade. English, French and Victorian reproductions and antiques can add a touch of class to anyone's decor. Just don't expect to get away cheap. It does look like you get a lot of bang for your buck though, when you consider the reproductions. If you're serious about your antique collection, you'll recognize their period pieces as the next major museum contribution. Containers from France or Belgium are often unloading as you shop, with beautiful ensembles of dining room suites and armoires often dating back to Louis XVI. Browsing is encouraged, questions are answered, negotiation is possible and it's a pleasure shopping in a one-owner, 3,000-square-foot antique shop for a change. *CK, MC, V*

★★★★ Texas Antique Connection, The — 817/429-0922

7429 E. Lancaster — *Mon-Fri 9-5; Sat 9-Noon*
Fort Worth, TX 76112

The Texas Antique Connection can be your connection to living the good life amid beautiful antiques and reproductions. No longer a full-blown antique mall, they now specialize simply in antique furniture from Belgium and France, with hand-carved mahogany reproductions from Indonesia and other foreign ports. They sell to dealers and the public, meaning you'll find furniture for any taste, for any room in the house, at prices that should fit your budget. Next door is soul mate store Classic Designs (www.classicdesign.com), where you'll find furniture, accessories, bronzes, pottery reproductions, autographs, books and more. This wholesaler sells off their million dollar inventory periodically. When you see their sale advertised, don't waste a minute in deciding if, when, or how you're going to get there. Just go! Although it is not affiliated with Texas Antique Connection, just to the west, you'll find Somewhere in Time, home to country reproductions and custom-made designs. The district is brimming with antique stores, little mini-malls and galleries, so it's well worth a trip back in time. *CK, MC, V, AE, D*

★ Texas Auction Academy 972/661-0313

7075 Elm Street *By reservation only*
Frisco, TX 75034 *www.texasauctionacademy.com*

Since helping train the 1998 International Auctioneer Champion, they've moved their digs and gone country. If you're interested, saying "Going... Going...Gone!" is just one of the things you'll learn by going to this school. Call if you'd like to learn the ins and outs of auctioneering, as well as how to run your business once you've called out, "Sold!" The start of the deal begins with 10 days of intensive classes (scheduled periodically). You have to give them a big hand (though it might cost you an arm), because the cost for the two-week cram course, plus materials, is $695. Once you pass the state's exam, you'll be licensed and ready to face a bidding storm. *Ask for catalog*

★★★★★ Unlimited Ltd. Antique Mall 972/490-4085

15201 Midway Rd. *Mon-Sun 10-6*
(Midway just past Belt Line) *www.unlimited-ltd.com*
Addison, TX 75244

With more than 150 vendors, Unlimited Ltd. could be the beginning, middle and end-all for something big. With unlimited possibilities, just wind yourself up and walk, baby, walk to the building with the pink trim and covered awning. Smart shoppers and antique lovers (with sturdy soles) appreciate the concentration of antique dealers all under one roof. Surely, you won't come home empty-handed. They have more than 40,000 square feet of classic old furniture, artwork and miscellaneous collectibles in climate-controlled splendor. For brides who believe in acquiring something old for their dowry, consider antiques for the bridal registry. What a perfect contribution to your hope chest–something you want, can use and may actually appreciate with time. Like that four-poster burlwood bedroom suite–what a perfect gift for the intended couple. Then, when you think you can't take another step, relax and kick up your heels in The Garden Tea Room, Tue-Sun, 11:30-3:30. Then for dessert, visit the Showcase Gallery with more than 135 cases of prized antiques. Yum-m-m. *CK, MC, V, AE, D*

★★ Wynnwood Antique Mall 940/325-9791

2502 Hwy. 180 East *Mon-Sat 10-5:30; Sun 1-5:30*
Mineral Wells, TX 76067

Across from the Brazos Shopping Center, consider this old favorite, literally. Antiques shouldn't have to be investment-priced to turn your head. Just ask

Joy, 'cause what you want, Joy can get. Within this 20,000-square-foot building, she has spent a decade selling antiques via 20 (give or take a few) dealers who continue the tradition of collaborative savings. The variety could create a whirlwind. From Depression glass to birdcages, primitives to jewelry, roll-top desks to chandeliers, you can expect to see it all, somehow, somewhere. This former Gibson Building has been home to stand-up desks from town, stained glass from the old depot and memorabilia from the old Baker Hotel and the Crazy Water spring festival. As the story of Mineral Wells goes, the man who founded the town brought his wife here to treat her dementia. After drinking the water, she was cured. Maybe that's the reason I've always felt at home in Mineral Wells. *CK, MC, V, Layaway*

Apparel: Children's

★★ Carter's For Kids 972/724-6770

3000 Grapevine Mills Pkwy.
Grapevine Mills #242
Grapevine, TX 76051
Mon-Sat 10-9:30; Sun 10-8
www.carters.com

This 100-year veteran of the kids' biz is famous for its full line of sleepwear, playwear, underwear and layette items. A favorite at outlet malls across the country, Carter's features some of the most-trusted names in the children's clothing business at discounted prices. Sizes newborn to size 7 in boys; newborn to size 6X in girls (and occasionally larger in pj's). The store is an equal opportunity purveyor–one side of the store is pink and the other side is blue. Savings are in the 20-30 percent range on first-quality items, escalating to greater discounts as the season and the irregulars move on. We found an entire rack of end-of-season buys for almost 70 percent off. Kids, mommies and strollers abound on Saturdays, so shop during the week if you want a calmer, quieter atmosphere. Visit also at Fort Worth's Outlet Square and Gainesville Factory Stores. *CK, MC, V, AE, D*

★★★★★ Chelsea's Tea Room & Boutique 817/276-8100

2421-C Westpark Row
Pantego, TX 76013
Mon-Fri 10-6; Sat 10-5:30; Sun Noon-5

Catering to children and their moms, Chelsea's Tea Room & Boutique has something tasty for everyone to try. Choose from girls' 0-14, boys' 0-7, even maternity samples and gifts. Happy Days are here again. Save 15-20 percent off both boys' and girls' wardrobes, including the preemies who arrived before their time, all boasting many of the most sought-after labels: CHICKEN NOODLE, COTTON COLLECTION, NANETTE, WEEBOK, ZOODLES are noodling their way to more kids' closets than ever before. If you want to dress 'em to the nines for their birthday party, don't overlook Chelsea's afternoon tea party clothing. *CK, MC, V, AE*

★★★★★ Children's Orchard 972/612-7177

3000 Custer, Suite 106 *Mon-Fri 10-7; Sat 10-6; Sun Noon-5*
(SE Corner Parker & Custer)
Plano, TX 75023

There's plenty to pick from at this resale shop (no consignments). You'll find a fresh selection of popular brands, including GAP, GYMBOREE and TOMMY HILFIGER, to name just a few. The clothing selection is varied, with all seasons represented year-round, but in A-1 outstanding condition. Prices are 60-70 percent off retail and more than half of the items are priced under $8. Going out on a limb, let me also rave about their wide range of accessories, though they didn't have a car seat or baby bathtub on the day of our visit. Check directory for their closest location as they branch out across the Metroplex. *CK, MC, V, AE*

★★★★ Children's Store, The 972/442-2708

101 S. Ballard *Tue-Fri 10-5:30; Sat 10-5*
Wylie, TX 75098

You may use a little gas to get there, but what you save on children's, preteen and mom's clothing will be worth the drive. Save 20-50 percent on nearly every name-brand children's line made under the sun. Names like ANITA G, CASH-CASH, COTTONTAILS, HEARTSTRINGS, KC PARKER, KNITWAYS, LITTLE ME, MAGGIE BREEN, MONDAY'S CHILD, NAUTICA, NICOLE, RUTH OF CAROLINA, TICKLE ME and VIVA LE FETE just tickled me. If you're looking for girls' clothing up to size 14, as well as some preteen and ladies' sizes, you've come to the right place. Boyswear is not forsaken, but not nearly as extensive. When it comes time to dress 'em in a wardrobe that they soon become accustomed to, land here. Looks like they're about to capture the hearts of moms, too. Each year they add a little more to the women's line. They now carry LUCIA, MALIK, PINECOVE, SHARON YOUNG, and TELLURIDE for women and COTTONTAIL for mother and daughter dresses. They also carry dress-making fabric, buttons, lace, braid trim, ribbons of all sizes and colors and all sewing supplies. Go north on Central to the 544 exit. Go right or east to 78 then go left. Second red light on the left-hand corner of Oak and Ballard and you have arrived. *CK, MC, V, AE, D, Layaway*

Apparel: Children's

★★★ Chocolate Soup

214/363-6981

1214 Preston Royal Plaza
Dallas, TX 75230

Mon, Thu-Fri 10-8; Tue-Wed, Sat 10-6; Sun 1-5

No slurping your soup in these fine digs, but don't let the upscale feel steer you away. With items direct from the CHOCOLATE SOUP factory in Kansas City, you'll find clothing for your favorite girl or boy at prices around 25 percent below comparable designer lookalikes. On the southeast corner of Preston and Royal, near Borders and Linens 'n Things, the refurbished neighborhood shopping center is ready for action with a huge selection in girls' sizes 0 to 12 and boys' to size 7. Off-season and sales, expect savings to soar to 60 percent off. If you're thinking you'll go into sugar shock if you ladle out another CHOCOLATE SOUP label, you can select from the approximately 25 other brands of clothing they carry: BUSTER BROWN, CARRIAGE BOUTIQUE, HEART STRINGS, LE TOP, NAUTICA, S.F. BLUES and others in the pot for extra flavor. *CK, MC, V, Layaway*

★★★★ Consolidated Clothiers

214/678-0060

2246 Vantage
Dallas, TX 75207

Mon-Fri 9-5

When one outlet goes, another one moves in to take its place. And for Underground Shoppers, that is good news. Not long after Children's Factory Outlet, 2239 Vantage, left the landscape, Consolidated Clothiers opened a store just a few doors down the same street for infants through sizes 4 bargains. They carry some apparel for the entire family, but their true specialty is in better children's clothing, at prices well under wholesale. When available, they stock manufacturer closeouts of brands such as HOUSE OF HATTAN, KATHERINE REBECCA, LAVENDAR, MONDAY'S CHILD, SAN FRANCISO BLUE, TOO TOE PICCOLO, VIVA LE FETE and more. Call before you go to see what the current stock holds. *CK*

✔ Funtasia Too!

214/634-7770

4747 Irving Blvd., #230
Dallas, TX 75247

Open for 4 sales per year only

Getting better designer kids' clothing for well below wholesale is no fantasy here. But this manufacturer only opens her doors four times a year, so call to have your name added to the mailing list. Then and only then does the fun begin. Expect to save 75 percent off the lowest wholesale price during fall/holiday clearance sales; for the spring sale, expect to pay 10 percent less than wholesale on in-season togs. Girls can choose from 9-12 months up to preteen sizes, and boys can be covered mostly in toddler sizes. What's leftover, discontinued or moved to their outlet clearance sales are always worthwhile. Then again, you could head to the department store and pay full price. *CK, MC, V*

★★★★★ Just Kidstuff — 972/240-5500

4125 Broadway, Suite 120 — *Mon-Sat 10-6*
Garland, TX 75041

It may be Just Kidstuff, but with 200 items arriving daily, there's *lots* of kid's stuff to choose from. And just for knowing about Just Kidstuff, you can reap up to 70 percent savings from this cream-of-the-crop harvest. For school clothes to party dresses, you can exit La Prada off LBJ (it turns into Wynn-Joyce almost immediately) and shop 'til somebody drops. From newborns to junior 7s for girls and up to size 20 in boys, Just Kidstuff won't let you leave empty-handed. At its nice prices, shopping here should also leave a little something in your pockets. And babies-in-waiting can get outfitted too (in maternity fashions). Baby gear is another specialty, including toys, cribs, high chairs and walkers; if it was meant for junior, they've got it in all the right brands. How can you miss–they're located between Subway and The Donut Shop, between Oates and Wynn-Joyce. Consignments taken for in-season only, cleaned and gently-worn. Tickets with a hole punched under the price are half the ticketed price, based on how long the items have been on the floor. Every month they punch another color of tickets. There is always something happening, so make them a regular stop on the resale circuit. *CK, MC, V, AE, D*

★★★★★ Kids R Us — 214/373-1383

9500 N. Central Expressway — *Mon-Fri 10-9; Sat 10-9; Sun 10-6*
Dallas, TX 75231

Crowds of kid-toting parents shop here and save 20-30 percent less every day. If crowds don't bother you, then you'll enjoy the 20,000 square feet of one-stop shopping for brand names like BUGLE BOY, CARTER'S, CHEROKEE, L.A. GEAR, LEE, LEVIS, MICKEY MOUSE CO., NIKE, OCEAN PACIFIC and OSHKOSH B'GOSH to boot. Not to mention the clearance racks. Check directory for other locations. This one is below the new Gateway Computer superstore at Central and Walnut Hill. Now that they've bought Baby Superstores and converted them to Kids R Us, new parents have another reason to rejoice. Wall Street did, and the chain's stock jumped enough to buy baby a new pair of shoes. *CK, MC, V, AE, D*

★★ Kids' Alternative — 817/377-4988

2823 Alta Mere *Mon-Sat 10-5; Sat 10-5:30*
Fort Worth, TX 76116

Bless the children, and dress them here. Another smart alternative to paying retail, Kid's Alternative is a unique children's resale shop that sells name brands for less. They've cornered the market on GAP, GUESS?, GYMBOREE, POLO, THE LIMITED, TOMMY HILFIGER and more. But well-rounded children don't just live by school clothes alone. Kid's Alternative also turns out dance apparel for after-school activities; sizes infants through 16, plus baby accessories and toys. A little toddler sweatsuit was $5, but expect the designer duds to sport price tags from $16-$24, on average. They buy and consign; either way, it's up to you. What was once Yours, Mine & Ours is now Kid's Alternative and just up the street from where the old shop used to be. It is barely a block away at Alta Mere and Calmont. *CK, MC, V*

★★★★★ Mudpuppy — 817/731-2581

5714 Locke *Mon-Sat 10-6*
(Locke at Camp Bowie)
Fort Worth, TX 76107

For the richest labels in children's clothing, smart fashion hounds clean up big at Mudpuppy, which sells sought-after children's labels that have been lovingly worn once before. There are even toys, shoes and maternity clothes, all on expanded racks to accommodate their burgeoning inventory stocked for nine months' worth of activities. Girls' sizes 0-preteen (16) and boys' sizes 0-20 are all neatly lined up to perfection. Owner Jana Minter knows how to attract the cast-off's of the rich and not-so-famous brands bearing NEIMAN's labels, of course. GAP, GAP KIDS, GYMBOREE, POLO and the like close the gap on high retail prices. Now comfortably settled in their new location directly behind the Mexican Inn Cafe, unless you want to continue to wallow in the mud of high prices, scamper in here, puppy, where you'll pay at least a third less than retail. *CK, MC, V*

★★★★★ Once Upon a Child — 972/618-5800

7200 Independence Pkwy. *Mon-Fri 10-7; Sat 10-6; Sun Noon-5*
Plano, TX 75025 *www.ouac.com*

Once you happen upon this resale store on the northeast corner of Independence and Legacy, you'll be happy that you did. Once Upon a Child is bigger and better than your run-of-the-mill resale shop. One reason is cash up front. No consignments. No hassles. No wait for your money. "Kid's stuff with previous experience" is their tag line. New this year is the increased new product line–about 20 percent of their inventory is now brand, spankin' new. Still lots of GAP and GYMBORE clothes, and lots of your better brands of upscale children's clothing and equipment are all discounted, like the new CENTURY Bravura Booster seat for $49.99; or a custom-made new child's padded rocking chair that was snatched up as I showed it on "Positively Texas" by an anonymous Channel 11 anchor. (She was expecting her second child and it showed!) A delightful hand-painted wooden chair was perfect for baby's room at only $15. And a new INSTEP JOG-ABOUT jogging stroller was $89.99–about half of what you'd pay elsewhere. So hit the road, Jackie, for name-brand apparel, toys, cribs, strollers and more in sizes infant to 7 in mint condition. Even a mint-condition JENNY LIND crib was looked upon with disdain–a meager $25 was its price–but if you bring in a BELLINI, well, that's a whole different story. Other locations at the SW corner of Trinity Mills and Midway in Carrollton and the on Cross Timbers and Morriss Road in Flower Mound. *CK, MC, V, AE, D*

★★ Rabbit's Recycle — 972/298-9819

320 N. Main — *Mon-Fri 10-6; Sat 10-5*
Duncanville, TX 75116

It's good to recycle and the recycling's still good at this resale store. Just a short hop to North Main from Camp Wisdom Road, where the store used to be, Rabbit's Recycle keeps rising costs in check. Children's and maternity steal the focus, though new market samples are included in the mix. Baby furniture, nursery bedding, books, everything for the layette in just two little words: Rabbit's Recycle. For hare-ied moms-to-be, expect everything to be in good working order, and brand-spankin' new or at least spiffy-clean, in sizes newborn to 14-plus (some junior sizes, some boys' 18s and 20s). We paid almost nothing for cute samples (still with the original wholesale price tags on and marked down another 20 percent). So let your ears down, and get your tail over here. *CK, MC, V, D*

★★★★ Runt Rethreads — 972/686-7007

1220 Town East — *Mon-Sat 10-6; Sun Noon-5*
Mesquite, TX 75150

Maybe they don't have the most flattering name, but the store itself is clean, bright, well-organized and comes complete with a safe, inviting play area to keep kids entertained while you get down to serious shopping. Located between Town East Mall and The Dusty Attic Antique Mall, this children's resale shop sells infants' through size 16 clothing. Bring in whatever your little bundle has outgrown and enjoy a 50/50 split. Consignments are accepted daily. Clothes will be offered for sale for 60 days without taking a mark-down. If they don't sell, you have 10 days to pick up your items or they will donated to Buckner Children's Home. Now they have opened a second location at Broadway and Colonel in Country Club Square, 972/271-1251. Here you will find ladies fashions from juniors to plus sizes and maternity. *CK, MC, V, D*

★★★★★ Small Fry — 940/387-9915

330 Sunset — *Mon-Sat 10-6*
Denton, TX 76201

For a small fry, this store has a big big selection of some of the finest department and specialty store labels around. Don't confuse them with Small Fry World, or you may miss out on big first-quality savings. Get as much as 50 percent off on market samples, promotional goods and current fashions in girls' preemies to 16, boys' preemies to 7 and infants' clothing, bedding and gifts. Dress your small fries in top brands like ALLISON ROSE, AMY BYER, BABY TOGS, BISCOTTI, CALVIN KLEIN, CHICKEN NOODLE, CITY KIDS, CLAIRE LYNN, COTTON COLLECTION, DORISSA, FELTMAN, GOOD LAD, KC PARKER, KNITWAVES, LE TOP, LITTLE ME, MICHAEL SIMON, MONDAY'S CHILD, MULBERRIBUSH, SCHWAB, SIMI, TICKLE ME, TODDLE TYKE, ZOODLES and ZYNO. Shipping is available nationwide. For grandmas, this store is but one phone call away for every birthday and holiday gift–without leaving home. But for those who like to shop first-hand in Small Fry's boys and girls separate-but-equal cottages, head north on I-35, exit Hwy. 377 (which turns into Carroll), Exit 465B. Turn right on Sunset, and you're ready to get those kids in designer clothes for a lot less. *CK, MC, V*

★★★★★ Sprouts Children's Boutique — 817/788-8020

1101 Cheek Sparger — *Tue-Thu 10-6; Fri 10-4; Sat 11-3*
Tara Village Shopping Center
Colleyville, TX 76034

Thanks to those stylish Colleyville kids who keep outgrowing their fashionable wardrobes, this upscale resale store has sprouted up right between highways 121 and 26. Designer special occasion apparel for both kids and moms-to-be including hard-to-find dancewear and costumes–like children's costumes (Dorothy from "The Wizard of Oz", new tap and ballet shoes as well as leotards. Hip, hip hooray! Winter coats, baby gifts (layette sets), lest we forget the important stuff in a child's life, and children's wear in sizes 0-14. New market samples and designer consignments, first communion apparel plus shoes, designer maternity, toys, dancewear, dance costumes, baby items and more. Boy's sizes newborn and up 0-14, girl's sizes also 0-14. Consignments accepted. *CK, MC, V*

★★★★ Too Little For Me — 214/341-8144

11411 E. Northwest Hwy. — *Mon-Sat 10-6*
Dallas, TX 75218

Considering it's the largest children's consignment store in the Metroplex, Too Little For Me hides pretty well. Tucked into the back corner of the strip shopping center at Northwest Highway and Jupiter, this store has it all in infants up to size 16 in girls' and up to size 20 in boys'. Moms can get outfitted too. Look for the maternity sample clothes and save at least 20 percent in new and 40 percent in resale. The store is brimming with clothing bargains at every turn mixed in with furniture and equipment, such as swings, toys, games and videos. What more could you ask for when it gets to be–too little for you? Come swing with the best of them. Consignments welcome. *CK, MC, V*

★★★★★ Yesterdaze Kids — 817/284-5437(KIDS)

7269 Glenview Drive — *Tue-Fri 11-6; Sat Noon-4*
Fort Worth, TX 76180

When you want a great children's resale clothes' shopping experience, this is your home away from home. To find this welcomed newcomer to children's closets, look for this store's light brick house, which is just minutes from North Hills Mall. Quality kids' resale, in sizes newborn to 18 for both boys and girls, are waiting to be discovered. Look for designer duds, toys, gifts, books, baby accessories and more. And get this: They will either buy your items outright or you can consign them for a 50/50 split. How's that for generosity? Sandy Parrent (how telling!) is the mother in charge. One room is designated the kids room so kids can play while parents pay. This 1,300-square-foot converted house is the kind that won't come tumbling down on your budget. There's no place like home. *CK, MC, V*

Apparel: Family

★★★ American T-Shirt — 972/289-8262

1228 Scyene Rd., #209
Mesquite, TX 75149
Mon-Fri 9-5; Sat 10-3
www.american-t-shirts.com

In 1988, American T-Shirts started with 1,000 square feet and a very American idea–to give the competition a run for their money. Now 79,000 square feet larger, today American T-Shirt still gives customers the shirt off their back–from names like ANVIL, FRUIT OF THE LOOM, GILDAN, HANES, JERZEES, LEE, OUTER BANKS, RAWLINS and VAN HEUSEN. They also offer hard-to-find and custom orders, too. Some of their best-sellers include Van Heusen golf shirts, retail $32.99-up, their wholesale price $20.99-$29.95. Order by the piece, the dozen or by the case. This wholesale distributor has no minimum orders, but the more you buy, the more you'll save. They will even custom embroider most products. With so many companies instituting casual Fridays, you can buy T-shirts, athletic apparel, outerwear, caps and golf shirts to dress the part. Glad to see that some American values are alive and well. Call for a free brochure or their $5 catalog, or visit them online. *CK, MC, V, AE, D, CB*

★ Andor's Dollar Store — 817/531-3225

3700 E. Lancaster
Fort Worth, TX 76103
Mon-Sat 9-5; Sat 9:30-5

The panty patrol has just issued a citation for shockingly low prices on men's BLOOPERS, FRUIT OF THE LOOM and JOCKEY briefs and boxers. So pull over and pull some on. Even HANES HER WAY were stacked up for savings of almost 40 percent. BERKSHIRE pantyhose, from sizes small to extra large, were spotted at $.99 to $2 per pair. The owner travels all over the country to find the best deals in close-outs, irregulars and the like. Boxers for 3/$6.99 and ultra-sheer pantyhose for $1.99 would do in a pinch. Good choice for men's dress socks and women's sleepwear, too. Some store brands, like JC PENNEY, MONTGOMERY WARD and others were also seen. Selection changes regularly, so if you don't see it the first time, try again later. Cash or checks only, so leave the credit cards at home. *CK*

★★★★ Bugle Boy

940/665-6988

4321 I-35 North
Gainesville Factory Shops
Gainesville, TX 76240

Mon-Sat 10-8:30; Sun 11-6
www.bugleboy.com

Sound the trumpets, because nothing at this store is ever priced at more than $25. That's their policy. And most items are $15 or less. Men's sizes, boys' to size 7, and women's clothing is how the band plays now. Little boys' dress shirts were $3.99, so if you are a fan of BUGLE BOY, you can really toot your own horn. Slacks, jeans, button-up shirts, zippered-down jackets–it's worth the drive to outfit the entire ensemble.The 30-50 percent savings on clearance items are still marching on. Other stores in the area: Fort Worth Outlet Square, 150 Throckmorton, Suite 214; Grapevine Mills, 3000 Grapevine Mills Pkwy., Suite 236; Prime Outlet Center in Hillsboro, 104 I-35 N.E., Suite 160; North East Center, 873 North East Mall Blvd., #E05, Hurst; Plano Market Square, 1717 E. Spring Creek Pkwy., Suite B7, Plano; Richardson Square Mall, 501 S. Plano Rd., Suite L141, Richardson; and Tanger Factory Outlet, 301 Tanger Blvd., Suite 224, Terrell. *CK, MC, V, AE, D*

✔ Colbert's Warehouse Sale

214/638-4580

1295 Majesty Drive
Dallas, TX 75247

Thu 11-7; Fri 10-6; Sat 10-5

It happens twice a year, and when it does–run–do not walk, to the Colbert's annual warehouse sale. The prices are unbelievably low on the store's more than 2,000 pairs of ladies shoes, missy and large size dresses and sportswear, outerwear and accessories and some men's apparel and shoes, too. Watch for the announcement in the paper around March/April and September/October. Brands include BREEZE, CITY GIRL, FAITH, PETER POPOVICH, RICHARD & CO., SANDY STARKMAN, ST. GERMAINE and many more. *CK, MC, V, AE, D*

★★★ Dickies Factory Outlet

817/877-0387

521 W. Vickery
Fort Worth, TX 76104

Mon-Sat 9:30-5:30
www.dickies.com

You just gotta love a man in overalls. But at prices 40 percent or more off, everyone can take advantage of the fine work clothes, caps, gloves and socks made by DICKIES. Here you can salute the savings, since everything is categorized as an irregular (meaning something indiscernible is wrong with it). The dye lot might not be exactly right, maybe it was sized incorrectly...whatever it is, something's not kosher, but it's still very wearable. Closeouts and irregulars, so what? Really, can you tell the difference between last year's bib overalls (for $24.99) or this year's? At their outlet shop, you can find irregular bargains, as well as their first-line products. Selection changes often and there's usually lots to choose from, including jeans up to size 56/32. Like Dickies, good prices never go out of style. *CK, MC, V, D*

★★★ Emeralds to Coconuts — 214/823-3620

2730 N. Henderson — *Tue-Sat 11-6*
Dallas, TX 75206

Just as the name implies, this eclectic corner shop sells everything but the same old thing. If donning the unusual is your bag, you will be able to fill your bags to overflowing here. Not to mention, chapeaux, peasant blouses, woven vests, concho belts and Turkish sandals, even jeweled elephant collections. Lots of interesting textures and colors. Selling "culturally enriched" unisex clothes (what a great description!), this funky little house-store has the corner (literally and figuratively) on imported clothing from Guatemala, Indonesia, Turkey, India and China. Just right for today's environmentally concerned fashion consumer, at Emeralds to Coconuts you get the feeling you're saving the world when you shop. Jewelry accents for that one-of-a-kind conversation piece are hard to resist. Puppets and masks and other doodads surprise you at every turn. The stock changes frequently, as do the styles! *CK, MC, V, AE, D*

★★★★★ Hale's Costume — 817/838-7126

2902 Race — *Tue-Fri 10-6; Sat 10-4; Mon by Appt.*
Fort Worth, TX 76111

This costume place is so good it's scary. Whether your goal is to spook or spoof, Beverly Hale and her daughter have been helping you dress the part since 1947 and can make a believer out of anyone. In Fort Worth, off Hwy. 121 and Sylvania Avenue, look for a black and yellow free-standing building. Hale can custom-make anything you want–even if it's out of the ordinary. One of their specialties is non-traditional bridal dresses, such as styles in medieval, Western or surreal. Some of their all-time favorites standards include Batman, Snoopy, Lucy, saloon girls, Dracula, Grim Reaper, Pocahontas, Little Red Riding Hood and the Big Bad Wolf. Hale's sells lots of sequins, fabrics and other oddities–including eyeballs. Adult-sized costumes range from $35-$55 for 24 hours; children's costumes rent for $25 (though you can buy one for $39.95).

Bring in a picture of what you want to play dress-up in and by the end of the month you can be the belle of the costume ball for as little as $70. *CK, MC, V*

★★★★ Harold's Outlet Store

254/582-0133
104 N.E. I-35
Hillsboro, TX 76645
Mon-Sat 10-8; Sun 11-6
www.harolds.com

If you love Harold's of London, you'll adore Harold's in Hillsboro when they open their doors to their multi-million dollar warehouse sale, held each year around Valentine's Day. If you are a Highland Park devotee and would rather not pay the price of success, don't hold your breath for a periodic sale. Shop seven days a week for the least expensive way to climb the corporate ladder. Both men and women can get outfitted. They consolidate men's and women's merchandise from their many Southwestern locations and price them as low as they go. All items appear in-season and current, though you can't expect alterations at these close-out prices. Harold's also has outlet stores in Austin, Katy and San Marcos. *CK, MC, V, AE, D*

★★★★★ Jeans Warehouse

972/247-2800
11171 Harry Hines
Dallas, TX 75229
Mon-Sun 9-7

Don't let anything come between you and your jeans, especially not a high price. Locate "the" place to buy jeans just south of Royal Lane, next to Wolf Camera and Video's clearance store. Here, you'll find men's, women's, juniors' jeans and shirts with all the stellar names. Buy your current LEVI'S elsewhere and you'll pay $44; here they're $29.95. Slip into a pair by BOSS, CALVIN KLEIN, COSMO, GUESS?, JNCO, POLO, SOUTHPOLE, TOMMY HILFIGER, WRANGLER...seen enough? Pay less. Sizes to fit any man, woman, teen or child. *MC, V, AE*

★★ Socks Galore

254/582-9439
Hillsboro Outlet Center
I-35 South (Exit 368)
Hillsboro, TX 76645
Mon-Sat 10-8; Sun 11-6

Where do designer socks come from? From the same major mills that Socks Galore gets them from before the designers slap their labels on them and jack up the price. Now that you know, you won't ever have to be embarrassed again by paying more than you should. At Socks Galore, you can save on more than 60,000 pairs of socks for anybody who wears shoes. From knee-highs to anklets, scrunch to athletic, buy direct and save 10-20 percent. Dive in feet-first in Hillsboro or at their location in Conroe. *CK, MC, V*

Apparel: Family

★★ Wearabout Factory, The

214/350-4722

5710 W. Lovers Lane
Dallas, TX 75209

Mon-Sat 10-8; Sun Noon-6

It may call itself a "factory", but low priced it's not. However, if you're young and svelte, you can find something in vogue for any occasion, be it baggy grunge, '70s or current contempo. This unisex trendsetter has a few deals on sample sizes, but most of the stock is retail, and you know how I feel about that. Of course, the clothing selection, especially for the young and the hip, is inviting. Beyond the more expected garden varieties like CALVIN KLEIN, LEVI'S, MASSIMO and more, The Wearabout Factory also has street smart names like DIESEL, ENERGY and LUCKY'S. If you're ready to assume a new ATTITUDE, they can help in that department, too. The sample items were all mediums, so when we tried to fit our tootsies into a size 9 (UK 8) pair of DOC MARTEN's, well, let's just say it wasn't merely our attitude that needed adjusting. The meek shall inherit the earth, but the size skinnies shall do well at The Factory Wearabout. Ladies' shoes and sandals by 2LIPS, CHINESE LAUNDRY and STEVE MADDEN. Word to your mother, smart shoppers will do better elsewhere. *CK, MC, V, AE, D*

★★ Wilson's Suede and Leather

972/681-5731

Town East Mall
Mesquite, TX 75150

Mon-Sat 10-9; Sun Noon-6

Warm leatherettes will like Wilson's year-round selection (unlike the slim pickins you get at most other leather clothing stores in Texas during the warmer three-fourths of the year). For leather coats, jackets, shirts and accessories, or for that oh-so-hot little leather dress, you can count on Wilson's to keep the price under wraps. Most of the big items were priced from $99-$349. Items are very competitively priced; save 20-30 percent for sure. Labels and brand names like ANDREW MARK, LIZ CLAIBORNE, NINE WEST along with their own stuff. Scope out other locations at the Parks Mall in Arlington, in the Dallas Galleria, in the Collin Creek Mall in Plano and the Irving Mall. *CK, MC, V, AE, D*

Apparel: Men's

★★★ Apparel World

214/887-8999

4949 Beeman Ave.
Dallas, TX 75223
Mon-Fri 8:30-5

If jumpsuits are your thing, this true manufacturer's outlet has them priced as low as wholesale prices go. It just can't get much better than that. Offering a much bigger selection of men's jumpsuits than at their previous location, Apparel World sells jumpsuits in all sizes from 38-short to 60-long–and all at factory direct prices. Knits and long-sleeved shirts (small to 2XL) were abundant, plus a menagerie of other menswear items from socks to sweaters. Men up to size 60 can shop successfully and get in and out quickly. *CK, MC, V, D*

★★★ Barry Mfg. Co.

972/298-3366

4141 Independence Drive
Dallas, TX 75237
Mon-Thu 9-7; Fri 9-8; Sat 9-7; Sun Noon-5
www.bettermenswear.com

Same day alterations for great suits at 50 percent below retail? Sounds good to me. Men sized small through size 60 will think so, too. We found single- and double-breasted suits, rayon/linen blends, polyester and wool, all priced up to 50 percent off retail, from $99-$169. Your guy will like the selection and the fact that the pants are un-hemmed. Ties, socks and underwear bottomed out their inventory. Formal wear was also ready to take the walk–tuxedos were $99.95 and up. No rush charge on same-day alterations. Sizes in short, regular, long and extra-long. In Fort Worth, 5700 Airport Hwy, 817/834-8413. *CK, MC, V, AE, D*

★★★★★ Big and Tall Fashions for Less

817/468-5900

951 W I-20, Suite 105
Arlington, TX 76015
Mon-Fri 10-8; Sat 10-7; Sun Noon-5

Save big and walk tall at this chain. When it comes to outfitting the tall, the big and the handsome, Texas-sized Texans can live large on name brands like ADOLFO, ARROW, DUCK HEAD, HAGGAR, HARMONY, IZOD, LEVI'S (545s up to size 60), PALM BEACH, RALPH LAUREN and WRANGLER for less. Some jeans are available up to size 66. Suits ranged from $229-$299 in sizes up to 70. Easy to shop layout, new improved stores, sizes to 6X; XLT-5XLT. Check directory for one of eight locations near you. This one has easy on and off between Matlock and Cooper. Just remember, life is too short to be small. *CK, MC, V, AE, D*

★★★ Casual Male Big and Tall, The — 817/468-8224

3200 S. Cooper, #101 — *Mon-Sat 10-7; Sun Noon-5*
Arlington, TX 76015 — *www.thinkbig.com*

Reasonable men will like the reasonable prices and the fact that finding the casual wear they love to wear is a no-brainer. Beyond the khaki, big and tall hunks can cover their work-wear needs, too, with a handsome selection of slacks and ties. And yes, there are jeans for casual wear and underwear for either. LEVI'S and WRANGLER were a big hit with our most happy fella, but the HARBOR BAY slacks (they look just like DOCKERS) were a runaway best seller. Prices are competitive and reasonable. Sizes run from 1X-6X and XLT-4XLT. Choose from many locations in the Metroplex. *CK, MC, V, AE, D*

★★★★★ Corporate Traditions — 214/638-5050

1140 Empire Central — *Mon-Fri 9-5; Sat 9-2*
Dallas, TX 75247 — *www.corptrad.com*

This best-kept secret is indeed a corporate tradition, but no secret handshake is required to get into this well-heeled establishment. Whether you're on your way up the corporate ladder, or have already arrived, you'll appreciate the good old-fashioned service in the relaxed, elegant surroundings. Within the 4,000-square-foot showroom space you'll find personalized service and designer names straight from the market at "value" prices (and you know what that means). You will probably follow in the tradition of lots of other corporate types who've jumped ship and gone underground. Custom shirts, business attire, golf wear, casual wear, formal wear, shoes and more are part of their traditional offerings along with company seminars, closet audits and assessments and a personal shopper if you're too pooped to participate. Pardon me if I drop a few brand names here: get business wear from AUSTIN REED, JACK VICTOR, TALLIA, TERZO; business casual from BALLIN, BARRY BRICKEN, COOGI, HAUPT, JHANE BARNES, ST. CROIX; golf attire from ASHWORTH, AXIS, CUTTER & BUCK, DESCENTE; formal wear from LORD WEST, MR. NIGHT TIE'M; custom shirts from IKE BEHAR, INDIVIDUALIZED; and shoes by ALLEN EDMONDS, COLE HAAN and TIMBERLAND. *CK, MC, V, AE, D*

Apparel: Men's

★★★★ David's Big and Tall Shop

817/731-3691

6730 Camp Bowie
Fort Worth, TX 76116
Mon-Sat 9:30-7
www.hardtofit.com

After 28 years in business, this old-timer is better than ever. Expect the discounts to be big and tall. On one visit, suits and sport coats were 30 percent off. Compare and you will discover that this is quite the place if you are big and tall. Although they carry a few 46s, expect the majority of the inventory to be in hunk sizes 48-70 in coats and jackets. Let Michele, the store manager, be your guide to the wonderful world of keeping up with the Too Tall Joneses. Labels linger on while the memory of not finding clothes that fit dwindle from your mind. Relax in a pair of DOCKERS (up to about a 56) or the comparable SALMON RIVER or CREEKWOOD in sizes 36-70; play a round or two of golf in something from IZOD; and if you are a member of the clergy, the additional 10 percent discounts are heavenly. Amen, brother! *CK, MC, V, AE, D, DC*

★★★ Far East Outlet

214/637-6828

1336 Inwood Rd.
Inwood Trade Center
Dallas, TX 75247
Mon-Sat 10-5:30

After a quick detour into women's wear, Far East has returned to doing what they do best: selling men's clothing. Since 1972, the men in your life have been able to get outfitted for less. Expect to see discounts of 30-50 percent off retail–every day–and expert alterations. Men's brand names such as CLASSICO UOMO, EUROPA COLLECTION, GINO CAPPELIO and LINEA CLASSICA were hard to pronounce but easy on the budget. Boys' suits regularly $99/their price $39 and up. Men's suits, all wool, regularly $360/their price $165. Dress shirts $31/$16.50, silk shirts $50/$12.50, shirts and pant sets $90/$45.50. Boys' suits sizes 4-20 (slim/reg), men's suit sizes 36-60 (reg/long) and 36-44 (short), men's shirts sizes 14 1/2-20, dress slacks 27-42. So few stores cater to little boys these days, so grab a few outfits while the iron is hot. Don't, however, use a hot iron if it's polyester. Not bad, considering the alternative of paying retail! *CK, MC, V, AE, D, Layaway*

★★★★★ Gent-ly Owned Men's Consignery

972/733-1115

17610 Midway, #108
Dallas, TX 75287
Mon-Fri 11-7; Sat 11-5

The minute you walk in the room, you can tell that it's a place of distinction, but not for big spenders. This upscale resale store for men sells an attractively-priced selection of European and designer labels from ARMANI, CANALI, COLE-HAHN, COOGI (those wonderful rainbow sweaters are tops on the list), HUGO BOSS, NICOLE MILLER, PERRY ELLIS, POLO, TOMMY HILFIGER, VERSACE and ZEGNA. Business attire, casual, formal wear and business casual, as well as incredible market samples at wholesale prices can all be found here. The other outstanding feature of this store is their customer service. They are always working to make your shopping experience better, including keeping records of merchandise you might be interested in and calling when it arrives. Mr. Shevlin has also been known to turn his customers into consigners and vice versa. Their name says it all, gentlemen. *CK, MC, V, AE, D*

★★★★★ Haggar Clothing Co. Warehouse 214/956-4431

6113 Lemmon Ave. *Mon-Sat 10-6*
Dallas, TX 75209 *www.haggar.com*

When it comes to dressing for casual Fridays, these guys beat the pants off other men's outlets. Texas-born HAGGAR is the brand that does it. Shop their warehouse outlet and forget paying retail. For slacks, sport coats, suits, shirts, shorts, jackets and jeans, Haggar dresses you for a whole lot less. Slacks here from $14.99-$19.99 were as good as it gets. They stock sizes up to 54, so everybody's happy and dressed for work or play. Look for the Alexis Body Shop and go left up the ramp into the parking lot. Head for the tower and you're in like Flint. Women's clothing are back in stock, so come on down and save, whether you wear the pants in the family or not. *CK, MC, V, AE, D*

★★★★★ International Suit & Shoe Warehouse 972/780-2599

4030 W. Camp Wisdom Rd. *Mon-Fri 10-8; Sat 10-7*
Dallas, TX 75237

You don't need a spreadsheet to spell out savings this obvious. This huge liquidation center (comparable to T & C) and owned by Big and Tall Menswear for Less offers savings on private-label suits and sportswear as high as 70 percent off. People in the know, know a good suit when they see it, label or no label. Prices start as low as $89-$329 on suits, from polyester blends to virgin wools in sizes 36-60. Add slacks, sport coats and all the accessories (ties and shirts from sizes 14-22, 32-37 sleeve length) and STACY ADAMS and GIORGIO BRUTINI shoes, and you're looking sharp and spending smart. Some alterations can be made on the spot, $4 for a hem and $5 for a cuff. Second location in North Dallas in the old Vantage Show location at 635 Preston Rd., 972/239-1984. *CK, MC, V, AE, D*

★★★ Jos. A. Bank Clothiers

972/248-4330

1713 Preston Rd.
Dallas, TX 75240

Mon-Fri 10-8; Sat 10-6; Sun Noon-5

Goodbye ladies, Jos. A. Bank's makes clothes exclusively for men now. Serious about quality, this direct-merchant catalog store has no doubt sharpened the images of many successful white-collar executives. Pinpoint and more pinpoint shirts, button-down everything if the man in your life is looking to open doors and close deals. With sizes from 37S-50XL and additional sizing available through their catalog, expect to shell out $375-$575 for a suit, unless there's a sale (which is often). Not your everyday, cheapo career clothing store, but if classic dressing is in the cards, pull up to this bank and make a deposit. Your bottom line will appreciate it. Famous for their "Business Express" program, which consists of a 100 percent wool suit coat (two-, three-button or double-breasted) with a coordinating pant, pleated or plain, for $375. Now, that's a clever way to get rid of suits that haven't sold. Mix 'n match 'em. Alterations are extra and ready in seven days. The Valley View store is closed, but you can find this Jos. A Bank's at Preston and Park, across from Borders, or look for them at 4025 Northwest Highway, Dallas, 214/691-9199, and in Lewisville at Vista Ridge Mall, 972/315-2577. Be sure to request their catalog to keep you abreast of all the latest suits. *CK, MC, V, AE, D, DC*

★★★★★ K&G Men's Center

972/438-6100

3417 E. John Carpenter Frwy.
Irving, TX 75062

Fri 10-9; Sat 10-7; Sun Noon-6
www.kgmens.com

What was T&C is now K&G and, if the crowds at this liquidation center are any indication, this is the start of something even bigger. K&G Men's Stores out of Atlanta has 29 locations, and buying suits has never been this easy or this cheap. Wool suits at $99 each (compared with $250-$325); leather bomber jackets, wool blend tuxedos, cashmere blend topcoats, $99. Expect to save 30-70 percent throughout their plain vanilla warehouse in sizes 36 Short to 54 Extra Long (almost every man has his limits). At K&G, 100 percent wool and fine wool-blend suits were priced anywhere from $119.90-$179.90 (up from a low of $79.90 last year) compared with $350-$450; sportcoats and blazers were $79.90 (compared to $165) and up. Oxford dress shirts (100 percent cotton) were a steal at $19.90 and their tie collection (values to $30-plus) for $7.90 chokes most of their competitor's pricing. Wool gabardine dress slacks $39.90, compared to $80, or famous-maker dress shoes, $49.90-$64.90, compared to

$72-$100. First-quality, name-brand, in-season ... what more could you ask? Well, they could advertise their brands, but they don't. We did see ADOLFO, CHAPS by RALPH LAUREN, CHRISTIAN DIOR, PIERRE CARDIN, PURITAN and more. They're located 1/2 mile east of Texas Stadium at the Grauwyler exit. Look for the associated T&C Men's Centers at 4400 Little Road, #104 in Arlington, 817/561-5100, and at 1050 N. Central Expressway, Richardson, 972/234-8688. *CK, MC, V, AE*

★★★★★ Men's Wearhouse, The 214/369-1841

8239 Preston Rd. *Mon-Fri 10-9; Sat 9:30-6; Sun Noon-6*
Dallas, TX 75225 *www.menswearhouse.com*

George still guarantees it, but at this point, who cares? If you can cringe and bear the advertising campaign, seeing is believing. Men can save 30-40 percent off retail on name brand suits from designers such as BOTANY 500, CHAPS BY RALPH LAUREN, EVAN PICONE, GIVENCHY and PIERRE CARDIN. Their reputation definitely precedes them, but they seem to deliver on their brash promise, which might explain why they have 17 stores in the Metroplex alone. This year, a visit to the Lewisville store and the South African sales person who waited on us, I must congratulate them on their fine customer service...no, *great* customer service. Step out putting your best foot forward in men's dress shoes in sizes 7-13 with such stellar names as BOSTONIAN, FLORSHEIM and STACY ADAMS. To save an additional 10 percent off their already well-below department store pricing, join their V.I.P. Corporate Program. Just call 800/776-SUIT (7848) to get on their list. Amenities such as 24-hour tailoring upon request, free lifetime pressing of your garments, Corporate Dress for Success seminars, free delivery to your office and free re-alterations of seams that have been previously altered, all suited to your good taste. You have to be a member of the club, however, to enjoy these perks. Regular folks can still shop for suits, sportcoats, slacks, shirts, ties, formal wear, shoes or dress casual wear at any one of their 500 locations nationwide. Check directory for a location near you. Their website will tell you, too. Unfortunately, the only thing you can buy online is a gift certificate. After all, they can't guarantee that you look good until they see you. *CK, MC, V, Men's Whs. CC*

★★ REPP Big & Tall 817/784-8091

4100 S. Cooper St. *Mon-Sat 10-9; Sun Noon-5*
Arlington, TX 92110 *www.reppltd.com*

If you have trouble finding clothes that fit at any price, this store will suit you fine. REPP Big & Tall fills the barren closets of over-the-top men measuring 6'4" or taller or men with waists 36-58. If you're a BMOC, you will enjoy a wardrobe befitting a king in sizes to 8X or waists to size 70-72. The stores in the Dallas area are all their "Premier Stores" with brands such as: NAUTICA, POLO, RALPH LAUREN, their own REPP label and TOMMY HILFINGER in all the classic fashions and colors for men. Designer shirts in-store run from $50 to $69.50. Available also, for catalog order only, are brands including CUTTER & BUCK, ENRO, GANT, HEARTLAND, IZOD, LEVI'S, NEW BALANCE , PALM BEACH, RALPH LAUREN, SEBAGO, WORLD CLASS TRAVELLER and more. ENRO dress shirts were $34.50, WORLD CLASS TRAVELLER cotton trousers were $52.50, LEVI'S 545 jeans were $49.50 and cotton pocket T-shirts were $14.50. For these sharper price points, be sure to ask for their "REPP Catalog," where those who want to look sharp can be sharp for less. And if you need your pants hemmed, alterations are very reasonable. Their no-hassle return policy is another plus. The other Metroplex locations are: 1025 N. Central Expressway, Plano, 972/423-4215; and 1725 N. Town East Blvd., Mesquite, 972/270-4476. *CK, MC, V, AE, D*

★★★★★ S&K Famous Brand Menswear 972/874-1927

3000 Grapevine Mills Pkwy. *Mon-Sat 10-9:30; Sun 11-8:30*
Grapevine Mills Mall
Grapevine, TX 76051 *www.skmenswear.com*

They don't give you S&H Green Stamps with every purchase, but S&K does help stamp out high prices. If you want to get into some current designer fashions for 20-50 percent off, get into S & K. We found ROBERTO VALINI suits, which usually retail for $550, for $299 here. You may select from more than 1,000 suits in stock for $139-$299 with names like DANIEL HESTER, FENZIA, JOHNNY BENCH and NINO CERRITO (just to name a few) in sizes 36 short to 52 long. Then check out their sportswear lines, featuring BILL BLASS, EVAN-PICONE, JONES NEW YORK and PIERRE CARDIN, all at the same great discounted prices. S&K buys direct from the manufacturer, who often has created a line of menswear just for them. Unlike many men's discounters, S&K doesn't carry manufacturer overruns or seconds; these are current fashions only. To whip your wardrobe into shape, try S&K. Other locations in the area include Fort Worth Outlet Square Mall, Fort Worth, 817/335-6305; and Prime Outlets, Hillsboro, 254/582-0082. *CK, MC, V, D*

♥♥♥♥♥ Tie-Coon Trading Co. 214/369-8437

4015 Villanova St. *Mon-Sat 10-5:30*
Dallas, TX 75225

This tie store is to-die for. And not just for ties, which they have in every flavor from conventional to designer to novelty. Here you can also select from Hawaiian print and LACOSTE shirts, all the while consulting with a Magic 8-Ball Financial Advisor to see if you can swing more than one. They also have fun items including a '50s martini shaker, a clock shaped like a PC and vintage books on subjects you never imagined, such as art photos of 1900s wax anatomy models. But perhaps one of the best finds here is the large selection of men's vintage and novelty cufflinks. You'll find something here to satisfy most any taste, hobby or vice, with prices averaging $55. Cufflinks include Brooklyn Dodger logo reproductions, gold-filled black and white enamel skunks from the 1950s, pin-ups and even glass eyeballs. They also have watches in the same vein. Just about the only thing you won't find are run-of-the-mill styles. Still the oldest tenant at Preston Center Plaza, but now in a new spot cattycorner to the plaza fountain. *CK, MC, V, AE, D*

Apparel: Resale

★★★★★ ACO Upscale Resale Shop 972/727-4751

801 E. Main St. *Mon-Wed, Fri 10-6; Thu 10-8; Sat 10-5*
Allen, TX 75002

Get top brand names for bottom-of-the-barrel prices and help people in need all with one purchase, all from one place. Every time you buy something from the ACO Upscale Resale Shop, your donations benefit programs of Allen's Community Outreach, a United Way affiliate. And at this shop in the Plano-Allen-McKinney corridor, you find the likes of top names, such as ANNE KLEIN, CACHE, CAROLE LITTLE, GAP, HILFIGER, IZOD, LITTLE TIMES, LIZ CLAIBORNE, OSHKOSH B'GOSH, PERRY ELLLIS, POLO and TALBOTS for less. Fashions (men's, ladies', infants' and children's wear) line up proud and clean. All men's suits, $18, can do a wheelie out the door in a stroller. Find baby gear like car seats and toys; collectibles and housewares; small appliances and bridal wear. At last, they've given new meaning to being a "Bag Lady!" Once a season, help them clean out the store during their infamous "bag sale" when for $15, you walk out with whatever you can stuff into one bag. Donations accepted daily. Tax receipts are provided. *CK*

★★★★ Allure Upscale Resale 972/866-0935

6959 Arapaho Rd., Suite 121 *Mon-Fri 10-7; Thu 10-8; Sat 10-6*
(Arapaho at Hillcrest)
Dallas, TX 75248

Would you pay $150 for a new COACH purse? How about $90 instead? Prices as low as these for name brands as hot as these is the lure of Allure Upscale Resale. And prices are even more alluring for used items. Owner Chris Furrate has outdone its allure and proud of it. If you're looking for upscale clothing from top designers, why not ogle CHANEL for a change ranging from $38-$68 or eyeball an ARMANI and walk out in style? Everything from the GAP to LIZ, MAGGIE LONDON to you never know who you'll be hob-knobbing with from $28-$48. Pairs of ANN TAYLOR pants flew out the door from $18-$24.

Sizes from 1-16 (a few larger sizes, but not much). Lots of accessories, such as shoes, handbags, hats, belts, scarves–even a DOONEY & BOURKE handbag drew one shopper to the register for $50. *CK, MC, V, AE*

★★ Almost New 972/231-6333

2141 E. Arapaho Rd., #140 *Tue-Sat 11-7*
Richardson, TX 75081

Two-year-olds are prized at the Kentucky Derby, but at Almost New they barely make the cut. Resale clothing at this store is fresh, clean and literally almost new. Variety distinguishes–and is the reason for the success of–Almost New. Primarily ladies' sportswear and career–clothing generally from sizes 2-26, but they are more than willing to take even larger or smaller sizes as the case may be. If you're PG, not to worry as there was a good selection of maternitywear, small through large, play and dress clothes for girls, newborn to preteen, and boys' newborn to 14, as well as bedding, toys and a little furniture. It's impossible not to buy something...well, almost. *MC, V, AE, D*

★★★★ Backroom Raggs 972/227-4600

129 Historic Town Square *Tue-Fri 10-5:30; Thu 10-8; Sat 10-5*
Lancaster, TX 75146

What first Mondays mean to Canton, third Thursdays are at Backroom Raggs, where their fashionable mix of names and sizes fly off the racks for an additional one-third off already half-off prices. You'll find a good mixture of consignment clothing and some new accessories from BRIGHTON (belts, watches, key fobs and bracelets). Shine on wardrobes from DANA BUCHMAN, GAP, LIZ CLAIBORNE, NEIMAN MARCUS, SEVENTH AVE. PLUS SIZE OUTLET and more, from $10-$100, and lots of accessories to coordinate. Career or casual clothing, evening or after-5–the selection changes constantly, so shop often. Sizes 2-28 are equally accepted for consigning women. *CK, MC, V, D*

★★★ Champagne Taste 972/233-9999

5211 Forest Lane, Suite 115 *Mon-Wed, Fri 10-6; Thu 10-7; Sat 10-5*
Dallas, TX 75244

For furs, jewels and couture, this upscale resale shop has been the toast of Dallas' smart shoppers for 18 years and counting. Find women's upscale clothing in sizes from 2-26, as well as furs, jewelry, bags, collectibles and more. Designer and couture clothing, shoes, purses, belts, hats, scarves, jewelry (costume, fine and antique), fragrances and furs (year around). They also have gift items, collectibles, small antiques and some art. Sizes range from 4-44 plus some 2s. Business to ballgowns, casual to cocktail in names like ADRIENNE VITTADINI, ANDREA JOVINE, ANNE KLEIN, BICCI, CALVIN KLEIN, CAROLE LITTLE, CHANEL, CHRISTIAN DIOR, COACH, COLE-HAAN, DANA BUCHMAN, DAVID DART, DKNY and many more. Layaway available. Plenty of enclosed dressing rooms and helpful salespeople. At least when you are inside their door. They could do with a few tips from Miss Manners on telephone etiquette, however. *CK, MC, V, D, Layaway*

★★★★ Chapter Two — 972/594-7722

1111 W. Airport Frwy., Suite 123 *Mon-Wed, Fri 10-6; Thu 10-7; Sat 10-5*
(183 at MacArthur)
Irving, TX 75062

If your closet could use some new material, or slightly used material, turn to Chapter Two and get it for less. Just down the sideline from Texas Stadium, Chapter Two scores big with Irving and Las Colinas women. Lots of casual sportswear, after-5 and dressy dresses, business suits, shoes, jewelry and accessories are brought in by designing women for you to check out. Save up to 75 percent off, if new, in everything you need to dress rich. Plenty of inventory to choose from and most items are in excellent shape. Consignments are accepted by appointment only (minimum five pieces, cleaned, in-season and on hangers). Another satisfying chapter in the saga of The Good-Buy Girl. Lots of options, from CAROLE LITTLE, ESCADA, EMANUEL, LIZ CLAIBORNE and, new this season, an emphasis on the "Dallas Style" with brands like BMW and DOUBLE D RANCHWEAR. Sizes 4-18 with an occasional plus size is held for 90 days. The last 30 days, they relocate to the backroom where everything is marked half price. Look for market samples woven in between and don't close the book until you've at least read Chapter Two. Move over, Loehmann's. End of story. *CK, MC, V, AE, D*

★★★★ Chic to Chic Designer Resale — 972/713-7733

7529 Campbell Rd., #303 *Mon-Sat 10-6*
Dallas, TX 75248

If you're going dancing cheek to chic, you can't wear rags. Wear high-class, designer resale clothing. It feels and looks better, right? Clothing sizes range from 0-16, shoes sizes 5-10. And at discounted prices, who cares if you dance your shoes off because you know where to go to get another pair. Don't overlook the accessories and new samples, but don't expect to return your purchases either. If buying resale is wrong, I don't want to be right–at least not if it means I'd have to go barefoot to the ball. *CK, MC, V, AE, D*

★★★★★ Clothes Circuit, The 214/696-8634

6105 Sherry Lane *Mon-Fri 10-7; Thu 10-8; Sat 10-6; Sun Noon-6*
Dallas, TX 75225 *www.clothescircuit.com*

Life in the social circuit can never be dull when it's paramount to never wear the same thing twice. To make it easy on the pocketbook and the eyes, head to this Park Cities' circuit. Everthing is decidedly upscale resale here, and the majority looks as though it had never been off the hanger. Dresses, suits and weekend wear with names like ANN TAYLOR, ARMANI, B.C.B.G., CALVIN KLEIN, DKNY, DONNA KARAN, ESCADA, RALPH LAUREN, ST. JOHN'S KNITS are run-of-the-mill and marked at a fraction of their original price. Racks of better sportswear and separates sporting tickets with automatic price markdowns. Hundreds of items go on the revolving price reduction rack faster than a New York minute. Typical sizes range from Scarsdale-skinny to 14; however, they have expanded to include women's sizes and maternity. When something catches your eye, buy...'cause it won't be there for long. We found a few outfits we couldn't pass up–they looked as if they'd never been worn and quite likely hadn't been. An expanded accessory department made us all want to be bag ladies: BOTTEGA, FENDI, GUCCI, LEIBER and PRADA. Belts, too, by BRIGHTON, COACH, DKNY and JUDITH LEIBER. Bid adieu to the bridal area as it has been discontinued. In its place, they now carry better furs. (Avoid in the interest of PETA, please.) Sale events here require their own social calendar. Whenever neighboring Foley's holds its Red Apple Sale, The Clothes Circuit thumbs its nose at retail with its own Yellow Banana Sale, when prices already 30-40 percent off retail are reduced an additional 20 percent. Twice a year, in late January and late July, The Clothes Circuit has its Back Room Sale, where prices are slashed to a pittance while last season's goods on the floor are marked 50 percent off. (Prices as low as $5.) They also mark down items an additional 10 percent off during their Random Tuesdays sales, which are unannounced and decided ... at random. Maybe I'll see you there, dahling. *CK, MC, V, AE, D*

★★★★★ Clothes Haven 817/861-2373

3100-C W. Arkansas Lane *Mon-Fri 10-6; Sat 10-5*
Arlington, TX 76016

For top-of-the-line labels at below-the-belt prices, go north in Arlington to

Terry's Clothes Haven. Without skirting the issue, this is where some of the best deals are transacted in resale shopping. One whole room is devoted to children's wear. Kids, pay attention: Take mom and dad by the hand and spend the day. Hide and seek out designer and name brands for women's clothes in suits, sportswear and dresses. And they carry menswear, too. Expect to see an expanded selection in this department, including men's clothes, shoes and after-5. If you are looking to outfit the family, this is the house that savings built. Gently worn resale clothing is where it's at. Retreat to this Haven for a real treat. Amen. *CK, MC, V, D*

★★★ Consigning Women — 972/732-8770

6205 Coit, Suite 324 — *Mon-Fri 10:30-6; Sat 10-5*
(Spring Creek and Coit)
Plano, TX 75026

Formerly Accent on Designers on Campbell, now turn your attention to Consigning Women. Turn from being Designing Women into Consigning Women and you won't lose out on a starring role. At Consigning Women's, upstage those paying full price in a size range from 2-24, Delta could find a wardrobe here for any of her lesser or greater roles. Since 1981, they've been outfitting North Dallas women in designer resale, though today, you'll also find an occasional market sample. Notable nods went to CAROLE LITTLE, CHRISTIAN DIOR, JONES/NEW YORK to name drop a few. Consigning Women has clothing for every season and for every reason. Cheers! Brand names at up to 50-70 percent off, who "Wants to be a Millionaire?" From "Liz", "Jones", "Ralph" and "better" maternity for moms-to-be, Consigning Women has something nice for any woman who refuses to pay retail price. *CK, MC, V, AE, D*

★★ Crissa's Closet — 214/361-5008

10455 N. Central Expressway — *Tue-Sat 11-4*
(Royal Lane exit)
Dallas, TX

For goodness sake, go shopping...at Crissa's Closet. And why not? You'll find a closet full of designer labels for less and and when you buy you help. Proceeds from Crissa's benefit the women at the Hope's Door Women's Shelter. Donating clothes and other good merchandise is another way to help. The clothes must be cleaned and on hangers *s'il vous plait*. Depending on the season and donations, Crissa's offers casual, careerwear, dresses, jeans and more in sizes 2-28 accompanied by jewelry, accessories, boots, shoes, collectibles and housewares. Shop nice. *CK, MC, V*

★★★ Dot's Closet — 214/826-4099

5812 Live Oak St. — *Mon-Fri 10-6; Sat 10-5*
Dallas, TX 75214

Founded for the sole purpose of raising money to help the terminally ill, Dot's Closet offers one of the area's largest selections of everything: clothing, collectibles, household items, furniture, jewelry...you name it. They accept donations or consignments, but either way, you can bet that when you buy, you'll be making a worthwhile contribution to guilt-free shopping. *CK, MC, V*

★★★★★ Double Exposure — 817/737-8038

6205 Sunset — *Mon-Sat 10-5*
Fort Worth, TX 76116

Double your shopping pleasure by heading to Double Exposure. This benefit / thrift shop is located just behind the Ridglea Presbyterian Church and you just might do a double-take when you see the savings. Men's clothing is 25-75 percent off, but it's their womenswear that bring on the rave reviews. Fort Worth closets have always been a source for fashion finds! Clothing is their mainstay for saving from the friends and family of Fort Worth's Junior League. Designers like ARMANI, CHANEL and ST. JOHN'S KNITS visit regularly. Wrap up in someone else's jewelry – it's like having permission to help yourself to your mother's jewelry box. Picture-perfect home furnishings, too, like books, accessories and artwork, can easily find their way to your home. Furniture is a rare find here. But if you happen to find something in-stock, don't delay if you are interested as it is quick to make an exit. Donations, which are tax deductible, are welcome. Do your good deed of the day and help someone else in need. This group's one of the best in the charity business and there is something for everyone. *CK, MC, V*

★ Encore Resale Boutique — 817/292-4927

5358 Wedgmont Circle N. — *Mon-Sat 10-5*
Fort Worth, TX 76133

Act Three can be as good as the First the Second time around. At this Fort Worth consignment shop, savings are front and center. Specializing in reasonably priced ladies' garments, Encore Resale offers gently-worn women's fashions in all sizes. Consignments are taken Mon-Thu 10-4 only (so if you have a lot, try to make it by early in the day). Clothes are kept for 60 days for a 50/50 split. Applaud when they make their exit. *CK, MC, V, AE, D*

Apparel: Resale

★★★★ Encore, Encore 972/317-3772

1301 W. F.M. 407, Suite 104 *Tues-Sat 10:30-5; Thu 10:30-7*
Lewisville, TX 75077

Shopping at Encore, Encore is like attending a command performance of a big show. It's still a hit even though it's been around before. After more than ten years in business, they just keep getting better and better. Encore, Encore's best feature is "Hot Tuesdays", when they take half off everything in the store on the first Tuesday of each month (everything, that is, except coats, evening wear, better leather and sterling silver, which is reduced by 30 percent). We cheered when we saw ANN TAYLOR, ARGENTI, CALVIN KLEIN, ESCADA, ESPRIT, GOTEX, LIZ CLAIBORNE, NIPON and more with some retailing from $80-$110 (with the tags still on) slashed to $36-$42. (Hey, since when did others start wearing their price tags? That's MY trademark!) Sizes 0-22 were priced $5 and up. The store is clean and spacious, with the scent of potpourri greeting you as you walk in the door. We saw lots of jewelry, accessories (a few designer bags priced $20-$60) and teen things, too. After seeing this performance, you'll shout "Encore! Encore!" Markdowns occur every five weeks with tag colors up to 50 percent off. This does not include better leather, eyewear, coats or eveningwear. These items are 30 percent off and never go for less. Enjoy three sidewalk sales per year, in mid-February, mid-July and mid-October, when they open and close early. Otherwise, always come early and shop fast because it's often a two-hour wait to get inside one of their two dressing rooms. They were voted #1 by *Lewisville Leader* for Denton City Resale 1996-99. Located on F.M. 407, 1/2 mile west of I-35 E, just north of Main St. in Lewisville. Consignments accepted by appointment only. *CK, MC, V*

★★ Family Treasures Resale Shop 214/823-3600

6465 E. Mockingbird Lane *Tues-Wed, Fri 10-5; Thu 10-7*
Dallas, TX 75214

Your treasures can be somebody else's pleasure. Be generous and donate what you're not wearing or using and then buy something else to enjoy. Proceeds from your purchase provide shelter for a family in need. At Family Treasures Resale on Mockingbird, name brand children's, men's and women's apparel, books, collectibles, housewares and furniture are available at unbelievably discounted prices. (How does $5 and up sound for clothing?) Proceeds benefit Family Gateway-Homeless Families, providing shelter and training for mothers with young children. *CK*

★★★ Fashions For Fractions Boutique — 214/630-5611

5554 Harry Hines Blvd. — *Mon-Sat 10-5:30*
Dallas, TX 75235

Look like a million without spending one at this specialty boutique. Here, you can rummage through racks of CALVIN KLEIN, CHAUS, GLORIA VANDERBILT, GUESS?, LIZ CLAIBORNE, POLO and even a few ex-hometown favorites including VICTOR COSTA. Gently worn and some perfectly new is you–with a new dress on! But don't forget, women do not live by clothes alone. While you're at it, don't forget to wade through the treadmills, the housewares and other buried treasures in their showroom. And, if you want to donate a car, a boat or a motorcycle, press 3 on their voice messaging system. The auto auctions are nationwide but some times will vary depending on the quantity of cars. Also look for stores in Farmers Branch, Irving, Grand Prairie and two in Oak Cliff. *CK, MC, V*

★★★★ Fifth Avenue Rags — 972/248-7337

17610 Midway Rd., Suite 132 — *Mon-Fri 11-6; Sat 11-5*
Dallas, TX 75287

One of the finest resale boutiques in Dallas hands down, Fifth Avenue Rags has done things right for 16 years and is still selling strong. From others' closets to yours, names like CASABLANCA, EPISODE, MODA, RAMPAGE, SAVILLE and ST. JOHN'S KNITS should strike a familiar chord. The only difference is the price. Catering to working women dressing for success with some evening apparel thrown in for a dinner on the town, if you are looking to walk in and turn heads, this is the place. Funky stuff, too. Whatever the occasion, from strictly business to happy hour, cruises to casual fare, this resale shop's a fast fix for anyone with champagne taste and a beer budget. Sizes 2-20 in clothing plus jewelry, belts, bags and shoes are in stock. Consignors have a ten item minimum. Items should be clean and on hangers. Seasonal consignments accepted daily with free pick-up available. *CK, MC, V, AE, D*

★★ Flock Shop, The — 817/834-2503

2908 Layton Ave. — *Fri-Sat 10-2*
Haltom City, TX 76117

One block north of N.E. 28th St. between Beach and Belknap, follow the flock to Asbury United Methodist Church Mission's resale boutique and gift shop. What a nice source of inspiration. Specializing in "gently used merchandise",

Apparel: Resale

The Flock Shop has everything from household items to men's, women's and children's clothing. They also have some furniture, occasional collectibles, toys, children's items and some crafty notions. Their inventory changes frequently, so shop often. Saving more than just grace, their prices are admirable and their philanthropy likewise. *CK*

★★★★ Gavrel Consignment Furs — 817/335-3877

2735 W. 7th St. — *Mon-Sat 10-5*
Fort Worth, TX 76107

Can't get past the fur issues myself, but if you have, try this consignment shop and pay only 10-50 percent of the value of these pre-owned furs. Vintage furs at yesterday's prices. A Lunaraine mink stole, circa 1955-1965, just like one you might have seen Laura Petrie wearing on "The Dick Van Dyke Show" was only $199. Full length minks made in 1995 were as good as new for only $299. These same jackets sold for $3,000 new. A Russian broadtail vest with fox trim, if made new, would cost $2,000, but their cost was $795. A great-looking stenciled cowhide and mink vest, retailing in a catalog for around $1,500, was $795. This concept at least takes the old and makes it do for today with something new. Also, if you have a fur and prefer to keep it, they will bring it up to contemporary fashion styles. Look for the only sign visible, "Fur Storage," and take cover. *CK, MC, V, AE, D*

★★★★★ Genesis Encore — 214/351-6298

5417 W. Lovers Lane — *Mon-Fri 10-5:30; Sat 10-5*
Dallas, TX 75209

Help a sister start a better life when you shop at Genesis Encore. Like its sister-store, Genesis Thrift on Oak Lawn Ave., Genesis Encore is one of the best. Rather than accepting donations, it's a consignment store. When you donate or buy, all proceeds go to the Genesis Women's Shelter. Genesis Encore carries clothes from Senator Kay Bailey Hutchison, Channel 8 news anchor Gloria Campos, Channel 4 anchor Clarice Tinsley, Channel 5's Ramona Logan and state Sen. Florence Shapiro. Only problem, I'm not their size. Note the two racks of designer clothes referred to as the "couture racks". (That means, those are the dresses of the rich and ultra rich.) Located across the street from the Inwood Theater in a small strip center with Pier 1, Dunston Steaks and PrimeCo, this is no clinging vine (though their decor has stenciled vines on the wall leaning toward an Italian vineyard motif). Come check them out. You won't be the only one pleased that you did. *CK, MC, V*

★★★★★ Gentry Men's Resale

817/428-4196

8218 Grapevine Hwy.
North Richland Hills, TX 76180
Mon-Fri 10-6; Sat 10-5

Aspiring to be part of the Gentry? If your man is a Tarrant County man, this is the place to begin his education. As the one and only resale shop in Tarrant County devoted to menswear, Gentry takes exclusive top billing as the area's best priced men's clothing store. No store is better than this little-known but sharp source in North Richland Hills. Their labels are heavenly: ALEXANDER JULIAN, AUSTIN REED, BROOKS BROTHERS, HART SCHAFFNER & MARX, HICKEY FREEMAN, NEIMAN MARCUS, PERRY ELLIS, POLO, TOMMY HILFIGER (just to name-drop a few) and others. Of course, there's always room for GAP, IZOD or LEVI'S. Sizes run the gamut from 36-Short to 54-Long, including boys sizes 12 and up. Stock up with suits, sportswear, shirts, sweaters, shoes, jeans, vests, tuxedos, etc. They carry a great selection of market samples and special buys of extra-nice leather wallets, watches, ties and men's gifts. Regular Joes pay retail. Smart gents shop at Gentry. So guys, which will it be? *CK, MC, V, AE, D*

★★★ Grand Thrift

817/560-1800

3100 Las Vegas Trail
Fort Worth, TX 76116
Mon-Sat 9-8

It's a grand night for shopping and the moon was shining bright. But now it's time to get down to business...big business for those who like to shop thrifty. Head to the grandpappy of thrift stores, Grand Thrift, a place that seems to have it all at discounted prices. When you buy the donated items from this non-profit organization, you are also helping a child. Browse through furniture (sofas range from $30-$100), men's, women's and children's clothing, shoes, housewares, books, collectibles and pictures throughout their jam-packed 21,000-square-foot warehouse. Our shopper said all the merchandise was in good to grand condition with bargains jammed into every nook and cranny, grandy. Watch for the red tag sales when you'll save an additional 25-50 percent off. Their kids will thank you. *CK, MC, V, D*

★★★★★ Hope Chest Resale Shop

214/520-1087

4209 McKinney Ave., Suite 200
Dallas, TX 75205
Tues-Sat 10-5

Whether you choose something borrowed or something blue, you can leave knowing that your purchase brings hope to pregnant women who elect to give birth. Appropriately, Hope Chest Resale Shop is a family place. The store offers maternity, baby and children's resale items, as well as market samples. For example, the showroom of Ross Barrie at the World Trade Center donates seasonal, decorative and gift items for your next bargain buy. Also, find resale clothing for men, women and children as well as furniture for your home. Proceeds benefit the Hope Cottage Pregnancy and Adoption Center. Begin your day with giving a little hope to those who'd appreciate it most. *CK, MC, V*

★★ Joyce's Shop — 972/296-3055

1210 N. Duncanville Rd. — *Tue-Fri 10-5:30; Sat 10-5*
Duncanville, TX 75116

Find Joyce's and rejoice.This mother-daughter duo will treat you like one of the family. If you're part of the regular clan who congregate to buy and sell clothes, they'll even call you by name. We found ladies' and children's new and pre-owned apparel sporting designer labels such as CHANEL, LIZ CLAIBORNE and PIERRE CARDIN. Little boys' clothing was scarce, but they did have some in sizes infant to 12. Girls' clothing was more abundant, with sizes for females ranging from infants to teens to women's. Accentuate the positives with jewelry, shoes and purses. Ladies' sizes 4-16 will enjoy shopping here, and larger sized women will, too, when larger sizes and plus sizes are on hand. You'll always find joy inside Joyce's. *CK*

★★★ Just Once and More — 817/488-3480

140 N. Main St. — *Mon-Sat 10-5:30*
Grapevine, TX 76051

Just once in this upscale resale boutique is all it takes to get used to the personal, friendly service. Ladies' clothing, market samples and accessories, many designer and boutique labels are all featured here. DANA BUCKMAN, ELLEN TRACY, GAP, STAHL and YORK are just some of the brands that make their way into this store in sizes 0 to Plus. Some maternity and evening wear are also available. Clothes must be clean, pressed, gently worn and on hangers to be accepted. All new jewelry, shoes, handbags, sunglasses, giftware and fantastic items from estate sales are on display. Going once, going twice, whatever, just get going to this juicy little Grapevine store. *CK, MC, V, AE*

★★ Kidswap — 214/890-7927

6728 Snider Plaza — *Mon-Fri 10-6; Sat 10-5*
Dallas, TX 75205

No parents, you can't swap out your kids, but at least you can dress them nicely for less at this resale swap-shop located on Hillcrest Ave. near Lovers Lane. Kidswap now carries infants through high school clothing as well as maternity clothes on consignment. We saw lots of gently worn (if that's possible with kids) clothing, including DKNY and GAP for girls and POLO and TOMMY HILFIGER for boys. Some infants' clothing with French-sounding names appeared royally endowed. Recent additions include overruns and brand new clothes from FLAPDOODLE. Clothes are swapped and crowded into this hideaway down the street from SMU. Though there was plenty from which to choose, everything was really packed in. Some prices seemed a little on the high side, others were right on the money. Their proximity to the Park Cities should pique your interest. Expect to divvy up 60/40 when they sell your consigned items. (By the way, 60 percent is *their* take.) If it's not sold after 90 days, either pick it up or they'll donate it to charity. *CK, MC, V*

★★★★★ Labels Designer Resale Boutique 972/713-8600

18101 Preston Rd., Suite A105 *Mon-Fri 10-7; Sat 10-6; Sun Noon-5*
Dallas, TX 75287

If you must label yourself with something, this resale boutique places a premium on some of the very best. Hang with ANN TAYLOR, CHANEL, DONNA KARAN, ESCADA, FENDI, GUCCI, JILL SANDERS, LIZ CLAIBORNE, PRADA or ST. JOHN'S KNITS. If you have lots of acceptable clothes to consign, they offer free pick-up and a 50/50 split. Sizes 2 to a few 16s with some petites thrown in. The store is located at the northwest corner of Frankford and Preston, next to the Mediterraneo Restaurant. They work with The Family Place, a charity for abused women, in helping them make a fresh start. Your consignments help, too. Dress the part with the labels that impress. Even your best friend won't be able to tell. *CK, MC, V, AE, D*

★★★★ Larger Than Life—Rubenesque Resale 214/342-8550

10233 E. Northwest Hwy., Suite 435 *Mon-Sat 10-6; Thu 10-8*
Northlake Shopping Center
Dallas, TX 75238

It's a big city, but there's not always an abudance of choices for big and beautiful women. Larger Than Life just celebrated their fifth anniversary, and Dallas' grande dames couldn't be happier. Larger Than Life carries upscale fashions from size 14 and up at 1/3 to 1/2 off retail. Casual dressing as well as evening wear, career suits and separates are plentiful. For damsels in distress when stylish clothes are scarce or priced out-of-sight, relax and take a deep breath. There is hope on Northwest Highway. Live the large life, save big, and update your wardrobes often. Life is good. Many new items, too. *CK, MC, V, D*

★★★ My Sister's Closet — 214/826-6977

6434 E. Mockingbird Lane., Suite 105 — *Tues-Sat 10-5*
Dallas, TX 75214

Sisters unite. After 27 years in the business, My Sister's Closet is still one of the best deals in Dallas. Comfortably situated at the corner of Mockingbird and Abrams with continued emphasis on service and selection, women of independent means in sizes 4-20 empty their closets and recycle their clothes here for a 50/50 split. All the top labels, such as CAROLE LITTLE, CHANEL, EVAN PICCONE, LESLIE LUCKS and LIZ CLAIBORNE were seen, but we didn't hear whose closets were ravaged. Accessorize with jewelry, shoes, belts, bags and scarves. Consignments are accepted and kept in the store for two - three months. Keep an eye out for their colored tag sales. And don't forget to call your sister. After all, what is family for except to share and share alike. *CK, MC, V, AE, D*

★★★ Nearly New Shop, The — 972/245-6144

2105 N. Josey Lane, Suite 322 — *Mon-Thu 10-7; Fri-Sat 10-5:30*
Josey Ranch Shopping Center
Carrollton, TX 75006

What's in a name if the name says it all? At this resale shop, only the nearly new gets chosen. And with price tags so low, you can go to town. Don't worry, be happy with the quality of their suits and dresses. All roads lead to the intersection of Keller Springs and Josey at the Josey Ranch Shopping Center. See suits priced around $40-$45. KASPER suits, for example, were as low as $50 and dresses were priced from $20-$105. Some samples even had their original price tags still on. On the day of our visit, prices were slashed another 20 percent off. A nice selection of good-as-new clothes arrive daily. All sizes, including some for fuller figures, have a consignee split of 50/50.
CK, MC, V, Layaway

★★ North's Plus Size Fashions — 817/737-2174

5405 Birchman Ave. — *Tues-Sat 10-5:30*
Fort Worth, TX 76107

In Tarrant County, fuller-figured women with a sense of style and a mind for saving money head North. This resale and consignment shop near I-30 and

Camp Bowie Blvd. has the larger ladies' fashion niche sewn up, so in these parts, North's has them coming and going in sizes 16 and up. Browse through racks of slacks, tops, blazers, suits, dresses, skirts and sweaters. They don't carry much in the way of formal wear but they can pull together some cute outfits. They have a variety of activewear and some evening wear, although most of their dressier items don't appear until the holidays. This would make you think big girls don't party but once a year...not true! *CK, MC, V, D*

★★ Pretty & Practical Consignments — 817/284-2333

1113 W. Pipeline Rd. — *Mon-Sat 10-6*
Hurst, TX 76053

First came Pretty and Practical. Then came the fans. Then came the spin-off. Carrying clothing for men, women, boys and girls, this consignment store offers a full size range plus toys and furniture, too. To get there from Dallas, the Mid-Cities and northeast Tarrant County, travel on Highway 183 to Precinct Line Rd. Then go south two miles to Pipeline Rd. Turn right, go one mile and look to the right just before the Melbourne Rd. light. From Fort Worth take Highway 121 to I-820 north. Then take the Pipeline/Glenview exit, turn right and look left just past Melbourne Rd. Make some extra spending money by consigning your outgrown children's clothes, then save some money by buying your children's "new" clothes here. Enjoy a 50/50 split once the clothes sell. You will come across a large selection of brand names from almost every quality store out there including GAP, LIZ CLAIBORNE, POLO and TOMMY HILFIGER. Throw your newly bought clothes through one wash cycle and they're ready to wear. *CK, MC, V*

★★★★★ Resale Gallery — 817/285-0633

724-A E. Pipeline Rd. — *Mon-Sat 10-6*
Hurst, TX 76053

Spending more on a wedding dress won't make your marriage better, but starting out with a little more cash on hand might. Who cares if the dress has been worn once before? (As long as it wasn't by you of course.) Even "new" dresses have been tried on by lots of brides. Not really much difference if you think about it. Head to Highway 183, go south on Brown Trail to where it dead ends into Pipeline, then left for two blocks and look for the Resale Gallery on the south side of the street behind Grandy's in the Village Square Shopping Center. Get the most for your money at the largest bridal resale shop in northeast Tarrant County. Bridal gowns, bridesmaid gowns, flower girl dresses, mother-of-the-bride gowns, tuxedo rentals, pageant dresses and evening attire all priced way below the Mason-Dixon line. No bridal gown was seen for more than $300. Now, that's the kind of train to hop aboard. They also offer consultations with their designers for invitations, flowers and made-to-order veils, pillows, garters and baskets. So, put that in your pipeline and start married life with a lot of bang for your buck. *CK, MC, V, D*

★★★★ ReThreads 972/233-9323

411 Preston Valley Shopping Center *Mon-Wed, Fri 10-6:30; Thu 10-8;*
Dallas, TX 75205 *Sat 10-6; Sun 12-6*

Rethink the way you buy clothes by shopping at ReThreads. Tired of the same ole, same ole clothes? Trade them in, trade up, trade around and chances are you'll wind up at ReThreads. Consignment women's and men's apparel, some designer labels, as well as some shoes and accessories are crammed onto the racks and stacks. Equally divided they stand, this large repository houses both men's and women's apparel and accessories. Some plus sizes, too, but the pickings are slim. Tailor available if alterations are needed. Don't expect just any ole garment to make the grade at this Preston Rd. and I-635 shop. They are very particular about what they take in, so check carefully before schlepping your entire wardrobe into the store. Stains, tears, etc. are unacceptable. Great brand names to applaud were ARMANI, LIZ CLAIBORNE, GAP and POLO. Selection of men's clothing is one of the best in the Metroplex. Often times, you'll even find something that still has the original price tag on it...and it, too, will be marked down. For the men's store, call 972/233-1684. *CK, MC, V, AE, D*

★★★★★ Revente-Upscale Resale 214/823-2800

5400 E. Mockingbird Lane., Suite 113 *Mon-Thu 11-7; Fri-Sat 10-6*
Mockingbird Central Plaza
Dallas, TX 75206

Reinvent your wardrobe for less at Revente, across from the old Dr Pepper site (and now home to upscale apartments). This high-end resale shop offers designer and better labels for the working woman or the party gal, including hard-to-find petite, and the full complement of sizes from 2-18. Consignments with the previous wearers are split 50/50 and remain in the store for 60 days. They specialize in designer clothing. Bearers of good tidings report that names such as ANN TAYLOR, BCBG, CALVIN KLEIN, CAROLE LITTLE, DONNA KARAN, ELLEN TRACY, ESCADA, KENAR, LIZ CLAIBORNE, NEIMAN MARCUS and more are quietly hanging around this jam-packed resale shop. If hospitality counts for anything these days, this shop wins the Cordiality Contest. Shop in a beautiful and spacious environment and don't leave without getting decked out in jewelry, shoes, handbags, belts, scarves and hats, too. *CK, MC, V, AE, D*

★★★★★ Ritzy Raggs Ladies Resale — 817/377-1199

6714 Camp Bowie — *Tue-Sat 10-5*
(Town West Center)
Fort Worth, TX 76116

Considered the Rolls-Royce of Ladies Resale in Tarrant County, Ritzy Raggs indeed caters to the hoi polloi. Put on the Ritz with the glitzy crowd who only wears things once or twice. At last, more of us can enjoy the savings on barely worn items from the best closets in town. Designer apparel, shoes, bags, accessories and even new fashions can be bought for less at Ritzy Raggs. Of course, you have to make do with what comes in, but names like ADOLPHO, AFTER FIVE, ALBERT NIPPON, ANNE KLEIN, ARMANI, BIZ, CHANEL, CRISSA, DIANE FREIS, ESCADA, HARI, KASPER, LIZ CLAIBORNE, RALPH LAUREN, ST. JOHN'S KNITS, TERI JON and UNGARO certainly whetted our appetites. Lots of dresses, shoes, belts, purses, suits, casual ensembles and separates, but in the midst of prom season, they were plum running on empty. Also, they're one of the best sources for a great used fur coat (in season) if you would like to pick up something foxy for a fraction of new. Consignments (cleaned, pressed and on hangers) are accepted Thu-Sat 11-4. Whether you're selling or buying (or both), this Town West Shopping Center addition is well worth the drive. *CK, MC, V*

★★★ Robin Hood Designer Resale — 214/360-9666

6609 Hillcrest Rd. — *Mon-Fri 10-6; Sat 10-5*
Dallas, TX 75205

Hit Robin Hood Designer Resale on the right day, and the deals here are a steal. Lucky maidens will score with these women's designer suits, pants, jeans, T-shirts, suits, dresses and blouses. An occasional couture label hits the bullseye, like a ST. JOHN'S KNITS. The other names banded together included ANN TAYLOR, BANANA REPUBLIC, GAP and GAP EXPRESS, J. CREW, RALPH LAUREN and others. After all, they *are* across from SMU. You won't find much larger than a size 10, however. Most of their clothes are in sizes 2 - 8, with a few 10s here and there. *CK, MC, V*

★★★★ S&P Trading Co. 214/369-8977

6104 Luther Lane *Mon-Sat 10-6*
Preston Center
Dallas, TX 75225

Some of Dallas' best-dressed have a secret they aren't sharing. But I will. They aren't just shopping at the tony boutiques about town. No, siree. Some of their most stunning ensembles come direct from this consignment shop. Here you'll find apparel and accessories for women in sizes 2-16 for a fraction of what they were new. They have a great selection of clothing from most of the popular designers in the country but it all depends on the day you visit. Shimmy into more than 1,200 square feet of clothing and accessories–it's a gimme. Consignments are accepted for 60 days with a 50/50 split, unless your item sells for more than $100, then you get 60 percent. S-tylish and P-riced right is this trading company's moniker. *CK, MC, V*

★★★★★ Second Glance 817/581-1909

6304 Rufe Snow Drive *Mon-Sat 9-5*
Fort Worth, TX 76148

When you shop at Second Glance, it means a second chance for abused women and their children. Proceeds go directly to the haven that this shop tirelessly supports. At the stores, you'll find terrific prices on mostly new and gently used children's clothes, men and women's career wear and casual and formal designer-label clothing. You can also find some antiques, furniture, accessories, household items, appliances and collectibles. Every Saturday, at the corner of Watauga and Rufe Snow, there's a gigantic rummage sale where prices are reduced even further. Visit, too their other locations at 2400 W. Pioneer Parkway in Arlington, 817/277-8658, and 1629 Northwest Hwy., Grapevine, 817/416-2953. Volunteers unselfishly renovated and refurbished a house that provides a safe haven for women who have been abused. This non-profit agency, funded by private donations and proceeds from the resale shop, provides homes for the homeless, sanctuary for the battered and bruised, and acceptance for innocent victims of abuse. Volunteers and donations welcome. *CK, MC, V*

★★★★ Spankie's Rethreads 972/227-8822

169 Historic Town Square *Tue-Sat 10-6*
Lancaster, TX 75146

Find Spankie's in an historic building with prices so low, you'll think you're back to the future. Spankie's caters to better children's resale clothing from newborn to size 16 in both boys' and girls' designs. Close the GAP on HUSH PUPPIES and it's over and out in a pair of OSHKOSH B'GOSH overalls. Does CARTER'S still have a toehold on those sleeping buntings? You bet! If you see the yellow and orange tags, slice 50 percent off the price; if you see purple and pink, then it's 75 percent off. They also take a minimum of 10 consignment items (Tuesdays and Saturdays from 10-5) that are clean and on hangers for a 50/50 split. They are only kept on sale for three months. Any stragglers who have not joined Spankie's gang should head down to this cornucopia of second-time-around wardrobes if they want to be part of the "in crowd." Labels are a barometer of tastes from GUESS?, GYMBOREE, LEVI'S, MONKEY WEAR, OSHKOSH B'GOSH and TOMMY HILFIGER. Other items include maternity, baby accessories, toys and more. *CK, MC, V, D*

★★ St. Michael's Exchange — 214/521-3862

#5 Highland Park Village — *Mon-Sat 9:30-5*
Highland Village, TX 75205

Want a good deal on kid's clothes? Go to church. St. Michael's Episcopal Church sells retail gifts and consignment children's clothes to benefit the church and other supported charities. Merchandise is not too expensive, but you will find one or two high-end items. Bargains in children's clothes is the big draw. Want to do a good deed? Go shopping! *CK, MC, V, AE*

★★★ Sweet Repeat — 972/241-7790

3068 Forest Lane, #121 — *Tue-Sat 11:30-5:30*
Dallas, TX 75234

If I've said it once, I've said it a million times. (Need I repeat myself again?) For a bargain shopping experience you'll want to repeat, head to Sweet Repeat, located on the southwest corner of Forest and Webb Chapel, south of the Cinemark and next to Aladdin Beauty School. Don't be afraid to be picky. Choose the best from this resale and consignment shop for children, ladies, men, plus sizes and maternity, as well as decorative items and other sweet things for your home and closet. A repeat performance always commands my attention. *CK, MC, V*

★★★★★ Thrift Mart — 972/721-1861

1131 E. Irving Blvd. — *Mon-Sat 10-8; Sun Noon-6*
Irving, TX 75060

Million dollar babies will love this five and dime. Men's, women's and children's clothing in names that spark the imagination (BUGLE BOY, CALVIN KLEIN, GIRBAUD, NAUTICA, POLO, TOMMY HILFIGER, UNION BAY) were all worn once upon a time, but who knows and who cares? We found pre-owned furniture, exercise equipment and stereos, too. If you're just interested in furniture, call 972/721-9635 for the direct information. For the thrift-concious and the fashion wise, you can't go wrong with any of their buys. *CK, MC, V, AE, D*

★★★★★ Tinka's — 972/716-9944

7989 Beltline Rd., Suite 142 — *Mon-Sat 10-6*
Dallas, TX 75248

Inka, Dinka, Tinka's, too. If you wanna good deal, come on-a this house. Tinka's consignment boutique offers an elegant shopping atmosphere and women's clothing for all occasions with lots of designer labels, after-5 and prom dresses, suits, skirts, blouses, pants and much more. Tinka carries both new and used inventory so, either way, you can save the day. They also have a fantastic selection of jewelry, shoes, handbags, belts, hats and scarves. Buy one piece or a collection in sizes 2-22 with such names as ELLEN TRACY or ESCADA. Give them an A for selection and an E for excellence. *CK, MC, V, AE*

★★ Wardrobe Anonymous — 817/924-1441

3506 Bluebonnet Circle — *Tue-Fri 10:30-6; Sat 10-5:30*
Fort Worth, TX 76109

If you're looking for a four-leaf clover in this Bluebonnet Circle, chances are you won't find any. As luck would have it, we found no name brands either. The good news, though, was there was nothing priced at much more than a few dollar. We found jeans, skirts and lots of blouses in good condition. Not too many suits, but there were tons of Sunday-go-to-meetin' dresses. Consignments are taken by appointment only. If you're looking to add to their collection, they prefer current fashions with name brands. Exit University and go south past the zoo, past Texas Christian University about six or seven blocks until you end up at Bluebonnet Circle. Look for them next to Hardie's Jewelers, just past Fishmonger's Restaurant. *CK, MC, V*

★★★★★ Western Wear Exchange — 817/738-4048

2809 Alta Mere — *Mon-Sat 10-6*
Fort Worth, TX 76116

Grab your partner and promenade home to this good old standby for resale and consignment westernwear. Specializing in gently-worn (but not worn out) jeans, shirts, boots, belts and buckles, vests and hats for the entire family, you can clean up real nice here, yes ma'am. And you sure as heck won't be paying anything like the rustlers down the street have been charging! Bring in your tired jodhpurs, your too-tight jeans or the hat from western days gone by and let this shop sell them for you. Trade in, trade up, but always look the part. Brands including CINCH, JUSTIN, NOCONA, PANHANDLE SLIM, RESISTOL, ROCKY MOUNTAIN, ROPER, STETSON, WRANGLER are just a few to lasso here. *CK, MC, V, AE, D*

Apparel: Vintage

★★★★ Ahab Bowen

214/720-1874

2614 Boll St.
Dallas, TX 75204
Mon-Sat Noon-6; Sun 1-5

Cool cats and groovy chicks can flash back in style at Ahab's. For vintage couture as well as eclectic head-turning stoppers at a fraction of the original price (even without inflation), this funky boutique is the hippest, baby. The early bird gets to wait outside here, as Ahab doesn't open till noon. You'll find a full size range, small to large, with antique purses and women's hats, men's suits and accompanying accessories. Old clothing, funky clothing, trendy clothing–it's all part of Ahab's repetoire. Most prices are under $40–nothing was too pricey. Put a definite time warp on your next semi-formal occasion with a '50s prom dress. Here's looking at you in a Bogie-style fedora, kid. Vintage clothing from the 1940s through the 1970s as well as hats, handbags, costume jewelry, scarves and ties. Both men's and women's clothing have been hanging out here since their opening in 1984. Their best-selling items include men's shirts circa 1970 and women's dresses from the '40s, '50s and '60s. Fast turnover, so shop often, shweetie. *CK, MC, V, AE, D*

★ Casa Loco

214/748-5626

2639-B Elm St.
Dallas, TX 75226
Sun-Mon 2-6; Tue-Sat 2-9

Going to Deep Ellum tonight, but don't have a thing to wear? Here's a loco idea. Make Casa Loco your first stop and step out in something with sass. Tuesdays through Saturday evenings, the store's open until 9. Trendy, somewhat vintage clothing in sizes 1-10 and S-L in alternative, hip clothes similar to those found in Barney's (such as BETSEY JOHNSON.) Though Dallas' hottest nightlifers hang here, sale priced items don't. If you're looking for a deal, you'd be loco to spend too freely here. *MC, V, AE, D*

★★★★★ Just Pennies Vintage Resale — 817/784-2332

3115 S. Cooper — *Mon-Fri 11:30-3, 4-7; Sat 11:30-7*
Arlington, TX 76015

Vintage costumes at vintage prices. For whatever age or occasion, from Halloween getups to flashbacks in fashion, some things do get better with time. If you're into vintage, retro or modern wardrobes for either men or women, this is the place where you can get into a '40s '50s, '60s or '70s look–for just pennies. Just Pennies also has some '80s and '90s looks for those seeking a more contemporary statement. Pull it all together with accessories including jewelry, hats, ties, shoes and purses. Unlike most vintage stores, they carry a full size range from XS to XL. Located one mile north of the Parks Mall and I-20 next to CD Warehouse. When it rains it rains pennies from this resale shop. *MC, V, AE, D*

★★★ Puttin' on the Ritz — 214/369-4015

6615 Snider Plaza — *Tue-Fri 11-5; Sat Noon-5*
Dallas, TX 75205

For beautifully restored vintage clothing and wedding gowns, million dollar troopers shuffle-step it here. From Victorian vintage to '60s funk, the diverse collection of wardrobes at Puttin' on the Ritz is pure perfection. When the occasion calls for a great wedding dress, a drop-dead party look or an elegant costume for the ball, they'll have something really super-duper. Wedding dresses date back as early as the 1880s up to the '60s and sell for $200-$3,000; don't plan to walk down the aisle in one of their vintage gowns, however, unless you're a size 1-10. Whatever the occasion, this shop does its part in helping make you look the part. *CK, MC, V*

★★★★ Ragwear — 214/827-4163

2000 Greenville — *Mon-Sat 11-7; Sun Noon-7*
Dallas, TX 75206

Got the oogie boogie in your socks? Then you've gotta map this joint on lower Greenville. Ragwear's got some of the coolest vintage frocks in town, so don't let their name fool you. Ragwear specializes in clothing 20 years old or older, with most priced under $40. They carry some new repro's, but most clothing is authentic. From top to bottom, they have everything from hats to shoes that are sure to stop the clock the minute you walk in the room. We also found lots of jewelry, bags, sunglasses...even gloves and lacy underthings. New innovative lines that you must check out because they are too cool for school. Across the street from the Arcadia Theater and by Lula B's restaurant, this is Lower Greenville at its best. *CK, MC, V, AE*

★★★★★ Rose Costumes **940/566-1917**
521 N. Elm St. *Mon-Sat 10-6*
Denton, TX 76201 *www.dentononline.com/rosecostume*

The deals are so sweet at this Rose, you can practically smell 'em as you pull up. If you need a visual cue, look for the palm tree awnings and the flamingo mural that greets shoppers. From funky to avant-garde, thousands of costumes from every time period are available. You can rent a 1970s sherbet-tinted tux for $50; 1920s-styled gangster suits for $45; Scarborough Faire-era clothing to become gypsies, knights, faire maidens and scoundrels in the $45 range plus hundreds of hats, shoes, wigs, capes and other unusual costume accessories that are sure to turn heads. For today's Bohemian look, check out Miss Mona's boutique with vintage-inspired clothing for sale. Look for expanded hours near Halloween. Here's just a sampling of costumes: Captain Hook, Elvis, Cher, Minnie Pearl, Zorro, Sherlock Holmes, Darth Vader, Lady Godiva (can't be MUCH of a costume), Keystone Cop, clowns, royalty, fireman, old-time bathing suits, bag lady, calypso, Rhett Butler, Wizard of Oz, Pinocchio, Flintstones, poodle skirts, cheerleaders, gorilla, Easter bunny, pilgrims, nativity, gamblers, can-can dancers, a beer can, belly dancer, witch doctor, devil, rabbit, chicken, cow, wolf, pink elephant and much more, including couple costumes such as Abraham and Mary Todd Lincoln, Marilyn Monroe and Joe DiMaggio, Mickey and Minnie Mouse, Dallas Cowboy cheerleader and Troy Aikman, Lucy and Ricky Ricardo, John and Lorena Bobbit, Father Mulcahey and Hot Lips Hoolihan and more. Wait a minute. John Bobbit??? *CK, MC, V*

Apparel: Women's

★★✯ A&A Fashions — 972/241-858?

11363 Denton Drive — *Mon-Sat 10-6*
Dallas, TX 75229

Gather 'round here if western wear is your thang. Located just a hop, skip and a long-jump from Harry Hines, A&A sells a high-scoring selection of women's sportswear from all across America. How patriotic! Overall, the selection is plentiful and the gentleman in charge was a real charmer. After all, theyíre devoted to selling all-American clothing, and at prices that'll make you feel proud to be in America. *CK, MC, V, AE*

✔ Amy Alexandra — 214/688-5235

1231 Wycliff — *July & December weekend sales*
Dallas, TX 75207

It happens twice a year, and if you're one of the few in the know, these sales are your V.I.P. pass to 50-70 percent savings on designer clothes that rival those displayed in the best specialty boutiques in the country. Three-day-only sales and no phone number means you need to get on their mailing list. Their summer sale is held in July. Look for their fall clearance early December. No dressing rooms–bring a friend and a tape measure. No retail amenities. On this showroom floor, you'll find casual denim to elegant chiffon dresses, from black tie to casual chic, there's a large enough selection in both casual sportswear and career dresses to justify a few days off. We bought a long crepe jacket and short skirt with black piping for $44 that would run four or five times that in a specialty store. Now, that's my kind of dressing. *CK, MC, V, AE, D*

★★★★ Apparel World — 972/247-9692

11363 Denton Drive, Suite 205 — *Mon-Fri 10-6; Sat 10-5*
International Plaza
Dallas, TX 75229

Experience the real difference between retail and wholesale when you walk into this real outlet. Slink out in acetate, garment-dyed, linen, cotton and knit casual wear in the spring or velvet garments, dyed sweater sets and denim in the fall–apparel-ly the selection is staggering. At last, one of the country's leading wholesalers has opened its warehouse doors to the public and sells a full size range of specialty ladies' fashions–dresses, blouses, slacks and more–from juniors to plus sizes, priced at $15-$75. You can outfit yourself from the bottoms to the tops in sportswear, dresses, sweaters, activewear, separates and denims. And it's all honest-to-goodness wholesale. *CK, MC, V, AE, D*

★★★ Avenue 214/358-5642

3701 W. Northwest Hwy. *Mon-Sat 10-8*
Dallas, TX 75220

THE AVENUE is now its own private label. Formerly Plus Sizes, Plus Savings, that means out with the brand names, and down with the prices on clothing for fuller figures. Sportswear, dresses and coats all figure in the inventory in sizes 16-30/32. Looks like a retail store, they treat you like you're in a retail store, but they'll still save you money like a discount store. Nice, big, sales personnel complete the picture. Also visit their location in Red Bird at 3265 W. Camp Wisdom and across from Vista Ridge Mall on I-35 in Lewisville. *CK, MC, V, D*

★★★★★ Bierner & Son Hat Factory Outlet 214/634-1286

3120 Commonwealth *Mon-Thu 8:30-4; Fri 8:30-Noon*
Dallas, TX 75247

Texans have never been shy about expressing themselves. So when it comes to finding the perfect statement for the occasion, this place is a-head of the crowd. Climb the back iron steps into one of the largest (if not the only) hat manufacturers in the country. This outlet makes any dame dizzy for derbies, or for whatever style is you. Choose from straws and organza, feathers or boas, buttons and bows for the Easter Parade. Save up to 50 percent over department store prices (even more on out-of-season styles). From felt to straw (depending on the season), this outlet has more than 300 hats for you to try on. So, grab your coat, and don't forget your hat. *CK, MC, V ($25 min with credit card)*

★★★ C'est la Vie! 214/939-0074

163 Cole Ave. *Mon-Fri 7-5*
Dallas, TX 75207

Guess what lucky ducks? Now you can buy the lovely clothes you see in

Coldwater Creek catalogs direct from the source. One of their clothing contractors has an outlet store in Dallas. How lucky can we be? Take I-35 south to Oak Lawn. Turn west and then south on Industrial, then right on Cole. Call before you go as there are times when stock is so low, it's hardly worth your while. When production picks up, run. Then you can pick up samples and overruns on fabulous-looking women's apparel, casual sportswear, fun dresses, pant sets and jackets in misses 4-14, Petite, S-XL. They also have Plus sizes. If you're a fan of the catalog or website (www.coldwatercreek.com), you'll love fanning yourself with the dollars you'll be saving. C'est la Vie! *CK*

★★★★★ Carolyn's Boutique — 972/724-1457

2900 Chaparral Drive — *By Appt. Only*
Flower Mound, TX 75022

People will think your outfit cost $1,000. The fact that you most likely paid less than $100 can be our little secret. But you must meet Carolyn, who will see that you are waited on hand and foot in this personalized boutique. But by appointment only do you get the privilege of being catered to and saving money at the same time. This Flower Mound hideaway offers wholesale prices, some appeared less than wholesale. Sizes Small to 3X covers the Metroplex in knock-out outfits and accessories (scarves and jewelry) from BLUE FISH and VERSACE lookalikes and name brands. Simplify your life with styles that are wash-and-wear, no-iron, cut-off-the-hem-to-shorten-and-go, man, go! From the Junior League to the League of Women Voters, dressing the part is half the fun. This former school teacher now dresses others for the classroom or nights out on the town. A black acetate pants set with leopard trim for $85.99 by TANUJA DIOR was the cat's meow! *CK, MC, V, AE*

★★ Cato — 972/436-7885

724 W. Main — *Mon-Sat 10-9; Sun 1-6*
Lewisville, TX 75067

Fair maidens will find fair prices at Cato.This women's apparel specialty store carries misses, junior and plus-size sportswear, careerwear, coats, hosiery, shoes and accessories priced for those shopping on a budget. You'll get the right look at this national chain offering the right price on Juniors, Misses, Girls (in select locations) and Plus sizes. Anything goes (as long as it's at a discount) in sizes 7-16 children's, juniors and misses, as well as 14-28 plus sizes. Clothes made especially for their stores with names like CAROLINA COLORS and STUDIO C.

This Cato never took the stand, but if you shop here, you could be dressed to kill. Tops were the tops at $10; dresses at $20; and shorts and pants for $15. What fun. What fervor. What fabulous prices you have, my dear. *CK, MC, V, D*

★★★★★ Clothes-Out 817/731-0086

3710 W. Vickery *Thu-Fri 10-6; Sat 10-5*
Fort Worth, TX 76107

For more than eight years, Fort Worth's finest fashion brokers have been working hard to help us fight inflation. They only work three days a week, but if everything we bought was 50-80 percent off like it is here, the rest of us would only have to work three-day weeks, too. *The Fort Worth Star-Telegram* says Clothes-Out is one of the top 15 places to shop in the Metroplex, other than the malls. Oh dear. What a distinction. What do they mean other than the malls? In any case, at Clothes-Out, you can get great deals on designer dresses and suits, separates, sportswear in sizes 2-26 and accessories. Sweaters, vests, purses, belts and lots more round out the opportunities. Sterling silver and costume jewelry also caught our eye. ON THE VERGE denims were plentiful, too. New inventory every week (close-outs, of course!) Also visit their location at 4201 W. Green Oaks Blvd., #400 in Arlington, 817/483-7418. *CK, MC, V*

★★★★★ Designer Group, The 972/335-9176

6991 Main *Tue-Sat 10-5*
Frisco, TX 75034

The fashion capital of Frisco is downtown at The Designer Group, where room after room is filled with choice selections from casual to dressy-country and a category we like to call "North Dallas Society!" An expanded stock awaits you–lots of separates and casual pieces in cottons, linens and blends. Lots of fun and funky labels like BARBARA LESSOR, FAITH & SURYA, FRESH PRODUCE, IRIS SINGER and SOFTWEAR. You'll also be dazzled by accessories, gifts, shoes and special buys. Go north...far north. Past Plano. Past Highway 121. And when you hit Main, you've reached the end of the road. Turn left. Shop often, as the stock changes frequently. What you see may be it, so grab it while you can. Look for the cream and green building at the corner of Fifth and Main. Whenever we shop here, we're amazed at the low prices. Eliminate the Crisco and you'll save in Frisco. *CK, MC, V, AE, D*

Apparel: Women's

★★★★★ Discount Dresses

214/634-3366

1304 Inwood Rd.
Dallas, TX 75247

Mon-Sat 10-7
www.discountdressesonline.com

This sibling of Seventh Ave. Plus Sizes outlet is off and running. Now you can dress up at dressed down prices–at Discount Dresses. Here you'll find the perfect prom or mother-of-the-bride dress for as low as $99. This place also has an extensive selection of plus formal and casualwear for the full spectrum of dressing at a discount. You'll save up to 75 percent off retail prices with their guaranteed low prices. How can you lose? *MC, V, AE, D*

★★ Dress Barn

972/437-0967

1361 W. Campbell Rd.
Richardson, TX 75080

Mon-Fri 10-8; Sat 10-7; Sun 1-5
www.dressbarn.com

You can lead a shopper to water, but you can't make them drink. You won't go thirsty at this Dress Barn. At least they try to give you something to slip on. The lessons to be learned are plain and simple: you don't have to offer the biggest discounts in town to have folks coming back for more. Stop stall-ing around and see for yourself why women are somehow satisfied with the unimpressive 20 percent discounts (and more so as the season wanes.) An adequate selection of career and casual wear brings 'em to the barn at a full gallop. Name-brands were sporadic, but we did see ATRIUM (a KASPER knock-off), ISAAC HAZEN, LEE DAVIS, SIGNA and WESTPORT (the name they used to use on their store signage). They also have accessories including necklaces, pantyhose and belts for 20 percent off. Nine other locations in the DFW area, including Terrell and Gainesville. Open a Dress Barn charge account and receive an additional 10 percent off your first purchase. Whoopee! *CK, MC, V, AE, D, Dress Barn*

★★★★ Escada, Co.

972/355-8186

3000 Grapevine Mills Pkwy.
Grapevine Mills Mall
Grapevine, TX 76051

Mon-Sat 10-9:30; Sun 11-8
www.escada.com

Sorry, but I can't just up the star ante when it comes to the Escada outlet. Anyone paying almost $3,000 for a suit combo just because its label oozes of Hide and Sleek needs to have their head examined. But if it's this fabled label you're after, this is where Escada-seekers meet Underground Shoppers. So what if it's last season's style–who can pass up an Escada blouse, jacket and slacks combo, regularly priced at $2,885, but here for $1,727? For donning snob apparel, head to their outlet but expect last season's leftovers to evoke the rave notices. What you'll see are big shoulders, bright colors and short skirts from past collections reduced 40 to 60 percent. Even saw a few LAUREL brands. *CK, MC, V, AE, D*

♥♥♥♥♥ F.L. Malik — 214/638-0550

8303 Chancellor Row — *Special sale hours only*
Dallas, TX 75247 — *www.flmalik.com*

The doors fly open eight times a year at this manufacturer of department and specialty store clothes. Buy two items at wholesale, get the third one free, for unlimited possibilities. Get a leg up during their periodic warehouse sales when year-end liquidations can net huge savings. Clothes from department and specialty stores make their final exit out the back doors of their warehouse. But be aware that only the ladies on The List get in. Call to get on their mailing list to receive an invitation or to find out the date of the next sale. All it takes is a phone call. Prices are 40-50 percent off retail. Twice a year they offer seasonal blowouts where everything is $16.99 or less. *CK, MC, V*

★★★★★ Fashion Corner Discount Boutique — 972/991-9366

5519 Arapaho, Suite 110 — *Tue-Fri 10-6; Sat 10-5*
Dallas, TX 75248

What did one wallflower say to the other wallflower? Meet me at Fashion Corner, of course. At up to 80 percent below retail every day, drab closets can spring into season fast. Fashion Corner offers a small boutique atmosphere with friendly fashion consultants to help you coordinate great looks from their fresh selection of career and casual apparel, dresses, sportswear and separates, grouped in misses sizes 4-20 (S-XL). Now for the best part. Discounts average 60 percent off, but soar to 80 percent when the spirit moves them. New arrivals hang out weekly. The accessories here start as low as $7. They also have a terrific selection of jewelry, belts and handbags to complete the fashion look. Look for a new fashion overhaul on Arapaho between Preston Road and the North Dallas Tollway. Their Mockingbird location has closed, so all sites converge in North Dallas. *CK, MC, V, AE, D*

★★★★★ Fast Fashion — 214/634-4181

1321 Regal Row — *Mon-Fri 8:30-6; Sat 8-3*
Dallas, TX 75247-3615

No one but you has to know how cheap (or is "economical" a nicer way to say that?) you are. Thousands of dresses, pants, pant suits and tops that you see in retail stores all over the country (and plenty on Harry Hines) are sold here at the lowest prices seen anywhere. Row after row of wholesale shopping for the casual Metroplex lifestyle. It's almost an endless assignment, but someone's got to do it. You can shop 'til your feet blister (I did!) because the warehouse seems endless. If you find a lower price within 30 days of the invoice date, they'll refund the difference or give you credit. Get a copy of their catalog and reorder without the stranglehold of full price. Plenty of knit tops and matching pant sets with appliques that can take you from the ballpark to a bunko. Dig through the massive cartons of imported handbags and find yourself a few hundred lookalikes at $15-$20. No one will know but you. Across from the Mary Kay Building, see ya! *MC, V, D, MO*

★ House of George — 214/630-1631

2610 Irving Blvd. — *Mon-Fri 9:30-5:30; Sat 9:30-1*
Dallas, TX 75207

Before you go into another house of prayer, visit House of George. Specializing in church dresses and suits, this manufacturer of dresses, sportswear and rompers in misses sizes is rumored to save you 50 percent or more. Pray you see more than we did though–only one rack and it was so dark, we probably couldn't tell white from wrong anyway. Specialties of the House include career garments and suits sizes 6-22. Remember, bring cash (and a flashlight) as they don't take credit cards. *C*

★★★ Inlook Outlet, The — 214/630-5320

1431 Regal Row — *Mon-Sat 9:30-5*
Dallas, TX 75247

Real outlets come in all shapes and sizes. This one is small, but the savings are a true 50 percent and more on moderate missy dresses and sportswear to size 24 from the Jerell Company (now part of the Haggar empire). Save on dresses, pantsuits and a few accessories. Lots of denim, khaki, handkerchief broomstick skirts and vests spotted on our last visit. First-quality samples and some irregulars can be found in misses, petite and plus sizes. The outlet on Regal Row is where the corporate offices are housed and is little more than "two walls, two aisles." Visit their slightly larger stores at 6245 Rufe Snow, Watauga, 817/428-0115, and in Waxahachie at the corner of highways 77 and 287. *CK, MC, V, D*

★★ Kay's Kloset

972/436-6543

1106-A W. Main
Lewisville, TX 75067
Mon-Fri 10-8; Sat 10-6; Sun 1-5

At Kay's Kloset, you will find everything you'd want for your own closet but didn't know who to ask. But it's their dynamic sales that bring the crowds out of the closet. Can't reveal some of the brands of shoes and purses 'cause if I speak, they'll freak! At Kay's Kloset, they make the deals with clothiers in the market so that they can pass the savings on to you. Brand names include AMBITIONS, CAROL ANDERSON, CALIFORNIA IVY, FOCUS 2000, GINA PETERS, LIV, MAC & JAC, MY WEEKEND CLOTHER, TRIBAL and more. At Kay's, they don't skirt the issue when it comes to offering a great selection of women's shoes. If you like the sound of periodic 50 percent off labels you never see at a savings, then add Kay's to your shopping "must-do's." *CK, MC, V, AE, D*

★★★★★ L'eggs-Hanes-Bali-Playtex

972/881-1006

1717 E. Spring Creek Pkwy.
Plano, TX 75074
Mon-Sat 9-9; Sun Noon-6
www. Myfavoriteoutlet.com

Got legs? Walk this way. Supporting every popular brand from BALI to HANES, L'EGGS and PLAYTEX, this outlet dresses legs for less. Find first-quality and irregular men's, women's and children's socks and pantyhose, including full-figured varieties. Save 20-50 percent, plus lots more during sales. The price for SHEER ENERGY was only $7.54 for three pairs. We also picked up some first-quality HANES HER WAY panties for $1 less than seen at Wal-Mart. Seeing is believing, so let's see those legs get moving. *CK, MC, V, AE, D*

♥♥♥♥♥ Legends Boutique

972/250-0502

17390 Preston Rd.
Dallas, TX 75252
Mon-Fri 10:30-6; Sat 11-5

Direct from Seventh Avenue to you, Legends is making a name for itself by bringing New York and California's trend-setting best to Dallas. This is the place to find knock-their-socks-off after-5 looks for high school reunions and Carribbean cruises. Dressed-to-impress big-city suits and sportswear can go home to create your legendary wardrobe, all priced right for the value represented and punctuated with the perfect accessories. A full size range is available from 2-12 sporting labels such as BETTE PAIGE, BIANCA-NERRO, CUSTO, ESSENDI, TEMPESTA, WAYNE ROGERS and other notables too numerous to mention. Add coordinated gorgeous fashion jewelry, handbags and terrific gift items like TRAPP CANDLES and it spells a Legend in their own time. So, why not, "Make my day!" *CK, MC, V, AE, D*

★★ One-Price Clothing Store — 972/399-1434

231 Plymouth Park — *Mon-Sat 10-7; Sun 1-6*
Irving, TX 75061

Do your closet a favor this week. Get to One-Price Clothing and save 50 - 80 percent in casual sundresses, slacks, blouses, knits, shorts, biker shorts with matching tops, T-shirts, rompers, earrings, sunglasses, hair clips, socks, belts and more. In small sizes up to 3X, this is the place to stock up on closet-fillers without emptying your bank account. New shipments arrive every Wednesday. There are several other locations in the Metroplex, so check directory for the one nearest you. *CK, MC, V, D*

★★★★ PS Plus Sizes — 972/239-3517

13309 Montfort Drive — *Mon-Fri 10-8:30; Sat 10-6; Sun Noon-5*
Dallas, TX 75240 — *www.catherines.com*

P.S. The pluses are obvious here. You can dress with panache for 20-30 percent less. During promotional events and seasonal sales, which are often, mature fashions, lingerie and hosiery for the fuller figure are discounted up to 60 percent. This offshoot of the Catherine Stout retail stores caters to the shopper who just happens to like discounted prices. In sizes 16W-34W and 16WP-26WP, you can find casual to career outfits for all seasons; name-brand and designer sportswear, dresses, pantsuits and dressy garb abound. With the exception of some Omar-the-Tentmaker type outfits, most were both camouflaging and chic. P.S.S. Check your directory for other locations. *CK, MC, V, AE, D*

★★★ Pursley Discount Fashions — 972/298-3384

208 N. Main — *Mon-Wed, Fri-Sat 9:30-6:30; Thu 9:30-8*
Duncanville, TX 75116

If you want to experience first-quality bargains from someone with experience, you've come to the right place. Since 1955, this fixture in fashion has been delivering the bargains in dresses, sportswear, sweaters, fabrics and notions from the same Main Street location in Duncanville. First-quality and some seconds (all clearly marked) are available at each of their stores (though their Duncanville store is still the grandest). Dresses ranged from $5-$125 with lots of dresses in the $60 range, but we like them best when their closeout or end-of-season shipments arrive. We found ANN TOBIAS, JENNIFER JEFFRIES, LESLIE LUCKS, MELISSA and REBECCA HARRIS priced to keep us laughing all the way home. (It also put a smile on our bank account.) Also look for locations in Lancaster, West and Hubbard. *CK, MC, V*

★★★★★ Rhodes Collection 214/342-9400

1621 S. Jupiter, Suite #102 *Wed-Sat 10-5:30*
Garland, TX 75042

You don't have to be a Rhodes Scholar to know a fantastic deal when you see one. One of the few remaining local women's apparel manufacturers that has survived and prospered, Rhodes Collection sells career fashions so low it defies logic. Smart shoppers know to buy direct and bypass needless retail markups. Case in point, when you shop at Rhodes Collection, you save 50 to 80 percent (and even more during their warehouse sales) across the board. Their repertoire is extensive: suits, coordinates, separates and accessories in the fullest spectrum of sizes, from 2-34. Need a new suit? Find them here in petite, misses, tall and plus sizes. Across from E-Systems, they're an easy jaunt off LBJ and Jupiter. Thought you'd want to know. *CK, MC, V, D*

★★★★ Secrets 972/239-5822

14315 Inwood, Suite 106 *Mon-Fri 10-5:30; Sat 9-5*
Farmers Branch, TX 75244

I love sharing secrets, especially when I can help you find really great stuff at underground prices. Secrets is just such a place. You used to have to size up the Apparel Mart to find this great stuff, but now it's laid out for you in all its 2-14 slinky-sized glory. One room of samples, another room of competitively priced merchandise and lots of jewelry and one-of-a-kind artsy stuff. Look for the turquoise awning and enter a boutique of bargains. Prices on clothing started around $21–better suits priced to $400. Some of the brands noticed were ALBERTA MACAULEY, ESSENDI, FORWEAR OF NY, GARFIELD & MARKS, JACKET REQUIRED, LIA, TELLURIDE and others. Chi-chi, smart and perfect for patrons and matrons. Look for their biannual sales when prices are slashed to 75 percent off. Now there's a deal you can't refuse. In the jewelry department, don a man-made azurite gemstone that has been cut in Belgium and see if you can spot it from the real McCoy–even with a jeweler's loop. All the jewelry here is set in 14- or 18-Karat gold or platinum, and each stone comes with a lifetime guarantee against discoloration, fading or breaking. Then, continuing the faux de grace, try the gloves trimmed in fake fur or take a peak at the line of SYDENSTRICKER glass. Artists and collectors have been fascinated by this product for years and now it's right here in Big D. Pieces are on exhibit in many major galleries and museums, including the Toronto Museum of Art, Winter Park's Tiffany Museum in Florida., the Chrysler Museum and the Museum of Modern Art in New York. Complimentary coffee and colas served to shoppers. If you're a real friend, tell a friend about this place. *CK, MC, V, AE*

★★★★★ Seventh Ave. Plus Size Outlet 214/638-9033

1331 Inwood Rd. *Mon-Wed 10-6; Thu- Fri 10-7; Sat 10-6; Sun Noon-5*
Dallas, TX 75247

If your bra cups runneth over, cheers! Seventh Ave. Plus Size Outlet boasts 11,000 square feet of the best plus-sized fashions in the world. Take one whopping step for womankind and soar with this selection of plus sizes. From suits to sequins, you'll never be left out in the cold if you are a size 14-32. One line, made exclusively for Seventh Ave. by R&B WOMAN, fits up to size 5X. Top it off with a hat, a pair of earrings (some as low as $1.99), a scarf or belt, and you've got the whole shebang under one roof. Located off Stemmons where all twains meet, watching the friendly sales ladies work the dressing rooms is a sight worth seeing. Of course, it's the customers who are knee deep with buys at the cash register who know the real draw. Finally, there's a place where zaftig babes can bargain shop at the guaranteed lowest prices. Save 40-60 percent (and more) on designer clothes such as embellished suits, career suits, evening suits, career dresses, evening dresses, sportswear, jeans, blouses, hats, accessories, earrings and more. Needless to say, I'm big on this place. *CK, MC, V, AE, D*

★★★ Sheryl's Basement 214/630-9499

9011 Carpenter Frwy. *Mon-Sat 10-7; Sun Noon-6*
(Carpenter at Regal Row)
Irving, TX 75247

The store on Carpenter is referred to as "Sheryl's Basement" and the other stores are just plain Sheryl's. By either name, there's a reason to shop here for clothing in women sizes 4 - 24. For one, Sheryl's offers a good selection of dresses and sportswear, career apparel, business suits, casual clothing, misses, juniors, petites and plus sizes. Their stock changes rapidly, so the early birds gather the cream of the crop. Save big at their end-of-season sales. Additional Metroplex locations: Duncanville, 972/298-9855; Mesquite, 972/288-9048; and Fort Worth, 817/292-6373.

In former lives, Sheryl's, which has been around Dallas for an eon or two–since the first edition of *The Underground Shopper*–was first called Original Manufacturer's Outlet when it was on East Grand, then Suzanne's, now Sheryl's. Owner Tom Spiegel continues to reign supreme. *CK, MC, V, AE, D*

★★ Simply Fashions — 214/946-8929

257 Wynnewood Village — Mon-Sat 10-7; Sun 1-5
Dallas, TX 75244

Guilt-free splurging goes on at this place, because while the quality varies dramatically, the prices are always dirt cheap. That's the Cliff's Notes version, plain and simple. If you feel the need to shop even when your better sense tells you to wait, treat yourself to a closet full of jeans, shorts, T-shirts, skirts, jumpers and dresses in sizes 2-52 for next to nothing. In our test shopping run, some of the cotton blends lost their shape and color after a few washings, while our shorts from last year are still looking good. Lots of clearance items for even better deals. The highest priced item was around $35–and not worth more. If you are looking for a junior miss, miss, plus or super plus, this is Simply Fashions to consider for its "Cents and Sensibility." *CK, MC, V, AE, D*

★★★★★ Special Occasion Dresses — 972/732-8900

19009 Preston Rd. — Mon-Thu 10-8; Fri-Sat 10-6
Dallas, TX 75252

Glitz and glamour for 70 percent less than retail? Sounds special enough for me to check out. When you do, choose from more than 30,000 outfits in stock per store (three locations and one outlet store in Fort Worth). If it's romance that you want to wear, this is the spot. Save on dinner dresses, evening dresses, semi-formal wedding dresses, dresses for the prom, dresses for that black-tie affair, dresses for the club meeting, dresses to wear on the cruise–if it's a dressy occasion, your salvation lies in Special Occasion. Sizes 2-24 to snare off the racks and racks of beaded and sequined dresses to fit every occasion, shape, season and style. If you have seen it in a department store, buy it here for less. They have a large number of dresses for under $100, with markdowns each week. Also save up to 70 percent with such pearls of wisdom as an off-white wedding dress by PRECIOUS FORMALS with pearl, lace and mesh inlays, sheer sleeves with seed pearls, regular price $400, their price $249; or a navy dress by JOVANI, regular price $500, their price $299; and a burgundy dress by SHARON TOP, regular $250, their price $199. Special Occasion has the largest selection of mother-of-the-bride dresses in the

Metroplex. Big dressing rooms add to the special services without feeling compromised. Accessorize with sequin jackets, evening shoes, jewelry and handbags, too, even dyed to match when necessary. More Special Occasions in Arlington in Lincoln Square, 817/226-0100, and in Dallas at the southwest corner of Walnut Hill and Central Expressway, 214/691-1300. Their outlet store in Fort Worth at Hulen Square Center, Hulen and Granbury, 817/361-9200, has dresses priced from $19.99-$99.99, regularly up to $400. P.S. Shoppers tell me while other stores' prices went up this past year, Special Occasion Dresses prices actually went down. See, I told you. *CK, MC, V, AE, D*

★★★ Suzanne's 214/638-8429

1335 Inwood *Mon-Wed, Fri-Sat 10-6; Thu 10-7; Sun Noon-5*
Inwood Trade Center
Dallas, TX 75247

Suzanne's can save you money, but on which name brands depends on their catch of the day. Some days you might see fancy names like ANNE KLEIN or DONNA KARAN, and on other days (as was the case the day we visited), you might see ONYX NIGHTS, PAPILLON and VIANCO. What you will find every day are moderately-priced garments that will have you looking like a million bucks. They specialize in career-wear and suits starting at $75, but you'll also find better sportswear and casual separates. They offer 30-day layaway so if you see a name you like, you better lay it away, 'cause you may not see it again until a later rainy day. *CK, MC, V, AE, D*

★★★★★ Talbot's Outlet 972/315-5900

500 E. Round Grove Rd., Suite 101 *Mon-Fri 10-9; Sat 10-6; Sun Noon-5*
The Shops at Vista Ridge *www.talbots.com*
Lewisville, TX 75067

If you love their catalog, their outlet store will be a best seller. Great selection, great prices and great service are top drawer with our dressers. How is all this possible? When a shirt doesn't sell at one of the Talbot's regular retail stores, it reunites with similar fashions, which are consolidated into one of Talbot's Outlet shops. Happily for local ladies, one of the three outlet locations in Texas is right up the road in Lewisville (the others are in Houston and San Marcos). Items here are at least 50 percent off their original retail price. Next to the Vista Ridge Mall off FM 3040 at the corner of Round Grove and MacArthur, you'll see the gamut of women's and children's clothing from petite and children's wear through size 24W. No occasion goes undressed. They specialize in conservative tailoring (nothing far-out or trendy) in the basics. Suits, dresses, evening attire, bridesmaid's dresses and even coats are found in this jammed-to-the-gills repository that has taken the Metroplex by storm. *CK, MC, V, AE*

★★★★★ Tiny Thru Plus Size Outlet 817/265-DRESS

705 Secretary Drive *Tue-Sat 10-5; After 5 by Appt. Only*
Arlington, TX 76015

One of the area's true wholesale locations, Tiny Thru Plus Size Outlet in Arlington sells the same clothes that many popular retailers do, just without the label and the fatter price tag. Many Dallas area manufacturers are contracted for private label merchandise that is sold to department stores; then the stores affix their own labels. If you want to save on them, and I mean thousands of them, go 1.5 miles north of I-20 off Matlock, and turn left at the Texaco. Dresses, suits and pantsuits in sizes 2-34, plus petites with thousands of brands to choose from, direct from the manufacturer. Expect to shell out $29-$69 instead of retail prices of $90-$350. According to those in the know, this is the best fashion warehouse in the mid-cities. A word of caution. If you are planning a special trip just to visit here, call ahead. On occasional weekends, when they take their show on the road (Janie's Traveling Dress Outlet), they're only open three weekdays, so make sure they are open for business before you head out. Fortunately, they always return and don't leave us naked in the aisles. They have two huge local sales a year, the second through the third weeks of January and July where everything is marked down again, with an extra $10 off on whole outfits. *CK, MC, V, D*

★★★★★ Wycliff Dress Factory Outlet 214/634-8444

1305 Wycliff *Mon-Fri 10-5:30; Sat 10-5*
(Wycliff at Monitor)
Dallas, TX 75247

Another sibling was born from Seventh Ave. Plus Sizes, only this outlet caters to the smaller figures in the fashionable spectrum. Thousands of dresses with savings skyrocketing to 75 percent off. Party dresses, career dresses, special occasion dresses, suits, separates–priced as low as $10. Samples, overruns, irregulars, dogs...in sizes 2-14. Tons of clothes for dirt cheap. What else can I say except, "Wy jump off the Cliff over high prices?" Shop at the Wycliff Dress Factory Outlet instead. The end. *CK, MC, V, AE, D*

Appliances

★★★★★ Allen's Wholesale Appliance Outlet 972/727-4798

103 N. Austin Drive *Mon-Fri 8-5:30; Sat 8:30-3*
Allen, TX 75013

When parent company Rodenbaugh's Appliances takes its brand-name appliances out of the box for display, only to finds a dent or scratch, or simply needs to move the older inventory out, Allen's gets them, in turn selling them for 15-30 percent less. Once run as more of a sideline to its retail store, Allen's Wholesale Appliance Outlet now stands alone and all we can say is, "Yeah!" Name brands like AMANA, JENN-AIR and WHIRLPOOL in cook-tops, ovens, refrigerators (some side-by-side), dishwashers, washers and microwaves priced to cook 'em hot but sell 'em low. If by chance you can't find it at the outlet, check with their parent company next door. Prices are even acceptable there. This family-owned and operated business stands behind everything they sell and service everything they sell. All appliances carry a full warranty. *CK, MC, V, D*

★★★★★ Appliance Builder Sales 972/701-8181

4550 McEwen *Mon-Fri 8-5; Sat 10-2*
Dallas, TX 75244

Looking for that built-in look in your kitchen? Picture them snug as a bug in every nook and crevice thanks to Appliance Builder Sales (down the street from the Gabberts Furniture Outlet.). Look for the blue awning, and let these people bring your mental picture (even if it is torn out of a magazine) to reality. The appliance brands include SUB-ZERO refrigerators, JENN-AIR, MAGIC CHEF and MAYTAG stoves, cook tops, free-standing ranges and microwaves, as well as washers and dryers. The best names join your remodeling project or find a new home in a custom cabinet. These are the folks to seek and you shall receive. *CK, MC, V, D*

★★★ Appliance Concepts

972/235-4231

4614 Princeton Drive
Garland, TX 75042
Mon-Fri 8-5

Total Home Service is now Appliance Concepts, which now sells new and refurbished appliances, not electronics. Appliance Concepts also services the appliances they sell for a $40/service call. Catering to those who squeak on a dime, they have washers and dryers, microwaves, dishwashers, ovens, cooktops, microwaves, and can fix you up, one way or another. Washer/dryer sets were around $400 and these include MAYTAG and WHIRLPOOL. Refrigerators were $300 and up. All products came with at least a 30-day, and up to a six-month, warranty. Many of the appliances were between 5 and 10 years old; while a few sneaking in under 5 years old. A concept whose time has come. Aren't you believers yet? *CK*

★★★★★ Arrow Appliance

817/465-5660

2902 W. Pioneer Pkwy.
Arlington, TX 76013
Mon-Fri 9-6; Sat 10-4

Best brands. Bulls-eye pricing. And the only place in the Metroplex where we could find practically brand new 30-inch, built-in stovetop and microwave for just $399. Sure, we could have paid $1,100 for it somewhere else, but if anyone can smell a deal, the Underground Shopper's nose can because it is one finely-tuned sniffer. Yes, it even comes with a 1-year warranty. So, if used and reconditioned will do, this place is right on the money. Owner Chuck Friberger has been buying and selling used appliances (washers, dryers and refrigerators) for years and he only carries the best brands like: GE, KENMORE, MAYTAG, WHIRLPOOL and more. Washers started as low as $99 and refrigerators were $159. Whether you need appliances for your second home or your first, when you want it for less, these guys hit the mark. *CK, MC, V, D*

✧✧✧✧✧ Broward Factory Service

metro 817/640-1772

1225-F Corporate Drive E.
Arlington, TX 76006
Mon-Fri 8-5

Buying a house that has been lived in before? Always insist the sellers throw in a home warranty. Don't you know, two weeks after you move in, the A/C will run hot as the oven runs cold? Well, here's the answer to the house you're already living in. Before your 4-year-olds get into trouble, get with the plan, Stan. For $199 a year, you can insure your older appliances in case they have a breakdown. That's what Broward Factory Service does. This is what they cover: central air conditioning, refrigerators, heating (gas or electric), wall thermostats, ovens/ranges, water heaters, freon recovery, dishwashers and disposals. Not a bad investment when you think about all the blips in the night. *CK, MC, V, AE*

★★★ Direct Maytag Home Appliance — 972/404-0040

13536 Preston Rd. — *Mon-Fri 9-6; Sat 10-5*
Dallas, TX 75240 — *www.maytag.com*

Want a MAYTAG washer, dryer, refrigerator, dishwasher, range, wall oven, cook top or microwave? Buy it direct. Direct Maytag carries all MAYTAG products and they stock the parts and accessories, too. The prices are retail, but competitive. The real bonus is the longer warranty and the direct connection should you ever need to use it. Three Metroplex locations. *CK, MC, V, AE, D*

✧✧✧✧ Gunn Appliance Repair — 214/823-2629

Dallas, TX 75214 — *By Appt. Only*

Dishwasher down? Fridge on the fritz? You might want to shoot 'em, but get Gunn to fix them instead. The guys and gals at Gunn Appliance repair all makes and models of major household appliances with the greatest of ease. Washers and dryers, too. *CK, MC, V*

★★★ Hoover Co., The — 972/503-9494

13536 Preston Rd., Suite 100 — *Mon-Fri 9-6; Sat 10-5*
Dallas, TX 75240 — *www.hoover.com*

All HOOVER, all the time. Listen to the sound of savings to the tune of 30-50 percent off on discontinued models, demos, reconditioned models and those with damaged cartons. (You don't vacuum with the carton anyway, do you?) No trade-ins, but at these prices, both new and refurbished models can keep you grounded in reality. The new upright cleaner called the "Windtunnel" offered a 100 percent allergen filtration system with a long (20-inch) attachment hose. A new carpet cleaner, the "Steamvac Ultra," contained five revolving brushes that is purported to clean all sides of the carpet fiber with a power brush attachment for furniture. Have your carpets dry in two hours! As the only all-Hoover station in the Metroplex, The Hoover Co. at Preston and Alpha also offers excellent repair service on all makes of HOOVER. *CK, MC, V, AE, D*

✧✧✧✧✧ InterCell+ 972/492-7807

3030 N. Josey Lane, #101 *Mon-Fri 9-6; Sat 10-2*
Carrollton, TX 75007 *www.intersell.com*

Want more bang for your battery? Compared with the $70 cost of buying a new battery for your cell phone, Intersell+ can revitalize your old one for $9.95. Most cell phone batteries will hold up to 350 charges, but are quick to de-juice once they hit 150. Think of it as a 150 charge tune-up for your phone! Look for accessories, too, like digital battery analyzers, hands-free units and PULSETECH batteries, which boost battery life by years. Our U.S. military tanks and rocket launchers wouldn't leave home without them. And even though most people leave analog phone users high and dry, InterCell+ comes through again. And let us not forget to mention that everything here is priced way below what you'll find anywhere else. Over and out. *CK, MC, V, AE, D*

★★★★★ Oliver Dyer's Appliance 817/244-1874

8201 Hwy. 80 West *Mon-Fri 9-6:30; Sat 9-6*
Fort Worth, TX 76116

In the market for a washer, dryer, refrigerator, dishwasher, room air-conditioner, stove, oven or cooktop? In Fort Worth, get all of them at Oliver's. The prices are nice and if you wait for their final close-outs, you can save even more. Save up to 50 percent on seasonal items, as well as on models that have been used for display or demo, or got scratched or dented. All the names in the business, a 5-year guarantee and a $30 charge for delivery plus installation charge for the built-in models. Brands such as CARRIER, JENN-AIR, KITCHEN AID and MAYTAG are all party of the Dyer family. They also service all makes and models of appliances and guarantee used washers and dryers with a 1-year limited warranty. *CK, MC, V, D, Financing*

★★★★★ Robert Kent Television & Appliance/Repairs 817/923-1973

4944 James Ave. *Mon-Fri 8:30-6:30; Sat 9-6*
Fort Worth, TX 76115

If it's a TV or appliance, these guys will service it, whether you bought it from them or not. If you do buy it here, they back it with a 5-year warranty. Family-owned and operated since 1953, Robert Kent also knows the ins and outs of selling it for less. Washers, dryers, refrigerators, stoves, TVs, VCRs, microwaves, bedding and furniture with names like CARRIER, GE, KITCHENAID, LANE, MAYTAG, RCA, WHIRLPOOL and ZENITH capture the essence of their roster alongside POSTURE BEAUTY bedding and RIVERSIDE furniture. *CK, MC, V, D*

★★★ Speedy Service Appliance Co. 972/907-2000

401 S. Sherman, #217 *Mon-Fri 8:30-5; Sat 9-3*
Richardson, TX 75081

As you would expect, Speedy Service Appliances services all makes and models of refrigerators, stoves, washers, dryers, dishwashers, trash compactors, disposals and air-conditioners. What you might not know is that you can also buy refurbished appliances here for really cheap. Each refurbished model comes with a 30-day guarantee. For an additional $25, there's a 6-month warranty and for $50, a year's warranty. On one visit, Speedy had one free-standing stove and microwave combo that was priced at $250 (but it was 10 years old, and I like only toddlers). Nevertheless, they did have plenty of washer-dryer sets in the $250-$325 range with names like GE, KENMORE, SPEED QUEEN (no relation to Speedy) and equal numbers of refrigerators (as the stock is used, the brands vary). One in particular struck our fancy: A 25-inch, side-by-side FRIGIDAIRE with ice water and cubes on the outside for $324 was one cool buy. *CK, MC, V, AE, D*

★★★★★ Texas Appliance & Builders Supply 817/460-5252

3401 W. Pioneer Pkwy. *Mon-Fri 8-6; Sat 9-6*
Arlington, TX 76013

The appliances have been scratched or dented. As a result, the prices have been slashed. Hundreds of units in otherwise perfect condition arrive daily from major manufacturers. To find them, head through the main showroom and enter their famed backdoor warehouse where you'll see name brand appliances such as SUB-ZERO. Who cares if there's a scratch in the back? There are also odds 'n' ends, one-of-a-kinds, freight-damaged, display units and close-outs from major manufacturers waiting to be delivered to your front door and all available with the manufacturer's warranty. You'd be hard pressed to find anyone who sells refrigerators, washers, dryers, freezers, microwaves, cooktops, dishwashers and ovens–all for less. Call for prices before shopping anywhere else. We found a HOTPOINT built-in dishwasher for only $189, a large capacity ROPER washer for $188 (same for the dryer), and refrigerators all day long for $299 (one that swept us off the floor during our research was a GE at $289). Servicing any brand they sell, they have all the parts, too. Don't be surprised to find contractors and builders vying for the same items you are. Enjoy 90-day, interest-free financing. It just doesn't get better than that. *CK, MC, V, D, Financing*

★★★★ Thompson's Appliances 817/277-1131

2408 S. Cooper *Mon-Fri 8-7; Sat 9-7*
Arlington, TX 76015 *www.metroplexpages.com/yp/817/277/1131/*

If paying retail really cooks your goose, Thompson's in Arlington can help. No matter what your taste and style, Thompson's has the brand-name appliance to match and the prices to please. Choose from top names including BOSCH, KITCHENAID, SHARP, SUB-ZERO, THERMADOR and WOLFE, which they offer alongside other performers such as AMANA, FRANKE, JENN-AIR, MAGIC CHEF, MARVEL, MAYTAG and WHIRLPOOL. If you buy the entire kitchen package, expect a lot of wheeling and dealing, just like the builders do. Expect superb service from the time you walk in the door until your machine is humming on its own. They also offer a 3-year warranty on anything they sell because they also service them. Laura is one of the most knowledgeable salespersons in the business. She even suggested we consider the new front-load MAYTAG washer and dryer because it uses half the water, is much gentler on your clothes, and has a delayed timer so you decide exactly when you'd like your clothes to take a bath. For those of you remodeling or planning a new home, they have a complete built-in department (at builder pricing) that includes custom hoods, under-counter ice makers, refrigerators, freezers, hot water dispensers, custom sinks/faucets, ice machines, beer taps, commercial-style ranges, cooktops/hoods, built-in ironing centers, toasters and can openers. Just south of Arkansas Lane and west of Cooper. *CK, MC, V, AE, D*

★★★★★ Vac-Mobile, The 972/247-5838

12895 Josey Lane, Suite 122 *Mon-Fri 9-6; Sat 9-5*
Farmers Branch Shopping Center
Farmers Branch, TX 75234

For 28 years, these people have been making vacuums hum and customers smile. They tell it like it is and sell 'em for less. We shelled out $149 for a clean and dependable SHARP, but there were also several models as low as $39. Brands from DIRT DEVIL, EUREKA, HOOVER, PANASONIC, RAINBOW, SANYO and SHARP stand tall and at some of the best prices in town. Trade-ins are welcome because they can fix them up like new. We even saw an upright ELECTROLUX, a brand you rarely see on the "used" market, at a sensational price. All the best brands and a few we've never heard of were waiting to cut a rug. Whether it's new or used, why pay top dollar for vacuums when you can snag a top-quality machine for less here? At the southwest corner of Valley View and Josey. *CK, MC, V, AE, D*

Appliances

★★★★★ Walt's Appliance

972/263-3751

2336 E. Main *Mon-Fri 9-6; Sat 9-4*
Grand Prairie, TX 75050 *www.waltsappliances.com*

With 35,000 square feet of name brand merchandise for sale, and 40 years of service under its belt, Walt's is a legend in its own time. But don't let that mystify you. Ask for Rick and take them to task. They won't guarantee the lowest price, but they'll try their best. You can save 10 percent on new appliances, and even more on close-outs and "last-one" deals. But the real steals are on rebuilts, which these folks know how to do better than anyone. Choose from names such as AMANA, FRIGIDAIRE, HOTPOINT and MAGIC CHEF. More than three acres of appliances in working order can be delivered to your front door. If you are looking for a new or rebuilt appliance, Walt's has it. Walt's also services ailing washers or other home appliances, and runs a parts division, too. *CK, MC, V, AE, D, Layaway, Financing*

Arts & Crafts & Collectibles

★ Aidaworks

972/436-5999

1134 W. Main
Lewisville, TX 75067
Mon-Fri 10-6; Sat 10-4:30

The cross-stitch capital of the country is right here in Lewisville. One of the few shops to specialize in cross-stitching, Aidaworks stocks lots of threads and fabrics, including AIDA fabrics and linens, and plenty of patterns and supplies. Of particular note is their custom framing of cross-stitch designs. Aidaworks has how-to books, leaflets and personalized instruction, too. Neighborhood friends congregate here to work on their own cross-stitch patterns. If it was meant to be cross-stitched, these are the folks to needle. *CK, MC, V, AE, D*

★★★★ American Needlewoman

817/551-1221

2944 S.E. Loop 820
Fort Worth, TX 76133
Mon-Sat 10-4

American Needlewoman won't let it be retail anymore than I would. If you're a Wal-Mart shopper, you'll love this shop 'cause they're even cheaper. Since 1976, this catalog company has been sending out signals of a small crafts warning. Their 2,500-square-foot outlet is attached to their warehouse fulfillment center and offers everything that's found in their beautiful 72-page, four-color catalog at outlet prices. Items that have been discontinued are sold for up to 50 percent less than their already low prices. For instance, the 8-ounce PERFECT MATCH yarn was $1.99 a yard and VERELLA $1.88/yard. An additional 10 percent off is available to any senior citizen. Kits, books, craft supplies and yarns are all cross-stitched and ready to sew. Cross-stitching kits, needlepoint tapestries imported from Europe, latch-hook kits and even wood paintings and supplies are found here. Don't wait until the last minute to start those crafty projects. Get with the program and get on their good side for their four-times a year catalog mailings. To get there, look for where 820 meets I-20, go west to the Wichita exit (if you get to the Campus exit, you've gone too far), go under the freeway to the first right after the Fina station (across the street from the TCJC campus) to the second row of warehouses. *CK, MC, V, D, MO, C*

★★★★ Art Encounter

972/726-7220

230 Spanish Village
Dallas, TX 75248
Mon, Wed-Thu, Sat Noon-5; Tue, Fri 10-6
www.artencounter-dallas.com

Maybe it's not the Moulin Rouge, but the Art Encounter at the corner of Arapaho and Coit is a surprising gathering of artists and artwork all the same. Here, 150 artists offer an expanse of thousands of original works of art and on-premise custom framing. Prices appeared fair, but with additional overhead for the gallery owners, someone's got to pay. On the other hand, for the quality shown, prices seemed very good. This non-traditional approach to fine art begins with the artist leasing a space and displaying their talents in this most appealing and aesthetic environment. Almost every medium and variety of art is represented–oils, pastels, modern, Southwest, ethnic, jewelry, pottery, wood carvings, sculpture and bronzes. Some museums should be this varied. Prices started around $8 for jewelry, $35 for pottery and around $40 for art works and ascended from there. Then again, what price art? As Picasso said, "Art is a lie that enables us to realize the truth."
CK, MC, V, D, AE

★★★ Art USA

972/491-2441

7000 Independence
Plano, TX 75025
Mon-Fri 10-7; Sat 10-6; Sun Noon-5

At prices this democratic, the framers of this country would be most pleased. Located at the northeast corner of Independence and Legacy (next to Kroger), you can frame your art for 25 percent less than anywhere else. Just bring in your quote and Art USA will match the materials, then chop down the price by 25 percent. Gotta love that free enterprise system. There's always a promotion going on, so strike while the sale is on. For example, they would frame any poster (up to 24-inch x 36-inch) for $39.95, plus tax, with regular glass, dry-mounted in metal, round top frames in your choice of 25 colors. Usual turnaround time is six days on framing. Critique their already framed artwork for sale, too. Check directory for location nearest you. There are eight in the Metroplex. *CK, MC, V, AE, D*

★★★★ Art-Frame Expo

214/824-1214

5620 E. Mockingbird
Dallas, TX 75206
Mon-Sat 10-7; Sun Noon-6

If it's all in the presentation, this is the place to go to get your art ready for its debut. Frame a poster for $34.95, or use their "buy one, get a second at half-price" deal for custom framing. Of course, Art-Frame Expo also offers a gallery's worth of more than 1,000 oil paintings, mirrors, prints and posters at low, low prices. Three other locations: 3501 E. McKinney Ave., 214/219-2242; 17390 Preston Rd., 972/373-8449; and in Plano, 1725 N. Central Expwy. *CK, MC, V, AE, D*

★★★★ Audria's Art & Craft Supplies 817/346-2497

6821 McCart Avenue *Mon-Tue 9-9; Wed-Fri 9-7; Sat 9-6*
Fort Worth, TX 76133

Not only have these guys been selling arts and craft supplies for 35 years, they also can teach you the craft of making art. From jewelry-making to cake decorating, needlework, framing and silk-flower arranging, there's an artist who can share their secrets with you. Just give Audria's your name, the craft you're interested in and an artist will contact you when a class becomes available. Audria's is also the largest supplier in the Metroplex for homecoming mum accessories. Rah! Rah! Sis-Boom-Bah! *CK, MC, V*

★★★ Binders Discount Art Center 214/739-2281

9820 N. Central Expwy. *Mon-Fri 10-7; Sat 10- 6; Sun Noon-6*
(Central at Walnut Hill)
Dallas, TX 75231

You don't have to be a starving artist to shop smart. When it comes to getting the supplies to create and present art, Binders displays some appealing prices. For paint and brushes, paper, posterboard, mats, X-ACTOs, ready-made frames and presentation binders, Binders sells them for 30 percent less. For those who need to cover up and hand out the best, Binders has a knack for custom framing, too. Bring your work of art in to be museum-mounted and expect a quality job at a fair price. When this Atlanta-based company opened their discount art supply store, they made their mark with many local artists who now know where to shop and save up to 30 percent off list on NEWTON and WINSOR paints, brushes, canvases and other accouterments to complete their life's works. *CK, MC, V, AE, D*

✧✧✧✧✧ Brush Strokes 817/247-9678

By Appt. Only

It will take little more than a few expert brush strokes from these two talented ladies to turn your eyesore walls into a work of art. Invite them into your home for a visit and they will quickly be able to determine the best course of refinishing for your boring expanse of sheet rock. They specialize in unique and extraordinary glazing, torn paper and all types of faux finishes. Murals, too. For a list of references that include the rich and famous, restaurants and kitchens not open to the public, call Nancey (817/247-9678) or Charlotte (817/798-7119). Despite the Tarrant County phone numbers, they will paint the Metroplex in a marbelized look that will even fool Mother Nature.

★★★ Cabin Craft Southwest — 817/571-3837

1500 Westpark Way — *Mon-Sat 8:30-5*
Euless, TX 76040 — *www.ccsw.com*

Are craft projects taking their "toll" on your budget? Well, consider this source for "tole" and other decorative painting supplies as a way of keeping costs in line. Classes and seminars are ongoing, so keep ahead of the class by signing up. Selling all the tools of the trade, they are located about two miles south of Highway 183 in a warehouse district, allowing them to keep their overhead down and their prices low. If you're looking to find the perfect wood wall piece, without paying the toll, tag along here. Mail orders welcome. *CK, MC, V*

★ Castle Collection, The — 817/645-5415

137 S. Ridgeway — *Mon-Sat 10-5*
Cleburne, TX 76031

Over the woods and through Cleburne, head onto North Main going south 'til you get to the courthouse. Then turn right on Henderson. About two-plus miles down the road you'll discover the shopping center where the Castle Collection resides. Fortunately, you'll not have to cross any moat to enter this little shop of decorative arts and gifts. No castles in sight, either. The owner's family name just happens to be Castle. You'll be right at home with the items here–perfect for viewing and collecting. Ceramic villages, for example, were shown with lots of home, building and other miniature replicas complete with lights that are shining bright at holiday time. Lots of SNOW VILLAGES and SNOWBABIES. Instead, we ogled the last three Beanie Babies ($6 each) in preparation for a favorite little girl's birthday. While we loved the selection, this Castle needs a refresher course from Miss Manners. They treated us like we were remnants from the Dark Ages. *CK, MC, V*

★★★★★ Coomers Craft Mall — 972/554-1882

900 W. Airport Freeway — *Mon-Sat 10-7; Sun Noon-5*
Irving, TX 75062 — *www.coomers.com*

Variety is the operative word here. Many talented people display their usual and not-so-usual wares in the creative collections at these specialty malls. If you're looking for a gift you won't see coming and going to every occasion, welcome to Coomers. All hand-crafted and imaginative, you'll need a truck after a few hours of well-spent browsing. Like the fishing pole holder, $16.75, that we bought for dad; the leather belts, $23-$24, that went to our best friend, Bob; the pen and pencil set, $30, that now resides on our desk; and the sculpture of a golfer, $25, that went to the winner of the "hole-in-one" contest. This is the granddaddy of the crafter mall craze and your link to all things to consider. If you're looking for porcelain dolls, one craftsman has them for as low as $54. Looking for birdhouses? Well, this is like a forest (and none were seedy.) For those that prefer to do for themselves, they carry a comple line of AILENE craft supplies. Coomer's is still the place to applaud others' handiwork and with so many locations, there are plenty of hands across the Metroplex working their fingers to the bone. Check directory for additional locations. *CK, MC, V, D*

★★★★ Dallas Visual Art Center 214/821-2522

2917 Swiss Ave. *Mon-Fri 9-5; Tue 9-9; Sat Noon-4*
Dallas, TX 75204 *www.startext.net/interact/forums/dvac/dv*

Leave it to the Swiss to be culturally enriched. This non-profit art center is located in the hub of the Wilson Historic District and houses some of the best cultural bargains in the Metroplex. The center is free and open to the public. See original works of art by up-and-coming Picassos and Monets. Don't miss their annual Critic's Choice Juried Show that features artists from all over the state of Texas. This year more than 300 artists entered with almost 900 works of art. From this bank of talent, 21 artists were selected representing different mediums, from pottery to iridescent photography. From '40s retro images to minimalist abstract paintings, be sure to check out this center for art on the move.

★★★ Deck The Walls 972/315-1808

2401 S. Stemmons, #1122 *Mon-Sat 10-9; Sun 11-7*
Vista Ridge Mall
Lewisville, TX 75067

All you need to turn blah into AHH! are the services of Paul Pechacek and his artwork at Deck The Walls. From custom-framing to a large variety of original, limited editions, framed prints and out-of-stock paintings, it won't be hard to add the perfect touch to the décor of any room. Framed prints start as low as $30 and framed orginal oils were $75 - $3,000. Don't forget their selection of framed limited editions that cost anywhere from $500 - $5,000. February,

September and October are sale months, and corporate discounts are welcome. But the masterpieces at this shop are their customer service and personal attention to all your framing needs. *CK, MC, V, AE, D*

★★★★★ Decorators Warehouse 817/460-4488

1535 S. Bowen *Mon-Fri 10-6; Sat 9-6*
Arlington, TX 76013

Formerly at 1844 W. Division Street, their new Garden of Eden is growing at the southeast corner of Park Row and Bowen. If ever there was a greener pasture of silk flowers from $3.99 to $6.99, I haven't seen it. Sales bring out their roots for stems that are (sans) dirt cheap–$1 to $1.50, plus another 20 percent off. It's practically a free-for-all. Everything in the store is at least 20 percent-50 percent below retail. Once you walk into the store, its like coming across a "secret garden" with their huge selection of floral displays, silk flowers and silk trees (from only $89) They also have gifts items and furniture. For instance, they had a glass-top dining table with four chairs and a lamp for only $299. Watch for ads in the newspaper. A sister location is in Plano at 1441 Coit Rd., 972/964-0499. Quality silk plants at tremendous savings, silk arrangements, artificial trees, plants, vases, flowers, cabinet toppers, and other arrangements are always 40-70 percent off. Plants run anywhere from $15 to $500 depending on the size and quality. This large nondescript store is right next door to Dickey's Barbecue and behind Cathy's Wok. *CK, MC, V, AE, D*

★★★ Emporium, The 214/320-2222

950 Big Town *Mon-Sat 10-7; Sun Noon-5:30*
U.S. 80 and Big Town Blvd.
Mesquite, TX 75149

Have a big time at the Emporium in Big Town Mall. Now, three experiences under one roof within an expanse of 38,000 square feet. Look for the red signs facing Highway 80 that say, "Craft Mall and Consignments." Then wander down the aisleways and buyways of furniture (both new and old) and crafts. From wooden creations to ceramics, booth after booth features T-shirts, pillows, Victorian bric-a-brac and Southwestern folk arts and crafts. Turning to the other half of the emporium, you'll find market samples, seconds in new furniture and consigned inventory for the major living areas of your house. In between, you'll even be able to appreciate the antiques, glassware and collectibles. Lots of booth spaces available, so if you want to make a few extra bucks, and if Grandma's attic is overflowing, you might consider transforming a retirement project into a second career. *CK, MC, V, AE, D*

♥♥♥♥♥ Florence Art Gallery 214/754-7070

2500 Cedar Springs *Tue-Fri 10-5; Sat 11-5*
Dallas, TX 75201 *www.florenceart.guidelive.com*

Florence Art Gallery has a wide selection of artwork of the original kind. Their primary focus is on paintings and sculptures made of both stainless steel and iron. Don't overlook their contemporary glass-top iron tables or miss their showings held five or six times each year. The gallery is 4,000 square feet and features a variety of artists, including Henrietta Milan, J. Miller and Peter Max. Their consignment service can help you take home a painting or sculpture, regardless of your price range. In business for the past 26 years, enjoy a glimpse into the art world, and who knows, maybe you'll take a piece of it home with you. They are located at 2500 Cedar Springs Rd. at Fairmont in uptown Dallas. *CK, MC, V, AE*

★ Frames 'n Graphics Warehouse 817/488-5511

6301 Colleyville Blvd. (Grapevine Hwy.) *Mon-Fri 10-6; Sat 10-2*
Colleyville, TX 76034

Though "warehouse" is in its name and Deanna has been known to be $200 less than a Bedford competitor's price, she prides herself in being competitive–but "not discounted." Since we don't like frame-ups and we aren't chintzy, we can tell you she's good, but be prepared to pay the price. Don't fret though, because she is worth it. If you pass the Bluebonnet Cemetery, you've missed her. This non-descript little frame hideout has a lot more inside than what meets the passerby's eye. Lots of frames, of course, but also original art by G. Harvey, Sky Jones and Cynthia Bryan, limited editions and posters. In fact, they are a poster manufacturer. A one-stop place to hang out if you're into moldings, mat boards and all things artistic. *CK, MC, V, AE, D*

Framing Studio and Gallery 972/404-8899

6959 Arapaho Rd *Mon-Fri 10-6; Sat 10-5*
Dallas, TX 75248

If the crime is saving you money, then the people at Framing Studio and Gallery will frame you. Come in and save 50 percent and more on framing, shadow boxes and custom matting. The selection here is huge. You will find more than 2,500 moldings to choose from, as well as canvas transfer, quality framing and affordable art. The trained and experienced design staff will help you find what you need and save 10 percent and more off Michael's and MJD prices. *CK, MC, V, D, Debit Cards*

★ Framing Warehouse 972/416-3626

2760 Trinity Mills *Mon-Fri 10-6; Thu 10-8; Sat 9-5*
Carrollton, TX

There is nothing like a frame and at the Framing Warehouse, you can expect to see plenty of frames (metal and wood ones are the frames of choice). The difference, though, is the Framing Warehouse offers custom-made frames tailored to the object d' framed. If you are struggling with your Frame and Fortune, you won't be lost in the stuffle. A painting that needs special attention or special protection for the diploma that you sweated bullets over–Framing Warehouse will see to it that it's all done with attention to detail. *CK, MC, V, AE, D*

★★★ Garden Ridge Home Décor Marketplace 972/681-5006

2727 Towne Center Drive *Mon-Sat 9-9; Sun 9-7*
Mesquite, TX 75150 *www.gardenridge.com*

This monstrous marketplace puts most others to shame–by intimidation. It's so big, with prices that are so formidable, others can't take the heat. A 6-foot ficus tree and other specialty trees were $18.88 and up. Go ahead. Make my day. Then, for school, kids were loading up baskets with stackable file crates and bins and 20-gallon hinged lid totes. What about those barren walls? Why not hang up some framed artwork? Sure makes it simple. Too bad it wasn't closer to Christmas when we shopped, as their doors stay open 'round the clock. Room decorating is made easy at this place. Add several porcelain fish bowls, a bean bag and silk greenery. What else could anyone need? And this was just down one aisle ... there are hundreds more to travel before you sleep. Garden Ridge runs promotions, sales and specials on various items throughout the year, so check in often and find some great buys. Visit also in North Richland Hills at highways 121 and 820, North Central Expressway at Spring Creek in Plano, Southwest Loop 820, Fort Worth, and I-35 Exit FM 3040 in Lewisville. *CK, MC, V, AE, D*

Arts & Crafts & Collectibles

✧✧✧✧✧ Go With The Faux 817/265-3289

2304 West Park Row, Suite 28 *Mon-Fri 9-5; or by Appt.*
Arlington, TX 76013 *www.gofaux.com*

For faux that's the real thing, you won't go wrong with Go With The Faux. Create beautifully painted decorative finishes made with techniques ranging from rag rolling, marbleizing, crackle, stone, wood graining or by adding imbedded art. They have classes to teach paper hangers, painters and faux-finish artisans on how to start their own business or improve an existing one. Or ask for a recommendation and they'll put you in touch with one of their guild members. Classes start at $25 for a one-day introductory class and go up to $1,195 for the Full Faux. If only your walls could talk they'd be screaming for something new and interesting. Enough of that plain vanilla treatment. Their schooled artisans do some breathtaking effects for walls and furniture. This is the only hands-on decorative painting school in North Texas featuring Aqua Finishing Solutions by FAUX EFFECTS. *CK, MC, V*

♥♥♥♥♥ Handmade & Company 972/480-9202

1455 W. Campbell *Mon-Sat 10-6*
Richardson, TX 75080

What a difference a year makes. Now housed in their new and expanded location next to the Richardson Bike Mart, bigger in this case really does mean better. What a doll! If you're looking for LITTLE SOLES, this is the place to say, "Sold." These wooden doll faces are darling, loved by school girls to moms, and they're all dressed the part. But that's not all. If you are looking for unique and interesting gifts and collectibles, this little shop has just what the doctor ordered. Candle lines by ASPEN BAY, TRAPP, VILLAGE DAY and YANKEE; all the TY products and the full CAMILLE line of hand and body products. Also admired was the JEEP COLLINS sterling, gold and brass jewelry made in Fredericksburg and treasured by many little angels. Collect SCARBOROUGH & CO. wooden houses or light your bath area with candles and sprinkle in bath crystals and powders. Inventory changes frequently. Travel directly to the back area for what's priced according to *Underground Shopper* standards. Open Sundays during the holiday season. *CK, MC, V, AE*

♥♥♥♥♥ Helene's Fine Art and Framing 972/867-1733

2001 Coit Rd., Suite 305 *Mon-Sat 10-6*
Plano, TX 75075 *www.helenes-fine-art.com*

Looking for the perfect frame-up? Helene's is one fine source for original fine art, paintings, limited edition prints and custom framing. Since appreciation is as important as the artistry involved, this combination makes for fine bedfellows. Then if your cupboards are bare and you must fill it with collectibles, Helene's is one of the best sources to get your started. GIUSEPPE ARMANI sculptures and MARK HOPKINS bronzes, along with SWAROVSKI crystal, WALT DISNEY Classic Collections and more are part of her landscape. Larry Dyke is America's most collected golf artist. His work can be found in the collections of Pope John Paul II, Ronald Reagan and even Jack Nicklaus. Go to Helene's and you can add his work to your collection as well. Helene's is also a source for local and national artists' original oils, water colors, lithographs, sculptures and bronzes. Expect custom framing and museum mountings. A local artisan whose line is called "Pocket Dragons" has made a believer out of me with their expressive little faces. I'm hooked. Pay attention to these last few lines because the Pocket Dragons are going places. *CK, MC, V, AE, D*

★★★★★ Hobby Lobby — 972/772-5021

2004 South Goliad — *Mon-Sat 9-8; Sun Noon-6*
Rockwall, TX 75087 — *www.hobbylobby.com*

This is one giant step for the artistic kind. Stretched-to-the-max shoppers will find a hobby to lobby all the way to Congress. Keep it all in the House, though, as this is one of the chains that will save you the most on arts and crafts supplies and everything else that smacks of making your house beautiful. For all your kitsch and kaboodle, make way for Hobby Lobby. Find supplies for any craft imaginable: from single-stemmed silk flowers, dried flowers, vases and silk trees to unfinished wooden shelves and quilt racks. Needlepoint pillows if you've got creativity to burn. Crocheted baby coverlets. Decoupage. Faux finishes. Refinishing. It's all here. The newest Hobby Lobby just opened its doors in Allen to join the other area stores in Arlington, Burleson, Carrollton, Cedar Hill, Dallas, Irving, Lewisville, Mesquite, Plano, Rockwell, Sherman and Southlake. When they're running their 50 - 90 percent off sales, don't even think of shopping anywhere else that day. From picture frames and furniture to wicker baskets and painting supplies, the variety is monumental and gives the hometown boys a run for their money. Check their homepage at www.hobbylobby.com and make sure to sign up to have the weekly coupon e-mailed directly to you. For even more savings, apply for their Hobby Lobby Visa card. It will save you an additional three percent on all your Hobby Lobby purchases and one percent on all other purchases. *CK, MC, V, AE, D*

♥♥♥♥♥ Joel Cooner Gallery 214/747-3603

1605 Dragon *Mon-Fri 10-5; or By Appt.*
Dallas, TX 75207 *www.joelcooner.com*

You don't have to have a Goliath budget to slay the dragon. But, it doesn't hurt to know you're not throwing your money away to mythical monsters, either. Joel Cooner is the man who can buy it right so your collection of fine tribal, pre-Columbian and Asian art is right on the money. You can also find antiques and one-of-a-kind items here. He's got exquisite taste, knows his art and works hard at buying–and selling–it. For a conversation piece or an investment, his clients are worldwide and his expertise and gallery are in the heart of the Design District. *CK, MC, V, AE, D*

★★★★★ Julie's Custom Frames 214/341-1631

Dallas, TX 75243 *By Appt. Only*

Julie Forsyth will frame anything–but you. Her handiwork has been seen hanging out with Mary Kay and The Black-Eyed Pea Restaurant chain, and you know *they* stay in the pink. Since she operates out of her home, the overhead is limited. But that doesn't mean your choices are too. The selection is every bit as big and varied as chain craft stores, but her prices are a whole lot less without sacrificing one bit of quality. She started 20 years ago framing needlework projects for friends who wouldn't trust their works-of-labor to anyone else. Now, she's a full-fledged craft industry, churning out custom-framed works one picture at a time. *CK*

★★★★ JW Sports Cards & Collectibles Superstore 972/788-5487

14902 Preston Rd., Suite 410 *Mon-Fri 10-8; Sat 10-6*
Dallas, TX 75240 *www.jwsportscards.com*

Were you one of those crazies who stood in line for days just to buy a Furby? Well, fur goodness sake, if you'd known JW, you could have saved yourself a lot of wear and tear. (Plus he would have saved you hundreds of dollars.) At the southeast corner of Preston and Belt Line, you can start counting your blessings. Whether you're buying or selling trading cards or collectibles, chances are, they're in the right hands...theirs! Buy them, and they'll be in your hands. How about some autographed sports memorabilia? Babe Ruth, Pudge Rodriquez, Troy Aikman, Michael Jordan and others can be found here. For the non-sports crowd, find Pokémon, Star Wars, G.I. Joe and other collectible figures. Collectors will be in good hands with JW. So from now on, don't throw your hands up and bid for a Beanie Baby or a Barbie at an online auction. That could be a fiscal mistake. To err is human but to shop JW's divine. It's the ultimate store for buying sports cards and collectibles–without losing an arm and a leg. *CK, MC, V, AE, D*

★★ K's Klassic Knits — 972/306-2536

4300 Charles Rd. — *By Appt. Only*
Hebron, TX 75010

If she's not out working in the hay business with her husband, K's spinning yarns at a discount. Quality yarns such as BRAMWELL, DELAINE, HEIRLOOM, NOMIS, PLYMOUTH and SCOTT MILLS, plus special orders from lots of other specialty companies are available at this house-bound business. One of the largest selections of coned yarns in the North Texas area, this machine weaver can even magically deliver a custom knit designer outfit, sweater or baby gift for a pittance of retail value without pricking a finger. She sells linkers, too. But don't expect her to take you "skein-diving!" Call for directions. We always find it somehow, but we could never tell you how we did it. *CK*

★★★★ Kangoo Gallery — 817/329-8500

304 S. Park Blvd, # 200 — *Mon-Fri 10-7; Sat 10-6*
Grapevine, TX 76051

Formerly Warehaus Gallery, now hop to Kangoo Gallery if you're tired of searching the outback for in-stock mounting and mats, technical assistance and framed art at bargain basement prices. Take a few hours to wander through their stock of thousands of prints by G. HARVEY, KINCAIDE and others. Then have it framed at prices lower than fair on all frames and framing materials, including matting, glass, etc. Custom framing also is available. Kangoo works almost entirely in wood frames, with a wide variety available. Low prices and good workmanship keep the customers coming back. *CK, MC, V, AE, D*

♥♥♥♥♥ Legacy Gallery — 972/772-9967

910 Steger Towne Crossing — *Mon-Fri 10-6:30; Sat 10-5:30*
Rockwall, TX 75032

Customer service is the difference that sets Legacy Gallery aside from other stores selling memorabilia, antiquities, fine art, as well as award winning custom picture framing. Creativity and quality are also what customer's can expect. Throw in a fair price for a great product, and we believe this store is a winner. They handle selections from well known artists such as G. Harvey, Bev Doolittle, Bob Byerley, and in memborabilia, the selection is huge in golf, baseball, football, basketball, track, auto racing, boxing, music celebrities, historic and more. In adding to the heritage of this legacy, they'll track down anything you might be searching for in any of their product categories. That's service, now smile. *CK, MC, V, AE, D*

★★ Lone Star Sportscard Co. — 972/245-8884

2150 N. Josey, Suite 100 — *Mon-Fri Noon-7; Sat 10-6; Sun Noon-5*
Carrollton, TX 75006 — *www.lonestarsportcard.com*

In a strip shopping center on the northeast corner of Josey and Keller Springs in Carrollton, next door to Albertson's, is this one-stop shop if you are combing the world for sports cards, POKÉMON and autographed memorabilia. Others will find them to their liking, too, if they're buying or selling major trading cards such as STADIUM, TOPPS and UPPER DECK. Little and big kids like to collect signed sports memorabilia such as jerseys, baseballs and footballs, so trek to Lone Star because they're a store that names names. On one incredible treasure hunt, we found the autographed #0001 card three from the Pinnacle's 1993 five-card Joe DiMaggio set selling for $400. By the time you read this, they may even have a Troy Aikman jersey and football all signed, sealed and ready to be delivered. *CK, MC, V, AE, D*

★★★★★ Marshall Moody — 214/631-5444

2910 N. Stemmons — *Mon-Fri 8:30-5; Sat 8:30-Noon*
Dallas, TX 75247 — *www.marshalmoody.com*

Get in the mood and shop for seasonal ornamental and decorative accessories at Marshall Moody's. Even if you're in a bad mood, you'll smile all the way to the bank. The selection is spectacular. To celebrate Christmas (even in July) and other holidays, shop year 'round for decorative ideas and holiday cheer (except during market weeks, when MM closes its doors). From Santa's (mechanical and stationary), ornaments and chandeliers to Christmas trees and other holiday displays, you will be in holiday heaven, regardless of the season. The same displays you see in retail stores are sold off by the truckloads at prices almost too good to be true. From the smallest ornaments to the largest displays, Marshall Moody fits the bill. A catalog is available if you can't find something that fits your party plan, but the catalog only reflects about 15 percent of their inventory. Haven't you always wondered about this shop on Stemmons, at the Inwood exit? Custom orders accepted with pleasure. *CK, MC, V, AE, MOC*

★★★★★ Marshall Pottery

903/938-9201

4901 Elysian Fields Rd.
Marshall, TX 75670
Mon-Sat 9-6; Sun 10-6
www.marshallpottery.com

This Marshall has a better Plan–but be sure to allow plenty of time to plot out this shopping expedition! Marshall Pottery manufactures their pots on the spot. They've got more than 100,000 square feet of space to display their wares with a product mix unlike anything you've ever seen. Seasonal decorations, florals, baskets and garden center items are a drawing card for shoppers all over the country. As a destination stop on the interstate of bargains, expect to also enjoy a delicious repast in their attached restaurant called The Hungry Potter. If you're thinking about ordering pots for shipping, sorry, they only ship by pallet quantities. Then again, maybe you're the caller who requested that acre of pots for his own Killing Fields. *CK, MC, V, D*

Metro Home Warehouse

214/426-4663

2234 Cockrell Ave.
Dallas, TX 75215
Thu-Sat 9-6

The largest framing manufacturer in the Southwest has just opened a retail outlet in their factory–just minutes from downtown Dallas. They offer the absolute lowest price in custom framing, as well as hundreds of square feet of mirrors, photo frames, furniture, samples and world-wide imports. In furniture you'll find an ever-changing array brands and styles including chrome, barnwood, couches and more. *CK, MC, V, AE, D*

★★★★ Michaels

972/691-1355

2705 Grapevine Mills Circle
Grapevine, TX 76051
Mon-Sat 9-9; Sun 10-6
www.michaels.com

America's largest, billion-dollar craft chain (arts, crafts, framing, floral, decorative wall decor and seasonal merchandise) has been embraced by crafty shoppers across the Metroplex with open wallets. For the hobbyist or do-it-yourself home decorator, Michaels and you can create projects for the rest of your life. They typically carry 36,000 items, including a wide selection of hobby and art supplies, creative crafts, party supplies, framing materials and services, silk and dried flowers, and lots of seasonal and holiday merchandise. Imagine life without something to do! They have plenty of in-store classes and demonstrations, special kids' clubs and activities, and enough tools to let your imagination soar. Watch newspapers for sales on their already low prices (you will typically be able to find a 40 percent off any one item coupon each Sunday.) They carry LOEW CORNELL artist brushes, straw wreaths, DECOART patio paint, everything and anything you need to frame a work of art or photo, whether you do it yourself or let them do it for you. Scrapbookers will revel in the large selection of acid-free stickers from MRS. GROSSMAN and others, paper, books, markers and more. Now it's party time and time for party supplies–from streamers, AMSCAN streamer strings, ribbon, paper, candles, silk plant cleaner, glue guns, GOO GONE to SNAZAROO face paint. Bake a cake with WILTON cake decorating supplies or create a Winter Wonderland and Enchanted Village, it's all in the making. Call for the class dates and away you go. Check the directory for additional locations. *CK, MC, V, AE, D*

★★★★★ MJDesigns — 214/696-5491

810 Preston Forest Shopping Center
(Forest at Preston)
Dallas, TX
Mon-Sat 10-9; Sun Noon-6
www.mjdesigns.com

Reorganized under new ownership, one of the Metroplex's favorite craft stores is back in business. But the road back is a long one and it has to start with baby steps. In this case that means just eight stores in the Metroplex, but MJDesigns continues to be synonymous with savings and sensational looks for your home/fashion. An expanded home decor inventory means great selections of silk and dried flowers, wicker, vases, rockers, cushions and more. Don't stop there–balloons, cards, art supplies, ribbons, wrapping paper, needlework, T-shirts (and paint to apply). We had to stand in line to have one of those gorgeous bows made for our balloon bouquet, but it was worth the wait. Want to create a memory book that'll last for generations? Here you can chronicle your whole life story and your family history without having to secure a major New York publisher (chances are, they wouldn't talk to you anyway!) If you need an idea, why not capture the creation of the new bisque pottery piece you created here? Crafting classes available to help you learn to do-it-yourself for dozens of projects. DFW locations include: 1250 William D. Tate, Grapevine, 817/251-0099; 1400 Green Oaks Rd., Fort Worth, 817/737-3668; 2325 S. Stemmons, Suite 106, Lewisville, 972/315-9046; 3407 Trinity Mills Rd., Carrollton, 972/662-3402; 6120 E. Mockingbird Lane, Dallas, 214/827-2965; 600 W. 15th Street, Plano, 972/578-9600; and 335 S. Cedar Ridge, Duncanville, 972/780-8913. *CK, MC, V, AE, D*

♥♥♥♥♥ Moses Gallery 214/528-7983

4253 Cedar Springs Rd. *Wed-Fri Noon-6; Sat 11-6; Sun 1-5*
Dallas, TX 75219-2691 *www.mosesart.com*

At the southwest corner of Cedar Springs and Wycliff, one block off the North Dallas Tollway, you've probably passed this clapboard house a million times and didn't think to stop. Holy Moses, what a gallery! Known just as Moses, this Dallas artist, armed with a BA in painting and illustration, has developed an imaginative and broad spectrum of styles, including contemporary as well as impressionist, and has surrounded himself with several other talented exhibitors all under one artistic roof. This original art can go up to $6,500 (none higher) would be perfect hanging in the most prestigious homes, corporate lobbies or museums, for that matter. Dale Moses, proprietor and artist, has color in his corner. Vibrant, rich and deliciously painted, one of my favorites is titled simply "Duckies" (one of his signature themes). His animals, flowers and "Tillie in Her Sunday Best" were irresistible and sure to become sought-after commodities worldwide. Giclée prints are available from $200-$750. So, before the rest of the world catches wind of the potential of a windfall, budget some time to check out the Moses Gallery. *CK, MC,V, D*

★★★★★ Nostalgia Crafts and Antiques 972/613-6622

971 W. Centerville Rd. *Mon-Fri 10-8; Sun Noon-5*
Garland, TX 75041 *www.nostalgiaca.com*

Memories were made from stores like this. With three locations in the Metroplex (you will also find them in Lewisville and Plano) you can't forget them. At the Garland location, there's a '50s diner and an old-fashioned soda fountain; in Lewisville, there's the Cameo Tea Room and a full-service florist. Highlighting the Garland location is Cathy's Closet, your "one-stop" Lucy shop. They were reportedly the first store anywhere to offer "I Love Lucy" collectibles exclusively. There's something to suit any fan's taste. There are small address books as low as $4, figurines for $25-$30, cookie jars for $70 and more. I fell in love with the MADAME ALEXANDER character dolls for just $160. Cathy works hard to have the lowest price possible and will happily match a lower price found elsewhere. You'll find her on the internet at www.lucystore.com as well. All in all, there's antiques and old stuff, ceramics, hand-painted apparel, jewelry, stained glass, silk flower arrangements, original art, porcelains, dolls, bird houses–after all, isn't variety the spice of life? Also look for Nostalgia Crafts and Antiques in Lewisville at Highway 121 at I-35 (next to Tia's in case you shop up some hunger pangs), 972/434-8004, and Plano (in the back of the Plano Outlet Mall, Central at Spring Creek), 972/424-2995. *CK, MC, V, AE, D*

★★★ Old Craft Store, The — 972/242-9111

1110 W. Main St. — *Mon-Sat 10-5; Thu 10-7*
Carrollton, TX 75006 — *www.flash.net/~oldstore*

For the dedicated Queen Bee, this is the hive to flock to. After nearly 30 years in business, their philosophy remains the same: Offer the latest items at the best prices while educating customers with all the current trends and timely traditions in the art of quilting. They have a knowledgeable staff, a quarterly newsletter filled with new patterns and swatches and a calendar of classes and tips. Expect down-home, old-world service and a warm, "Y'all Come In" welcome. That alone is sweet enough to tweek anyone's interest, but the "Discount Quilting Club" will really have you buzzing. Join for $25 a year and receive discounts of 20 percent off the prices of all fabric and notions, plus 25 percent off patterns, magazines, books and most classes. During your birthday week, enjoy savings of 30 percent, honey. *CK, MC, V, AE, D*

★★ Prime Time Treasurers — 214/369-7446

9845 N. Central Expressway — *Tue-Sat 10:30-4:30*
Dallas, TX 75231

Attention all Grannies and Peepaws: Looking for something to do in your well-deserved free time? Well, consider showing your crafty side at this store on the northwest corner of Central Expressway and Walnut Hill. The over-the-hill gang gets their creative juices flowing by displaying these one-of-a-kind crafts and selling them through this non-profit Assistance League of Dallas store. Quilts, oil paintings, denim purses, appliquéd T-shirts, ceramics and toys are all hand-crafted by senior citizens. And, if you're looking for something for yourself, see good-looking furniture, baby and children's gifts and toys and pictures, then throw your support to this deserving group. *CK, MC, V*

★★ Richard Marmo — 817/536-0128

Fort Worth, TX 76103 — *By Appt. Only*
www.tricky.com/model-builder

For more than 30 years, this inventive model builder has built everything from a motorized toilet paper dispenser to a Continental Trailways bus with wings.

His client list spans the panorama from private collectors to advertising agencies, courtroom models for accident scenes to room interiors (such as a saloon and a brewery). Since 1967, this craftsman has virtually created any 3-dimensional project the mind can imagine. With his low overhead, budgetary restrictions can be honored, just remember his motto, "Quality and speed are not synonymous." A photographic portfolio is available upon request. He also has built custom furniture and, for us, he created a floating letter design with individual letters hanging on a Plexiglas rod. If you can describe it, he can build it–or help you design it to fit your needs. *CK, MO*

♥♥♥♥♥ Rock Barrell, The 972/231-4809

13650 TI Blvd., Suite 104 *Mon-Tues, Thu-Fri 9-6; Wed 9-8; Sat 9-5*
Dallas, TX 75243 *www.rockbarrell.com*

Rock hounds will go nuts over these 4,000 square feet of stone-age fun. There are counters full of books and reference materials for the beginner and the pro. Shelves full of tumblers, grits and saws to fit any budget, and if you want the big stuff, they can order it. And you never saw so many rocks and beads. OK, beady eyes, we saw semi-precious stones, metal, glass, sea glass and Greek ceramic models as well as African tribal beads. Precut, polished and raw stones or cabochons, they have it all. Agate, aventurin, carnelian, goldstones, hemitite, howlite, jasper, leopard skin, malachite, mother of pearl, onyx, paua, quartz, rhodonite, snowflake, sodalite, tiger eye and unakite are all here in sizes running from 5 by 3 mm up to 38 mm in most cases. Of course, they offer all stringing supplies from silk and "polymid" (nylon) to leather and waxed cotton cords. Don't vascillate between a rock and a hard place, this IS the place to shop. *CK, MC, V, D*

★★★★★ Sandaga Market 214/747-8431

1325 Levee St. *Mon-Fri 9-5; Sat 10-5; By Appt.*
Dallas, TX 75207

Darrell Thomas' Sandaga Market is a one-man show but don't let that dissuade you. This is one small step for the artistic kind. After one dose of his African imports, you'll be drunk with pleasure. Offering probably the biggest and no doubt the best selection of African imports in the Metroplex, he features a distinctive selection of tribal art and textiles from Ghana, Ivory Coast and Mali. Dogon stools, masks, mud cloths, sculpture, fetishes and fine art are all bought direct and priced to sell. To find him, take I-35 E southbound to Continental, turn right, turn right again at Industrial, go four blocks to Cole, then turn left to the end of the block and look for a big white sign with red letters proclaiming, "Sandaga Market." *CK*

♥♥♥♥♥ Sports Legacy, The Gallery of Sports Art 817/461-1994

1000 Ballpark Way, Suite 122 *Mon-Sun 10-6*
Arlington, TX 76011

With a true gallery of sports art right at The Ballpark in Arlington, why would you run all over town for a home run? When you go out to the ballgame, save your money buying peanuts or Cracker Jacks and visit Sports Legacy instead. (They close the doors to the outside at 6 P.M. on game days, but those with a game ticket can visit until 30 minutes after the last pitch is thrown). Don't settle for a walk without scoring a Bart Forbes "First Season" print or a Mickey Mantle portraiture by Cliff Spohn. Besides, if Jody Dean was reduced to tears when he received his favorite Brent Benger's print of a boy and his father attending their first ball game together, there's no need to belabor the point. Remember, your investment may appreciate to a grand slam. However, to fully appreciate the selection of art from all sports, make it a point to come on a day when the Rangers aren't in town. The rooms won't be packed tight and the service will be more personalized. *CK, MC, V, AE, D*

★★★★★ Squadron Mail Order 972/242-8663

1114 Crowley Drive
Carrollton, TX 75011

Say tanks to this defender of discounts on model airplanes, motorcycles, bombers, battleships, tanks and other "militaria." Win the war on boredom with savings of 30-70 percent off retail. This is one of the country's foremost dealers of airplane kits, with a selection that ranges from a simulated World War I biplane to an exact replica of a Navy fighter detailed down to the cockpit and decals. A fascinating selection of books for the model builder is also available, many concerning a particular branch of the armed services. Squadron owns their own publishing company and markets publications though their mail-order business. Minimum order is $10. Bombs away! *CK, MC, V, AE, D*

★★★★★ Stained Glass Overlay by Glass Solutions 972/570-4685

2814 N. O'Connor Rd. *Mon-Fri 11-4; Sat by Appt.*
Irving, TX 75062

I think that I shall never see a stained-glass shower as lovely as thee. Their patented technique of making stained glass overlays brings great beauty and dimension to your home's decor and windows. One look and you're hooked. Well, what is it? It's actually a work of art that is created for your doors or windows. Or you can add it to a skylight, a ceiling panel, a room divider, a cabinet door insert, a sliding glass door, a shower door–the list is endless, but don't expect masterpieces to come cheap. Do you think anyone had the nerve to negotiate with Michaelangelo while he was hanging from the ceiling? Since it's a secret how they do it, the only way you can enjoy it is to buy it. Seeing is believing. They also carry a selection of nifty gift ideas, such as gift boxes, Austrian crystals, decorative bevels, Lava Lace perfume bottles, shells and eggs made from Mount St. Helen's ash and Victorian enameled bells. Drop by their studio to behold a work of art. The studio is at O'Connor and Rochelle, which can be confusing to some first-time visitors. The two streets intersect twice. Glass Solutions is two lights north of 183 on O'Connor, not in the Las Colinas area where O'Connor and Rochelle also intersect. *CK, MC, V, AE, D*

♥♥♥♥♥ Stitch Art Embroidery 972/247-6697

Farmers Branch, TX *By Appt. Only*
www.stitchartembroidery.com

With satisfied customers across the country, this Farmers Branch-based company will please even the most discriminating tastes when they put your name, logo, number or the design that catches your eye on T-shirts, caps, towels, jackets and more. In addition to embroidery services, they have access to other advertising specialty printing as well. They take orders as small as one, but price breaks begin to kick in at 12 or more. Be ready with information about what you want, and samples are helpful. Another plus at Stitch Art Embroidery is working with the Celia. She's a stitch!

★★★★ Wholesale Art & Frames 972/864-0278

2480 S. Jupiter Rd., Suite 1004 *Mon-Fri 9:30-5; Sat Noon-5*
Garland, TX 75041

Next to Vikon Village, picture this: your favorite picture being skillfully custom-framed at wholesale prices near one of the largest flea markets in the Metroplex. You can choose from a variety of oil paintings, posters, prints and limited editions in contemporary, Southwest or classic designs. Ready-made frames and custom framing and matting done to your specifications. Decorators and designers are welcome, but they have a special fondness for Underground Shoppers. *CK, MC, V*

Arts & Crafts & Collectibles

★★★★ Woodworks Outlet Store

817/581-5240

4521 Anderson Blvd.
Haltom City, TX 76117
Mon-Fri 8:30-5
www.woodwrks.com

Looking to "pig out"? This is the place not only to carve out your own creative niche, but to also paint it. Carved-out wooden pigs, cows and apples, for starters, can be seen and then painted. Enjoy the fruits of your own labor without paying for the finished product. This is the place to put your finger on the pulse of your imagination and paint these wholesale-priced wood cut-outs. Need other craft supplies, books, patterns, kits or items such as paints and jewelry components? The store is a little section of their warehouse that is open to the public. Woodworks Outlet Store is at the corner of Anderson and Murray. Take I-35 W to Meacham Boulevard, head east and where it dead ends, take a left. Then take another left on Anderson That should get you there. *CK, MC, V, D*

Audio/Video/Stereo/TVs

★★★ Audio Concepts

214/360-9520

11661 Preston Rd.
Dallas, TX 75230

Tues-Fri 10-7; Sat 10-6
www.dalaudioconcepts.com

Their systems only sound expensive. While it's true you can spend $50,000 or more, you can also spend as little as $2,000 and get a system that takes you to the next level in music and film reproduction. Worried that it won't sound as good in your home as it does in their store? Not to worry. They deliver and set up every system they sell and can even wire your entire home for the sound of music. Have questions but not sure where to start? You'll find no-pressure sales, where professionals can talk high-tech or simply let the music do the talking. Listen to these brands: ARCAM, AUDIO RESEARCH, AYRE, GRADO, JPW, KIMBER, KIMBER SELECT, KONTAK, LINN, MAGNEPAN, MISTRAL, NAD, NAKAMICHI, PROAC, PROCEED, PROTON VIDEO, QUADRASPIRE, REGA, ROTEL (not the tomatoes), RUARK, RUNCO, SOUND ORGANIZATION, THETA, THEIL, ZOETHECUS and EKORNES chairs and sofas. Heard enough? There's more, but "hear" is where I get off. But before we leave you completely, we did leave with a LINN CD player (top-of-the-line) that sounded like a 40-piece orchestra in the showroom. If you want a complete room stereo system, they will even come to your house to set up your hearing aids. *CK, MC, V, AE, D*

✧✧✧✧ Bayard Electronics

214/828-1422

5706 E. Mockingbird Lane
Dallas, TX 75206

Mon-Fri 10-7; Sat Noon-5
www.bayard.com

If your VCR goes on the blink, don't automatically trash it! It's not cheaper to buy a new one. At Bayard Electronics, located on the bottom floor of a two-story red brick building near the Java Jones Coffee Shop, you can have it fixed–a lot cheaper. Here they'll give you an estimate and a pre-approved fee, not to be exceeded (similar to a car repair). You're in the driver's seat if you choose to trash it or not. But think repair, first. Bring in your tired and worn–anything electronic. TV-VCR service, camcorders, audio systems, car stereos and radios, big screen TVs, NINTENDO systems...and if need be, they make house calls. If you need a second opinion on this place, the *Dallas Observer* has voted Bayard best electronics repair center in Dallas for the last few years. *CK, MC, V, D*

★★★★ Best Buy — 972/239-9980

4255 Lyndon B. Johnson Frwy. — *Mon-Sat 10-9; Sun 11-6*
Dallas, TX 75244 — *www.bestbuy.com*

Just because they're the big guys, don't overlook some of their Best Buys. This supermarket-style showroom concentrates on the most popular items–TVs, stereos, VCRs, home office equipment, computers, photographic equipment, cellular phones, car audio and installation, and more. We walked for hours, checking out prices on refrigerators, gas grills, cellular phones and computers. Their large selection of CDs, cassettes (audio and video), and computer software are priced as good as it gets for new merchandise. In fact, this category may be their strongest suit. Check the directory for other area locations. *CK, MC, V, AE, D, Best Buy*

★★★★★ CAM Audio — 972/271-0006

2210 Executive Drive — *Mon-Fri 8:30-5*
Garland, TX 75041 — *www.camaudio.com*

Since 1968, CAM has been a distributor of 3M audio products. Over the years, they've expanded to other audio, video and sound amplification products (tapes, albums, storage units, video cameras, decks, monitors and blank videotapes). Located near Jupiter and Miller, if you're looking for sound equipment, including microphones, speakers, mixers and amps, CAM is your man! Tune in to such brand names as AMPLI VOX, ASTOUND, BOSE, BRAVO, BRETFORD, BUHL, DA-LITE, DOLBY, DRAPER, EIKI, ELECTRO-VOICE, ELMO, GEM, HAMILTON, JVC, LUXOR, MARANTZ, MAXWELL, MOTOROLA, OTARI, PANASONIC, PELICAN, SANYO, SHARP, SURE, SONY, TDK, TEAC, TECHNICS, TELEX, ULTIMATE SUPPORT and VIDEONICS. Discounts are offered off manufacturers' suggested retail price and even more is discounted from "house" brands. Looking for bulk audio and video cassettes? Even audio and video duplication is discounted. For professional users, shop here for supplies if you want custom boxes, labels or albums. You'll also find high-speed cassette (16x) duplicators, audio and video recording equipment, and sound amplification. Returns are accepted if in new condition. Merchandise is shipped via UPS within 24 hours. If you prepay with a check, the freight is free. *CK, MC, V, AE, D*

Audio/Video/Stereo/TVs

★★★ Circuit City

817/738-1796

4820 W. I-20
Mon-Sat 10-9; Sun 11-6
Fort Worth, TX 76132
www.circuitcity.com

Often offering no interest and no payments for six months on big ticket items, don't short circuit Circuit City. Camcorders, stereos, televisions, computers and accessories, appliances, videos and music, telephones and cell phones are part of the package from AMANA, BOSE, CANON, COMPAQ, HEWLETT PACKARD, KENWOOD, LEXMARK, MAYTAG, PANASONIC, ROPER, SONY, WHIRLPOOL...well, the beat goes on. Thousands of CDs for under $10 every day. Perennial sales, so check their web page and newspapers for current events. We like the catchy jingle. We like the huge selection. We like the prices. The only thing we don't like are the salesmen who tried to get you to buy up (that means to a more expensive item). In our case, we wanted a plain-Jane camcorder and asked for the SONY Handycam for $599, but, "No," he moaned. They were so many better. Nevertheless, we got what we wanted, which included a ZENITH 19-inch color TV with remote for $189. We were tempted, but resisted the MAGNAVOX two-head VCR with remote for only $159, because it was the last one and there was no box. (Well, who plays the box anyway?) And we held firm in shopping for computers elsewhere though FREE Six Flags tickets were an additional incentive to buy without getting electrocuted. Circuit City, like all the category killers, offers a low-price guarantee, so check around before making the final plunge. (They'll also refund 110 percent of your money within 30 days if you find it cheaper elsewhere.) Check the directory for one of nine other locations in the Metroplex. With 600 locations across the country, their power speaks loud and clear. (Remember, they're also the founders of CarMax.) They have a toll-free technical help line called "Answer City," but so far, we've never gotten through. Lines were always busy. *CK, MC, V, AE, D, Circuit City*

✧✧ Dr. VCR

214/748-6955

By Appt. Only

If you can't program your VCR, please don't call Bill. However, if your VCR has called it quits, or has eaten your "Jurassic Park" tape, call on this doctor. Bill Springer. He only makes house calls. For less than the cost of a movie, drinks and popcorn for two, you can get a clean bill of health by having your VCR cleaned and repaired (minor only). When you leave a message, let him know the brand, its age and the nature of the problem to ensure a prescription that will effect a cure. Also, ask him if it's even worth repairing. Yes, sometimes it's better to let sleeping dogs lie in the trash. Expect to pay $32.50 to fix, clean and get it in working order (sure beats paying for a new one). He'll try to fix your VCR, but he lives up to the old adage, "Honesty is the still the best policy." *CK*

★★★★★ Ed Kellum & Son

214/526-1717

4533 Cole Ave.
Dallas, TX 75205
Mon-Sat 9-6; Thu 9-8

Located behind Weir's, next to Hoffbrau Steak House in the heart of the chichi Knox-Henderson marketplace, their new home is bigger and better, standing all by itself in a contemporary beige building. They're still pulling the same old shtick–they pay you $1,000 cash if they don't beat another's deal. But, if you show them an ad for an item at a lower price, who wouldn't meet or beat it? Nevertheless, it sure beats paying you a thousand "smackaroos". This Dallas tradition has been selling appliances and electronics since 1948. An RCA big screen 56-inch stereo TV, picture-in-picture with universal remote, was reduced from $2,999 to $1,189; a 35-inch stereo TV was marked down at $887 from $1,499; a 27-inch traditional stereo console TV was no longer $949 but $487; and an 18X zoom VHS compact camcorder was $447 instead of $899. From big screens to a little MAGIC CHEF 30-inch electric free-standing range, they also have refrigerators, freezers, built-ins and super-capacity deluxe washers and dryers. Expect the prices to be right in line with the best discounters in town. With all the best brands, from AMANA to MAYTAG, KITCHENAID to JENN-AIR, you can't go wrong with this family's contribution to saving you time and money. *CK, MC, V, D*

★★ Freedom Appliance Town

214/388-8585

7016 Military Pkwy.
Dallas, TX 75227
Mon-Fri 9-6; Sat 9-4

Bordering Mesquite, this is no wildfire, nor is it a place to blow caution to the wind. Since they buy all their refrigerators in working condition, there are some pretty cool buys here. Scott makes sure everything's in tip-top shape before leaving the floor. Refurbished appliances allow you to assert your new-found freedom from ever paying full prices again. So, if it works, don't knock it. Furthermore, you won't have to fix it. Used GENERAL ELECTRIC, HOTPOINT, KENMORE, WHIRLPOOL and other washers, dryers, stoves and refrigerators are sold at decidedly discounted prices from new, but you have to shop often as the inventory blows hot and cold. One day, there were 70 refrigerators, one stove and no dishwashers. Another day, they were loaded with washers and dryers. But the gentleman in charge is always on the prowl and will no doubt find what you're looking for. Prices will free you from bondage and a 60-day warranty makes it easier to swallow. Same-day delivery is also available if you're in the area. *CK, MC, V, AE, D*

★★★ Fry's Electronics

214/342-5900

12710 Executive Drive
Dallas, TX 75238

Mon-Fri 8 A.M.-9 P.M.; Sat 9-9; Sun 9-7

Fry's is a disappointment in their overall appearance, sorry to say, but you've got to give them credit for coming into such a competitive market as Dallas/Fort Worth without batting an eyelash. Trouble is, they are not seeing that clearly that in spite of full-page color ads–you still have to be minding the store. Nevertheless, there's a huge selection and low prices on computers, software and hardware (internal and external parts), PANASONIC and other vacuum cleaners, washers and dryers, refrigerators and freezers, small appliances, phones, pagers and answering machines, CDs, movies and tapes, receivers and players, sound systems, camcorders, cameras both digital and film-types make Fry's a super mercado of good buys. One savvy shopper drives to their Northwest Highway at Jupiter Rd. area location from Austin just to check out their prices whenever he can. Most times they will equal or beat what he can get over the internet. The prices are ever changing to keep ahead of the competition. Look for their full-page ads and weekly inserts in newspapers to keep up with current prices. Be sure to beat a path to their doors so you don't miss out when quantities are limited. Their lowest price guarantee is nothing to sneeze at. Plus, no rebate hassles and friendly and knowledgeable salespeople are definite pluses as well. Visit their other location at 102 E. I-20 (at Matlock Rd.) in Arlington (817/784-5800). *CK, MC, V, D*

★★★ FuncoLand

972/385-0422

12817 Preston Rd
Forest Village Shopping Center.
Dallas, TX 75230

Mon-Fri 11-9; Sat 10-6; Sun Noon-6
www.funcoland.com

Are you bored with your old Mario Brothers game? Check out FuncoLand for the latest in new video games. They sell new and previously played video games reconditioned and with a 90-day warranty. FuncoLand also offers you the opportunity to come in and play the games before you buy. What do you have to lose? They'll even pay you to turn loose of your old games or provide you with an in-store trade-in credit. Get about ⅓ to ½ of the original price with trade-in credit. We found a SONY PLAYSTATION, refurbished by Sony, for $79.94. New they were $99.95, but get this: If you buy the reconditioned unit and the extended warranty for $14.95, you've got a practically new unit with a one-year warranty instead of Sony's usual 90-day warranty. Be prepared for the store to be packed with 10-year-olds on Saturday, all wanting to play the same game you came in to try. Check the directory for many locations throughout the Metroplex. *CK, MC, V, D*

✧✧ GARC (Garland Amateur Radio Club) — 972/272-4499

Monthly Meetings
www.qsl.net/garc

If you're a ham radio fan, join the Garland Amateur Radio Club. Meetings are held on the fourth Monday of every month at 7:30 P.M. at the Garland Women's Activity Center, located at 713 W. Austin St. Dues are $15 per year. For classes, call 972/495-9654, and for testing sessions, call 972/475-9407. Calling their 800 number above is a great source for finding used equipment, and if you have a scanner, tune in every Monday night (except on club meeting nights) for the GARC Information Net. Here, you can listen in to local and national amateur radio news, a technical help session, a "swap-shop" of used gear for sale and public service events.

♥♥♥♥♥ Hillcrest High Fidelity — 972/392-7636

13400 Preston Rd. — *Mon-Fri 10-7; Sat 10-6; Sun Noon-5*
Dallas, TX 75240 — *www.hillcresthifi.com*

Hillcrest High Fidelity has been the cream of the crop in sound systems since 1947. The finest audio and video equipment is offered at fair prices, but be warned, this is serious high-tech stuff and is priced accordingly. Staffed with knowledgeable salespeople who are available to answer even the most complicated or mundane questions, shoppers may audition new and previously-owned audio gear from such prestigious companies as ANTHEM by SONIC FRONTIERS, AUTOQUEST CABLES, B&W, KIMBER KAIBLE, KLIPSCH, KRELL, LEXICON, MARANTZ, MCINTOSH, NAKAMICHI, PARADIGM, PIONEER ELITE, ROCKUSTICS, ROTEL, SONY ES, TRIBUTARIES, VELODYNE and YAMAHA for starters. They also offer a wide range of video systems from CHANNEL MASTER, CHANNEL PLUS, ELITE by PIONEER, FUJITSU, LOEWE, PIONEER, RCA 18-inch DSS systems, SONY ES, STEWART, WINEGARD and more. For serious movie buffs, Hillcrest offers the LUCASFILM THX audio system for the home! They even offer a "sound architect," who will create your in-home design and install the system. Also visit their Plano location at 3309 Dallas Pkwy. (at Parker Rd.) or call them at 972/473-2248. *CK, MC, V, AE, D*

♥♥♥♥♥ Home Entertainment 214/373-0600

8414 Preston Rd. *Mon-Fri 10-8; Sat 10-7; Sun Noon-6*
Dallas, TX 75225 *www.tweeter.com*

Home Entertainment is a purveyor of high-tech toys from quality companies such as ACOUSTICS, BOSTON, KLIPDVH, MACINTOSH, NAD, PHASE TECH, VELODYNE, YAMAHA and others. The store is divided into several spacious listening areas that make it easy to critically audition equipment. You will find MITSUBISHI 50-inch big screen TVs along with bookshelf speakers and many other home entertainment products for pictures and sounds that will blow you away. From basic to extravagant, the sound systems are the focus here but it's their in-home design and custom installation that we sing their praises. Also hear them at the Galleria–Level 3 (972/934-8585) and in Plano at 3400 Preston Rd. (at Parker Rd.; 972/985-9945). *CK, MC, V, AE, D*

♥♥♥♥♥ Home Theater Store 972/404-9500

13330 Preston Rd. *Mon-Sat 10-8; Sun Noon-6*
Dallas, TX 75240 *www.hometheaterstore.com*

Even if the Cowboys didn't score the big one, that doesn't mean you can't. Root for the Boys and maybe you can really see their moves clearly (on screen, not off!) on a big screen TV. Though not always the lowest price, you can't fault Home Theater Store for their selection. Audio and video systems from CINEMA SERIES by TOSHIBA, ELITE by PIONEER, MITSUBISHI, RUNCO, SHARP, TRINITON by SONY and XF by PANASONIC are the brand highlights here. You'll also find a wide variety of speakers by BOSE, PARADIGM and POLK AUDIO, as well as furniture by CONTOUR, DRAPER and LEXINGTON, to name a few. Their claim, "Guaranteed Low Prices!", is no big deal. Everybody's doing it! But same-day delivery is a plus, as well as the fact that they specialize in home theaters. Don't be a killjoy and put some lowly 13-inch TV in your new media room. What will the neighbors think? Tune into the Home Theater Store across from Valley View Mall. *CK, MC, V, AE, D*

★★★★ Panasonic Factory Service Center 972/385-1975

13615 Welch Rd. *Mon-Fri 9-4:30; Thu 9-6*
Dallas, TX 75244

Whether it's PANASONIC, QUASAR or TECHNICS, it's all under one roof here, waiting for a new home. New or refurbished, dropped or dented, who cares as long as it works and looks good. Everything this service center sells comes with a 90-day warranty and if you're still squeamish, you can always purchase an extended warranty. The line-up of electronics and small appliances is extensive. Small and large screen TVs, bread machines, VCRs, microwaves, console and portable stereos, boom boxes, telephones and faxes can all be found here. Prices–well, what did you expect? Retail? Not even close! If you want a deal, this is where you'll have to appeal. Whether it's a big screen TV or a pocket-sized Walkman that has been factory refurbished, returned, or set out because the box was dented, as long as it's running, looks good and comes with a warranty (or you can buy an extended warranty), who are you kidding? You can't beat it. If you need parts for anything, just call their 800 number. Inventory fluctuates, so if you see something that is appealing, grab it before it gets away. *CK, MC, V, AE, D*

Pro Audio Video Systems & Satellite Technology — 214/341-DISH

10201 Plano Rd., Suite 110 — *By Appt. Only*
Dallas, TX 75238

Tired of waiting for your cable company to get its act together? Go for a satellite dish–it's 25-60 percent cheaper over time than a cable subscription. See football games minus the commercials with raw feeds, watch live concert performances and get instant pay-per-view with video quality comparable to that of a laser disc player and CD-quality sound. DISH Network, DirecTV and 4DTV satellite dishes for residential and commerical use are offered from $99 and up. Pro Audio can also provide you with a complete home theater system. Complete turn-keys are offered and no subcontractors are used, as the owners install and service each and every time themselves. *CK, MC, V, AE, D*

★★★★★ Radio Shack Outlet Store — 817/654-0337

900 Terminal Rd. — *Mon-Sat 9-8; Sun Noon-6*
Fort Worth, TX 76106 — *www.radioshack.com*

Tune into the radio–Radio Shack, that is. Take a look inside one of Radio Shack's retail stores and then shop here. Though the stock includes scratched and dents, seconds, imperfects and some items sold "as-is," who cares when the quality, value and selection is where it's at anyway? Save up to 50 percent and more at their spacious outlet, located near the historic Fort Worth Stockyards. From TVs to computers, CD players to car stereos, mobile phones to scanners and much more, this outlet bats a thousand! At Christmas time, this place is humming with the sound of...batteries. In the summer, find toys and other goodies at 50-80 percent off retail, just the perfect opportunity to stash away in a Christmas stocking. Two remote-control cars fit perfectly–trust me. And that, folks, is the end of the story. *CK, MC, V, AE, D, Store Card*

RCA

www.rca.com

Are you looking to get a high quality entertainment center? If so then you have come to the right place. We are happy to tell you about RCA and their website at www.rca.com. You can start with an EX5 5-disc CD carousel changer. It has a dual-layer four-color vacuum, fluorescent display with spectrum analyzer. It has 60-watts of total power, four-way speaker systems with KEVLAR woofers for only $199.99. A 36- inch RCA direct-view high resolution television is great for any entertainment system. You can find them here for around $2,499. The deals are flourishing at RCA so call them toll free at 800/835-8316 or visit them online at *www.rca.com.*

✧✧✧✧ Satellite Guy, The 972/243-3838

Dallas, TX *By Appt. Only*

Mike Allen's the Satelite Guy. He'll hook you up in his spare time when he freelances from his regular satellite set-up job. Or, if it's a total audio experience you're looking for, he also does surround sound. *CK*

★★★★★ Starpower, The Ultimate Home Theater Source 214/522-2000

3927 Oak Lawn Ave. *Mon-Sat 10-8; Sun Noon-6*
Dallas, TX 75219 *www.star-power.com*

Big screen and high-definition TVs, hi-fi audio, custom entertainment centers, DVD players, indoor and outdoor speakers, phone systems, cabinetry, theater and leather seating are all part and parcel of this giant home theater source. Automatic low-price guarantees make shopping a sure-fire lesson in saving money. If you find the same item for a lower price elswhere within 30 days after your purchase, you'll find a check in your mailbox. Specializing in custom designs and installation, brand names are impressive: ATLANTIC TECHNOLOGY, B & O (BANG & OLEFSUN), CITATION, ENERGY, FAROUDJA, HARMON KARDON, HITACHI, KENWOOD, MONITOR AUDIO, PIONEER, RUNCO, SONY XBR and TOSHIBA. They also feature audio systems with DOLBY DIGITAL and DTS sound. They'll work hard to provide the best solutions for all of your home entertainment needs. Financing is available, as well as immediate delivery for in-stock products. Also visit their other location at 15340 Dallas Pkwy., Suite 1000, 972/503-6000. *CK, MC, V, AE, D, Financing*

✧✧ U-Edit 972/690-3348

1002 N. Central Expwy., Suite 689 *Mon-Thu 9-8; Fri 9-6; Sat 10-4*
Richardson, TX 75080 *www.u-edit-video.com*

Budding Steven Spielbergs can try their hand at directing their own edited version of the next award-winning film by heading to the closest location of U-Edit. Bring in your video footage, old photos, music, etc., and make a memory last forever. The equipment is all here, and if you don't have your own tape, they will provide you with one. Editing charges are $18-$75 per hour and some instruction is available to beginners. Call for details on how to prepare for the big day. Add titles to your video for $5 each. Machines are also available to convert 8 mm film to VHS videotape. They'll also make copies of tapes and copying charges start from around $8. This is a great way to make that perfect wedding tape or chronicle baby's first years. Additional locations are in Arlington, 817/261-3348 and Lewisville, 972/459-0086. Appointments are preferred. *CK, MC, V, AE, D*

✧✧✧ Video-Sat TV & Satellite 972/617-8600

2509 Ovilla Rd. *Mon-Fri 9-5:30*
Red Oak, TX 75154

Wayne Rose has been tuning in area viewers with TVs and satellite systems since 1972. Both sales and service are his method of Staying Alive, Staying Alive! You don't need to be John Travolta to learn the ropes of the satellite business, though. And if your TV, satellite or VCR goes on the blink, Wayne's World is where to land. View the world of hundreds of channels 24 hours a day, seven days a week, as Wayne offers Dish Network, DirecTV and C-Band satellite systems. He'll even recommend a programmer for the channels and will special order what you're looking for, too. Consumers keep him pretty busy, so he serves primarily northern Ellis and southern Dallas counties, including Red Oak, Ovilla, Cedar Hill, Lancaster, DeSoto and Duncanville. Look for the metal building out in the country near I-35 E and Ovilla Rd., next door to the Granson Feed Store. *CK*

Baby & Mom

★★★★★ A Little Behind

972/769-2229

3001 E. Plano Pkwy., Suite 400
Plano, TX 75074
Tues-Sat 10-6
www.alittlebehind.com

Call the corporate offices for the closest local delivery reps and have the dirty job cleaned up without getting behind on your budget. Stay ahead of the game and save money on keeping baby disposable diapers bought factory direct. A case of 320 small diapers, delivered, was $46, or in-store, $38.99; medium (per case of 252), $51, in-store, $41.99; large (per case of 216), $51, in-store $41.99. Also Wet Wipes, Training Pants and the "can't be without" Diaper Genie refills are available. You can also get adult incontinent diapers on request. Cloth diapers are PH balanced, and whether it's their brand or a national one, you'll save 40-70 percent. Have them delivered to your front door or pick them up for less at one of their area stores. Either way, it's hard not to dry a hard bargain. This year they've expanded their merchandise to include baby fashion gear, cribs, car seats, children's furniture and more. Everything is at close-out prices and only the top name brands are represented. Also check out their stores in DeSoto, Gun Barrel City, Lewisville, McKinney, Mesquite, Tyler and Weatherford. *CK, MC, V, COD*

★★★★ Babies R Us

972/247-4229

3850 Belt Line Rd.
Addison, TX 75244
Mon-Sat 9:30-9:30; Sun 10-7
www.babiesrus.com

When Toys R Us gobbled up the former Baby Superstores, it's now (with the exception of Burlington Coat's Baby Depot) the powerhouse for bargain bambinos. Apparently, that has made stockholders very happy since toys have been teetering lately. No doubt, they're probably the largest baby store presence in the country catering to parents who are singing the blues over the high prices of baby buntings. Within 40,000 square feet of selling space, you'll not want just a single thing if babies are on your mind. First-time expectant mothers (or grandparents) and those who have babies in tow, this store targets that niche. Like other "category killers", the selection, variety and discounted prices are staggering. Outfit the nursery with cribs and related furniture (their forte), stock the shelves with discounted diapers, Tylenol for babies, rattles, toys, and clothing, all at everyday low prices. Though these superstores may be the biggest, they are not always the lowest prices. Check the directory for other locations. *CK, MC, V, AE, D*

★★★★ Babies 'n' Bells Announcements & Invitations — 972/416-2229

2110 Springwood St. — *Mon-Fri 9-5*
Carrollton, TX 75006 — *www.babiesnbells.com*

One stay-at-home mom, with years of advertising and marketing experience behind her, found a way to fulfill her needs to have a home-based career without sacrificing time spent with her young and growing family. Babies 'n' Bells was born and is now franchising. This local resource offers thousands of designs available with new inventory arriving weekly. All orders are printed within 48 hours with fast delivery, so there are really no labor pains at all. Whether it's birth announcements, wedding invitations, christening invitations, shower invitations, calling cards, thank-you notes and birthday party invitations, if it's a printed piece of paper, this company does it all for less. *CK, MC, V, D*

★★★★★ Baby Bedding — 817/419-0088

3415 S. Cooper St., Suite 102 — *Mon-Sat 10-6; Sun Noon-6*
Arlington, TX 76015

This factory outlet is another of the growing list of workrooms catering to the booming baby business. Located at the corner of Cooper and Mayfield with "nobody beats their prices...guaranteed" as their slogan, this is a one-stop shop worth a look-see. Everything for your baby (except the nanny and the live-in pediatrician) helps make those first few years a little easier on the budget. Outfit the entire nursery with custom bedding, round cribs, standard cribs, cradles, highchairs, changing tables, rockers, chests, mattresses, gliders and more. JENNY LIND, a popular line of baby furniture, was a highlight for $369.99, a price which included the crib, cradle, changing table, chair and a child's rocker. Baby cribs started as low as $99 and included the bedding. Brand new, in the box, these prices can't be beat (even at resale shops). High-quality fabrics are also in stock for your own design, 100 percent cotton. Visit their other location that is open on weekends at the Traders Village Flea Market at 2600 Mayfield Rd. in Grand Prairie. *CK, MC, V, AE, D*

Baby & Mom

★★★ Baby Delights — 972/291-7844

608 Cedar St. — *Tues-Fri 10-6; Sat 10-5*
Cedar Hill, TX 75104

Located across the street from the Cedar Hill City Hall west of Belt Line Rd. and U.S. Hwy. 67, baby (and parents) will delight in the hand-made bedding and bumper pads found here. Darling duds, furniture and more, the stock includes crafty knickknacks for the nursery and clothing for baby to 6X. Delight in traditional cribs in cherry, oak, white or natural finishes starting around $250, as well as matching furniture and accessories from MILLION DOLLAR BABY. Also be sure to sign-up your little gals for their "dress-up tea parties" for girls ages 4 - 9. They'll all have a wonderful time. *CK, MC, V, AE, D*

★★★★★ Baby Depot — 972/613-1333

2021 Town East Blvd. — *Mon-Sat 10-9; Sun 11-6*
Mesquite, TX 75150

Choo-choo your little caboose over to the Baby Depot inside Burlington Coat Factory. This expanded section carries almost as much inventory as other baby stores. If you're making a list and checking it twice, get a load of these stellar performers: APRICA, BASSETT, CHILD CRAFT, GRACO, LAMBS & IVY, NOJO and SIMMONS. Aren't you impressed yet? In terms of quality, we were told that SIMMONS is the best because they hand-make all of their furniture. CHILDCRAFT and BASSETT come in a close second. Everything for the baby's room, except the baby, is here. Choose cribs, changing tables, chests, dressers, rockers, strollers, layettes, accessories, bedding, high chairs, car seats, play yards, carriers, swings, walkers and more. We cooed over a wonderful wicker bassinet and a two-piece bassinet skirt set in white lace, but were wooed instead to the mother-to-be gift registry, which is certainly a high-brow service for an off-price department store. Check the directory for the Metroplex location nearest you: Webb Chapel and Forest; Plano, Central Expressway and Parker; Euless, Industrial Blvd. and 183; Grapevine Mills Mall; and Arlington, I-20 and S. Cooper St. *CK, MC, V, AE, D*

★★★★★ A Baby's Dream — 817/795-2366

2205 W. Division St., Suite A-6 — *Mon-Sat 10-6*
Arlington, TX 76012

Mommies and grannies-to-be have found heaven at this custom workroom for a baby's nursery, including matching bedding, window treatments, canopies, wall hangings, chair cushions, cradles, dressers and chests, dressing tables, lamps, rocking chairs, mobiles and gliders. Meet me and my mouth, because I've just blown her cover. Pearley Terry is the reason to celebrate giving birth. The custom, hand-painted lamps that match the bedding that match your decor are the way to decorate. Whether it's a circular crib like those chosen by movie stars or a more traditional crib or cradle (your fabric or theirs), your baby will look great in it. The brand name they carry is called MILLION DOLLAR BABY. It's a wonderfully made brand of baby furniture. Don't miss the TOWNE SQUARE glider-rockers made in Hillsboro. They are the ones everyone is clamoring for. Custom orders and nine-month layaways available. The workroom is right next door so you can't get closer to the factory than here. A Baby's Dream is in west Arlington on Division St. between Fielder and Bowen. It's worth the drive if you're expecting or if you know someone who is. *CK, MC, V, AE, D*

★★★★★ Be' Be' Maternity — 214/742-2229

1644 Irving Blvd. — *Mon-Fri 11-6; Sat 10-5*
Dallas, TX 75207 — *www.bebematernity.com*

From Here to Maternity, it's important to keep your budget in check. From dressy to casual, this is the place that allows you to keep growing, and growing and growing. Beautiful maternity fashions in Tencel denim and Pima cotton are especially comforting (and comfortable) for mothers to be and their babies. They also have a large variety of maternity accessories including jacket clips, panty hose, and bras. This source is a top notch maternity outlet with the BE' BE' MATERNITY label. Experience the Great Expectation and save 50-75 percent over anything remotely close in quality. Endorsed by Organized Labor! *CK, MC, V, AE, D*

★★★ Beary Cute Kids — 817/370-0058

5352 Wedgmont Circle N. — *Tue-Fri 10-6; Sat 10-3*
Fort Worth, TX 76133

Want quality children's, infants through pre-teen in girls and through size 14 in boys clothing? Then head to Trail Lake Dr. and Wedgmont Circle. N. behind the credit union building if you're looking for beary, beary cute clothes. Some brand names, some non-name brands are featured here. TOMMY HILFIGER was spotted at beary, beary good prices. Their shop is small (700-800 square feet.) to complement their small (in stature) clientele, but savings and variety are huge. In toys, they carry new and used market samples with an especially good selection in L'IL TYKES. For example, a L'IL TYKES picnic bench was $20 and new BOYD'S BEARS were $12-$20. They usually have a sale on all winter clothing in the spring with savings of up to 25 percent. The owner's personality adds another plus to our round of accolades. *CK, MC, V, AE, D, Layaway*

★★★ Big Baby Boutique (BBB) 940/381-3095

1720 W. University Drive *Mon-Sat 10-5:30*
Denton, TX 76201

This resale children's shop located near the Subway sandwich shop on University Drive just east of Bonnie Brae recycles wardrobes from newborns to size 8. After all, no kid can tell the difference. Even moms-to-be wardrobes can be expanded if budgets are stretched to the max. Outfit the nursery from cribs to changing tables (though changing tables fly out the door as fast as they come in), cradles to full-size car seats, walkers, children's videos, swings and toys. Rock the baby to sleep without those nightmarish prices. See what "roll models" your kids can be by downsizing your budget. *CK*

★★ Dan Howard Maternity Factory Outlet 972/233-4077

13323 Montfort Drive *Mon-Sat 10-6; Thurs 10-8; Sun Noon-5*
Dallas, TX 75240 *www.imaternity.com*

Let's face it, spending money on maternity clothes is not a long-term investment. So why go for broke? Granted, you can just by-pass this expansion mode when it comes to a mother-to-be growing pains. If you're an expectant career woman or fashionable mom-to-be looking to climb the corporate ladder, bypass the middleman and head straight to this manufacturer's outlet. You can certainly expand your wardrobe by filing into the Chicago-made maternity options here. But don't expect Dan to be your man for saving money. Apparently, they used to sell to department and specialty stores, but decided that their bread was buttered on the side of the consumer. Claims of saving 25-50 percent may be true, but they must have started on the high end of the price scale. Three other locations in the Metroplex: Loehmann's Plaza on E. Northwest Highway (near Jupiter) in Dallas; Collin Creek Village in Plano; and in Hurst at 936 Melbourne Rd. They also own the Mothertime stores, which are strictly retail, so stay away. Selection is certainly admirable with the addition of plus sizes 1X-3X. Watch for sales for your best bet. *CK, MC, V, AE, D, MOC*

★★★★★ Diaper Mart Superstore Warehouse 214/358-1499

2600 W. Mockingbird Lane *Mon-Fri 9-6; Sat 10-6; Sun 11-5*
Dallas, TX 75235

Factory direct, you can't get a better price, even if you tried. Play diaper derby without the diapers soaking you. This is the perfect place for those who "go leak in the night." Newborn diapers go for $10.99 (case of 96) and Ultras (with liner and gathered waist) were $16.99 for the large size. They even beat Wal-Mart's prices. All diapers are the disposable kind. Some kids' clothing, too, is here as surplus from major department stores. Disposable training pants were $13 for a 50-count, while diaper bags started as low as $4. We also snagged shoes, T-shirts and more for less than $2 each. Baby girls' dresses and baby boys' closeouts and overruns are also priced right. Located near Love Field on Mockingbird with a discounted furniture store complete with cribs, changing tables and custom gifts right next door. If you're still sweating the small stuff, they've got boxes of baby wipes, too. Cry all the way home to their Arlington/Grand Prairie outlet, Diaper Mart II at 2424 S. Carrier Pkwy., 972/606-0180; Diaper Mart III, 2825 Valley View Lane in Farmers Branch/Carrollton, 972/484-2880; or Diaper Mart IV in Garland at 1030 W. Centerville Rd. *CK, MC, V, D*

★★ Diaper World 817/459-3843

1417 E. Abram St. *Mon-Sat 9-6*
Arlington, TX 76010

Translated, this may be the start of something big. Look for the Diamond Shamrock station on E. Abram between Collins and Browning even if you don't need gas and fill'er up if you want to buy diapers direct from the factory. A package of 100 diapers for newborns for $15.99 is the straight poop, but everything else needs someone who is conversant in Sudanese. The gentleman in charge was a trip–funny and engaging–but his English was limited to a few mono-syllabic words (tell him to slow down and you will better understand him). We did understand that diapers at the lowest prices guaranteed can be delivered the same day–but from then on out, you wash and dry on your own. Interspersed with their main business, they also have baby clothing, toys, shoes, swings, bikes, walkers, cribs, bedding, strollers and more, but the selection is lean. *CK, MC, V, AE, D*

♥♥♥♥♥ Father Goose 972/985-3111

5100 Belt Line Rd, Suite 796 *Mon-Sat 10-6; Sun 1-5*
Addison, TX 75240

Okey, dokey, artichokey. From the creators of the Beyond Conception store, this is a place conceived by parents who had a better idea. With four stores (Addison, Austin, Houston and Scottsdale, Arizona), how can anyone with kids not feel a kinship to them? Children are waiting to be dressed (but no dressing rooms–you know how they hate to try anything on). Fill up with darling clothes from premi to 4T in AGABANG, HEAD OVER HEELS, KID SKINS, LETOP, MINI BASIX, MULBERRY BUSH, PETITE PATOE and VICTORIA KIDS. In furnishings, check out LE PINE, MARIGEAU, STATUS and PRIVATE LABEL with BLUE MOON and CHERBINI bedding. Twin beds and bunk beds are on display, too, for double the pleasure. If they don't have a specific item, they will order it for you but what else is there besides EVENFLO? *CK, MC, V, AE, D*

★★★★★ Kid to Kid 817/468-1995

1201 W. Arbrook Blvd., Suite 115 *Mon-Sat 10-8; Sun 1-5*
Arlington, TX 76015

Chocolate doesn't just melt in their mouths and on their hands, it also melts on their shirts and dresses! Kids outgrow all their clothes before they wear them out anyway, so why spend lots of dollars on a outfit that will only be stained or outgrown before you know it? Kid to Kid sells quality used kids clothes, furniture, toys and equipment at amazingly low prices. (Call ahead, 'cause they can't keep the furniture in stock. So many babies...so few bargain cribs.) This resale shop is proud to accept recycled clothes and will pay cash on the barrelhead for them. They also have new and used maternity wear, infant toys, baby furnishings, nursery sets and linens, car seats and strollers, cribs, cradles, bassinets, play pens and port-a-cribs, infant swings and walkers, swimwear, shoes–and the list goes on. For the best prices on TOWN SQUARE GLIDERS, check here before you head elsewhere. In fact, TOWN SQUARE GLIDERS is the only brand deemed safe for children. They buy your gently used children's items six days a week. Call for an appointment. Located across from The Parks of Arlington Mall, get a grip on reality if you know what's good for your budget. Check out their other locations in Fort Worth at 4750 Bryant Irvin Rd. (817/263-4660) and in Bedford at Highway 183 and Central Drive (817/283-6364). *CK, MC,* V

♥♥♥♥♥ Kiddie-Guard (Aquata-Tech) 972/931-7555

17811 Davenport Rd., Suite 43 *Mon-Fri 8:15-5*
Dallas, TX 75252 *www.gtesupersite.com\aquata-tech*

Relax while you're snoozing by the pool. If you don't want your little ones falling head-over- heels into the water without supervision, think protection from Aquata-Tech, an authorized KIDDIE-GUARD removable pool fence dealer. This easily removable pool fence is made of a transparent mesh barrier, powder-coating aluminum poles and molding, and a 2-inch long deck hole cover which is easy to roll up and be put out of the way while allowing peace of mind with double latches when in place. The fences are durable, easy to maintain and come with a five-year limited warranty. Aquata-Tech also offers professionally trained estimators and installors to do high quality work at a fair price. Call them for a free estimate. *CK, MC, V*

★★★ Kiddo's Kloset — 817/460-1746

2223 W. Park Row Drive, Suite E — *Mon-Sat 10-6*
Arlington, TX 76013

Hand-picked children's and maternity resale is a nice combination for baby and mom. After all, mothers know best–that is, until the teenage waifland. Boys' sizes from 0-16, girls' 0 up to Juniors, even "regular" mom's and maternity wear in sizes 4-16, S-XL, were all found here. At least while you're waiting, you don't have to go naked. Shoes and bedding for babies were in stock, too. Other important accoutrements to the kiddo's closet include toys, hair bows and other accessories. After all, how can anyone leave the house looking like plain Jane? Take I-30 to Fielder and go south. Just past Allan Saxe Stadium (UTA's baseball field), turn right on Park Row and Kiddo's Kloset is at the bottom of the hill in a strip center with CiCi's Pizza. If you get to Bowen Rd., you've gone too far. *CK, MC, V*

★★★★ Kids Too — 817/656-2919

8214 Grapevine Hwy. — *Tues-Sat 10-5*
North Richland Hills, TX 76180

Two lights north of I-820 on Grapevine Highway just before Harwood Rd., you can pare your budget to the bone for both baby and older kids. Back-to-school doesn't mean taking out a second mortgage. It does mean learning the ropes to Shopping 101. Think "resale" in clothes and uniforms–who will know the difference? The labels are the same on those with perfectly attired wardrobes–only these have been worn before. Who cares? We cheered when we saw BUGLE BOY, GAP and ZOODLES in girls' sizes 0-16 and boys' 0-12 at a fraction of the price sold new. Make money, too, by recycling last season's outfits that were worn once and outgrown quicker than a New York minute. Not to be forgotten, moms-to-be can get all decked out with a great selection of new and used maternity clothing. Pre-bundle, buy your shower invitations here; apres-bundle, send out your custom birth announcements and save. Every last penny counts from this day forward. They also feature MEDELA breast pumps for sale or rental from Lactation Connection. You really can't improve on Mother Nature, now can you? CK, MC, V

★★ Lik-Nu

817/428-9400

8053-A Grapevine Hwy.
North Richland Hills, TX 76180
Mon-Wed, Fri-Sat 10-5; Thu 10-6

If you want a complete overhaul of your kid's clothes, have them try on something from Lik-Nu. The average price of each item isn't like new, though–$5.99. Everything's clean and all clothes are steam-pressed before they're displayed. They also carry used beds in good to excellent condition. We saw a crib for $135 that had more than a good night's sleep, cheap. Clothing for infants through size 12 and a large selection of children's shoes are also available. Lik-Nu also buys used dressers, high chairs, strollers, walkers, toys and other accessories. Find this place just north of I-820 on Grapevine Highway between Bedford-Euless Rd. and Harwood near Chuck E. Cheese's Pizza. *CK*

♥♥♥♥♥ Magic Pen, The

817/424-4207

422 S. Main St.
Grapevine, TX 76051
Mon-Fri 10-6; Sat 10-5:30
www.themagicpen.invitations.com

Pen those magic announcements when your baby arrives. Create them loud and clear and custom-printed in less time than you've spent in delivery (hopefully no more than 24 hours). DISNEY characters, Classic Pooh or traditional CRANE papers and more are the basic facts, ma'am, and nothing but. This little shop in historic downtown Grapevine is hardly filled with horrors. Rather, it features a wonderful selection of collectibles, baby books, photo albums, children's stationery, calling cards, unique gifts and picture frames for the perfect mother's inscription. Choose from a vast selection of party invitations with coordinating thank-you notes, and the best part is, they're personalized FREE. Now put that in your pocket and say "thank you" to The Magic Pen. *CK, MC, V, AE*

★★★★★ Maternity Designer's Outlet

214/630-2327

1219 Conveyor Lane
Inwood Trade Center
Dallas, TX 75247
Mon-Sat 10-5:30

Expecting? What do you expect? This five-star maternity outlet boasts bargains for every trimester: dressy, casual and evening wear in sizes petite through 3X (also in tall sizes). You can KISS high prices goodbye because this manufacturer sells nothing but good buys. They even sell leftover fabric, in case you have nothing to do for the next nine months. Save 50-75 percent across the belly on CODY PATRICK, HALEY MICHAELS, OH, MA MA and, of course, the

KISS label. What this all means is that you will be paying wholesale prices or below for your entire maternity wardrobe. Now, take a deep breath and push! And when push comes to shove, visit their full-retail store in Fort Worth near Hulen Mall called Maternity by Design at 4969 S. Hulen St. (817/346-1662). *CK, MC, V*

★★★ Metroplex Diaper Service

Metro 972/445-6550
9119 Diplomacy Row
Mon-Fri 8-5
Dallas, TX 75247

Keeping them high and dry is no small feat, so saving some money on diapers is what Metroplex Diaper Service is all about. Come clean with clean diapers without lifting a hand. Since these folks also own Metro Linen Service, which delivers linens to health clubs and other commercial establishments, they've got cotton to spare and diapers to bare. Prices for newborns are 80 diapers for $14.95/week or 40 diapers are $11.85/week. A member of the National Association of Diaper Services, these 100 percent cotton didies can be picked up and delivered for just $64.73/month. Compared to disposable diapers, it might be the start of keeping your little one high and dry. Delivery is available throughout the Dallas/Fort Worth area. *CK, MC, V, AE*

★★★★★ Motherhood Outlets

972/539-2154
3000 Grapevine Mills Pkwy., Suite 239
Mon-Sat 10-9:30; Sun 11-8
Grapevine Mills Mall
www.motherhood.com
Grapevine, TX 76051

Well, at last, for mothers who work (and those who don't), you can enjoy an entire nine months of dressing to the hilt without the guilt. Here you'll see closeouts, discontinued styles, last season's cast-offs and overruns from some of the best in the business: MATURNITEE, MIMI, MOTHERHOOD and PEA IN THE POD for starters. Skirts as low as $1.50, outfits for as little as $3-$9 and designer MOTHERHOOD dresses for $138. No, this was no miscarriage of justice. We also saw cotton knit short dresses for $19, a two-piece career knit dress with short sleeves with a matching long jacket that was $49. Savings of 30-75 percent are nothing to sneeze at. Would you rather pay full price? Who are you kidding? Visit their other locations at Gainesville Factory Shops, 940/665-9924; Prime Outlet Center in Hillsboro, 254/582-0770 and San Marcos Factory Shops, 512/392-2855 for continued savings throughout the state. Then you can boast, "Born and dressed in Texas!" *CK, MC, V, AE*

Baby & Mom

★★★★ Neighborhood Diaper Delivery 817/652-0477

1226-B Corporate Drive *Call to set up deliveries*
Arlington, TX 76006

For moms on-the-go, finally a disposable diaper service that delivers! Neighborhood Diaper Delivery delivers first-quality disposable diapees anywhere in the Metroplex for free (the delivery is free, not the diapers). Outside the Metroplex, deliveries are handled by independent dealers or by mail. Never again worry about running out when your baby has the runs. They carry small, medium, large and extra large as well as training pants and baby wipes. We found newborn diapers as low as 14.6 cents each in case lots! They deliver to day-care centers, too. Expanding nationally, referral fees are paid. Small diapers are $22.95 for a package of 136, extra large diapers are $31.99 for 120 and training pants go for $32.99 for 90. Swim diapers and baby keepsakes are also available. Wee! Wee! all the way home.

★★★ Oh Baby! 817/460-2229

612 Lincoln Square *Mon-Sat 10-6*
Arlington, TX 76011

While not noted for their grand baby discounts, the large selection alone makes it a slam dunk. Oh Baby, Oh Baby, Oh-h-h! This North Arlington (on N. Collins St. just south of I-30) store is always doing double duty. First priority, get the mother-to-be covered–then we'll worry about the baby. What to wear to that gala event when you're eight months along is right up their alley. How about a gorgeous formal dress? Why buy when you can rent it from Oh Baby? It'll be a one-time fee and then it doesn't have to hang in your closet 'til you're pregnant again. Who wants to pay mega-bucks for something you only wear once anyway? You'll be able to stomach the nice selection of clothes for mothers-to-be including lingerie, work, play and even workout clothes. And now, it's baby's turn. You'll find unique baby clothes and gifts, along with the largest selection of career and casual maternity clothes in the Mid-Cities. Plus, you'll find some good prices on sizes 0 through 4T for both boys and girls, as well as on new furniture and a few toys. Additionally, they carry a full line of MEDELA products including breast pumps and bras. A nice neighborly approach to service also makes this a worthy pregnant pause that refreshes. *CK, MC, V, AE, D*

★★★★★ Once Upon a Child 972/618-5800

7200 Independence Pkwy., Suite 240 Mon-Fri 10-7; Sat 10-6; Sun Noon-5
Plano, TX 75025

At the northeast corner of Legacy and Independence, a legacy of children's stuff with "previous experience" is front and center. If you're looking for bargains for your bundle of joy, this store has it all. Name brand clothing for both boys and girls in boys' sizes 0-7 and girls' sizes 0-6 are all here. Their prices are very competitive compared to other resale stores in the same category. The difference, as always, is in the selection and the savings. Offering a large selection of name brands labels that you'd be proud to send them off to school in including GAP, GUESS?, JAMBOREE, LIMITED and OSHKOSH B'GOSH. Besides the great selection of clothes, you'll also be able to get your hands on baby furniture, strollers, cribs, toys and swings. *CK, MC, V, AE, D*

♥♥♥♥♥ R.B.J. Manufacturing

PO Box 353 *www.johnny-light.com*
Burleson, TX 76097

The boys at R.B.J. (Richie, Bill and Jack) came up with a DHC (domestic harmony commodity) in 1996 that they call the Johnny-Light, an easily installed light to help eliminate late-night fall-ins and help in toilet training. The battery-powered device lights up when the seat is down, helping remind users to return the seat to its full down position after late-night use. The light also reportedly helps potty-training efforts by giving a visual aide. Available only through the mail (batteries are included). No tools are required for installation and the $12 cost is a mere drop in the bucket. The Johnny-Light has become visible in more ways than one, as the trio's product has received national exposure on the "Regis and Kathie Lee", "Leeza" and "The Howie Mandel Show" TV programs, as well as in magazines and newspapers across the country. *CK, MC, V, D*

★★★★ Wee Resell It 972/446-8189

2150 N. Josey Lane, Suite 316 Mon-Wed 10-5; Thu 10-7; Fri-Sat 10-5
Carrollton, TX 75006

Selling all the Right Stuff for kids, this is the store to shop if you need children's clothing at discounted prices. There's always a sale going on somewhere amidst this Romper Room. Good quality clothing at unbeatable prices is the rule of thumb here. HEALTH TEX and OSHKOSH B'GOSH are just a few examples of their quality apparel. But children do not live by clothes alone. Also see a good selection of cribs, toys, shoes, walkers, high chairs and books. New clothing, too, is here at less than retail prices. Now we're talking! *CK, MC, V, D*

★★★★★ You & Me Babe

972/669-2110

870 N. Coit Rd., Suite 2651
Promenade Shopping Center
Richardson, TX 75080

Mon-Fri 10-6; Sat 10-5
www.youandmebabe.com

You've got me, babe, lock, stock and bargains. But in today's shopping scene, this is harmonic heaven for baby and children's (sizes 0-10) along with maternity clothes, saving you 50-70 percent off retail. In maternity, we found all new items in sizes 2-26 (petites-3X), including hosiery, lingerie and undergarments often overlooked in other outlet stores. Whether it's a casual dress or pantsuit, career dressing or a special occasion, they can get you covered for at least the full term. Going on a cruise? Need a bathing suit? Don't bypass your maternity months just because you've got nothing to wear. They also sell nursing apparel and supplies, such as the MEDELA breast pump (you can rent them from $39.95 or buy them, it's your option). Children can get their just desserts in yummy labels like MARIMEKKO, NEW POTATOES, REBECCA'S RAGS, SAN FRANCISCO BLUES, SOPHIE'S DRESS, TICKLE ME and ZOODLES. And don't forget the accompaniments of a proper bedroom suite with a crib, bedding and accessories. You can't go wrong whether you're a kid or the maker of one, two, or three! *CK, MC, V, D*

Beauty & Drug Stores

★★ Aladdin Beauty College — 940/382-6734

407 Sunset — *Walk-ins Accepted; Appts. Suggested*
Denton, TX 76201

The secret is out. You can get your toes polished for $9 and look like the rich ladies. And, that's just the beginning. For a great 'do, (you know "just a little trim") or a perm, you can't beat the price. There are always specials going on. In August, all $36 perms were $25. The senior class of the beauty school gets to cut, clip and curl under the watchful eye of supervisors while you sit back and reap the savings. For example, a prescription perm (regularly $30 on Mondays) was $17.88 and included a shampoo, haircut and style. Prices go from cheap-cheap to almost a cut below. Some big bargains on overlays for $10, $15 with sculpted nails; then, while you're in the mood, have your eyebrows shaped. Ouch! Check directory for many other Metroplex locations. *CK, MC, V*

★★★ Beauty Mart — 972/596-2673

3100 Independence, Suite 213 — *Mon-Sat 9:30-7; Sun Noon-5*
Plano, TX 75025

When it comes to beauty, we still like to save money. And at up to 40 percent off, you can forget putting that bag over your head. Beauty Mart is the source for mainstream and also unusual hair and beauty products. We saw lots of brand names, like L'OREAL, PAUL MITCHELL, REDKEN and TONI & GUY. On the day we stopped by, they were having a 50 percent off sale. A full-service salon inside completes your beauty makeover. Shoppers take note. Come armed to buy. *CK, MC, V, AE, D*

★★★★ Beauty Store & More — 972/867-6888

1900 Preston Rd. — *Mon-Fri 9-8; Sat 9-7; Sun Noon-6*
Preston Park Village
Plano, TX 75093

Mirror, Mirror on the wall, who's the most beautiful of them all? Try to figure it out. Well, here's a place to begin your quest. (Besides, you'll get $1 off selected products if you bring in your empty containers and have them refilled.) Taking the lead from The Body Shop's concern for the environment, this is a surprisingly good place to get–not only the "works"–but also to buy the "works," too. Salon products plus salon services for both men and women are available. (Children, too, if you must know everything.) The lineup's impressive because of both the familiar names, like BAIN DE TERRE, BIOLAGE, BROCATO, JOICO, MATRIX, NEXXUS, PAUL MITCHELL, REDKEN, SCHWARZKOPF, SEBASTIAN, VAVOOM and for those we haven't seen anywhere else, like JINGLES, LANZA, TRI, UPPER CANADA. Then, it's on to cosmetics, hair accessories, brushes, nail products and more. What really stung us, though, was the BUMBLE & BUMBLE line. We've been flying around looking for it for months. It's a honey! You can find this treasure at Preston and Park Blvd. or beautify in another location at Willow Bend Market, next to Tom Thumb on the southeast corner of Parker and the Tollway, Plano, 972/608-4444. *CK, MC, V, D*

★★★ Beauty Supplies, Etc. 972/231-8848

718 Lingco Drive *Mon 9-4:30; Tue-Fri 9-6*
Richardson, TX 75081

Discounts on more than 3,000 nail- and personal-care products are right at your fingertips. Beauty Supplies, Etc., offers 10 - 20 percent off (25 percent less if you happen to hold a beauty license) on big names for your big 10, such as ALPHA 9, DEVELOP 10, JESSICA and ORLY, among others. Products you never see discounted, period! Who says you have to go to a professional manicurist to nail down great polishes and nail-care accessories? Their hottest sellers are nail tips, CALVERT nail dryers and polishes. No catalog, so you'll have to visit, call or write for a price quote. Hold out your hands for brands such as ESSIE, FORSYTHE, OPI, PRO FINISH, STAR and more. One of the largest selections of fingernail products in the country. Beauty Supplies, Etc. is, hands down, the biggest in the Metroplex. Hair brushes, rollers, coloring agents, shampoos, conditioners and many other professional beauty supplies that are not seen anywhere else but here. Some products are sold only to salon owners and professionals. They deliver, they ship–the only thing not available is Saturday service! So don't break a nail on Saturday. *CK, MC, V, AE, PQ*

Beauty & Drug Stores

♥♥♥♥♥ Big State Drug

972/254-1521

100 E. Irving Blvd.
Irving, TX 75061

Mon-Fri 8-7; Sat 8-4

Big State is a throw-back to the days when Irving was a small town and downtown was the meeting place of the local yokels. This 50-year-old drugstore in old Irving center boasts a bustling soda fountain and grill that turns out breakfast, lunch and dinner, as well as ice cream treats, that will take you back through time. Look for malts made with real malt powder, old-fashioned ice cream floats and sodas, and bottled sodas in flavors such as cream-ale, orange cream, key lime and root beer. The counter and six booths also evoke the good old summertime. Maybe, if you play your cards right, you'll be the next major Hollywood starlet discovered sitting at the soda fountain. But don't primp too long at home, the grill hours are 8-5:45 during the week and 8-2:45 on Saturdays. While you wait, they have a large greeting card and gift selection (including Beanie Babies) and a full-service pharmacy along with scaled-down drug store offerings. The selection will never rival the big chains, but here you'll find the basics fast. *CK, MC, V, AE*

★★★★★ CBI Laboratories

972/241-7546 x 335

2055-C Luna Rd., Suite 138
Carrollton, TX 75006

Tue-Sat 10-6

Want beauty–at the least? CBI is the warehouse of wonders. Several Mercedes blocked our view of the front door every time we decide to bathe in our fantasies. Why? Because these are the folks who make beauty lotions for major department and specialty stores. Be it skin care or bath gels, gift sets or shampoos, you can double the bubble without getting soaked. Save 50-90 percent off retail–worth every sudsy cent. Products retailing for $10-$15 can be had for $.50. I'm not kidding. At the corner of Luna and Valwood Parkway, bring a truck, trailer or semi–'cause just a back seat won't do. Shop at their outlet store in the front of their warehouse and load up on lotions, potions, body oils, body salts, bubble baths, shower gels, shampoos, specialty soaps, skincare items and baskets filled with animal-shaped sponges. Solve major stocking stuffing dilemmas at Christmas or any other gift-giving time. Gift boxes are $10 each; bath salts, $1; and soap bars, $.25. Doesn't it make scents? Watch for periodic warehouse sales when the doors to their big distribution warehouse open to the public. Then, bring out the helpers to pack it all in. *CK*

★★ Debbie's Fragrance & Gift Shop — 972/278-9747

2840 S. Jupiter, #103 — *Wed-Sat 10-5; Sun Noon-6*
Garland, TX 75041

Where do "scents-ible" gals find a pal at the cosmetics counter? Want to save 20 percent on the most popular fragrances? Debbie knows. And Debbie is here to help. Find almost every scent on the market: ESCAPE, GIORGIO, JOOP, PASSION, RED, WHITE DIAMONDS, WINGS and stop spreading your budget so thin. Men's fragrances, too–COOL WATER, HALSTON, LAGERFELD, POLO, etc. Debbie's prices were lower on some and comparable on others. Gift baskets, cosmetics and those "gift with purchase" offers are plentiful, especially around holiday times. Located next to Vikon Village, stop in for an aroma break. Exit from LBJ going east onto Jupiter-Kingsley and turn left on Jupiter. CK, MC, V

★★★★★ Drug Emporium — 972/492-5300

3065 N. Josey Lane, Suite 65 — *Mon-Sat 9-9; Sun 9-6*
Carrollton, TX 75007

Pack up the kids. Pack up the car. Pack up the cart. The savings are so big, you need a big one to wheel and deal down this grocery-store-sized emporium. Most shoppers swear by Drug Emporium. They also swear, when they see how much they could have saved if they had been loyal to Drug Emporium. Besides, where else can you go to save on toilet paper, travel-sized toothpaste, face powder, favorite colognes, greeting cards and diapers? Save 10-50 percent in the usual and customary sundry departments–pharmaceuticals, health and beauty aids, cosmetics, hair care, cards/paper products, housewares ... the works. We found big savings on nail polish and shampoo on our visit–both under $1 in their bin of closeouts and fantastic savings on salon-type products. Sometimes, you get lost in the maze of aisles and find yourself in the holiday candy when you only came for cough drops, but both were at mouth-watering savings. Ranked one of the best pharmacies in the country according to the October '99 issue of Consumer Reports. Check directory for location nearest you. CK, MC, V, AE, D

★★★★★ Fazio's Discount City — 972/986-2984

135 Plymouth Park Shopping Center — *Mon-Sun 9-9*
Irving, TX 75061

Fazio's has moved into the world of category killers. Keeping up with the

Joneses is part of their new modus operandi. Now carrying meat, produce, dairy and frozen foods along with more than 45,000 other items to save you money, this supermarket superstore requires enough dexterity to navigate with two shopping carts. They have everything you've ever needed or wanted in the following categories: health and beauty aids, housewares, electronics, groceries, pharmaceuticals, cosmetics, car care, jewelry, office supplies–seeing is believing. This family-owned chain knows its business, having been a powerhouse in the grocery-store business in Chicago ... or was it Cleveland? Nevertheless, they're in Texas now and that's all that counts. While prices were competitive with other deep discounters, many shoppers thought they were "outstanding," having bought five frames for much less than Michaels was selling for just one. One case of SIMILAC with iron ($2.90 per can here versus $3.25 per can at Wal-Mart) should make shopping down their baby aisle worth the walk. And according to the powers that be, the ambiance is no longer plain vanilla and bor-r-r-ing. You'll find this chapter at Story and Irving Boulevard, but you can also visit the original DFW location at 5101 Gus Thomasson in Mesquite, 972/681-9862. *CK, MC, V, D*

♥♥♥♥♥ Forbess Corp. 972/867-5313

Mon-Fri 8-5
www.solefood.net

Call if your feet are taking too much of the heat. Since 1988, Jack Forbess has been standing on Easy Feet. But, if your feet can't take it anymore, try feeding them with Sole Food, developed by Forbess, a drug and cosmetic chemist. Perfect for feet (or hands) to soften skin, protect against the elements and help heal minor cuts and irritations. A small amount is all it takes to massage tired toes and even can be applied through pantyhose. This non-irritating, non-prescription cream also contains anti-fungal and deodorant agents. Product eliminates dry skin; softens cuticles and calluses; has a long massage time; and is non-greasy. For your hands, try their Finger Food Hand Cream. Both sell in a large jar (4.25-ounce) for $20; small jar (2/3-ounce) for $6. Their free brochure details the ingredients and its healing agents. Note that no credit cards are accepted–you pay upon receipt of product. Full refund within 30 days, but in 12 years, that has never happened. Mailing charges: $4 UPS shipping and handling; expected delivery time 2-5 days, depending on distance. And if you mention the *Underground Shopper*, you can take a 20 percent discount. *CK*

Fragrance World/Fragrance Outlet

972/241-9696

2588-A Royal Lane
Dallas, TX 75229
Mon-Sat 9-6:30

Come up smelling like a (tea) rose at this fine fragrance and cosmetics wholesale outlet. Yes, all the big names in the beauty biz are lined up. A little spritz of this, a little splash of that–for a whole lot less. Save 25-60 percent on cosmetics and skin care products from CLINIQUE, ELIZABETH ARDEN, ESTEE LAUDER, LANCOME, LA PRAIRIE, YSL and save up to 70 percent on fragrances such as Liz's WHITE DIAMONDS and PASSION or ESCADA, GIORGIO, LAUREN for women or for men, ARAMIS, LAGERFELD, JOOP!, PHOTO, even old MACKIE's back in town–so what's your POISON? Men and women can enjoy all the scent-sational trappings of success. Heaven scent us to this out-of-this-world fragrance outlet. And why not? Savings are substantial. Why pay department and specialty store prices? Just west of Harry Hines, you can find the sweet smell of success. Let's face it, now you can take a powder without ever paying face value for beauty products again. *CK, MC, V, D*

♥♥♥♥♥ Mimi's Wig Boutique

972/380-5306

7522 Campbell Rd., #112
Dallas, TX 75248
Mon-Sat 10-6

Smart women know that they don't have to settle for limp locks anymore. At Mimi's Boutique (named one of the five best wig salons in the country by *Vogue*), you'll find an assortment of wigs, hairpieces and accessories that can take your hair from faded to fabulous in no time at all. What's even better–it's as wash and wear as the real deal. Wash it whenever it gets dirty. Hang it up to dry. After a few brushes, you're ready to go. To the PTA meeting, the tennis match, the debutante ball, your company picnic, the Super Bowl, Deep Ellum–anywhere. All the fixings, styled by professionally licensed hairdressers who really know their stuff, can transform you into a beauty queen. We were amazed at how well the hair blended with ours. And believe it or not, your best friend won't be able to tell (except that your hair looks sooooo much better). Not discounted, but cheaper than regular visits to the hair salon when a quick makeover will do. Southwest corner of Coit and Campbell. *CK, MC, V, D*

★★★★★ Miracle Wrinkle Cream/Spiritus

972/476-2853

PO Box 443
Seagoville, TX 75159
By Appt. Only
www.mywrinklecream.com

Looking for a miracle cream to magically erase the wrinkles? Well, as sure as I'm sitting here, I've found it! For plastic surgery in a jar, this magic formula really works. For only $39.95, you can minimize years of tears, hard work, aggravation and the normal aging process. Just think about all those sleepless nights you suffered when your teenager didn't come home on time; or the years you were working two jobs struggling to make ends meet. It ultimately shows up on your face. Isn't it about time you turned back the hands of time? This cream doesn't need any guarantees because in two days, I started to see results; in two weeks, my deepest frown lines not only had diminished, they were gone. Also available are moisturizers, tanning lotions for tanning booths, cleansers, all-over body renewal cream, scar cream, arthritis cream, eye cream and more. All are made the old-fashioned way–one jar at a time. Call for a price list/brochuret. $5 shipping for the first item and $2 for each additional item. *CK, MO*

★★★★ MJ Cosmetics — 214/814-4248

PO Box 113041 — *By Appt. Only*
Carrollton, TX 75011

Martha Jackson is my kind of entrepreneur–she's a Ph.D. turned make-up artist and cosmetics distributor. Who better to turn the other cheek than one who can cover up the lines, blemishes and unslightly scars? Call for your make-over appointment and see why women have been bombarding her for her BOBBI BROWN and MAC look-alike lipsticks, foundation, powders, brushes, eyeshadows and more. Customers can now order cosmetics through e-mail and be cyber beautiful, too. What's another lipstick ... especially one at half-price? No one will know the difference when they kiss you. But then again, if you kiss and tell ... well, that's another story. We'll leave it to the history books. *CK*

★★★★★ Nails USA — 972/418-8221

1906 E. Belt Line Rd. — *Mon-Sat 10-7:30*
Carrollton, TX 75006

Why pay $30-$40 and more for that full set of nails? What about tips of $15? The battle of the nail files ends here as the revolution in price cutting hit the Metroplex with the onslaught of talented Vietnamese. Most of the low-price leaders in a field that was ripe for a takeover. The high price of elegant nails has just hit the bunkers. Walk-ins welcome, but sometimes there's a wait. Make an appointment. Get your hands and feet coifed from you fingertips to your tipi, toes. At last, the masses can be Dragon Ladies, too. *CK, MC, V*

★★ Ogle School of Hair Design 214/821-0819

6333 E. Mockingbird, Suite 201 *Tue-Fri 8:30-5:30; Sat to 5;*
Dallas, TX 75214 *Appt./Walk-ins*

We all like to get Ogled–and we mean that figuratively and literally. The Ogle School of Hair Design offers services by senior students at very age-retardant prices. Get a manicure for $6, a haircut for $8.25, a perm for $27 or a machine facial for $16. Get the massage? Students of this school (there are others in Arlington, Hurst and Fort Worth) are cosmetologists-in-training and are supervised every step of the way. So, what do you have to lose but a few gray hairs? *CK, MC, V*

✧✧✧ Oriole Barber Shop 214/651-0019

1923 Commerce *Mon-Fri 7-5:30*
Dallas, TX 75201

Here's something we thought was lost forever–a $7 haircut. No manicures. No facials. No vanity fares. Just a decent–inexpensive–haircut! Seven's the operative number here and it looks like it's here to stay. (Now, if you want a shampoo, that's another $7.) If you enjoy the buzz of razors and the smell of talc, this is the place for you. Definitely a step into the past. A popular spot with men who miss the barber shops of old. No quartet on the premises, though, so bring your own baritone. *CK*

♥♥♥♥♥ Parfumelle 817/731-6633

6441 Southwest Blvd. *Mon-Sat 10-6*
Fort Worth, TX 76132 *www.parfumelle.com*

If you are hooked on a fragrance that has gone bye-bye (out of style, out of stock or out of your mind), these pros can find it for you. Their selection of perfumes and colognes is great. They carry almost every brand you have every sniffed. The variety of products here is the primary value of this beauty tracer, because prices are not cheap. But, you can order your mom's favorite cologne or your aunt's must-have sachet and wait for the wizards seek it out from the farthest reaches of the planet. Free shipping, but perfumes are not discounted. *CK, MC, V, AE, D, DC, PQ*

★★★★★ Perfumania 940/665-4124

4321 I-35 N, #285 *Mon-Sat 10-8; Sun 11-6*
Gainesville, TX 76240 *www.perfumania.com*

Are you practicing safe scents? Catch just one whiff at Perfumania and I promise, you'll have a scent-sational out-of-body experience. The Scents of a Woman (or man) can make you crazy, so a shopping trip to Gainesville is just what the shrink thinks. With savings of 20-60 percent on designer fragrances, you won't be satisfied with just one. With hundreds to choose from, they provide you with three different card sniffs at a time; then, to clear your olfactory senses, they ask that you take a whiff of some coffee beans. Supposedly, that dilutes the smell of the previous scents so you can smell with a fresh approach as you move on. We saw most designer names and some oldies, too: OMBRE ROSE, OSCAR, PASSION, POISON, etc. They even had more than 500 men's fragrances to choose from. Good Life by DAVIDOFF, a new cologne, retails for $45 but sells here for only $28.99. ESCADA Light retails for $42, but sells at Perfumania for only $26.99. Dune by CHRISTIAN DIOR retails for $35, but sells here for only $24.99. Check out their promotions all year long, as well as gift baskets around Christmas for extra savings. Visit also at the Fort Worth Outlet Square, 6441 Southwest Blvd. in Fort Worth. *CK, MC, V, AE, D*

Pro Brushes/The Makeup Academy — 972/307-5949

Dallas, TX

By Appt. Only

www.probrushes.com

One of the most essential makeup tools is a good brush. If you haven't bought one lately, well let's just say they're the makeup industry's equivalent to a mink coat–except at Pro Brushes, they sell quality, name brand brushes like, M.A.C., MAKEUP FOREVER, NARS and STILA for 40-50 percent off retail. A deluxe fan brush, $30 elsewhere, is just $16.50 here. A sable lip and liner brush retails for $12, but is $7.25 here. Complete sets are also available, with discounts of 20 percent off pro sets and 15 percent off personal sets. You will also receive 10 percent off any additional brushes you buy at the same time. One of the personal sets includes deluxe powder, blush, fluff, flower tip blending, angled brow and liner brushes for only $112.32. Compare that with the retail price of $132.15. Randy Harris, owner of The Makeup Academy, is selling the brushes because he got mad at how much he was paying retail–so he found a better source. Good for him. Now he's sharing. Better for us.

★★★★ Sally Beauty Supply — 214/350-7363

9751 Webb Chapel Rd.
Dallas, TX 75220

Mon-Fri 8:30-8; Sat 9-7; Sun Noon-6
www.sallybeauty.com

Buy your hair, nail and skin products where the pros shop. At Sally Beauty Supply, based in Denton, professional hair and nail care products are in abundance (a lot you never see except at the salons) and often in bulk sizes so you can save even more. All sales personnel are licensed cosmetologists, so they can instruct you on product use. We've never seen more choices in brushes. Great savings on perms and rollers. Good buys on curling irons and nail tips, and the source for those great tweezers that never miss a hair (Twizzerman). For expert advice on hair and nail care (what to buy and how to use it), their professionals can guide you every strand of the way. Call the number above for the location nearest you (and with more than 2,000 nationwide, the chances are very good that at least one is near you). *CK, MC, V, AE, D*

✧✧ Salon Suites — 972/250-1884

2650 Midway Rd., Suite 140 — *Tue-Sat 9-5; Walk-ins welcome*
Carrollton, TX 75006

If shopping the malls makes your hair stand on end, try making waves at this 12,000-square-foot beauty emporium. You will be in for a hair-raising experience. One central phone bank downstairs where the offices are will direct you to a tech upstairs–each with a different phone number. Beauticians and technicians have their own salon, but they share the building and receptionist. Still, get ahead by making "do" at this beauty salon concept where there are more than 48 beauty professionals ready to do you over. What can be confusing is there's also 48 price lists, at least one price list for each salon. Want your ears pierced? Hair styled or replaced altogether? Knead a massage ? A touch-up? A wax job? Or some tips? Then, this is a suite deal. Next to CiCi's Pizza. For nails, for example, you can call: Kimberly Hawkins, at 972/732-1168, Charlene at 972/248-0003 or Danny Phan 972/732-7766. Check directory for other Salon Suite concepts. *CK*

✧✧✧ Salons Unique — 972/516-4000

1301 Custer, Suite 482 — *Tue-Fri 10-7; Sat 9-5; or By Appt.*
Plano, TX 75075

Now you can have your 'do 24/7. Their store hours, however, are above. And if you buy a membership to their price club (cost $5), you can take an additional 15 percent off the products in their store (does not apply to services). This is a beauty mall with 12,000 square feet of individual booths filled with beauticians, barbers who give old-fashioned razor cuts, massage therapists, nail technicians, facialists, make-up artists, plus hair extenders, non-surgical facelifts, jewelry and accessories–the works of artisans of beauty all under one roof. With a super-store mentality operating under the premise of saving you time (but not always money), this place is certainly something to see. The in-store product selection includes, ABBA, ARTEC, BIOLAGE, DEVELOP 10, ICE, JOICO, KENRA, LOGIX, MATRIX, NIOXIN, OPI, PAUL MITCHELL, REDKEN, SEBASTIAN and lots more to take you from salon to home along with collectible dolls and fabulous gifts. Visit also at 401 West I-30 in Garland. *CK, MC, V, AE, D*

✧✧✧✧✧ Star College Of Cosmetology — 817/329-0222

120 N. Main — *Tue-Sat 8:30-5 (Appt. Suggested)*
Grapevine, TX 76051 — *www.starcollege.com*

Looking for a star performer? Then look to the heavenly future stars here. If you are thinking about a career in cosmetology, this college was half the price of the others we sampled. Consider that your first lesson in cost-cutting! And for those in search of bargain haircuts, look no further. Senior students can fix you up with a new 'do for $5 (shampoo included) or a perm for $20. Facials, manicures and more are available by appointment only. They were rated as the number-one cosmetology school in Texas in 1998. CORNELLA and REFLECTIONS products are used and sold. They provide job placement assistance and are licensed by the Texas Cosmetology Commission. *CK*

✧✧✧ SuperCuts — 972/385-0575

14902 Preston Rd., Suite 928 — *Mon-Fri 9-9; Sat 8-8; Sun 10-6*
Pepper Square
Dallas, TX 75240

Really, now, just how much better does an expensive haircut look than an inexpensive one? Maybe in some cases a lot, but the chances are slim that it will look much different if you have it done here. It might even look better because you'll be glowing, knowing you only spent $11. ($16 for a shampoo and cut; add a blow dry for $5 more. Conditioners are extra.) But even with the works, you can walk right in and sit yourself down for less than a fancy salon. Don't forget to sign in or they will pass you by. Coming soon is "SuperCall," where you call-in before leaving home to have your name put on the list so it could be your turn when you arrive. Our best tip for hair snobs? Get an expensive 'do from your favorite designer, then have it trimmed to stay in shape at SuperCuts. Your hair-do will never know the difference. On previous visits, we've enjoyed watching stylists shave designs into a (willing) customer's hair or French-braid a ponytail for a prom. Other times, it's just a plain old cut and go. We've even found, at times, 30 percent off promotions on SEBASTIAN hair care products. On the downside, you'll sometimes see a crowded waiting room (like at the Wailing Wall) because the "word" is out that you get a "super deal" at SuperCuts. Check directory for area locations. *CK, MC, V, D*

✧✧✧✧ Toni & Guy Academy 972/416-8396

2810 E. Trinity Mills *Tue-Sat 9:30-3:30 (Last Appt.)*
Carrollton, TX 75006 *www.toniguy.com*

Don't curl up and dye when you see what it costs to getting your hair in order. At Toni & Guy, expect to pony up $33 to $58 for a haircut (the price is dependent on the expertise level of the stylist.) Partial color is $44 to $78 for medium-length hair; full color, $63 to $103. Perms run from $53 to $98. *But,* here's the good news. At the Toni & Guy Academy, located at Marsh and Trinity Mills in the Mills Point Shopping Center (look for Tom Thumb and Mr. Gatti's on the southeast corner) you can get it coifed for much less. Unlike area cosmetology schools, all of the academy-goers are licensed operators who have been brought in for specialized training. Since they've grown to such proportions, the Academy now is open full-time. For a hair-blowing experience, haircuts are $15, $21 for highlights, $41 for coloring short hair, perms are $44–but for chemical treatments, you should come in for a consultation ahead of time as the price depends on hair length. Call for appointment and wash those retail prices right out of your hair. *CK, MC, V, AE*

✧✧✧✧✧ Top Nails 817/451-8530

6741 Bridge St. *Mon-Sat 9:30-7:30*
Fort Worth, TX 76112

On your way to the studios of Channel 11, you never know where your next break will come. Mine came just as I turned the corner onto Bridge Street and took a chance. Boy, was I in good hands! Buff, rough, scuff, file, clip, dip, soak, dig deep and have your nails or feet done for less. Great nails. Great toes. Acrylics, tips, sculpts, pedicures–if it's a top nail, they could be the tip of the iceberg. Specials Mondays through Wednesday take the price down a bit–$18 for a full set of tips and $12 for fills. Pedicures are $15. Not bad, when your tips are down. *CK, MC, V, AE, D*

✧✧✧ Touch of Heaven Day Spa 972/680-1337

2007 N. Collins Blvd., Suites 203 & 205 *By Appt. Only*
Richardson, TX 75081

When it comes time to contemplate the pearly gates, why not get a headstart and enjoy a Touch of Heaven on earth. Jeri Randall, formerly of Neiman Marcus Salon, Cosmopolitan Lady and Medical City has opened her doors to hours, even days, of beauty bliss. Do something nice for your health and well-being by indulging in a therapeutic massage. Add a seaweed or sea salt rub-down or relax under the care of an European facial (Sothy of Paris) or all three. Then, as a first-time Underground Shopper special, you'll receive a FREE gift of a bottle of avocado body lotion with your purchase of a one-hour massage or facial or a $10 discount, whichever you choose. A series of treatments will net you a bonus–$10 off each hour when you purchase a series. Specialized treatments such as Shiatsu and Tragger are also specialties of the house. Call for appointment early as crowds start to form at the end of each week. *CK, MC, V*

★★★★★ Ulta — 972/612-6031

2432 Preston Rd., #320 — *Mon-Sat 10-9; Sun 11-6*
Dallas, TX 75093 — *www.ulta.com*

We can get lost at Ulta. Three hours just doesn't do justice to our hair, ladies. Though no longer a secret, they're still a great place to buy department store fragrances and cosmetics as well as professional hair salon products. More than 1,500 of them wind their way to an Ulta store. Cosmetics to hair care, nail polish to tips, it's here. Hair care products included GOLDWELL, IMAGE, JINGLES, NEXXUS, PAUL MITCHELL, PETER HANZ, TIGI, TRESSA and more. Naked nails get covered in CREATIVE NAIL, OPI, PEAU DE PECHE or ZOOM. And other brands such as FRANCIS DENNY, ULTIMA II and more. Knowledgeable sales staff guides you to their recommendations for fine limp hair or callused heels. (Oops, did I speak out of turn?) Salon specials are, well, hair-splitting. For example, a professional manicure was $29 and a man's haircut, style and blow dry for $27 seemed a cut above the rest. Check directory for additional locations and look for their newspaper inserts for money-saving coupons. *CK, MC, V, AE, D*

Bed & Bath & Mattresses

★★★★ Adjustable Beds — 972/671-5551

1002 N. Central Expressway, #559 — *Mon-Fri 9-5; Sat 9-2*
Richardson, TX 75080

This is the way to go Beddy Buy! With more than 25 years in business, Adjustable Beds has the PANASONIC Shiatsu massage chairs and beds–the same ones you line up to sample each year at the State Fair en masse. They also carry brands by INTERACTIVE HEALTH and PRO-MED. At their new location at the northeast corner of Arapaho and Central, take it easy for a change and experience the next best thing to a full body massage. Save up to $500 on a Dual King Adjustable Bed model that lets you and your bed partner adjust to each of your individual comfort zones (even if you shake, rattle and roll!). They've also added lift chairs to their list of options. So, if you're having trouble getting up, let them show you the way do it in to an easy-does-it lift chair. They also offer replacement mattresses for adjustable beds. Whether you're an over-the-rim basketball player or a tiny 4-foot gymnast, their beds are made to fit and induce an even deeper sleep state because most people sleep better with their head and legs slightly elevated. And, if you want a state-of-the-art dual massage system, don't forget to ask for the rub. *CK, MC, V, AE, D, DC*

★★★★ American Wallbeds/Off the Wall — 214/350-9895

2530 Electronic Lane, #702 — *Mon-Sat 10-5*
Dallas, TX 75220

If you're looking for the components for a do-it-yourself wall bed, this is the only place to shop. Similar to a Murphy bed in that they disappear into the wall, these beds, however, are spring-loaded whereas Murphy beds use a hydraulic lift system and much more elaborate cabinetry. For a basic queen-size wall bed, for example, expect to pay $569 (if it were a Murphy bed, the cost would be around $1,600) or $499 for a full-size bed. Price includes frame and bunky board (a 1-inch board, covered with

3-inch foam, then wrapped). One style of cabinet is offered for an additional $895 and comes unfinished so you can stain it yourself. Perfect for that weekend "honey-do" list. In a field of few players whose specialty is turning your empty room into one of usefulness (be it a home-office, study, sewing room, guest bedroom or exercise room), this company has the lowest prices for your off-the-wall projects. *CK, MC, V, AE, D*

★★★★★ Bedroom Shop, The — 817/274-2222

2012 W. Pioneer Pkwy. — *Mon-Fri 10-7; Sat 9-6*
Arlington, TX 76013 — *www.bedroomshop.com*

Beds...beds...beds, that's what you'll find here. Arlington-based, this manufacturer has been sewing up a storm, making beds for more than 33 years. Fully adjustable electric beds (some with massagers), juvenile bunk beds with full-size futon mattresses on the bottom and a twin-size mattress on top and even brass beds that weren't tacky. Prices were pretty snoozy, too. But the only name brand carried is SEALY POSTUREPEDIC, along with the claim that nobody sells it for less ($499 for a king and up). Waterbeds were available at prices duly noted as good buys. Complete waterbeds from $249 and adjustable beds, a twin XL, started at $749. But the real claim to fame at The Bedroom Shop is that they also manufacture their own line of premium bedding and that's where the savings can really be extended. Top-of-the-line pillowtops were $899 and included a 20-year, non-prorated warranty (most companies issue 10-year warranties). The Bedroom Shop has been manufacturing mattresses in Arlington since 1966, which tells you experience counts. Other locations in Duncanville, Fort Worth, Richardson, Hurst, Wichita Falls, Temple and Longview. *CK, MC, V, AE, D*

★★★★★ Bunkbed & Mattress Place — 817/572-7126

624 W. Mansfield Hwy. — *Mon-Sat 8-6*
Kennedale, TX 76060

This is no bunk! With more than 20 different styles, all with unique features, there isn't a kid out there who could ask for anything more. Look for the two red buildings; showroom's in the front building and the factory's behind. But don't look for them on Sundays 'cause that's when they set up shop at Traders Village. BEAUTYREST, CMF, NOAH, POSTURA and SIMMONS factory-seconds (nothing's wrong with them, really) serve their purpose and lifetime guarantees comfort you the rest of the way.

They even make matching chests of drawers, night stands and matching pieces to accompany the beds. Double-up in the same room, pile 'em on for a sleepover, hide out on the top bunk when you want some peace and quiet. This manufacturer builds them all, from A-frames to stackables (unstackable to L-shaped models). They also sell to other distributors who then mark up the price. Bypass them all and go directly to Bunkbed & Mattress Place. Priced from $250-$1,050, including mattresses. This might be the least expensive way to bunk down for the night. Don't forget their other location at 1275 N. Main, Suites 101-102 in Mansfield, 817/477-0664. Just to sum things up to make sure there is no bunk, they build their own beds and specialize in name brand mattress seconds, minor blemishes and those with discontinued fabrics. *CK, MC, V, AE, D*

★★★★★ City Mattress Factory — 817/834-1648

900 S. Haltom Rd. — *Mon-Fri 9-6; Sat 9-3*
Haltom City, TX 76117

Off 121, exit Haltom Road and go south for a half-mile–across the railroad tracks, then around a curve. It's worth it. I promise your back will be grateful. City Mattress is the second warehouse on the left. Born and bed in Fort Worth, this manufacturer has taken mattress-making to new heights. Making their own version of European mattresses, natural latex beds called the DUNLOPILLO SLEEP SYSTEM (considered state-of-the-heart). Save plenty of restless nights figuring out how to pay for a mattress that is handed down for generations. Instead, buy their version and stop counting sheep. Besides a great selection of mattresses, you'll also find futons for as low as $159, custom mattresses, air mattresses, adjustable beds, the amazing new sleep sofas, soft-side waterbeds, inner spring mattresses...for at least half the price and twice the value. When you snooze, you win. Buy direct and save up to 70 percent. Are you in a deep sleep yet? *CK, MC, V, D*

★★★★★ Dallas Mattress — 972/423-7173

301 W. Parker, #118 — *Mon-Sat 10-7; Sun Noon-5*
Plano, TX 75023

From bed to toe, Dallas Mattress is your mattress comforter at the guaranteed lowest prices. Serving the Metroplex for the past 15 years with quality futons and matresses, you can rest assured in top brands like KING KOIL, SEALY (futon collection) and SERTA. Make this a preferred stop on your journey to dreamland. Prices vary, but there's always a good selection and plenty of mattresses in stock for quick delivery, although you'll pay about $25 for the service. You can get futons for as low as $149, and a queen-size pillowtop set starts at $249. Free delivery or a free bed frame with the purchase of a premium set. At these prices, and great mattresses, a good night's sleep should be the least of your worries. Shop also these Dallas locations at 11333 E. Northwest Hwy. at Jupiter, 11441 Stemmons at Royal and 18111 N. Dallas Tollway at Frankford. Night. Night. *CK, MC, V, AE, D*

★★★★★ Factory Mattress Outlet & Futons 817/346-4893

6236 McCart *Mon-Sat 10-6; Thu 10-8; Sun 1-5*
Fort Worth, TX 76133 *www.factorymattressoutlet.com*

Located one mile south of I-20 on McCart (second exit past I-35 South, go left over the bridge for one mile), come see how the Factory Mattress Outlet has grown. They've expanded to an even larger selection of futon frames and mattresses as well as bunk beds, daybeds, lamps, accessories, iron beds, brass beds and more. Some of the best bedding buys and showroom samples on nine brands from major mattress manufacturers. Factory Mattress Outlet & Futons has one of the biggest selections of futons in the Metroplex, with prices starting as low as $139. Rest easy on a SEALY POSTUREPEDIC, SERTA and SPRING AIR mattress to start the evening in style. We almost z-z-z-oned out on our visit but were jarred into action when we saw savings of 30-60 percent across the inner springs. They will pick up your old bedding and deliver and set up your new set. We enjoyed bantering with the owner, who thought he had us pegged as Underground Shoppers during our visit, but we eluded his interrogation by saying "goodbye" after we heard that the extra-firm SIMMONS BEAUTYRESTset was $449 ($100 cheaper than last year). Make sure when comparing mattresses that you compare apples to apples, wool to wool, silk to silk. Mattress covers vary. *CK, MC, V, AE, D*

★★ Heavenly Sleep Shoppe 817/595-4205

1133 W. Pipeline Rd. *Mon-Sat 10-6; Sun 1-5*
(Pipeline at Melbourne)
Hurst, TX 76053

Heavenly bodies shop here as this is the "nobody sells for less" store. Sorry, Charlie, but sometimes promises cannot be spoken out of bed. The savings are not quite heaven-sent, but every little bit helps. This SEALY dealer sells the Posture Premier for $299 (double) and $499 for a king. Not bad, unless of course you prefer paying retail. You'll save at least $50-$100 on every buy and now it's time to say, goodbye. Oh, I almost forgot to mention they also have a futon gallery. Gee, sleeping on a Sealy may just be like sleeping on a cloud. *CK, MC, V, D*

★★★★★ Kayan's — 972/238-9835

102 Dal-Rich Village — *Mon-Sat 10-5:30*
Richardson, TX 75080

Are you a stickler for coordinated accessories for your home? Kayan's has been creating beautiful bedrooms since 1985 including their award-winning bedcoverings–all are bed winners at 25 percent off. Comforter and duvet ensembles, bedspreads and daybed sets, headboards and bed benches, window treatments and wallpaper in contemporary, transitional and traditional styles. Upholstery, too. Expect your bedcoverings to take about four weeks to complete the picture-perfect custom accompaniments. Now just don't cover-up your pride in knowning which way to sew. *CK, MC, V*

★★★★ Lone Star Mattress — 214/630-0798

2348 Irving Blvd. — *Mon-Fri 9-6; Sat Noon-6*
Dallas, TX 75207

Are you lonely tonight? If so, at least do your mind a favor and go to bed with a good book. But first, buy yourself a good night's sleep. Go south on I-35 toward downtown Dallas, exit Motor/Wycliff, turn south on Motor Street. Motor dead ends into Irving Boulevard. Turn left and it's about a half-block down. You can't miss it. Just look for the big truck with "Lone Star Mattress" emblazoned on the side. Their motto is, "We don't sell cheap beds. We sell beds cheap." They carry BASSETT, EASTMAN HOUSE, KING KOIL, SIMMONS, SPRINGWALL, THERAPEDIC, THOMASVILLE and more. An EASTMAN HOUSE mattress started at $299. Granted the mattress is a mismatch, but who'll notice? There's a limited supply, so first come, first to sleep. Save money the warehouse way on name-brand mattresses, some mismatches, floor samples and discontinued lots coupled with lower overhead, no commission sales personnel and no frills. I mean it! A twin set was $99; full set, $129; queen set, $149; king set, $199. Now a second location, 13502 Floyd Circle, Dallas/Richardson, 972/234-5231, open daily 11-6. *CK, MC, V, AE, Dl*

★★★★★ Mattress Firm, The — 972/401-9665

10699 N. Stemmons Frwy. — *Mon-Fri 10-9; Sat 10-8; Sun Noon-6*
Dallas, TX 75220 — *www.themattressfirm.com*

They only carry SEALY and Sealy's top-of-the-line STEARNS & FOSTER brand. This location on North Stemmons is a regular Mattress Firm and their clearance store with blemished, clearance and mismatched sets on which you can save even more than an arm and a leg. Shop 21 store locations throughout the Metroplex, all with three-hour express delivery, same-day, next-day, *any* day delivery, have it your way–we still continue to be firm supporters of The Mattress Firm. For attentive service and competitive prices, free delivery or your choice of a bedframe with premium purchase, plus free set-up and removal of old mattress, their service policies are firm. We firmly support their "beat any price or your mattress is free plus $500!" policy. For example, a SEALY Posturepedic queen set began as low as $299 and a king-size set started as low as $450 for the basic bed; Pillowtops started at $809. Though many mattresses today come with 15-, 20- and 25-year warranties, industry standards recommend changing mattresses every seven years (I guess when you get the itch). Check directory for their multiple locations in the Metroplex and get a firm grip on your bedding budget. If you have access to the internet, you can print out additional money-saving coupons that you can redeem at their stores for $25-$100. *CK, MC, V, AE, D*

★ Mattress Giant — 972/960-2337

4900 Belt Line Rd., #100 — *Mon-Fri 10-9; Sat to 10-8; Sun Noon-6*
Addison, TX 75240 — *www.mattressgiant.com*

Thanks in large part to several reports of "used-car-like" sales tactics, this giant has fallen a few notches this year. Now owned by Simmons, it's a shame since you're not buying something to drive, but rather something to sleep on. Driving a hard bargain should be *your* m.o., not theirs. With more than 50 mattresses in stock to choose from, we certainly can't fault their selection. In fact, Jim, our salesman, indicated that in the 18 locations throughout the Metroplex, they sell 2,500 mattresses a week. (And he wasn't dreaming.) So, if you're looking for name brands like SIMMONS, SERTA and SPRINGAIR, you can "ooh and aah" or you can shop elsewhere for better prices and softer sells on mattresses, box springs, day beds, brass and iron beds. Mattresses ranged from around $300-$2,000 depending on the coil counts and other inner workings. They claim to never be undersold but it's up to you to figure out what they are selling. We couldn't get a straight answer from two different salesmen. Free delivery and set-up still an option. Check directory for the location nearest to you. *CK, MC, V, AE, D*

★★ Mattress Max 972/315-1060

500 E. FM 3040, #113 *Mon-Fri 10-9; Sat 10-8; Sun Noon-6*
Lewisville, TX 75067

At the southeast corner of MacArthur and Round Grove, keep those mattress savings to the max. Forget counting sheep. Instead, count on Mattress Max for being pretty reasonable. Twin beds started as low as $84 for each mattress. You can get a queen size pillow top mattress and box spring for around $599. The prices are not set in stone, though. The owner was willing to do a little negotiating, so don't take the prices as firm. Then, roll over to the SPRINGWALL pillow top queen sets for $409-$695 and sleep like royalty. Looking for a queen iron or brass-plated headboard? They started as low as $129. Futons can be ordered through a catalog and air beds (the kind you hear commercials about on the radio) started at $1,000. "Now I lay me down to sleep..." *CK, MC, V, AE, D*

★★ Mattress USA 972/424-0474

811 E. 15th St. *Mon-Sat 10-7; Sun Noon-6*
Plano, TX 75074 *www.mattressusa.com*

See the USA flat on your back in a mattress that's 50 percent off and more. Head to Plano, one red light east of Central Expressway, in downtown on the northeast corner and sign up here. Uncle Sam wants you! Just look for his sign and enlist the services of factory-direct, first-quality mattresses with names like CHIROPRACTIC by SPRINGWALL, KING KOIL, POSTURE BEAUTY and SIMMONS BEAUTYREST. Choose also futons, daybeds, bunk beds, iron canopy beds, custom-order mattresses, futon/sofa accessories and bedroom suites for moderately-priced house calls. Great bunk beds start at $299 in your choice of four colors. There's a nice neighborhood feel to the shop–it almost puts you to sleep. *CK, MC, V, AE, D, Financing*

★★★★★ Mattressland 972/423-5656

6000 N. Central *Mon-Fri 10-7; Sat 10-6; Sun 12:30-5*
Plano, TX 75074

Not Fantasyland, not Adventureland, but Mattressland. Maybe they should call it Dreamland. Dream on. Featuring factory blemishes, seconds, liquidations and closeouts with names such as BASSETT, KING KOIL, SIMMONS, BEAUTYREST, SPRING AIR and SPRINGWALL, savor the savings on queen-size pillowtops selling from $250-$599. The $999 model was out the door for $499, so we would say, a savings of this magnitude, puts them in a class all their own. Don't expect a fancy showroom or fancy headboards to distract you. These folks are strictly mattresses. And with Shaun's accent, we think we'll go back and try out a few more. Same-day delivery from this land of mattresses. Sleep tight, too, at their other location at 12115 Self Plaza, 214/320-2500. *CK, MC, V, AE, D*

★★★★★ North Texas Mattress & Futons 817/274-1266

1615 W. Park Row *Mon-Sat 10-7; Sun Noon-6*
Arlington, TX 76013 *www.ntxmattressfuton.com*

Top-of-the-line at bottom of the barrel prices is why North Texas Mattress & Futons gets rave reviews. You gotta sleep, don't you? And you want to sleep on the best at the lowest price, don't you? Then park your car on Park Row and see what a top-quality mattress sleeps like. Trust you'll sleep like a log and feel great when the alarm goes off. The futons, too, are the best. The "Sleigh Arm" futon holds the record for being the strongest futon frame in the industry; it converts to three positions and is available in mahogany and medium oak-finished hardwood. Or what about the "Portafino" futon, available in golden oak, American oak, dark walnut or black finishes with convenient arm storage. All futons are available in chairs, loveseats, full- and queen-size. They not only look good, they also perform great. You can also shop for bedroom furniture at shaved-down prices. An OLIVE GROVE sleigh bed and bedroom suite would be a beautiful addition to any bedroom. They also have latex mattresses, adjustable air mattresses and the "memory foam," therma-sensitive mattresses made famous by NASA astronauts. *CK, MC, V, AE, D, Financing*

★★ Original Mattress Factory, The 817/334-0361

912 E. Vickery Blvd. *Mon-Sat 10-6*
Fort Worth, TX 76104

The Original Mattress Factory has been bedding down for 100 years and it's still a Duncan family tradition. Buying direct from the manufacturer makes for a good night sleep. Look for their warehouse clearance sales, when they get very competitive. We saw their premier luxury firm set for $399 and the king for $499 with a 20-year warranty at one of these sales. Now, that's more like it. The competition is stiff out there in the big city and being a mattress manufacturer holds promise but should be scruntinized as any other mattress retailer. So be it. It's up to you to try and decide if sleeping on their mattresses is like sleeping on a cloud or if there's so much turbulence that the bumps are keeping you awake. The original warehouse site is still standing with other locations in Arlington and Dallas. *CK, MC, V, AE, Layaway*

★★★★ Rick's Bedrooms — 972/840-3000

3010 S. Jupiter — *Mon-Fri 10-8; Sat 10-7; Sun 11-6*
Garland, TX 75041 — *www.ricksbedrooms.com*

Take note. It's not just Rick's Waterbeds that's making waves in the Metroplex. It's now Rick's Bedrooms–in fact, if it's a sleeping surface, Rick can get you covered. Whether you'd like to ride the tide with a waterbed, or jump on the bandwagon with a futon, or any other kind of mattress, Rick has not been lying down on the job. No sir. His salesman at Vikon Village couldn't have been nicer or more enthused without even trying to close a deal. In fact, even if we perspired (or did we sweat?), he made shopping a pleasure. If you're thinking of a waterbed, especially one that doesn't look or act like the old waterbeds, Rick is the Olympic gold medal winner. Choice of finishes included ash, pine, oak, and metal, but black lacquer seems still to be a favorite. Futons and mattresses should not be ignored either. Brands such as BEAUTYREST, KING KOIL and SIMMONS could keep you in bed for days. A waterbed queen set was $499.95. They also carry BOYD, out of St. Louis, Mo., waterbed mattresses starting at $399 for queen-size and air beds from $699.95 ($1,999.95 for the king). Check directory for other locations in the Metroplex and watch for perennial promotions. Ninety-days same as cash, free layaway and immediate delivery another plus. Four more locations: 901 W. Parker, #117, Plano, 972/422-4401; 15300 Midway Rd., Addison, 972/991-9811; 3501 Gus Thomasson, Mesquite, 972/681-5878; and 2544 E. Abrams, Arlington, 817/265-8144. *CK, MC, V, AE, D*

♥♥♥♥♥ Sico Room Makers — 214/361-7160

4508 Lovers Lane — *Mon-Fri 8:30-5; Sat 10-4*
Dallas, TX 75225

Make the move to the Park Cities, and expect the customers to flock in, but you can expect to pay higher prices. Sico's room makeovers are not for cheapos. Creating two rooms into one doesn't come cheap. But then again, have you priced a room addition lately? Turn your spare bedroom into a guest room when needed AND an office when you don't. Slide that mattress back into the wall and you've got possibilities. Wallbeds and organization keep all things in their proper places. And, you'll get a good night's sleep, too. Workmanship is guaranteed top-quality, and top quality is not bargain basement stuff–you pay for what you get! The quality makes it a fab find and an extended value for crowded lifestyles. *CK, MC, V, AE*

★★★★★ Simmons Mattress Outlet — 214/631-3257

1200 Conveyor Lane — *Mon-Fri 10-7; Sat 10-6; Sun Noon-5*
Inwood Trade Center — *www.simmons.com*
Dallas, TX 75247

Off Inwood and Stemmons, in the Inwood Trade Center, say "good buy" to paying retail for a SIMMONS mattress. For more than 125 years, this company has been bedding down those looking for a good–no, great night's sleep. Give them credit for inventing the Hide-A-Bed sofa in 1940. During the war, they made 2,700 different items, from parachutes to bazooka rockets. Simmons became the first mattress company to introduce a Super Size mattress in 1958. By 1960, Simmons was boasting a king- and queen-size mattress. In 1995, Simmons introduced its Advanced Beautyrest Coil–the tallest coil in the industry. They also have the Backcare mattresses, designed to help the sleeper maintain proper spinal alignment by giving proper support and comfort in all five zones of the body. I wonder when they're going to introduce the "zoo" mattress–where my dogs and cats can comfortably zone in between. Can you imagine all this innovation at outlet prices? Don't re-coil...these are genuine Simmons mattresses: they have BEAUTYREST (The "Do-Not-Disturb" mattress), BACK CARE, MAXI-PEDIC and ULTIMATE SUPREME. Savings of hundreds of dollars is commonplace. Queen sets started as low as $199; king sets started at $350. They also just opened a second location at 1144 Plano Rd., Suite 100, Richardson (Arapaho Station), 972/690-4270. Same hours and same great products. Dallas is lucky to have one of only 13 Simmons outlets nationwide. *CK, MC, V*

★★★★★ Sweet Dreams Bedding Co. — 817/790-8510

4125 S. I-35 W — *Mon-Fri 9-5*
Alvarado, TX 76009

Sweet Dreams Bedding Company is a manufacturer of SWEET DREAMS, futon and hospitality industry mattresses. The bargain that you get from this company is available because you're buying direct from the manufacturer. You know the old adage, eliminate the middleman and go direct to the source. They sell their products to major hotel chains such as Marriott. Their quality and specifications meet or exceed the standards set by the major brands (SEALY, SIMMONS, etc.). They also carry bedding to dress up your new mattress. You won't have any trouble catching your ZZZs if you buy from Sweet Dreams Bedding. Call for quotes. Free delivery in the Metroplex.

Big Stores & Catalogs

American Needlewoman Catalog

817/293-1229

2944 S.E. Loop 820
Fort Worth, TX 76133
Mon-Sat 10-4

Stop needling the competition. This inexpensive catalog (about $2) should tickle your creative fancy and keep you in stitches for years. If you're a Wal-Mart shopper, you'll love this catalog. Since 1976, this company has been sending out signals of a small crafts warning. Everything you've ever wanted in needlecrafts but didn't know who to call is found in their beautiful 72-page four-color catalog. Low prices throughout, where your fingers not only do the shopping but do the crafting, too. Kits, books, craft supplies and yarns are all cross-stitched and ready to sew. Cross-stitching kits, needlepoint tapestries imported from Europe, petit-point kits, latch-hook kits, even wood paintings and supplies are all available. Don't wait 'til the last minute to start those crafty projects. Get with the program and get on their good side for their quarterly catalog mailings by writing PO Box 6472, Fort Worth, TX 76115. *CK, MC, V, D*

★★★★ Big Lots

972/889-9815

1400 W. Spring Valley Rd.
Richardson, TX 75080
Mon-Sat 9-9 P.M.; Sun 10-7

When it comes to odd lots of most anything, consider Big Lots your saving grace. Holy Cow! There were so many aisles to navigate, we wished we had a computer program to guide us. This converted grocery store offered a supermercado selection of closeouts from housewares to sporting goods, gifts to jewelry, comforters to hard candy, name-brand toys, lawn and garden equipment, furniture, and much more. Brand name furniture includes ASHLEY and SAUDER. On the day of our visit, they were offering $48 off any couch set that was bought. Big Deal at Big Lots. Couch sets start at around $398-$698. Visit them in Mesquite (972/613-2455) as well as Fort Worth, Haltom City and Irving. *CK, MC, V, D*

★★★★★ Burlington Coat Factory

817/571-2666

1201 W. Airport Frwy.
Euless, TX 76040
Mon-Sat 10-9; Sun 11-6
www.coat.com

With almost 250 warehouses coast-to-coast including, several in the Metroplex (Dallas, Euless, Fort Worth, Arlington, Mesquite and Plano), this Burlington is a train to catch. Contrary to popular opinion (and the name), the 65-year-old Burlington has much more than just coats. But don't get me wrong, they have coats! Lots of them. 10,000 of them for the entire family. Furs and leather ones, too, plus clothing and accessories for men, women and children. Their expanded baby collection has spun off into its own identity called Baby Depot with BABY TREND, CENTURY 4-in-1 travel systems for babies and toddlers, DELTA/LUV walkers, GRAECO strollers, KOLCRAFT, SIMMONS cribs and more. Think you're outta there, yet? Guess again. Say hi to maternity and plus sizes, lingerie, athletic apparel, shoes, designer fragrances, jewelry, linens, towels, blankets, housewares, gifts–well, it's a big store. (See category listing above). Also baby furniture, linens, home accessories and more and most priced 25-60 percent lower than retail. Wore out a silk washable slack set for $20 and a NYPD suit for $40. *CK, MC, V, AE, D, Layaway*

★★ Clearance Center, The

972/387-0700

5812 LBJ Frwy.
Dallas, TX 75240
Mon-Fri 10-7; Sat 10-6

The Clearance Center clears the path to savings. How do they do it? By being scavengers, that's how. And their store looks like they've hit rock bottom. An occasional windfall, like a SONY large-screen TV that retailed for $1,999 was $999 was so impressive after I showed in on TV, that I called in an order for one, too. Sorry, Charlie, we only had one and it's been sold. Well, so be it. Customers, then, flocked to the store in search of the big B...only to come away empty-handed and disappointed. Somewhere between a warehouse that needs a little TLC to a garage sale is how they described it. Perhaps, they will have cleaned up their act and you will be the benefactor of factory closeouts, overstocks and liquidations of brand name stereos, VCRs, computers, camcorders, clothing, groceries, hardware, sporting goods, lawn and garden and more. They get new shipments weekly. We got lucky on a recent trip with a HITACHI VCR four-head with remote for $69.95, regularly $170. Also BILL BLASS khaki cargo pants for $9.99, retail $58. Even if I hate GATORADE, finding it for $.49 compared to $1.19 made us thirst for more. Located off 635 between Preston and the Tollway. *CK, MC, V*

★★★★ Dillard's Clearance Center 817/649-0782

3000 E. Pioneer Pkwy. *Mon-Sat 10-7; Sun Noon-6*
Arlington, TX 76010

Dillard's, Dillard's, we can all scream for Dillard's. One of only two Dillard's outlet stores in Texas, if it was meant to be discounted, it is meant to save you 40-75 percent. Smart shoppers know where to find this department store outlet to see first-hand the art of the deal. But first, be patient. The floors are crammed with stuff everywhere, but unearthing the ultimate bargain may be worth it. ELLEN TRACY walking shorts originally priced at $100-$150 were snatched up for $10. This huge clearance center is packed with seasonal close-outs and discontinued merchandise from more than 50 stores–but you definitely have to have an eagle's eye. Not everything that meets the eye is a bargain. We're not talking two or three racks here. We're talking more than 50,000 items, including misses' skirts, pants, more than 9,000 dresses, 18,000 pairs of women's shoes plus children's clothing, men's shirts, formals–the selection is astronomical. Now that furniture has joined the racks, it's practically a free-for-all. Though they were the winner of a past year's Shoppers Choice Award, they didn't even attend or acknowledge their accolade. This time, they were only a finalist. Maybe shoppers are trying to tell them something? *CK, MC, V, AE, D, CB, Dillard's*

★★★★ Goodwill Industries 214/638-2800

2800 N. Hampton Rd. *Mon-Sat 9:30-6; Sun Noon-6*
Dallas, TX 75212

There is no shame in shopping at the Goodwill Store. Goodwill = Good Deals, plus you'll be benefiting a very worthy cause. We have always gotten lucky at the Goodwill stores. All kinds of odds and ends, small appliances, dishware, glassware, family clothing and toys. No pick-up service, though, since there are drop-off donation centers around town. Goodwill provides jobs for those who may not otherwise be able to work. Check directory for the closest location and lend a helping hand. Every little bit helps. Remember, generosity begins at home. CK, MC, V

★★★★ Horchow Finale 972/519-5406

3400 Preston Rd. *Mon-Fri 10-7; Sat 10-6; Sun Noon-5*
Plano, TX 75093

Have you drooled over the pages of The Horchow Collection? Well, now you can have some of the same wonderful goodies that didn't make it to someone's mailbox, for whatever reason, from this Neiman-Marcus sibling. Nobody bought it, or somebody bought it and returned it, or it was damaged in transit, or they produced too many–whatever the reason,it's yours here at a savings of 30-75 percent. Clothing, jewelry, shoes, linens, china, crystal, furniture, rugs, decorative accessories and more line their Plano repository. You'll find FIELDCREST, LANE, MARTEX, MIKASA and more name brands as well as the private HORCHOW label. Some of the items were fairly pricey to begin with, so even at a discount you might not bite. Others are right on the money (and below!). Their second location is closer to the Park Cities (hey, everybody likes a bargain!) at 3046 Mockingbird Lane (at the northwest corner of Mockingbird and Central Expressway; 214/750-0308). *CK, MC, V, AE, Neiman-Marcus, Bergdorf Card*

★★★★★ JCPenney Outlet Store — 972/874-0578

3000 Grapevine Mills Pkwy.
Grapevine Mills Mall
Grapevine, TX 76051
Mon-Sat 10-9:30; Sun 11-7
www.jcpenney.com

When you think it just doesn't get any better than this, you turn the corner and are hit with another surprise. That's if you're a JCPenney fan. A penny saved is a penny earned, said Mr. Penney when he developed his billion-dollar empire. And if you shop their outlet store, you can reap immediate gratification in inventory that is closed-out, discontinued, returned or overrun from their catalog offerings. Save 40-60 percent off suggested retail prices. Look, see what your pennies will buy: family apparel, athletic apparel, family shoes, athletic shoes, petite, misses, and tall women's clothing, home furnishings, home accessories, electronics and even big and tall men's apparel–a lost bastion in the bargain arena. Forgo the retail ambiance and get down to the bare prices. On one of our trips, we saw a men's LEVI'S silver tab hidden pocket plaid shirt for only $23.99. For the ladies, an embellished skirt cost only $28. They also have a great selection of women's accessories. A Crazy Horse leather belt was a cinch–only $9.99. *CK, MC, V, AE, D, JCPenney*

★★★★★ Just-A-Buck — 972/287-5669

129 Hall Lane
Seagoville, TX 75159
Mon-Sat 9-8; Sun 11-6

What-a-bargain! What-a-deal! Supersize it behind the Whataburger if you want to spend-a-buck. At Just-a-Buck, that's where it's at. It's practically a free-for-all. The owners buy from auctions, closeouts from manufacturers or stores, wherever they can get their hands on a deal, then lots-a-luck. Luscious silk flowers-for-less including mums and roses with dew drops. Party supplies and Halloween masks. For your bed or bath, lovely-looking cloth-covered trash cans for $4.99, cloth-covered jewelry boxes with compartments, $3.99 or cloth-covered shower rings for $2.99. Originally made for JCPenney, shower rings in hunter green or burgundy were their namesake, just-a-buck. DUNDEE 100 percent cotton bath towels, Made in the USA, were $3.99. You never know what's going to be Just-A-Buck or a lot of bucks, but you can rest assured, it's going to be a lot less. Decorative wooden garden wells were $32.50 and Igloo-type pet cases with fur inside that retail for $19.97 were barking at-$7.97. You never know what you will find, so go take a look. A second Just-A-Buck in Canton on Hwy. 243, 903/567-0966. *CK MC, V*

★★★★ Kohl's 972/939-2887

4120 Old Denton Rd. *Mon-Thu 9-11; Fri-Sat 8-11; Sun 10-7*
Carrollton, TX 75010 *www.kohls.com*

This value-oriented, family-focused department store offers attractive pricing on name brand merchandise such as ADDIDAS, CANDIES, DOCKERS, GLORIA VANDERBILT, KEDS, LEE, LEVI, NIKE, UNION BAY and VILLAGER. In addition to clothing, they carry shoes, housewares, home décor accessories (from frames to candles), jewelry, toys, cards and much more. Frequent sales include additional hours on the weekends. There are 16 locations in the DFW are including: Valley Ranch, 214/574-5750; Plano West, 972/309-0004; Plano East, 972/309-0080; Plano North, 972/309-0080; Flower Mound, 972/691-1106; Lewisville, 972/353-3438; Keller, 817/431-4437; North Richland Hills, 817/498-1808; Garland, 972/495-6756; North Dallas, 972/309-0608; Cedar Hill, 972/299-9001; Hulen, 817/569-7550; Grand Prairie, 972/263-1009; McKinney, 214/544-3535; Rockwell, 972/772-5920; and South Arlington, 817/417-6540. Well organized and displayed and ready to take on the day. *CK, MC, V, AE, D, Kohl's Card*

★★★★★ MacFrugal's 972/484-4821

2865 Valley View Lane *Mon-Sat 9-9; Sun 10-7*
Farmers Branch, TX 75234

Move over, Mac, there's a new game in town. We don't intend to give you the knife, but you've got some closeout competition. Still, you're a top contender. Looking for Games People Play? Do they have games? Yes, sir, and plenty of other stuff that makes shopping here a slam-dunk for deals. When we saw the bird clock for $19.95, we knew it was cheep, cheep. (It was long before the department stores started selling their versions for $29-$39.) Unfortunately, when we got to the store, the birds had sung their final swan song. That should tell you something. If you wait it out, you'll be out of luck. Today, that same bird clock is selling for bird seed and now it's the dogs who are barking the time out. Every Tuesday, new merchandise arrives. If they don't have it, as they say, you probably don't need it. One day we lingered over to the lingerie department for BALI bras closed-out from Macy's. Then, we were off to the children's department for DISNEY clothes (the highest priced item was $6.99). Fleece tops and bottoms were a measly $3.99. Tons of seasonal decorations (do you care if it was last year's?) including Halloween and Christmas supplies that are usually in-stock from springtime on. Porcelain Christmas balls for $9.99 and a 20-piece set of dishes for $14.99 were crystal-clear steals. In the gift department, we were swept off our feet with a FANTOM vacuum cleaner (Service Merchandise has one marked from $350 down to $299); MacFrugal's had it for $159. Where else can you get a punch bowl with 12 glass cups for $8.88, an OSTER rice cooker for $16.99 or a PROTER-SILEX can opener for $8.88? And in the toy department, we'd be remiss if we didn't scream over their selection of the CALIFORNIA ROLLER GIRL for $12.99 (every place else had it for $19.99) plus a huge selection of Barbie dolls and her jewelry collection. What a babe! Check for the location nearest you: Carrollton, 2865 Valley View Lane, 972/484-4821; Garland, 825 W Centerville Rd, 972/270-2498; Richardson, 1322 S Plano Rd,972/480-0921; Lewisville,2325 S. Stemmons Frwy, #501, 972/315-0559; Mid-Cities, 1201 Airport Frwy, (metro) 817/540-4946. *CK, MC, V, D*

★★★★ Marshall's 972/248-8494

7609 Campbell Rd. *Mon-Sat 9:30-9:30; Sun 11-7*
Dallas, TX 75248 *www.marshallsonline.com*

Marshall's has been going strong for years and is now part of the TJ Maxx family, so even in the off-price world, mergers and acquisitions are running wild. Bargains are plentiful from this Boston-based giant, who has been saving you green for decades. They have expanded their giftware and housewares presence and expanded their Women's World for plus sizes since TJ Maxx decided to fade out that department. Name-brand fashions (still stronger in men's sportswear, children's apparel and ladies' lingerie) plus shoes and accessories, giftware, gourmet food items, jewelry, hosiery, linens and more. We saw designer fragrances (CHLOE, FENDI, PALO-

MA, PASSION, POISON, SHALIMAR, SUNG and more) for $19.99 and great junior dresses and broomstick skirts for $19.99 (retail $39) on one visit. Selection ranges from staggering to close to sparse, so shop often. Check directory for nearest location. *CK, MC, V, AE, D*

★★ Mervyn's

972/270-8800

1201 Centerville Rd.
Garland, TX 75041

Mon-Sun 9-10
www.mervyns.com

This jewel in the chain of stores from Dayton-Hudson has lost some of its glitter this year, but it still maintains some of the most loyal followers. With the California influence as part of their marketing strategy, things were supposed to improve. Well, maybe they are just California dreamers. Maybe there's just too much retailing in this town and everything looks alike after a while. Both private label and name-brand clothing and domestics at up to 20 percent off everyday are part of their core merchandising strategy. (Sales, though, make the bargains more tempting.) The quality of goods passes our white-glove inspection, but it's really just another store, another dollar. Slip into a pair of CHEROKEE jeans or men's DOCKERS, which seem to be their mainstay. Casual and comfortable BILL BLASS stretch jeans, men's T-shirts and LEVI'S were easy on and easy off. They seem to be catering to aging Baby Boomers, but don't want to own up to it. Not much to rave about, except the better buys seem to be on lingerie, baby items, jewelry, shoes, housewares and gifts. Their mall stores carry a much bigger inventory, especially on housewares. Check directory or call 800/MERVYNS for a location nearest you. *CK, MC, V, Mervyn's*

★★★ Off Rodeo Drive

972/724-7860

Grapevine Mills Mall
Grapevine, TX

Mon-Sat 10-10; Sun 11-8
www.bernini.com

Right in the heart of the biggest mall in the State, forget hitting the high road. Shop On Rodeo Drive and you'll shop 'til you've dropped a bundle. Shop Off Rodeo Drive, and you'll only shop 'til you drop. Why foot the bill to Hollywood when Grapevine Mills is just around the corner. Save on the star-studded line up for less from the chi-chi store Bernini for exclusive menswear. More than 50 Off Rodeo Drive stores with savings up to 70 percent off designer fashions for menswear, dress shirts, dress pants, accessories like belts and cuff links. Almost 30,000 square feet of shopping heaven including those that were heavenly scent (perfumes for men and women). *MC, V, AE, D*

★★★ Ross Dress For Less

972/247-1228

3046 Forest Lane *Mon-Sat 9:30-9; Sun Noon-7*
Dallas, TX 75234 *www.rossstores.com*

This national chain (more than 350 stores in 17 states) with 1998 revenues of $2.2 billion is nothing to sneeze at. They have certainly blown their way into the Metroplex. Unfortunately, bigger is not always better. Some stars do not always shine brightly. Some days, it's heaven; other days doom and gloom. There are some stores that never have a customer in sight while others (like the one in Lewisville) are always busy. Nevertheless, with regular visits, you can dress for less. In fact 20-60 percent less. Not much in the designer realm, but prices are compatible with frugal shoppers. First quality, in-season, name brand apparel, accessories and footwear for the entire family. Watch for the summer opening of a new store in the Richardson Square Mall. *CK, MC, V, AE, D*

★★★★★ Sam's Wholesale Club

972/436-6684

751 W. Main St. *Mon-Fri 10-8:30; Sat 9:30-8:30; Sun 11-6*
Lewisville, TX 75067 *www.samsclub.com*

Welcome to this Wal-Mart division for wholesale shopping. A membership gets you in the door (and just in case you thought your passport ID photo was bad, wait 'till you see your Sam's picture!). A tow truck may be needed to cart you off from this mart at the end of your shopping journey. Forget the amenities–no plush carpeting, no carry-out help, no sacks, limited brands, often bulk sizes, and sometimes long and frustrating waits at the check-out counter, but not to worry–you will be saving $$$$. Warehouse atmosphere complete with low lighting and concrete floors, Sam's is continually adding more and more resources, including a photo-developing desk, an eyeglass counter, a pizza kitchen, a fresh bakery, car sales, mobile phone service, travel, and more. Wear comfortable shoes and come for an afternoon to load up on TVs and TV dinners, bargains in best-selling books and blue jeans, food and furniture, office supplies and equipment, faxes and floorcare, carpet and Christmas wrap. Check directory for other locations throughout the Metroplex, most located next to a huge Wal-Mart. And, when shopping for a new car, pull out your Sam's Club Membership and there's a chance they'll negotiate. Soon you will be able to join, renew or upgrade your membership to Elite status and also be able to shop on-line 24 hours a day. Just what I need. *CK,MC, V, D, Sam's*

Big Stores & Catalogs

★★★★★ Sears Appliance Outlet 972/418-8445

1927 E. Belt Line Rd. *Mon-Thu 10-6; Fri 10-8; Sat 9-6; Sun Noon-6*
Carrollton, TX 75006 *www.sears.com*

This Sears Outlet is the repository for appliances and a few odds 'n' ends, such as big screen TVs. Hey, what's odd is that there weren't a lot. Everybody wants one these days. Are you listening, Sears? But if you're looking for an appliance that has been returned, discontinued, out-of-the-carton by mistake, damaged in transit, used, abused, one-of-a-kind or a floor sample, chances are it winds its way to this central clearing house for a quick getaway. Save 20-60 percent on a vast selection of appliances (they no longer have furniture). What pushed our button in no time flat was a big screen TV that was reduced 30 percent with an additional 30 percent off. (Add it up, friends, that's 60 percent off!) If it's great brands that you are looking for, you'll find them here, including AMANA, FRIGIDAIRE, GENERAL ELECTRIC, KENMORE, MAYTAG and WHIRLPOOL. Since merchandise moves out the door fast, if you want to see the softer side of Sears, run fast to the outlet. Tons of refrigerators (over 400 at last count) and 200 washers and dryers were corralled starting around $289. Weekend sales are whoppers–often 50 percent off the original price. Choose any appliance–from washers, dryers, ranges, refrigerators and more. Visit them also in Grand Prairie at 2985 S. Hwy. 360 (972/988-3036). Bear in mind that the Grand Prairie outlet sells furniture only. *CK, MC, V, AE, D, Sears*

★★★★ Service Merchandise 214/361-1202

11250 N. Central Expressway *Mon-Sat 10-9; Sun 11-6*
Dallas, TX 75243 *www.servicemerchandise.com*

With more than 350 stores nationwide, Service Merchandise has fallen on hard times. But, if you haven't shopped their new and improved stores lately, you're missing the book. Despite its antiquated beginning as a catalog showroom, their turnaround is finally seeing the light of day. Concentration on their strengths like jewelry and small appliances has improved their image. If you need something now or want good choices for a gift, you'll strike gold at your closest Service Merchandise. They have a superb selection of jewelry including diamonds, gold, pearls, gemstones, watches, and silver for men, women and children. Watch out: names included ARMITRON, ELGIN, GUCCI, MOVADO, PULSAR, SEIKO and TAG HEUER just to name a few. This store is a good source for patio furniture, large screen TVs, stereo systems, phones, home office furniture, home accessories, binoculars, telescopes and yes, toys and games for the kiddos. *CK, MC, V, AE, D*

★★★★★ Stein Mart 817/735-4533

6385 Camp Bowie *Mon-Sat 10-9; Sun Noon-5:30*
Fort Worth, TX 76116 *www.steinmart.com*

Wal-Mart, Kmart, Mini-Mart–here a mart, there a mart, everywhere a mart, mart. But their resemblance to Stein Mart ends at the door. This is the best off-price specialty store for your upscale statements including apparel, shoes, accessories, gifts, linens, home decorative items and more, no doubt about it. We saw plenty of designer dresses and sportswear including plus sizes at 30-50 percent off (and more during special sales and promotions). The ladies' shoe department is a shoe-in and the men's designer and contemporary collections, especially knit and woven shirts, is a nice addition to all-around fashion firsts. Purses, wallets, necklaces, bangles and the earrings, well, expect these to be shown at the finest specialty stores–only here, they're half the price. Be sure to ask for one of the "Bou-Ladies" (previously Fou-Fou Ladies) who will see that you are included on their mailing lists. The ambiance will floor you. You think you're at Saks Fifth at a fifth of the price. Eleven area Stein Marts and no relation, unfortunately, to Gold-Stein. *CK, MC, V, AE, D, Panache Card*

★★★★ Syms 214/902-9600

4770 W. Mockingbird Lane *Mon-Fri 10-9; Sat 10-6:30; Sun Noon-5:30*
Dallas, TX 75209 *www.symsclothing.com*

Here an educated consumer is a Syms shopper with savings of 25-40 percent throughout the store on family apparel, luggage and other leather goods, pantyhose, linens, shoes, lingerie, coats, furs and more. Names to bargain with include BALLY, COLE-HAAN, PERRY ELLIS, REEBOK, STANLEY BLACKER, RALPH LAUREN and more. Automatic markdowns were posted everywhere, providing additional savings as time goes by. The men's department, occupying 60 percent of the selling space, is definitely their forte in sizes from 36S-54XL with brands such as ADOLPHO, BILL BLASS, CALVIN KLEIN, DKNY, GEOFFREY BEENE, HUGO BOSS and STANLEY BLACKER just to mention a few. Remember, their early beginnings were in men apparel. Visit them also in Hurst on Airport Freeway (183) just west of Precinct Line Rd. near Abuelo's Mexican Restaurant. *CK, MC, V, AE, D, Syms*

Big Stores & Catalogs

★★★★ TJ Maxx

972/437-1842

12 Richardson Heights
Richardson, TX 75080

Mon-Sat 9:30-9:30; Sun Noon-6
www.tjmaxx.com

Aside from their catchy jingle, there's almost always something to sing about at TJ Maxx. This department store off-price powerhouse (who also owns Marshall's–the store that founder Bernie Cammarato once worked) is a Mecca for name brands at 20-60 percent off. Men's, women's, and children's apparel, fragrances, domestics, shoes, handbags, gifts, jewelry and more. We liked the selection of watches for under $40 and the women's workout suits for only $19.99. There's always a good selection of potpourri, bath soaps, and oils on display and a host of must-have's that you didn't know you needed until you saw the price. And believe it or not, it's a great Saturday night people-watching source. The Diva has often run into stars shopping with the verve of a Saturday Night Fever. (Perhaps they, too, are sick of paying retail!) Call 800/2-TJMAXX for a location nearest you. *CK, MC, V, AE, D*

Boats & Supplies

★★ Barber Boats

214/357-8294

10220 Harry Hines Blvd. *Mon-Sat 9-6*
Dallas, TX 75220

Though we all didn't come over on the same ship, we all kinda wind up in the same boat when all things are said and done. So, after 40 years in the boat biz, don't you know there's safety in numbers (and years of experience). This Barber sells quality boats, boating accessories, and repairs at better than excellent prices to his customers. The parts and service department maintain the standards that a-fish-ionados are accustomed to when traveling by boat. Keep yourself afloat on the high seas by not paying retail. You can get cookin' in a BAYLINER, MISTY HARBOR, RANGER and other great brand name boats or even get that pontoon boat for the company outing. Check out the outboard collection, too. And by the way, in case you haven't noticed, my favorite winter sport is looking at the pictures I took last summer (on the boat!). *CK, MC, V, D Financing*

★★★ Boater's World

214/750-6819

9100 N. Central Expwy., Suite 115 *Mon-Thu; Fri 9-9; Sat 9-6; Sun 10-5*
Caruth Plaza Shopping Center *www.boatersworld.com*
Dallas, TX 75231

Before you head for the lakes, you'll want to make a stop by Boater's World. That way you'll be prepared for every situation encountered away from shore. These folks have 80 locations nationwide and surely know the difference between a DOCKSIDER and a SHAMU. If you must know, they even sell all the sophisticated navigational systems that can keep you headed in the right direction. Grab an O'BRIEN SUPER SCREAMER tube–that'll keep your boat on course. So much work. So much fun. So much money. But here, wave goodbye to paying full price. For example, a pair of O'BRIEN celebrity water skis retailing for $179.99 was off the dock for $149.95. A TALARERA fishing rod retailed for $98, but BW had it for only $64.95. They also carry a full selection of electronics including boat sound systems, radars, radios and speakers. If you are looking for fishing equipment, they have lures, rods and reels. For all of your water sports, they carry skis, ski ropes, tubes and toys. Since they buy in bulk, they pass on the savings and will guarantee to at least match anyone competitor's price. Located next to Oshman's, maybe a sail is worth it. *CK, MC, V, AE, D*

★★ Marine Max 817/465-9595

808 W. I-20 — *Mon-Sat 9-6*
Arlington, TX 76010 — *www.marinemax.com*

Marine Max is floating on water. This south Arlington shop is the place of choice for boating enthusiasts. After all, what better wave than to show off your craft than on the water. They carry BAJA, BOSTON WHALER, CENTURY, HATTERAS, LOWE, MALIBU, SEA RAY and STRATOS–from fishing boats to yachts. A 19-foot LOWE deckboat with 115 horsepower was $17,000. They have a service outlet at Lynn Creek Marina on Joe Pool Lake where they deliver, service and demo boats. (Ever thought about the fact that it's a crime to catch a fish in some lakes, and yet a miracle in others?) They also resell boats and periodically offer close-outs on last year's models. Ever wonder when's the best time to buy a boat? Answer...in the fall. Knowing when to shop for a boat may be your best route. For example, a LOWE'S pontoon/deck type boat, 17-foot, aluminum, 115 hp that was regularly priced at $19,000 was reduced to $16,900. We also found a good deal on a 19-foot, 130 hp gasoline injection engine plus trailer that was $17,900. Lifejackets are a necessity and they start around $18. This hobby doesn't come cheap, but shopping here may be one way to catch a whale of a deal. With better than average prices, great service and easy financing, why not hit the water with smooth sailing? Yacht are you waiting for? Check out the manufacturers' websites for more detailed information if you are a novice mariner. *CK, MC, V, AE, D, Financing*

★★★★★ Travis Boating Center 972/436-BOAT (2628)

1320 S. Stemmons Frwy. — *Mon-Fri 8-5:30; Sat 8-5*
Lewisville, TX 75067 — *www.travisboatingcenter.com*

Considered the largest discount boating chain in the country, lucky Lewisville water lovers can say hello to BEACHCOMBER, LARSON, POWER QUEST, SEA ARK, SPRINT and VIPER brands, plus parts and service that go along with maintaining your water vessel. Drop your anchor here for less. If you're looking for a marina-size selection, you can count into the hundreds. It's like a dry dock from the San Diego Yacht Club. If you're not wanting to part with all your money, here's another reason to shop here. They have an outlet in front of their showroom where last year's models and some used boats are closed-out and priced even lower than their regularly discounted inventory. Factory-trained mechanics, financing, trade-ins, accessories...the works can be accessed without drowning in debt. Then again, with all the upkeep, you may just want to rent a yacht and leave the driving to a hired hand. Aye, Aye, Captain. (If you're asking about the annual upkeep of a yacht, you probably should consider renting the Titanic instead.) They are a member of BUCNET Worldwide where if they don't have the boat you want, they can find it through their database. Winter hours are above; when warmer weather comes, their hours and days expand. *CK, MC, V, AE, D, Financing*

Boots & Westernwear

★★★★★ Beads Beautiful/Wanted

940/627-7394

106 W. Walnut St.
Decatur, TX 76234

Mon-Sat 10-5

Looking for something to wear to the Cattle Baron's Ball? Westernwear for less is their modus operandi at Beads Beautiful Factory Outlet. High-tail it to Decatur (a hop, skip and a jump from D/FW and Denton) if you want factory pricing on dresses, skirts, jackets, vests, fringed outfits and silk broomstick skirts, all hand-painted or decorated by on-site artists. If you want a western twist on your nuptials, they will even customize bridal ensembles, from white dresses to tuxedo shirts or hats for you and your betrothed. Usually found only in specialty shops on Rodeo Drive (that's not even in Texas), you can shop here and save up to 75 percent. The only thing left to do is accessorize. Waltz out with earrings and things (pawn and new Native American sterling silver), scarves, bandannas and hats, all with a western flair. Started by two women 16 years ago in a garage, Beads Beautiful has grown into a multi-million dollar business with their "WANTED" label. *CK, MC, V, AE*

★★★★ Boot Town

972/243-1151

2821 LBJ Frwy.
Farmers Branch, TX 75234

Mon-Sat 9-9; Sun Noon-6
www.boottown.com

Dallas is a boot town, so kick up your heels in a pair of ACME, DAN POST, DURANGO, JUSTIN, LAREDO, LARRY MAHAN, LUCCHESE, NOCONA, RIOS, TONY LAMA–more than 30 top brands from plain to exotic skins (lizard, snake, ostrich, antelope, cowhide and more) in sizes that'll knock your socks off! Justin calfskin and bullhide western boots were $99 and full-quill ostrich ropers were $369. Sizes 6 ½-13 for men, 4-10 for women and children's sizes, to boot. They also carry popular brands and styles of belts, hats by RESISTOL and other major brands, as well as a variety of buckles, including CRUMRINE. We also noticed western shirts and jeans by LEVI'S, PANHANDLE SLIM and WRANGLER. Ever worn a pair of WOLVERINE Durashocks? They're guaranteed to be the world's most comfortable boot–you be the judge, old bunion toes. They've been kicking up their western heels for the past 20 years, with seven locations in the Metroplex. To rope your boots and westernwear by mail, order from their free catalog. *CK, MC, V, AE, D*

★★★ Cavender's Boot City 817/589-7311

857 W. Pipeline Rd. *Mon-Sat 9-9; Sun 11-6*
Hurst, TX 76053 *www.cavenders-boot-city.com*

You won't have to be a scavenger when you look for boots at Cavender's. Though huge, it's easy to pick a pair or two from their well-organized racks. You'll find ACME, ARIAT, DAN POST, JUSTIN, LUCCHESE, NOCONA and TONY LAMA (just to kick around a few) starting at just $49 and up, up, up. DAN POST lizard boots were $219 and a pair of bull-hide western boots were $99 (retail $129). Racks and racks of famous-name western duds, too, complete the look. We wrangled men's shirts and jeans by CINCH, LAWMAN, PANHANDLE SLIM, ROPER and WRANGLER as well as women's duds by LAWMAN, ROCKY MOUNTAIN and WRANGLER. Straw hats, belts and buckles, and workboots by DOUBLE-H, DURANGO and WOLVERINE made our workout almost effortless. Selection rates a big "Yee Ha," and their prices are fantastic on sale days. Check the directory for additional Cavender locations in the Metroplex. It's been rumored that if you make them an offer, they usually don't refuse. (No horse's head on my pillow, please.) *CK, MC, V, AE, D*

★ Circle C Western Wear 817/237-7111

7640 Jacksboro Hwy. *Mon-Wed, Sat 10-8; Thu-Fri 10-9; Sun Noon-6*
Fort Worth, TX 76135

Looking for clothes in all the wrong places? Well, head away from the city down Jacksboro Highway just northwest of I-820 if you want a detour from high prices on westernwear. Not only that, they sure are friendly in them thar parts. In boots, strut out in COWTOWN, DIAMOND J, DOUBLE-H along with JUSTIN, RED/WING, RHINO and WOLVERINE. In westernwear, you'll find a nice selection of LEVI'S, CINCH and ROCKY MOUNTAIN. Oh well, "clothe us and shoe us ... just keep us on a horse, and we'll be happy," said one shopper with a Madonna-like smile. *CK, MC, V, AE, D, Layaway*

Boots & Westernwear

★★ Foster's Westernwear/Saddle Shop

940/383-1549

6409 N. I-35
Denton, TX 76207
Mon-Sat 9-6:30; Sun 1-6

Foster's has really cornered the market in Denton County. This family-owned and operated western store just keeps getting bigger and better. JUSTIN Sportsrider shoes, JUSTIN and TONY LAMA ropers and lace-ups, and full quill ostrich boots from DAN POST should give you room to roam. Then, hop in the saddle wearing a pair of WRANGLER or LEVI'S 505 jeans which are usually priced-to-go. Though not everything is discounted, you are sure to find your size and color, and that counts for a whole lot these days. One tall guy found five pairs to satisfy his 38-inch inseam and was proud as punch to not call them shorts. Top it off with a felt hat by BAILEY, RESISTOL or STETSON. Lots of choices for the little folks, too. Saddles, tack, down-coats, dusters and belts to round out the posse. Located just north of Denton Factory Stores and Loop 288 on I-35, drop by and say "Howdy" while heading north to the ranch. *CK, MC, V, AE, D*

★★★ Horse & Rider

972/542-4162

123 N. Central Expwy.
McKinney, TX 75069
Mon-Sat 10-8; Sun 1-5

America's largest saddlemaker makes hay when the sun shines, Nellie. More often than once in a blue moon, there are thousands of items closed out during their sale, priced at wholesale or below. Otherwise, they're just a rid-'em-cowboy kind of store. Saddles by ABETTA, ACTION, BILLY COOK, LONGHORN, SADDLESMITH and others are waiting to be harnessed, both western and English styles. But what's a saddle without a rider in a good-looking pair of boots, hat, jeans, shirt and belt? Everything for the horse and rider is at the Horse & Rider: bits, blankets, halters and saddles for the horse; the rest is for you. This store is now their "consolidation" store. Get matching bridles, boots and clothes so at least you'll ride out in a cloud of dust and make a few heads turn. Check for other locations in Lewisville (972/436-8742) and Mesquite (214/328-2731). *CK, MC, V, AE, D*

★★★ Just Justin

214/630-2858

1505 Wycliff Ave.
Dallas, TX 75207
Mon-Fri 9-8; Sat 9-7; Sun Noon-6
www.bootsforless.com

Are high-priced cowboy boots about to put you on Boot Hill? Get some relief!

Discounts run 40-70 percent off list here–that should spur you on to action! The selection's great (they have more than 20,000 pairs of boots in stock), but when they say "Just" Justin, they really mean it, as they've discontinued carrying other brands. To catalog order, send your size in regular shoes (men's or women's) and JUSTIN will send you the size you need in boots. Shipping's preset at $10 for each pair of boots; you'll probably receive your order in about a week to 10 days. They'll exchange or give refunds if you can JUSTIN-fy your problem. *CK, MC, V, AE, D, C*

★★★★ Justin Boot Outlet Store — 817/654-3103

717 W. Vickery Blvd.
Fort Worth, TX 76104
Mon-Fri 9-5:30; Sat 9-5
www.justinboots.com

You're practically in the back seat of the JUSTIN Boot Outlet Store when you careen off I-30 in downtown Fort Worth. Take the Commerce exit and go to Jennings, then turn left. Continue on to West Vickery and turn right. That's how we got there and you gotta go, too. You can't help but get a kick out of their outlet. It's a brick building with a big red boot on the outside. Giddy-up to the maker, whose name is synonymous with Texas. Just south of downtown Fort Worth, the entire family can try them on, buy them and wear them out. And the prices, well, it just doesn't get better than shopping at the outlet. Though you'll get a kick out of the selection, there's nothing but irregulars, small blemishes and defective boots. Sure could have fooled me and be grateful that they didn't move the outlet to El Paso like the rest of the plant. *CK, MC, V, AE, D*

★★★★★ Justin Discount Boots & Cowboy Outfitters — 940/648-2797

101 F.M. 156
PO Box 67
Justin, TX 76247
Mon-Sat 9-6
www.justinboots.com

Ready for Boot Camp? Then Justin line. Check out their free color catalog for a discounted hoedown. Learn how the West was really won–from work boots, ropers or exotic skins (bullhide, lizard, ostrich and shark). For men, women and children, you can wear your Justin desserts. Since 1978, this Texas favorite has been rustling up the boots-by-mail or in person (in the old Wallace Building in the small town of Justin). Rumor has it they sell about $60 million worth of boots worldwide. They carry family westernwear, including all the famous brands and styles, from jeans and belts to jackets and purses and boots, boots and more boots. They also feature STETSON hats, WRANGLER shirts and jeans, COMFY and TEMPCO goosedown jackets along with silver buckles, belt tips, leather-care products and more. Just don't expect everything to be discounted. Some first-quality items are full price, some irregulars are up to 30 percent off and some other items are priced up to 60 percent off. Everything's all under one roof and you can check out prices by mail, phone or letter before heading to the ranch. Unworn returns are accepted. *CK, MC, V, MOC*

★★★ Lone Star Boot Outlet — 972/445-0277

3209 E. Carpenter Frwy. — *Mon-Sat 10-9; Sun Noon-6*
Irving, TX 75062

Not a star was in sight at the Lone Star Boot Outlet when we were shopping, but certainly a celestial selection was in store, so who cares? With 15,000 pairs for the entire family (men, women and children) as low as $39, we roped some nice JUSTIN ropers for $80 while lace-ups were $90. Just around the bend from Texas Stadium on Highway 183, Lone Star Boot Outlet gets our praise for a great selection bursting with traditional and contemporary westernwear, from boot-scooting ropers and lace-ups to skin-tight jeans, kinky broom skirts and Southwestern accessories. All, of course, priced for less. You will find star-studded names like CODE WEST, DAN POST, DURANGO, JUSTIN, LAREDO, NOCONA, RESISTOL, ROCKY MOUNTAIN, ROPER, STETSON and WRANGLER to kick around a few. If you don't find the brand you are looking for (say, something by ARIAT), ask and they will be glad to special order for you. Go for the total western look, or just add just a little Texas accent with a pair (or two) of boots, y'all. Look over the special Texas gifts and souvenirs for those greenhorns back east. Visit them also in Dallas on I-30 just west of Buckner Blvd. (214/320-2453) and in Hillsboro near the Prime Outlet Center on I-35 (254/582-0716). *CK, MC, V, D*

★★★ Master Hatters — 972/276-2347

2355 Forest Lane — *Mon-Sat 10-6*
Garland, TX 75042

Owned by the Cook family of Garland, you can find the perfect shade from the Texas sun at this hat factory. Straw hats for men and women are their specialty, starting as low as $24.95, but they carry all types of cowboy hats. Hats off to their full size range, from 6 ¾ to 7 ⅝. Anybody, even those with a swelled head, can get covered for less. You'll also go wild for the westernwear selection. From the ubiquitous WRANGLER brand to less familiar names, you'll find first-quality jeans for $20-$25, with irregulars as low as $15. You'll find Master Hatters on Forest just east of Shiloh. *CK, MC, V, Layaway*

★★★★★ Mistletoe Boot Shop

214/946-0049

942 E. Jefferson Blvd.
Dallas, TX 75203
Mon-Sat 9-6

We thought we'd kissed this Mistletoe goodbye, but lo and behold, there they were, right where we left them back in '72. Nothing's changed in love and westernwear when the subject of boots is raised. This shop has been catering to cowboys since World War II. You, too, can do battle without the bulge of retail prices. Boots for the entire family, from babies to men's size 16, were at prices that run the gamut–from $25-$300 for top-of-the-line ostrich and emus. Mistletoe has been a leader of the pack selling closeouts, merchandise from stores that are going out-of-business, manufacturers' rejects, etc., in brands such as ACME, DAN POST, JUSTIN, LAREDO, PANHANDLE SLIM, TONY LAMA, WRANGLER and more, even an occasional DOUBLE-H work boot. The brands and sizes are sporadic, so call first for large sizes and brands to see what's in. Don't expect elegant surroundings. This old Oak Cliff beige-brick building has stood the test of time with a firm foundation of remnant carpeting in some rooms, vinyl in another, wooden benches to sit upon in another...but what the heck? There are plenty of boots to try on and you don't wear the structural amenities anyway. Located at 7th and Jefferson, take I-35 south towards Waco across the Trinity River Bridge. The second exit is Jefferson; bear right. It's one block down on the left hand side at the corner. Yes ma'am. *CK*

★★ Nancy's Square Dance Boutique

972/359-9330

Mon-Fri By Appt.; Sat 10-5; Sun 1-5

Allen, TX 75002

This cottage industry isn't square, but it takes a few stitches to make it 'round the dance floor. Doe-si-doers can save a little dough by checking out the squares at Nancy's. This is one of the few sources for square dancers in the Metroplex. Cut a rug and a few dollars off the outfits, fabric and shoes. And if you're a student of square dancing or belong to a square dance club, she'll cut another 10 percent off so you can cut a rug. Some clothes have been around the floor a few times; some are brand new. Call first to check for selection and sizes. Since she operates out of her home factory, you'll need to make an appointment, but not for Saturday nights! . *CK, MC, V, Layaway*

Boots & Westernwear

★★★★★ Resistol Hats Outlet Store/Arena Brands 972/494-0337

721 Marion Drive *Mon-Sat 10-5:45*
Garland, TX 75042

Who can resist a cowboy hat when you need to dress the part? We used to visit this spot when it consisted of just a few shelves of seconds. Today, I may even tip my hat for their turnaround and expansion. Since word has gotten out, this downtown Garland area store has spiffed up and spoiled shoppers everywhere. Now it's a full-fledged western store as big as Texas. Top off your outfit with a RESISTOL hat made right at this factory site. Save 20-75 percent, especially on seconds. And once one of their experts gets their hands on your new hat for an on-the-spot shaping, few people will ever guess it wasn't first-quality. Straw hats started at $39.95. You'll also find a large selection from CHARLIE 1 HORSE and STETSON. Expect millions of dollars in cowboy and dress hats for pennies on the dollar at this western hometown favorite. They also have a full line of westernwear including CINCH, ROCKY MOUNTAIN and WRANGLER in jeans, shirts, belts and jewelry, but expect prices that are closer to retail on those items. Catch them during sales for bigger savings. *CK, MC, V, D*

★★★ Rowan's Western Wear 903/887-3618

Highway 90 at 175 *Mon-Sat 9-5:30*
PO Box 571
Mabank, TX 75147

Row, row, row your way to Mabank. Somehow, the more you have to drive, the lower the price. Just a scenic drive down U.S. Highway 175, turn at Highway 90 and head into Rowan's. Featuring a nice selection of boots including TONY LAMA, NOCONA and TEXAS with savings in the 20-25 percent range. JUSTIN lace-ups were a steal at $89.99 and ropers were just $79.99 (at least $20 less than most Dallas stores). Straw hats started at $29.95 and went up from there. For $99.95, you could head off to work wearing your new RED WING work boots. Wait 'til you hear this, they have 13-MWZ and 936 DEN jeans by WRANGLER for $17.95. I can see the road getting crowded now. They are going to have to put up three more red lights in Mabank to handle the traffic. And for the listener in Killeen who wanted Red Wing work boots, here's looking at you! *CK, MC, V AE, D*

★★★★★ Sergeant's Western World

972/484-9988

13600 Stemmons Frwy. *Mon-Sat 10-9; Sun Noon-6*
Farmers Branch, TX 75234 *www.sergeantswestern.com*

Now that the best privately-owned westernwear store has gotten wind of discounting, there's no one better. Look for the cowprints on everything, as they leave an indelible mark on the western front. Outfitting you from the hooves up, if you weren't born with a silver spoon in your mouth, you might want to consider silver shoes for your horse, and silver earrings and silver-accented saddles for you. Serious rodeo shoppers and those who want to look like they're serious, shop here. Dr. Laura in her white limousine shopped here and Dale would, too, the next time she's in town. And why not? They guarantee the lowest prices, no ifs, ands or bull! JUSTIN Chukka's for men and women, $89.99, compare with POLO boots for $250. JUSTIN Double-Comfort Work Boots that are very hard to find, $119.99. LUCCHESE smooth ostrich ropers usually $244, $199.99. All in all they have the most comprehensive selection of western apparel, show clothing, custom saddles, tack and horse equipment. SILVER MESA SADDLES, the finest custom saddles available on the market today are only found at Sergeant's. Match your outfits with your horse's and even if you don't win any ribbons, you'll look like a winner. Also visit their superstore in south Arlington just south of I-20 at 4905 S. Cooper St. (817/784-6464). Their Lewisville location is history. *CK, MC, V, AE, D*

★★★ Shepler's Westernwear

972/270-8811

18500 LBJ Frwy. *Mon-Sat 10-9; Sun Noon-6*
Mesquite, TX 75234 *www.sheplers.com*

Best sales in town, according to one rodeo queen, which is why she keeps galloping back for more. Racks of $10 shirts, jeans, closeouts on hats and boots–nobody can touch them, according to another cowboy. Even if you're not part of the circuit, it's important to look the part. So, if your purses are not overflowing with money, consider the alternative–going naked! Or as Godiva should have done, dress up and impress your out-of-town relatives. Sales racks are where it's at. Another don't-miss is their Texas-size gift selection of western artifacts and knickknacks. It's all here at this Town East Mall area store. Visit also at 2500 Centennial Drive in Arlington (817/640-5055). One lucky shopper bought a glitzy lace $100 shirt for $10 and trotted all the way home. *CK, MC, V, AE, D*

Boots & Westernwear

★★★★ Western Warehouse 214/634-2668

2475 Stemmons Frwy. *Mon-Sat 9-9; Sun Noon-6*
Dallas, TX 75207 *www.boottown.com*

Traveling down Stemmons, we couldn't resist stopping at the neon lights and checking out the savings on jeans, westernwear and a huge selection of boots at Boot Town's sibling store, Western Warehouse. We found ABILENE, ACME, ARIAT, JUSTIN, LARRY MAHAN, LUCCHESE, NOCONA, PANHANDLE SLIM and TONY LAMA boots standing tall as well as LEVI'S and WRANGLER waiting to begin the two-step out. ROCKY MOUNTAIN jeans for women in every color imaginable were found here, too. DIAMOND J ropers were as low as $39 and a smooth ostrich Nocona boot was $179 (retail $249). Boasting more than 50,000 pairs of boots in stock, you are sure to find something to fit over those tootsies. Boot up also at 10838 Central Expwy. in Dallas (214/891-0888), 2501 Centennial in Arlington (817/640-2301) and Grapevine Mills (972/355-8312). *CK, MC, V, AE, D*

Bridal

★★ Al's Formal Wear Outlet — 817/284-9165

8708 Airport Frwy.
Hurst, TX 76053
Mon, Wed, Fri 10-6; Thu 10-8; Sat 10-5
www.alsformalwear.com

When your tails are wagging behind you, it's time to shop Al's Formal Wear. Tuxedo rentals start at $49.95 for the basic suit. (If you rent six, the groom's is free. And for more than six, rather than getting egg rolls, they'll give you $10-$30 off per tux.) Complete the rentals with a vest for $15 and shoes from $13-$15. If you want to keep that suit on hand for special occasions, you can buy a new or previously used (the tuxedos are retired after a predetermined number of rentals) tux. Prices on a new suit (coat and pants) are about $200, shirts go for $20 and up, and vests start at $40. For the used suits you are looking at $60 and up for jackets, $25 for pants, and shirts that start at $10. Cummerbund/tie combinations start at $5. There were other items such as bow ties from $1-$9.95, but by this point, I didn't think I'd make it to the church on time. Check the directory for one of the 15 Metroplex locations near you. At Al's, look for the word Outlet in the name if you want to buy new or used tuxes; otherwise, Al's is strictly rental. New owners, too. See Ascot and BridesMart. *CK, MC, V, AE, D*

★★★★★ All for Less, Wedding Invitations and More — 972/509-5368

By Appt. Only
allforlesswedd.cceasy.com

Sharon Nichols, now a member of the Association of Wedding Professionals International, is your liaison for one-stop bridal shopping. A wedding specialist and special events coordinator, Sharon and her team keep it lean to save you green. Start with the invitations and crown it off with a custom bridal headpiece (bring in a picture and they'll do it for less). Invitations everyday are from 20-35 percent off retail. You'll also find tuxedos, dyeables, gloves, wedding albums, bridal shoes and slippers for less. Wedding flowers that'll last a lifetime (fresh or silk), along with reception favors and personalized napkins are all here for less, too. Add jewelry, decoration services, free engraved monogramming, men's gifts and any other accessories you may need at considerable savings, and you'll be all set to have that perfect wedding. The father-of-the-bride seldom objects to giving her away, right? What he does object to is her being so expensively gift-wrapped! Help dads during this very emotional time by holding costs in check. Sharon and her staff will match almost anyone's business quote on the same product lines. All merchandise is new and first quality. Leave your name on her answering service and she'll return the call–to get you to the church on time! *CK, MC, V, MO*

★★★★★ Anonymously Yours 214/341-4618

204 Abrams Forest Shopping Center *Mon-Fri 10-6; Sat 10-5:30*
Dallas, TX 75243

Wedding woes start with the budget. That's why smart brides know where to look for some of the best resale gowns in Dallas. They look in this shop at the corner of Abrams and Forest in northeast Dallas. From business to bridal, you'll find anonymously worn dresses to fit any occasion. Bridal gowns, veils, slips, evening dresses, careerwear, accessories and some sample gowns all beg for a try-on at this small but stylish store. Save as much as 60 percent with lots of gowns to choose from–most almost new and *very* in-style. Sizes range from 4-24 (with lots in the sample size 10). Don gowns from the low-end $24 to $2,000 from designers such as ALFRED ANGELO and VERA WANG. The more than 350 gowns here average in the $199 - $399 range. They had a whole wall of sample dresses straight from market, as well as a huge selection of bridesmaid's dresses and formals (some brand new) from $25 - $200. One of the best places to shop for a chic going-away suit and some barely worn shoes and jewelry. Just remember, though, it's not politically correct to throw rice anymore. *CK, MC, V, AE, D, Layaway*

★★ Ascot 214/520-8897

3400 Oak Lawn Ave. *Mon, Thu 10-8; Tues, Wed, Fri-Sat 10-6*
Dallas, TX 75219 *www.ascottuxedos.com*

From weddings to debuts, make your entrance from the Ascot group (from Houston)–the same folks that call themselves BridesMart. Carrying all the popular labels like AFTER 6, ALPHA, BLACK RAINBOW (in 10 trim colors), ANDREW FEZZA, BILL BLASS, CHAPS by RALPH LAUREN, CHRISTIAN DIOR, DONI BARRASI, FUBU, PERRY ELLIS and OSCAR DeLaRENTA, the selection is most admirable. Most tuxes started at $49.95 and average prices were $75-$80. Find sizes from a boys' 3 to men's 70. Lots of trendy colors and styles in cummerbunds and ties if your man is one in a million (aren't they all?). Talk about a deal, they have a tone-on-tone pinstripe tux for as low as $39.95 and a solid black for as low as $59.95. You'll find 12 locations in the Metroplex, so check for the nearest to you, but their warehouse outlet at 4300 Spring Valley Rd. is where the action is; 50 percent off and more; call 972/404-8897. Call 972/423-6733 for the Plano store. Rent five or more and the groom's tux is free. For seven or more you get $25 off each of the other tuxedos. *CK, MC, V, AE, D*

Barbosa Studios — 972/620-1443

3840 Belt Line Rd. — *Tues-Sat 10-6 By Appt.*
Addison, TX 75001 — *www.barbosastudios.com*

Creative Images with a "Personal Touch". For more than 15 years, their mission has been photo finished: provide photographs that will be treasured for a lifetime and beyond–no matter how unique the event. Record those memories with a professional touch at this full-service studio. Do you know someone who is getting married or graduating soon? Barbosa Studios will take the pictures. For parties, weddings and any other special occasion, it's point and shoot. They also offer photo restoration and other special packages. Check out their website for monthly specials, such as 50 percent off on any sitting. *CK, MC, V, AE, D*

★★★★★ Bridal Co. Outlet — 940/484-2660

5800 N. I-35, Suite 505 — *Mon-Tues, Thu-Sat 10-7:30; Sun 1-6*
Denton Factory Stores — *www.bridalco.com*
Denton, TX 76207

The minute he proposes and you've committed to taking the plunge, rid yourself of paying retail prices. Located in the Denton Factory Stores, you will see more than 20,000 dresses from ALFRED ANGELO, MARY'S, MORI LEE BRIDALS, SINCERITY BRIDAL, SWEETHEART GOWNS and many more sought-after designers. Bridal apparel in sizes 4-44 covers the subject perfectly. Their huge selection suggests that anybody, any size, any shape, can turn heads when they take the walk down the aisle. Save 20-70 percent and buy it right off the rack, in fact. One of the largest selections of gowns and veils in the D/FW area is here, with wedding gowns starting as low as $149; bridesmaids' dresses, $49; and veils at $49. Now, here comes the bride! Closed Wednesdays for restocking. *CK, MC, V, AE, D*

★★★★ Bridal Fashions Unlimited 817/589-1272

7290 Glenview Drive *Sat 10-6; Sun Noon-6*
Fort Worth, TX 76101

Sometimes weddings can be an uncontrollable spending spree. It doesn't have to be that way, though. Not with sources like Bridal Fashions Unlimited. The bridal gowns here (sizes 2-28) are the same ones you see in the magazines (some simple, some encrusted with seed pearls and sequins), but they are 40-70 percent off. The bride and the glory here is in their in-stock bridal gowns (selection is limited, but prices are A-1). Almost any gown in the bridal magazines can be ordered, including bridesmaids' dresses and suits, so the sky's the limit. Special orders are also discounted, so now the sky may not be the limit. Always crowded on Saturdays, this shop features plenty of dressing rooms, huge mirrors and enough room to browse without bumping elbows. Don't drop by on weekdays, though–your days to buy white satin are limited to the weekend. Don't expect a live person to answer during the week. *CK, MC, V, AE, D, Layaway*

★★★★ Bridal Secrets 817/346-4848

6138 Westcreek Drive *Tue-Fri 1-5; Sat 11-5 By Appt. Only*
Fort Worth, TX 76133

This secret of "modern dresses at old-fashioned prices" is becoming common knowledge. Bridal gowns can be rented in sizes 1-44 here at this southwest Fort Worth shop. For more than 14 years, this secret has been known to smart brides who demand a bargain. For a small deposit (about $100; refunded when items are returned unscathed), why buy it when you can rent it? Gowns that retail for $500-$2,000 can be rented starting as low as $50. A complete package of a formal gown, slip, veil, jewelry and all the trimmings can be rented for as low as $350 (a value of nearly $1,600). You can also buy gowns ($50-$290), headpieces, shoes, slips, gloves and even jewelry without paying through the nose. Attendants' inventory is not as extensive, but prices are worth noting. Some bridesmaids' and mothers' dresses rent for $65 and up. For bridal try-on's on Saturday, appointments are heavily encouraged. Their twice-annual cash-only inventory clearance sale is worth waiting for–each spring and fall, gowns retailing for up to $1,800 fly out the door from $200-$400. Gowns are also taken in on consignment, though rental is still their specialty. They also have a nice selection of black-tie/prom/formalwear for rent or purchase. Bid adieu to high-price wedding ensembles and formalwear now that you know what's behind closed doors. Alterations are also available on site. *Cashier's Check*

Bridal

★★★ Bridal-Tux Shop 972/303-9022

6527 Duck Creek Drive *Mon-Thu 10-7; Fri 10-6; Sat 10-5*
Garland, TX 75043

The sun is shining, oh happy day! Every bride deserves to be beautiful on that special day. No matter how tight your budget, it'll still cost you a pretty penny. Save some pretty pennies here, though. Gowns started at $149 with a sale rack full of bridesmaids, prom and formal dresses for only $39. We didn't throw rice at the brand names, either: ALFRED ANGELO, AMY LEE, BILL LEVKOFF, BRIDAL ORIGINALS, FOREVER YOURS, MA CHERIE, MORI LEE, T.R. THORNTON and more in sizes 2-28. When one of our shoppers needed a gown in size 26, this shop delivered! Bridesmaids' dresses (starting at $98), formals, veils and the invitations are all covered here, too. They now have a tuxedo rental department ($59.95 and up with vest) and their direct tux department phone line is 972/240-0655. Alterations are done on the premises. *CK, MC, V, AE, D, Layaway*

★★★ Bridals by Sue Ann 817/926-0297

2612 W. Berry St. *Mon-Sat 10-6*
Fort Worth, TX 76109

No, we are not related. I haven't been associated with bridal gowns since 1964. This Sue Ann, though, has the distinction of being one of the few wedding discounters in the Fort Worth area. She can outfit the bride, the groom, the bridesmaids, the mothers, even provide the invitations. Sue Ann has quite a few gowns in stock–we saw least a 20 percent savings off retail–and, best of all, they are all well-known names, no off-brands. Special orders are available but prices go up accordingly. Tuxedo rentals at $45 and up, and the usual–rent six, pay for only five. We were a little bemused to see a "Mr." trying to sell our sister a wedding gown, though. Prices usually run about 20 percent off on bridals, bridesmaids' dresses and veils. Sizes 4-46 in stock. They have more than 500 nationally-advertised gowns to choose from and layaway until the date of the wedding. You can take your bridal pictures at the salon, and they offer in-store alterations. They also handle quinceañeras dresses. *CK, MC, V, AE, D*

★★★★ BridesMart 817/784-1171

4648 S. Cooper St. *Mon-Thu 10-8; Fri-Sat 10-6; Sun Noon-5*
Arlington, TX 76017 *www.bridesmart.com*

Dumb, de-dumb dumb if you pay retail for your bridal gown today. With more than 700 gowns in stock, this is truly a bridal bouquet. Prices began as low as $199-$699 (regularly $450 to $1,000) with names like ALFRED ANGELO, BRIDAL REPLACEMENTS, FOREVER YOURS, ILISSA BY DEMETRIOS, MON CHERE, MORI LEE and more than you see at traditional (retail) bridal shops. Savings soar to up to 70 percent on dozens of styles, including hundreds of sample couture gowns in sizes 1-44. Bridesmaids, whether they catch the bouquet or not, can still be dressed to impress from $39. All the accoutrements including headpieces, slips, bras and jewelry add to the selection. All gowns are in stock and ready-to-wear; magazine gowns are available by special order. There's also a complete selection of bridesmaid dresses, flower girl dresses, party dresses and bridal accessories including veils, headpieces and shoes. Financing is available with an interest-free, 90-day layaway. They also have locations in Dallas (972/233-5200), Mesquite (972/681-4100), Hurst (817/284-9555) and Fort Worth (817/731-7218). *CK, MC, V, AE, D*

✧✧✧✧ Dallas Arboretum, The — 214/327-8263

8525 Garland Rd. — *Mon-Sun 10-6*
Dallas, TX 75218

Autumn and spring weddings at the Arboretum are breathtaking. What bride hasn't fantasized about a gorgeous garden wedding? These 66 acres of gardens, lawns and shaded walks along the shores of White Rock Lake provide some of the most sought-after ceremony locations in the Metroplex. The Dallas Arboretum is truly one of the most breathtaking sites, especially for your bridal portrait if you come already dressed for just a regular admission price. The changing facility can be rented for a two-hour minimum for $50 and nobody will see your dress until you are ready to take the walk. In the gardens, you will think you've left Dallas for some dreamy hideaway. Lush foliage and walkways of all the blooms the season will allow. The 8,000-square-foot Camp House and several of the gardens may be rented for weddings or receptions. Fees run from $175 for the gazebo to $1,500 for the Camp House or Women's Garden. For garden availability call 214/320-1268. In the right season, you can take your vows amidst more than 15,000 chrysanthemums and blossom while you say, "I do." In the fall, the foliage rivals that of New England. Even if you're not thinking of tying the knot, there are lots of fun things to do at the Arboretum year 'round, such as a children's adventure maze, nature make-and-take activities and, for parents, there are weekend gardening tips, exhibits and demonstrations. For what's happening now, call their hotline at 214/327-4901. Winter hours are 10-5. *CK, MC, V, AE, D*

★★★★★ David's Bridal

972/458-2211

5525 Arapaho Rd.
Dallas, TX 75248
Mon-Fri 11-9; Sat 10-6; Sun Noon-6
www.davidsbridal.com

With more than 1,400 bridal gowns in stock, including designer knock-offs from $199-$800, you can reasonably expect the average dress here (all new and improved) to be around $500. At times, the gowns are cut to $99. Now who wouldn't be impressed? They also have mothers-of-the-bride, bridesmaid and flower girl dresses, too, as no one is forsaken. During clearances, on the full size range of 4-26, thousands of gowns are reduced even further from their regularly discounted prices. No special orders are necessary, as there's an extensive inventory. No waiting. No ordering. No worrying. Top it off with headpieces, jewelry, shoes, gloves, handbags, hosiery and undergarments–so now all that's missing is the groom! They even have gifts for your wedding party. How thoughtful! Just one block east of the Dallas North Tollway and north of Prestonwood Mall, their Dallas store's at the Prestonwood Village Shopping Center. Also check out their locations in Arlington (I-20 at Cooper, next to The Parks Mall; 817/472-2211) and Hurst (804 NE Loop 820, in front of North East Mall; 817/595-3094). *CK, MC, V, AE, D*

★★★ Designers Encore

817/656-9354

8216 Grapevine Hwy.
North Richland Hills, TX 76180
Mon-Sat 10-5:30

We applaud the savings of up to 65 percent on gowns, veils, bridesmaids' dresses and mothers-of-the-bride cnsembles as well as dresses for all special occasions. At Designers Encore on Grapevine Highway just north of I-820, you will find the perfect outfit in many designer names such as ALFRED ANGELO, BIANCHI, DEMETRIOS and ILLISSA. They will help you put together an outfit or an entire wardrobe and then help you accessorize with their selection of jewelry. And just as we bid farewell, we overheard them say, "We love our customers to death!" *CK, MC, V, D*

★★★★ First Impression Formals

817/459-3773

2304 W. Park Row Drive, Suite 21
Arlington, TX 76013
Tues-Sat 10-6

I think they've heard of The Underground Shopper because their slogan is "Never Pay Retail". Sound familiar? So kudos for them, and kudos for you if you need a prom or bridesmaid dress for less. From beaded (starting at $111) to simple chiffon from DAVE & JOHNNY, JESSICA MCCLINTOCK and SCALLA, expect a line-up in rows of wonderful choices (priced from $80 up). After you've chosen your gown, move into the accessory mode and check out their jewelry, purses, even gloves. Dress sizes 2-4X are featured here so everyone can go to the party in high style. Special orders are available, but no returns are accepted. *MC, V, AE, D*

★★★★ Gladis Bridal Boutique 972/783-9643

1617 Centenary Drive *Mon-Sat 10-6; After 6 By Appt.*
Richardson, TX 75081 *www.gladisbridalboutique.com*

Aren't you glad we know Gladis? Nestled just a few blocks north of Richardson Square Mall, we were delighted to find designer-quality bridal gowns and veils. Custom-designed gowns, alterations and minor changes are available in-house. This Argentinean artisan can craft some of the most stunning headpieces we've seen walking down the aisle. In fact, we found more than 150 custom headpieces in stock. Accessories, such as bridal bouquets, communion dresses, head pieces, photo albums, unity candles and lots of specialties items including cake tops, ring bearer pillows, flower girl baskets, gloves, garters and toasting flutes were also available. Unique brides should be "gladis" to make this their first stop. *CK*

★★★ Invitation Warehouse 214/381-6367

Dallas, TX 75227 *By Appt. Only*

This enterprising entrepreneur can get your guests to the church for less. And I do mean less. A superman's savings of 30 percent off on wedding invitations and all the other printed matter help you get what you'll need to make the occasion etched in time. Call on this Lois Lane for a superwoman collection of more than 35 albums to choose from in all the popular brands. CARLSON CRAFT, CHECKERBOARD, CLASSIC, KREPE KRAFT, MASTERPIECE, REGENCY, STYLEART and others are waiting to be engraved R.S.V.P. Graduations, anniversaries, thank you notes–any paper invitation–is just waiting to be approved. Monogrammed stationary is available here, too. One of the largest selections of invitations in the Metroplex. But getting a call back is like pulling teeth. Let us know how you fare. *CK*

★ Isis, Bridal & Formal 972/681-5939

1032 Town East Mall *Mon-Sat 10-9; Sun Noon-6*
Mesquite, TX 75150

Next door to Foley's, this bridal and formal shop is begging for a commitment.

While it's not a discount store, they do run extra special specials. Specializing in quincea...eras dresses and coronas, you can expect a one-stop shop for your bridal package. Tuxedos, too, to say, "I do". A dream bridal deal included the headpiece, veil, gloves, petticoat and shoes for free when the gown is $500 or more. Now, who can fault them for trying? They are importers and manufacturers, so trade accounts are welcome. Also look for their locations in Golden Triangle Mall in Denton (940/243-3305), Irving Mall (972/255-8550), Six Flags Mall in Arlington (817/640-7757) and in Richardson at the northeast corner of Central Expressway and Arapaho (972/235-4774). *CK, MC, V, D*

★★★★ Lasting Impressions Bridal Boutique — 972/991-7498

15056 Beltway Drive — *Mon-Thu 11-7; Fri 11-6; Sat 11-5*
Addison, TX 75001

One block south of the intersection of Belt Line and Midway, why not pay and play rent-for-the-day? Make a lasting impression in a bridal gown and rent one from $185-$500. An entire wedding package started as low as $300. Frankly, renting your bridal gown is the best idea for coming down the aisle and Lasting Impressions latched onto it quickly. Why pay megabucks for a one-time grand entrance? Wedding gowns for rent or sale in sizes 4-44 could cover any bride's requirements. Rentals, however, are only on wedding gowns. ALFRED ANGELO and WATERS & WATERS were names that stood out from the crowd. Add veils, shoes, jewelry and invitations from their stock, and your list is complete. *CK, MC, V, MOB*

★★★★ Le Renaissance Wedding Facility — 214/692-8442

8041 Walnut Hill Lane, Suite 820 — *Mon-Fri 10-7*
Dallas, TX 75231 — *www.lerenaissance.com*

This place will do your wedding right and for the right price. Call Penny and discover this neat little secret to making your list and checking the price. If you're the marrying kind, they can house just about every bride as long as she invites fewer than 200 guests. The staff includes some of the most well-known and experienced bridal consultants in the Metroplex. Prices are often 30-60 percent under comparable facilities. This family-owned business can supply everything to make your wedding special without adding any additional stress to your big day. They access caterers, bakers, limos, florists, paper products, make-up experts, musical and video artists–whatever it takes to make your day an affair to remember. And the selection of food! Do they have food! You can choose from barbecue, chef carving stations, pasta stations or the deluxe south of the border bar. There are enough choices to make your day as appetizing as possible. Watch for bridal photos on their home page soon. *CK, MC, V, D*

★★★★★ Luong Bridal 972/276-8786

799 N. Jupiter Rd. *Mon, Wed, Thu10-6; Fri-Sat 10-8; Sun 11-5*
Garland, TX 75042

The complete wedding shop is almost complete if you're the one waiting to say, "I do". They offer a large selection of designer bridal gowns for the bride and her maidens, flower girls' dresses and wedding accessories (tiaras and headpieces) at a discount of 30 percent and more. Manufacturers include ALFRED ANGELO, BONNY, BRIDAL ORIGINALS, LILI, MON CHERE, MOONLIGHT, MORI LEE, SAN MARTIN, SWEETHEART and others. But never on Tuesday. That's their one day off. On the remaining six days, if you're a bride, this can be your one-stop life-saver. They have one of the largest selections of bridal gowns, but is it Loo-on? Lu-own? Who cares, as loo-ong as they keep offering great prices and selection. Take the walk for less. During our visit, you could receive a pair of satin shoes free with any gown purchase. *CK, MC, V, D*

★★ Milliners Supply Company 214/742-8284

911 Elm St. *Mon-Fri 8:30-5*
Dallas, TX 75202 *www.milliners.com*

Walking down the aisle? Try a trip downtown first if you're thinking of saving money by making your own dress, veil, or accessories. This "picture of the past" shoppe has it all. Nothing seems to have changed in 50 or 100 years. Walk through and around the carved oak doors, shelving, and gleaming glass showcases. Up and down the long, narrow aisle, on either side, top to bottom, caress the bridal ribbons, flowers, and accessories for bridal hats and accessories. Then buy the forms for the hats and wrap up your own toppings with a Sunday going-to-meetin' chapeau for the bridal party. Lace appliqués, flower headbands, tiaras, boas, petticoats, garters, ring pillows, and yes, even hoop skirts are all here for your viewing and buying. No dress fabrics, though, so stop asking. Though this company has been doing business nationwide as a mail order source for other bridal shops, they welcome the public gingerly. If you don't have a million questions, they'll be happy to sell to you wholesale primarily items in their clearance section. There you'll be saving at least 35 percent off in dozen lots. *CK, MC, V, MO*

✧✧ Perfect Wedding Guide, The

972/418-6193

2810 E. Trinity Mills Rd., Suite 209
Carrollton, TX 75006
www.perfectweddingguide.com

For the seasoned veteran to the completely confused, the Perfect Wedding Guide may well be all the help you need for the big day. This wedding and honeymoon service company provides wonderful guidelines and checklists (tailored for your home city) for those who need a little help in the wedding plans. It takes you step-by-step from proposal all the way to the honeymoon. It even gives you guidelines on who is supposed to pay for what. There are also incentives to pick this up because of the chances to win great prizes along the way. Published four times a year, be sure to get your hands on it or check out their website today (where you can request a free copy of the magazine).

★★★★★ Resale Gallery

817/285-0633

724-A E. Pipeline Rd.
Hurst, TX 76053
Mon-Sat 10-6

Spending more on a wedding dress won't make your marriage better, but starting out with a little more cash on hand might. Who cares if the dress has been worn once before? (As long as it wasn't by you of course.) Even "new" dresses have been tried on by lots of brides. Not really much difference if you think about it. Head to Highway 183, go south on Brown Trail to where it dead ends into Pipeline, then left for two blocks and look for the Resale Gallery on the south side of the street behind Grandy's in the Village Square Shopping Center. Get the most for your money at the largest bridal resale shop in northeast Tarrant County. Bridal gowns, bridesmaid gowns, flower girl dresses, mother-of-the-bride gowns, tuxedo rentals, pageant dresses and evening attire all priced way below the Mason-Dixon line. No bridal gown was seen for more than $300. Now, that's the kind of train to hop aboard. They also offer consultations with their designers for invitations, flowers and made-to-order veils, pillows, garters and baskets. So, put that in your pipeline and start married life with a lot of bang for your buck. *CK, MC, V, D*

✧✧ Rouhier Photography

972/333-0876

6308 Bradley Lane
Plano, TX 75023
By Appt. Only

Do you need a professional photographer for a big event? Rouhier Photography has the right person for the job. They are available for all weddings and parties.

Whatever event you have planned, why not capture the moment in pictures? They charge $250 dollars for the first hour (which is very respectable) and $50 for each additional hour. Once your pictures are developed, they charge just $10 a print for 5 X 7 pictures for ever-lasting memories. *CK*

★★★★★ Saleplace, The 972/557-7747

3641 Shepherd Lane *Mon-Fri 10-8; Sat 10-6; Sun Noon-5:30*
Balch Springs, TX 75180 *www.weddingsuperstore.com*

Located just east of the Elam Road exit off of LBJ Frwy. (I-635), this unique store combines perhaps the largest selection–22,000 square feet–of wedding-related merchandise in the country with great prices, making it an incredible find for the bride-to-be or anyone involved in planning a wedding. The Saleplace has a large selection of confetti, heart-shaped bubble bottles and wands (the new no-mess trend), ring pillows, flower baskets, garters, gloves, veils, headpieces, unity candles, cake charms and other wedding essentials. Everything that is needed for a wedding can be found at The Saleplace, your guiding light. *CK, MC, V, D*

★★★★★ Sample Shop 817/268-0311

718 W. Pipeline Rd. *Mon-Fri 11-7; Sat 10-6*
Hurst, TX 76053

An occasional 50 percent off regular prices, in sizes 2-44, almost makes me want to get married again. Then again, I come to my senses and turn my attention to the tuxedo rentals, which started at $39.99. Some bridal gowns were as low as $150. This matron of the bridal world has been helping bridal parties walk down the aisle for 32 years. That's quite a record in retailing, wouldn't you say? They also sell prom, bridesmaid, party, debutante, quinceañera and mother-of-the-bride dresses (as low as $99), plus shoes and accessories to complete the picture. You could say they supply everything but the groom. Their closeout department brings rave reviews. From room to room, this is a one-stop shopping source to protect your dowry with decidedly discounted prices. Both wedding and formal-wear make their grand entrance in the full spectrum of sizes and selection. And yes, the entire bridal party will be able to celebrate the savings. Enter through the huge selection of formal, prom and flower girl dresses, then wind your way back to the special-order and bridesmaids' dresses, the mothers-of-the-bride section, the sequined pageant collection (behind glass) and, of course, the wedding gowns and veil salon. It keeps going, and going and going. For a nuptial agreement that's fair, shop where you both can save. *CK, MC, V, AE*

★★★★ Schmalzreid Formal Wear 972/423-4233

1201 E. Plano Pkwy. *Mon-Wed, Fri 9-5:30; Thu 9-8; Sat 9-2*
Plano, TX 75074

One mile east of Central Expressway on Plano Parkway, park your car at the gray and burgundy-trimmed warehouse if it's time to shop for a penguin suit. (That's a tuxedo for birds in this neck of the woods.) If you want to shop where the pros shop, shop at Schmalzried and ask for Curt Gumberling or John Scott. They are both excellent salesmen. Working at a name like Schmalzried, they've got to be good. Schmalzried is the national supplier for most tuxedo rental shops. Tuxes, shirts and more start at almost wholesale prices. Our favorite buy was an elegant notched-collar, 100 percent wool ensemble for $224.95 (included coat, pants, shirt, cummerbund, studs, cufflinks, bow tie and garment bag). Sizes ranged from 36-60. If you are renting, order six and the groom's tux is free. The basic black tux with coat, pants, shirt and cummerbund rents for $59.95, shoes extra, plus tax. If you choose one of their designer lines from CHRISTIAN DIOR, PIERRE CARDIN or OSCAR DE LA RENTA, for example, rentals are only $79.95. Schmalzried's is a great choice for proms and wedding parties. An extensive inventory and selection is an understatement–over a mile of tuxedos is your road to dressing to the nines. An in-house laundry and repair facility keeps merchandise in good to excellent condition. Their periodic sales of rentals net your greatest savings, so visit or call often. *CK, MC, V*

♥♥♥♥♥ Special Arrangement by L.L. 972/578-5189

1422 Ave. K *Mon-Wed, Fri-Sat 10:30-4; Sun Noon-2*
Plano, TX 75074

Don't throw the bouquet away–preserve it. This latest craze of freeze-drying flowers for a lasting full-size and color-enriched memory (retaining 80-90 percent of the original color and shape) has hit the bridal scene with a splash. The highly technical process of removing water from an object without disturbing its structure is accomplished by Linda Lee Sirmen and her trusty freeze-dryer. A bridal bouquet (or any other floral arrangement) is photographed and then taken apart and placed into the freeze-dryer. The process takes 2-3 weeks and costs $185-$450. Then, when the items are completely dry, they are sprayed with a poly-coat sealant and reconstructed as close to the original arrangement or bouquet as possible. Lastly, it's placed in a sealed container.

There are lots of containers from which to choose, such as domes and oval wall mounts. To preserve your bouquets right after the wedding, seal them in a plastic bag with wet paper towels and refrigerate promptly after the ceremony. Special Arrangements by L.L. will pick up your flowers for a small fee and the rest is history. Well worth the wait (as it was for your mate). They can also freeze-dry fruits and vegetables–perfect for seasonal wreaths. Even if you're not a new bride, freeze-dried flowers and arrangements make perfect decorative accents. *CK, MC, V*

★★★★★ St. Pucchi 214/631-4039

2277 Monitor St. *Mon-Fri 9-5:30*
Dallas, TX 75207 *www.stpucchi.com*

This apparel district manufacturer is home to those exquisite silk and pearl encrusted gowns straight from the pages of *Brides* magazine. Not your usual bridal fare, we're talking shantung silk, imported lace, pearl-encrusted, hand embroidered–the whole nine yards. They have some of the most beautiful gowns you've even seen–expensive even–at wholesale prices (in the thousands), but still exquisite in every detail. Located in the heart of the Market District, shop like the pros and pay wholesale (and sometimes below). This manufacturer sells directly to the public as well as to bridal salons, so lucky you, you get to pay the same price as they do! Some sale racks and market samples are below wholesale. Once a year, they have a great warehouse sale. Sizes 4-20 are available, but expect to wait 4-6 weeks if the gown you want is not in stock. *CK*

Stanley Korshak 214/871-3600

500 Crescent Court, Suite 100 *Tue-Sat 10-6*
The Crescent (Cedar Springs at Maple) *www.stanleykorshak.con*
Dallas, TX 75201

Yes, even the Hunts know a good thing when they build it. And for those who want to see stars without paying out-of-this-world prices, wait for Stanley Korshak's blow-out bashes and one-day sample sales. For example, Ulla Maiji held a trunk show November 4th-6th last year in The Bridal Salon (214/871-3611); at other times (once in March), they offered an exquisite collection of gowns, bridesmaid dresses, veils and underpinnings by such stellar designers as BOB EVANS, RON LOVECE and VERA WANG at up to 75 percent off. Watch their website for up-coming events. Aisle buy that. *CK, MC, V, AE, D, Stanley Korshak*

★★★★ To Have and To Hold (Discount Bridal Service) 817/424-1559

Grapevine, TX *Mon-Fri 10-6 By Appt.*

Discount Bridal Service from this day forward can save you 20-40 percent on bridal gowns, veils, bridesmaids' dresses, mother's gowns and lots more. On top of this, they provide undivided attention. Freda McKenzie, the top local representative, will be glad to quote you prices over the phone and assign you a personal counselor if she has one closer to your location who could better assist you. Pick out the "gown of your dreams" from any of the top bridal magazines and call Freda for a price. All gowns are guaranteed, new, first-quality made by nationally-advertised bridal gown manufacturers. Your gown will be made, inspected and sent directly to you. Freda is entering her fifth year as a DBS representative and can help you with so much more than just your gown...and save you money at the same time. Some of the other "discount" items available through DBS are: veils, shoes, accessories, invitations, tuxedos and favors/gifts, etc. *CK, MC, V*

♥♥♥♥♥ Wedding Cottage, The 972/771-2340

730 S. Goliad St. *Tues, Wed, Sat By Appt.*
Rockwall, TX 75087 *www.theweddingcottage.com*

A wedding day is stressful enough, so why add to it by trying to make all the arrangements yourself? Forget your worries and let The Wedding Cottage handle all the gritty details. They have different packages available, but perhaps the most economical is the most-inclusive dream package. With this one you get the Victorian-style wedding chapel and reception area for up to 2 ½ hours (depending on the number of guests), bride and groom cakes, punch, coffee, nuts, mints, engraved toasting glasses and napkins, the groom's tuxedo and shoes, a Victorian-style wedding certificate, birdseed, bubbles and limousine service to one Metroplex location. The owner started this business after retiring from the floral industry and it shows: flowers are the hallmark of the dream package. You receive a fresh bridal bouquet, one attendant bouquet, boutonnieres for the groom and best man, single roses for the mothers, flowers for the cake top and the throw-away bouquet. The best part is, since this is their facility, all clean-up is taken care of for you. Costs are based on the number of guests. For 50-75 guests, cost is $2,400, and $200 extra for each 25-guest increment up to 150 guests. A la carte catering service is available for an additional charge and a $200 deposit is required. The only two things not included in the packages are the minister and photographer, although they can provide you with a list of possible photographers. Weddings can be scheduled for any day, with up to three weddings scheduled each Saturday. *CK, MC, V, AE, D*

★★★ Yvonne's Bridals 214/467-2870

2550 W. Red Bird Lane, Suite 410 *Mon-Fri 10-7; Sat 9:30-5:30*
Dallas, TX 75237

Yvonne has been dressing Red Bird area brides for nearly 20 years. You could not find a friendlier, warmer atmosphere to ease the wedding blitz pressures that are par for the course when planning a wedding. If you've seen your favorite "look" in the bridal magazines, she probably has it in stock. ALFRED ANGELO and SWEETHEART are just a couple that can take you down the aisle in style. Prices started at under $200 and go up from there. Expect, too, that Yvonne has all the accessories you'll need to complete that look you want. Save 40-50 percent if you decide to rent instead of buy. Even flower girl dresses, mother-of-the-bride and formal selections are ripe for the picking. Layaway is available with as little as a 25 percent deposit. *CK, MC, V, AE, D, Layaway*

Cameras & Optical

★★★★★ Arlington Camera

817/261-8131

544 West Randol Mill Rd.
(Randol Mill Road at Cooper)
Arlington, TX 76011

Mon-Sat 9-6
www.arlingtoncamera.com

Maintaining a complete inventory of cameras and darkroom supplies at discount prices, Arlington Camera has one of the best selections of used cameras around, plus, we like the friendly and knowledgeable service. Co-owner Bill Porter reveals that a lot of his business comes from pros who favor used equipment because you can often get more bang for your money! Remember, older can mean better. Used, but not abused, is their camera mode. Choose also from such noted names as CANON, KODAK, KONICA, FUJI, HASSELBLAD, LEICA, MAMIYA, MINOLTA, NIKON, OLYMPUS, PENTAX and YASHICA for starters, along with lenses and every accessory imaginable. They also rent, repair and trade, and can process prints or slides from prints in minutes. Arlington's staff knows their stuff and will not (shutter) bug you. They will lead you on the path to a perfect camera, lens or other photographic accessory for your needs. They maintain a complete inventory of cameras (including digital cameras) and darkroom supplies at discounted prices. Call for a free brochure or price quote. Arlington Camera is also a regular vendor at the Greater Metroplex Camera Show. (To get on the camera show mailing list, call Donald Puckett at 214/824-1581.) *CK, MC, V, D*

★★★★★ Competitive Cameras

214/744-5511

2025 Irving Blvd., #107
Dallas, TX 75207

Mon-Fri 9-5:30; Sat 9-4

Since 1982, this store has been providing personalized service at almost unbeatable prices. Now comfortably situated in their new location, owner Ramsey Jabbour continues to direct you to the latest in camera gear from BRONICA, CANON, CONTAX, HASSELBLAD, KODAK, MAMIYA, MINOLTA, NIKON, OLYMPUS or PENTAX, including cameras, film, lenses, flashes and lighting supplies. They have a complete line of darkroom equipment and carry KODAK and FUJI professional film and paper. Located nearer to the Market and Design Center, this is your first stop for CANON video cameras (try out the high-tech features for first-quality filming) and those fantastic "underwater" cameras by OLYMPUS. We snapped on a waterproof CANON Sure Shot with built-in flash and red-eye reduction for only $169. Other Canons eyed included a 35-80 zoom for $449 and an 80-200 zoom for $609. Bring in your used equipment for trade-in, or find a great deal on some pre-owned models. And shutter at the thought of paying retail. *CK, MC, V, D*

★★★★★ KEH Camera Outlet 972/620-9800

3767 Forest Lane, Suite 126 *Tue-Fri 9:30-5:30; Sat 10-4*
Dallas, TX 75244 *www.kehoutlet.com*

Savings is in the eye of the beholder. But when it comes time to shop for a beauty of a camera, used camera equipment at picayunish prices, KEH is your one-stop salvation. Whether you're a pro, a serious amateur and/or a collector, you can see all the major top-quality and medium-priced cameras, lenses and accessories at this camera consortium of service and savings. They have a large inventory and will even keep up a personal "wish list" for you. Smile, even if you can't be candid, and lens us your ear. Choose CANON, HASSELBLAD, LEICA, MINOLTA, NIKON and PENTAX just for starters. About 99 percent of the equipment is used but in good-to-mint condition. There are no point-and-shoots; only top-of-the-lines for your serious takers. Also find a wide range of accessories, such as tripods, wide-angle lenses, enlargers and flashes. There is a second location in Atlanta, GA. Shipping nationwide is done by UPS and FedEx. *CK, MC, V, MO*

✧✧ Masterpiece Multimedia 214/336-3439

1717 Piedmont *www.photosinmotion.com*
Irving, TX 75061

Give your family a piece of you on the information highway. Masterpiece Multimedia will place your photos on a CD-ROM. You control how and where each picture is placed, and all service is customized to your needs. If you are in the DFW area they will even pickup and deliver. Photos 5 by 7 and smaller run $1 each; Images over 5 x 7 and up to 8 x 10, are only $1.50 each. If you bring them less than 50 images, expect an additional $15 set-up fee. If there are more than 250 images, you will receive two CD's, one will be your digital album and the second will be in bitmap format, which allows you to e-mail your photos. Now that's a novel idea. *CK, MO*

Cameras & Optical

★★★ Ritz Camera — 214/361-4928

9100 N. Central Expwy. Suite 115
(Caruth Plaza)
Dallas, TX 75231

Mon-Thu 9-7; Fri 9-9; Sat 9-6; Sun 10-5
www.ritzcamera.com

The exposure for Ritz must be set extremely high, 'cause this photography chain, with more than 75 years in the business, keeps growing and growing. Ritz guarantees a low, competitive price (but not the lowest), so check around before plunking your money down. On their website, there was a CASIO QV300 digital camera with a list price of $600 selling for a mere $200. Got a broken camera? Well, if it's worth fixing, bring it here and let them show off their repair skills. Great buys on film are developing fast at Ritz, too. Don't overlook the fact that they've got an extensive supply of lenses, binoculars, digital imaging, wireless communications, video and accessories, too. At this particular location, show your Ritz card and get a roll of 24 single prints for just $6.99, double prints for $8.99. With more than 800 one-hour labs nationwide for film processing, putting on the Ritz is everywhere. With multiple locations in the Metroplex, even if you blink, you'll probably find a Ritz near you. *CK, MC, V, AE, D, Ritz, MOC*

★★★★ Warehouse Photographic — 972/416-7110

2255 E. Belt Line Rd., Suite 301
Carrollton, TX 75006

Mon-Fri 9-6; Sat 9-5
www.warehousephoto.com

Smile! You'll be shopping with the pros. One of the largest selections of new and used camera equipment, studio lights, darkroom equipment, chemicals and photographic accessories, this may be your photo finish. They carry about 80 different models of point and shoot cameras by CANON, KODAK, KONICA, MINOLTA, NIKON, OLYMPUS, POLAROID, VIVITAR and more. Prices run anywhere from $7.49-$399.99. Prices may vary between the store and the website, so be wary. They also carry some excellent digital cameras and equipment. Commercial photographers and hobbyists alike recommend this source because of the vast darkroom supplies, plus there's a full-service photofinishing lab on the premises. The new KODAK Create-a-Print machine lets you do your own enlargements in minutes, and the latest machine from KODAK does "picture-to-picture" up to a final image of 8 x 10, all in seconds, no negative required. *CK, MC, V, AE, D*

★★★★ Wolf Camera Clearance Store — 972/241-0582

11171 Harry Hines Blvd. — *Mon-Fri 9-6; Sat 10-6; Sun Noon-5*
Dallas, TX 75229 — *www.wolfcamera.com*

Ever since the Wolf gobbled up Barry's Camera, we wondered if they would continue the tradition of quality service and decent (though not always the cheapest) prices. Well, things seem to be settling down now, as their prices are getting better. Service has always been pretty good and, for the most part, these guys know what they're talking about. When we visited the Old Town store, we found deals on POLAROID One Steps for $29.99. The PENTAX IQ Zoom 140 was a steal at $299.99 and the little KODAK Funsavers were dirt cheap. They even had some plain old cameras (like in the old days of 15 years ago) such as NIKON and CANON SLRs. Also, camcorders galore at some stores. Check directory for other locations. Main store location at 5500 Greenville Ave, Dallas, 214/691-3430. Or call their clearance center hotline for the latest product availability at 972/241-4688. They pay top dollar for used quality photo equipment and also take trade-ins at any location. Call the hot-line for a quote. *CK, MC, V, AE, D*

Carpets & Floors

✧✧✧ Amazing Surfaces — 817/459-4112

2506 S. Cooper Street, Suite B-1 — *Mon-Fri 9-5; Sat By Appt. Only*
Arlington, TX 76015

Amazing, amazing, amazing is all that can be said about Amazing Surfaces. For your pool, driveway, entryway, floors, patios, walls, bath–create a look-alike surface that is truly amazing. They have just expanded their business to include architectural resurfacing on outside walls. Be it slate, tile, flagstone, stained concrete...in more colors than Joseph's coat (and he had many). If you've got a solid surface anyway, it can be covered by another. That's why it's called an Amazing Surface. Jack Smith's the creator of this wondrous surface and since it's better than anything else out there in the marketplace, we have no complaints. We used it on our front porch at the old offices on Belt Line. It still looks like new; They sure made believers out of us. Try it, it's amazing! *CK*

★★★★★ Apex Carpets — 972/986-9161

119 Plymouth Park — *Mon-Sat 9-6*
Irving, TX 75061

When you climb to the apex of the mountain, it will be a more comfortable trip if you have carpeting on the way up. Even so, when you can save up to 70 percent on it, you will fall to your knees and bless the ground you've walked on. Formerly Pennell Carpets, this company has more than 45 years in the carpet business and the only thing new is the name and location change to bigger and better digs. Carpeting that normally sells for $50-$60 a square yard starts here as low as $12.99 and goes up to only $29.99. Other carpet can start as low as $3.99. The inventory includes name brands but I've been sworn to secrecy. All I can say is that you'll recognize them...thousands and thousands of square-yards in inventory for immediate installation. Pick from rolls and rolls in a palette of colors. Laminates, wood floors, tile–go ahead, price them elsewhere, even at the big home centers, then shop here. One shopper selected a $48/square yard carpet at another "discount" store; then saw it here for

$19.95/square yard. Do I need to spell it out any further? *CK, MC, V, D*

★★★ Bargain Carpets

214/948-9449
200 N. Lancaster Ave. *Mon-Sat 9-5*
Oak Cliff, TX 75203

A bargain, is a bargain, is a bargain... but why pay for the ambiance? At Bargain Carpets, what you see is what you get. Rolls and rolls of closeout carpet, from bankruptcies and liquidations to mill overruns and seconds, some as low as $2.99/square yard (even lower for just one room). Featuring carpet from some of the best mills around, choose from more than 30,000 square yards of carpet. Save 50 percent and more. Ralph Cole is a merry old soul and King of the Karpets in the Oak Cliff area, but his castle may be a little hard to find on Lancaster near 8th Street in South Dallas, Mapsco 55-A. Shop around, then go to town. If you don't see something you like, they can special order. However, it's worth the trek to shop here before paying for expensive overhead at one or another upscale carpet stores around the Metroplex. *CK, MC, V, D, Norwest Financing, WAC*

★★★ Belt Line Carpet

972/399-1033
1224 N. Belt Line *Mon-Fri 9-5:30; Sat 9-3:30*
Irving, TX 75061

Hugh O'Neal had a better idea. Cover your floor with tile or carpet from Belt Line Carpet and make it fair and square. Located just south of Airport Freeway, they offer CONGOLEUM vinyl flooring for $17.99/square yard. If you prefer the feel of a nice soft carpet on your bare feet instead of vinyl, look into footprint-free Berber carpeting for $11.99/square yard. Weardated carpet started at $14.99/square yard, and a heavy 65-ounce carpet for $18.99/square yard. The prices all include installation. You can finance your purchase for 90 days same as cash. Now why not stand up for low prices? *CK, MC, V, AE, D*

★★★★ Big Bob's New & Used Carpet

972/283-6600
638 E. Hwy. 67 *Mon-Fri 9-6; Sat 9-5*
Duncanville, TX 75137

Big Bob's not so bad after all–though anyone selling new carpet remnants for $2.99-$6.95 can be just what Grandma was afraid of. Trust me. Big Bob doesn't cry wolf. Rather he sells carpet and vinyl cheap. Would you believe vinyl as low as $3.95 a square yard and used carpet as low as $.99/square yard? Some remnant carpets are in such mint condition, you wonder if its occupants walked on water. How can you not consider new and used carpets (remnants of 14-15 feet) for $.99 up to $4/square yard? Why not stand up for your convictions? Thousands of yards (more than 200 new rolls) line up at discounted prices alongside remnants with names like CORONET and PHILADELPHIA. Seconds from $2.99-$12.99. Installation costs $3.50/square yard and comes with a lifetime warranty. This Big Bob's is off Highway 67 and Danieldale, but there is another in North Richland Hills, 817/788-8447. *CK, MC, V, AE, D, Six months same as cash*

★★★★★ Carpet Mill Outlet — 817/481-3551

401 N. Kimball — *Mon-Fri 9-6; Sat 9-3*
Southlake, TX 76092

Look for the 15,000-square-foot white metal building with the red lettering if you want to make it a red-letter day. This is a heavy hitter in the carpet business, but wear your walking shoes to take in the lineup of CORONET, MOHAWK, QUEEN, SHAW and TUFTEX, to name just a few. The Carpet Mill Outlet is also the home of SUTTON'S new COUTURE line. Prices are quoted any way you want–just the carpet, carpet with installation, furniture moved, whatever is necessary to make you a happy camper. Indoor/outdoor carpet was priced as low as $5.99/square yard; installed at $10.99/square yard, including padding. Sheet vinyl started at $6.99/square yard and installed at $15.99/square yard. All brands of ceramic tiles starting at $1.99/square foot or $4.99/square foot if installed. Lay out the laminates by MANNINGTON, SHAW AND WILSONART or stand tall on hardwoods floors by BRUCE and HARTCO along with an expanded wood area. The Carpet Mill Outlet has the reputation and motto of being "Large enough to compete but small enough to care." *CK, MC, V, AE, D*

★★★★★ Carpet Mills of America — 972/283-9241

4353 Gannon — *Mon-Fri 10-7; Sat 10-6*
Dallas, TX 75237 — *www.carpetmillsofamerica.com*

Roll out the red carpet (tile, vinyl, laminates and wood too) or any color for that matter and you'll be seeing the world of savings from the ground floor up. Located across from Target, you can hit the bullseye on flooring for any budget and need, from plush Berbers to a trackless dorm room, rental properties, to a cabin hideaway, tract home or custom–crafted. Expect the price quoted to reflect the carpet, pad, installation, removal of old carpet, moving furniture and vacuuming. No hidden costs. The Dallas and Carrollton stores also sell hand- and machine-made rugs. Choose Persian, Oriental, Turkish and contemporary styles made of 100 percent wool. The remnants are another good buy, reduced an additional 30 - 50 percent. They back all installation with a two-year guarantee (twice that of the industry). Check directory for location nearest you. *CK, MC, V, D, 90-day same as cash with approved credit*

★★★★★ Carpet Outlets of Texas 972/279-4800

5200 Gus Thomasson *Mon-Thu 9-7; Fri-Sat 9-5*
Mesquite, TX 75150 *www.carpetoutletsoftx.com*

For nearly 30 years, Bruce Moreland has been blanketing the Metroplex with carpet and floors, be it commercial or residential. Beginning with his superstore in Mesquite, he has since opened four other locations and continues to be a leader of the pack. He keeps thousands of yards of carpet in stock, along with vinyl, wood and laminates like PERGO, all with the guarantee that nobody beats his prices, period! Carpet Outlets of Texas features first-quality name brands only in the latest styles and professional installers. Remember what your mother said, "You'd better shop around." They encourage you to do just that so you know you're comparing apples to apples. Also, check out their supply of remnants and seconds for second-homes, small rooms, rental property and kid's dorm rooms. It's practically a free-for-all. Visit also in Red Oak at 274 Ovilla Rd., 972/617-7847; in Denton at 216 W. University at Elm, 940/243-9000; and in Dallas at 2842 S. Buckner, 214/275-9300, and at 909 Regal Row, 214/638-1188. Shipping nationwide. *CK, MC, V, AE, D*

★★ Carpet Town Discount Center 972/438-4056

3309 E. John Carpenter Fwy. *Mon-Sat 8-5*
Irving, TX 75062-4937

Between kids, pets and an occasional Texas flood, you need to consider carpet that will stand up to heavy wear. Carpet Town was the choice for those who really *use* their floors. We priced some great commercial-quality carpeting (great for offices or lake houses) at $7.95/square yard and residential carpeting at $9.95/square yard–installed with padding. Installation by an in-house team can be arranged within a week. Better lines started as low as $11.95/square yard. A selection of vinyl was also available to slick up your worn-out kitchen or bath. *CK, MC, V*

★★★★★ Ceramic & Marble Tile Outlet 214/951-9525

909 Regal Row *Mon-Thu 8-7; Fri- Sat 8-5; Sun 10-3*
Dallas, TX 75247

You might be more familiar with them as the Ceramic & Granite Trading Company, but with savings this good, what's in a name? This is the 72,000-

square-foot outlet that bends over backwards selling marble and tile cheaper than anybody else in town. All tile and marble is organized on slant boards so there's no bending over rummaging through boxes and bins. The selection is stupendous; the quality and the prices, likewise. Though it does take some effort–especially if it's hot outside, you'll sweat it–but it's worth it. Ceramic floor tile, first quality, from $.84/square foot to $1.94/square foot, marble at $2.48/ square foot and granite, $10.78 (selling elsewhere like Home Depot and Home Expo for $22-$24) sets the standard throughout the warehouse inside Seconds and Surplus. How they do it? Well, they sell off the last of the dye lots on tile orders from retail stores. Imported marble, including solid granite countertops, can also be glazed at with savings of 50 percent less than the competition. Where else can you tile out at $1.50 a tile? If it's more convenient, shop their Mesquite outlet at 5200 Gus Thomasson, 972/681-1300 and in Denton at 216 W. University at Elm, 940/243-9000. *CK, MC, V, AE, D*

★★★★ Charles Sharp's Carpet Creations — 214/749-0216

1515 Dragon — *By Appt. Only*
Dallas, TX 75207 — *www.charlessharp.com*

For more than 40 years, Charles Sharp has been creating custom carpets and rugs, so you might as well put your foot down on one of them. Though additional discounts are granted "to the trade," there's still enough savings to lay one on in your home, too. One-of-a-kind custom hand-crafted carpets and rugs can be created by this sharp artisan. Inscribe your logo, create a special pattern from fabric used elsewhere or create a wall-hanging–you're in their hands. Create a Sharp addition to your home or office by hanging carpet or wall art, add a border to your stairwell, or a monogram to your entry hall. Charles Sharp's credentials and reputation within the industry are impeccable. This has been a designer's secret for years, but now you, too, can go directly to the rug-maker and see art in the making in his studio/workroom. A full 95 percent of his business is wholesale to businesses, but he is always happy to work with individuals and help them out in any way possible. Custom colors and borders are a specialty. Consider this to be a "Rugs Gallery." *CK*

♥♥♥♥♥ Clanton's Tile & Etc. — 214/341-0070

9675 Wendell Rd. — *Mon-Fri 8-5; Sat by Appt.*
Dallas, TX 75243

Every tile-related need you have can be met here at Clanton's Tile & Etc. Clanton is the only showroom in Dallas that not only displays under one roof every major brand and style of ceramic tile, marble, granite and slate imaginable, but also does the installation, too. Headed up by their own certified tile consultant, hop to the trained staff here and don't pay for the gravy. Just north of LBJ off Skillman, you can while the day away while the pros lay the tile. Better you let them do the work. All the major tile manufacturers are represented including: AMERICAN MARAZZI, AMERICAN OLEAN, AMERICAN TILE, CEPAC TILE, CERAMIC TILE INTERNATIONAL, DAL-TILE and VILLEROY & BOCH. *CK, MC, V, Financing*

★★★★★ Dungan's Floors/Blinds & More 972/562-9444(metro)

1434 N. Central Expwy., Suite 109 *Tue-Fri 8:30-5:30; Sat 10-4*
McKinney, TX 75070 *www.ccvm.com/dungan's_floors/index.html*

McKinney has a corner on the home decor market and the Jenkins family has been handling home interiors for more than 20 years. Carpet is just part of their family tree, with roots in only name brands such as ARMSTRONG, BRUCE, MANINGTON, PHILADELPHIA and SALEM. You will also find a huge selection of tiles, brick, adobe, ceramic, hardwoods and laminates. If it was meant to cover your floors, you can find it here for less. Don't forget to ask for the newest in stain-resistant fibers and custom ceramic tile and counter tops to match your flooring. During our visit, the wait for installation was two weeks, so shop early during sales. Check out the full spectrum of window and wall coverings: blinds, shades, duettes and decorating accessories. Dungan's is a full-service/one-stop shop for the three S's: Style, Selection and Service, which all add up to $$$avings. Installation crews are exclusive to Dungan's Floors and not some pick-up, fill-in, work-for-food tagalongs. Of course, free estimates will save you money because they know what they are doing, and they do it right the first time around. *CK, MC, V, AE, D, 90 days same as cash*

♥♥♥♥♥ Esfahani Oriental Rugs 214/749-4000

1505 Oak Lawn Ave. *Mon-Sat 9-6; Sun Noon-5*
Dallas, TX 75207 *www.esfahani.com*

Fabulous authentic rugs from the Middle East and Asia abound at Esfahani Oriental Rugs. This 20,000-square-foot showroom is filled with a multi-million dollar inventory of rugs. Choose from new, antique and masterpieces from around the world. Esfahani specializes in hand-woven rugs from Persia, Pakistan, China and India. Rugs of this quality are not cheap, mind you, but the beauty and durability are remarkable. Prices range dramatically, depending on the size and quality of the piece. A 4 X 6 starts at $120 and goes up to $850, while a 6 X 9 runs from $200 - $3,000. For those with vast amounts of money and space, consider getting a 12 X 18 rug from $2,000 - $40,000. (That's not a misprint.) Be prepared to be overwhelmed.

★★★★★ Factory Outlet Rugs 817/417-7847

3605 S. Cooper *Mon-Sat 9-6*
Arlington, TX 76015 *www.bstrading.com*

Factor in your bare floors and cover up with Factory Outlet Rugs for less. No doubt, they lay out the largest selection of good-looking inexpensive area rugs from worldwide origins like China, Egypt, Pakistan, Spain, India, Belgium and the good ol' USA. Row after row, stack after stack, thousands of styles and sizes to choose from at savings of 20-50 percent every day. Closeout specials and continuous roll runners (perfect for hallways and staircases), even stair rods, make shopping here a roll-away hit. From Belgian art silk rugs to hand-made Chinese wools, at least you can look like you're living the plush pile life. Rugs made exclusively for them include the Texas collection, featuring the state, boots or lariats. From animals to seasonal offerings, a kids' collection to novelty rugs, you can't let the rug be pulled out from under you. Visit in Plano at 1717 E. Spring Creek Pkwy. at the Plano Outlet Mall, 972/423-0745. This location's open Mon-Sat 10-9 and Sun Noon-6. *CK, MC, V, AE, D*

★★★★★ Feizy Clearance Floor 214/747-6000

1949 Stemmons *Mon-Sat 9-6; Sun Noon-5*
Feizy Center *www.feizy.com*
Dallas, TX 75207

Don't miss an opportunity to own an Oriental rug at a fraction of its market value by shopping at the world-famous Feizy's 4th Floor Clearance Center. Their building rises from the Stemmons corridor like a tabernacle to saving money. Choose from thousands of authentic, imported, hand-made, new and antique Oriental rugs in every size and color imaginable–all clearance priced. Nowhere else will you find rugs of this quality at prices this low. None were as fine as a Chinese 230 line wool/silk 9 X 12 foot, 6-inch rug listed at $10,500 for $3,950; a Kashan runner 2 foot 7-inch X 14 listed at $1,500 for $395; a Kerman 4 X 6 listed $1,050 for $295; an Aubusson 8 X 10 listed $3,000 for $795; a Nepal 10 X 14 listed $7,000 for $1,950. Get the picture? Across I-35 from the Infomart and next door to Medieval Times, from a Chinese Needlepoint to a Persian Tabriz, you can take a magic carpet ride without being taken. They have one of the largest selections of one-of-a-kind Oriental rugs selling direct to the public found anywhere in the country. A vast array of styles, designs, colors and sizes, and all are first-quality and handwoven. They make it their business to shop the world's weaving marketplace for antique, classic and fresh new designs. Treasures that have been handwoven in wool or silk can be found here for a lot less than at designer or collector's boutique. But don't tell the designers you've found their secret cache. What a Turkish Delight! *CK, MC, V, AE, Financing*

★★★ First Floors/Carpet One 214/340-8611

10771 Estate *Mon-Thu 8-8; Fri-Sat 8-5; Sun Noon-5*
Dallas, TX 75238

First Floors is part of the mammoth Carpet One buying group founded in 1985 as the carpet co-op of America. Its intent was to help independent carpet retailers provide a better selection, lower prices and better service to customers. They must be doing something right, as there are now more than 1,000 Carpet One stores worldwide, including locations in Australia and Guam. They feature major brands of carpet and floor coverings at a discount of 20-50 percent the prices you'd pay elsewhere, but they are not considered to be the lowest price guarantor. Residential carpet did start as low as $7.99/square yard but escalated to $106/square yard for high quality wool Berbers. Commercial grades were lower, starting around $5-$7/square yard plus padding and installation. Value is the name of the game here. Only the best lines of quality carpet, like BIGELOW ($15.99 Berber installed) and KARASTAN, wood flooring, laminates, tile and vinyl at competitive prices will do. In fact, you can only get Bigelow here (except for the Bigelow outlet stores called Stone Mountain). They also display some exquisite bath designs for the quick bath makeover. Remember, this is no Tile and Error kind of store. In Southlake, visit also at Highway. 114 at the Wall Street exit, across from Stacy Furniture, 817/421-2539, and in Denton at 420 South Bell Ave., Metro 940/243-2131. Check directory for locations in Plano and Fort Worth, too. *CK, MC, V, AE, D, Six months same as cash*

★★★★ Floor Expo 972/315-5114

Shops at Vista Ridge *Mon-Sat 10-6*
500 E. FM 3040, Suite 301
Lewisville, TX 75067

Formerly Redi Carpet, now Floor Expo, but still the same opportunity to choose from their huge flooring inventory. They make house calls, too. At no charge, they will come to your home and measure to ensure proper quantities are provided from the same lots for uniformity. Their prices will be right on and the quote will not have anything hidden to surprise you later. All prices quoted included installation, cushion padding, old carpet and pad removal, normal furniture moves and their best-price guarantee. Choose ceramic tile as low as $3.99/square foot installed; PERGO was priced at $5.69/square foot installed. They will guarantee the installation for 24 months on carpet and 12 months on hardwood floors. Get WILSONART laminate plank for $5.79/square foot (floating). A favorite of most lawyers' offices, BRUCE hardwood flooring, was $5.99/square foot installed. Now, are you ready to walk the plank? Four area locations: Grapevine at 1469 State Hwy. 114 W., 817/251-6676; West Plano at the northeast corner of Preston Road and Park Blvd., 972/964-6871; and in Plano at Collin Creek Mall, 972/881-0212. *CK, MC, V, D, Financing*

★★★ Ged's Carpets — 817/275-7631

2633 S. Cooper — *Mon-Sat 10-7; Sun 10-5*
Arlington, TX 76015

After 23 years carpeting the Metroplex, Ged's has covered all the bases (except for those at The Ballpark in Arlington). Call in any brand of carpet and, gee whiz, it's either at Ged's or it's dead! Some of their biggest sellers are rolled out from COLUMBUS, MOHAWK and SHAW INDUSTRIES. Rolls to butter up to include those retailing for $1.50/square foot installed. For their outlet store, visit it at Highway 360 and Mayfield in Grand Prairie where they're open Mon-Sat 10-7 and Sun 10-5. First–quality mill closeouts in carpet, Berber, textures, ceramic, vinyl, laminates and wood with installation at $.44/square foot. Now, that's in the Ballpark. *CK, MC, V, AE, D, Financing, 90 Days Same as Cash*

★★ Henry's Carpet and Furniture — 972/238-9755

1815 N. Plano Rd. — *Mon-Fri 10-8; Sat 10-6; Sun Noon-6*
Garland, TX 75042

A bargain's a bargain, and they make their bargain better with that include prices for full service. That includes moving furniture, hauling off old carpets and installing the new. They carry name brands, like MONSANTO for less. A 26-ounce continuous filament plush carpet was $1.11/square foot, installed. A 40-ounce Monsanto Wear-Dated II trackless carpet with a 1/2-inch, 6-pound pad costs $1.75/square foot. Don't forget they carry contemporary and traditional furniture also, making this a one-two punch of good prices. Prices rise in the spring, just like the flowers. Pick your bouquet keeping in mind the long, cold winters. (HA!) CK, MC, V, D

★★★★★ Interceramic USA 214/503-5500

2333 S. Jupiter Rd. *Mon-Fri 9-5; Sat 9-1*
Garland, TX 75041 *www.interceramicusa.com*

Interceramic actually began south of the border in Chihuahua and found its way up to Garland in 1995. Since arriving, they have been helping you save up to 70 percent on ceramic tile. On their website, you can find out everything you ever wanted to know about tiles, including things you never even thought about, including a tile glossary, tile ratings, tile standards and more. Handyman hopefuls can attend special how-to clinics on the weekends on how to install floor tile, wall tile and counter tile, so you will know all the little tricks of the trade. Discontinued, closeouts and seconds give you plenty to choose from. Recently, they added several new lines, including the PASSPORT line, in a wide array of shapes, colors and textures. *CK, MC, V, AE, D*

✧✧✧✧✧ Interior Treatments & Cleaning (ITC) 972/671-0211

Dallas, TX *Mon- Fri 8-5, By Appt. only*

For professional residential and commercial carpet cleaning, turn to ITC and trust your fine interiors to the experts. They handle furniture cleaning, best quality steam cleaning, and also take care of area and Oriental rugs. Got a stain, call on the eradicators! These folks are also known around these parts as the ultimate stain removal specialists. Their staff consists of expertly trained, clean-cut technicians, and their service is affordable. They even offer a 10 percent discount if you tell them The Underground Shopper sent you. They office in North Dallas but clean up the entire Metroplex. *CK*

✧✧✧✧ J.M.P. Tile Co. 214/762-7107

Plano, TX 75023 *By Appt. Only*

How many generations does it take to make an expert floor installer? Ask Joe. This fourth-generation floor installer has been on his hands and knees practically since childhood. A master of interior and exterior floors, he only lays his hands on tile, hardwood and marble, so no carpet requests, please. Since 1979, this craftsman has stood the test of time with a standard price for labor and installation at $3/square foot. He also does patios. For anything involving hard flooring, Joe Petreola and J.M.P. Tile Co. are the way to go. *CK*

Carpets & Floors

★ Klemm's Furniture & Floors — 972/542-4221

1109 N. Tennessee — *Mon-Fri 9-6; Sat 9-4:30*
McKinney, TX 75069

Head north to McKinney to visit your ol' cousin Klemm for savings on furniture and more. Mattress sets, sofas, tables, all major furniture pieces, flooring and appliances at very affordable prices. No famous names, but we were told the folks that make Congoleum floors are the same ones who make the mattresses. Now that should guarantee you a firm night's sleep! Selection varies, but special orders (from catalogs) usually can be had within a week. Carpet, vinyl, tile and PERGO floors are part of their "Can Do" list. *CK, MC, V, D*

★★★★ Lee's Carpet — 214/941-5521

116 W. Jefferson — *Mon-Fri 8:30-5; Sat 9-Noon*
Dallas, TX 75208

New carpet can brighten your home delightful-LEE! Bill Lee has all the famous brands: ALADDIN, ARMSTRONG and L.D. BRINKMAN are just a few that stand out amongst the crowd. STAINMASTER for $7.99/square yard plus $2.50/square yard for installation (you move the furniture) are reflective of the prices and namebrands that Lee stands behind, on top, underneath–every which way but up! Parquet flooring began at $2.97/square foot, plus $1.75/square foot to install. That in itself is a world-class Underground Shopper price tag. Tile, ceramic, vinyl, laminates, wood–as Hazel Lee says, "If it's flooring, we have it!" Work can usually be completed within a few days. Free in-home estimates complete with samples another plus. *CK, V, MC, D, AE*

★★★★★ Massey Distributors — 972/394-7617

911 N. Mill St. — *Mon-Sat 9-6; By Appt.*
Lewisville, TX 75057

Call and let's get going. This multiple (15) mobile showroom gets its samples and takes them on the road. With no showroom overhead, this carpet dealer can offer savings up to 40 percent on carpet, vinyl, laminate and wood floors and ceramic tile. Priced distributor-direct with $0 down, $0 interest and 90-days financing with approved credit, you can sit home and let their feet do the walking. Serving the entire Metroplex, they also are the distributor for HOWARD MILLER clocks, be it an alarm, marine, wall, mantle or grandfather clock. Tick retail prices goodbye and relax. *CK, MC, V, AE, D*

★ Mill Direct Carpet

214/333-0208

618 S. Westmoreland — *By Appt. Only*
Dallas, TX 75211

Turn west on Stemmons and Mockingbird, past Fort Worth Ave, past Jefferson (landmark, the fire station) to this little store where the salesman is often on the road. There's a barber shop and a florist next door just in case you have to wait for him. It's better to make an appointment so you won't have to wait. The PHILADELPHIA Experiment. That's just one brand of carpet represented. Either cash and carry, or have it installed with padding and you'll save even more. Plan on "kilim" time while you wait for a call back. *CK*

✧✧✧✧ North Texas Bomanite

972/484-8465

11107 Morrison — *Mon-Fri 6 A.M.-7 P.M.*
Dallas, TX 75229-6608 — *www.bomanite.com*

Concrete–it's not just for walking on any more. Now it's a big part of indoor and outdoor home and office decorations. Bomanite floors from North Texas Bomanite can provide high-quality paving and concrete products. Now settled into their new offices between Ables and Shady Trail, off Walnut Hill and Stemmons, you will be able to see a sample of their floors by stopping by their showroom. Stand in awe on their BOMANITE, BOMACRON, stenciled concrete, textured risers, thin-sets, GRASSCRETE, MICRO-TOP, PANTENE ARTECTURA, stains and hardeners. Forget being between a rock and a hard place. This is better. *CK*

★★ Oriental Rug Gallery of Texas

972/991-5757

4519 LBJ Frwy. — *Mon-Sat 10-6; Thu 10-8; Sun 1-6*
Dallas, TX 75244 — *www.rugstudio.com*

It never fails to happen; the more wood and tile floors around, the more rugs are needed. The Oriental Rug Gallery of Texas has all the styles and sizes, including round and unusual shapes. Their special selection of handtufted rugs are known for their quality and great looks. Handmade, all wool rugs from India feature designs exlusive to this merchant and run from $70 - $2,000. Tibetan and Parsaman rugs are hand-spun and all wool. Styles also include Dhurries, the Adobe Collection or antique designs. Choose from Oriental weaves, machine-made, vegetable dyed, knotted and more. Rugs are available from $7 all the way up to close to $13,000. Other locations in Houston and San Antonio. Better hop aboard this Oriental Express as the train's leaving soon. *CK, MC, V, AE, D*

Carpets & Floors

★★★★★ Peek's Carpet Warehouse

972/245-0077

2450 N. I-35
Carrollton, TX 75006
Mon-Fri 9-6; Sat 9-5

Take a Peek at this warehouse store in Carrollton. The prices seemed, well, maybe a bit high until we investigated further. Then we learned that every price included measurement, moving furniture, removal of old carpet, of course, the new carpet, cushion and professional installation! Well, what a Floor Show! Ask for Mike if you want the whole nine yards. TARKETT was $6.50/square yard, CONGOLEUM was $6/square yard and KARASTAN and MOHAWK were as low as $12/square yard installed. We also saw PHILIDELPHIA and TRUST-MARK by SHAW–wonderfully plush stain-fighters in soft colors for $13.99/square yard. A patterned Berber (just beautiful!) was $15.99/square yard. Believe me, even the Rank and Tile could save here. Ceramic tile available and also ARMSTRONG vinyl was $7.98/square yard. Check directory for other retail locations, but this is their only outlet. *CK, MC, V, AE, D*

★★★★★ Persepolis Oriental Rugs

214/599-9966

3926 Oak Lawn
Dallas, TX 75219
Mon-Sat 9:30-6; Sun Noon-5

Across the street from Park Place Mercedes, this Oriental rug dealer is right on the money. As a direct importer, you can cut out the middle man and cut out high prices. Individual rugs (not thousands of the same kind) are laid out snug as a bug in a rug. More than 7,000 antique and new Oriental rugs are guaranteed to sell at the lowest prices. How you price–shop is a whole different bag. Can't say it's easy, but our experts tell us this source offered one of the largest selections of master-crafted rugs from Persia (a.k.a. Iran), Pakistan, India and China she'd seen in the Metroplex. They also offered professional rug cleaning and repair, just in case. There are two other showrooms: 4100 Oak Lawn (office is located here) and 19129 Preston Rd, Dallas 75252, 972/732-8400. *CK, MC, V, AE, D*

★★ Price Carpet Outlet

214/350-4951

2601 W. Mockingbird
Dallas, TX 75235
Mon-Fri 8:30-7; Sat 8:30-6

Over 30 years of laying carpets around town is something you can stand on. Don't let the name fool you. This might have started as a surplus and seconds business, but these pros now offer all the best names in the biz: LD BRINKMAN, MONSANTO, QUEEN, just to name a few. Their years of experience should count for something and ensure a new carpet you will be proud to show off. Give them a call–they floored us. Formerly Combie Salvage Carpets. Same folks. Different name. *CK, MC, V, D*

★★★ Pro-Flooring Centers 972/353-3500

1655 Waters Ridge Dr *www.ldbrinkman.com*
Lewisville, TX 75057

Call toll-free, it's easy. Connect to the nearest Pro-Flooring Center where selection, style, value and service combine to make shopping for floor covering a snap. For the latest in laminates, try "Fibo-Trespo" laminate flooring. A Norwegian wood-type creation made up of three layers of craft paper, one decorative paper layer and a melamine film that is fused together under high pressure and heated to create a durable, crimp-resistant surface that sure looks like wood or marble, depending on which you choose. The core of this wonder floor is a high density fiberboard which ensures the strongest impact resistance. With a 12-year warranty, you can stand on it for years. And if it's carpet, ceramic, tile, marble, granite, vinyl or more, a Pro-Flooring Center is just a phone call away. *CK, MC, V, AE, D, Financing*

★★★★★ Reese Interiors 817/292-9191

3861 S.W. Loop 820 *Mon-Fri 8-6; Thu 8-8; Sat 9-5*
Fort Worth, TX 76133

Exit Granbury Road, loop around to the south side of the service road, and you have made the best decision your home will ever know. Under one roof, this is your one-source showroom for home decorating–for lighting, floors, rugs, drapery and wallpaper. The fun begins, starting at the bottom of the alphabet with carpeting, every kind of flooring is grounded on their low-price guarantee and includes installation over premium padding, moving of furniture and vacuuming. No hidden costs. We saw pecan flooring (the most durable in the woods) and knew we were nuts to ever pay retail again. Next, on to lighting–on DALE TIFFANY, the Tiffany-authorized reproductions, you not only get substantial discounts, you can be assured that they have the largest selection of Tiffany in Fort Worth (that means lamps, pendants, chandeliers and fixtures). Another winner is their FRANK LLOYD WRIGHT lighting interpretations ... close to museum-quality, just not the real McCoys. They also feature professional lighting design and planning. Their lighting lab showcases energy-efficient fixtures that illuminates your home or office properly. Call for a free energy-audit for your home and let them shed some interesting light on the subject of saving you money. And lastly, custom draperies made in their own workroom ensure the perfect window treatment. Six months same as cash with no interest or payments with approved credit. And we didn't even make it to the 1,000s of rolls of wallpaper and borders. This is a go! *CK, MC, V, AE, D, Six mo. Same as cash.*

★★★ Rems & Rugs Carpet Outlet

214/630-8005

8888 Governors Row
Dallas, TX 75207
Mon-Fri 9-5

Once the carpet is installed, can anyone tell it was a remnant? I think not. At Rems and Rugs, you could choose from a large selection of roll ends and remnants of top-quality commercial and residential carpeting. We're not talking tiny little pieces of carpeting either, but enough to do one room or an entire house. Any of these "rems" can be made into an area rug of any size. They also carry sisal and seagrass area rugs. Lower overhead is one of the reason Rems and Rugs can bring you such low prices, but there are no in-house installers. They can recommend to you a host of trusted contractors, however, to do the work. You will find them at the intersection of Governors Row and Profit. *CK, MC, V*

★★★★ Rug City

972/488-0101

11111 Harry Hines
Dallas, TX 75229
Mon-Fri 9-6; Sat 10-6; Sun Noon-5

Located on Harry Hines just north of Walnut Hill to the light at Southwell, look for Rug City at the northwest corner in a big building sharing the spotlight with three or four other shops. There are more than 1,000 rugs in the showroom and, if you don't find exactly what you want, the owners are happy to special order any size or style. They offer many custom services, such as removing or adding fringe to any rug to make an area rug and custom-cutting rugs to fit any unusual spaces. They even stock a wide selection of hard-to-find sizes. Expect to ride out in rugs from all over the world (America, Saudi Arabia, Egypt, Belgium, China, Turkey or Russia) with mostly machine-made rugs. Rug City manufacturers many of its own rugs and are direct importers. You won't find lower prices anywhere,but if you do, let them know and they will match it. Rug City offers free delivery on all over-sized rugs. *CK, MC, V, AE, D*

★★★★★ Rug Mart

972/387-0235

6045 Forest Lane
(Forest at Preston)
Dallas, TX 75230
Mon-Fri 9-6; Sat 10-6
www.rugmart.net

If you want to get the most bang for your buck, shop at Rug Mart on Forest

Lane (they're next door to D-Ray's) at Preston. In fact, if it goes on the floor, you can find it here for less. Wall-to-wall carpet savings, professional installation and 90-days same as cash with approved credit are just some of the reasons shoppers stand behind this company. We jumped for joy with their revolutionary 30-day "No Questions Asked" replacement warranty...you can even take it for a test walk. With a motto like, "If you change your mind, we change the carpet," how can you go wrong? Find big names in carpet like CORONET, GALAXY. MOHAWK, WORLD and more. Find flooring by ARMSTRONG, MANNINGTON, PERGO and WILSONART. In fact, Rug Mart is the largest retailer of Pergo in the Metroplex with the lowest prices, even up against Home Depot. Wear-dated carpet at blowout prices is another option. Monthly specials cut prices even further. Armstrong vinyl was 30 percent off and ceramic tile was marked 25 percent off on one visit. They also have a shop-at-home service if you'd rather stay put. Rug Mart has been family owned and operated since 1983. Owner Eddy Phillipson says if you see a lower advertised price on an identical item, they will sell it to you at a lower price. If within 30 days after you buy, you find the exact carpeting (manufacturer and style) advertised for less, take them the ad and they will refund the difference. Shop also in Farmers Branch at 3350 Belt Line Rd. just west of Marsh Lane. The telephone number there is 972/243-0973. *CK, MC, V, D, Financing*

★★★★★ Russell's Carpet — 972/242-8556

1609 South I-35 — *Mon-Fri 9-6; Sat 9-5*
Carrollton, TX 75006 — *www.russellscarpets.com*

Keeping it in the family has always been the way to go. At Russell's, the whole family is working to keep prices low, low, low! Isn't it nice to find a store you can depend on? This one has the very best in "family values". (Kind of a nice plank to walk, wouldn't you say?) Choose from an enormous selection of first-quality carpets by CORONET, MOHAWK, SHAW and more, plus laminate flooring, hardwoods, ceramic tile (CERAMIC TILE INTERNATIONAL, DAL-TILE and MARAZZI as examples) and vinyl at up to 50 percent off what you would expect to pay at the typical retail showroom. The newest ALLOC laminated floor that's designed for do-it-yourselfers is what we chose for our office floors. Made to install without any glue, you simply snap it together. It's a snap! Edges are treated with wax to prevent moisture damage, and it's made of a solid high-density fiber board. Another innovative choice for flooring is the frieze carpet that wears like iron and lasts forever. It's similar to a Berber or a California Berber but for heavy-duty wear and tear, it's unflappable. You can find Russell's on the service road off I-35 south on Stemmons, between Crosby and Valwood exits. Russell's gets our highest rating for customer service, too. Expect the owners to come out and measure. They are in and out in a heartbeat, and our carpet was done quickly and professionally in less than two days. Paying close attention to your budget, floorplan and specific needs, Russell's can help you make the best possible choice for your lifestyle. Rolls of remnants are available, too, to help carve away every last penny from the total cost. *CK, MC, V, D, Financing*

★★★★★ S & H Carpet Distributors — 214/638-3311

8717 Directors Row — *Mon-Fri 8-5:30; Sat 9-3*
Dallas, TX 75247

Finally, they've landed. S & H is a carpet distributor selling to the trade for years, that has now opened their doors to the public. How much more direct can you get? Brands line up like the infantry, but they feauture COLUMBUS, CORONET and MOHAWK. The ever-popular PERGO flooring at up to 70 percent off, along with PICKERING and WILSONART.That's right. Wholesale prices–from 40-70 percent off–is how low the carpet goes. No fancy showrooms, no major advertising campaigns, just good old-fashioned service, professional installation and down-to-earth prices. Rock bottom prices are more like it. Some of the area's elite have unearthed this underground gold mine and with this S & H have stamped out high prices on carpet. You will find them between Regal Row and Mockingbird, exit Mockingbird off Stemmons, west to Ambassador, then north to Dividend. Turn south over the railroad tracks and past several four-way stops, and you'll run into Directors Row. Turn right and it's two buildings down on the left-hand side. Look for a free-standing brick warehouse with maroon trim and you have, at last, arrived. Visit also at 7395-A Grapevine Hwy. in North Richland Hills, 817/581-7777. Open Mon-Fri 9-6, Sat 9-3. *CK, MC, V, AE, 90 days same as cash*

★★★ Salvador's Carpet — 972/216-3606

2120 St. Augustine — *Mon-Fri 8:30-5; Sat 8:30-3*
Mesquite, TX 75227

Formerly Fabric Care, Salvador's now offers an equal balance of sales and service which is what it's all about. First of all, cover your bases (and floors) with carpet for less than at the big superstores. BRINKMAN is their specialty. We found a special of three rooms (up to 400 square feet) of carpet with pad for only $499, and up to 600 square feet for only $699. Don't forget the kitchen and bath–vinyl was $10.95/square yard. Now then, sit back and enjoy those floors. When they get dirty, they'll clean it for you at a discount. Call back and order their special of two rooms and a hall of carpet cleaned for only $49.95. These friendly folks will come to your home for a free estimate on carpet and vinyl, too. Is that your Vinyl answer? *CK, MC, V, AE, D*

✧✧✧✧✧ Servpro — 972/986-7677

2490 Joe Field Rd. — *Mon-Fri 8-5*
Dallas, TX 75229 — *www.servpro.com*

Want to get your ducts in a row? Or have your carpets clean as a whistle? These are the folks to call. A minimum charge of $55 is assessed to come out, and then they charge $.25/square foot instead of by the room, saving you a few shekels. Upholstery, too, by the linear foot rather than paying for a three-seater sofa when you only have a two-seater. Duct cleaning starts at $25 per duct. I know of one customer who saved thousands–yes, thousands–off an estimate from another duct-cleaning company that spends a zillion dollars advertising how wonderful they are. Plus, these guys are good, real good. Read about them in the latest edition of Spot News! There are 26 franchises in the area; visit their website at www.servpro.com to find the franchise nearest to you. *CK, MC, V, AE, D*

★★★ Southwestern Carpets — 214/634-0320

1130 Inwood Rd. — *Mon-Fri 8:30-5:30; Sat 8:30-1:30*
Dallas, TX 75247

Want something new on your floors, but aren't quite sure what? Then head over to Southwestern and they'll help point you in the right direction, whether that means carpeting, area rugs, wood, vinyl or any other kind of flooring. And the choices don't end there. Consider area rugs. They have wool, synthetics, Berbers, textures and more in a multitude of colors and patterns. You can select a ready-made rug in the color and pattern of your choice in a pre-cut size, or have one custom made. They do carry bargain buys with pricing comparable to Home Depot or First Floors. They carry wall-to-wall carpeting up to an 80 ounce weight, which is pretty decent. *CK, MC, V, AE, D, Financing*

★★ Stone Mountain Carpet Mill Outlet — 972/219-2221

1165 S. Stemmons, #130 — *Mon-Thu 9-7; Fri-Sat 9-5*
Lewisville, TX 75067 — *www.stonemountainflooring.com*

Big, big, big spells BIGELOW. Stone Mountain is the Bigelow carpet mill outlet, but they now represent more than 50 different mills. Stone Mountain has made its mark in Dallas in a big way. Get first-quality carpets with savings of 20-70 percent without traveling to Stone Mountain, Ga. The mountain has come to the Metroplex. More than 2,000 colors and styles are available. Come in during sales to get even greater savings. Heavy trackless was $.77/square foot; Berber started at $.49/square foot; heavy Berber as low as $.96/square foot and hardwood was as low as $2.49/square foot. Whether you choose ceramic, wood, vinyl (ARMSTRONG or MANNINGTON), laminate (PERGO) or carpeting (BIGELOW), Stone Mountain has it for less. When you're ready to stand on something solid, climb to the mountain and take the vow. Remember the 11th commandment: "Thou shalt not pay retail!" Check directory for other locations: 11413 LBJ Frwy., Garland, 972/840-3200; 825 Airport Frwy., Hurst, 817/590-2113; 5999 Woodway Drive, Waco, 254/772-8453 and 4501 S. General Bruce Drive, Suite 60, Temple, 254/773-6400. *CK, MC, V, AE, D, Financing*

♥♥♥♥♥ Style Weavers 972/243-2226

13675 Stemmons Frwy. *Mon-Sat 10-7; Sun Noon-5*
Farmers Branch, TX 75234 *www.styleweavers.com*

Cut your rug in style with custom-made rugs, floors, furnishings and window treatments from Style Weavers. They have a 27,000-square-foot showroom filled with competitively priced flooring, including slate, tile, marble and exotic woods (finished and unfinished hickory maple, mesquite, bamboo, hardwoods and more), ceramics, carpets, fabrics, furniture, accessories and a customer-oriented trained staff. They feature more than 75 styles of handmade, antique and machine-made Persian and Oriental rugs, along with floral, tapestry and hand-hooked rugs. They have a large selection of oversized and odd-sized rugs. If you don't see what you are looking for, they can create any flooring or rug you can imagine. Draw it. Then they'll make it. One of the most impressive well-priced furniture and high-end decorative accessories imported from Indonesia, Mexico, Europe and the Far East. They have leather and upholstered chairs, sofas, end and side tables, lamps, candles, African art reproductions, stone, bronze and copper urns and more. Located off I-35 between the Valwood and Valley View exits, one-stop home shopping just got better. *CK, MC, V, AE, D*

★ Texas Discount Carpets 972/484-8051

11265 Goodnight Lane, Suite 1012 *Mon-Fri 10-6, Sat 10-3*
Dallas, TX 75229

Instead of buying your carpet off the back of a truck, come to this warehouse setting and get a great deal. Then again, if they hang up on you, (like they did us), you might give it second thoughts. For carpets, let's lay it on the line: CABIN CREST, BRINKMAN and SHAW were front and center, from 20 ounces up to 100 ounces. Prices range from 99 cents a yard on up. But on up only means so far. A luxury 63-ounce carpet sells for $16/yard. A 55-ounce carpet sells for $14/yard. All 30-ounce carpet and above and builders' grade came in stain resistant. Free delivery, installation, repairs and restretching available. Go two blocks west on Walnut Hill off of I-35. And have a Goodnight. *CK, MC, V, AE, D*

★★★★★ Tile America 817/595-7900

7337 Dogwood Park *Mon-Fri 8-5; Sat 9-2*
Richland Hills, TX 76118

Give Fort Worth credit for having this terrific tile company in town. The tile itself is not from in town, because Tile America represents manufacturers from all over, including Spain, Italy and Indonesia. By eliminating the middle man (has anyone ever actually seen a "middleman"?) they can offer exceptional prices. You would not want to side step a huge selection of wall and floor tiles as low as $.89/square foot. They have their own brand of all-glaze tile, from 8 X 8-inch squares all the way up to 18 X 18-inch. Though they do not install, they will give you names of tile contractors they do business with, you do not wish to tackle the job yourself. When they offer their periodic closeouts, make a beeline to Dogwood Park, because they will have deals you can not afford to pass-up. *CK, MC, V, AE, D*

★★★ Tim Hogan's Carpet Outlet of Dalton, Ga 817/831-4167

5724 Airport Freeway *Mon-Fri 9-7; Sat 9-5; Sun Noon-5*
Haltom City, TX 76117

Want MONSANTO Wear-Dated Carpet II? Try calling this a Georgia peach of a carpet store. Tim Hogan's Carpet Outlet is not only about carpets. You can also find floor tiles in wood, vinyl and ceramic. They carry all the major brands for carpets and floors, so you will be able to find what you are looking for. A six-months same as cash finance program and a 30-day replacement warranty caught our eye, along with the offer of in-home sample shopping. Visit also in Grapevine, 817/481-8950 and Rhome, TX, 817/385-5540. *CK, MC, V, AE, D, 6 months same as cash*

★★ True Discount Carpets 972/276-0348

1403 S. Jupiter Rd. *Mon-Fri 9:30-6; Sat 9:30-5*
Garland, TX 75042

Across from E-Systems, truer words were never spoken. How many rooms could you carpet with 100,000 square yards of carpet? We don't know either, but what we saw was definitely a landlord's delight at $1.11/square foot and may not suit your purposes for a long–term commitment. A mid-quality Berber was going for $1.65-$2.10/square foot and the top-of-the-line Berber was $2.22-$3.33/square foot. Nothing to sneeze over. Brands were plentiful, including CORONET, MOHAWK and SHAW. We found a great plush pile for $1.55/square foot installed. Visit also in Plano, 972/238-9755. *CK, MC, V, AE, D*

★★★★ Verona Marble Co. 214/381-8405

8484 Endicott Lane *Mon-Fri 8-5; By Appt. Only*
Dallas, TX 75227

Choose your truly impressive decorating ideas side-by-side with Dallas' most selective decorators. Marble and granite close-outs in various sizes, starting as low as $1.90/square foot are usually available, but hard to predict in large quantities. This factory outlet brings in tile directly from Italy and passes the high quality and low prices on to you. All the supplies you need to lay the tile are also stocked at the same low prices during their once-a-year sale. Now be sure your work of art will stand the test of time and not start leaning like the Tower of Pisa. By appointment only, so call first before traveling. *CK, MC, V*

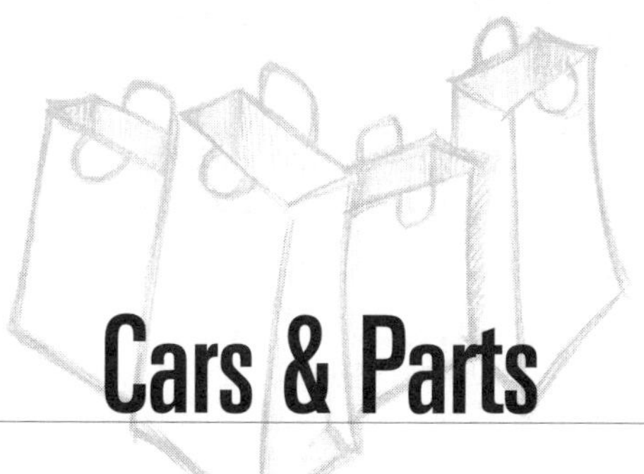

Cars & Parts

✧✧✧✧✧ A-1 United Transmissions — 972/278-9807

2201 W. Kingsley
Garland, TX 75041
Mon-Fri 7:30-6; Sat 9-Noon

When it comes time to tune the transmission, take a look at A-1 United Transmissions. If it has a transmission, they can handle it, and they deal with both American and foreign models. (The four-wheeled kind, silly!) The mechanics are all ASE–certified, so they know what they are doing. Having computerized diagnostic equipment helps too. Just to make sure the work is up to snuff, take a free road test and evaluation. No gimmicks. A-1 has been family-owned and operated since 1976, by the Easley family. Ask for Mike; he will treat you right. Just straight talk, man. *CK, MC, V, AE, D*

★★★ Atomic & Import Auto Salvage — 214/371-6020

8835 S. Central Expressway
Dallas, TX 75216
Mon-Sun 8-7

Looking for a carburetor for your Corvette or a part for a Porsche? Import Auto Salvage is your salvation. Let them unearth the missing links. Need a transmission? Get one here. Give them yours in exchange and it will cost you only for $59. Even though they don't handle antique auto parts, they were willing to chase them down through their hotline. Car crushing also available, if heaven (or hell) awaits your beloved Chevy. Winter hours are Mon-Sun 8-5. *CK, MC, V, AE, D*

★★★★★ Auto Buyers Assistance — 214/361-0090

14001 Dallas Pkwy., Suite 1200
Dallas, TX 75240
Mon-Fri 8:30-5
www.autobuyersassistance.com

Looking for a little help from your friends in the new car business? Call this ABA and leave the lawyers out of it. This service will direct you FREE of charge (see, I told you they had nothing to do with lawyers) to some hot deals without the fast-talk. You can get one low price on any new vehicle (buy or lease), from participating dealers statewide just by picking up the phone and talking to Ronnie Shipper. Domestic and foreign car seekers are equally served. He will then direct you to the fleet managers, where the dealers will give the lowest possible price. Thousands of cars, trucks and vans have been sold through ABA since 1989. Aren't you tire-d of paying retail yet? AARP, AAA customers and credit union members are the majority of their customers, but anyone and everyone is welcome. *Financing*

✧✧✧✧ Auto Critic — FW 817/460-8388

740 Newport — *Mon-Sat 8-5; and By Appt.*
Fort Worth, TX 76120 — *www.usedcarinspections.com*

When the transmission fell out of Josh's '82 ESCORT an hour after he drove it off the lot, I knew we had bought a lulu. Call Auto Critic before you get stuck with another lemon. (You should, at least, be able to drive off the lot without an unnecessary bump in the road.) Their mobile vans come to you with a 150-point checklist, bumper to bumper, examining the body, frame, electrical and all the major systems. They will give you a comprehensive, unbiased written report by a certified ASE technician on the true condition of the vehicle you are considering. They'll even take it for a spin to detect any operational or performance problems and compare the mileage on the odometer to the car's handling. This is a sound investment to ensure a smoother ownership ride. And since they have no vested interest in finding faults in your four wheels, you can bet they tell it like it is. Give 24-hour notice for your appointment. No referrals to mechanics are made, ever–even if asked! Franchises available nationwide; call 800/765-1857. *CK*

✧✧✧✧✧ Autoglass Plus — 972/222-2323 or 817/222-2323

By Appt. Only
www.autoglassplus.com

Have your windshield replaced at no cost to you, the clear truth, the whole truth, and nothing but! With Autoglass Plus, you save big-time. You save money. You save time. And you save effort. Don't waste valuable time taking your car to some auto body shop to repair those cracks and chips in the windshield. This mobile service gets the job done while you get your job done at your home, office or wherever–and they will even handle the paperwork and phone calls to file your insurance claim. Most jobs can be done at no cost to you (but your insurance company may not tell you that); so let the customer service people help with that exchange. No hassle, no double-talk, just quick, reliable service. Indianapolis, St. Louis, Dayton and Cincinnati locations as well. Just think, I knew them when. *CK, MC, V*

★★★ AutoZone — 972/221-1433

1106 W. Main — *Mon-Sat 8 A.M.-9 P.M.; Sun 9-6*
Lewisville, TX 75067 — *www.autozone.com*

Whether you do your own auto repairs or take it to the shop, AutoZone has "the best parts in auto parts." Sale prices on auto parts are their everyday low prices. From water pumps to anti-freeze, fan belts to fuel filters, wiper blades to brake pads, the discounts are a result of their enormous buying power. And they're even bigger since the buyout of Dallas-based Chief Auto. Along with parts, AutoZone offers a host of free services. They can test your alternator, battery and starter while they are still on the car. If the battery is already kaput, they can have it recharged for you in 30 minutes. All for free. They are even willing to give tips on basic repairs to save you the labor costs. Check directory for other locations. There are 2,796 locations in 40 states; 54 just in Dallas alone. *CK, MC, V, D*

✧✧✧✧✧ Bergman's Paint & Body — 972/247-0925

2316 Havenhurst — *Mon-Fri 8:30-6; Sat By Appt. Only*
Farmers Branch, TX 75234

Since 1979, Bergman's Paint and Body has been the plastic surgeon of area cars. Should you encounter any superficial dings or scratches, hail to the chief! If your car suffers from hail damage or you need quality color matching, auto glass, frame and body straightening, fiberglass or plastic repair, call on this doctor who cares for your car's woes without putting a significant dent in your pocketbook. They can handle all cars, be they American or foreign. You can see them from Stemmons Freeway, but pulling up to their front door is a little confusing. Call for directions. They're the best! *CK, MC, V, AE, D*

★★★★★ CarQuest Auto Parts — 972/790-4775

115 S. Belt Line Rd. — *Mon-Fri 8-6; Sat 8-5*
Irving, TX 75060 — *www.carquest.com*

When it comes time for your car to quit because of a bad part, don't part with any more of your money than you have to. Dealers who tell you the part is available only through them are often far from the truth. Fact 1: Most parts are available through CarQuest at a fraction of the dealer's price. Fact 2: The dealer does not want you to know that! After all, if we could get a coil pack for $48 rather than $259, then what is there to think about? Call this computerized search firm (be patient, lines are often busy) and tell them what part you need. Isn't it worth the wait on the phone if the savings are significant? Remanufactured, rebuilt and new parts for any car, truck or van are available. Also, your typical automotive supplies are sold here at a discount, like oil, filters and spark plugs. Check directory for the location nearest you. (There are 3,000-plus franchises worldwide.) *CK, MC, V, AE, D*

✧✧✧✧ City Garage — 972/434-4340

475 N. Valley Pkwy. — *Mon-Fri 7-7; Sat 8-5*
Lewisville, TX 75067 — *www.city-garage.com*

With 27 locations in the Metroplex, you can hardly miss a good thing when you drive by. Their appealing storefronts only make you stop; the friendly and capable service makes you come back. One-on-one personalized service is what makes this service chain a throwback to the good old days. You can even talk to your mechanic while your car is being worked on. They can handle most automotive services, from simple tune-ups and oil and lubes to emissions, heating and cooling, transmission and brake systems. They'll even help keep your new car warranty in force. The ASE certified mechanics are just part of this fast-growing neighborhood garage. Pay another $1 for all used oil, transmission fluid and anti-freeze to be disposed of properly. How nice, an environmentally-conscious company that puts the money where it'll count most. They do it all. Full-service automotive repair and maintenance with the highest quality parts. They'll even pick up and deliver the clunker as long as it's operational. Warranties, too, on parts and labor–12 months/12,000 miles. How's that for assurance? Locations all over the Metroplex, from Arlington to Watugua and parts in between. The downside? They make almost 100% profit on all parts. *CK, MC, V, AE, D, Napa card*

★★★★ Classic BMW Clearance & Trade-in Center — 972/918-1100

300 N. Central Expressway — *Mon-Sat 8:30-6*
Richardson, TX 75081 — *www.classicbmw.com*

The latest collector's craze is not Beanie Babies, it's the Beamer Babies. To get a great deal on one, check out Classic BMW Clearance and Trade-in Center for new or pre-owned BMWs. It's the only game in town and it's the only BMW clearance and trade-in center in all of Texas. They have the service, selection, deals and facilities to make you just say, "WOW"! Check their website at www.classicbmw.com to find deals on service and maintenance and-monthly BMW selections. A '00 Z3 convertible was this month's WOW

Choice, with 15 other cars among the WOW selections. But it was the Z3 and Z8 models that really got us drooling on the laptop. The location on 75 between Arapaho and Belt Line provides easy access for all of north Texans who'd rather drive a BMW...or walk! *CK, Financing*

✧✧✧ Comedy Defensive Driving School — 214/8-COMEDY

5500 Greenville Ave. — *Classes By Reservations Only*
Dallas, TX 75206

It's no laughing matter to have to attend a defensive driving school, but if you have to go, you may as well exit laughing. Courses are usually held from 9-3:30 each Saturday and every other week Sunday, also 9-3:30. In Addison and Mesquite only, evening classes are available on Monday or Tuesday. In "Old Town" classes are split over two days, Monday/Tuesday or Wednesday/ Thursday. Classes are $30, and after completion, you will be able to have one traffic ticket dismissed as well as receive certain discounts on auto insurance. While traffic regulations are hardly exciting topics of discussion, at least relieve the tedium with a joke now and then. Some of the instructors are animated and some are hilarious, according to many successful graduates. Check for a location nearest you. Classes are booked every 24 hours. For an alternative to attending in person, go to your nearest Blockbuster's and rent the Defensive Training Video, a six-hour video that requires you to check-in hourly with call-in questions and answers. *MC, V*

★★★★ CycleSmart — 972/712-0712

6427 Main St. — *Tue-Fri 10-6; Sat 10-4*
Frisco, TX 75034

Rev up those motors and stop being taken for a ride. This company sells cycles the smart way...used. If you're looking to buy or sell, they cater to every biker's taste. Hop aboard a previously-ridden motorcycle from BMW, HARLEY-DAVIDSON, HONDA, KAWASKI, MOTO GUZZI, SUZUKI, YAMAHA and others. From street or touring bikes (as opposed to dirt or ATVs), this company can propel you to greater heights at lower prices. Get those bikes out of your garage and onto the streets. Don't sit still. If you're looking to sell your bike, this company is consignment only. New and used parts and accessories, in-stock or ordered. Bob Sutton's your man behind the machine, and a full-time seasoned mechanic/racer is under the machine. Either way, between the two of them, they can get you up and riding. *CK, MC, V, PQ*

★★★★ Dallas Can! Academy 214/943-2244

325 W 12th St., Suite LL *Auctions the last Sat of each month 9 A.M.*
Dallas, TX 75208 *www.dallascan.org*

Buying or donating, this can be your salvation. Free towing, whether the vehicle is running or not, should count for something. About 100 cars, trucks, vans, motorcycles, tractors, golf carts and boats go on the auction block the last Saturday of each month at 9426 Lakefield Blvd. Call 214/824-4226 for information on the auctions. Registration (with $100 deposit) and vehicle inspection starts at 8 A.M., with the auction action beginning promptly at 9. If you want the list of vehicles in advance, available Thursdays before the auction. Expect to pay wholesale prices and below if you buy one; donating your vehicle to the Dallas Can! Academy helps an at-risk youth get a chance to finish high school and get a job. You get the benefit of helping and a tax deduction all rolled into one. All proceeds of the sale go to help area kids. Downtown location is 2601 Live Oak, 214/824-4226. *CK, MC, V*

✧✧✧✧✧ Dent Doctor 972/434-2254

808 E Hwy 121 *Mon-Fri 9-6; Sat 9-2*
Lewisville, TX 75057 *www.dentdoctorusa.com*

Dear Doctor: I have this bruise on my passenger side fender and I hate hospitals. Furthermore, I'm terrified of anesthesia and have no insurance. Any place where I can go for a quick fix without being completely put under? Dear Fearful: Never fear, there's a Dent Doctor in Lewisville. Call on this cosmetic medicine man for an on-location operation that should alleviate the pain without major surgery. Dents and door dings are their specialty. They offer repairs without painting, hence no mismatching of paint. No long waits, either. Same-day service and estimates, but like any other doctor, they require an appointment. Since they use no silly putty, their technique is more like dermabrasion. And I'm for that! They now have a truck accessory store with bed rails, bed mats, bumpers, hitches, tool boxes, running boards, vent shades and can spray a bedliner protection coating like PERM-TECH to keep your truck looking gooood. *CK, MC, V, AE*

★★ Discount Auto Salvage 972/263-3388

3965 E. Main *Mon-Sat 9-5:30*
Grand Prairie, TX 75051

Does your VOLVO need a bumper? Could your MAZDA use a new motor?

Discount Auto Salvage can help you find the part without draining your wallet. BMW, HONDA, NISSAN, TOYOTA, too, as well as domestic parts. Auctions run weekly, so call and find out when they are to score some points. Call for availability and see what kind of deal you can muster up–especially on expensive transmissions. They also buy cars if yours has reached the end of the line. From I-30, exit Loop 12, then go south to Davis where you'll go right one mile to Main, but don't try this route on days when there's an auction going on as they're apt to close the streets. Call ahead if you're missing a part. *CK, MC, V*

★★★★★ Discount Tire Co. 817/571-2341

3233 Harwood *Mon-Fri 8:30-6; Sat 8:30-5*
Bedford, TX 76021 *www.discounttire.com*

Down-to-earth prices (save 25-40 percent) on all tires, mounting, rotation and flat repairs are the way to go round and round with the best deals in town. All makes and models of tires are available: ARIZONIAN, BF GOODRICH, CENTENNIAL, CONTINENTAL, DUNLOP, GENERAL, GOODYEAR, KUMHO, MICHELIN, NITTO, PIRELLI, UNIROYAL and YOKOHAMA. Speedy service with a smile on all of them. Custom wheels from AMERICAN EAGLE, FITTIPALDI, ROH and many others are available. Special orders, too. The warranty, rotation policy and FREE flat/air check has kept one of our shopper's cars in tip-top shape for years, but we're devoted because they fix flats–FAST and for FREE. (Need I say that again?) Check newspapers for current sale prices. Expect superb customer service every time and at every location...and you won't have to throw the tire through the window to get their attention, I promise. Every employee knows what he is doing; they're professional, knowledgeable and courteous. They even sell used tires (great for spares) as low as $5. Check directory for more than 30 Metroplex locations. Ninety days same as cash. *CK, MC, V, AE, D, Financing*

✧✧ Du-Good Services 817/478-4842

3604 Fort Hunt Drive *Mon-Fri 8-4; By Appt.*
Arlington, TX 76016

Want to wash your car, clean it, polish it, protect and seal it in one fell swoop–sans water? Then this is the product to buy if you want the best that is also environmentally correct. Spray on a coat and wipe it off. It's as simple as looking into a mirror (and you will with the shine that is delivered). Can you imagine never having to wait in line at the car wash again? Or caring whether it rains after you have washed the car? Or schlepping all those hoses and soap buckets out to the driveway and flooding the neighborhood? Once you've applied the washless car polish, all you need to touch up is an occasional dirt spot with a damp rag and dry cloth. Even your tires will look brand new, mile after mile. These and other miracle cleaners (home appliances, leather and vinyl, carpet and upholstery and metal polish–all waterless) are available through Ron Hicks at Du-Good Services. And if you're really good, he might throw in a free demonstration. They also offer a lawn service now; call Ron for details. *CK, MC, V*

✧✧ Fantasy Limousines 214/351-0610

1055 Regal Row — *Mon-Fri 10-6; By Appt.*
Dallas, TX 75247 — *www.fantasylimos.com*

Hoity-toities love impressing clients and friends. Now you can, too, by taking advantage of this company's weekday special. You can rent a limo for $199 for four hours Sun-Wed. Grab five of your closest friends and shop in style in this six-person limo. Each additional hour is $65, and extra stops along the way don't come cheap. Isn't it so-o-o-o much better to drive up to an outlet store and have all heads turning? Extra charges for eight or 10 passenger limos, but hey, it's your shopping spree. Call at least one week ahead to reserve. Now merged with First Impressions Limos, they're even better equipped to handle your wildest fantasies. Besides, don't you hate people who drive around all day and have nothing to chauffeur it? *MC, V, AE, D*

♥♥♥♥♥ Fred's Foreign Car Service 214/350-6787

5915 Peeler St. — *Mon-Thu 7:30-6; Fri 7:30-5*
Dallas, TX 75235 — *www.dwfnetmall.com/freds*

Fred's Foreign Car Service specializes in fine European automobiles such as BMW, FERRARI, JAGUAR, MERCEDES, PORSCHE, RANGE ROVER and VOLVO. Fred's is not a "R&R" kind of place. They will not remove and replace items until they determine the problem. They find the cause of the problem and fix it, instead of treating symptoms at your expense. No matter what kind of mechanical repair you need, Fred's will take care of it. They are not "cheap", but they are honest. You get your money's worth, and they do exceptional work on foreign bodies. *CK, MC, V, D*

✧✧✧ Friendly Detail Car Wash on Wheels 214/871-9274

By Appt. Only

Wow! A Wash on Wheels? Don't leave home (or your office) ever again to wait in line at the car wash the minute the sun is shining. Wash those cars and woes, here they go. Britt Jackson's the guy with the better idea. He will wash, wash and wax, or wash and detail your car for almost the same amount of money you'd spend at the corner car wash. For a basic wash, it costs $12.50 up to $35 for a wax job. Count the savings, convenience and a clean car. Besides, a clean car always seems to drive better, right? It all adds up to a happier you behind the wheel. *CK*

★★★★★ Hub Cap Annie — 972/669-9898

11648 N. Central Expwy. — *Tue-Sat 9-6*
Dallas, TX 75243

Are your hubcaps looking like Orphan Annie's? Well, wheel on over to this source for completing the tire connection. Since they are a sought-after burglar's choice, you might find yourself in need of a few replacements. If they have your hubcap in stock, there is no one better. Chances are no one will beat their prices. A set of four was seen as low as $30-$35 (for a trade-in special) to the average price of $50. These are not "hot" wheels, but strictly good deals. Trade-in specials were even cheaper. Selection varies–call before you come to see what's in stock. A fun and original place to shop! Going north on Central, exit Royal Lane, and stay on the service road. It's one mile down the road. *CK, MC, V, AE, D*

✧✧✧ Maaco — 972/702-8877

4103 Lindbergh Drive — *Mon-Fri 8-8; Sat 9-1; Appt.*
Addison, TX 75244 — *www.maaco.com*

Maaco can make it all better if your car has a boo-boo. From quality dent, ding or collision repair to expert painting, they do it all. We found a Gold Pages coupon offering $75 off a Maaco Supreme Paint Service which included Primaseal. This included a chemical cleaning, thorough surface sanding, machine sanding most chips and scratches, priming and block sanding, feathered areas as required, applying a full coat of primer sealer, refinishing with durability plus catalyzed enamel and lastly, an integrated coat of gloss-extending UV sunscreen is applied. Then, it's off to the ovens for a baked finish. How about their presidential paint service which usually costs $349.95 for only $249. Check directory for location nearest you. There are 14 locations in the area. *CK, MC, V, D*

★★ McClain's RV Superstores — 800/497-3586

I-35 E., Exit 460 — *Mon-Fri 9-7; Sat 9-5*
PO Box 969 — *www.mcclainsrv.com*
Corinth, TX 76205

Hit the road, Jack, and pack your bags for a year. You don't have to have the luck of the Irish to save some green–like thousands of dollars on the best brands of recreational vehicles (RVs). Choose from hundreds, but don't expect life on the road to keep you on Easy Street. These guzzlers are expensive. A 2000 DISCOVERY Super Slideout 6-speed with awning, air brakes, front entry door, full air ride, exhaust brakes, 275 HP, chassis, 22.5 Alcoa wheels and America's #1 selling diesel recreational machine goes for $125,910, plus tax, title and license. Whoa! Want to ride something less elaborate? Try a 1999 WINNEBAGO Brave 35C with jack, awnings, fiberglass roof and many more options for a measly $69,997 plus tax, title and license. A 1999 SOUTHWIND Storm with living room/kitchen/double slideout, island queen bed, private toilet, swivel chair with a table, sofa and table with chairs could keep you on the road for a lifetime for only $73,490 plus tax, title and license. Sure beats a stationary condo! McClain's pays top dollar for trade-ins and up to 100 percent financing with approved credit. They have 15 service bays with factory-trained technicians to service what they sell, and they are the largest RV dealer in North Texas. Your best buys are in the used RV department. New fifth-wheels and travel trailers are also a lot less expensive and often do the trick. A 2000 SPORTSMAN 2456P, perfect for a half ton pickup, with a big slideout was $15,995 plus tax, title and license, or about $189 per month. Another McClain's location is at South I-35W, Exit 24, in Alvarado, Texas, 800/303-2330. Roger and out. *Financing*

★★★ National Tire & Battery (NTB) 972/387-7966

14107 Inwood *Mon-Fri 7:30-8; Sat 8-6; Sun 10-5*
Farmers Branch, TX 75244

Owned by Sears and formerly called National Tire Warehouse, you can still count on these guys to give you good prices on tires and service. The salesman was able to quote prices on the phone, and he also offered several recommendations for replacing the tires on the old Jeep. Low-price guarantees (they even compared favorably with Sam's) and the full range of motion: BF GOODRICH, BRIDGESTONE, DUNLOP, MICHELIN, PIRELLI, UNIROYAL, YOKOHAMA plus their own house brand of NTW. From basics to high performance, they rotate and fix flats for free (if you buy the $9 lifetime package). A set of four BF Goodrich tires would run anywhere from $51-$89 per tire. Check the newspaper ads for current sale prices. There is always a sale running and posted there in the store. Other incentives included a senior citizen's discount of 5 percent (for drivers over 65), an early-bird drop off service, a 30-day ride guarantee and courtesy inspections. They also do alignments, brake work, shocks, struts and course carry DIEHARD batteries. Check directory for other locations. There are at least 14 in Dallas and the Mid-Cities and more in Fort Worth. *CK, MC, V, AE, D, Sears*

✧✧✧✧✧ Oliver's Automotive — 972/221-5583

1244 S. Stemmons — *Mon-Fri 7:30-6*
Lewisville, TX 75057

When it comes to recommending a mechanic, my hair bristles on the back of my neck. In this case, though, I have never been left with a frizzy perm. At Oliver's, expect your car to be treated with tender loving care. They'll even tell you when something *doesn't* need to be fixed. As honest as the day is long, they do the full workload when it comes to fixing your car or truck. How else would they have stayed in business for more than 20 years? They are ASE-certified technicians for domestic and foreign vehicles, brakes, tune-ups, carburetors, fuel injection, A/C and heat and all electrical work. Exit Hwy. 121 and stay on the I-35 service road going north into Lewisville. *CK, MC, V, D*

★★★ Pep Boys — 972/242-3136

1455 W. Trinity Mills — *Mon-Fri 7-9; Sat 7-8; Sun 9-6*
Carrollton, TX 75006 — *www.pepboys.com*

The Pep Boys, Manny, Moe and Jack (no, they aren't the Three Stooges) rotate some of the best names in tires–BRIDGESTONE, FUTURA, GOODRICH, GOODYEAR and MICHELIN as well as all major brands of air, oil and fuel filters, spark plugs, headlights...you name it, they've got it. Lots of specialty items for the pernsnickity driver as well as the handy home mechanic. We had to have help choosing between the umpteen brands of car wax (MEGUIRS, we were told, was the best). Service was fast and friendly when we needed it in the aisles, but oh, those long cashier lines! If you don't know how to maintain your own vehicle (or just don't want to), let their service pros handle it for you. Locations all over the Metroplex, look for the three guys outside who look like the Kip's Big Boy's long lost uncles. To find the Pep Boys nearest you, call 800/737-2697. *CK, MC, V, D, AE*

✧ Precept Transportation — 972/238-8884

13539 Method St. — *24 hrs./7 days*
Dallas, TX 75243

Mergers and acquisitions are even spilling over into the limousine business. Precept has bought Lone Star Limousine and now has "spare tires" in every ZIP code in the Metroplex. The hours above are office hours, but you can call 24 hours a day for information and reservations. If you want to pay by check, though, you have to drop it off a week ahead of time to give it time to clear. (They don't want to tote any bouncers to the airport.) If a limousine seems a little pretentious to you, you can also catch a stately ride to the airport in a Lincoln Towncar starting at $65 (including gratuity, airport costs, etc.) each way if you're traveling from the 75248 ZIP code. The charges are based on distance or zones. Not bad if you like to ride in style (and safety), considering most shuttles and taxis aren't that cheap anymore. For other occasions, you can also rent the car and driver for $45 an hour plus gratuity (two-hour minimum); limo drivers command $70 to the airport and rental changes, car and driver, start at $65 per hour (two-hour minimum). *CK (prepaid), MC, V, AE, DC*

★★★ R.V. World of Texas — 940/320-4098 or 99

5201 I-35 N — *Mon-Sat 8-7; Sun Noon-5*
Denton, TX 76207

OK, shoppers, if you're a travelin' man, consider shopping at this superstore (next to Camping World in Denton) for some of the best prices on four-wheels. Want to buy a BEAVER or a SAFARI at "wholesale" prices? Here's the place to trek, including the two new diesel models under $150,000. Oh me, oh my. Such a deal! This is the headquarters for "pushers" like BEAVER, CHALLENGER, CONQUEST, INTRUDER, SAFARI & MINI, TOURMASTER, TRADEWINDS and "towables" like COLEMAN, COLLINS, SAVANNA and SEABREEZE. More than 150 new and used RVs to choose from. Sales, service, financing, insurance and trades are always welcome. Take the 470 exit northbound or 471 exit southbound. *Financing*

★★★ Radiator Express Warehouse — 800/252-1313

320 S. Belt Line Rd., #112 — *Mon-Fri 7-5:30; Sat 9-4*
Irving, TX 75060 — *www.radiator.com*

When it gets hot under the hood, call the radiator hotline and cool down. They will get you the radiator; but you have to install it. Wait in the shade while they bring it to you–there's free delivery. You can have it shipped directly to you or to an auto shop for someone else to put in. They have a huge inventory and offer a lifetime warranty on all their new radiators. Learn to not sweat the small stuff and save money, too. At $120, you won't get too hot under the collar. Plus, you never hear about one of their employees fired for–taking a brake! *MC, V, AE, D, MO*

Cars & Parts

★★★★ Rent-A-Wreck 214/398-7368

2025 S. Buckner *Mon-Fri 9-6; Sat 9-3:30*
Dallas, TX 75217 *www.rentawreck.com*

For just plain get up and go, nothing beats the reliability of a vehicle from Rent-A-Wreck. With more than 400 locations nationwide, this company offers all of the expected courtesies of a full-price company, without the full price. Since Rent-A-Wreck is franchised, you get friendly, personal service and the backing of the corporate honchos–the best of both worlds. Choose from a wide range of reliable, clean cars, trucks, vans (great for a weekend jaunt to Canton) and convertibles (for a leisurely drive through the countryside.) Rent-A-Wreck provides free local pick-up and delivery and is even recommended these days by some insurance companies. There are locations in Plano, 972/881-8142; Lewisville, 972/420-6305; Irving, 972/258-8260; Garland, 972/840-6531; Richardson, 972/669-2450 and Northeast Dallas, 972/620-1505. Another plus is that these folks accept a rental with cash and lots of ID. Can you believe it? *CK, MC, V, AE, D*

★★★★★ Self Sell Auto Sales 972/219-1803

1035 S. Mill St. *Mon-Fri 8:30-7; Sat 8:30-6*
Lewisville, TX 75057

For a flat fee of $39, take the hassle out of selling your car yourself. From their humble beginnings, Self Sell Auto Sales went from selling 25 cars a month to about 60 today. They take your asking price, add a little on top of it for themselves and for negotiating purposes. When they sell your car, you get the amount of money you were asking, and they get the amount above and beyond your asking price (minimum of $300). They even offer buyers a warranty on cars. From a variety of cars to choose from to several financing possibilities, they welcome repeat business by trading up to an even newer or fancier model. Trade-ins are encouraged. And get this, they will pay the seller's price for a trade-in. Unheard of at other dealerships. The average car sells here within 30 days. In a world of doing-it-yourself, sometimes it pays not to. And at this auto lot, you auto let them do it for you. They'll show your vehicle, handle all the negotiations, advertise in the local papers, offer multiple in-house financing options, take trade-ins and offer warranties. Put this task in the hands of a professional. You will save time and make money. *CK, Financing*

★★★★★ Texas Mustang Sales 972/243-3400

2718 Forest Lane *Mon-Fri 10-6*
Dallas, TX 75234 *www.texas-cars.com*

Believe it or not, Texas Mustang Sales doesn't sell Mustangs. They do sell BMWs, JAGUARs and MERCEDES. But on the day of our visit, they had nothing but Jags. Sedans, coupes and convertibles. Well, who's complaining. Buy your next previously-owned luxury Jag at wholesale prices. All the Jaguar and BMW models listed during the week of Feb. 23 were from 1994-1998, with the lion's share coming from 1996 and 1997. For those interested, you can also find a few domestics, such as Chevy Blazers and Lincoln Navigators. Get a bank loan on site, by fax or phone, with terms up to eight years with approved credit. Bumper-to-bumper extended warranties on most vehicles; up to seven years and 100,000 miles are also available, and trade-ins are welcome. Even though the vehicles are used, the sales people do not apply the pressure normally associated with used cars. In fact, they don't apply any pressure at all and will only offer assistance if you ask for it. Check out the vehicles each day on their website or wheel and deal at their showroom, I-635 to Josey, south 100 yards on Josey to Forest and go west one block. *Financing*

♥♥♥♥♥ Truly Texas Limousines 817/430-9989

13725 Bates Aston Rd. *24 Hours*
Haslet, TX 76052 *www.texaslimo.com*

For a unique ride, Texas style, call Brad Goodbread and he'll show up with a Chevrolet crew cab dually stretch-truck limousine. You won't believe it until you see it, but you can believe us when we say people will know they're in Texas when they see this fabulous limo driving down the street. This 31-foot monster seats eight and comes with a host of features. They provide three crystal decanters, eight crystal champagne flutes and high ball glasses, iced soft drinks and bottled water. If you want–ahem–*adult* beverages, you have to provide your own. It also has two color televisions, a VCR and a 10-disc CD changer. You can ride in style in this bad boy for just $95 an hour, plus a 20 percent gratuity. Brad also has traditional sedans and limousines if that's what you're lookin' for, but the stretch truck has to be experienced. Whether it's a ride to the airport or going to Bass Hall, say yeeeeeehaw and enjoy the ride. *CK, MC, V, AE*

★★★★★ United Liquidators 817/613-9191

3404 Fort Worth Hwy. *Mon-Fri 8-6; Sat 9-2*
Weatherford, TX 76087 *www.unitedliquidators.com*

Whether it's an auction or sold on their lot, expect prices to be straight from the book–the NADA book, that is. This is the book that banks use to loan you money on your car. That means, you'll be able to get financing, with good credit, right there on the spot. Two auctions on Feb. 26 featured cars from '86 up to '99. Select from CHEVY, CHRYSLER, DODGE, FORD, INFINITI, LEXUS, MAZDA, MERCURY, TOYOTA and more. If it has been repossessed, you can buy it here for less. (Price variations based on mileage and condition of car, of course.) Check website or call 800/698-4623 for locations and times for auctions. *CK (*Cashier , Bank Guarantee), *MC, V, D*

★★★★ Vehicles-in-Motion 972/242-BIKE

1000 W Crosby, Suite 100 *Mon-Fri 9-6*
Carrollton, TX 75006 *www.v-i-m.com*

Rev up the motors, grab a helmet and head for the wide open roads of ... Carrollton. At the Vehicles-in-Motion auctions, you can bid on all types of motorcycles, all-terrain vehicles and watercraft. Find cruising bikes such as NIGHTHAWKS, REBELS, VIRAGOS and VULCANS. Touring bikes include GOLDWINGS, VALKYRIES and VOYAGERS. Trip the bike's fantastic and find sport bikes, dirt bikes, ATV's, snowmobiles, golf carts and more. There's a $35 fee to gain admittance, plus a $300 deposit (refundable) for non-dealers, which allows you to bid. The $35 and the $300 is credited towards your purchase. If you do not buy, you lose the $35 but not the $300. Consignments are taken until noon on Tuesday the week of the auction. Public inspection is from 3-6 on the Thursday before the auction. Look for sales in the classifieds under "Motorcycles" six times a year. *CK (Traveler's, Cashier's, Bank Guarantee)*

China & Crystal

★★★ China Chasers — 972/660-4760

4613 Chalk Court — *24 Hours Online*
Grand Prairie, TX 75052 — *www.swchinasilver.com*

Did the movers drop the box with Grandma's china, leaving you with a broken piece or two? Then let China Chases chase down a replacement. To get the ball rolling, e-mail them with the specifics of what you are looking for or visit their website. They are also wizards at locating discontinued patterns. They buy and sell crystal and silver, too, so if your glass-conscious, this is a place to set on speed dial. If you're worried about the prices, they are quick to tell you, "They price to sell, not retire!" *CK, MC, V, AE*

★★★★ China Teacup, The — 254/876-3453

509 Texas Ave. — *Mon-Sat 10-5:30*
Mart, TX 76664 — *www.chinateacup.com*

The China Teacup buys leftovers from store warehouses and fills in the blanks with estate items. Don't dismiss this as a way to bypass paying retail for Grandmother's exquisite old china. Since moving to Mart (near Waco), this teacup has changed hands from mother to daughter. Do you need one more piece to complete your favorite LENOX pattern? Or ANSYLEY, CASTLETON, DANSK, DENBY, FIESTA, FLINTRIDGE/GORHAM, FRANCISCAN, JOHNSON BROTHERS, LENOX, METLOX, MIKASA, MITON, NANCY CALHOUN, NIKKO, NORITAKE, ONEIDA, OXFORD, PICKARD, ROSENTHAL, ROYAL DOULTON, ROYAL WORCHESTER, SPODE, SYRACUSE, VILLEROY & BOCH or WEDGWOOD? Finding pieces of silver, discontinued china or pottery patterns is this store's cup of tea. Pricing them nicely is another sugar cube. Not only do they fill your china cabinet, they will also give you a fair price for pieces from your own heirloom collection. *CK, MC, V, D, MO*

✔ Dallas Sample Sale

214/749-5491

2200 Stemmons Freeway
Dallas Market Hall
Dallas, TX 75207

Fri Noon-6; Sat 10-6; Sun Noon-5
www.dallasmarketcenter.com

When the doors to Market Hall open in November for this year's Dallas Sample Sale, run with checkbook in hand and watch what develops. Wholesale showrooms sell their samples of gifts, apparel, home decorative accessories, priced at wholesale or less and who wouldn't consider them a Glass Act. It's music to our ears and a boon to our budget. Watch newspapers for sale notices and contact Dallas Market Hall for information. Enjoy the same wholesale prices or less on men's, women's and children's clothing and accessories, picture frames, collectibles, figurines, framed art, luggage, shoes, jewelry, toys, lamps, books and much more. As if low prices wasn't enough of a reason to go, proceeds of the admission charge of $5 for adults benefits charitable causes. Children under 12 enter free. Pay the admission price once and you can shop all three days. *Credit Varies By Vendor*

★★★★★ Dishes from the Past

817/737-6390

3701 Lovell Ave.
Fort Worth, TX 76107

Mon-Sat 10-5
www.dishesfromthepast.com

No more excuses for not setting the perfect holiday table, or any occasion's table, for that matter. The owners of Dishes from the Past, Jennifer Marcell and Ida May Fleet, have a 6,000-square-foot showroom that may be the solution to your blue plate specials. If your gravy boat is no longer sea-worthy, call them, you'll lock horns with the gravy train. Each member of the staff works with the inventory, so they are knowledgeable and know what's in stock. If they don't have the piece you are missing, they can put you into the database and notify you when it comes in. Recycle those wedding dishes from your ex-mother-in-law. They buy and sell sets or partial sets of china, but they must be in good condition. They offer a 30-day return policy on anything if you're not satisfied. Everything is sold by the piece in more than 1,400 patterns. What a high-glass establishment. *CK, MC, V, D, AE, PL, PQ*

★★★★★ Fitz & Floyd

972/458-1471

4240 Alpha
Dallas, TX 75244

Mon-Sat 10-6; Sun Noon-6
www.fitzandfloyd.com

Save as much as 60 percent off retail on everything from the fanciful manufacturer FITZ & FLOYD. With savings like this it's no wonder shoppers line up to save some cash on their distinctive fine china and home decorative gifts. You'll find closeouts, discontinued lines, rejects, last year's models, one-of-a-kinds–whatever they can't sell through their regular retail channels winds up here at substantial savings. Seasonal merchandise is one of their fortes. Find specialty items for Mother's Day, Easter, Halloween, Thanksgiving and more. They continually add new merchandise from their manufacturing division and offer select closeouts from other manufacturers to broaden the scope. Moving at the end of May, so check directory assistance so you don't throw a fitz if you don't find them at the above location. *CK, MC, V*

★★★★ House of 1776 — 972/226-1776

610 E. Highway 80 — *Mon-Sat 10-6*
Sunnyvale, TX 75182 — *www.houseof1776.com*

Here you can have your cake and eat it, too. Normally they are just a mail-order resource to save on china and crystal, but an occasional windfall happens in their parking lot. An unprecedented clearance sale was held during the pre-holiday season with additional discounts saving you 40-60 percent. Load up on brands such as FIESTA, JOHNSON BROS., LENOX, LUNT, MIKASA, NORITAKE, ONEIDA, REED & BARTON, ROYAL DOULTON, TOWLE, VILLEROY & BOCH, WALLACE, WATERFORD and WEDGWOOD. Is there anything left on your plate? With a hearty high-ho silver–and china and crystal, take Highway 80 to Sunnyvale, exit Collins Road and stay on the service road. You will arrive without the silver spoon in your mouth after the long drive, but that's what they want to sell you...and more. Normally, without special sales, you'll be saving 20-30 percent. Not bad, considering the alternative is paying full price. *CK, MC, V, AE, D, MO*

★★★ Mikasa Factory Store — 972/881-0019

6100 Ave. K, Suite 100 — *Mon-Wed 10-6; Thu-Sat 10-9; Sun Noon-6*
Plano, TX 75074 — *www.mikasa.com*

Every time we checked out a new MIKASA outlet location, they had our pattern in the window! How could we resist? We always were a sucker for a discount. The same beautiful patterns you see in the department stores can be found at MIKASA outlets at savings of 30 percent and more. This manufacturer's outlet expresses the Orient's attention to beauty and detail. Choose from dinnerware, stemware, flatware, giftware, housewares, crystal serving pieces and frames. Enjoy the warm colors of their Garden Harvest line of dinnerware. It is microwave and dishwasher safe and dozens of pieces were available in this pattern. Serve your drinks in one of the 13 flutes, goblets and glasses in the Flame d'Amore line. These are among the most popular lines, but many others are available. Check directory assistance for the outlet nearest you; then call for a price quote. Authorized returns accepted for exchange, refund or credit. Other area outlets include: Tanger Outlet Center, 301 Tanger Drive, Terrell, 972/524-0066; Prime Outlets, 104 I-35, Hillsboro, 254/582-7453; Grapevine Mills, 3000 Grapevine Mills Parkway, Grapevine, 972/539-5363; Prime Outlets, 4321 I-35, Gainesville, 940/665-3064; Fort Worth Outlet Square, 100 Throckmorton St., Fort Worth, 817/335-1533; and 13710 Dallas Parkway, Suite C, Dallas, 972/385-6183. *CK, MC, V, AE, D, MO*

★★★ Neha's China and Crystal — 972/783-9151

521 W. Campbell, #300 — *Mon-Fri 10-6:30; Sat 10-6*
Richardson, TX 75080

Neha's China and Crystal serves up the savings on china and crystal on a silver platter, and then sells you the platter, too. All this and discounts of 20 - 50 percent. For more savings, check out the back room of the store. If you're planning a big dinner party and want to serve it on name-brand china, crystal and silver, this is the way to go. They also handle bridal registries and special orders. Phone orders welcome–just call with the item and pattern. The china, glassware, flatware and giftware come in all the major brands including MIKASA, NORITAKE, ONEIDA, ROYAL DOULTON, WEDGWOOD and dozens more. Cheers! *CK, MC, V, AE, D, MO*

★★★★★ Oneida Factory Store — 254/582-7449

I-35 South (Exit 368) — *Mon-Sat 10-8; Sun 11-6*
Southwest Outlet Center — *www.oneida.com*
Hillsboro, TX 76645

Oh me, Oneida. Their factory outlet stores can beat department store prices by 25 - 75 percent on the very same patterns you've admired from afar. They feature last season's merchandise, discontinued lines and some seconds in silverware, flatware and crystal. And while we were giving them the hungry eye, we observed that everything in the store was 50 percent off their already discounted prices. Now, put that on your shopping list when you're ready to entertain for the holidays. ONEIDA outlet prices can be a lifesaver for budget-minded hostesses or bridal-gift-giving guests. The outlet centers are only for buying full sets, not individual place settings. Mail order is available, too. Other Oneida outlets in Texas are at the Conroe Outlet Center, 409/756-1889 and the Tanger Factory Outlet Center in San Marcos, 512-353-4159. If you're thinking we missed the Denton Factory Store location, we didn't. Sorry to say, they closed. *CK, MC, V, PQ*

★★★★★ Oriental Outlet — 214/638-8382

2250 Monitor — *Mon-Fri 10-6*
Dallas, TX 75207

The Oriental Outlet provides the best prices by buying direct from China. Their 20,000-square-foot showroom and warehouse is filled with great deals on authentic Chinese crafts and gift items of all sorts. They specialize in custom-made lamps, which you are sure to love. Cloisonné, silk screens, figurines, antique porcelain, jade, furniture, woodcraft and more are all available to be shipped nationwide. Did I miss anything? Oh yes, you can save a fortune, Cookie, on both hand-carved and painted items. Some of the items are manufactured here by the owners, which means even more savings. Visit the Far East right in your own back yard. The Oriental Outlet is the place to purchase that coveted prize to spruce up your home decor. *CK, MC, V, AE, D*

★★★★ Southwest Gold & Silver Exchange — 817/735-1451

5722 Locke Ave. — *Mon-Fri 10-6:30; Sat 10-2*
Fort Worth, TX 76107

Don't expect to find silver saddles at the Southwest Gold and Silver Exchange. What you can look for is discount prices on such sterling names as GORHAM, LUNT, REED & BARTON, TOWLE and WALLACE, to name just a few. Pieces from previous estates are available if you only need one or two items to complete a set. For the coin collector, buy and sell rare coins, gold and silver, (American and foreign). Silver baby gifts, hollow-ware, silverplate–the list goes on. They will also do appraisals. And, for extra incentive, they offer a 90-day layaway program. It's like uncovering a silver lining. One look and you'll be hooked on his excellent prices. Ching-aling. *CK, MC, V, AE*

Computers & Online Services

★★★★ Altex Electronics — 972/267-8882

3215 Belmeade — *Mon-Fri 8-6:30; Sat 9-5*
Carrollton, TX 75006 — *www.altex.com*

If you were not born with a silver disc in your mouth, here's the place to part ways with your frugal heritage. Parts, parts and more parts is the part we liked best about this place, especially for electronic buffs who like to rough it! Capacitors, transistors, diodes, connectors, wire and cable assemblies, hardware, peripherals and accessories-find them all here. Those who were blessed with right-brain overload can probably assemble their own computers without a hitch. Or let them custom-design a system for your requirements. There is a $10 minimum order and any order under $99 is assessed a $3 handling charge. There are six locations in Texas, two in San Antonio, one each in Austin, Corpus Christi, Dallas and Houston. *CK, MC, V, AE, D*

✧✧✧✧✧ CCLIK- CCLIK — 972/934-2545

3961 Belt Line Rd. — *Classes available seven days a week*
Addison, TX 75001 — *www.cclik.com*

Networking and computer skills lay at the very heart of communication in the 21st century. E-commerce is the future. And if your current technical skills and knowledge won't cut it , take control of your lifetime earnings now. Get your foot in the door and be up to speed. Be in demand in the marketplace and command a top position. Like a diamond, get "certified" for instant credibility, respect, self-confidence; get better assignments and job options and earn more money. This is the age of the computer, and will continue to be so for the next millennium. That doesn't mean that everyone is up and racing down the kilobyte highway. If you're still in the slow lane, jump on board the CCLIK train. At CCLIK you can receive the training you need in A+, CCNA, LINUX, MICROSOFT MCSE and NOVELL'S CNE5. In other words, learn whatever you need to know about computers, from the guts out, in an attractive classroom setting with hands-on, attentive teachers. CCLIK provides "Quality, Value and Results." Networking is key for today's and tomorrow's business. The network is like the "veins and arteries of any organization, enabling vital information to flow where it's needed." (Internet, e-commerce, intranets, business partners, customers, employees.) Why choose CCLIK? Their program offers what you need to know to pass all tests the first time (97 percent do!) and the skills to excel in the field (including unlimited hands on "practice 'til experienced" labs). The instructor-led activities are usually evening or evenings/weekends. In addition to classroom training, CCLIK offers Test Readiness Sessions, Tutorials, Multimedia Computer Based Training and Simulated Practice Tests. CCLIK instructors work in the field, and are themselves certified. Interested? Call 972/934-2545 to schedule a free meeting with a CCLIK Career Consultant! Life is a series of choices. CCLIK ("Computer Certification Learning Institute for Knowledge") is a good one! *MC, V, AE Financing*

★★★★ Clone Computer Corp. 972/934-2200

14839 Inwood Rd. *Office Mon-Fri 9-6; Showroom Mon-Sat 10-5*
Addison, TX 75244-3241 *www.clonecomputer.com*

Wanna be a clonehead? Then shop straight from the factory for these clones that have all the right stuff. Pick up a variety of computer components and accessories without paying for a huge advertising schedule and wall-to-wall marble floors. Basic network cards and hubs were as low as $50. Tell them what you want and watch them put together a system that will knock you over with features but won't bowl you over with prices. Warranties on computer equipment were for one year with additional five-year options. All service is done on the premises. Don't be a bone-head, clone it. *CK, MC, V, AE*

★★★★★ CompUSA 972/233-4510

15250 Dallas Parkway *Mon-Sat 9-9; Sun 11-6*
Dallas, TX 75248 *www.compusa.com*

You'll have to stop by one of their stores to pick up a catalog (they offer several) or call for a price quote, but it may be well worth it. You can save 30-80 percent from this giant, who has its fingers in a web of more than 5,000 computer-related products. It's certainly worth going out of your way for. Desktop, laptop, whatever you're topping off, the prices bottom out here. And their technical assistance can be invaluable when you hit a glitch. Save your budget and retrieve your sanity with discounts galore. There are more options here than from anyone else in the USA, or on the planet for that matter, for computer training and repair. They also offer installation and on-site repair now, making them even more compelling. Check the "Ask PC Modem" archives on their website if you have computer questions. Check directory for the outlet nearest you. There are 29 in Texas with 11 in the Metroplex. *CK, MC, V, AE, D, CompUSA*

★★★ Computek Systems — 214/503-6500

10703 Plano Rd., Suite 300 — *Mon-Fri 9-6:30; Sat 11-4*
Dallas, TX 75238 — *www.zdsparts.com*

Consign your computer and equipment and see what documents materialize. About ½ mile off of I-635 at the Plano/Miller intersection, you can compute your savings on both new and pre-owned computers and peripherals at this full-service computer source. Accentuate the positives and pay attention to the accents here as they are all international. Budget-conscious computer users can take the byte out of paying mega prices. A real find–this ZENITH service center sometimes has nothing but computer antiques and sometimes you can find the latest technology...just visit Chris and inquire as to his current stock. It's all consignment, so the early bird catches the hard drive. A 60-day guarantee is the a la mode atop the APPLE pie. *CK, MC, V, AE, D*

★★★★ Computer Recycle Center — 817/282-1622

303 E. Pipeline Rd. — *Mon-Sat 9-6*
Bedford, TX 76022 — *www.recycles.com*

Your budget will beg you for more once you've shopped here. Selling both new and refurbished computers (PENTIUM 300s were going for peanuts) and that would be a welcome relief in any home, office or academic environment. Don't want to buy new? Why not consider a computer upgrade or a fix-up of the old one? No prices were listed on the website except for monitors–SVGA monitors from $119.95–which is not that great compared with Resource Concepts, for example. A rule of thumb, according to their resident geek: Pentium 100 systems, including monitor, about $195. P133s, $350. P166s, $400. Their printer prices were in the process of being updated but they had some dot matrix models starting at $49.95; lasers were not showing any prices but they did have some used HEWLETT-PACKARD LaserJet's I, II, III & III D in stock along with an ALPS LSX 1600, TOSHIBA PAGE LASER 12 and a MITSUBISHI G 650-10 Thermal. No doubt about it–you get more action by shopping the recycled route. So boot up. Knowledgeable and personable staff do make it easier to swallow when the hard drive goes down. *CK, MC, V, AE, D*

★★★★★ Computer's Worth

972/487-8922
120 Lavon Drive | *Tue-Fri 10-6*
Garland, TX 75240 | *www.computersworth.com*

Hello surplus. Hello liquidations. Hello deals on software, hardware and accessories. Your discount CD-ROM Source and some of the best applications by BORLAND, COREL, LOTUS and others. Looking to get your ACT 4.0 OEM together? It was $85. Or what about ADOBE PHOTO DELUXE 2.0 for $35? Then again, keep up-to-the-minute with the Ultimate Desktop Collection for WINDOWS, which includes 32-Bit Enhancement, Screensavers, Icons, Cursors, Fonts and Utilities and designed for Windows '95, '98 and NT. Also, get with the program with children's educational games, publishing, application tools, custom systems, upgrades and hardware repair. "The hottest titles at the lowest prices–from 30-70 percent off" is how this company grows. We checked Windows 2000, their price was $140. Pretty good as some places are offering it for $300. For the largest outdoor computer sale in the nation, access their sale information at www.sidewalksale.com (updated weekly). Also seen at "First Saturday" from midnight Friday 'til noon Saturday on the first Saturday of every month. (See First Saturday) *CK, MC, V, D, AE*

★★★ Computize

972/437-3100
1365 Glenville Dr. | *Mon-Fri 8:30-5:30; Sat 9-5*
Richardson, TX 75081 | *www.computize.com*

Since 1983, Computize has been on top of the computer competition. We found the prices on printers, plotters, scanners, toner cartridges, and, oh, yes, computers to be right in line with most discounters. Name brands were front and center–NEC, APPLE, HEWLETT-PACKARD and others, but what impressed us was the competency of our salesperson–he didn't bat any eye or run for a manual or supervisor after each question. And no high-pressure sales tactics, either. They seem geared mostly toward corporate accounts, but don't let that scare you. Sales are one-on-one. There is no showroom, but they're glad to help you fight the computer wars. They have consolidated all their offices at this location, but their online site offers a wide selection of products. *CK, Financing*

★★★★ Cyber Exchange

972/316-3030
360 East FM 3040, Suite 850 | *Mon-Sat 10-9; Sat Noon-5*
Lewisville, TX 75017 | *www.cyberexchangedfw.com*

Nestled between eyeglasses and a soccer shop, Cyber Exchange will help you see clearly to kick high prices goodbye. They're one slick franchise. They take used software (like games you've played to death, educational titles that are no longer teaching you and productivity applications that are collecting dust) at a percentage of the original purchase price. Trading in your software generates credit that you can then use toward the purchase of any of the new and recycled software titles they carry. Hundreds of titles, both new and recycled for the PC and MAC, including hard-to-find software for 386s, 486s and Apple's. All software is virus-checked and guaranteed against defective media. They also custom-build open architecture systems as well as perform upgrades and repairs. Current specials on equipment included new 19-inch monitors for $369, and installation of Windows '95 for $79, Windows '98 for $99.99. Businesses can lease equipment through their Business Leasing Program. *CK, MC, V*

★ Dal-Tex Computers — 972/312-8181

1717 Spring Creek — *Mon-Wed 10-8; Thu-Sat 10-9; Sun Noon-6*
Plano, TX 75074 — *http://members.aol.com/daltexcom*

Let these guys call the shots. They promise to save you 10-50 percent on all your computer needs. Fax them your configurations and specifications, and check the fax back. Buy used computers from as low as $600 without monitors. On the day we called they had a used Pentium processor 586/133 with 16m of ram for $199. For an investment of about $500, you can get a decent and serviceable computer, keyboard, and mouse. For $897, you can get a brand new notebook with DVD and wireless keyboard. They aren't hi-tech when it comes to updating their website, and claim they are just too busy making sales to bother. Oh brother! And they're in the computer business? *CK, MC, D*

★★★★ Dell Factory Outlet — 512/728-5656

8801 Research Blvd. — *Mon-Sat 10-6*
Austin, TX 78758 — *www.dell.com/outlet*

DELL COMPUTER is a chip off the old block. Since they've recently retrenched and returned to being primarily a mail-order business, shoppers from around the world can take advantage of their outlet store. Selling factory-reconditioned computers with a 3-year limited warranty, the outlet offers a variety of products at all levels of skill and budgets. The Dell Factory Outlet has great deals on their website. It's located at www.dell.com. All you have to do is click on "Refurbished Systems" to enter their factory store. Current technology and 24-hour toll free hardware technical support is part of the package. They're proud, too, that they ship refurbished products in new boxes (I guess to impress the UPS man). All products have been reconditioned, tested, re-tested and guaranteed. Check back often on their website for outlet specials. They seldom have anything below a P266, and those start at around $1,300 without monitor. Call for specials that change daily. *CK, MC, V, D*

★★★ Doctor PC 972/235-3772

209 W. Main Street *Mon-Fri 9-6; Sat 10-6*
Richardson, TX 75081

Have a slipped disc? How about a soft hard-drive? Well, drive to Belt Line (Main Street in Richardson), and take your problem to an appropriate healer. When our laptop was giving us a major pain, this doctor was our prescription to a full recovery. He can fix almost any computer problem, plus set you up with a host of new or used computers and accessories. They can build a system to your specs or sell you a pre-configured system for a dynamite price. Used systems, too. Brand names like APPOINT, EXPERVISION, LANTASTIC, MICROSOFT, MICROTEK, SOUND BLASTER and others too numerous to name. Add more memory or upgrade your computer's CPU to a newer, faster chip starting at under $200, depending on which old model is being changed. Call the doctor for your computer prescription today and worry about an aspirin in the morning. *CK, MC, V, AE (Extra 3 percent for AE)*

★★★★★ Electronic Discount Sales 817/548-1992

908 E. Pioneer Parkway *Mon-Sat 10-7*
Arlington, TX 76010 *www.discountsales.com*

When it comes to laptops, and we're not talking purring kittens, the answer is perfectly clear, my dear. For laptops, and other computer configurations, monitors, parts, memory and all the components to build your own, this computer outlet store has it made in the shade. Grab your shades and read the following: 14-inch color monitors, $29 and up; COMPAQ PENTIUM II, 35 MHz computers as low as $600; keyboards, $19.99. If you want a good deal, even if a part is trashed, this is the place to start from the bottom and work your way to the top. It's also the home of the "100 percent off sale". (Inquire within.) They also buy, sell and trade all computers and parts. Visit also in Irving at 4070 N. Belt Line Rd., 972/570-7393. *CK, MC, V, AE, D*

Computers & Online Services

★★ Electronics Boutique
972/783-6416

501 S. Plano Rd. *Mon-Sat 10-9; Sun Noon-6*
Richardson, TX 75081 *www.ebworld.com*

Just software and game cartridges, but for most of us, that's plenty. Located inside Richardson Square Mall, there were enough high-tech games to keep even a 14-year-old busy for...at least a few days. You'll also find accessories for better gaming. joy sticks, sound cards, Game Shark, even a faster mouse can be had from this collection. For a mall store, the prices are not too bad. Check out the sale bin for the best bargains. Check your directory for other area mall locations. *MC, V, AE, D*

★★★★★ Felix-Holland Computer Auction
214/350-1391

2551 Lombardy, #100 *Check Newspaper for Sale Dates*
Dallas, TX 75220 *www.netauction.com*

Check it out. Wrap it up. You'll need your driver's license and social security number or $500 cash deposit to register, as this company means business. You can expect to save 35-75 percent off superstore pricing, and in this high-tech day and age, that's a real byte. Liquidators of computer products for national distributors and mail-order companies, their inventory includes customer returns, overstocks, discontinued, freight-damaged and capital asset acquisitions. Somehow, they acquire the latest in cutting edge technology in desktops, notebooks, printers, peripherals, networking product and software, but if you're a novice, their auctions are probably not for you. The auctions are held once a month, usually on Saturday, but they're thinking about having one on Tuesday, too. Preliminary inventory lists are published the week before the auction; pre-auction purchases are available on a limited basis, check their site for details. Their website is not one of the easiest sites as they cater to more experienced end-users. So take time to get your bids in order and buy, buy, buy! *CK, MC, V, D, AE*

★★★★★ First Saturday

Ross Ave. & N. Central Expwy. *Midnight 'til Everyone Leaves*
Dallas, TX 75201

On the First Saturday of every month, the seven acres of parking lots on Ross Ave., just west of Central Expressway, become a hybrid traders' bazaar full of hams and cyber-geeks. This started almost 30 years ago under several bridges of North Central Expressway by ham radio operators. Now, almost 25 vendors show up on a regular basis at two distinct locations, and dozens more converge for a garage sale-like atmosphere for electronics, computer and radio supplies. On the north lot, you'll find a garage sale meltdown of bytes and pieces run by former State Senator John Leedom, who owns the Wholesale Electronics Building. There, you can expect more spartan surroundings (like no electricity) but just as much enthusiasm. Being first on First Saturday is no idle recommendation. Shoppers start the process in the wee hours of the morning just to get a jump on the competition. The south lot is an interesting mix, and might be the place to begin your computer search. Vendors set up at midnight, and many are gone by 9 A.M. Try to get there around 6 or 7 A.M. A vendor table on the south side costs $50 and $15 on the north side, and you will need a resale certificate to sell. All you need to buy, though, is money. Bring cash just to be sure, but keep it tucked inside your shoe. *Credit varies with vendor.*

★★★★★ Fischer Micro — 972/881-1171

2202 Lakeview Parkway, suite 102 — *Mon-Fri 9:30-6:30; Sat by Appt.*
Rowlett, TX 75088 — *www.fischermicro.com*

Fischer Micro moved into larger facilities in order to serve you better. Their reputation around town for being the "cheapest as well as the best," has expanded to include Internet and networking services. "We sincerely believe that we offer the best value equation (quality+price=value) in the Metroplex." Well, seeing is believing. These two brothers, Gary and Scott Fisher, are believers in delivering you a lot of bang for your byte by building "clone" computers to customer satisfaction. So for old clones' sake, can you hack it? They also buy large lots of surplus inventory of new or refurbished computer equipment and sell it to you at rock-bottom prices. Check out their website and order online. Saw a 4.3 gig Ultra DMA hard drive for only $169.95. All are sold with a minimum one-year on-site warranty on both parts and labor. Even "refurbs" are sold with a factory warranty. Whether it's motherboards with CPU, drives, components, accessories, or new memory, don't count them out of the picture. Yahoo named their website one of the seven best computer sales sites on the Internet. *CK, MC, V, AE, D*

✧✧✧ FlashNet — 972/299-9399

1812 N. Forest Park Blvd. — *24 Hours Online*
Fort Worth, TX 76102 — *www.flash.net*

Are you ready to deal for Internet and e-mail service? They are, and their service seems to have improved, perhaps due to hardware upgrades. Now serving most major markets, the basic plan is $17.95 per month, and includes 56K analog and 64K ISDN, two e-mail addresses and five megs of web space. Pay the $25 setup fee and get 99 days of free service. Or strike a deal for waving the set-up fee. Of course, the new buzz is all about DSL. Talk on the phone while you are surfing the net. Up to five people can be online at the same time with just one DSL service. The only downside is slower response time. The cost is $49.95 per month, with a $198 one-time charge, plus $14 for installation by SW Bell. Their new "Daytime" plan is only $6.95 per month, plus a $35 set-up fee, and it assumes you only want to surf between 7 A.M. and 5 P.M., which is fine if you only have a computer at work. *CK, MC, V, AE, D*

★★★ Gateway Country Store — 817/788-2979

4900 Oakridge Terrace — *Mon-Sat 10-9; Sun Noon-6*
North Richland Hills, TX 76180 — *www.gateway.com*

How are things down at the farm? Well, see for yourself. This country store has grown into a big city Internet slicker. Complete with tractor seats and wallpaper to welcome the cows when they come home. The Gateway Country Store, based in North Sioux City, SD, has opened more than 200 outlets nationwide since 1996. Gateway is the largest manufacturer and seller of computers-by-mail, building each PC to customer specifications. Hey, that's a novel idea. Bypass the middlemen, such as retailers, and you can make more money while we save more money. At their stores, you'll have a chance to try out each of their models in a showroom complete with Internet access. Because the machines are custom-built, they can't be bought at Gateway stores, but you can place orders at the store or from home, by telephone or through Gateway's website. Their other two Country outposts are in Arlington at 4701 S. Cooper St., 817/557-2192, and 9600 N. Central Expwy. 214/775-0243. *CK, MC, V, AE, D, MO*

★★★ Half Price Computers — 972/250-3332

Coit and Campbell — *Mon-Fri 9-7; Sat 9-6*
Richardson, TX — *www.halfprice.com*

Get rid of all that pent-up frustration shopping for computers with one key stroke. Start by shopping for half-price computers at Half Price Computers. Everything's in a name and everything's half price (or more; or close). All makes and models, refurbished and new and software galore. They were updating their website when we checked, so prices were unannounced (why have a site if your not going to post prices?) Never mind. They still have deals on computers-whether you're buying, renting, or needing service plus all the parts in question. Want to upgrade and exchange yours for something bigger and better? No problem. Just knock on wood and whisper low, "Vito sent me!" The inventory changes everyday, so check often. *CK, MC, V*

★★★★★ Hardin Electronics 817/429-9761

5635 E. Rosedale *Mon-Fri 9:30-5:30; Sat 9-1*
Fort Worth, TX 76112

Looking to reduce the fat in your diet? How about a refurbished big MAC? At Hardin Electronics, you won't have to digest any of the full-priced spreads. Don't look any further on the menu, because they are it for the lowest prices on Macs this side of the Pecos. This location deals in used and refurbished, plus a few games and accessories. If you're looking for new MACINTOSH computers and paraphernalia, and you still refuse to pay retail, you'll have to visit their parent location at I-20 and Green Oaks in Arlington. That's all there is to it. Nobody does it better. Further into other high-tech wizardry, ham-radio buffs converge on the scene. Bargain hunters tune in to Hardin for all kinds of parts and party lines. Professional audio sound systems, too, whether you're buying, selling or trading. *CK, MC, V, AE, D*

✧✧✧ Home & Business Computers 972/234-1228

885 E. Collins Blvd., Suite 103 *Mon-Fri 9-5:30*
Richardson, TX 75081 *www.habc.com*

Keeping up with the Joneses may be tough, but keeping up with the Davises is getting pretty busy, too. With all the PC price wars, they've decided to move their business to service only. Starting February 2000, they will no longer sell PC's. Most of the family has moved on, and even though they were established in 1983, say "Hasta la vista, baby" to anything having to do with sales. It's strictly service with a smile, and they'll install network connections on site, even though they aren't going to be a provider any longer. Upgrades with a chip or two; or they'll special order if not in stock. Customer satisfaction is still their #1 priority. *CK, MC, V, AE, D*

★★★ ICS Computers 972/509-8000

2301 Central Expressway *Mon-Fri 9-6; Sat 10-6*
Plano, TX 75075 *www.icspc.com*

If the chips are down, head to the northwest corner on Central Expressway, between Parker and Park Boulevard in Plano. Here another computer connection awaits. Surge up the super highway and upgrade, repair, order parts or network your office. This is strictly build-to-order computers and upgrades on existing systems, though they'll also make on-site service calls. Jump aboard the DSL or ISBN lines and connect to rapid-fire speed. They not only install, they provide. Computer buffs know enough to know what I'm talking about, even if I don't! From Pentiums to SoundBlasters, you will have a blast at this neighborhood congregation of bits and bytes. They were changing Internet hosts when we checked their site, so we can't say with 100 percent certainty they're up and running. *CK, MC, V, AE, D*

✧✧✧ ImagiNet Communications — 817/516-0040

PO Box 172977 — *Mon-Fri 9-5*
Arlington, TX 76003 — *www.imagin.net*

ImagiNet is a good and bordering great Internet service provider choice for small business accounts. Check this out: With a $75 setup charge and $40/month, you get two dial-up accounts (use only one at a time) with up to 64K ISDN access, 12 e-mail addresses, and a web server with 20 megs of storage using your domain name. It's a small outfit, though, and if you need tech support or have a problem with your bill, you may have to leave a message and wait for a call back. But the wait is usually short and the help is quick to come. They have new 56k FLEX modems capable of the fastest speeds available on the Internet today and their new e-mail SPAM filters can correctly identify and discard 99 percent of all SPAM or unsolicited commercial e-mail (UCE). Imagine that! *CK, MC, V, D, AE*

★★★★★ IMS Computers — 972/416-4000

2741 Belt Line at Marsh — *Mon-Fri 9-6; Sat 10-5*
Carrollton, TX 75006 — *www.imscomp.com*

Steer to this custom computer company that guarantees the lowest price, absolutely. Right on the information highway, they have parts, upgrades, repairs, hard-to-find PC parts, and a 24-hour service turnaround. Start with the hard shell, add name brand parts that are top-of-the-line all at the lowest prices, guaranteed, and it spells IMS. Add software, they'll even design you a web page. Put it all together and you have your own customized computer to meet your online and data needs. Written quotes came promptly as advertised over the fax. Check for the latest pricing and join the others on the road to the 21st century. Other locations in Plano, Dallas and Lewisville. *CK, MC, V, AE, D*

✔ Infomart's Super Saturday 214/746-3365

1950 Stemmons Freeway *Days and Hours Vary*
Dallas, TX 75247 *www.dfwxchange.com*

It's a bird...it's a plane...it's the largest monthly heated and air-conditioned computer show in Texas. It's Super Saturday! If you're selling, you can be a vendor for as little as $35 per table plus power and phone line charges. Thousands of computer users from all over North Texas meet at the Dallas Infomart to swap ideas, questions, hardware and software. The DFW-Xchange Corp. sponsors this forum each month but days varry. User groups include Apple Corps of Dallas, Atari Users of North Texas, DalCOGS–Dallas Computer Oriented Geoscience Society, Dallas Personal Robotics Group, Dallas Small Computer Society–Timex/Sinclair/Amstrad, Dallas TI Home Computer Group–99/4, North Texas PC Users Group, and SCOPE (Society of Computer Owners and PET Enthusiasts). Many vendors set up tables downstairs with everything from old PC juniors to new state-of-the-art systems. Admission is free–but bring cash anyway. For more information, contact the North Texas PC Users Group at 214/746-4699 or Apple Corps of Dallas at Metro 817/355-0797. Payment *Varies By Vendor.*

✧✧✧✧ Lanop Corp. 972/580-8582

2401 Gateway, Suite 103 *By Appt. Only*
Irving, TX 75063-2743 *www.lanop.com*

If you want to beat the cost of NOVELL CNE certification and save up to 50 percent over the costs for Microsoft's MCPS certification, have I got a secret! Go to Lanop, one of the few independent CNE training centers, and get the best hands-on CNE program available. They also offer MCPS (Microsoft) certification. This is the only Lanop campus in Texas. Besides classroom sessions, you'll get exam reviews, individual tutoring, video and computer lab training, and simulated testing at no additional cost. It's the only school that offers the "First-Time Pass Guarantee". If you fail to pass an exam after following their program, they will pay for you to retake it. Convenient evening and weekend classes with unlimited hands-on practice, small instructor-led classes, videos, pre-test quizzes, all manuals and workshops. If you want to move up to a high-tech, higher level position, this is the way to do it. The Lanop way. You'll earn more and your colleagues may even be envious of your newfound respect. *CK, MC, V, AE, D*

Computers & Online Services

★★★★ Micro Center

972/664-8500

13929 N. Central Expwy.
Keystone Plaza
Dallas, TX 75243

Mon-Sat 10-9; Sun Noon-5
www.microcenter.com

Since 1995, Micro Center has opened 15 stores nationwide that average about 45,000 square feet each. Make a weekly stop for a better-than-average selection of technical and computer books (especially since Pro-Tech bookstore went under), PCs, MACs and accessories. Choose from APPLE, COMPAQ, EPSON, HP, IBM, IOMEGA, NEC, POWER-SPEC and NEC for your PC needs. More than 700 product categories and sub-categories and nearly 36,000 products, including more than 6,500 software titles alone. Don't forget them for service, technical or computer furniture needs as well. Plus their knowledgeable sales clerks actually know their stuff. Next to the new Loews Theater at Spring Valley and Central, word of mouse advertising has certainly put them on the map. *CK, MC, V, AE, D, Micro Center, Leasing*

★★ MicroStar Computer

972/380-0811

15902 Midway
Addison, TX 75001

Mon-Fri 9-6; Sat 10-5
www.microstar-computer.com

Now located across the street from the Beauty Control building, expect beautiful deals on PC computers. A recent deal for a Pentium III 500, with 128MG memory, 10.2 gig of hard disk, keyboard, mouse, modem and Windows 98 was $1,199. Leasing programs are also available, which makes sense for almost immediate trade-ups if you're in business and need state-of-the-art computing. Watch for a change in websites as they're moving to www.microstarpc.com in the near future. *CK, MC, V, AE, D, Financing*

★★★★★ NEXT International

972/481-1113

3214 Belt Line Rd., #446
Farmers Branch, TX 75234

Mon-Fri 8:30-7:30; Sat 10-2
www.neqx.com

You've heard of the Terminator, now meet the Configurator! One of the unique features of this mail-order/website company is the Configurator page where you pick your PC components. Start with a basic configuration, then delete or add the features you want. Offering the best names at wholesale prices, pick from a variety of choices in motherboards, hard drives, monitors, printers, video cards and more. Don't forget their repairs and upgrades, or opt for a maintenance contract, and you'll be safe rather than sorry. No on-site service available, but you will get a one-year warranty on parts and a 30-day "no-questions-asked" money-back guarantee. Big names you can count on at this site include INTEL, MICROSOFT, SUPERMICRO and VIEWSONIC. Check their specials, and expect turn-around within six business days. *CK, MC, V, AE, D*

✧✧✧✧✧ OnRamp Technologies — 214/672-RAMP

1950 Stemmons Frwy., Suite 2026 — *24 Hours*
Dallas, TX 75207 — *www.onramp.net*

When you hit this OnRamp, expect to be speeding. Founded by two out-placed Superconducting Super Collider geeks, they were one of the first locally-based Internet service providers (ISPs) in the area. Now they're in several cities and are part of a much larger national business called Verio, Inc. With that kind of money behind them, there's only one way but up. Located in the Dallas Infomart, OnRamp has been one of the most reliable ISP's in the Metroplex. Even though they're NOT the cheapest, dial-up service is $24.95 per month, the time you save by not having busy signals or dropped and slow connections might make the extra few bucks per month worth it. And so does the excellent tech support. They were even named the "Best Regional Provider" by *SmartMoney* magazine, partly because of their "legendary tech support". Since Underground Shopping is about value, not just price, they're a favorite in our book. Check out their service, now available in Dallas, Fort Worth, Austin, Lubbock and Houston. *CK, MC, V, AE*

★★★★ Past & Present Computers — 972/233-6684

4128 Billy Mitchell Drive — *Tue-Fri 9-5; Sat 10-4*
Addison, TX 75244

Where have all the good re-sellers gone? Into the service business, that's where. Past & Present Computers (aka, 911 Mobile Computer Service, 972/233-4911) has thrown in the towel on resale. (Guess they couldn't hack-er!) Nevertheless, they still provide custom-built systems for both business and residential users, plus operate a repair shop at their Billy Mitchell Drive address. When you need to upgrade, they're pros, offering onsite networking upgrades and repair. Give Eric a call so he doesn't remain idle for long. *CK, MC, V, Financing*

✧✧✧✧✧ PC House Call — 972/234-0655

14001 Goldmark Drive, Suite 101 — *Mon-Fri 8-5:30; Sat 10-2*
Dallas, TX 75240 — *www.pc-housecall.com*

What regular doctors gave up years ago, this technician has turned into a business. For troubleshooting, upgrades, networking, training, or a simple tune-up or set up, contact PC House Call. In-home computer support at $79/hour was the lowest we've found. Unless you have a geek wizard living next door, this company is your new next best friend. How many times have you schlepped your TV to the shop only to discover it works fine there? Same with your computer. When your computer goes into a tail spin, settle down knowing these guys make house calls. If they can't fix it on-site, they carry it to their shop. If they can't fix it THERE, you don't pay. Period. Now they take drop-offs during regular business hours. Check out their upgrade prices before you buy elsewhere. *CK, MC, V, AE*

✧✧✧✧✧ Professional EDGE — 214/637-0787

2343 Lone Star Drive — *By Appt. Only*
Dallas, TX 75212 — *www.professionaledge.com*

If you're looking for a goldmine, these are the experts in this sales support, software field. Professional EDGE's mission is to provide superior value, excellent service, unquestionable ethics and focused, individual attention to each of their customers. They are a fast-growing consulting firm that will show you how to make your business ideas go further. Areas that they focus on include application development, contract programming, data conversion, project management and strategic planning. Their other strong point is training. Have their trainers teach you and your entire company the tricks of the trade. They are your Guiding Byte.

★★★★★ Resource Concepts — 972/245-5050

2940 Eisenhower, #130 — *Mon-Sat 9-6*
Carrollton, TX 75007 — *www.outletcomputer.com*

Attention Techno Shoppers...Resource Concepts sells refurbished computers lower than a junkyard dog. So low, they are downright hitting below the belt. They have refurbished thousands of computers in their 153,000-square-foot facility for the past decade and have finally opened their doors to the public. Since many are DELL and COMPAQ factory-refurbished computers, you won't have to worry about a thing. They all come with a 3-year RCI warranty. The inventory is staggering; the prices are, too. Give a look: 17-inch monitors start at $169; a Dell Inspiron 3700 Pentium III 450 notebook for $1,995; Compaq Deskpro PIII450 from $799. Keyboards and mice for $1.50. Add CD ROMS, hard drives, tape drives, speaker...what more do you want? A house like Bill Gates? Don't answer. *CK, MC, V, AE, PQ*

★★ Seabrook Computers — 972/480-0060

12101 Greenville Ave, #110 — *Mon-Fri 9-6; Sat 10-5*
Dallas, TX 75243 — *www.seabrookcomputers.com*

Don't let the high-tech wave of the computer age leave you drowning in misinformation. Grab Seabrook Computers as a lifeline and expect smooth sailing. No clones here. Seabrook likes to wheel and deal with the big boys as an OEM provider of Microsoft, Intel and AMD products. Don't forget to check out their lines from COREL, CREATIVE LABS, EPSON, HEWLETT-PACKARD, NEC, OKIDATA, PANASONIC, and several others. A basic Pentium III 450 with 32 RAMS, 13 GB on hard drive, mouse, keyboard, speakers, Windows '98, sells for $849. At the time of this writing, that's a pretty good deal that could change in a week or two. Most of Seabrook's customers are Fortune 500 companies, so they buy in high volume and can usually pass the savings downlink. Ninety days same as cash on most purchases. Seabrook also excels at upgrading and finding parts for your existing systems. *CK, MC, V, AE (+3 percent for credit)*

★★★★ Software, Etc. 972/727-9695

801 S. Greenville Ave. *Mon-Fri 10-8; Sat 10-5; Sun Noon-5*
Allen, TX 75002 *www.software-etc1.com*

Scroll through their software list online before you head to your local computer store. Or give them a call, they'll check the stock. Just don't confuse this great pre-owned and used computer software and component company with the mall store (are they even around any more?). This is a whole new ball game. Find software like Easy Family Tree, CAD packages, virus scans, games and screen savers for a fraction of their retail cost. Both software and hardware are available on consignment, as well as a selection of video games. New this year is the addition of used paperback books for those technically-challenged needing a step-by-step guide to mastery. One shopper found e-mailing them for a price quote was worth it. They came back with a $7 price on some software that would have cost $35-39 new. Growing pains this past year have justified expansion to 3,500-square-feet with computer bar-coding for faster check-out service. *CK, MC, V, AE, D*

Entertainment

☺ Air Jump Moonwalks 817/453-5867

610 Cretien Point Drive *Mon-Fri 8:30-5:30; By Appt. Only*
Mansfield, TX 76063

Want to have a blast jumping, Jack? This is where it's at. Great for birthdays, company picnics, festivals and all special events, the Air Jump Moonwalk comes in perfect condition (it is all new equipment). Don't worry, be happy. They also set up and deliver for free. *CK*

☺ Anointed Clown Ministry 817/446-6659

Fort Worth, TX *By Appt. Only*

Face painting, sculpture balloons and more with the average cost of $65-$75 an hour is a small price to pay for success. Call for quote. Minimums fees are based on group size and acts to be performed. Call Phyllis Dunk for details. She will return your call to confirm dates or offer additional information generally after 6:30 in the evening. *CK*

☺ Beltline Station 972/399-8008

1503 N. Belt Line Rd. *Mon-Thu 10-11; Fri-Sat 10-Mid; Sun 1-11 P.M.*
Irving, TX 75061

All aboard at the Beltline Station for miniature golf, video games, batting cages, go-carts and more. Hidden behind the Golden Corral, pawn shop and Sonic, you can make an all-day outing of the two 18-hole miniature golf courses, batting cages, arcade, go-carts and snack shop. Birthday parties, for eight kids, includes use of the party room for an hour, invitations, plates, napkins, cups and other paper products, soda, ice cream, 18 holes of golf per guest, 10 game tokens per guest and 20 game tokens for the birthday child. You supply the birthday cake, decorations and guests, they supply the fun for $59.95 (additional children are $3.50 each). For an extra $25 you get all that, plus 10 additional tokens for each child and pizza in the caboose out back ($4.50 per additional kid). Hours vary with the season, so call first. *CK, MC, V*

Birthday Ranch, The
817/790-8587

2701 FM 2738 *By Reservation Only*
Alvarado, TX 76009

Shawn and Beth Gibson do the work while the parents relax! Now that's the way to go. For a unique way for children to celebrate their birthdays, head to the Ranch for pony rides and a petting zoo, birthday cake, hot dogs, games, chips and drinks, face painting, party favors and more. Start riding in March because they are totally outdoors. Cost is $100 for up to 15 kids, but adults are free. Yippee! *CK*

☺ Brass Register, The
972/231-1386

610 James Drive *Mon-Sat 9-5:30*
Richardson, TX 75080

Looking to rent a jukebox for that next '50s sock hop? Look no further. This could be the start of something great. From jitterbugging to the bump, the Macarena to the mamba, if it's a sound machine, this is where to rent it. Between Spring Valley and Belt Line off Central Expressway, whether you're a fan of the Golden Oldies or contemporary rock, both new and antique jukeboxes sit side-by-side with barber chairs and Poles (Czechs welcome here, too). The jukeboxes come with more than 300 records, so if you don't find, "It's all Over," or "The Party's Over," that's fine, the party will be jumping anyway. Slot machines were hands-down winners and the video poker machines got a hands-up on the competition. In fact, next to Be-Bop, their prices are peanuts by comparison. When the sale is made on any one of their antique cash registers, you'll be saving 30 percent and more off retail prices. So why not "Kunkle" down at discount prices and join the top brass. Jukebox rentals are $150, $200 and $250, depending on the model. There are also one-day rentals with pick-up and delivery available. *CK*

☺ Carbon Copies
972/644-6660

9801 Cross Creek Court *By Reservation Only*
Dallas, TX 75243

Have the passion, but not the smashing good looks of a Liz Taylor? Well, at your next gathering, convention, party or store opening, have a Carbon Copy show up. It is usually about $200-$250 an hour depending on what all is involved to hire this celebrity lookalike to come visit. Janie Minick is a seasoned actress, but found that her resemblance to the other Diva was uncanny (the difference, folks, is also in the number of husbands). Everywhere she goes, she is besieged for autographs. It will be hard for you to know for sure. Right down to the voice, the mannerisms, the dress, the diamonds and the cleavage, she's a ringer. Unless you see for yourself, you won't believe your eyes (or hers, either). As a great luncheon or after-dinner speaker, she wins the White Diamonds Award. *CK*

☺ Celebration Station 972/279-7888

4040 Towne Crossing *Mon-Thu Noon-11; Fri-Sat 10-Midnight; Sun 11-1*
Mesquite, TX 75150 *www.celebrationstation.com*

Splish-splash! Kids will love the bumper boats during the summer. For landlubbers, try the batting cages or the go-carts, then top it off with a round of miniature golf to beat the band. They even have laser tag. Wind up your day in the arcade, where you can collect tickets toward prizes. You can play here for one low price–all day, Monday-Thursday, $10.99 for kids under 56 inches tall; $14.99 for taller kids and grownups. Special group rates are available for parties. They also have a party room for groups. When you get tired of playing, grab some pizza, nachos, hotdogs and ice cream to cool off. Exit Town East Boulevard, follow the access road to Towne Crossing, past Restaurant Row to this brightly lit amusement center. *CK, MC, V, D*

☺ Dallas Arboretum, The 214/327-8263

8525 Garland Rd. *Daily 10-5*
Dallas, TX 75218

World renowned for beautiful buds and interesting landscape designs, the Arboretum has more than 60 acres of flowers, gardens and beautiful grounds. We loved the toad fountain and the mist garden. Located on the shores of White Rock Lake, it's a great morning or afternoon outing anytime. The gardens and all facilities are available to be rented for a wedding, reunion or party. Bring your camera and get some incredibly colorful shots. Admission $6 for adults, $3 for children 6-12, free under 6. Seniors 65 and older get a $1 discount. Bring $2 extra for parking. *CK, MC, V, AE, D*

☺ Dallas Museum of Natural History 214/421-3466

3535 Grand Ave. *Mon-Sun 10-5*
Dallas, TX 75210

Always interesting with standing exhibits of dinosaurs and fossils, this is The Lost World, for real. Located inside Fair Park, it's a wonderful day-long expedition with a few hours reserved for frolicking around the Lagoon. Admission $4, adults; $2.50 kids 4-18; free for kids under 4. Free admission from 10-1,

Mondays. Parking is free for all the museums at Fair Park. For group rates and reservations, call 214/823-7644. *CK*

☺ Dallas World Aquarium

214/720-2224

1801 N. Griffin Street — *Daily 10-5*
Dallas, TX 75202 — *www.dwazoo.com*

Join the Marines and sea this World Aquarium, Dallas' other aquarium, located near the West End Marketplace. Vicariously fish the saltwater tanks full of marine life from Australia, the Bahamas, the Philippines and other remote locales. This sea world has beautiful colors and species rarely seen. For the after-5 formal-look, don't miss the black-and-white suited penguins. They're unflappable. Vampire bat, piranha, shark and eel feedings highlight each day. If watching them dine whets your appetite, you can enjoy the "eighteen-O-one" restaurant from 11:30 to 2:30 or the Jungle Café from 11 to 4. Adults $10.95; kids 3-12 and seniors 60 and over $6; and those 2 and under are free. No free parking, but plenty of parking lots and meters. *CK, MC, V, AE, D*

☺ Dallas Zoo

214/670-5656

650 S. R.L. Thornton Freeway — *Daily 9-5*
Dallas, TX 75203 — *www.dallas-zoo.org*

If the traffic on I-35 is a bear or your kids are driving you batty, hop over to the world-class Dallas Zoo to check out the tigers, apes and other assorted finned and furred animals. Founded in 1888, the zoo has been in a growth-spurt of late, adding new primate and tiger habitats. The 25-acre walk/ride through the Wilds of Africa was recently named the Best African Exhibit in the United States by "The Zoo Book: A Guide to America's Best". Make sure to stop in to say hello to Jake, the zoo's baby gorilla. The North Zoo includes birds, reptiles, elephants, giraffes, big cats, wart hogs and more. Thanks to a 67 ½-foot giraffe ambassador standing alongside I-35, the zoo entrance is practically a no-miss proposition. Admission: $6 for adults 12-64; $4 seniors 65 and up; $3 children 3-11; children under 3 and Dallas Zoological Society members are free. Parking: $3 per car, or avoid the hassle and take the DART light rail. It has a stop at the zoo's doorstep and an all-day pass is $2 per person.

☺ Fort Worth Nature Center

817/237-1111

9601 Fossil Ridge — *Tue-Sat 9-5; Sun Noon-5*
Fort Worth, TX

Over by Lake Worth and Eagle Mountain Lake, you can get back to nature at this natural wonder. Roam the woods or take a hike through more than 3,500 acres of prairies, forests, hills and dales. (It can get a little marshy in the spring, so watch where you step!) Experience Texas as it was when the pioneers settled it–just don't look too hard for the Fort Worth skyline. Open year 'round. Admission is FREE though donations are not only accepted but also greatly appreciated. *Free*

☺ Fort Worth Zoo — 817/871-7465

1989 Colonial Parkway — *Daily 10-5*
Fort Worth, TX 76110 — *www.fortworthzoo.com*

The oldest continuous zoo site in the state is wearing its age beautifully. More than 5,000 exotic and native animals call the zoo their home. Enjoy the World of Primates, Asian Falls/Asian Rhino Ridge, Raptor Canyon, Cheetos Cheetahs Exhibit, African Savannah, Komodo dragons, Penguin Island, Meerkat Mounds, Thundering Plains, the James R. Record aquarium, the herpetarium and the Koala Outback. And if you happen to fall in love with an elephant, flamingo or even a warthog while you are there, remember animals are available for adoption. Zoo Parent packages cover the cost of the feeding and care of that animal for a year. Admission is $7 for adults; children 3-12, $4.50; seniors $3; and 2 and under are free. Wednesdays are half-price days for all guests. Parking is $4. Strollers, wagons and motorized carts are available for rental. Wheelchair rental is free with proper identification.

☺ Fun Fest — 972/620-7700

3805 Belt Line Rd. — *Sun-Thu 11 A.M.-Midnight; Fri-Sat 10 A.M.-2 A.M.*
Addison, TX

What a fest for sore eyes! This huge place is full of fun for the entire family! Racing, pool tables, virtual reality games, 30 bowling lanes, darts, laser tag and a huge penny arcade (OK, so it's not pennies anymore). Pizza Hut Express, Ginger's Grill and a full bar make this a fun place for everyone. Their arcade machines use the party card system instead of coins or tokens, everything else is "you pay as you go". No charge at the door, ever. Located behind Joe's Crab Shack, they have several different party plans to choose from for all age groups. They range from $78 up to $148.95. *CK, MC, V, AE, D*

☺ Funny Business Clowns and Characters — 817/265-5696

Fort Worth, TX — *Tue-Fri 9-3*
www.fun-bizz.com

Let's get down to business, funny business. Professional high-energy shows for all occasions are provided by more than 50 costumed characters and theme shows.

Looking for the perfect entertainment for a corporate event, day care, birthday party, grand opening, etc.? Bring on the clowns. If that isn't your cup of tea, why not pony rides, a petting zoo, animal acts, cartoon characters, balloon art/decorations, jugglers, stilt walkers, unicyclists, puppet/magic shows, caricature artists and face painting. Just smile–and let's get on with the show. *CK*

☺ Granada Movie Grill — 214/823-9610

3524 Greenville Ave. — *Call for show times*
Dallas, TX 75206 — *www.granadamoviegrill.com*

It's show time at the Granada! This beautifully restored theater in the heart of lower Greenville opens its doors to grandeur and thrift. A combination cinema and drafthouse, you'll have a grand night for viewing and having fun. Children's matinees in the summer just can't be beat; otherwise, no admittance for them unless accompanied by an adult. Call for daily specials. Originally built in 1946 with murals of Grauman's Chinese Theater, its restoration is part of the ambiance of splendor for the masses. Also look for the second Granada Movie Grill at Prestonwood. Tickets are $6.50 for evening shows, $4.50 for matinees. *MC, V, AE*

★★★ Half Price Tickets (Ticketmaster) — 214/696-4253

Foleys @ Preston Center — *www.ticketmaster.com*
SE corner, Northwest Highway and Preston
Dallas, TX 75225

What do you do with left-over tickets? Sell them for half-price the day of the performance. Head to the lower level of Foley's Customer Service area and check what's available. Call first. Ticketmaster sells off half-price tickets on the day of the performance only. For evening performances, they are open Tue-Sun Noon-3; for matinees, Saturday 10-1 and Sunday 11-1, but you must show up in person. First come, first served on a very limited basis. Call ahead and they'll let you know if anything's available. Roll the dice, you might come up a winner. *C, MC, V, D, Foleys*

✧ Little Gym, The — 214/515-0800

410 Hillside Village — *Hours Vary*
Dallas, TX 75214

Tumble with the best of them. From gymnastics to karate, hundreds of kids are having fun and staying fit at these mini-gyms with what they call "total development programs." Want to jump on the bandwagon and learn to twist and shout as a cheerleader? At this gym, they can teach you all the right moves. Want your child to learn better sports' skills? Call the Little Gym. Ages 4 months to 12 years is ripe for development; call for details. Locations also in Richardson, 317 Dal-Rich Village, 972/644-7333; Plano, 3115 W. Parker, 972/985-4545, Arlington and Fort Worth. *CK, MC, V*

☺ McKinney Avenue Trolley — 214/855-0006

Stops at Hard Rock Café and along McKinney Ave.
Fri-Sat 10 A.M.-Midnight; Sun-Thu 10-10
Dallas, TX — *www.dallassites.com/trolley*

Lunch at the Hard Rock and then go clang, clang, clang on the trolley. Enjoy the breeze and great people-watching as you go. Get off and shop at some of the glorious antique and specialty shops along the track, or just ride, ride, ride. Only $1.50 for the 30-minute round trip; children 2-12, $1; seniors, infants and handicapped, $.50. *C*

☺ NRH$_2$O Family Waterpark — 817/656-6500

9001 Grapevine Hwy. — *Seasonal*
North Richland Hills, TX — *www.nrh2o.com*

Here's a spring, summer and fall idea that's all wet: Take the kids (that's little AND big ones) to the park. The water park, that is. Slip-sliding away is fun in the sun with swimsuits and water all over the place. They have four water slides, a wave pool, volleyball and a great kiddy area. If you live in North Richland Hills, get in for cheap. Normal admission is $12.95 for the big kids (those taller than 54 inches) and $10.95 for the smaller ones. Children 2 and younger are free. The really little ones (under 3) are free. Season passes and seasonal specials make NRH2O an even better value for a full day of fun. Season passes $79.95 (for one); $149.90 (for two); $194.85 (for three); and $229.80 (for four). Groups are $9.95 per person, with bigger price breaks the larger the crowd. *CK, MC, V*

☺ Pines, The — 214/522-6533

3519 Cedar Springs, Suite A — *By Appt. Only*
Dallas, TX 75219

The Pines offers fun and entertainment for the entire family. The camp for the Dallas-based group is on 4,500 acres of rolling hills overlooking Lake Lewisville. This is a premiere party site for anyone living in the DFW area. They sponsor corporate parties, daily horseback rides, kids' birthday parties, a petting zoo, trail rides, old-fashioned barbecues and company picnics. If you are into horseback riding, saddle up at River Riding Stables which offers daily horseback riding tours throughout the lovely countryside. City "sickers" revolt. You'll be glad that you did! *CK, MC, V, AE, D*

☺ SpeedZone — 972/247-7223

11130 Malibu Drive — *Sun-Thu 11-11; Fri-Sat 11A.M.-1A.M.*
Dallas, TX 75229 — *www.speedzone.com*

This place was fun when it was known by a different name, but since it became SpeedZone there's been no stopping the thrills. The bright colors you see to the west of Stemmons at Walnut Hill are the new SpeedZone tracks. Race your heart out throughout the twists and turns, from the slick track to drag racing, then if you still haven't gotten your fill, go inside for Electric Alley video simulators and video games. Then have a bite to eat and play some golf on either of two miniature courses with racing themes. If you haven't been here lately, you haven't been here. Keep a sharp eye out...NASCAR superstars such as Mark Martin have been spotted enjoying the thrills. *CK, MC, V, AE, D*

☺ Tarantula Train, The — 817/251-0066

707 S. Main St. — *By Reservation Only*
Grapevine, TX 76051

"Come and ride a little train that is going down the track!" The beautifully restored Tarantula Train CHOO-CHOOs its way from downtown Grapevine to the Stockyards and back each day. Step into the golden age of steam and ride this rejuvenated remnant of Texas history. Daily round trips depart the 8th Street Station at Noon and return at 1; Sundays 3-4. Adult fare is $11 for a roundtrip, seniors ride for $10 and kids under 12 for $8. Also there is a longer ride from Grapevine to the Stockyards Wed-Sat 10-11:15, returning 2-3:15; Sun 1-2:15, returning 4:45. Cost is $22 for adults, $20 for seniors and children over 12, and $11 for children 2-12. For reservations, call the Grapevine Station. *CK, MC, V, AE, D*

☺ Texas Queen Riverboat — 972/771-0039

I-30 at Dalrock — *Office Hours Mon-Fri 10-5*
Lake Ray Hubbard
Dallas, TX

You can either go jump in the lake–or take a ride on one. The latter is Texas Queen's specialty. Dine on fine food and dance under the stars to the vocal style of Ms. Cali McCord. Or, take the Jazz Cruise, the Blues, Country/

Western, Reggae, South-of-the-Border–whatever turns your rudders can be provided with a band or DJ. Or, to laugh 'til you cry, the Comedy Killers or a murder-mystery play that tickles your fancy. This riverboat is also available for private parties, cruises, personalized murder mysteries, weddings, maybe even an Underground Shopper sail! Cruise on Wednesday, Thursday, Friday or Sunday. Price depends on the particular meal they're serving and the type of entertainment, but usually runs between $38-$54 per person for two- or three-hour cruises. For $2,000 and up they can do an entire wedding party for you. Board at 7 P.M., cast off at 7:30. *CK, MC, V, D*

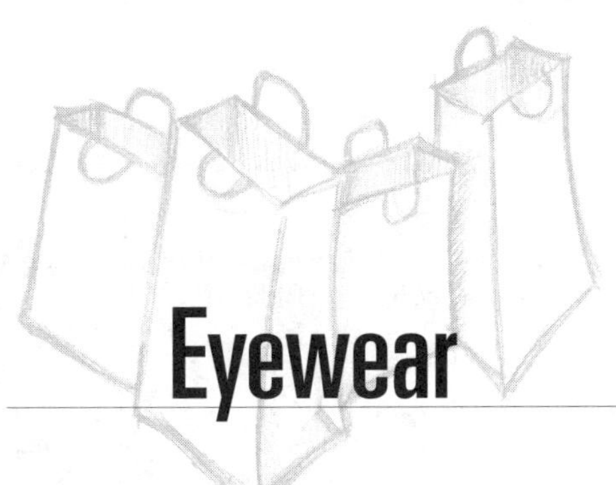

Eyewear

1-800-CONTACTS 800/266-8228

51 West Center *24 Hours Online*
Orem, UT 84057 *www.1800contacts.com*

With more than 1 million contact wearers ordering direct, why don't you? Call, fax, mail in your orders or order on-line and pay less. All major brand of contact lens – including ACUVUE, BIOMEDICS, FOCUS, NEWVUES, OPTIMA and SUREVUE – at up to 50 off. Gas permeable, toric, hard and colored contacts are available. ACUVUE six-packs or OPTIMA FW/SEEQUENCE II are just $79.80 each for four boxes; an additional $69.90 for four more boxes on the same invoice. You'll find NATURAL TOUCH opaque lenses for $79 a pair or $148 for two pair. Give them a call and see what they can do for you. Free shipping with mail orders and internet orders. Buy in quantity for a bigger discount. You receive $10 off orders of more than $140; spend up to $230 for another $20 off; and orders of more that $350 are discounted by $30. No membership fees are assessed to get a cheaper pair of contacts. *MC, V, C*

★★★★ 20/20 Eyecare Center 972/596-2250

4721 W. Park Blvd. *Mon,Wed,Thu 9:30-6; Tue,Fri,Sat 9:30-4*
Plano, TX 75093

Watch for specials if you're looking for the best buys "four" eyes. This one-hour service eyecare center is visible one-half block east of Preston by the United Artists Theater. For more than a decade, Bonnie Noyer has been delivering a clearer picture of the world in glasses by ARMANI, FISHER-PRICE (for kids), GUESS?, JORDACHE, LIZ CLAIBORNE, NINA RICCI and VOGUE to keep your viewpoint in vogue. If you work in the immediate area, you're in luck because all employees are given a 20 percent discount. This 20/20, though, primes their customers by guaranteeing to sell their products at 10 percent lower than anywhere else. During limited special events, you can even get an eye exam plus eye glasses for $79 complete. And talk about frames. There were about 1,000 frames to see; or soft contacts for $29–up to

$179/pair. A current doctor's prescription is required and as luck would have it, they have a doctor standing by–Dr. Haislip. *CK, MC, V*

★ Adair Optical 817/377-3500

3210 Winthrop Ave. *Mon-Fri 9-6; Sat 10-4*
Fort Worth, TX 76116 *www.adairoptical.com*

Eye dare you to find more fashionable frames than at Adair. In fact, seeing is believing since it appears all of their frames are exclusive. Featuring CARTIER, DANIEL DUPONT, LUNOR, MATSUDA, KEISEL STEIN-CORD, SWAROVSKI, YAMAMATO and YONJI to name drop a few, these frames can make a statement on their own. After almost 20 years in business, this Fort Worth eyewear source ought to be able to pick 'em like they see 'em. And the prices are right in line with their exclusivity, from $100-$2,500. Contacts must be ordered so expect a few days' wait. Located near La Madeleine and Pier 1 in the Ridglea Village Shopping Center, all major brands are represented, but don't think of Adair as a discount store. There is a second location in Sundance Square, 310 Main St, 817/870-2221. *CK, MC, V, AE*

★★★★ Contact Lens Center, The 214/739-2020

6921 Snider Plaza *Mon-Fri 9-5; Sat 9-3*
Dallas, TX 75205

Just down the road a bit from SMU, these contact specialists know their stuff. You don't need to matriculate or enter the Ph.D. program to secure the contacts here. This is the place for contacts, especially if you want them (or need them) today. ACUVUE disposables were $89 for four boxes, $45 for two boxes and $23 for one. Most lenses in stock, so no waiting. Gas permeable, colored, soft lenses, etc.–the works. Contact exams were priced at $99. Good prices were consistent at all three locations so you can readily see what a difference the savings make. *CK, MC, V, AE, D*

★ Discount Optical 972/620-9242

2880 LBJ Frwy., Suite 155 *Mon-Fri 9-6; Sat 9-5*
Dallas, TX 75234

At the corner of Josey and LBJ, you will see a wide selection of frames at a discount. Though small, our eyes opened wide when we saw single-vision eye glasses starting at $29.95 and bifocals at $59.95. Contacts, too, but the discount isn't clear–six pairs of ACUVUE disposables for $69. Your prescription must be current (that means 12 months or less since you last visited the eye doctor) or you'll have to be retested by a professional. The sales gal was not very fluent in English so we had to read lips and point in order for her to quote us prices. Maybe a refresher Berlitz course would have helped. *CK*

★★★★★ Experts on Sight — 972/459-0555

360 E. Round Grove Rd. — *Tue-Thu 9-7:30; Fri 9-5:30; Sat 9-3:30*
Lewisville, TX 75067

Our favorite Singing Doc relocated to Lewisville and I'm so happy I can hardly see straight. This is a sight for sore budgets. Frames including eye exam–$49.99. More than 100 years combined experience in the store that sells: ANNE KLEIN, ARMANI, BROOKS BROTHERS, CAZAL, EYETELL, FRATELLI LOZZA, LUXOTTICA, NEOSTYEL (my personal favorite), RALPH LAREN, TOMMY HILLFINGER and more. It's amazing that I can see straight after eyeballing their selection. Bifocals at guaranteed lowest price. The new progressive bifocals, daily wear soft contacts, O.S.I. and disposable contacts are all available here. *CK, MC, V*

★★★★★ Dr. George Orm/Eyesite.com — 972/233-4113

13243 Montfort Drive at LBJ Frwy. — *Mon-Fri 9-6; Sat 9-3*
Dallas, TX 75240 — *www.eyesite.com*

Quality, value, and personal service are the three ingredients that go into each prescription here. But designer frames at the guaranteed lowest prices can't be seen in any other light. Brand names such as ANN KLEIN, ARMANI, BROOKS BROTHERS, CALVIN KLEIN, CHRISTIAN DIOR, DONNA KARAN, EVAN PICONE , GUCCI, GUESS?, LAURA ASHLEY, LIZ CLAIBORNE, MARCO POLO, NBA, OTTO KERN, POLO, RALPH LAREN, SWANK, TURA and a stunning jewel-like collection from Germany, NEO-STYLE (worn by the Queen ... and now worn by the Diva). If it's good enough for Liz Taylor, Oprah, Stallone, Madonna and Elvis, why not? RAY-BANS worn by Tommy Lee Jones, Will Smith, and Nicolas Cage were eyed and ... well, my son couldn't live without them. Soft contacts were $99 for exam and two pair Tinted disposables were $34.50 for a box of six. Clear disposables were $19 a box of six. Exam and six pair of extended wear were $139 complete. Laser vision correction surgery available. Dr. Orm performs the free screening test to see if you're a candidate. He did mine and now I'm seeing fine ... without my glasses. One-hour service on glasses and contact lenses and the lowest price equals the best value in the Metroplex. *CK, MC, V, Third Party Insurance Accepted*

★★★★★ Fashion Discount Optical 972/416-8200

1912 E. Belt Line Rd. *Mon-Fri 9-6:30; Sat 10-4*
Carrollton, TX 75006

Seeing is believing. This optical outfitter sells most any name-brand optical frames without getting framed. Expect to lens me an ear. Hear this. They are all 50 percent off retail. Typical price ranges for most frames are $49 and up but average around $89. Eye see ARMANI, CALVIN KLEIN, CHAPS, ELLE, ESPIRIT, JESSICA McCLINTOCK, LAUREN HUTTON, NAUTICA and POLO, just to name a few. After more than 25 years in the optical business, their experience and buying power net a very clear picture. Also look for a second location at 3430 Oak Lawn Ave. (at the corner of Lemmon; 214/526-6006). *CK, MC, V, AE, D, PQ*

★★ LensCrafters 972/991-9940

13331 Preston Rd. *Mon-Sat 10-9; Sun Noon-6*
Valley View Center *www.lenscrafters.com*
Dallas, TX 75240

These crafty folks can take your single-lens prescription and turn out some great looking glasses in about an hour. Some of the name-brand frames they carry are exclusive to them; others are not, and include such eye-openers as ANN KLEIN, ARMANI, BROOKS BROTHERS, LUXOTICCA, MODO, RAY-BAN, SAKI and YSL. Designer sunglasses from GUESS, PERSOL and SERENGETTI and others are carried here, too. Don't expect to see cheaply, though. Progressive lenses started at $185 and frames were as low as $49.95, but the only way you're going to save is to find the coupons in *The Dallas Morning News*, for example (they also accept competitor's coupons), or on their website. Be sure to check in at least 90 minutes before they close to ensure same-day delivery. Check the directory for other locations. *CK, MC, V, AE, D*

★★★★★ Luck Optical 817/738-3191

7108 Camp Bowie Blvd. *Mon-Fri 9:30-6:30; Sat 8:30-5:30*
Fort Worth, TX 76116 *www.luckoptical.com*

With more than 60 years of quality, fast service, low prices and guaranteed satisfaction, this optical clinic certainly doesn't rely on luck. They earned their stars the old-fashioned way–one year and one patient at a time. Since their humble beginnings in downtown Fort Worth on Houston Street, Dr. L.H. Luck originated the "glasses in an hour" concept in 1938 when he added an in-house lab to his practice. Luck Optical prides themselves on offering the best selection (thousands of frames in stock), complete eye exams using the latest technology and, most of all, value. Their "price beater guarantee" promises to beat the competitors prices by 10 percent as long as it's comparing eyeglasses to eyeglasses (it also applies to exams and contact lenses). Exams for kids are only $33 (age 12 and under) and adults, $38. No membership fees charged for their low-price contact lenses. No appointment necessary because there are six doctors on staff. *CK, MC, V, D, AE*

★★★ Lux Eyewear for Less — 972/686-0595

1020 W. Centerville Rd. — *Mon-Fri 9-6; Sat 9-5*
Garland, TX 75041

Formerly Eyeway for Less, now it's the Lux of the Irish. See clearly with single vision glasses starting at $44.95 for two pairs of glasses or two pairs of flat bifocals for $44.95 from their SmartBuy frames. Now, smarty pants, what if you want those no-line models? Two pairs of no-line bifocals, with clear plastic lenses, were $102.95. A pair, a spare and all frames from their SmartBuy selection, this is your lucky day! Eye see. You're cheap. So here's the place to act on your genetic disposition. Check directory for the location nearest you. Glasses are ready in five working days (or sooner). Bring in your current prescription and you'll be seeing through rose-colored glasses in no time. *CK, MC, V*

★ Marx Eye Care/Dr. Jack Marx — 214/324-1100

3302 N. Buckner Blvd., Suite 111 — *Mon-Thurs 9-6; Sat 9-3*
Dallas, TX 75228

As long as you don't suffer from Fatale Vision, you'll be seeing in no time. Just don't expect to see discounted prices. Contacts for $119 for extended wear, plus the $59 exam fee is just the beginning to an above-average selection of frames for men, women and children. Through the Looking Glass lightly, we saw frames by AUTOFLEX, GUCCI, POLO, RAY-BAN to name a few, including those great ultra-thin lenses that weigh practically nothing! Appointments were readily available when we called. If you can get through, you might be able to book an appointment at any one of their six locations in the Metroplex. *CK, MC, V, AE, D*

★★ Optical Clinic — 214/521-5775

4309 N. Central Expwy. — *Mon-Fri 8:30-5:30; Sat 8:30-Noon*
Dallas, TX 75205

You will be able to see multiple locations in the Metroplex since Optical Clinic has been one of the most visible home-grown eyewear chains for years. The special this year cost $109, which included an exam for contacts, glasses and sunglasses. But they are very precise in this offer. One pair of regular daily-wear clear-view contact lenses, clear single-vision glasses with light weight Herculite lenses up to a certain correction, frames from a certain collection, same with the non-prescription sunglasses, 30-day unlimited checkups and an eye exam for contact lenses or glasses. Hurry. This offer may not be in effect forever. So what this all boils down to is this: there may be some folks who probably won't need what they're offering ... so chances are, it might cost you more. You may need bifocals, or you won't like the limited frame selection, or you'd prefer to try a progressive lens, or something. Isn't it always something? Seniors enjoy everyday discounts, though, and Medicare/Medicaid is accepted. *CK, MC, V*

★★ Optical Dispensary — 972/285-8941

3914 Hwy. 80 — *Mon-Fri 8:30-5:30; Sat 8:30-1 (Walk-ins on Sat)*
Mesquite, TX 75150

This optical lab can save you up to 50 percent on frames and more on contacts. A special on daily-wear contacts plus glasses (including the exam) was only $88; single-vision lenses were $29 and the same for an eyewear exam. A small price to pay to see the small print, wouldn't you say? Bifocals started at $44. But don't expect designer or brand-name frames. But, at least you'll be able to see straight paying the bill. Same-day service has an extra charge. Walk-ins are taken on Saturdays, but they only take the first 20 patients and appointments are booked every 20 minutes ... so if you're a looker or a talker, forget it. Pack a breakfast, get in line and enjoy the savings! *CK, MC, V*

★★★★★ Optical Factory, The — 214/741-6660

130-B Express St. — *Mon-Thurs 8-4:30; Fri 7:30-1*
Dallas, TX 75207

Buried in the subterranean network of back roads off Irving Boulevard, here's another example of how the factory can save you money. Eye spied glasses, all kinds of glasses, from single vision to bifocals, trifocals, lined, unlined–you call the shots. The clear plastic lenses and frames were priced lower than a junk-yard dog with hundreds of frames to choose from. And get this ... the frames are free. That's right. You can finally see the light. It's the lenses that will cost you. A doctor's prescription is needed or your current lenses are duplicated exactly. Some single lenses in plastic frames started at $48; adding ultra-violet protection and scratch-coating bring the charges to $54.95. If you prefer the thinnest lens with the polycarbonante coating and UV protection, expect to pay $68-$89.95. Bifocals, my nemesis, lined with the scratch protection were $64.50. Not many designer frames but plenty of metals and plastic models from which to choose, some plastic frames from $10-$40. Scratch-resistant lenses with ultra-violet protection no-line bifocals for $169.50. *CK, MC, V*

★★★ Optical Mart — 972/669-9648

804 University Village — *Mon-Fri 9-6; Sat 9-4*
Richardson, TX 75081

Let Elysia be your seeing-eye guide to keep costs within seeing-eye range. With 14 locations, one is sure to be close to home. More than 400 styles and colors to choose from with single-vision glasses only $28.95 and bifocals for $44.95. If you want a tint, UV coating, and scratch-proof, add another $25. See, sometimes it can be deceiving. Extras add up. No extra charge, though, for lightweight or oversized lenses. Some of the designer names included LAUREN BACALL, RODENSTOCK, TITANIUM, YORKERS, but most were no-names thereby keeping the costs down to the bare truth. Progressive lenses were offered in two forms: the basic (with much peripheral distortion, they claimed) for $114.50 and the elite model for $139.50. This location is across from Richardson Square Mall, but check directory for the one nearest you. *CK, MC, V*

★★ Pearle Vision Express — 972/239-8585

5549 LBJ Frwy. — *Mon-Fri 9-8; Sat 9-6; Sun Noon-5*
Dallas, TX 75240 — *www.pearlevision.com*

Hit the Target–the store, that is, at Montfort and LBJ and you'll find Pearle Vision. Stanley Pearle, the patriarch of vision, now is the face behind the glasses. As a TV spokesperson for his empire, he's to eyes what Lee Ioccoca was to Chrysler. Besides building a national chain of stores, Pearl has been generously philanthropic over the years, contributing glasses to area charities. When all is said and done, though, are you really saving money? On our visit this year, they were selling all their frames at 30-70 percent off ... but the discounts depended, of course, on the frames. The bigger the discount ... the less desirable were the frames. 'Course we were seeing stars like JOAN COLLINS, LIZ CLAIBORNE, SILHOUETTES, WRANGLER, some popular brands, no doubt about it. But, when it came to the lenses, they were regular price. That's a "gotcha!" After all, one just doesn't see through the frames. On the flip side, the selection was great, the service fast, and the nicest part of the experience was the salespeople, who were genuine pearls. Check directory for multiple locations. *CK, MC, V, AE, D*

★★★ Reading Glasses To Go

972/392-3111
5411 Belt Line Rd.
Dallas, TX 75240
Mon-Sat 10-6

First there was Chinese-to-go, and now there's Reading-To-Go so you can see what you're ordering. One from Column A, two from Column B. At last, it's perfectly clear. Change your glasses as often as you change your outfit. Get your magnification strength by taking their little reading test and you're ready to roll those eyes. These non-prescription glasses are not discounted, but at $21-$65, who cares? A trained staff is available to help you decide the proper strength and to point you in the right direction. There are even sunglasses, bifocals, no-lines, and progressive lenses. Perfect if you lose your glasses on the road. Perfect if you are a world traveler. And perfect if you're like me and can never find yours. Run in and pick out a few pairs-to-go. Also look for locations in Dallas on Oak Lawn and on Lovers Lane, as well as in Plano. *CK, MC, V*

★★★★ Southwest Vision Center

817/281-3386
7728 Mid-Cities Blvd.
North Richland Hills, TX 76180
Mon-Fri 9-6; Sat 9-2:30

They wowed us with great prices and, boy, do we love to get things free! First of all, they have more than 1,000 frames in stock, some as low as $10. Second, they have lots of contacts in stock, too. Extended wear contacts were $159 and that included a free spare pair! We also got a free pair of clear daily lenses when we ordered DURASOFT colored contacts for $199. Bring in a current prescription or have your glasses duplicated–obviously a better way to see your way clearly. Medicaid/Medicare and most insurance are accepted. *CK, MC, V*

★★★★★ www.Eyesite.com

972/620-7895
2925 LBJ Frwy., Suite 188
Dallas, TX 75234
By Appt. Only
www.eyesite.com

For the best in personalized care and attention for your eyes, you need a private practice eyecare professional. To locate the best private practice eyecare professional in your area, go to www.eyesite.com. While visiting, you will be also be able to find the area's best values in eye exams for 50 percent off, as well as other opportunities to save your hard-earned dollars. Learn valuable information about the care of your eyes without squinting between the lines. Now for those who want to throw away the glasses, meet Dr. Mark Suggs–and you will see clearly without a personal introduction from Barbara Walters. *CK, MC, V, Financing*

Fabrics & Upholstery

★★★ ABC Textiles

214/357-8700

2623 Perth St. *Sat 8-1*
Dallas, TX 75220

How does fabric priced from $1 per yard sound? Open to the public on Saturdays only at their store near Walnut Hill and Harry Hines, new fabrics are added daily to their outlet operation for dressmaking dilettantes. Get a grip on gabardines. Got a feel for wool? A handle on twills and frills? Care for cotton? Crepe de Chines? Silk? These are the same fabrics used by manufacturers of moderate to better women's sportswear–but no names spoken aloud here. Fabric on bolts is sold by the yard. Season permitting, they also have children's prints, challis prints, upholstery and drapery fabric, men's suit fabrics and denim. *CK*

★★★ Allied Fabrics

214/741-4431

163 Parkhouse St. *Mon-Fri 8-5*
Dallas, TX 75207

If the notion hits you that you should be paying wholesale prices, sample this showroom near I-35 E and Continental Ave. for all the trimmings. No fabrics, although the name implies it, but plenty of notions and embellishments are featured if you're into "Fringe Benefits." You'll find buttons, braids, lace, elastic, ribbon, rattail, rickrac and eyelet ... a million ideas just waiting to be developed. They also have many catalogs to choose from if what you need isn't in stock. Don't expect to be warmly greeted, but persistence pays off. This is a no-nonsense kind of operation. So, try to have a nice day anyway! *CK*

★★★★★ Best Fabric Outlet

214/350-2583

10901 Harry Hines Blvd. *Mon-Sat 9-5*
Dallas, TX 75220

This place is a madhouse on Saturdays, but who are we to be "knit pickers"? There is so much fabric bolting out the door, it's enough to tire even

Thumbelina. At the corner of Perth and Harry Hines, that's where East meets anybody who's anybody wanting to buy fabric. And the best place on the block is Best Fabric Outlet. The bolts are organized on tables by prices, by fabrication and by project. Dress fabric is separated from upholstery and drapery fabric, and all are priced at cut-and-carry discounts. Bring your bolt choices to the ladies doing the cutting, and they'll snip, snip away. *CK, MC, V*

★★★★ Calico Corners — 214/349-6829

12370 Inwood Rd. — *Mon-Sat 10-6; Thu 10-7; Sun 1-5*
Dallas, TX 75244 — *www.calicocorners.com*

What does "less than the designers charge" mean to poor little old me? Not much. But then again, every little cut counts. Regular fabric is discounted about 20 percent and seconds are slashed even more. Possibilities abound if you're looking for a fabrication makeover. Let them sew up a storm with a colorful trip to bountiful. Bolt into here for drapery and upholstery fabric and see what materializes. They have an in-house workroom where they can provide the sewers to whip up the goods to make your house a "Home and Garden" segment. There are hundreds of choices, attractively displayed and color-coordinated to make shopping a breeze. Then, let the pros sew. Custom pillows, window treatments, bedspreads, draperies, slipcovers and more can all be found here. Other locations to sew from, so check the directory for one nearest you. *CK, MC, V, D*

★★★★ Carousel Fabrics & Interiors — 817/926-4702

2300 Edwin St. — *Mon-Sat 10-5*
Fort Worth, TX 76110

Take a ride on the discount merry-go-round at this Fort Worth Zoo area store. Choose from all the famous fabric names–AMERITEX, ROBERT ALLEN, WAVERLY and WESTGATE, just to name a few. Discounts ranged from 40-60 percent off retail prices. Choose your drapery or upholstery fabric from stock or they will special order for you. They also provide custom services such as reupholstering, bedspreads, draperies, valances and headboards, and they are one of the few places that won't give you the runaround. Giddy-up and take a ride to this Carousel–one of the few custom workrooms in Tarrant County to hop aboard for serious savings without going 'round and 'round getting the run-around. *CK, MC, V, AE, D*

Fabrics & Upholstery

★★★★ Childress Fabric Outlet — 214/565-0900

2517 Ferris St. — *Mon-Fri 9-5; Sat 9-3*
Dallas, TX 75226 — *www.childressfabrics.com*

Across the street from the other Childress family business, Custom Upholstery Mart, visit this fabric headquarters near downtown for deals on RALPH LAUREN, ROBERT ALLEN, WAVERLEY and much more. More than 4,500 designs to choose from, with many running $5-$15 a yard, 50-70 percent off retail. Furniture, drapery and bed fabric are their specialties, but they also deal in trims and tassels. Then, when you pick out the fabric, go across the street and they'll reupholster your favorite chair, sofa or whatever. Owned and operated by the Childress family, serving the Metroplex since 1958. See listing for Custom Upholstery Mart: 2512 Ferris St. (214/821-4444). *CK, MC, V, AE*

★★★★★ Childress Upholstery — 214/698-1771

2900 Dawson St. — *Mon-Fri 7-5; Sat 7-1*
Dallas, TX 75226

The original, original Childress family patriarch is still sewing up a storm. In his cozy 4,000-square-foot warehouse, ring the bell and in seven-10 days, chances are you'll be sitting pretty on your new upholstered chair, bench or couch. Make your fabric selection at this small but genuinely dedicated family-run business. Gene will cover and his wife Dorothy will come out to your house and give you an estimate for free, along with free pick-up and delivery. Though they've been planning on being able to accept credit cards for some time, they're so busy and just haven't gotten around to it. See, they keep their noses to the grindstone. Besides, credit card companies charge so much, he would probably have to raise his prices. For a medium-sized chair, the labor would be $195-$295. It would take approximately 7 ½ yards of fabric for solids and approximately 9 ½ yards for prints–add it up and you've got your final price. They are located south of Deep Ellum near the I-30 and I-45 interchange. Go south on Hall St. and the next street after Canton will be Chestnut. Go right and then left on Dawson behind the police station. Feel safe and secure–your furniture is really in great hands. You can see I-30 out the window, so it's not so difficult once you get the hang of these directions. *CK*

✧✧ Come and Sew — 972/539-1948

Flower Mound, TX 75028-1056 — *By Reservation Only*

This home-based business is the place to call if you want to be called a sew-

and-sew. Kathy Arnold, one of the few sewing teachers around, offers a variety of classes from the basics of basting to advanced sewing techniques. Learn the rudiments from the Beginner's Series or enjoy how to create wonderful window treatments in an eight-week series. A practice garment is done in the class to give you a headstart on your future, baby. All materials, fabric and supplies are included in the packaged price. Kids' classes are also available for quilting and crafting, including an occasional class with children with ADD, dyslexia, etc. Classes are usually 12 hours over a six-week period–that's one night a week from 7-9, or she teaches during the daytime. Occasionally, she'll hold a class on making cathedral window quilts. The class costs $80 plus a $17 registration fee, which includes the materials and equipment needed for the project. Cheaper than ready-made and a whole lot more creative. *CK, MC, V*

★★★★★ Current Fabrics 214/353-2766

2655 Perth St. *Mon-Fri 9-4:30; Sat 8:30-2:30*
Dallas, TX 75220

Head to the fabric district on Perth St. and keep Current. Since shopping without getting fleeced is the current subject at hand, and you'd rather not pay full retail, this is the place to go for closeout fabrics. The rolls are priced up to 50 percent off with names you know, such as J.P. STEVENS and WAMSUTTA. A full line of fabrics could be the pick of the lot from cotton prints to bridal delicacies. If you want to buy the bolt, an even bigger discount is offered. Off Walnut Hill and Harry Hines, choose from more than 15,000 yards. An entire department this year is devoted to just bridal and bridesmaids' fabrics, and there is more drapery and upholstery than ever before. Remember, you don't have to travel to Australia. This Perth's in Dallas. *CK, MC, V, D*

★★★★★ Custom Upholstery Mart 214/821-4444

2512 Ferris St. *Mon-Fri 9-5; Sat 9-3*
Dallas, TX 75226 *www.childressfabrics.com*

This powerhouse has been going strong in the upholstery business since 1958, and they show no signs of slowing down anytime soon. Almost everyone here is related and has worked their fingers to the bone building the largest upholstery and fabric outlet in the Metroplex. Kind of like the Trade Mart of fabric, prices are generally wholesale and sometimes below. The Fabric Outlet across the street offers all the peak performers in fabric: DURAL, KRAVET, MARTEX, PENDLER & PENDLER, RALPH LAUREN, ROBERT ALLEN, SCHUMAKER/WAVERLY and more. Then, it's on to the tassels and trims, the down pillow forms–you just walk away shaking your head in amazement. Let's see ... how many yards will it take to upholster my couch, my dining room chairs? Throw in a few throw pillows and at these prices, it's an amazing one-stop festival of fabric finds. They do reupholstering, custom-furniture, custom headboards, custom draperies, custom pillows, custom shams, custom bed-spreads–guess that's why they're named Custom Upholstery Mart. More than 4,500 designers to choose from, with many running $5-$15 a yard retailing $50 and up. *CK, MC, V, Financing*

★★★★★ Cutting Corners 972/233-1741

13720 Midway Rd., Suite 200
Farmers Branch, TX 75244
Mon-Sat 9:30-5:30; Thu 9:30-8; Sun Noon-5
www.cuttingcorners.com

Cut as many corners as you like when buying fabric at Cutting Corners, located between Spring Valley and Alpha on Midway Road. Rub elbows with Dallas decorators and hobknob with the snobs. They're all vying for the same bargains. Drapery and fabric bolts line this 14,000-square-foot warehouse from as low as $3.99/square yard (but most higher). Current releases included cotton prints, $7.99/yard; chenilles, $12.99/yard; and a voluminous selection of tassels and trims. Save up to 50 percent or more on in-stock fabric at this mill outlet and say goodbye to high and mighty prices. Your only problem? Which to choose? Tartan plaid or the herringbone? Suede-like or chenille? New to the fold, custom furniture from $799-$800 for sofas, chairs from $199–you choose the style and fabric, they'll make it and deliver it in six weeks. You'd think we'd be a badge-carrying Scotland Yard by now. Cut it out, too, in Fort Worth at 5525 S. Hulen St. (817/262-6834). *CK, MC, V, D*

★★★★★ DRC Sales 817/244-9057

10005 Spur 580
Fort Worth, TX 76116
Tues-Fri 10-5; Sat 10-3

Get your fabric direct from the mills at DRC Sales. They're running bolts around the competition with their decorative fabrics with famous names. You don't need to be a believer in heaven sent, just know that they will ensure you're heaven spent. Plus, if you're cheap, it helps. All the biggies are represented: BLOOMCRAFT, CREATIVE, P. KAUFMAN, ROBERT ALLEN, SCHUMACHER/WAVERLY, WESTGATE, and that's just the tip of their thousands of yards of upholstery fabric discounted miles and miles apart from the nearest competitor. Take I-30 west, past Ridgmar Mall and go under I-820. Exit Chapel Creek and go left/south on Chapel Creek until it dead ends at Spur 580 (Weatherford Highway). Turn left, going east, and it is the first building on the right (south). Whether it's on cut orders or roll goods, expect to save 50 percent from book prices. Also they offer custom-made window treatments with a designer on staff. The cream of the crop, says chop, chop. *CK, MC, V, AE, D*

★★★★ Fabracadabra 214/357-3555

5370 W. Lovers Lane *Mon-Fri 9:30-5:30; Sat 10-4*
Dallas, TX 75209

With just a few strokes of the magic wand, your home can be transformed into a work of beauty forever. Expect to save money at this magic shop. How much you save depends on the deals they can cut, but it's usually up to 40-50 percent off. Plenty of in-stock fabric from the famous mills like FABRICUT, P. KAUFMAN, ROBERT ALLEN, WAVERLY–the whole nine yards are all a cut above the rest. For those who'd rather let others do the needling, their workroom can whip up custom drapery or other window treatments, bedspreads and coordinated ensembles, even fabric walls. Everything but paint and carpentry for your magical makeovers. All work is custom, so that effort is not discounted. After all, they are paying rent in Highland Park. *CK, MC, V, AE, D*

★★ Fabric Factory 972/720-1400

12330 Inwood Rd. *Mon-Sat 10-6; Thu 10-7; Sun Noon-5*
Dallas, TX 75244

We called Scotland Yard to solve the mystery of where to buy high-end fabrics. Purportedly at the lowest prices in town–sure could have fooled me. Though now the case (goods) is closed, they do have gorgeous fabrics and an enormous selection. This source can cover the Metroplex. If you're in the market for upholstery and drapey fabric, only the finest, first-quality inventory was rolled out to royalty. If you've not been born with a nimble finger, not to worry. They've got you covered. Thumbelina's would be impressed. Operating out of their own workroom, let them whip up a line of custom-made furniture that will soon be the talk of the town. One room in this vast expanse is devoted to trims, tassels and bows; another room is just for kid's fabrics. Finally, a one-stop source that will keep you in stitches. On the downside, though they buy "direct from the mills", their prices are not winning rave notices from Underground Shoppers. *CK, MC, V*

Fabrics & Upholstery

★★★★★ Fabric Source, The 972/267-3400

2385 Midway Rd. *Mon-Fri 9-5:30; Sat 9:30-5*
Plano, TX 75093

With more than 7,000 square feet of hundreds of first-quality drapery and upholstery fabrics at 40-60 off, they are now settled into their new and expanded headquarters. More space means more inventory. No doubt, this fabric source can enhance your lifestyle with a variety of textures and styles. Create custom sofas and loveseats with in-stock fabric for as low as $350, love seats for $325, and wingback chairs for $175 (skirts, tufting and nail trim extra). First-quality drapery damask was $8.99/yard; overlay prints, $9.99; and plaids, stripes or solids were $8.99. (I guess you could say we're "Plaid about them".) Drapery lining (54 inches) was shockingly sheared at $2.49/yard and tapestries were $14.99/yard. An expanded line of trim and tassels and comparable savings on custom slipcovers make this a fabric source to be contended with. Free pick-up and delivery are other pluses. This direct mill outlet has been making bed benches, headboards and ottomans for the past 25 years, so you can expect them to at least know how to sew a thing or two. *CK, MC, V, D*

★★★ Fabrics & Frames Furniture 972/385-4097

5322 Alpha Rd. *Mon-Sat 10-6; Thurs 10-8; Sun Noon-6*
Dallas, TX 75240

With thousands of rolls of fabric in stock, you're sure to find something to invest in. The DeCuir family stands behind their furniture made right on the premises. Since they're a stone's throw from Cantoni, expect to pay the price of quality and dependable custom furniture. Relish custom-built furniture that is proudly built one piece at a time, but your budget may be in a pickle. Reupholstery and slipcovers are in the picture here, too. From the simplest of upholstered chairs to the most exquisite fabrics to choose from, Fabrics & Frames can build your dream suite to match your style. An in-house design team is ready to help you define your needs with fabrics from tapestries to cottons, from parson chairs to plush comfortable sofas and chairs. Delivery, if all goes well, is in four weeks or less. They can also take your favorite furniture and refurbish it–making it stronger as well as more stylish. Clearance items at 50 percent off are your best buys, pricewise. Relax, they offer a 90-day, no-interest financing plan to cushion the blow. Now consolidated in their one 8,000-square-foot store, if you're looking for custom furniture, reupholstery and fabrics, this is a company we can stand behind (as they're the ones who stand on it). *CK, MC, V, D*

★★★★ Falk Fabric Outlet 214/855-0636

2633 McKinney Ave. *Mon-Fri 9-5:30; Sat10-5*
Dallas, TX 75204

One of the largest decorative fabric inventories in the Southwest, this is nobody's Falk except Falk's. Serving the Metroplex since 1951, this outlet offers shoppers a formidable fabric inventory. In fact, their reputation covers the Southwest. Located just down the street from the Hard Rock Cafe, this outlet has decorative and upholstery fabrics at substantial savings. We priced some exquisite Moiré Taffeta at $7.98/yard, which was hard to beat. We had a real dilemma deciding which gorgeous matching drapery fabric to pick, so we picked three for $6-$10/yard, seen elsewhere for $12/yard. A custom workroom is on the premises to help your fabric take shape. Watch for seasonal sales, when another 20 percent is snipped off through no Falk of their own. *CK, MC, V, AE*

★★★★ Golden D'Or Outlet 214/351-6651

10795 Harry Hines Blvd. *Mon-Sat 9-4:30*
Dallas, TX 75220

Open this D'or to saving on quality fabrics, even if your name's not Dior. Golden opportunities on linens, twills, knits, denim, poplins, satins, Lycra, challis, even decorator fabrics, all priced 50 percent and more off retail. Sew for less at this factory store for fabrics! Thousands of yards to choose from including the popular western and African prints from $1.99-$4.99/yard; drapery fabric, $4.50/yard; decorator fabric, $2.50/yard and remnants–plenty of remnants–in sheeting prints, twills, knits, denim, calicos, juveniles, craft prints, poplins, interlock and more from $.99/yard. Everybody's doing African prints these days, but then again, we couldn't decide between them and the sequins, Dupionii silks, satins, rayon or craft prints. (In the real world, I always thought there weren't enough prints ... and too many princesses!) Prices like these will make dreams of sewing machines dance in your head. All fabric is $.59 to $4.99/yard. Worth a trip just to see what you might find. We saw nothing for more than $4.99/yard, with most under $3. Shop around, then dig around the thousands of yards. Located on Harry Hines, between Walnut Hill and Lombardy, in the heart of the upholstery fabric district. *CK, MC, V, AE, D*

★★★★★ Interior Alternative, The 214/637-8800

1305 Inwood Rd. *Mon-Sat 10-5; Thu 10-6; Sun Noon-5*
Dallas, TX 75247

Can't keep a secret? Well, if you promise not to tell, I'll let the cotton out of the bag. WAVERLY/SCHUMACHER has an outlet and The Interior Alternative is its name! Hundreds of bolts line the walls in their showroom where every color, every print imaginable is on the cutting edge. Some day your prints may come but at these prices, who cares if he's a second! All seconds are clearly marked, and other first-quality runs are closeouts and remnants. All are wonderfully priced from $4-$15 for wide decorator widths. Most are in the $7-$9 range. Some trims and accessories, too, are in stock at discounted prices. Printed linens, chintzes, damasks and tapestries, comforter sets and bedspreads, decorative pillows, chair pads and acccessories, ruffles, pillow shams, even carpets and rugs are all under the umbrella of this alternative to high prices. And in the middle, you'll see a featured gallery of WAVERLY wallpaper. Walls on over to The Interior Alternative. Additional outlet stores in Boaz, AL; Newark, DE; Dalton, GA; Huntley, IL; Adams, MS; Jericho, NY; Morgantown, Pa.; and Richburg, SC. *CK, MC, V, AE*

★★★★★ J & D, Inc. — 817/626-2365

2015 N. Main St. — *Mon-Fri 8-6; Sat 9-4*
Fort Worth, TX 76053

Quality fabrics at J & D have become a cowtown custom. Near the Stockyards, more than 8,000 bolts line the walls and are stacked to the ceiling in more than 20,000 square feet of selling space. One of the largest inventories of decorative fabrics in the Metroplex. Decorative fabric for upholstery and drapes, tassels and trims, tapestries, prints ... you name it, they've got it. It's where Tarrant County shoppers have been saving 25-60 percent off retail on designing fabrics–and that's no bull! Let these pros sew a matching headboard, reupholster that aging sofa, hang up some new draperies, coordinate all of your design dreams and throw in some beautiful tasseled pillows to "gussy up" the entire look. *CK, MC, V*

★ Keeton Supply Co. — 817/332-7888

912 E. Vickery Blvd. — *Mon-Fri 8-5; Sat 8-Noon*
Fort Worth, TX 76104

If you take a notion to add a little oomph to your home life, Keeton may be able to provide some creative material. They specialize in upholstery supplies, including foam, dacron, padding, welt cord, burlap threads, staples, tools–everything you'd need for upholstering furniture. And while they aren't always discounted, they do carry a wide selection of vinyls to velvets. Call first for comparative prices and ask for the manager for the best service–we've gotten a cold shoulder from the staff before. Stock changes often and what isn't in can usually be ordered. *CK, MC, V, AE*

★★★★ Legacy Furniture

972/272-8427

626 Easy St.
Garland, TX 75042
Mon-Fri 9-5

Create a legacy in your own home by calling the number above. Legacy can update your current furniture and accessories, or you can start from scratch and have the artisans build it from the ground floor up. These are some of the finest craftsmen around who have been re-doing the town up 'til now wholesale to the trade only. Their legacy is to go direct to the public and now, those nips and tucks can be yours (for your furniture, of course). Fabric prices discounted, you ask? Of course. (This is not *Town & Country* magazine, you know.) Or, bring your own. Pick and choose from the myriad of options and design possibilities. Draperies, bedcovers, wall upholstery, and slipcovers, too. Want a sofa copied that you saw in *Architectural Digest*? No problem, amigo. Save a favorite wingback chair and recover it for $270 plus fabric. Add slipcovers for a fast makeover for the holidays. Choose accent pillows in tapestry or damask, add trim, rug fringe, cording, or tassels, and let your imagination soar. Transform your couch or chair into picture perfect with its new coat of many colors. Pickup and delivery available. *CK, MC, V*

★★★★★ M & M Upholstery

214/391-4085

8337 Lake June Rd.
Dallas, TX 75217
Mon-Fri 8-5; Sat 8-Noon

Since 1857, this third-generation family business has been known to decorators as THE place to take your tired and worn furniture. Now you, too, can shop where the decorators shop. They encourage you to bring your own fabric as their mastery is the art of upholstering. An antique sofa in its original condition was restored to mint condition after M & M got their hands on it. A typical six-cushion sofa with roll arms and skirt will need approximately 18 yards of fabric; labor to reupholster at M & M would be $425. More common projects, such as a wingback chair that would need about 7 ½ yards would cost about $250 in labor. Not bad, considering the alternative of buying a completely new sofa and chair. These folks are some of the best craftsmen in the business. Add $40 for pickup and delivery. For kitchen chair seats, it would take about ¾-yard of fabric and cost $35 per chair. Expect to be sitting pretty in two - three weeks. Look for the harvest gold, free-standing building with awning and bars with the blue and white banner in front. Between U.S. Highway 175 and I-635. *CK, MC, V*

Fabrics & Upholstery

★ Miracle Fabric — 972/579-7451

1720 E. Irving Blvd. — *Mon-Sat 9-5:15*
Irving, TX 75060

See what materializes for you at Miracle Fabric. We remember when this used to be a wholesale source for HABER, but now the store seems to be mostly retail (though you can save 20-50 percent on a select range of fabrics for dress-making needs). Fake fur and fleece got your goat? Many dress fabrics, bridal fabrics, trims and poly-cottons are a portion of the notions. Patterns, too, but all retail priced. No miracles found, but a few blessings were revealed by our dogged-determined digging through the remnant bins and s(t)ale rolls. *CK, MC, V, AE*

★★ Pete's Upholstery Shop — 817/274-2431

2620 W. Pioneer Pkwy. — *Mon-Fri 8-4:30*
Arlington, TX 76013

For Pete's sake, consider Bill Yeager if you're needing an uplift to your deep-seated future. Furniture reupolstery is his forte in up-to-the-minute styles and fabrics. In business since 1963, repeat business is really the secret as to how his garden of bargains grows. Expect to pay $395 for labor, plus fabric and tax. Fabrics start at about $15 or $16 and go up from there. If you buy the fabric from him and live in Arlington, then pickup and delivery are free. If you buy the fabric elsewhere, expect to pay $40. Once he's got it all together, expect to be sitting pretty in about three weeks. *CK*

★★★ Richland Sewing Center — 817/590-4447

850 W. Pipeline Rd. — *Mon-Fri 9:30-6:30; Sat 9:30-5*
Hurst, TX 76053

This is one store that can keep you in stitches for years to come. They carry JANOME, SINGER and WHITE sewing machines, as well as BROTHER, HUSQVARNA, JANOME and WHITE home embroidery machines along with a complete selection of design cards. Used machines start at $35, with new machines starting at $130. But wait, you say, you'd like to get a machine, but don't know a bobbin from a bird's nest. Never fear, they provide free machine operation classes with all new machines. And if anything ever goes wrong with your machine, you won't have to ship it off to some faraway land. All repairs are done in-house. Sew, there's a second location in Richland Hills at 6620 Grapevine Hwy., 817/284-0162. *CK, MC, V*

★★ Sewing Room, The 972/315-1489

420 E. Round Grove Rd., Suite 115 *Mon-Sat 10-6; Thu 10-8; Sun 1-5*
Lewisville, TX 75067 *www.sewingroom.com*

This sew-and-sew stopped by one night late, looking to replace some buttons. Since I didn't find what I wanted, I instead struck up a nice conversation with the husband whose wife was busy in the back teaching a class. How nice it is to be neighborly in a retail store. This is a one-stop sewing shop if you want to learn about the MEMORY CRAFT 9000 machine (and others). Can you believe one machine can embroider, quilt, and more *and* that this place discounts them considerably (during special promotions, as much as 75 percent). Then, I eyed a JANOME model sewing machine with one-step buttonholes and I knew what I intended to do the minute I had a day off. Learn to needle someone else rather than those at work. *CK, MC, V, AE, D*

★★ Super Textiles Fabric Outlet 214/353-2770

2667 Perth St. *Mon-Fri 9-5; Sat 8-2*
Dallas, TX 75220

Yet another entry in the fabric district off Harry Hines, Super Textiles offers a selection of bolts from HOWARD WOLF, SHARON YOUNG and other clothing manufacturers that will save you more than a just a few stitches. These are the same fabrics that are found in better womenswear outfits around the country. Prices on challis, prints, jacquards, poly-cotton, interlock and denim (at a low $3/yard) were all decidedly discounted. While stock was great and prices low, the reception was less than thrilling. Maybe they were having a bad fabric day! Or maybe their Fruits of the Loom were too tight! *CK, MC, V, D*

★★★★★ Upholstery Place, The 972/271-6669

2406 S. Jupiter Rd., Suite 2 *Mon-Thu 8:30-5:30; Fri 8:30-5;*
Garland, TX 75041 *Sat By Appt.*

Talk to Teresa Garner if you're in need of some reupholstering. That means, if you want to cover up and make it look brand new, even better than before, then consider the magical transformation by The Upholstery Place. In three-four weeks (not months, sometimes years at other places), they can have your old recliner, sofa or wingback chair looking brand spankin' new. They also sell fabrics for do-it-yourselfers or for use on your upholstery item. To reupholster a standard wing-back chair, the cost is about $250-$290. Fabrics run from about $15-$100. This is the place for restyling your oldies but goodies. And as they state, "Superior service sets them apart!" Now doing custom slipcovers, window treatments and bed dressings, too. (Hey, I thought you got "undressed" to go to bed!) *CK*

Flea Markets & Bazaars

★★★ All American Texas Flea Market — 817/783-5468

3004 S. I-35 W — *Fri-Sat 7-5; Sun 7-5*
Burleson, TX 76028

The fleas have left this dog as they've condensed back to about 250 vendors and put an emphasis on the tractor shows. You'll still find 75 more inside booths that are typically brimming with bargains, and you can still enjoy the variety–from crafts to antiques, junk to jewelry, hubcaps to baseball caps. Walk 'til dark or until you're ready to park it. Not as crowded or as commercialized as some of the other flea markets around, they also sport antique car shows periodically throughout the year. Antique tractor shows and tractor pulls are becoming the main attraction. When the tractor show is on, the cost per booth is $15 a day and $30 at the gate. Otherwise, regular admittance is $2 for adults and $1 for children over 6. The public market opens at 8 A.M. on Saturday. Friday is when people begin setting up. *Varies with Vendors*

★★★★★ First Monday Trade Days — 903/567-6556

I-20 East to Hwy. 19 and Kaufman Street — *7 A.M.-Dark*
Canton, TX 75103 — *www.firstmonday.com*

First Monday is legendary, come rain or come shine. Born in 1873 as Canton's Court Day, town folks began their mercantile efforts by horse trading while waiting for, "Here comes the judge!". In 1965, the city of Canton bought the two blocks north of the courthouse that now houses thousands of dealers (last count was more than 4,000) who set up shop. Both new and used items, arts and crafts, antiques and collectibles share the spotlight over Canton. A wonderful day's outing for individual scavengers or for the entire family. Definitely the place for those who prefer to "dicker", but remember to dress the part. Wearing a $15,000 watch and diamond stud earring are duds for negotiating the best prices. For information on dealer space, contact the City of Canton, PO Box 245, Canton, TX 75103, 903/567-6556. Admission is FREE; parking, $3.

They open the Friday before the first Monday of each month and stay open through Monday. *Varies with vendor*

★★ First Monday Trade Days 817/421-1778

303 Palo Pinto *Fri-Sun 7 A.M.-Dusk*
Weatherford, TX 76086 *www.firstmonday.com*

Happening the weekend before the first Monday of each month, Saturdays are still the best days to shop. Vendors start packing up on Sundays, ready to fold down the tents and head for the hills. Get there early during the not-so-hot days and enjoy the myriad of crafts, food and fun. You can buy anything here, including animals, so why bark up another tree? If you're looking for a second income, here's a place to start. Starting in November, reservations are in order if you would like to rent a space. Reservations should be made the first week of the month prior to the month you want. Reservations may be made by calling 817/598-4215 or you can go to City Hall, 303 Palo Pinto St. in Weatherford. Mailed payments should be addressed: First Monday Reservations, PO Box 255, Weatherford, TX 76086. Ask about their "Intent to Reserve" policy for ensuring the same place every time. To set up a food booth, it costs $150 for a hookup for wagons and $5 per day for electricity. A maximum of 10 spaces can be reserved by an individual/group/company, etc., and walk-up customers are accepted for $15 per day as long as space is available. *Varies with vendor*

★★★★★ Mountain, The 903/567-5445

Rt. 5, Box 605 *Weekend prior to 1st Monday 8-Dusk*
Canton, TX 75103

Look for Wild Willie now in a permanent home-on-the-range called The Mountain. Join in the live musical performances and take some time to recover from your shopping excursion. The Mountain is easy to navigate without an avalance of the mundane. If you're in the market for an artistic nature, collect your foundation here. Most of the shops are air-conditioned (a real plus) or tucked under the trees for your shopping comfort. It's your home-away-from-home for crafts, arts, antiques, food, Native American arts and crafts, music, street entertainment, demonstrating artists and craftsmen. To enjoy the free admission, head east on I-20 to Canton. The Mountain is home to a beautiful tree-shaded Old West atmosphere where one can turn back time and wallow in the history of the Wild West. More than 700 antique and crafts shops are open with new attractions opening all the time. Visit the two weekends prior to the first Monday of each month. *Varies with Vendors*

★★★★★ Old Mill Market Place 903/567-5445

Hwy.64 East at Mill Creek, Rt. 5 *Mon-Sun 9-5*
Canton, TX 75103

More than 800 vendors line the area at the Old Mill Marketplace. Old Mill Marketplace offers a friendly, clean and convenient marketplace complex for shoppers with more than 800 shops. This area is the newest shopping area in Canton and you will not be disappointed in the variety. At Old Mill Marketplace take the time to select only the BEST of vendors. They jury each and every vendor to assure you quality of his or her product as well as assurance that the vendor is reliable and stands behind his/her product. *CK*

★★ Second Monday Trade Days—Bowie 940/872-1680

304 Lindsey *Fri-Sun 7 A.M.-Dusk*
Bowie, TX 76230 *www.morgan.net/~a2ndmonday*

Visit the rodeo grounds on E. Wise Street in Bowie, Texas, the second Monday of each month for a taste of the country. Check out the antique shops and malls around the Wise County Courthouse Square, where about 200 vendors set up by Saturday. It's better to get there early if you want to haul it off without a sweat. Vendor booths go for $20 for the weekend plus $4 for electricity. Take 287 north, exit on US 81/Waurika Exit, and you'll run right into it. Easy on the budget for wise shoppers looking to draw some strength from "Collective Bargaining"! *Varies with Vendor*

★★★★ Third Monday Trade Days—McKinney 972/562-5466

4550 W. University *Fri-Sun 7 A.M.-Dusk*
(Hwy. 380, 2 miles west of Hwy. 75) *www.tmtd.com*
McKinney, TX 75069

One of the oldest county-wide markets, Third Monday Trade Days began more than 100 years ago when judges rode circuit from county seat to county seat. Recent improvements in the roads make heading north each Saturday and Sunday before the third Monday of the month a treasure-trove. Drive up Highway 75 to Highway 380 and go two miles west to the historic Buckner Community where, since 1966, McKinney's Third Monday Trade Days have laid claim to the bargain kingdom. With roughly 30 acres, more than 800 vendor spaces (and now 200 covered) and ample parking, this place rules the roost (especially if you're not royalty). The market has undergone many changes under the present ownership, so be sure to visit the new Trading Post section and the large pavilion. There is a fine array of food vendors with everything from snacks to full meals. Open-air space rentals are $35 for the first lot and $25 for each additional lot. Seeing is believing what was "Too good to be threw!" But some of your best buys were originally discards. *Varies with Vendor*

★★★★★ Traders Village 972/647-2331

2602 Mayfield Rd. *Sat-Sun 8 A.M.-Dusk*
Grand Prairie, TX 75052 *www.tradersvillage.com*

Take Mayfield Road off Highway 360 north one mile off I-20, park for $2, and walk, baby, walk. Bring a shopping bag or cart, wear comfortable shoes and clothing, dip yourself in SPF 15, do not drink a Diet Coke during the day (bathrooms are far apart) and bring cash. It's your only control to stop before you drop. (I take that back. Can you believe they've installed an ATM machine for those who can't get enough of a good thing?) This 106-acre complex has seen more than 35 million shoppers since its inception in 1973. More than 2,000 dealers, lots of ethnic food stands (we counted 20), rides for the kiddies, stroller, wagon and wheelchair rentals and RV parking make it accessible and fun for everyone. Compared with Canton, this is the bargain basement of the bargain bazaars. Enjoy more than 25 special events, such as rodeos, auto shows, swap meets, Native American Pow-Wows and barbecue cook-off. Lease space by the day, week, month or year. Houston has had their own Traders Village since 1989. *Varies with Vendors*

★★★ Vikon Village Flea Market 972/271-0565

2918 South Jupiter *Sat-Sun 10-7*
Garland, TX 75041

At the intersection of Kingsley and Jupiter, two blocks north of LBJ, one of the greatest little flea markets exists for your shopping pleasure. Whether you're looking for a Nolan Ryan baseball card or a new collar for your dog Spot, somewhere in this maze of marketers, you will find the perfect kitsch and kaboodle. More than 300-350 dealers converge weekly selling treasures and trash. Some impressive antiques, some new and exciting ideas, some funky and fab fashions, some total dogs. Since Iron Works left, not much in the way of furniture, but it's still a mixed bag. Some new, some not so, some samples, some you'd rather not. A 12- x 24-foot booth rents for $360/month. Check with Diane if you've got the itch to open shop. *CK, Varies with Vendors*

Flea Markets & Bazaars

★★★★ Whitewright Trade Days

903/364-2994

Sears Street
PO Box 566
Whitewright, TX 75491

Thu-Sun (times vary)

On the last Saturday and Sunday before the fourth Monday of the month, visit Whitewright's American Legion grounds in beautiful downtown Whitewright. This market has been open for more than 20 years and has about 250 vendors. Some dealers set up Thursday, and some leave around Noon on Sunday. Take Highway 75 to Highway 121; right on 121 to 160, turn left to the end of the road. Bring plenty of "Pine Soul" for dusting off the stash that you bring home for a lot less cash than at some of the more commercial flea marketplaces. Some real treasures can be unearthed. *Varies with Vendor*

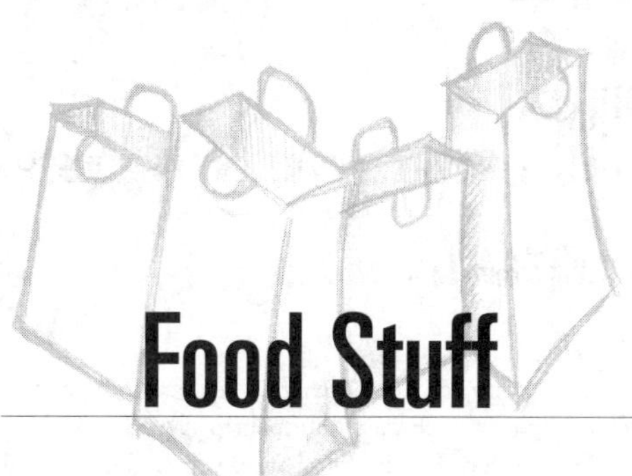

Food Stuff

★★★★★ Best Desserts 972/596-4858

925 22nd Street, Suite 108 *Mon-Fri 2-6; Sat 10-4*
Plano, TX 75074 *www.bestdesserts.com*

Want the best desserts? Get a taste of this Plano outlet ... where you'll be able to take a bite out of paying retail for gourmet cheesecakes, cakes, cookies, pies, tortes and ... diet beware! Located at Park and Avenue K in downtown Plano, expect to enjoy a slice of life at wholesale and often 15 percent below wholesale for what you'd pay for the same quality in a retail store or restaurant. Scrumptious temptations from many different gourmet bakeries are housed all under one roof and sold to individuals or corporate clients. They don't take the description "gourmet" lightly (though they do offer lighter offerings, such as a line called Natural Feast, which is safe for special dietary needs). Whether you lust for a luscious Princess Torte cake for a family gathering or 100 Marzipan Jewel Starbars for a major business meeting, you can place orders 24 hours a day and have it delivered to your front door (or pick it up at their outlet). It all tastes the same. Check with their website for special Internet deals. Yum-mmm! *CK*

★★ Big Town Farmers Market

U.S. 80 at Big Town Blvd. *Mon-Sun 8-8*
Mesquite, TX 75149

Cantaloupe this season for budgetary reasons? Then check off one more thing off your honey-dew list. Here, you can find savings on fresh fruits (the honeydew melon and seasonal veggies are given top priority) and other leafy matters. You'll be scooping out more than just melons, though, with the savings. Both indoor (covered barn) and out, there's a lot of everything for that homegrown recipe. Remember, variety is the spice of life. Produce your money and you'll come home with plenty of good stuff. Bed down in bedding plants and hanging baskets from $10-$15. On a recent Saturday, we had to compete for parking with a classic car show, but who says shopping has to be easy? *CK*

★★★ Blue Cottage Herb Farm

903/498-4234

8050 FM 4030 — *Mon-Sat 10-6*
Kaufman, TX 75142

No more dinners. No more Bed 'n' Breakfast. Just an herb shop and nothing but. Travel down Highway 175E past Kaufman to FM 2860 and turn left. Go three miles to the stop sign. It's the first gate on the right. Deborah will be your guide Mon-Thu and Regina, the owner and renowned herbalist, takes over Fri-Sat. You are cordially invited to enjoy their wide sampling of herbs grown right on the premises, tour the greenhouses and buy the dried and fresh herbs, including those from the herbal apothecary shop (for what ails you). This is the "Greening of Life" you don't want to miss. It's always better to be healthy, wealthy and wise. *CK*

★★ Candy in Bloom

214/363-2399

728 Preston Forest Shopping Center — *Mon-Fri 9:30-6; Sat 10-3*
Dallas, TX 75230 — *www.candyinbloom.com*

Some say flowers show how much you care. Forget that! Give me and my sweet tooth candy! But if you really want to score points for a birthday, holiday, bat mitzvah, graduation or "just because", don't just throw a bunch of Snickers and Crackles into a bag, call Candy in Bloom for a bouquet made of the sweetest treats available. From that simple bag of candy, these artists will create bright, beautiful arrangements that someone might think are too good to eat. (Not me, honey bunny). Bouquets are available with sugar free, low fat, specialty items, cookies, chocolate and hard candy. You can even have them include flowers if you can't break totally free from tradition. Prices range from $25-$150 depending on the size. You can get same-day local service or seven-day national processing. Local delivery starts at $6.95; national shipping is $12.95. *MC, V, AE, D*

★★★★★ Celebrate Cakes

972/271-4396

4310 Saturn Rd. — *Mon-Wed, Fri 10-6; Thu 10-7; Sat 10-3*
Garland, TX 75041 — *www.celebratecakes.com*

For the latest look in cake design, turn to Celebrate Cakes for all your needs. They can take a photograph and put it on the cake using icing, replicate your company logo, design a bridal fantasy, or sell you the supplies so you can make your own. Wedding cakes start at $1.75 a serving, and are worth every bite. They also have classes in cake decoration starting at just $35 for four 90-minute sessions. This family-owned company makes the kind of cakes your family will love to eat, so dig in. To get a sneak peek at the possibilities, long on to their website and view some samples. Only there, you can't have that cake and eat it, too. For that, you'll have to call in your order or stop by the bakery. *CK, MC, V, D*

★★★★★ Central Group 214/565-7888

1804 South Harwood Mon-Fri 4:30-3:30; Wed, Sat 4:30-12:30; Sun 7-10
Dallas, TX 75215

Two blocks south of I-30, check out a square block of freshness at Central Group and get the freshest veggies and fruits in North Texas. You don't have to be at the market at 4:30 A.M. to get the best deals, but it does help to get there early if you want the best selection. Even if you are not a restaurant or hotel, you are still welcome to choose from the best in fruits and vegetables around. Yummy! Only the freshest, luscious and juiciest are picked to begin with and then offered for sale. Add to your shopping list, frozen foods, domestic and imported cheese, canned items, dairy products, commercial chemicals, paper goods, and don't forget to ask for herbs and spices–is there anything on your list they don't have? Well, maybe home delivery. *CK*

★★★★★ Cheesecake Royale 214/328-9102

9016 Garland Rd. Mon-Sat 9-6
Dallas, TX 75218 www.cheesecakeroyale.com

Smile when you say cheese-cake! But don't expect to eat just one slice from this bakery. These cakes are sold in the finest specialty stores and catalogs in the country at $45, but they are available for half the price to individuals who order direct. All natural ingredients–real cream cheese, whipping cream, hand-squeezed lemon juice, dairy butter, sour cream and fresh fruits–are used with absolutely no added preservatives, artificial flavors, flour or gelatin. Scrumptious cheesecake choices include chocolate, key lime, white chocolate, amaretto, black forest, strawberry, raspberry and, yes, classic, plain New York style. Then, if cheesecake is not your piece of cake, try their chocolate mousse, kahula, rum, black forest, rum raisin, chocolate, three-layer cake or carrot cake for additional decadence. What you forego in calories, you'll save in costs. For gift-giving, the cakes can be shipped overnight by FedEx. Each cake is pre-cut, with tissue separating the 16 large slices. Cakes weighs approximately 4-5 pounds. and are an over-generous 10-inches in diameter. You know the old saying, "Since life is uncertain, eat dessert first!". Well, the least you can do is not pay the price! These cakes should be considered a national treasure. *CK, MC, V, AE*

★★★★★ Classic Touch by Hedy Wilson 817/921-0365

3133 Cleburne Rd *By Appt. Only*
Fort Worth, TX 76110

Owner and chef Hedy Wilson serves up some pretty heady fare. In fact, if you want a delicious spread without spreading yourself too thin in the budget department, call her. Bar mitzvahs, weddings, lunches, brunches, dinners, business functions, if the occasion calls for a scrumptious repast, don't pass her by.

★★★★★ Collin Street Bakery 903/872-8111

401 W. 7th Ave. *Mon-Thu 7-5:30; Sat 7-6; Sun Noon-6*
Corsicana, TX 75110 *www.collinstreetbakery.com*

You don't have to be nutty to love one. I'm talking fruitcakes, fruitcake. You can have your patty cakes and chocolate cakes, just send me a fruitcake from the Collin Street Bakery. They range from $17-$41. Four million pounds worth are sold every year. A deluxe version is still circling the earth aboard one of the Apollo spacecraft. If it's good enough for Vanna White, Princess Caroline and Nolan Ryan, it's good enough for me. Founded, owned and operated by the McNutt family, *Consumer Reports* ranks its customer service and product satisfaction #1 (even over L.L. Bean and Land's End). They even own their own plantation in Costa Rica, which supplies them with their pineapple and papaya, and they own the second largest pecan-shelling facility in the world. As if that weren't enough, they founded a computer company that helps keep track of customer information and order fulfillment. So, load up the clover honey, honey, and batter away. The onsite bake shop has a wonderful assortment of cookies, pies, cakes, breads, brittle, muffins and pastries. And there are always free samples and cups of coffeefor a dime. These cakes are never sold in stores–only direct from the maker. Say Happy Birthday when you're there. They are celebrating their 101st year. *CK, MC, V, AE, D*

★★★★ Cookie Bouquet 972/245-5010

3044 Old Denton Rd. *www.cookiebouquet.com*
Carrollton, TX 75007

Save a fortune, Cookie. Why expend the labor running around looking for the perfect delivery? Try a deliciously different gift from Cookie Bouquet. Colorfully decorated cookies are arranged in fun baskets, creating a bouquet that not only looks good enough to eat, you can. Nibble and bits go along way to welcome new employees to the Diva Team. Say "I Love You", "Congratulations on the New Baby", "Thanks for the Delicious Evening" or any other endearment that lasts longer than flowers and tastes a whole lot better. Enjoy your Cookie Banuqet 'til the very last crumb. Known, too, as Cookies By Design, they also offer gourmet, hand-decorated cookies. Choose from sugar, peanut butter, chocolate chip, fudge, snickerdoodles, oatmeal raisin, maccarroon, Neiman Marcus, and on several–with or without nuts. Go online to find the store nearest you, or czu 800/945-2665. *CK, MC, V, AE, D*

★★ Cooper Street Farmer's Market 817/276-8810

1606 S. Cooper St. *Mon-Sat 9-7; Sun 9-5*
Arlington, TX 76013

If you've spent too much time at Krispy Kreme, take a detour just down Cooper for a healthier alternative. In season, you'll find fresh-from-the-farm local produce that will have you jumping for joy. But even in the "off season", there's no reason to avoid this market. Starting each April, area farmers begin bringing in the freshest tomatoes, peaches, melons, squash, zucchini, peas, beans and much more. When those sources stop, Cooper Street heads to market, bringing in fresh produce from South Texas, California and Florida at better than grocery produce quality. Prices vary, but if you know what the squash is going for at the grocery store, you'll be able to make wise buys. *CK, MC, V, AE, D*

★★ Cowtown Natural Food Co. 817/531-1233

3539 E. Lancaster Ave. *Mon-Sat 10-6*
Fort Worth, TX 76103 *csf.colorado.edu/co-op/cowtown/*

Go green and get healthy the natural way at this cowtown favorite. Specializing in old-fashioned remedies and "good for you" foods, customers come to Cowtown from as far away as Mineral Wells, Alvarado, Arlington, Irving and Burleson. This co-op has the market cornered on organic foods, bulk grains and beans, fresh fruit and herbs. Our shoppers rave about all the healthy possibilities as well as reaping the fiscally healthy benefits. What's more, they offered environmentally-safe laundry detergents to clean up and contribute to the "Greening of America". *CK*

★ Culligan 972/233-1646

11910 Preston Rd., Suite 212 *Mon-Fri 10-7; Sat 9-6*
Dallas, TX 75230 *www.culligan.com*

Water, water everywhere, but not a decent pure drop to drink. Well, make an event of it and get thee to the watery. You can get bottled water right at your kitchen sink by renting a reverse osmosis drinking water appliance for $10.95/month and $1.95 for refills. Or, if you take the water cooler for six months, it's only $9 a month; on a 12-month lease, it's $8 a month. Got it? Get it? Water is the stuff of life and half the battle is having ice cold water at your fingertips. Other locations near the Inwood Trade Center at Irving Boulevard and Turtle Creek, and in Bedford at Harwood and Central. *CK, MC, V*

★★★★★ Dallas Farmers Market 214/939-2808

1010 S. Pearl Expwy. *Mon-Sun 7-6*
Dallas, TX 75201

The downtown Dallas Farmers Market shines heads (of lettuce) and shoulders (pork loins) over all the others. The grande dame of direct-from-grower, this metro marketplace attracts even world-famous Rio Grande grapefruit and oranges just minutes away from being picked. Pecans, more than seven varieties of them, in the shell, shelled or cracked ... you're nuts if you don't stop by. They have Christmas trees when the season permits, flocked or au natural; fruit baskets, lush and plump, and a whole host of specialty shops to wander and wonder in and out. Taste Daniel's Gourmet Coffees and The Mozzarella Company. Very few taste buds are left unattended. Open 364 days a year (closed Christmas and New Year's Day), this farm-to-you source is the one to take for the trip to bountiful. They have the freshest fruits, vegetables and florals in the area. Call the Produce Hotline to hear the latest offerings. Is it English peas, pickled cucumbers or black-eyed peas today? True farmers are a minority, though. Most stands are run by dealers who buy produce wholesale and resell it. Look for signs in the corner of each stall that identify the occupant as "farmer", "dealer" or "farm merchant" (farmers who purchase and resell produce). Shed 3 (the orange shed) is all dealers. Shed 4 (red) primarily holds dealers selling watermelons. For real farmers, head for shed 1 (yellow). Bet you didn't know that! My favorite still-on weekends only in Shed 2, gourmet foods and decorative gifts. You'll taste it all, from fresh vegetables, fruits and flowers to different events to liven the pickings, such as children's activities and musical entertainment–all at home at Dallas Farmers Market. Free parking. *CK*

★★ Dallas Food Depot 214/942-3201

909 S. Tyler *Mon-Sat 9-6*
Dallas, TX 75208

Want to scrounge around a grocery clearance center? Forget pristine aisleways and epicurean displays, this is where the bottom meets its match. But if price is your consideration, this is Nirvana for underground cheap. Dallas Food Depot is a major buyer of overruns on all name brand chicken, fish and beef, a large variety of frozen food, dry groceries, health and beauty products and general merchandise. No means a Sam's, a far cry from Whole Foods and a lifetime away from Simon & David, but it you go the distance, you may win the war on high prices. There is no way to tell what you might find on any given day. Food is still a big staple here, with the shelves full of canned goods and undamaged (as far as we could tell) bottles of brand-name condiments. Take I-35-E south to I-30. Cross the Trinity River. Exit 12th and Beckley. Stay on 12th Street for four or five blocks to Tyler. But since Tyler is a one-way street, go to Polk and circle back. On the right-hand side, you'll find this unclaimed grocery freight depot. Worth a trip if you're in the area, but I wouldn't go out of my way. It's a bummer to find if you're not familiar with the Oak Cliff/South Dallas neighborhoods. Then again, three big bags of Doritos for $1 was worth it. *CK, MC, V, AE, D, Food Stamps*

★★★ Dallas Tortilla — 214/821-8854

1418 Greenville Ave. — *Tue-Sat 8-8; Sun 8-6*
Dallas, TX 75206

Muy bueno. It doesn't get any better than this. This tortilla source is a delicious way to get your fix of freshly made tortillas (made in their Oak Cliff factory), as well as handmade tamales, tostadas, chips and taco shells. If you're getting ready for a party, don't forget to pick up a batch of fresh or frozen tamales, with or without jalapenos, in your choice of beef, pork or chicken filling. If it's hot today, it may be better tamale. At the corner of Greenville and Bryan, expect to shell out $4.75 for tamales per dozen and $1 for a pack of 100. Holy mole! *CK, MC, V*

★★★★★ Delicious Cakes — 972/233-2133

14819 Inwood Rd. — *Mon-Sat 9-5*
Addison, TX 75244

You can probably smell the raspberry liqueur wafting one block south of Belt Line in Addison. No doubt, at Delicious Cakes they are whipping up another sublime batter that will ultimately rise to the occasion. Straight from the bakers who are baking as fast as they can, you can even sample a taste before you buy any one of Elaine Luttrell's delicious cakes. They are fabulous. Rich, moist, succulent–they melt in your mouth (and sometimes in your hand). From birthdays to wedding cakes, or other special occasions, the bakers are like artists with a pastry brush. From traditional to exotic, fresh flower decorations to artistic designs, these cakes are not just a pretty face, they're delicious, too. Texas turtle cake, Mexican chocolate, orange marmalade and lemon, raspberries and liqueur, all frosted with cream cheese or fudge frostings. Well, yum-m-m-m! *CK*

★★★★★ Diet Gourmet 972/934-0900

4887 Alpha, Suite 285 *Mon-Thu 9-4; Fri 7-7; Sat 10-4*
Dallas, TX 75244

At last–gourmet, heart-healthy, low-cal meals delivered to your front door, home or office. You'll love staying on a diet with food like this. It's convenient. It's affordable. It costs $63 for four days, Mon-Thu; three days, Fri-Sun, $47.25. Freshly prepared meals are ready to store in the refrigerator. Breakfasts are a favorite. Scrumptious muffins, granola, oatmeal with fruits and nuts, crepes, pancakes, French toast. They are delicious and almost too good to be true. Lunch and dinner, too. Meals are delivered twice a week, or are available at their kitchen location. Everything is clearly marked as to when to eat it and how to heat it up, if needed. Choose from just plain healthy and delicious to very low-cal and still yummy. And if it's just a few items you're wanting, stop by for a quick muffin or cookie snack pack. Even their packaging and carry-all bags are first class. New this year are their additional dietary considerations such as those on Weight Watchers will be able to order according to preferred plan. *CK, MC, V*

★★★ Dolly Madison & Wonder/Hostess 972/399-0770

584 S. Belt Line *Mon-Sat 8-6; Sun 11-5*
Irving, TX 76060

Good grief, Charlie Brown, we've run out of Zingers! All of the unsold DOLLY MADISON sweets and HOSTESS/WONDER bakery treats are packed up and shipped to these outlet chain locations for a quick and cheap sale. Pick up a dozen cupcakes for your Girl Scout Troop, or supply a party tray for your next get-together. Who can tell between today's batch and a few days old anyway? (The package keeps them fresh.) Hot dog and hamburger buns (eight pack) were $.39 each and LAYS chips were $.99. Then, too, we winked for the Twinkie multi-packs for $1.59. Watch for coupons for even more bitten off, and if you qualify for the senior citizen's discount, don't hesitate to pull rank and ask for the additional 10 percent off their already low prices. And for those younger, be sure to ask for your free cards (Snacking Card at the Dolly stores and the Sweet Treat card at the Wonder Hostess stores). Check your directory for additional locations of Dolly and Wonder Stores. *CK*

Food Stuff

★★★ Enchanted Garden, The — 972/926-8924

2485 Merritt Drive — *Mon-Sat 10-6*
Garland, TX 75041 — *www.theenchantedgarden.net*

Take a deep breath, enjoy the aroma, take a sip, a-h-h-h! Be swept away to England, Ireland, South Africa or India with the best selection in the Metroplex of teas, or enjoy dinning by the light of Olde New England or Aspen candles. Be enchanted at this quaint little store with tea kettles, cups, sweets and tea for sale. Tea for two or 200, remember your roots! Cheerio. *C*

★★★★★ Entenmann's/Oroweat Bakery — 972/231-3487

1419 E. Spring Valley — *Mon-Fri 10-6; Sat 10-5*
Richardson, TX 75080

Now part of the Best Food Baking Company, this is the only remaining Entenmann's/Oroweat Bakery thrift store in the Metroplex. Their former location at 3068 Forest Lane is now a Mrs. Baird's Thrift, but you will see some of their products still available for sale. And that's good because their no-fat coffee cakes are too good to be threw. We just can't get enough of them! The cheese Danish makes you want to go Home, Swede, Home. Whether a gourmet, a gourmand or a glutton, you don't have to eat your heart out here. Besides being better for your health, you'll be saving up to 50 percent on products ranging from almost right-from-the-ovens to just a few days old. Nothing second-quality about shopping at this yummy outlet. A real sweet for your Eyes. *CK*

★★★ Farmers Market — 817/838-8781

5507 E. Belknap — *Mon-Sat 8-6*
Fort Worth, TX 76117

Fort Worth's original Farmer's Market serves it up fresh every time. We've been waiting with baited breath for the fresh stock of sweet Vidalia and 1015 onions (great for making your own Bloomin' Onion), but we wound up swooning over the succulent selection of melons. Stock, of course, varies with seasonal choices, as do prices. Now read this Tomato Scoop! Be prepared to deal amongst the wholesalers, tourists and little old ladies who may get nasty if you try to reach for that eggplant before they do. Worth every scuffle, though. *CK*

★★★★ Fiesta Mart — 214/944-3300

611 W. Jefferson Blvd. — *Mon-Sun 7-11*
Oak Cliff, TX 75208

Turn your next fiesta into an international buffet by shopping at Fiesta Mart. This 50,000-square-foot food emporium is designed to serve an international community, including Hispanic, African-American, Asian and Anglo shoppers. What a neat entree to the supermercado taste treaty. Shop for a comprehensive menu of Hispanic favorites, like camarillas and mangoes, along with the more exotic but "flavorful" shitake mushrooms and yuppie lettuce like radicchio. A snack bar selling tacos and fajitas at the entrance entices the most reluctant shopper to drool and pull up a stool at a market that oozes with Heart and Sole. Check directory for other locations. *CK, MC, V*

★★★★ Fresh Express Dallas — 214/421-1947

2500 S. Good Latimer — *Mon-Fri 5-5; Sat 5:30-11*
Dallas, TX 75215

Stop being so fresh! It's time to call it a day. Why spend time as a human food-processor for your next get-together? No more! Call Fresh Express and let them be your chopping block. Call a day in advance and $31 will get you four trays of the freshest veggies: radishes, cherry tomatoes, broccoli, cauliflower, celery and baby carrots. Then invite your guests over for a healthy repast. A 5-pound bag of fruit containing cantaloupe, honeydew melon and grapes was a mouthwatering $8.50. Call in advance for availability. Add dressing or dunking material and you're ready, set, go-urmet! From north Dallas, take I-35 to I-30 E. Exit 46A South Central Expressway to the Harwood light. Continue past the light and stay to the right; the next light is Hickory; turn left and go two blocks. Stay to the left to Good Latimer and turn right. Go a quarter mile and it's on your left. *CK*

★ Fresh Start Market — 214/528-5535

4108 Oak Lawn — *Mon-Thu 7-7; Fri 7-6; Sat 9-6; Sun Noon-5*
Dallas, TX 75219

A luxury grocery store in *The Underground Shopper?* Yes, it's located across from a luxury car dealer (Park Place Motors), but why not get the skinny on where to shop? This is a full-service supermarket whose specialty is low-fat and fat-free items that are as delicious as they are healthy.

Dine in or take it out. Check out the wonderful selection of fresh produce and herbs (we cleaned them out of cilantro). Though not discount, what price do you put on good health? *CK, MC, V, D*

★★★★ Gene's Fruit Stand & Patio — 972/247-7301

2508 Forest Lane — *Mon-Sun 9-6*
Dallas, TX 75234

Open for more than 30 years on Forest Lane, this open-air, fresh produce stand for fruits and vegetables is also rooted in some of the best plants and herbs in town. You can enjoy the plums of seasonal fruits and vegetables seven days a week. Such delicacies as perfectly rounded shelled peas were direct from East Texas farmers. Airplane plants and Swedish ivy were hanging around in the biggest pots in town–for $13.95 (only during springtime). Check out their pottery, swings, fountains, statuary, gazebos, lawn furniture, hanging baskets, bakers racks, pole lamps, concrete benches and tables, willow furniture ... you won't have to take a birdbath when it comes time to call it a day. You will savor the quality and get your money's worth every inch of the way. (It's in your genes, isn't it?) For holiday decorating on the green, save yourself a bunch ... and shop here. *CK, MC, V, D*

★★★★ Georgia's Farmers Market — 972/516-4765

916 E. 15th St. — *Mon-Sat 8:30-6:30; Sun 9-5*
Plano, TX 75074

This Georgia's a peach. Her name is Georgia Machala Massey and she started in the business on the ground floor, at the downtown Dallas Market with her father and brothers when she was a mere 7-years-old. The Machala family still operates a stand in the No. 2 shed, but many of Georgia's brothers have migrated to her new stand in Plano, which she opened in March of 1997. This former body shop, with roll-up doors, creates a classic, open-air market atmosphere. She hand-picks her produce from Texas and elsewhere, and includes vine-ripened tomatoes, fresh peas and peaches from East Texas and Parker County, Collin County okra and squash, eggplant, peppers and new potatoes. To get a taste, head north on Central Expressway to the 15th Street exit and go down to the light. Turn right and go through another light. It's not far from the railroad tracks, approximatelyhalf a mile from the freeway on the right, across the street from City Park. *CK, MC, V*

★★★★ Goodie Basket, The

817/377-4222

4319 B Camp Bowie Blvd.
Fort Worth, TX 76107
Mon-Fri 8:30-5; Sat 10-4
www.yourgoodiebasket.com

The Goodie Basket is just this side of heaven, featuring some of the most delicious little gift items around. Creative boxing and unusual fillings add to the goodies that are packed inside. Choose from a bounty of scrumptious white chocolate truffles, white chocolate raspberries, cappuccino, espresso coffees, cookies and more, hand-picked by you or by one of their creative staff designers. Baskets can be made to fit any occasion. They aren't discount by any means, but they are one of the most imaginative sources for gift-givers in the Metroplex. And if you're looking for the exclusive MICHAEL SIMON sweaters and Michael Simon Lite, here's the place. Gourmet gift baskets for all occasions. Delivery and shipping anywhere in the Metroplex and beyond. *CK, MC, V, AE, D*

★★★ Grapevine Farmers Market

701 S. Main St.
Grapevine, TX
Sat 8-Sellout; Wed 3-6

Grapevine takes its historical image to heart, from the look of Main Street down to presenting a genuine seasonal farmers market. About 15 actual farmers roll into downtown twice a week with mouthwatering produce from peaches, tomatoes and corn to fresh from the nest eggs and honey. The market starts each year the weekend after Main Street Days in late May and runs through November when the produce turns toward pumpkins, gourds and the like. *CK*

★★★★ Greenberg Smoked Turkeys

903/595-0725

221 McMurray
P.O. Box 4818
Tyler, TX 75712
Daily 8:30-5:30

In business for 58 years, the Greenberg Smoked Turkey stays in demand across the country. Glowing reviews from *The New York Times, Esquire, Forbes, Family Circle, Connoisseur* as well as many satisfied customers attest to their plump and juicy credentials. Though they have no catalog, no website, no toll-free telephone number and take no credit cards, they bill their customer at $3.20 per pound plus shipping and handling. Birds run small, (6-9 pounds), and medium, (9-12 pounds), plus shipping and handling. Peak season is October-December and personalized cards can be included with the turkeys if sent as a present. Family secret recipe leaves birds looking black on the outside with meat darkened all the way through. Bones are recommended as soup bones. A real, down-to-earth bird worth its weight in gold. *Billing*

✧✧✧✧ Groceryworks.com — 877/505-4040

Carrollton, TX — *24 hour/7 Day*

www.groceryworks.com

Do your grocery shopping without the annoyances of shopping cart wheels that go in different directions, easy listening music, long lines and screaming kids. At groceryworks.com, you can do all your grocery shopping from the comfort of your home or office. One of the great features of groceryworks.com is the cartminder–a reminding service that remembers up to 10 of your previous grocery orders so you can quickly and easily purchase certain items again. Talk about high-tech Gingko. Expect a $25 minimum order for no delivery charge; but believe me, tips are appreciated. *CK, MC, V, AE, D*

★★★★★ Homemade Gourmet — 972/712-1885

Debbie Diaz, Distributor — *Mon-Fri 10-5*

Carrollton, TX 75010

Hate to cook? In a hurry? Faster than a New York minute, why not try Homemade Gourmet mixes and get cooking a meal that will take less than the Minute Waltz. Mixes for bread, soup, chili, bar-b-que marinade, desserts and more can be whipped up in no time flat. Cooking the old-fashioned way has never been this easy (or this much fun). Just add ingredients such as eggs, oil, water or milk. A few call for ingredients that are readily available at your local grocer. Cheese, sour cream, canned corn – be the "life of the Pantry"! Jump dump all the ingredients together, stir and heat. Eat a delicious meal that you thought impossible to squeeze into your already jammed-packed day. The mixes are the creation of Tami Van Hoy, who started by bringing mixes to family members, then to craft shows. Many of her recipes are adaptations from old family recipes from her Grandma's days. She has carefully preserved the rich flavors and "homemade" taste of these oldies but goodies. Try 'em. You'll love 'em. Call the distributor, Debbie Diaz, visit their retail store in downtown Frisco at 6943 Main St., 75034, 972/712-1885 or order online at their website. *CK, MC, V, MO*

★★★★★ IWA-International Wine Accessories 214/349-6097

10246 Miller Rd. *Mon-Fri 9-7; Sat 10-4*
Dallas, TX 75238 *www.iwawine.com*

It might be a little challenging to get through for directions and slightly intimidating once you've arrived (they have to buzz you in the front door). But, if you're a true wine enthusiast, it's well worth taking on the challenge. The closeout section of this catalog giant will leave you reaching for a bottle of wine to steady your nerves. (It's one of the conditions often exhibited by bargain shoppers.) Called by some, The Horchow Finale of wine, the closeout section features beautiful items from previous catalogs, samples, one-of-a-kinds, overstocks, blemishes/imperfections and canceled orders all at prices that are 10-to-50 percent below original cost. There are antique bottles, glassware, crystal, decanters, room dividers, sculpture, tables, rotisserie grills, books, videos, ties, wine-cellar units and more. L'chaim! *CK, MC, V, AE, D*

★★★★ Krispy Kreme Doughnuts 817/461-2600

2600 S. Cooper St. *Mon.-Sat.: 5:30A.M.-Midnight; Sun 5:30 A.M.-11P.M.*
Arlington, TX 76015 *www.krispykreme.com*

If you walk in the door when hot doughnuts are coming off the assembly line, you'll probably get a free sample. If it's an original glazed donut you're drooling for, be prepared for Nirvana; warm and meltingly sweet, the light pastry delivers full flavor with no oily taste. The North Carolina-based company, which recently opened the first of many planned locations in the Metroplex on Cooper Street, plans on a Grapevine site soon. The variety leaves no holes opened: cake-style chocolate, devil's food and blueberry for starters to filled doughnuts including custard-filled made without eggs or dairy products. Better for your health. *MC, V*

★★★★ L'Epicurien 214/747-5885

2025 Irving Blvd., #213 *Mon-Fri 8-5; Call for Sat Hours*
Dallas, TX 75207

L'Epicurien spelled any other way still tastes as sweet and I can assure you, I know what it means. It means, you must order in advance, but you can enjoy sweets from this caterer and food wholesaler that sells to area restaurants. (There's nothing just sitting out in bakery cases waiting for you to taste, however.) You've probably tasted their sumptuous sensations at such fine dining establishments as Marty's/Café Tugogh and Wine Bar or the Riviera Restaurant, but now you can go directly to the maker and save money. Baker,

baker, bake me three-layers of chocolate mousse cake resting on an almond meringue base as fast as you can. Operation Dessert Storm doesn't end with desserts, as their pates and sausages are big sellers, too. For fresh fruit tarts and other pasty creations (as in everything they make), it's tasteful to order 24 hours in advance. Call for a product list and bakers away! *CK, MC, V, AE*

★★★★ La Spiga Bakery 972/934-8730

4203 Lindbergh *Mon-Fri 7-3; Sat 7-4*
Addison, TX 75244

A freshly baked loaf of bread–what else is there in life worth turning your nose up for? Whether it's for the holidays or an everyday treat, head to Addison where the aroma wafts its way down Belt Line. At La Spiga's, they've been serving their artisan breads and pastries since 1994, when Donato Milano and Carolyn Nelson began selling their breads and pastries to many major hotels and restaurants. Soon they opened their ovens to the public. They make bread by hand, the old-fashioned way, for their early morning Italian breakfasts or daily lunch specials. So relax and enjoy every bitefull. Caesar salad with focaccia, quiche or lasagna, topped off with an exotic coffee and a swan Èclair, pecan/almond bar or fruit tart, it's enough to make you want to jump-start the rest of the day. Make your day. Their famous Italian Milano white bread is as good as their calamata olive, jalapeno cheese, pumpernickel, sfilatino baguette, sweet basil and rye. They also have the best "raisin challah" in town, biscotti cookies, ciabatta and panini rolls. Come to think of it, their chocolate eclairs and bread pudding for $2 aren't bad either. So enjoy! *CK, MC, V, D*

★★★ Margarita Masters 972/641-7926

PO Box 540502 *Call to Reserve*
Grand Prairie, TX 75054

Chill out with a frozen drink machine that you can rent for your next party. Margarita Masters is the oldest and largest company of its kind in the Metroplex, where they're also known for their unmatched service, attention to detail and reliability, not to mention their awards. For $125, plus $15 per Margarita mix (serves approximately 80), you just have to add the tequila to serve up delicious frozen drinks. Even better, try a Bellini, daiquiri, piña colada or swirls mix. Prices ranged $15-$20 for the mix. Different drinks call for different liqueurs. Call and ask for Carl, the friendly Margarita man. He can tell you exactly what to purchase for the party. The rental fee includes the machine, delivery/set-up, salt, straws and 80 glasses. Call a week in advance to reserve your machine. Isn't it about time you got on the road to Margaritaville? *CK, MC, V, AE*

★★★★ Mary's Sweets 972/221-7707

1114 W. Main *Mon-Fri 10-6; Sat 10-5*
Main Street Shopping Center
Lewisville, TX 75067

Native Texan Mary Jennings has been knee-deep in chocolate for the past 15 years. Only in Texas can you find your heart's desire, at least if it's chocolate. Her gift-giving talent has been shipped worldwide because she is one of the most delicious purveyors of Texas gifts and candy. Want a Mary's chocolate in the shape of Texas? Armadillo? Boots? Cowboy hat? These can be bought individually for $.99, or boxed in a Texas gift set for $5.50. Chocoholics who can't get enough of a good thing, love her half-lb. state of Texas made in white chocolate with almonds or milk chocolate with pecans. ($5.99–a small price to pay for a sugar rush). For the holidays, you can ship white chocolate states with red and green peppermint bits, as chocolates always do better when the weather is cooler. Y'all enjoy and order again real soon! *CK, MC, V, AE, D*

♥♥♥♥♥ Mozzarella Co. 214/741-4072

2944 Elm St. *Mon-Fri 9-5; Sat 9-3*
Dallas, TX 75226 *www.mozzco.com*

Say cheese! The selection at this factory is sure to make you smile, from goat cheese to more than 20 different kinds of cheeses–fresh mozzarella and mascarpone tortas (basil, tomato or pecan praline for starters). These award-winning cheeses are handmade daily from fresh milk and shipped from this tiny factory across the country. Special party platters and gift baskets are put together everyday, some even while you wait (and salivate). Offering the Cheese of the Month, a perfect gift, they'll send one of their cheeses each month for $240 for 12 months or $150 for 6 months, shipping included. A half-pound container of homemade heaven was $5. When you're in the area, for the Doubting Thomases, their tasting area could cultivate buds for new and exotic flavors. A beautiful Rhapsody in Bleu!, Italian cheeses (fresh mozzarella, mascarpone and scamorza); Greek cheese (feta); Mexican cheeses (queso fresco, blanco and oaxaca); French cheeses (chevre and creme fraiche); Southwestern cheeses (caciottas and montasios flavored with robust chilies and fragrant herbs); American cheeses (including cream cheese); festive cheeses (like mozzarella rolls); even party cheeses (especially mascarpone tortas)–all flavorful cheeses without additives or preservatives. *CK, MC, V* ($15 minimum)

★★ Mrs. Baird's Thrift Store

972/243-4050
14500 N. Josey
Mon-Sat 10-6
Farmers Branch, TX 75234

Save some dough on breads and dinner rolls when you shop for MRS. BAIRD'S goodies fresh from her ovens–just a day late. Stock up, put the extras in the freezer and enjoy the savings for weeks to come. We picked up some loaves of split-top wheat bread for $.89 each, and eyed the dinner rolls (two packages/$1.95)–but the dough has definitely risen pricewise. Never mind, we still loaded up for our next dinner party. (Our guests will never know!) Pop them in the freezer when you get them home and when warmed, you'll whip out the freshly baked rolls just like Suzy Homemaker. Check your directory for other locations. *CK*

★★★★★ Mrs. Renfro's

817/336-3849
PO Box 321
Mon-Fri 8-4
Fort Worth, TX 76101

Everything's fresh from the kitchens of Mrs. Renfro. More than 50 years ago, Mr. and Mrs. George Renfro began selling their relishes and sauces in and around the Fort Worth area. Now, they are legendary. Spice up your own bland cooking with something from their ovens. Serve up award-winning dips, sauces, relishes and syrups and experience perfection in a jar. Prepared with the finest ingredients, you can really have a hot time in the old town tonight. Order their jalapeno peppers, hot picante salsa, hot chow chow, nacho sliced jalapeños, or their hot tomato relish and you'll be whistlin' Dixie. Personally, we relish the black bean salsa, mixed with no-fat sour cream. It's our favorite late night snack (with no-fat crackers, of course.) Order by phone; four jars for $17 (includes shipping). Mix and match. Ask for their brochure and ordering instructions. *CK, PQ, PL, MO*

★★★ Omaha Steaks

214/368-7597
10854 Preston Rd.
Mon-Sat 10-6; Sun Noon-5
Dallas, TX 75230
www.omahasteaks.com

You can lick your chops, day or night in person, from their (800/228-9055), by catalog or order online. Either way, discriminating diners have been savoring Omaha Steaks since 1917. Corn-fed, Midwestern beef is the best (ask any Midwesterner) and these are the meat-packing best. They have six, 6-ounce, fork-tender filet mignons for $49.99 (a savings of $18) and took home a free calculator to boot (what one has to do with the other is your guess). If you finish the last bite and are still not satisfied, they offer a money-back guarantee. ('Course, you'll have to do some explaining if you ate every last morsel!) Check out the specials on quality seafood, pork chops and chicken, too. But don't expect the prices to come cheap. Watch for their newspaper coupons when products are offered at 50 percent off. Check directory for other locations in Dallas, Lewisville and Plano. CK, MC, V, AE, D

★★★ Pendery's 817/332-3871

304 E. Belknap *Mon-Fri 8:30-5:30; Sat 9-5*
Fort Worth, TX 76102

This paramour of spices has returned to doing what they do best ... and that is selling spices and custom-blended chili powders by mail through their beautifully illustrated catalog. You, too, can be a hothead with any of their blends. For example, you can pay retail for those little spice bottles in the grocery stores and pay $4-$5 for two-ounces; or you can forgo the fancy packaging and buy a one-pound bag for a whole lot less. Their Top Hat chili blend is their most sought-after item for just a slice more than $10 (and that is for a pound–which is 16 ounces, folks). Head south to their San Antonio–blend red for $8.63. Now, for any more spicier secrets, you'll have to call the numbers above. *CK, MC, V, AE, D, MOC*

★★★ Rainbo Bakery Stores 972/686-2330

2914 Centerville Rd. *Mon-Fri 9-7; Sat 9-6*
Dallas, TX 75228

You can fly on over to the RAINBO outlet and become a happy little bird when you find a box of donuts for as little as $1.25. We sprinkled powdered sugar all over ourselves before checking out the buys on day-old bread (from $.40-$.80) and the other goodies from the Rainbo Bakery. Check out daily specials on day-olds. Check your directory for other area Rainbo Thrift Stores. Then maybe you'll be able to see the light at the end of the other rainbow. *CK*

★★★★ Russell Stover Candies 972/563-8227

200 Apache Trail *Mon-Sat 9-6; Sun Noon-6*
Metrocrest Industrial Park
Terrell, TX 75160

Next time you're traveling on I-20 through Terrell, take the FM 148 exit and travel a mere-quarter-smile to the Best Little Chocolate House in Texas and the

#1 candymaker in the country. Russell Stover has set up their Southwest distribution center there and has accompanied it with a candy store open to the public. This is a fun little rest stop with friendly, helpful folks. (How can you have a bad day working in a chocolate factory?) On our visit, we found those sinful pecan rolls four/$1 and WHITMAN (now owned by Russell Stover) candy bars (all varieties) for $.15 each. And if it doesn't matter to you that the box doesn't weigh exactly the right amount, or that it might be a bit misshapen, you can save lots of money here. Even if you are buying first-quality merchandise, you will still save 15 percent off the retail price. Save on overruns or seconds up to 36 percent and on holiday left-overs up to 75 percent. We also sucked up to sugar-free and hard candies, like RUSSELL STOVER jelly beans and a former president's favorite, JELLY BELLIES. There's a different special every week, and don't forget, you don't need to wait until Valentine's Day to shower her with candy. (Even though Valentine Day candies ranged from $1.09 to $44.99.) *CK, MC, V, D*

★★ Susie B's Fruit Stand — 817/244-1888

8300 Hwy. 80 W — *Mon-Sat 8:30-5:30; Sun 9-4:45*
Fort Worth, TX 76116

Forget Susie Q. This Susie B knows her way around the produce trucks that will help you save money to the core. For the past 20 years, this family has been delivering fresh fruits and vegetables from the fields or right off the shipping trucks which saves you money in the end. How do they do it? Eliminate the middleman, that's how. Scoop up Vidalia onions for $.69 a pound and pack up the fresh black-eyed peas. Tomatoes were ripe and huge on our visit, but the peaches went out the door faster than we could grab a bushel or two. Visit early for the freshest choices. He or she who hesitates, hates when Susie makes a B-line and heads home when her baskets are empty. If you want giftbaskets, small or large with assorted fruits and nuts, you're nuts to pay retail. *CK, MC, V, D*

★★ Sweet Endings — 214/747-8001

2901 Elm St. — *Mon-Wed, Fri 7:30-1A.M.;*
Dallas, TX 75226 — *Thu 7:30-10; Sat 10-1A.M.; Sun 10-10*

Their hours are varied and go deep in the night, but deep in the heart of Deep Ellum, here's a real Sweet for sore eyes. Customized gift baskets or cookie tins can be filled to the brim with a collection of specialty coffee items, such as coffee beans, coffee makers, coffee mugs, coffee candies and coffee drinkers' T-shirts (sure to create a major brew-ha-ha for the recipient). Or try a dozen or so chocolate chip cookies like Mama used make for a fingerlickin' accompaniment. Sweet Endings starts early in the morning mixing and stirring the batter for their mouthwatering muffins, ready for you to serve at breakfast meetings to impress clients or to eat there and be intoxicated by the combination of brew and bakery. Taste a happy ending to a hungry eye. Located at the corner of Elm and Malcolm X in a hot pink building with white French doors, smell the sweet ending to cakes, cookies and muffins, then wash it all down with a smoothie. *CK, MC, V*

★★★★★ Texas Pecan Co. 972/241-7878

2850 Satsuma *Mon-Fri 8:30-5*
Dallas, TX 75229

Only a nut would pay retail for pecan halves or pecan pieces when you can get a pound here for $4.95. Looking for quality products that are guaranteed "new crop"? then forget buying them at the grocery stores. If you are already bucking the system, you might as well go for broke. Here you'll take the bite out of paying retail for almonds, Spanish peanuts, walnuts, filberts, Brazil nuts, pumpkin and sunflower seeds, pine nuts, trail mixes and roasted/salted nut mixes. Go to the source and satiate your taste buds with the best. Off Stemmons between Forest and Royal, it's especially delicious to buy them almost pound-free and fancy foolish. It tastes the same and it's time you straightened up and stopped all this craziness. You're nuts if you don't! *CK, MC, V, D*

✔ Vending Nut Co. 817/737-3071

2222 Montgomery St. *Mon-Fri 8:30-5; Sat 9-Noon*
Fort Worth, TX 76107

Though open year 'round for wholesale business, the public is invited to shop only occasionally. Watch for their sales, where you'll go nuts when they open their retail store to show off the owners' treasured collection of antiques as well as their supply of freshlyroasted nuts and gift baskets. You're nuts if you don't stash a few pounds away for the winter. These enterprising folks have been shelling out the roasted nuts for decades: cashews, Hawaiian macadamias, Southern pecans, almonds and pine nuts as well as gift containers of candy and nuts. Then, fix up a mix or two of grated coconut, pumpkin or sunflower seeds; or if you must, buy some already made. *CK*

Food Stuff

♥♥♥♥♥ Whole Foods Market — 817/461-9362

801 E. Lamar — *Mon-Sun: 8 A.M.-10 P.M.*
Arlington, TX 76011 — *www.wholefoods.com*

Shop with WholeFoods.com to discover thousands of natural and organic products at your fingertips! The newest candidate to go online for your shopping convenience. Grab your cart and start shopping! One of the newest locations to open this year is Tarrant County's first Whole Foods Market and it boasts 24,000 square feet of natural foods and related products. These include organic and conventionally-grown produce, fresh seafood, natural meats and groceries, including baby foods and pet foods. Whole Foods' bakery receives deliveries twice daily of freshlybaked European-style crusty breads. The bakery also carries a full selection of cookies, muffins, scones and fancy pastries. Whole Foods' bulk-bin section features hundreds of scoop-your-own products, including natural grains, nuts, dried fruits, spices, nut butters–even real maple syrup. Also look for prepared foods, a large selection of imported cheeses and specialty beers. Whole Foods also has a demonstration kitchen with a full slate of classes. Stop by for a schedule and enjoy the fruits of their labor. Though not discount by any stretch of the imagination, it's more of the most pleasurable and aethetically-appetizing places to shop in town. Check directory for location nearest you.

★★★★ Wonder Bread Thrift — 817/534-3152

5609 Wichita Ave. — *Mon-Sat 8-7; Sun 11-5*
Fort Worth, TX 76119

Be the HOSTESS with the most-ess when you buy Wonder-ful breads and snacks at the Wonder Bread Thrift Store. You'll be a day late but a dollar saved when you net loaves at 20-60 percent off. One pound loaves were selling for \$.33; 1 1/2 pound loaves for \$.49 and the split-top wheat loaves were \$.59. Satisfy your sweet tooth with TWINKIES and DING DONGS for just pennies on Wednesdays and Saturdays (those are bargain days). Boxes were headed out the door for half-price. Some of their stock is rerouted from the stores (day old) and some of it is right from the ovens. Who knows? Not my nose, that's for sure. If you're a native, you'll be delighted to know that a loaf of Texas Toast was \$.99. Hostess cupcakes were on special during our visit; buy one box of eight and get another free. Then, we went into sweet shock. CK

Furniture

★★★★★ 5th Avenue Dinettes & More 972/241-5565

14000 Stemmons *Mon-Fri 10:30-7; Sat 10-6; Sun 1-5*
Farmers Branch, TX 75234

When you're good, you're very, very good. When you're great, you come back for more. With more than 45 years combined retailing experience, 5th Avenue Dinettes & More has been reincarnated into a huge and visible specialty showcase featuring dinette sets and more. Hundreds of styles waiting for a new home (or an old home will do, too). Bar stools? Staggering selection. You can even pick out chairs and stools for your existing tables. Save 20-45 percent off manufacturer's suggested price in all your better brands: CHROMCRAFT, PASTEL, STONEVILLE and WHITAKER to name a few. They dare you to find them anywhere else, cheaper. The possibilities are endless but your bucks should stop here. For example, on their opening weekend, we found a five-piece iron table with glass top and four iron and wicker chairs for $499 (retail $930) and a ChromCraft glass table with four upholstered chairs for $582 (retail $897). If you're a card carrying game player, they have the largest selection of game sets in the Metroplex, pokerface. Leather sofas, too. When it came time to outfit our breakroom and media room, we headed for 5th Avenue and bought it all in one stop. Price, quality and service, how can you not want to put all your cards on their tables? Going north, exit Valley View and stay on the service road. *CK, MC, V, AE, D*

★ Aaron Rental 972/416-3111

1235 S. Josey Lane *Mon-Fri 10-7; Sat 10-6*
Carrollton, TX 75006

The former Clearance Center is kaput and now it's the same old story. Aaron will rent you just about anything and it's yours after the last payment. Not a bad deal if you're desperate but not a good deal if you're looking for major savings. Plans run for 12 months, with a lowest price guarantee, or you'll get

$. /CR from MAGNOVOX, RCA, SONY, ZENITH with payments starting .99 per month, ends up costing you at least $239. Then again, you could go to the $1 movies instead and save even more. At the southeast corner of Josey and Belt Line where the Sack 'n Save is, look for Aaron's in the corner. Refrigerators from GE or MAYTAG start at $64 a month, or find any other appliances. They will lease you jewelry, pictures, lamps, furniture for the living room, bedroom or dining room or most any kind of TVs, shelf stereos, entertainment center and more. Check directory for location nearest you. *CK, MC, V, D*

★★★ Adams Furniture 940/648-3145

417 N. FM 156 *Mon-Wed, Fri-Sun 9-6; Thu 9-7*
Justin, TX 76247

There's not a bad apple in this Adams' repertoire. Not exactly the Garden of Eden, but not the opposite direction, either. In fact, a trip here is Justin-fied. Since 1929, in the days of the Depression, they have been passing on the savings owing to their low overhead. Brand names that are planted firmly on their showroom floor include ACTION LANE, BROYHILL, CORSICANA, EAGLE INDUSTRIES, ENGLANDER, ALPHA MAYO, SEALY, LANE, TOWN SQUARE and more. Check out their "Texas Western" collection for down-home picks. These are special items (hand-made by Texas artisans and craftsmen) and are sure to become a "conversation piece" in your home. Most of their furniture comes straight from the factory with free delivery. *CK, MC, V, AE, D*

★★ Affordable Furniture 817/277-4481

629 W. Pioneer Pkwy. *Mon-Sat 10-7; Sun Noon-5*
Arlington, TX 76010

Affordable Furniture's philosophy is basically the more you buy, the more you save. Choose from DIXON, MEADOWBROOK, PASHLEY, PIONEER, PURDUE, RIVERSIDE and other brands that are affordable but not necessarily on everybody's "must-have" list. On the northeast corner of Matlock and Pioneer, sofas are so affordable, guess that's why it's their moniker. Sofas started as low as $399, though sitting on one wasn't as cushy on the tushy. But, for anyone setting up first-time housekeeping, you can't go wrong. Deals on mattress sets began with twins for $89.95; full $99.95; queen, $159.95; and king, $199.95. Financing and layaway available. *CK, MC, V, AE, D*

Furniture

★★★★★ AFFORDIT Furniture 940/566-3222

1802 Alice *Mon-Sat 9-7; Sun 1-5*
Denton, TX 76201

Students or families of students or friends of students need all the help they can get. Enter AFFORDIT Furniture, a family-owned enterprise that has finally settled into bigger digs across the street from their original, long-time University Street location. How about a futon bunkbed, complete with twin mattress and regular mattress for $288 in black, blue, white or red? Or a farm table dinette group, four chairs and a table, in a choice of three finishes for $158. Prices get better and better with four-drawer chests starting at $38, bookcases for $58, three-piece parquet table group for $68, a sofa and loveseat combination with several colors and styles to choose from for $488 and up, a metal futon sofa with regular futon mat for $148, and a papasan chair with cushion for $68. Sofa sleepers start at $588 and up. Another location in Watauga at 6535 Watauga Rd, 817/281-9140, Mon-Sat 9-7, Sun 1-5. Need more information? Call Don or Eldon Nicholson and find out about how you too can AFFORD IT. *CK, MC, V, D*

★★★★ American Furniture Warehouse 972/660-6660

2000 S. Great Southwest Pkwy. *Mon-Sat 10-9; Sun 10-8*
Grand Prairie, TX 75051

Wanting to strike it rich? Then head to the northwest corner of Great Southwest Parkway and Pioneer Parkway and shop at American Furniture Warehouse. Across the street from the bowling alley, when it comes to offering all American deals, you can count on this company to score big time. ASHLEY, CLAYBROOK, MAYO, PIONEER and SOUTHERN TRADITIONAL were just a few of the names that were ready to rock and bowl. Ashley sofas ranged from $459 and love seats were $419. Dinettes ranged from $79.99-$1,299.99, so you can sit down once in a while and enjoy the fruits of your labor during the ups and downs in your lifetime. Financing can be arranged through Norwest and they offer 90 days same as cash. Visit, too, their location at 4554 McEwen Rd. in Dallas, 972/866-6600. *CK, MC, V, D*

★★★★★ Anderson Martin Furniture 214/343-9752

10890 Bekay St., Suite 400 *Mon-Sat 8-5; Sun 10-4*
Dallas, TX 75238

What a novel idea–bookmark this company on the best-seller list. They're the ones who provide the furnishings for vacant houses waiting to be sold. The theory that a house sells better with that "lived-in" look is the basis for this business with you as the beneficiary. Expect houses in the $500,000 range and up to be the display showcase for furniture that ultimately winds up for sale at the Anderson Martin warehouse. Gorgeous custom furniture that has been seen but not used with price tags of 5-10 percent above cost. As good as new, a queen-size sleigh bedroom set, made from solid cherry, five pieces, hand-carved was $1,700. Hand-carved, ornate armoires, retailing for $5,000 were $1,200. How about a solid cherry dining room set, featuring a hand-carved table with two leaves, six chairs and a china hutch with light for $2,500. They also have living room furniture including leather pieces. Though they're being sold at a warehouse, remember from whence they came. If it once was displayed in a million-dollar mansion, it sure fits in more-down-to-earth house settings. *MC, V, AE, D*

★★★★ Armoire Store, The — 214/696-2684

10745 Preston Rd. — *Mon-Sat 10-6; Sun 1-5*
Dallas, TX 75230 — *www.armoire-store.com*

Armoires from $600-$2,000 is now how the mold is cast here. If you have special requirements for an entertainment center, no problem, they can transform it into a custom entertainment center because they have their own in-house woodshop. Nestled into a bricked corridor entrance, you're apt to pass right by, but when you find it, you're hooked on the look. Lots more antiques than in the past are priced accordingly. Choose from hundreds of highquality wood armoires such as French, country French, art deco, Chippendale, pine, Louis XVI, even Queen Anne–any shopper would be impressed with the artistic reformation. Whatever the conversion–from wine racks to computer stations, bookshelves to a pantry, you are only a stone's throw away. *CK, MC, V*

★★★ Arrangement, The — 214/748-4540

2605 Elm St. — *Mon-Sat 10-6; Sun Noon-5*
Dallas, TX 75226

If there was a category killer for southwest furniture, let me introduce you to "America's largest source." Housed in a 17,000-square-foot showroom in the heart of Deep Ellum, you'll be a washed in a field of solid wood furniture, white-washed and natural-finished pine chairs and sofas, dining room and bedroom furniture, office tables, armoires and more. The adobe look may be on the way out, but the rustic "Taos" look is going strong. And full prices are out, although for this quality, you can expect prices not to be cheap! Furniture appears to be handcrafted one whittle at a time. Artists and craftsmen are available to create whatever you may need and the staff is eager to show you the catalog of goodies for custom orders (but expect a eight-ten week wait). In addition to the Plano location at 2411 Coit Rd., north of Park Blvd., they have stores in Houston and Denver. *CK, MC, V, AE, D*

★★★★ Baker's Furniture and Accessories — 972/221-3252

176 Lakeland Drive — *Mon-Fri 10-8; Sat 10-6; Sun 1-6*
Lakeland Plaza Center
Lewisville, TX 75067

This Baker's no candlestick maker but a source to seeing the light on home furnishings. Does the name THOMASVILLE ring a bell? Since opening their first showroom in Garland, the Baker family has more than 75 years in the business but, believe it or not, does not sell BAKER furniture. (So stop asking me!) They do, instead, offer the largest selection of Thomasville (their specialty) furniture in the Metroplex. With five locations in Lewisville, Garland, Plano, Addison and the Knox/Henderson area, you also can save on other big names in furniture like ACTION, BRADINGTON YOUNG, BROYHILL, FLEXSTEEL, HEKMAN, HOOKER, HUNTINGTON HOUSE, LEXINGTON, MASSOUD, RIVERSIDE and more with the lowest price guarantee on everything they sell. Beautiful room-like settings highlight the possibilities, and with more than 1,200 custom fabrics, you can go from brushed denim to chintzy in no time. Leather sofas, home office furniture, entertainment and computer armoires and accessories from around the world make Baker a deal-maker worth checking out. The Renaissance Collection of bedroom, dining room and living room furnishings, for example, was an inspiration right from the sun-drenched Mediterranean. Check the directory for the location nearest you. Special financing packages are also available. *CK, MC, V, D, Financing*

★★ Bar Stools Etc. — 817/589-7055

2416 Gravel Drive — *Mon-Fri 9-5; Sat 9-3*
Fort Worth, TX 76118

You can sit around, twirl around, and pick your choice of barstools at this manufacturer's outlet near I-820 and Trinity Blvd. They don't even ask to see an ID unless you're paying by check. Choose either a wood base or metal, 24-inch or 30-inch, then pick from more than 82 different fabrics and more than 500 different vinyls and naugahydes–from $42.50-$300 is the norm depending on the style of the back. Custom bar tables and bar tops, too. Orders take eight-10 days. *CK, MC, V, AE, D*

★★★★★ Bassett Furniture Direct 972/315-9988

1915 S. Stemmons Frwy. *Mon-Sat 10-9; Sun Noon-6*
Lewisville, TX 75067 *www.bassettfurniture.com*

Can't be more direct that at Bassett Furniture Direct. Save time and money at this one-stop design retail environment created by the nationally-known Bassett Furniture folks. It's a cinch to envision total room possibilities as you meander through the furnished vignettes. Priced to sell with specials and decorative accents at low, low prices. Don't think, though, that you'll have to forgo service. It's superb. Bassett makes a home furnishing statement for those who'd like to shop for the coordinated total look. Bedroom sets for $699 in pine or cherry (including a headboard, footboard and rails, night stand and dresser with mirrors) are hard to beat. Their lowest-price guarantee (on exact matches) is a plus. You'll be sleeping like royalty on the many mattress styles without having nightmares about the bill. Take advantage of their in-house decorators if you're creatively challenged. See Bassett dining room, living room, bedroom, casual living and home-office furniture plus home accents like lamps, wall art, area rugs–the whole nine yards. Bassett has been making furniture for a century, so their pieces are meant to last for generations. We were aided in our search by Barbara Milwood, a design consultant, who is a U.N.T. grad with a degree in Home Furnishings Merchandising Service. Bassett is right on target. Quality. Price. Service are all right here. *CK, MC, V, AE, D, Bassett DC*

★★★ Bent Tree Resale Furnishing 972/250-2060

17610 Midway Rd., Suite 144 *Mon-Wed 11-6; Thu-Fri 11-9;*
Dallas, TX 75287 *Sat 10-7; Sun Noon-5*

The apple doesn't fall far from the tree. So when you're looking to bend the rules, trade in the old and trade up to something new (even if it isn't!). That's the beauty behind this resale repository of furniture and accessories, including antiques and collectibles, paintings and art, office furniture and prints. They'll even pick up items for a fee depending on the distance, but be sure to get a permission slip. This 3,000-square-foot sapling was born out of the creative energy of two former advertising guys who saw the potential in high-quality recycling. Merchandise is spic 'n' span in spite of having been previously owned. A 200-year-old antique dresser was snatched up for a pittance and it's now the perfect home for table linens. Lots of prints and paintings, antiques to contemporary to Southwest–at least you'll know how this tree was bent. Former furniture and home accessories can be bought at one-third off what their previous owners paid. Lots to choose from here, including sofas and love seats to armoires and art. Inventory changes weekly and new items arrive daily, so shop often. They also own a companion store called Le Garbage, located next to Bagelstein's at Spring Valley and Coit in far north Dallas. *CK, MC, V, AE, D, Layaway*

★★ Best Value Furniture — 972/480-0111

9025 Forest Lane — *Mon-Sat 10-8; Sun Noon-6*
Forest Green Shopping Center
Dallas, TX 75243

Value is value spent. Join in the savings at the corner of Forest and Greenville in the Forest Green Shopping Center if you're in the market for inexpensive furniture. OK, so cheap. Sofa groups start as low as $349, seven-piece bedroom groupings that include dresser, mirror, chest, headboard, footboard, nightstand and rails were rock-bottomed out at $697; a solid iron, five-piece dining set was only $347. Don't forget to check out their mattress deals–a king set for as low as $159 could give new meaning to the expression, "Sleep tight". Free six-month financing and layaway are also available. *CK, MC, V, AE, D*

★★★★ Bova Contemporary Furniture — 972/620-1367

15166 Marsh Lane — *Mon-Fri 10-7; Sat 10-6; Sun 1-5*
Addison, TX 75001

If you love to roam-a all over town looking for contemporary furniture, stop at Bova for deals like a top-grain leather PRESIDIO recliner and ottoman for $849. Not bad, considering you can pay that much for just the recliner elsewhere. If you want to put your feet up for even less, they offer the recliner in four other grades of leather that may be even smoother on your budget. Customer service is also contemporary, as well as 12 months interest free financing with the minimum purchase. Ease on down to their other location at 2160 N. Collins St. in Arlington, or call 817/261-9977. *C, MC, V, AE, D*

★★★★★ Brad's Factory Direct 972/986-0365

1718 N. Belt Line Rd. *Mon-Sat 9:30-8; Sun Noon-6*
Irving, TX 75061

Just south of Highway 183 at the Belt Line exit, Brad's no cad–though he does moo a lot. His building is one big cow print, but you'll never be given a raw (hide) deal. Within his 100,000-square-foot showroom and manufacturing space, you can have a free-for-all. For example, buy one of his cool leather top-grain sofas and get the love seat free. Choose from six colors and pay only $888. Cheap seats. They also build lodgepole beds and matching pieces for as low as $488. See them muscle their way into your house with iron futon groupings with 6-inch mats for $138; or a pine three-in-one futon lounge love seat and bed for $218. For a custom-built estate bed in all sizes, just say, "When?" A five-piece country dinette set that was retailing for $218 was on sale for $138. A waveless waterbed mattress, any size was $59. If you need financing, it's available with approved credit. Their manufacturing and bedding site is next door at 1414 N. Belt Line Rd. and if you're in East Texas, try their Tyler store at 3717 S. Broadway, 903/509-2150. *CK, MC, V, D*

★★★★★ Brooks Weir Furniture Outlet 972/503-3503

4515 McEwen Rd. *Mon-Wed, Sat 10-6; Thu-Fri 10-8*
Dallas, TX 75244

It's hard not to babble about this Brooks with its watered-down prices on discontinued, special orders, closeouts, market samples, canceled orders and overruns of furniture. But this is no tributary to the original Weir's stores. This Weir does his own thing and carries furniture from manufacturers such as BASSETT, BERNHARDT, RIDGEWAY, even some imported items to improve your home and garden, and sells it off at ridiculously low prices, six days a week–up from just three days a week last year. You'll find them one block north of LBJ between Midway and Welch. *CK, MC, V, AE, D*

★★★★★ Brumbaugh's 817/624-4123

140 E. Exchange Ave. *Mon-Thu 9-6; Fri-Sat 9-9*
Fort Worth, TX 76106

Something's mooin' in the Stockyards, and it's not just the cows. At this outpost of Wild West Furniture and Leather Gallery, make no bones about it, this place is like playing "hides and sleek". With the return of interest in the wild, wild west, you can visit Cowtown and stay overnight at a former bordello and wild west hangout (Miss Molly's). You can also shop for furniture that is being replicated from that era. Some of the most collectible furniture of that time was made by Thomas Molesworth, and his designs are now being reproduced and sold here. This replica of a Molesworth red and white cedar, keyhole desk was more than OK for our corral. But not to overlook Larry Brumbaugh's imaginative addition to his ole standbys such as leather furniture at 40-50 percent off suggested retail with names like CLASSIC, EXECUTIVE, LEATHERMAN'S GUILD, NATUZZI, OLD HICKORY, SHERRILL, VIEWPOINT, WHITMORE and more. Certainly one of the largest leather inventories this side of the Pecos, hundreds of items stretch comfortably from recliners to couches. Soft and luxurious cowhide dandies were lined up but remember, quality leather's still pricey. A good supply of area rugs at 50 percent off retail were stacked high and well-priced, due to Brumbaugh's bulk-buying capacity. A notable stop on the Chisholm Trail if making a visit to The Stockyards. Delivery is available throughout the Metroplex. Also check out their carpet store in west Fort Worth at 7714 Spur 580 (817/244-8034). *CK, MC, V, D, MOC*

★★★ By Consignment Only — 972/867-1592

2757 W. 15th St. — *Mon-Thu 10-5; Fri-Sat Noon-5*
Plano, TX 75075

New to town, but carrying on the tradition of selling antique furniture–By Consignment Only. Don't expect market samples and don't expect new furniture and home accessories and you won't be disappointed. Located in the Cloister Square strip shopping center at the northeast corner of Independence and 15th, this is an honest-to-goodness consignment store–castoffs from other people's homes come into yours with nary a snag in sight. But don't expect some ratty chair or some torn ottoman to make it past the scrutiny of their finely-tuned taste. Only fine furniture, collectibles, china, glassware, art memorabilia, antiques, unique gift items, silver, home accessories and estate jewelry show up boasting prices of yesterday. *CK, MC, V, AE, D*

★★ Cargo Factory Outlet — 817/861-0041

478 Lincoln Square — *Mon-Sat 10-8; Sun Noon-5*
Arlington, TX 76011

If you've decided to place an embargo on full price furniture, then transport yourself to Cargo Factory Outlet on N. Collins St. just south of I-30. At their mall locations, you order from a catalog and pay full price. But why, oh why, would you want to do that? At this outlet, what you see is what you can take home and save money, as well as time. Displays, scratch and dent, discontinued or close-out solid wood and upholstered furniture can be had at 20-30 percent off (sometimes more, depending on condition). Some pieces were in mint condition and priced accordingly (maybe retail, if the truth be known). Others from the "scratch and dent" collection were whitewashed and went to our car-to-go. A white-washed cottage-style daybed for $199 and a twin-bed ensemble for kids at 40 percent off retail were two good examples. Check here first before shopping at their mall location! (Did I say mall?) *CK, MC, V, AE, D, Cargo*

★ Carlson Furniture — 817/831-6116

2819 E. Belknap St. — *Mon-Fri 8:30-5:30; Sat 8:30-5*
Fort Worth, TX 76111

If you're just starting out on the road of life and don't have a brother or sister in the business, Carlson can help you furnish your home without a lot of fuss. Carlson stocks new and used furniture bought from individuals and other stores and sells it for less. Count on finding all sorts of home furnishings, dinettes, chairs, even appliances. A five-piece farm table set was just $159 with a 30-48-inch tabletop and four chairs in white. Delivery is available for a fee of $20-$35, depending on distance. *CK, MC, V*

★★★★★ Carolina Direct — 972/517-8733

111 W. Spring Creek Pkwy. — *Mon, Fri 10-9; Sat 10-6; Sun 1-6*
Plano, TX 75023

Stop beating around the bush and be more direct. Carolina Direct couldn't be any closer to the truth. Look for their sign out front, it says, "Furniture Direct." Plain and simple. To the point. Direct. They guarantee the lowest price or will beat any other price by 10 percent. Open four days a week (they are closed Tuesday through Thursday), this furniture retailer can take the sting out of your spending habits by saving you at least 33 percent off retail. Whether it's for your bedroom, dining room or living room, they can get you up to speed with entertainment centers, upholstered pieces, mattresses and more at prices almost too good to be true. Motion sofas, loveseats and sectionals in designer fabrics and tapestries can be had for a song. Sofas run $700-$1,800 and custom-made pieces cost no more than showroom-ready ones. In fact, about 50 percent of their business is custom. Living room groups by ROWE come with kiln-dried hardwood frames and upholstered seating with eight stitches per square inch plus your choice of more than 500 fabrics. Expect loveseats to cost about $40 less than sofas. Other brands included less familiar names like CAROLLAS and ELDORADO and more familiar names like KIMBALL, PETERS REVINGTON and STANLEY. The INDIGO RUN leather line is an eight-way, hand-tied mighty fine line as is ELITE LEATHER at 50 percent off retail. Next door to Albertson's, nothing could be finer than to shop direct from Carolina. *CK, MC, V, AE, D*

★★★★★ Carolina Furniture Co. 972/988-8560

2920 N. Hwy. 360, Suite 100 *Mon-Sat 10-8; Sun 11-6*
Grand Prairie, TX 75050

Once a wholesale outlet for designers, when the walls came a tumblin' down, the bargain shoppers dove in with both feet. Now, everybody's welcome to buy name-brand furniture at 50 percent off retail in their new 40,000-square-foot warehouse/showroom. Names like AMERICAN DREW, BROYHILL, HOOKER and STANLEY are universally popular sellers. With names like these and at *prices* like these, go ahead, make your day! They even have an additional section devoted to their "Clearance Outlet" for even further reductions. Period antique reproduction styles are another of their specialties along with KING KOIL mattress sets at unbelievable prices (queen sets for $237). Queen Anne and 18th century reproductions like a four-poster rice bed or a sleigh bed, china cabinets, dining room suites, bedroom suites and occasional tables all represent royalty for the masses. A recliner by BEST CHAIR that retails for $800 was seen with a price tag of $399. Built to last, with a limited lifetime warranty, it's almost impossible to tell the difference between this chair and a real leather one. At 50 percent off, available in many colors and fabric selections, why not put your feet up and relax? 90 days same-as-cash. *CK, MC, V, D, Financing*

★★★★★ Casa Bonita Mexican Imports 214/651-8284

905 Dragon St. *Mon-Fri 9-5; Sat 10-3*
Dallas, TX 75207

Come on a my house, come on a, come on. Just make sure your casa is furnished with furniture and architectural components from this designer 6,000-square-foot showroom with south-of-the-border imported treasures. Iron and glass furniture, custom stone tables and chairs, clay and stone sculpture and fountains, and a wide assortment of home furnishings all imported directly from Mexico and offered to you for less during frequent sales. Decorate la casa with authentic Mexican flavor and make your world muy bonita. Olé! Buenos Couches! *CK*

★★★★★ Changing Places 214/570-0077

101 S. Coit Rd., Suite 82 Mon-Wed, Fri-Sat 10-6; Thu 10-8; Sun Noon-6
Richardson, TX 75080

Old neighbors never die, they just resurrect. Does that have a familiar ring? Well, it should because this store is the brainchild of Louis Ring who has taken consignment shopping to greater heights. Consign or buy, either way it's running rings around the competition. Nothing but the best in resale and reconditioned furniture encircles the store, which is a large as most full retail stores. You don't have to be lucky to find furniture by BAKER, BOB TIMBERLAKE, CENTURY and HENREDON, it's a given. The selection varies as merchandise flies out the door the minute it arrives. Choose from great-looking framed art priced at a pittance to wood and metal bunkbeds for $149 or LEXINGTON bunkbeds with storage for $669. Turn the corner, straight ahead, wherever you look, they will ring up the savings on furniture that you'd swear is new. *CK, MC, V, D*

★★★★★ Charter Furniture Outlet 972/484-1102

13550 Stemmons Frwy. Mon-Fri 10-6
Farmers Branch, TX 75234

Exit Valley View to Chart-er your course to savings of up to 50 percent on the hundreds of couches, tables, chairs, lamps and mattresses housed in this 25,000-square-foot warehouse. Returns from their full-price rental operation are discounted accordingly depending on the age, condition of item and number of same units on the floor. Living room, dining room, bedroom, home office furniture–moderately priced–is sold for a song. We sang the praises of a four-piece wall unit, oak or washed finish, that was priced under $1,000. A bedroom ensemble by BROYHILL included a queen-size poster bed that retailed for $709, their price was $499. Fabrics, handcrafted furniture, unique accent pieces, everything that was used to fill a model home, brings buyers flocking to their doors, and is available and priced so low you'll want to take home a truckload. Couches started at $100 and some complete bedroom sets were as low as $100. Some pieces appeared more used than others, but all priced well below the early orange crate level. Since everything's "below cost", nobody's complaining. *CK, MC, V, AE, D, Financing*

Furniture

★★★★ Consignment Collection

972/788-4444

12300 Inwood Rd., Suite 116A
Dallas, TX 75244-8032
Mon-Sat 10-6

Whether you need to get a tolltag (on one side) or a taco (Mexican restaurant on the other), there's always room for more. Look for the large 4,000-square-foot beige stucco building with the blue awning that sells furniture and accessories on consignment. More than 5,000 items are on the floor with 200-300 new ones set out every day. And the best part? The average price of a sofa was $295. For an eclectic mix of furniture, antiques, gifts, accessories and more, with lots of fun in store, this is like scrounging around your grandma's attic! Whether you're buying or selling (they split it with you 55-45 percent), you'll wind up a winner. This showroom houses furniture and antiques wall-to-wall, but some of them needed collagen injections. What you see is what you get sofas, chairs, dishes, dolls, tables, and lots of home accessories and bric-a-brac priced accordingly. *CK, MC, V, AE, D*

★★★ Consignment Galleries

214/357-3925

5627 W. Lovers Lane
Dallas, TX 75209
Mon-Sat 10-5:30
www.themetro.com/02/consign

Located between Inwood and the Tollway on the north side of the street, this gallery can save you 75 percent off the retail price of "preciously owned" furniture and home accessories straight from some of the finest homes in Highland Park. Traditional and fine used furniture, antiques, area rugs, lamps, china, sterling and wicker make quicker getaways here than Bonnie and Clyde. Choose from paintings, mirrors, chandeliers, objects d'art, copper and bronze figures and collectibles. You may bring in smaller items or arrangements can be made to have someone visit your home for larger pieces of furniture. You also can bring in a picture for approval before you drag in an entire houseful for consideration. All items must be in good shape, and unusual, interesting items get first approval. If accepted, you get 55 percent of the split. Expect items to start off pricey, though. *CK, MC, V*

★★★ Consignment Store, The

972/991-6268

5290 Belt Line Rd., Suite 122
Dallas, TX 75240
Mon-Sat 10-6; Sun Noon-5

The matriarch of consignment furniture with prices rising as the years pass us by. This was one of the first consignment stores on the block that marketed new markets samples and consigned furniture together, arranged all in attractive room settings and coordinated vignettes. At The Consignment Store, why buy new when you can save up to 50 percent off someone else's gently used furniture, mirrors, Oriental rugs, pictures and frames, flower arrangements, bird cages, quilts, potpourri and more? To fill in the gaps, they also house new samples from the market in between those who are seasoned–just don't expect rock-bottom prices. A homey atmosphere complete with the scent of success tastefully arranged in an artful meandering of aisleways. Pickup, delivery and financing are also available. *CK, MC, V, AE, D, Financing*

★★★★★ Cort Furniture Clearance Center — 972/445-2678

250 W. Airport Frwy. — *Mon-Fri 9-6; Sat 10-5*
Irving, TX 75062

Want to go a-Cort-ing? Then jump on over to your closest Cort's Rental Return Clearance Center. Even the most reluctant shopper will be converted by the substantial savings on previously rented furniture. Check out the living room, dining room, bedroom or office full of furniture relocated from someone else's temporary digs. All is priced right ... right down to 70 percent off retail. We saw enough to furnish a small home for less than a grand. Small dinettes started at $148, a plush blue sofa was $199, and a cute living room set was only $249. At the intersection of Highway 183 and O'Connor, you don't have to abort good taste when shopping at Cort. Be as cheap as you want here or at their other locations in North Dallas at Spring Valley and Inwood as well as north Arlington and Fort Worth. *CK, MC, V, AE, D, Financing*

★★★★ Custom Oak Furniture Mfg. — 214/340-6656

10660 Plano Rd. — *Mon-Sat 10-6*
Dallas, TX 75238

Woodn't you know it? If you've got lots of unfinished business to attend to, this may be the place to start. An unfinished bookshelf, 36- x 48-inch, was $165. If they finish it, it would go for $245. During specials, the prices are shaved even more. If you're looking for a factory that carves out an end product one leg at a time and passes the savings on to you, then consider this manufacturer an option. Choose from plenty of in-stock bookcases, tables, chairs, wall units and the like; some are already finished, others can be finished in the color of your choice. They can

even match it to one of your existing pieces. These craftsmen can also design an original unit for you. Seeing is believing! *CK, MC, V, AE, D*

♥♥♥♥♥ D'Hierro **214/3357-7956**

7807 Inwood Rd. *Mon-Sat 10-6*

Dallas, TX 75209 *www.dhierro.com*

Press on to this iron man for a touch of elegance to your home décor. There's none like it in the Metroplex. Exquisite hand-forged wrought iron furniture, lighting and accessories are the norm, not the exception. They have beds, nightstands, armoires, dining tables, chairs, coffee tables, chandeliers, lamps, floor lamps, garden furniture, chaise lounges, fireplace screens, wine racks, candleholders, original framed art and accessories in styles including Greek, Lisboa, Gothic, Napoles, Hojas, Malaga, Nefertiti, Creta, Greca, Alluette and more. Not to appear ignorant, even if you don't recognize the style, you'll recognize the good taste. In any language, D'Hierro means quality. *CK, MC, V*

★★★★★ De La Garza Furniture Services **972/864-1933**

2901 National Drive *Mon-Fri 9:30-5*

Garland, TX 75041

For custom furniture and friendly service, call on these experts located just off Kingsley, between Jupiter and Shiloh. Family owned and operated since 1960, De La Garza gives on-site free estimates (absolutely no quotes given over the phone), and the estimate given is the firm price you pay. Choose from a large selection of fabrics in the comfort of your own home–they pick up and deliver FREE. Let's face it, even furniture is entitled to a change of wardrobe. So once you've completed your furniture fashion statement, let De La Garza give your wood furniture a face-lift. Same great quality and service for all refinishing with an average turnaround time of two to three weeks on both upholstery and refinishing. Your children's children will thank you for caring for their hand-me-downs. And you don't pay until the job is done by De La Garza. It also pays to visit the shop and ask if there are any great bargains on furniture. Sometimes pieces get left behind–and Jesse will offer these refurbished products to the inquisitive consumer at an indecent price! (So low, we can't even print it!) If you're nuts about cuckoo clocks, you can now special order the Black Forest cuckoo clocks, all sizes and all models, at very good prices. Coo-Coo! In celebration of their 40th anniversary, De La Garza has added wholesale carpeting, priced at $1 above cost. *CK*

★★★★★ Decorator's Reserve 972/620-8999

13970 Stemmons Frwy. Mon-Thu 10-7; Fri, Sat 10-8; Sun Noon-6
Farmers Branch, TX 75234

No need to make a reservation at this standing-room-only bargain haunt for would-be millionaires. Expect the best, the most unusual, the eclectic, the economical. As you enter the store, expect to be greeted with the latest finds in life-size replica statues. Carved wood and painted statues of a chef, policeman, Indian, pirate and several more welcomed us with prices starting at $450. A 10-foot bronze mermaid, right inside the door, was casting her charms for just $5,385. Wrought iron and bronze items were carved in our memories and priced to sell. All kinds of table and display shelving, stands, candelabras and decorative art pieces such as a rattan and iron baby carriage were $79. Most of the furniture was Far Eastern reproductions or reminiscent of pieces you might find in an English Tudor manor house–including carved chairs with a lion motif (they looked like they came straight from the Round Table) went for $849 each. A three-piece swan carved leather settee and chairs was $1,695. Walls of mirrors, sconces and art, including unsigned "original" oils sold for less than $200. Tiffany look-alike lamps started at $29, and an art-deco mirror, 39 x 49 inches, was $225. If you're looking for impressive lawn ornaments, look no further. Lions and hippos and planting urns, Oh My! If you feel faint, find the closest leopard print chaise lounge and catch your breath. Once you've got your second wind, you'll be ready to shop for more. Just don't make the mistake of expecting one of the life-like dog statues to fetch you your checkbook. *CK, MC, V, AE*

★★★★ Dinette Center 972/235-7626

2250 Promenade Center Mon, Thu 10-8; Tue-Wed, Fri-Sat 10-6; Sun 1-5
Richardson, TX 75080

For dining in, order some furniture to go from The Dinette Center. For informal and casual living, expect to see the full spectrum of dinette sets, barstools and game/party sets, perfect collections for cocooning. Save 20-45 percent on every type of dining table and chair (more than 200 to choose from), from casual rattan to extremely formal polished oak with stellar collections from ASHLEY,CHROMCRAFT, ELITE, JOHSON CASUAL, PASTEL, PACIFIC, RATTAN SPECIALTIES, WHITAKER and more. Dinette sets from $299 to $7,000; barstool (more than 200 styles) from $59-$800; game sets, party sets, set your mind to heading to their clearance department for rock-bottom buys. They guarantee to meet or beat any price. *CK, MC, V*

Furniture

★★ Dream House Furniture & Interiors

972/245-5842

1225 W. College Ave.
Carrollton, TX 75006
Mon-Fri 10-5; Sat By Appt.

If you're dreaming of a house full of brand name furniture, wake up and smell the bouquet of possibilities outside those limiting selections. Those who dream of dream-come-true décor know to come here. The real créme de la créme is often found in your own imagination, not in the mass-produced showrooms. Here, at the intersection of Belt Line Rd. and I-35 E, they will turn your dreams into a house full of reality. Stop daydreaming about what if! This full-service design service is not just for dreamers. They design their own furniture, offer repairs and reupholstering, an art gallery, custom metal and stone tables–the works. And don't forget the beautiful selection of custom-made draperies. Oh, they discount, too. *CK, MC, V, AE, D, Norwest*

★★★★ Durango Trading Co.

972/716-9898

420 Spanish Village
Dallas, TX 75248
Mon-Sat 10-7; Sun Noon-6

This is one of the Southwest's largest collections of furniture and accessories from Mexico at less-than-retail prices. (After all, with expensive real estate comes higher prices.) Housed in a 10,000 square feet at Arapaho and Coit, you'll score a home run on fabulous Southwestern, Western, County and Hacienda furniture and accessories at a fraction of inflated tourist prices. Handcrafted wood furniture from Mexican artisans, decorative folk art and accessories, armoires and entertainment centers, dining room tables and chairs, hand-painted masks, stone and handforged iron, terra cotta, Pueblo clay pottery–now you can stay home and look rich. This gallery setting is on a grande scale at scaled-down prices and is just what the game plan's about. Armoires (their specialty) were priced from $699-$3,000 (values to $4,000). Choose mesquite, cedar or pine as well as the finish and you're on your way, Jose. Six months with no interest financing with approved credit ($750 minimum purchase) makes it even more appealing. Custom work is also available. Second location in Preston Center at 6116 Luther Lane, open Mon-Sat 10-6 and Sun Noon-5, 214/369-3773. CK, MC, V, AE, D, Special Financing

★★★★★ Elegant Casual

972/669-9098

1621 N. Central Expwy.
Richardson, TX 75080
Mon-Sat 10-7; Sun Noon-6
www.elegantcasual.com

Between Arapaho and Campbell, a casual elegant emporium rises out of the ashes and peeks through like a zenith. Specializing in patio, rattan, and casual living furniture, this store has worldly proportions. Even if you do no al fresco dining, you can bring the outdoors in and still be cool. Savings throughout are a hot 30-50 percent off, but during sales, savings soar to 70 percent (check their outlet below, too). So what if you don't have a patio? It's still a coveted look for casual indoor dining! Brand names like BENCHCRAFT, HOMECREST, LANE/VENTURE, MALIN, RATTAN SPECIALTIES, WINSTON and WOODARD are partly to blame for our enthusiasm. More than 25,000 square feet brimming with cast aluminum, wrought iron, aluminum, steel, teak outdoor chairs and benches, plus other accouterments to accompany casual living. Lots of hammocks, umbrellas, replacement cushions, wind chimes, bird baths, outdoor candles, thermometers, even dishes and place mats. Dinette sets in all sizes, styles and price ranges are another plus. When the seasons change, fireplace accessories and gas logs appear. And, if you want to go even lower than low, their warehouse outlet can save you up to 80 percent off list (at or below dealer cost). We saw five-piece rattan dinette sets starting at $299; beach umbrellas, $59; spring chairs, $49; rattan sofas, $429; odds and ends in patio chairs at $59; lounge cushions, $10. Dinettes and bar stools, too at their outlet at 2125 Chenault in Carrollton (open in season only; 972/387-0505 or 800/440-0773). Same day delivery in the Metroplex and 90 days same-as-cash are also available. *CK, MC, V, AE, D*

★★★★★ Eurway — 972/386-0389

4720 Alpha Rd. — *Mon-Fri 10-7; Thu 10-9; Sat 10-6; Sun Noon-5*
Dallas, TX 75244 — *www.eurway.com*

The curvy but comfy HARLOW sofa retro-look was certainly avant-garde, yet it didn't exact a toll on my budget. For only $699, I had it my way at Eurway. Though there were dozens of fabrics and colors to choose from, we opted for the black suede-like version and laughed all the way home. This affordable sleek contemporary outpost is everything, including eco-affordable. A tubular steel base glass-top dining table including four chairs was the perfect counterbalance for contemporary and chic living quarters. And, again, you can have it your way since delivery and assembly are extra. Calling themselves a superstore, you can find everything from very simple designs to ultra modern additions, though they continue to shun any association with the "underground." With prices so low, maybe they think we just fell off a turnip truck? Or have bad breath? Or are cheap? A 90-day same-as-cash financing plan is available, too. Just three short blocks from the Dallas North Tollway, you can also partake of tubular steel beds made in Canada for a sleek appearance for a guest room or college dorm. What about workstations for the computer-centered office, the corner desk and options such as a pedestal drawer, monitor stand, hutch top and matching storage unit in black, white or cherry melamine laminate for $249? A real steal! If it's minimalist, sophisticated yet simple, functional yet fun, this 35,000-square-foot emporium represents almost 100 different manufacturers, so you can have most anything, and have it Eurway. Since their inception in 1980, their styles have "morphed," yet they continue to offer well-designed furniture, lighting and accessories at reasonable prices. If you're a fan of European styling and IKEA, you'll get the picture. *CK, MC, V, AE, D*

★★★ Expressions 214/522-7820

3101 Knox St. *Mon-Sat 10-6; Sun 1-5*
Dallas, TX 75205 *www.expressionsfurniture.com*

Express yourself with a wonderful custom-made sofa or entire living room suite to match your style. At this franchised Expressions, we found a huge selection of fabrics (over 700) to cover 150 different sofa and chair frame styles. Our visit coincided with a 30 percent off sale, so we went home for swatches of our carpet to match up. A lifetime warranty is offered on springs and frame, so rest assured, you are getting a quality performer. Expect to sit on your custom seats in 45 days. Lots of coordinating details are left in the hands of their personnel, making your job of shopping a breeze. Comparing them with Norwalk and Fabric and Frames (stores with similar concepts), they win hands down in the price department. If you don't find what you're looking for on the floor, they'll be glad to order it for you. Covered parking outside the front door was a big plus in this converted filling station in the trendy retail location on Knox at McKinney. Another franchised location of Expressions is in Fort Worth at 2900 S. Hulen St. (817/921-4100). *CK, MC, V*

★★★ Family Furniture Warehouse 817/498-8005

5230 Denton Hwy. *Mon-Fri 10-8; Sat 10-7; Sun Noon-6*
Haltom City, TX 76117

Formerly Discount Furniture Warehouse, now they've brought it into the family. Still, you can order in AMERICAN DREW, ASHLEY, BASSETT, BENCHCRAFT, CARLETON, COVINGTON, KEMP, LANE, LEA, MAYO, SIMMONS, SOUTHWEST ... come to think of it, hold the mayo, I prefer mustard. After you finished shopping for the main ingredients for a house full of furniture, bed down for the night on a GOLDEN or RESTONIC mattress made right in Fort Worth since 1938 by Sleep-eze. From I-820 look for the U.S. 377/Denton Highway (Exit 19) and it's one block on the right. You're looking for a two-story building sitting on four acres with 20,000 square feet (13,000 of it is selling space). Yes, they have no refrigerators but they do sell laundry centers and gas ranges. Sofas start at $398-$898, so are you ready to take your seat? They offer 90 days same as cash. *CK, MC, V, D, Financing*

★★★★★ Finfer's Furniture Outlet 940/484-1818

2100 Sadau Court *Mon-Sat 10-7; Sun Noon-6*
Denton, TX 76205 *www.finfers.com*

This lean, green furniture machine is belting out the great buys as never before. After all, the Finfer family name has a reputation to uphold and saving you money on some of the finest furniture in town is just part of their commitment. And providing bend-over-backwards service is also their middle name. Open seven days a week in Denton, there is no rest for the weary. Located near Golden Triangle Mall just north of the Loop 288 exit off of I-35 E and behind Taco Bell, they are selling in a bigger, better box–and you can continue to bark about the bedroom, living room, dining room and leather furniture and bedding from the same folks that supply some of the chi-chi-est stores and catalogs in the country. You'll love AMERICAN LEATHER. Nothing but the finest hides from Europe are used (called Elmo Boutique hides), eight-way hand-tied (a lost art) cushions, fully aniline hides (color that is soaked throughout so there's no scratches), down cushions, and Finfer's is the ONLY outlet store in the country for AMERICAN LEATHER at up to 65 percent off. A lifetime warranty on the frames with more than 700 color options, and all this for a whole lot less. Finfer's sells only the best furniture–no particle board, no paper wrap (wood with a paper wrap), and no fooling about the prices. Even the best negotiators won't overpower the crew of professional career salesmen. Prices are the lowest every day, period, end of discussion. Selling the old-fashioned way, this family has built a legacy in north Texas selling popular brand names like ALEXANDER JULIAN, CARLTON DESIGNS, UNIVERSAL and the world-famous POSTURE BEAUTY mattress line from Canada. Looking for that custom look in upholstery? Pick from over 250 fabrics in the ALIDA line and you've got it covered. And then, turn your addition to the Closeout Room, another 4,000-square-foot surprise waiting for your bid on closeout leathers. Drops descend until it sells. A kids' zone, coffee, drinks and savings up to 70 percent off are all highlights here, too. *CK, MC, V, AE, D, Financing*

★★★★★ Ford's Furniture Gallery 972/881-0084

3045 W. 15th St *Tues-Fri 10-6; Sat 10-5*
Plano, TX 75075

Ford's has a tradition of offering low prices on some of the better names in the industry. If you're looking for a traditional transition from paying full price, head to the northwest corner of 15th and Independence, because this Ford has a better idea! Look for the silver lining in names like AMERICAN DREW, BARCALOUNGER, BROYHILL, DESIGNER CHOICE, HFI, LEXINGTON, PULASKI and others. Wishing you knew where some of the model home furniture went? I wonder if it went to Plano? Then mix in clearance and sale merchandise with model home displays alongside their regularly-discounted prices and this Ford has a better idea! This design-studio look is deceiving. Prices are often 30-50 percent off retail, soaring to 80 percent if the spirit moves them. Shop for sofas, tables, chairs, lamps and accessories with new arrivals that come in often. *CK, MC, V, 90 Days Same As Cash*

★★★★★ Freed's Home Furnishings Clearance Center 972/233-6871

4355 LBJ Frwy *Mon-Fri 10-9; Sat 10-6; Sun Noon -6*
Dallas, TX 75244

It's taken my entire career to finally be able to award Freed's the coveted five stars. Though they've been a North Dallas institution for as long as anyone can remember and their sale tent seemingly has been a semi-permanent fixture in their parking lot, now that they've opened their clearance center in the back, I think I have died and gone to heaven. It's a sure bet that name brands like ASHLEY, CENTURY, HEKMAN, PULASKI, RESTONIC, SIMMONS, UNIVERSAL and others draw crowds to this massive markerplace. Having freeway frontage to LBJ doesn't hurt. Maybe it's the mammoth square footage inside that weakens the purse strings of eventje most reluctant buyer. Maybe it's the selection–or all of the above. Many styles to choose from–traditional dining rooms, living rooms, bedrooms, even some elegant office furniture can be found at below retail. Sale time brings the prices down even further, and brings shoppers to their knees. *CK, MC, V, D, 90 Days Same-As-Cash*

★★★★★ Freedom Furniture Rental Clearance Center 972/385-7368

13645 Welch Rd. *Mon-Sat 10-6*
Dallas, TX 75244

Want to escape the tyranny of high prices? Flee to Freedom Furniture, my beloved. At their clearance store, you can often find something from most all major manufacturers, including the LANE/VENTURE collection (with the name Eddie Bauer) in pine or cherry with natural finishes and leather accents. Previously-rented furniture, generous in scale, and in an eco-American style can be rented or bought outright; either way, it's a freeing experience. Don't see what you like? Browse through their catalogs. Other items caught our attention as well. An oak-finished chest with decorated front was $288, (and they threw in a free mini-chest). Churchill Humidors by Lane retailing for $655 were going for $388. A warm oak-finished chest with upholstered top and brass finished accents was $188 (retailed for $325); cedar storage chest in cherry finish was $288 ($525 retail). Head north of Alpha and shop often for there's an ever changing selection of sofas, chairs, beds, dinettes and office furniture at prices 50-70 percent off. At the Clearance Center, see thousands of items harvested from their rental store displays and returns. New furniture mixed with gently-owned are spread out in an easy-to-see showroom with low key, no-hassle sales personnel. Each week they bring out dozens of fresh furniture pieces in current colors and fabrics with names like BASSETT, BROYHILL, UNIVERSAL and more. It's a challenge to tell what is new and what is gently owned. *CK, MC, V, AE*

★★ Furniture 4 Less — 214/821-5128

5408 East Grand Ave. — *Tues-Fri 10-7; Sat 10-5*
Dallas, TX 75223 — *www.furniture-4-less.com*

Since you don't live in the Taj Mahal, you don't have to spend a fortune on furnishings. Fill your house with furniture you can live with–4 less. There are two locations in the Metroplex stocked with great buys that include a sofa and loveseat sets for $198, five-piece full or queen bedroom sets for $398, dinette sets for $99, or a futon and pad for $158. And if you're looking for an ortho-plus mattress, dreams can come true for just $98 for a queen set. Now that's king-size savings! Also located at 1841 N. Jupiter Rd. in Garland, call 972/272-6760 for directions. *CK, MC, V, AE, D*

★★★★★ Furniture Buy Consignment — 972/436-4389

1340 W. Main St. — *Tues-Sat 11-6*
Lewisville, TX 75067

Like any good consignment shop, the stock here rolls in and out the door at a pretty fast clip. But in spite of its rapid-fire exit, it's become a hideaway for folks looking for that perfect accent piece, that custom-made leather and acrylic dining room table and eight chairs that once sold for $6,000 for $12,000, that ETHAN ALLEN obelisk bookcase that was marked $90 or the wrought-iron bench and matching vanity chair for $55—get the picture? Last year, there were birdhouses that flew out the door; this year, it's floral arrangements and objects d'art. This store has a lock on the consignment furniture business in Denton county. They're the best for unique furniture, home accessories, antiques and more–the majority of which sells for less than $50. They have a second Lewisville location at 201 S. Mill St., 972/221-3878. Pickup and delivery are offered for a nominal fee. *CK, MC, V, AE, Layaway*

Furniture

★★ Furniture in the Raw

972/270-4469

1118 W. Centerville Rd.
Garland, TX 75041
Mon-Fri 10-8; Sat 10-6

Fortunately, Furniture in the Raw has smoothed their rough edges this year. The sales force obviously passed the course for manners, so you'll no longer be getting a raw deal in the customer service department. Our mission, should you decide to accept it, is to finish what they leave undone. Like Schubert's symphony, the furniture here is all unfinished, ranging from traditional to contemporary, French and English, to country or Southwest. One of the largest unfinished furniture stores in the nation, you can choose from hundreds of different options including the hard to find Adirondack chair, unassembled for $69.88; hardwood TV armoires for $199.88, oak bookcases from $49.88-$129.88 and a maple barstool for $19.88. Now, put that in your vise and sand it. *CK, MC, V, AE, D*

★ Furniture Liquidators

972/276-6834

3517 Dividend
Garland, TX 75042
Mon-Fri 10-7; Sat 10-6; Sun Noon-6

It's cheap, *really* cheap furniture on the block here. Like how does a sofa and loveseat sound for $188-$699? Don't expect their merchandise to win any beauty contests, but if you want something that's covered in fabric to sit on, this should do ya. Across from E-Systems, the sales gal was pleasant enough and gave explicit directions, which is good because they aren't the easiest shop to find. Coming west on LBJ, take the Miller Road exit. Turn right on Miller. At Jupiter turn left. Second street to left is Dividend. Go all the way to the back of the parking lot if you want to browse through inexpensive furniture at low prices. *CK, MC, V, AE, D*

★★★★ Furniture Source

972/243-8311

11545 Reeder Rd.
Dallas, TX 75229
Mon-Fri 10-7; Sat 9-6; Sun Noon-5
www.furn.net

Now settled into their 20,000-square-foot, two-story building, you'll have to rise to the top to shop. (They're on the second floor.) Exit Royal off Stemmons, go east under the overpass and between McDonald's and Wendy's, you'll see what they're serving at up to 50 percent off. Fast food finds in sofas, dining room sets and bedroom furniture, recliners, mattresses, occasional tables, lamps, accessories, fine carpet. You can outfit your home in some of the most sought-after names: AMERICAN DREW, ASHLEY, BROYHILL, BENCHCRAFT, BERKLINE, CELLINI, CHROMCRAFT, FLEXSTEEL, FREDERICK, HYUNDAI, KIMBELL, LANE, LEA, LEXINGTON, MAYO, MILLENNIUM, PULASKI, SCHNADIG, SEALY, SIMMONS, STANLEY, TOWN SQUARE, UNIVERSAL, VAUGHN BASSETT and more. Sweet dreams! Delivery with set-up available. Special orders welcome and the special treatment is a nice touch. *CK, MC, V, AE, D, Financing*

★★★ Futon Co., The — 972/458-1108

5000 Belt Line Rd., Suite 770 — *Mon-Fri 11-7; Sat 10-6; Sun 1-6*
Addison, TX 75240 — *www.futonco.com*

The largest futon company in Texas should need no introduction, but if you need one, head one block west of the Tollway on Belt Line. There, at the southwest corner of the shopping center, you'll find the solution to your dilemma if you need extra sleeping space, but don't want to give up the room (or the décor) for a bed. There are more than 35 styles of futons to choose from in more than 200 custom fabrics and in your choice of such finishes as pine, maple, oak, mahogany, ash—you name it. They manufacture it all—from the futon frame to covers and sofas—thereby eliminating the middleman. Another plus is that they offer a lifetime warranty. What a way to go. *CK, MC, V, AE, D*

★★★★ Futon Factory Outlet — 817/379-6921

2225 N. Pearson Lane — *Mon, Fri 11-7; Thu 11-8; Sat 11-6; Sun Noon-6*
Keller, TX 76262

Closed on Tuesdays and Wednesdays, but every other day you can be sleeping or sitting on a futon. Rest assured, this factory can sell them to you at wholesale prices (saving you from 20-90 percent). Heavenly layers and layers of supreme batting help create a futon's firm foundation with natural air flow. That means when you sit, sleep or just relax, you're cooler in the summer and warmer in the winter. More than 50 are in stock at all times and custom orders (at no additional charge) are welcome. More than 600 fabrics to chose from in beds, couches and lofts/bunkbeds. A twin futon bed with frame was only $99 complete, a twin-over-full loft was complete at $535 and futon sofas started at $270 complete. There's a lifetime warranty from head to toe. And if that's not enough, this company also manufactures custom furniture, offers refinishing, frame repairs, entertainment centers, platform beds, bunkbeds, custom wall units, tables, lamps and more. Hard to find, but worth it. You'll be surprised at how big this family operation between Keller and Southlake really is. Call for directions. *CK, MC, V, AE, D, Financing*

★★★★★ Gabbert's Furniture Outlet 972/385-9666

4610 McEwen Rd. *Thu Noon-9; Fri 10-9; Sat 10-6; Sun Noon-5*
Dallas, TX 75244

This four-day-a-week operation is better for your home than a face-lift. No scars, bruises, bandages or big bills to contend with while recovering from your home furnishings blues. In fact, if you like Gabbert's ... you'll love their outlet. There's a reason why they've been named by *House Beautiful* as the #1 furniture retailer in the country. The reason should be perfectly clear once you step into their warehouse environs. See chairs, sofas, loveseats, recliners, bedroom suites, dining room suites, bedding, area rugs, Oriental rugs, mirrors, lamps, pictures and objects d'art. If it's beautiful and for your house, it's wholesale priced here. Save 40-70 percent off showroom samples, items from their model home displays or from their main line store at LBJ and Midway, manufacturers' closeouts or discontinued items. However they acquire them, you will want to buy them. Be happy. Popcorn and snappily-dressed warehouse consultants are at your beck and call. Service and savings–what a winning combination! But remember, if you snooze, you lose. They're only open four days a week. Delivery is available seven days a week. *CK, MC, V, D, Gabbert's Charge*

★★★★★ Globetrotter 214/744-4732

1601 Dragon St. *Mon-Sat 10-6*
Dallas, TX 75207

Be sure to identify yourself as an Underground Shopper, otherwise they might think you're just looking and not a serious buyer of name brand furniture at substantial discounts. Divas of all kinds like a good deal and this source offers world-class examples. Located smack dab in the middle of the Design District, shop alongside professional decorators at Globetrotter and pay the same price (which is definitely not retail). Remember, you've taken the vow of sellibacy! More than 17,000 square feet of new, first-quality fine furniture and home accessories with names like AMERICAN DREW, BROYHILL, HOOKER, HYUNDAI, PAUL ROBERT, PARKER SOUTHERN, PULASKI, MILLENNIUM, RIVERSIDE, ROWE, SAM MOORE, VAUGHAN BASSETT and many more are on display. You can be selective from the hundreds of sofas, chairs, lamps, dining sets and area rugs in stock, or special order. Shop one of the largest selection of mirrors and framed prints for that perfect accent. A lifetime guarantee is offered on all their eight-way hand-tied sofas and chairs with more than 200 different frames and hundreds of fabrics and leather (at no additional cost). *CK, MC, V, D*

★★★★★ Goodfellow Furniture 972/248-3062

17194 Preston Rd. *Mon-Sat 9-6*
Dallas, TX 75248

Not associated with any other Goodfellow, nor do you have to be a member of the Gambordini clan to shop here, you just have to want to save 30-50 percent off award-winning manufacturers. Listen to the lineup of high-quality, traditional furniture makers: BERNHARDT, HARDEN, HEKMAN, HENKEL-HARRIS, HICKORY CHAIR, JEFFCO, LA BARGE, MAITLAND-SMITH, NATIONAL MT. AIRY, SHERRILL, TOMLINSON, WOODMARK and other luminaries line up, ready for their starring role in your decorator scheme of things. They'll even throw in free design service with your purchase. What good fellows they must be! Their only interior motive–to bring you the best, for less. *CK, MC, V, D*

★★★ H & K Furniture 972/709-8989

303 E. Camp Wisdom Rd. *Mon-Sat 9:30-8; Sun Noon-6*
Duncanville, TX 75116

After more than a dozen years, this family has expanded their scope to include furniture for every nook and cranny. Even for granny, this 43,000-square-foot store in Duncanville houses furniture for every room of the house. Low prices on brands like ASHLEY, MILLENNIUM, SEALY, UNIVERSAL and more can be found here. Six months free layaway with 10 percent down should help get you in the sofa's seat, though most rooms are covered–living room, bedroom, dining room, baby furniture (a real plus) and mattresses—all at low, low prices. Another location is at 11055-B Harry Hines Blvd. in Dallas, 972/484-8986. *CK, MC, V, D*

♥♥♥♥♥ Habitat 972/701-9800

13615 Inwood Rd. *Mon-Thu 10-7; Fri-Sat 10-6; Sun Noon-6*
Dallas, TX 75244

An interesting commune of a dozen or so artists make up this congregation at the corner of Alpha and Inwood. This unique upscale contemporary showroom displays the unusual and the exotic from the ground floor up, but imagination doesn't come cheap. Custom interior designers are on site; just give them your specs and they'll create the rest. They carry top-of-the-hide leather furniture at the lowest leather-grade price. Iron works, marble, murals, artwork, gifts, beds, custom furniture, collectibles, faux finishes, interior design, even stained concrete that looks like leather (one of my personal favorites) for your walls or floors can all be found here, too. Regardless of the grade of leather chosen, Habitat has one low price. This anomaly is smack dab in the middle of the Addison corridor and provides a unique contribution to function and frivolity. More than 20 styles and 70 leather colors to choose from, and a two-week turnaround time certainly qualifies as a grade above the others. Going through their front doors is a feast for the eyes. And the ayes have it! *CK, MC, V, AE, D, Financing*

★★★ Home Concepts — 214/761-1872

2900 Main St. — *Tues-Sat 11-7; Sun 1-6*
Dallas, TX 75226

The concept is perfectly clear. They sell minimalist furniture and accessories, cheap. TV stands, $79-$139; bar stools, metal chairs with ottomans, $199; full-size futons (8-foot) with black or white metal frames, $159; or a full-size hardwood frame with an 8-foot futon, twice as strong as pine, $259. Dreaming of a pine spindle bed with natural finish? You'll agree that $279 for a full-size is a small price to pay for such luxury; queen-size, $299. Serve up a scrumptious meal on a solid wood table with four chairs, natural top and black trim for $299; or a modern dinette with four chairs, $299. Stick the year's worth of *The Underground Shopper* magazines in a metal rack for $15-$25, or write your own book on a corner desk, $99. Relax in a steel rocker for $99 and put a light on the subject with a tripod lamp for $29. From barstools to etageres, wallgrabber desks to adjustable shelving, shoji screens to multimedia storage units, call this Deep Ellum shop your home away from home. *CK, MC, V, D*

★★★ Home on the Range — 972/562-9877

110 E. Louisiana St. — *Mon-Sat 10-5*
McKinney, TX 75069

Oh, give me a home where the bargains do roam and I'll steer you to McKinney and this shop. Specializing in handcrafted rustic, western and Southwestern furniture at affordable prices, you can choose from a variety of beds, tables, cabinets, pottery, rugs, lamps and accessories. Scouting the range for upholstered and leather furniture? Look no further than this eclectic cowboy heaven. The range of prices are probably the reason the West was Won! We left holding on to a bag of cast iron masonry stars from the '20s and '30s (priced from $2-$4.25) and dreaming about a solid, primitive, carved bookshelf for $295, all the while singing, "Oh, give me a home"... all the way home. "Whoopee!" *CK, MC, V, AE, D, Financing*

♥♥♥♥♥ Homteriors 972/239-3323

13619 Inwood Rd., Suite 340 *Mon-Sat 10-6*
Dallas, TX 75244

This new kid on the block is really an old-timer with a new name. Though they've been around the block before (at the old Sakowitz Village), you can return to the good ole days when beautiful furniture in a designing atmosphere could be rounded up and sold at 40-60 percent off during their sales or everyday at 20-30 percent off. Select your comfort–sofas, chairs, tables, consoles, dining room, bedroom furniture and accessories. Homteriors by the Gardner Group represent only the best. CASA STRADIVARI, CLYDE PEARSON, HEKMAN, LANE, MAITLAND SMITH, SWAIM–all brands indicative of the quality for which decorator Jane Gardner is noted. She recently received a *House Beautiful* award for a bedroom she designed in a Parade of Homes. Revel in the whimsical folk-art artistry of SUSAN SARGENT PLATT fine art lamps and other colorful designs. See hand-tufted rugs, bedding and hand-painted ceramics. Achieve the totally coordinated look with matching appliquéd bedding, pillows, shams and top sheets. They also have slip covers by DINO MARK ANTHONY. Delivery is included if it's not a sale item. They are tucked behind Costume World, at Alpha and Inwood. Watch for specials. Couches ranged in price from $800-$2,700. *CK, MC, V, Interiors By The Gardner Group Card*

★★★ Infinity Leather 972/490-3786

4816 Belt Line Rd. *Mon-Thu 10-8; Fri-Sat 10-6; Sun Noon-6*
Addison, TX 75240

Open wide and say, "Moo-ve over." Initially, we had an affinity for Infinity, but somehow their prices appeared out-of-our-worldly scope. Two blocks west of the Tollway in Addison, at the corner of Inwood and Belt Line behind Benedict's and several hides away from being out of our price range, leather was by HUKLA, but it looks like good prices went bye-bye. They now feature SEALY LEATHER and SEALY MOTION. You can still choose hides in 35 different styles, nine grades of leather, and more than 100 colors for one low price of $1,699, but one shopper felt it was overpriced to begin with; the others didn't want to choose the higher grade of leather just to save more money in the long run. A catch twenty-two and so the story goes. You might want to "dog-ear" this page and return on another rainy day. *CK, MC, V*

Inside Out/Clearance Outlet — 972/931-0626

17390 Preston Rd.
Dallas, TX 75252
Mon-Fri 10-8; Sat 10-6; Sun 10-6

HOMECREST is just one of the names you can enjoy inside or out. This bi-polar resource for both patio and fireplace equipment is the perfect combination of year-round living. But next door is where the best action is–their outlet. Two lights north of Campbell, you're a hop, skip and a jump to cushioning the blow to high prices on patio furniture–the kind with slings and such. Why not save a bundle on BROWN JORDAN, HOMECREST ALUMINUM, MEADOWCRAFT, SAMSONITE, TROPITONE, WINSTON, WOODARD and more. You'll also find all major brands of gas logs, including GOLDEN BLOUNT, HARGROVE, HEAT MASTER, PETERSON, RASMUSSEN and SURE FIRE. Load up on umbrellas and cushions without blowing the whole nine yards. Though their retail store discounts somewhat, the buys are next door. *CK, MC, V, AE, D*

Kathy Adams Interiors — 972/447-9231

1509 Preston Rd.
Plano, TX 75093
Mon-Sat 10-6

Wait for Kathy Adams' "buy one thing at full price and get another thing for $1" sale, and you could miss out on furniture from HANCOCK & MOORE, DREXEL HERITAGE, MAITLIN SMITH, LEXINGTON and PEARSON. Be sure and check out an extensive selection of pine furniture from England, French buffets, old world new construction furniture, leather and fabric sofas, as well as all the accessories, offered at 35–45 percent off the manufactures suggested retail price. They offer 90 days same-as-cash. *CK, MC, V, AE*

★★ Krause's Sofa Factory — 817/557-5520

1536 W. I-20
(I-20 at Cooper)
Arlington, TX 76017
Mon-Fri 10-9; Sat-10-6; Sun 11-7
www.krausesfurniture.com

Though this powerhouse chain entered the Metroplex with locations in Arlington, Fort Worth and Dallas, the reviews are in and they are not all good. Actually, nobody complained about the savings or the quality. It was their customer service that stunk. No beating around the bush here. In sofas, their specialty, you can choose from more than 50 different styles including a complete selection of leathers. You can, on occasion, buy one sofa and get a chair free. But, then, come time to deliver, well, that's a horse of a different color. Promises. Promises. That's what several shoppers got. This California charmer needs a few lessons in Communication 101 before we elevate them to a more prominent position in the hierarchy of star performers. Choose your fabric and hold your breath. More than 100 different sofas, chairs, loveseats, sleepers, or sectionals of your choice. Everything comes with a Lifetime Guarantee (frame, springs and exclusive innerspring cushions). Then again, if it doesn't break in your lifetime, who cares? Check out other locations in North Dallas at 4519 LBJ Frwy. and in Plano at 1001 Central Expway. *CK, MC, V, D, Krause's Credit*

♥♥♥♥♥ Kreiss Collection 214/698-9118

1628 Oak Lawn *Mon-Fri 9-5; Sat 10-4*
Dallas, TX 75207

If you have but one life to live, live it with something from the Kreiss Collection. Join the designers as they wing their way through the Design District, impressing clients with their showroom—the envy of every decorator's eye. Now, you too can shop with the big folks who like the big deals on the big designer looks. When they decided to open their doors to the public about three years ago, it was to clear out their exquisite showroom samples. Now that it's an everyday event, just don't get so blasé that you forget your humble beginnings. Run, baby, run for the finest furniture, plus fabrics, imported accessories and luxury bed linens this side of New York City. Don't tell them you feel like a voyeur peeking in on how the rich and famous live. After all, you can, too, at these prices. From Stemmons, exit Oak Lawn and it's the second showroom on the left. *CK, MC, V, AE, D*

★★★★ Le Garbage 972/437-6096

8074 Spring Valley Rd. *Mon-Sat 10-6; Sun Noon-5*
Dallas, TX 75240

There are no accents in their name, but plenty of accents were attractively displayed in this cozy home store. Furniture and accessories abound–

some new, some consigned, some antiques, some market samples–surely there's something appetizing for your home decor. And, if you can't truck it off for your home, put it on and wear it out. There is a back area devoted to men's and women's consignment apparel, with concentration in the smaller size ranges and some vintage clothing to squeeze into. Talk about the big squeeze! There's not much breathing room between merchandise, but if you work up an appetite catching your breath between items, stop in next door for a nosh at Bagelstein's Delicatessen. Kin to Bent Tree Resale Home Furnishings, now there's two North Dallas/ Carrollton ways to covet other's castoffs and come off looking like you've hit pay-dirt. *CK, MC, V, D*

★★★ Leather Center 972/458-0885

13460 Inwood *Mon-Thu 10-8; Fri-Sat 10-6; Sun Noon-6*
Farmers Branch, TX 75244 *www.leathercenter.com*

The Leather Center handcrafts all their furniture in a state-of-the-art factory and will deliver in two weeks or less, guaranteed. As one of the largest manufacturer/retailers of leather furniture in the United States, being the biggest does count for something, if not everything. They've been stitching up leather furniture for the past 16 years on Inwood, north of LBJ and south of Alpha. Their factory is in Carrollton so you can get your special order usually in 10 days. Made by hand the old-fashioned way, you have your choice of more than 25 styles in leather sofas, in 70 different colors (yes, you can have red, blue or maybe even one that's black and blue), plus six different grades of leather. Check directory for their other five locations (Oak Lawn, Lewisville, Plano, Mesquite and Arlington) in the Metroplex. *CK, MC, V, Financing*

Leather Country 972/404-9950

13881 Midway Rd., Suite 104 *Mon-Thu 10-8, Fri-Sat 10-6, Sun Noon-6*
Farmers Branch, TX 75244

"Moo-sy" on over to the kingdom of cowhide called Leather Country. Within two weeks they'll rustle you up a leather sofa for less than $1,200–and that's cause for a Couch Celebes! Sit down in your Home On The Range and stop being such a skinflint! Hand-crafted, made-to-order leather furniture with no down payment, no interest or payments for six months. Sounds like it's steal. Send in the posse and go direct to the Leather Country outpost. *CK, MC, V, AE, D, Financing*

★★★ Leather Direct Clearance Center 972/484-9900

3128 Forest Lane, Suite 241 *Mon-Fri 10-8; Sat 10-6; Sun Noon-5*
Dallas, TX 75229

Former leathermen reappear in the strangest places. They flit around like fireflies appearing, disappearing, flying off while metamorphosing into another store as the wind blows. This time they call themselves Leather Direct. If you believe in reincarnation, head to the southeast corner of Forest Lane and Webb Chapel next to El Fenix and say adios to paying full price. Expect to pay less 'cause this is their Clearance Center. After all, it is a factory store outlet with multiple locations in Dallas and parts unknown. No longer associated with Leather Showcase, it takes a Ph.D. to comprehend the rather abrupt separation. Here you can see 100 percent leather love seats, chairs, ottomans, sleepers, sectionals with free design service to help coordinate the lamps, coffee tables, end tables, sofa tables, rugs, pictures, mirrors and accessories. Offering a lifetime warranty on their furniture, Leather Showcase is the newest name with reported more than 50 years of combined experience in manufacturing leather furniture in their factory. Most items are in-stock and ready for immediate delivery or pick up. Sofas started at $700, loveseats from $600, chairs from $500 and Ottomans from $100 at the clearance center above. They are not only beautiful, but easy to care for and durable almost for a lifetime. And if you suffer from allergies, believe it or not, leather is easier on your nose. Choose from more than 50 styles, 200 colors and 12 grades of leather at their location in Plano, Preston and 121; Lewisville, 2240-B S. Stemmons; and Dallas, 4207 Simonton Rd. Watch for openings in Arlington, Southlake and San Antonio soon. *CK, MC, V, AE, D*

★★★★★ Leather Leather 972/458-9393

13465-B Inwood Rd. *Mon-Fri 10-8; Sat 10-7; Sun Noon-6*
Dallas, TX 75244

Leather Leather, who's got the leather? Across the Tollway from the Galleria, whether you like leather or not, you're going to love Leather Leather–especially if you love what you see at Cantoni, Roche Bobois and other chi-chi furniture stores. I do. And I did. My purple piano-style leather sectional is the talk of the town. With new ownership since 1998, the transformation has been startling. Cutting edge designs at prices you can afford. As seen on national television, after all, doesn't every lover covet a red leather with black piping, oversized chair and ottoman for Valentine's Day? If you want to see a leather work of art (by designer Brian Amos), Leather Leather is where it's at. The Diablo Curve is an exclusive six-piece grouping in a rich creamy brown that forms a semi-circle—perfect for conversations or curling up with a good book. Also, check the "Spitfire" grouping, another of Amos's original designs. Pick your color ... 300 beautiful leather-fashion colors made in their own factory, complete with a lifetime guarantee. With zero financing and a two-week delivery time, you could be sitting pretty in no time. The designer collections range from contemporary to transitional leather furniture in the best selection, highest quality in the Metroplex. It's your "best-ist-best" store for leather. *CK, MC, V, AE, D, DC*

♥♥♥♥♥ Lone Star Living Furniture — 903/886-8883

1304 Washington — *Tue-Fri 2-6; Sat 10-6*
Commerce, TX 75428 — *www.lonestarliving.com*

Give your living room and dining room the flavor of the Southwest with furniture and accessories from Lone Star Living. The unique iron and leather accessories from Texas and Mexico will give your home the feel of the untamed frontier. You will find an iron lamp with a cowboy (or a vaquero) on a bucking horse built onto the stand for just $185. Maybe you would like a table made from an authentic antique wagon wheel, a glass top and an iron base. These are in very limited quantity, so the price tags are mighty high. Then again, if you're living in the Lone Star State, life does begin at the time. Don't expect their merchandise to be hum-drum. There's nothing plain vanilla about them but this is the place where the West was won. For authentic Western décor, Lone Star Living is the place for more. *MC, V, AE, D*

★★★★★ Lone Star Trading Co. — 972/712-1669

6443 W. Main St. — *Tue-Sat 10-5; Sun Noon-5*
Frisco, TX 75034

Straight from the border, this old-fashioned Mexican marketplace has two locations—Frisco and Lewisville, so there's double the possibilities if you take the ride. Is it worth it? Are you cheap? This is the ultimate end-of-the-line for wholesale prices in American money. Save your pesos. This import emporium accepts weekly shipments direct from Mexico, but they don't accept the *other* green card (American Express). They do sell wrought iron and pottery—perfect accompaniments to any home or patio. Barstools, baker's racks, fountains and birdbaths are some of the surprises in between the furniture, accessories and traditional patio furniture. A large King Kong Mexican pot was seen elsewhere for $295 but here, $195; a wrought-iron tea cart was $149/their price $89, a wrought-iron bistro table with glass was $119, while the two matching chairs were $29 each. But, the party's not over 'til you've picked your finishes: black, pewter, verdé (greenish) or bronze. This year, they offered many versions of rustic armoires and great-looking, all-weather wicker sets (made of heavier forms of synthetics) that included a couch, two side chairs and coffee table from $269-$329. We also found some cute rustic animal statues made from old iron, such as a pig, rabbit and cow, really cute for country coffee tables. (from $39-$69). Also visit their second supermercado on Highway 121 in Lewisville, about a mile east of Stemmons on the south side of the highway, Tue-Fri 10-6, Sat 10-5, Sun Noon-5. *CK, MC, V, DC*

★ M&K Furniture Sales 817/329-0565

6605 Colleyville Blvd. *Mon-Fri 11-5; Sat 10-5:30*
Colleyville, TX 76034-0623

Factory-direct furniture means savings, you bet your sweet bippee. Just don't expect heirloom-quality. So if that's not what you're looking for then why pay more than you have to? Here you'll find a five-piece wood dinette set for $159, metal futons starting at $150 and a futon bunkbed (frame only) starting at $200. They also offer mattresses. Look for their second location at 606 Industrial Blvd. in Euless, 817/355-5100. Take Highway 26 to Colleyville Blvd., just past the swimming pool store. *MC, V, AE*

★★ McGannon "Interiors to Go" 214/748-1828

1525 Turtle Creek Blvd. *Mon-Fri 9-5*
Dallas, TX 75207

When this Design District wholesale showroom beckons, smart shoppers go. An occasional special tag sale means even bigger savings on samples from the floor. Run when you see their sale signs posted and wallow in the wondrous names right from the pages of *Architectural Digest*: ALEXANDER TAYLOR, ARTIFACT INTERNATIONAL, BERNHARDT, COUNCIL-CRAFTSMEN, COUNCIL OFFICE, FERGUSON COPELAND, LLOYD FLANDERS, OFS OFFICE, SOUTHAMPTON, SOUTHWOOD, TROPITONE and T.R.S.–some of the best names in residential and commercial furnishings. Casual and formal dining rooms await a sit-down dinner or informal buffet, your patio is panting for some new outdoor wicker, your office cries out for a new executive desk and chair and your den demands a new entertainment center. Show up when the gates open at McGannon "Interiors to Go." And go, go, go! *CK, MC, V*

Furniture

★★★★★ Media Furniture — 972/701-9003

5100 Belt Line Rd., Suite 850 — *Mon-Sat 11-6; Sun Noon-5*
Dallas, TX 75240 — *www.media-furniture.com*

The newest wave in home entertainment is media rooms. So where to go to catch the wave? Behind Bed, Bath and Beyond on Belt Line, facing the Tollway. Media Furniture carries entertainment systems at unbelievably uncustomary prices. Depending on size and quality, you could be viewing the Academy Awards on your large screen TV nestled into their ULTRA contemporary laminate TV cabinet for $1,999. (Compared elsewhere at $6,000.) An Italian maple, three-section entertainment center in different sizes started $699. For up-to-the-minute technology and style, Media Furniture is ready whenever you are, doing what they do best. *CK, MC, V, AE, D, Financing*

★★★★★ MF Industries — 817/795-2368

2110 W. Division — *Mon-Fri 9-5; Sat 10-2*
Arlington, TX 76012 — *www.mfteakwood.com*

Give me teak wood home and outdoor furnishings and I'll have my lasting legacy. Teak and company is why it's such a joy to have found MF Industries—the source for "wholesale" custom indoor and outdoor teak furniture. Their motto is "Our teak furniture has it all!" and they have lots of it. From benches to chairs–regular, rocking, folding–to tables of all shapes and sizes (coffee, end, even child- and doll-size furniture.) To round out their collection, their worldly ethic and eclectic pieces in seagrass, iron, bamboo and teak leave us with a titanic appetite to buy it all. A BATAVIA loveseat, 4- x 5-foot was $195. Other styles include BUCKINGHAM, COTTAGE, DEVON, EDEN, EDGERTON, MADURA and more. Since they own their own factories in Asia, they can sell their furniture at 75 percent below retail. Shop at their warehouse where you can get a taste of their entire line;. *MC, V, AE*

★★★★★ Monterrey Imports — 817/424-3480

314 S. Main — *Tue-Sat 10-5:30; Sun 1-5*
Grapevine, TX 76051

Why head for the border when Monterrey Imports is a main event in Grapevine? Find exotic imports where each piece is stripped down to the bare metal and repainted, refinished, touched up–including gold caps–where needed. Stripped down prices, too. Save 40-70 percent off retail at this Main Street emporium that specializes in wrought-iron furniture with a custom flair.

Located just south of the Palace Theater, wrought-iron furniture, for either your home or garden, can be incorporated into anyone's decor. Each piece is uniquely handcrafted. From baker's racks with built-in wine racks, tables and chairs with fish, moon, sun or daisy motifs, baskets for decorating, tall plant stands, candle holders, candelabras, wall-mounted pot racks, wall plaques, sofa tables, chandeliers, bar sets and bar stools, dining sets, love benches, wine racks, small gift items, glass bowls, iron candle sconces, most anything can be handmade with different finishes and coordinated with wallpaper or fabric. Finishes, though, are their forte–pewter, copper, bronze, filigree and special orders are welcome. Free delivery. Second location is now open at 804 E. Northwest Hwy. in Grapevine, 76051, 817/424-0099. Look for the small white house with rooms of wrought-iron furniture, outdoor fountains and garden art. It's something you wrought to do. *CK, MC, V, D*

★★ Nayfa's Furniture — 817/731-9828

6901 Camp Bowie — *Mon, Wed, Fri-Sat 10-6; Tue, Thu 10-8; Sun 1-5*
Fort Worth, TX 76116

OK, so there's nothing that comes between you and your weekend projects. Here's a good one for you: Grab a paint brush and start the old brush-off at Nayfa's. Unfinished furniture for perfect one nightstands. Tables and chairs, chests, cabinets, desks, entertainment centers, bedroom and dining room sets, outdoor furniture and, of course, bookcases of all sizes. An entertainment center was well-priced but looked to be a huge job for our busy schedule (and newly painted fingernails). A full-size bed with head and footboard could be ingrained into our handyman's schedule for $300; otherwise, expect to pay $600. Those who love the brush strokes will really enjoy the activities here. This is their one and only location, so if you're not as handy as Andy next door, you can also ask the pros at Nayfa's to do it for you, but prices escalate substantially. Exit I-30 going west and when you get to the "Y" in the road with Office Max and Highway 80 on the right and Denny's and Camp Bowie on the left, choose Camp Bowie. Go for a couple of blocks and it's on the left. *CK, MC, V, AE, D, Financing*

★★★★★ Neal's Unfinished Furniture — 972/418-7329

2760 Trinity Mills — *Mon-Sat 9:30-6; Sun Noon-5*
Carrollton, TX 75006 — *www.nealsunffurn.com*

At the southwest corner of Trinity Mills and Marsh Lane, get ready to complete some unfinished business. Knock on wood, this is your lucky day. A trip to Neal's should be at the top of your home improvement list of things to do. Add something from here and personalize it with your touch of class. Great prices for the do-it-yourself set that'll set you into the mood for love. Embrace a four-drawer pine chest for $99.95/retail $164.95; entertainment center with some adjustable shelves, one glass door and solid doors for $199.95/retail $299.95; a 30- x 48-inch farm table for $115.95/retail $178.95 or one with a drawer for $169.95. Other options included a modern chair $35.95; pine toy box $77/retail $115.95; a bowback chair for $39.95 instead of $52.95 and a pine TV/VCR entertainment table for $89.95. Lots of toy boxes, pine desks, Shaker tables, porch rockers to rock around in–all for less than other unfinished stores in the area. But, that's just for starters. Don't miss a thing. Of course, the way to save is to finish it yourself, or you'll have to shell out for refinishing but at least start off naked for less. Delivery available. Visit their new location in Plano on Independence and Parker. Other locations in Houston and Austin. *CK, MC, V, D*

Norwalk/The Furniture Idea — 972/490-4540

133520 Inwood Rd. — *Mon-Fri 10-8; Sat 10-6; Sun 1-5*
Dallas, TX 75244 — *www.norwalkfurniture.com*

You'll get the idea when you take the walk to Norwalk. But you'll run when you see the prices. Though you'll land in custom-furniture heaven, the stars featured were the more than 1,000 fabrics and 500 styles of leather to choose from. Sophisticated. Unique. Affordable. Well, think again. It's definitely a cut above the typical bread and butter custom furniture stores in terms of selection and possibilities, but you'll pay for the privilege. Don't expect these furniture ideas to come cheap. Your beat bet is to shop during sales for better pricing. Take the walk and shop also their Knox Street Village location at 4615 Cole Ave. in Highland Park. *CK, MC, V, D, Financing*

★★★★ Nude Unfinished Furniture — 817/577-1331

6242 Rufe Snow Drive — *Mon-Sat 10-9; Sun Noon-6*
Richland Hills, TX 76148

No, the salespeople aren't nude, just the furniture. The bare truth lies within the confines of this unfinished store. With a name like Nude, you can expect them to at least dress the part. Snicker just once, but after you see an oak entertainment center for $179.95 or a pine desk for $149.95, you might not believe you bought the whole kit and kaboodle. Solid wood furniture is just waiting for your Midas touch. Nice selection of children's furniture and dining room ensembles. Everything was reasonably priced and will keep you from painting the town upside down. Paint and stain brands included GENERAL FINISHES and PRELUDE making it easier to add your own creative juices and see the fruits of your labor materialize into a work of art. Check the directory for additional locations. Try not to stare. *CK, MC, V, AE, D*

★★★★★ O'Neal Furniture 817/337-0068

1711 Keller Pkwy. *Mon-Sat 10-8; Sun Noon-5*
Keller, TX 76248

You don't have to be Irish to find your lucky charmer. Homer O'Neal and family have been charming the Fort Worth furniture scene since 1935, and saving green has been their heritage. A new location and new offerings add up to a lot of things, but higher prices are not among them. While they still specialize in traditional, colonial and country furniture designs, they have added accessories, art and more to fill up the new, much larger, much improved store. They still offer some standard favorites such as AMERICAN DREW, DREXEL HERITAGE, FAIRFIELD, HFI, KIMBALL, LANE, RIVERSIDE, STANLEY, SUMTER CABINET and others at decidedly discounted prices. Any room in the house deserves a slice of your budget every now and then and O'Neal is the real McCoy. Sofas, dinettes, bedroom suites–this Homer just may make home run history. The best bet of the day? A wonderful solid wood coffee table on sale for $99. One shopper bought two. *CK, MC, V, D, Financing*

★★★ Oak Mill, The 817/263-4097

5531 S. Hulen *Mon-Fri 10-8; Sat 10-7; Sun Noon-6*
Fort Worth, TX 76132

"Oak-y, dokey, artichoky", if you'd like to save some green, tie a yellow ribbon 'round this old oak tree. With locations throughout the Metroplex, consider not going against the grain and try some of these all-oak offspring. This chain was rooted in California, but it has branched out to Plano, Addison, North Richland Hills and the Fort Worth location above. Items are finished in light or dark oak, so you're nuts if you pay full retail ever again. Solid oak cupboards for $299, 60-inch china cabinets for $599, a hall tree for $259 and an old-fashioned icebox end table for $69 could be the perfect ending to this story, except where to place your microwave? How about a microwave cart for $129? From entertainment centers to bookcases, computer desks to curio cabinets, you can't go wrong. Pick and take is their motto, but delivery is available. From the office to the bedroom, dining room to a media room, these folks guarantee the best prices. *CK, MC, V, D*

♥♥♥♥♥ Pacific Imports 214/303-0733

2600 Fairmount St. *Tue-Sat 11-5:30; or By Appt.*
Dallas, TX 75201 *www.pacific-imports.com*

If they were opened evenings, you might meet a stranger across a crowded room at this import furniture store specializing in handmade Indonesian furniture purchased in Bali. As it is,-(sigh),-you have to go during the day to shop for armoires, trunks, chests, painted wooden animals, iron candlesticks and candelabras, wood carvings, primitives, masks, bamboo wind-chimes, pottery, intricate model pirate ships, whimsical birds and boat kites, boxes, unique mirrors and more. Teakwood, coconut wood, spices, banana leaf and bamboo are some of the exotic materials used to make home accessories from this faraway land that one cries, "Bali Ha'i." Say "hi" to Pacific Imports. You'll fall in love with them, too. If you need something shipped, they'll be happy to contain your order and send it on its way. They also custom print logos on boxes, just let them know what you need. *CK, MC, V, AE, D, DC*

✧✧✧✧ R&R Custom Wood Designs 972/680-1414

739 S. Sherman *Mon-Fri 8-6*
Richardson, TX 75081

Rusty Brown is no newcomer to the design and crafting of custom wood designs. If your furniture calls for some R&R, or if you need some repair to a mortise and tendon joint in a pair of dining room chairs, this is the place to go. Each job is assessed when it walks through the door, but the prices are surprisingly low for anything from first-class restoration to custom designs. Real shoppers shop for real wood (oak, walnut and cherry); Formica laminates, too. Reproductions, touch-ups and light manufacturing with friendly service is a plus. Located just east of Spring Valley and 75, his artistry includes custom furniture, stripping services, refinishing and caning. Special color matching and repairs possible. Call before you go because, in their words, "We are in and out." *CK, AE, D ($50 minimum with credit)*

★★★ Rishers Furniture
817/274-7187

108 N. Collins
Arlington, TX 76011
Mon-Sat 9-6; Sun 1-5

At the corner of Division and Collins, the story here has been quality and dependability since 1956. Mrs. Rishers' house of furniture promises savings on names like BASSETT, CORSICANA, HIGHLAND HOUSE, QUALITY, STRATALOUNGER and others. Expect at least a 35 percent savings on beds, pictures, vases, tables, chairs, bookcases and the typical furniture tale recanting the "importance of being furnished." Free delivery. Returns are accepted if you don't like or if it doesn't fit. But, if a button's missing when you get the couch home, expect Mr. Rishers to come to the rescue. Low overhead (such as no carpeting and no air-conditioning) accounts for low prices. But–whew–what a way to make a living! *CK, MC, V, AE, D, Layaway*

★★★★★ Rooms to Go/Kids to Go
214/513-8550

2905 E. Grapevine Mills Circle
Grapevine, TX 76051
Mon-Sat 10-9; Sun Noon-6
800/ROOMS-TO-GO

Finally the doors have opened and with it comes the revolution in furniture retailing. Home furnishings at a price easy to understand is why their success is making history. Up-to-date styles on quality furniture at prices you can afford. ('Course, I knew about them for a long time and have shopped their cleatance store in Orlando every chance I get). Custom-designed room packages that is easy on your budget and easy on the eye. More than 95 percent of the furniture they sell is in stock and ready to go. Add accents, accessories, wall décor, rugs and more and it's your guess why the clock has been ticking a mile a minute. Three-piece sofa, loveseat and chair in your choice od colors, $999.99. That's practically an entire room-full. A five-piece denim package for the kids, $599.99 complete with bunk beds, dresser and mirror. It's too much to take in all in one visit. This is only the beginning. Watch them go, man, go! *CK, MC, V, AE, D, RTG/KTG Credit*

★★★★ Roomscapes
972/226-3993

4321 N. Belt Line Rd., Suite 100
Mesquite, TX 75150
Tue-Sat 10-5

This Ginger's the spice of life. As an owner who loves what she sells, you can see why shoppers are clamoring to get through her door. If you're going east on I-30, exit Belt Line and go right for one mile. When you see the Diamond Shamrock station on the right, turn right into the East Belt Plaza Shopping Center for a little bit of heaven. Unique furnishings and accessories offer a great escape from the humdrum of decorating. Save 20-30 percent off what others might charge, including prices on antiques. ALEX VALE end tables, white-washed on bottom and dark on top, started as low as $299, consoles for $499. Of course, we tried to restrained ourselves until we saw another 10 percent off the sticker price. Then we bought it quicker than a New York minute. Off we went. If you're looking to accessorize with conversation pieces rather than just small talk, this is the place to escape. *CK, MC, V*

★★★★★ RoomStore Clearance Store, The 214/358-7287

3546 Forest Lane *Mon-Sat 10-8; Sun Noon-6*
Dallas, TX 75234 *www.roomstore.com*

Besides their catchy rhythmic song, there's other melodic savings in store at the RoomStore Clearance Store–especially if you want to save tons of money. Shop for discontinued, floor models and the dent-and-scratch remains of the day from their other retail stores. Jump in near the Dolphin Pool Company and swim toward the northwest corner of Forest and Marsh. Clearance furniture from the RoomStore's warehouse and their multiple showrooms in town included sofas, sleepers, loveseats, recliners, sectionals, chairs and more–just waiting to be adopted. Shop early for the best selection such as a sofa and loveseat for as low as $397; sofas, with assorted fabrics, styles and colors (values to $499) as low as $199; living room chairs, assorted fabrics and styles compared at $299 were RoomStore priced at $99; a three-piece sectional leather group in teal or black was compared to $2,199 for $999; and 100 percent leather chairs in assorted colors and sizes compared at $599, for a low of $299. Frankly, you get what you pay for and you pay very little. Floor models and mismatched sets of mattresses were priced 30-70 percent off for SEALY, SIMMONS, SPRING AIR, including Posturepedic and Beautyrest. Lots of odds-and-ends and scratch-and-dents are the most fun, especially in bedrooms, dinettes, odd beds, odd headboards, odd dressers, odd is in. The many one-of-a-kinds include cocktail tables and end tables starting at $29, assorted dining chairs for $19, assorted Texas lamps for $9, assorted recliners as low as $99, odd ottomans as low as $19, three-piece bedroom sets only $399, a five-piece dinette set only $167 and a five-piece cherry dining set for $499. All close-out purchases must be carted off by Tuesday at 6 or you have to arrange delivery, which is available. *CK, MC, V, D, RoomStore*

★★ Rosewood Fine Furniture 972/233-3288

13460 Midway Rd. *Mon-Fri 10-7; Sat 10-8; Sun Noon-6*
Dallas, TX 75244

This gallery of gigantic proportions, two blocks north of LBJ, lets you enjoy the fruits of their labor in the largest rosewood furniture store in the U.S. They manufacturer direct and sell for less. A two-piece 84-inch French china cabinet retailing for $4,988 was $1,899; a 96-inch double-pedestal French dining set with two arm chairs and six side chairs retailing for $6,988 was $2,588. Still, my dining room can only accommodate a few TV trays so I was out of my league. But it's their thousands of hand-painted porcelain pots and figurines which we coveted from their Oriental expression. Surely, within their 40,000 square feet of showroom space, something will catch your eye. Just make sure you pay for it from the right account or you could be sitting in ruins, too. *CK, MC, V*

★★ Sam's Furniture & Appliance 817/838-6991

5555 E. Belknap St. *Mon-Fri 10-7; Sat 9-6*
Haltom City, TX 76117

Sam's the man. Around since 1946, he can save you about 10-20 percent on budget to moderate furniture, appliances, carpeting and mattresses–to lease or own. Frankly, Sam prefers to lease! Even mattresses. Yuck! Check out the lease plan on just about everything in the store if you aren't planning on making a permanent move. Spin out with a new AMANA or WHIRLPOOL washer/dryer combo at a competitive price. Lots of furniture big names, too—BROYHILL, LA-Z-BOY, SEALY and more. You'll find sofas, recliners, loft bunk beds, captain's beds, mattresses, refrigerators, televisions and more. This multi-level showroom was appealingly appointed with merchandise displayed in room settings and accompanying mood music, plus the sales help was friendly—very friendly. Financing options are also available. For even greater bargains, check out the clearance items just down the road at the second Sam's location at 6630 Grapevine Hwy. in Richland Hills 817/284-6300, Mon-Fri 10-7; Sat 9-6. *CK, MC, V*

★★★★★ Select Collections 972/492-2491

3733 N. Josey Lane, Suite 100 *Mon-Sat 10-6*
Carrollton, TX 75007 *www.angelfire.com/biz/antiqueman*

Located in an innocuous strip center in Carrollton at the northwest corner of Josey and Rosemeade, you will be bowled over with the incongruity.

Gorgeous antiques at prices so low, you might think they are too good to be true. An intricate, hand-carved secretary (the wood kind, not the plastic) seen at an antique store for $4,000 was $1,700 here. Inventory changes like a roller coaster, so if you find the WOODARD wrought-iron tea cart and four chairs for $495 and *don't* cart it off right then and there, chances are you'll be left holding just the bag. Need a deal on something that is older but only gets better? Charles and Barbara Holland and Associates are ready to strike one. They have a second location at the corner of Coit and Campbell, 972/248-7021. *CK, MC, V, Layaway*

★★★ Sell It Again, Sam! 214/340-6897

10233 E. Northwest Hwy., Suite 401 *Mon-Sat 10:30-6; Sun 1-5*
Dallas, TX 75238

What a hoot! Now overseeing two entrepreneurial efforts (the Book Rack is her other baby in the same shopping center), this Northlake Shopping Center resale shop is now home to plenty of used furniture and accessories that are sold off, cheap. Regardless of their history or worth, somewhere within this 20,000-square-foot surprise store, with a big yellow sign, you might be able to cart off a maroon leather sofa for $350; or possibly part of a dining room suite (table was in, but you might have to eat standing up as the chairs were in absentia). Then there was the bedroom set with no bed, but a chest, one night stand and little desk with chair. So be it. Who needs to sleep when you're shopping and having so much fun. Add glass dishes, collectors' plates and a pair of MERONA roosters that went home to roost with a collector for $50 to the mix. The specialty here is definitely household and garden furnishings on consignment with everything you'll need to set up housekeeping inside and out. Consignees get a 50-50 split. *CK, MC, V*

♥♥♥♥♥ Shortell Bros. Intl. 214/748-4233

122 Howell St. *Mon-Fri 8:30-6; Sat By Appt.*
Dallas, TX 75207 *www.shortell.com*

Whoa! You can lead a horse to water, but you can't make him–shop. Not with this ole mare. At this family-owned company offering Mediterranean, Southwestern and Colonial Spanish country-style furnishings and accessories, it was easy to quench my thirst. The product line includes handmade wooden furniture, wrought-iron, pottery, hand-carved stone fountains, table bases, figurines, pewter, glazed and unglazed ceramics, tile, marble, stone pavers and decorative accessories, including saints and angels. Then, rounding the last lap, we filly-ed up with Talavera pottery and hurricane lamps. If you don't find what you are looking for, they have a custom workshop on site. Located off Irving Blvd. between Oak Lawn and Industrial.

★★ Showplace On The Square — 214/742-6523

1645 Stemmons Frwy., Suite 200 — *Mon-Fri 10-5*
Dallas, TX 75207

Fantasying about creating a showplace? Have dreams, but little money? Well, hold your breath and exhale every few months when this "to-the-trade" only showroom opens it doors to the public for a three-day sale. Taste this: One-of-a-kind barstools and chairs from $25-$75 with values up to $700; or unique accessories that sell for $19-$349 with values to $700. OK, so there's limited quantities. Did you expect them to have thousands left over? Exit Oak Lawn Ave. *CK, MC, V*

♥♥♥♥♥ Simple Things — 817/332-1772

1540 S. University Drive, #110 — *Mon-Wed, Sat 10-6; Thu-Fri 10-7*
University Park Village — *Sun Noon-5*
Fort Worth, TX 76107

Simple is as simple does as this TCU area shop located just south of I-30. Incredibly soft, washable slip-covered sofas, deep sumptuous cushions, impressively constructed, generously-sized frame, and as comfortable and practical as your favorite pair of jeans. Select from 600 fabrics and guess what? You've just simplified you entire home furnishings shopping dilemma. *CK, MC, V, AE, D*

★★ Skillman Homefurnishings — 214/343-0400

9243 Skillman St. Suite 103 — *Mon-Wed, Fri 10-6; Thu 10-8; Sat 10-5*
Dallas, TX 75243

This store has endured more reincarnations than King Tut. And still, they keep going, and going, and going. From Bargains for Better Homes to Marilyn Sue's, it seems like these folks have an identity crisis, or amnesia, and can't remember what's in a name. Now with new owners, again, this multiple-personality consignment store for furniture keeps going, and going, and now, another owner, another name. Time to settle down and stick around. New furniture, market samples, one-of-a-kinds and custom furniture are replacing the old and gently used. But bowing down to their confusion leaves us dizzy. Got to give them credit for being a "skilled man". Time will tell what may happen next. *CK, MC, V, AE, D*

★★★★★ Stacy Furniture 817/481-1564

280 Commerce *Mon-Sat 10-8; Sun Noon-6*
Southlake, TX 76092 *www.stacyfurniture.com*

Don't you just hate it when someone refuses to acknowledge that they discount ... although they undercut everybody in the Metroplex! That's according to Randy, who must be in the know. But, I wonder if the Mayor knows? If you are a politically-correct shopper, shop where the honorable Rick Stacy sets up shop. Shopping throughout his three acres of name-brand furniture (close to 300 vendors are represented, including DUCKS UNLIMITED, HUNTER'S RUN, KINCAID, PULASKI, RIDGEWAY, ROWE, SINGER, UNIVERSAL and others) is like training for a marathon. Wear comfortable shoes and don't sweat it. They sell recliners, sofas, chairs, bedroom suites, mattresses by KING KOIL, everything in the category of "Gallery Furniture at Warehouse Prices." You'll find them two blocks behind the Texas National Bank, at the corner of Hwy. 114 and Southlake Road. Call before you head out to their new location which at the time of publication was not complete. *CK, MC, V, AE, D, Financing*

★★★★★ Stewart Allen Furniture 214/349-2140

11411 E. Northwest Hwy. *Mon-Sat 10-6*
Dallas, TX 75218

Stewart Allen Furniture is the big daddy when it comes to designer furniture and accessories at significant savings (often 40-80 percent off), but it's the back room where the action is. This manufacturer sells direct his high-end commercial line which he wholesales all over the country. Do not expect these exquisite pieces to be anything but chic. In the back room, however, bargains are rooted in years of experience and clout with other manufacturers. One-of-a-kind market and photography samples, hand-finished custom-made factory tables and chairs, overruns, close-outs, restored antiques and lots of custom solid Honduran mahogany, are a never-ending showplace for shoppers looking to save money. If you prefer a special finish, choose your own. Custom designer finishes, antique restoration and refinishing are just part of the finishing touches to a total makeover for your home, suite home. Get on their mailing list so you'll be first in line when their hold their famous auctions. Hands up! Sold! *CK, MC, V, AE*

★★ Style Weavers 972/243-2226

13675 Stemmons Frwy. *Mon-Sat 10-7; Sun Noon-5*
Farmers Branch, TX 75234 *www.styleweavers.com*

Cut your rug in style with custom-made rugs, floors, furnishings and window treatments from Style Weavers. They have a 27,000-square-foot showroom filled with competitively priced flooring, including slate, tile, marble and exotic woods (finished and unfinished hickory maple, mesquite, bamboo, hardwoods and more), ceramics, carpets, fabrics, furniture, accessories and a customer-oriented trained staff. They feature more than 75 styles of handmade, antique and machine-made Persian and Oriental rugs, along with floral, tapestry and hand-hooked rugs. They have a large selection of oversized and odd-sized rugs. If you don't see what you are looking for, they can create any flooring or rug you can imagine. Draw it. Then they'll make it. One of the most impressive well-priced furniture and high-end decorative accessories imported from Indonesia, Mexico, Europe and the Far East. They have leather and upholstered chairs, sofas, end and side tables, lamps, candles, African art reproductions, stone, bronze and copper urns and more. Located off I-35 between the Valwood and Valley View exits, one-stop home shopping just got better. *CK, MC, V, AE, D*

★★★★★ Sunnyland 972/239-3716

7879 Spring Valley Rd. *Mon, Thu 9-8; Tues-Wed, Fri-Sat 9-6; Sun Noon-5*
Dallas, TX 75240 *www.sunnylandfurniture.com*

Don't let their discount prices rain on your parade. Since 1970, this family-owned business has been written up in the *Underground Shopper* because they have more than 350 outdoor patio and casual sets and lots of umbrellas to shade you from the sun. Their 30,000-square-foot superstore represents all the stellar stars of casual living, most at 30-50 percent off (unless they're having a warehouse-sale when prices are slashed even further). The lineup of brand names is impressive–ALLIBERT, ARLINGTON HOUSE, BROWN JORDAN, CUMBERLAND, GROSFILLEX, HOMECREST, LLOYD/FLANDERS, MALLIN, SAMSONITE, WINSTON, WOODARD and others–are cushioned to help ease the blow of the patio breezes. And while we're at it, their outlet store is next door, where the living is even easier and the prices of patio furniture practically falls off into the pool. Their outlet store, I'm happy to report, has expanded with more cushions and umbrellas and a new wood section–with everyday discounts of 40-75 percent off. A full 3-year frame and finish conditional guarantee and a 90-day layaway policy with no interest make for a sunny day. *CK, MC, V, AE, D, Financing*

★★★★★ Tommy Snodgrass Discount Furniture 972/262-1507

505 E. Main St. *Mon-Sat 10-7; Sun 1-5*
Grand Prairie, TX 75050

While their unmarked trucks are pulling up unloading furniture in some of the finest neighborhoods in town, just remember, "I told you so." Why unmarked, you may ask. After all, if "they" let you in on "their" little secret, you, too, would know where to go to get some of the best furniture at the lowest prices in town. If you were shopping in 1945, you probably knew the Snodgrass family. They've become famous by outfitting the gentry in Grand Prairie and thereabouts for decades. The locals even know them on a first-name basis. If you don't already know them, now is the time to introduce yourself to their deep discounted prices on name brand furniture like AMERICAN DREW, ASHLEY, BERKLINE, FENTON HAND-BLOWN GLASS, GEORGIO LEONI, KIMBALL, LEATHER TREND, MAYO, PEOPLOUNGER, POWELL, PULASKI, RIDGEWAY CLOCKS, RIVERSIDE, SPRING AIR, UNIVERSAL, VAUGHN BASSETT and more. Leather couches started at $699. If you're a little cuckoo at gift-giving time, think about choosing time-honored clocks–from contemporary, traditional, curio, grandfather or anniversary. Even an outdoor weather and temperature-resistant clock was a coup. Choose from their stock or special order–be it living room, bedroom, dining room furniture or mattresses. And if you want to put it in layaway, listen to the Snodgrass plan: Pay whatever you can as a down payment, pay whatever you can per month for as long as you need to, and pay no interest. Period. And if you see the same item elsewhere, for less, they'll make you a better deal. Go see for yourself why even folks in $2 million houses shop here. *CK, MC, V, AE, D*

★★★ Ware Thomasville Home Furnishings 817/274-5521

222 W. Main St. *Mon-Wed, Fri-Sat 9-6; Thu 9-7; Sun 1-5*
Arlington, TX 76010

No Ware else but in Arlington can you shop this Thomasville Gallery. Though Haverty's may sell a few THOMASVILLE pieces, this is as close to North Carolina as it gets (without having to pay the freight or doing your own setup). This Thomasville Gallery has more Thomasville than there are cherries in a cherry jubilee (10 or 15 bedroom suites, for example). Watch for sales because it gets even juicier. Only two miles from Six Flags, this might be

"Ware" you should spend time waiting for the kids while they're taken for a ride. Free delivery and set-up within the Metroplex. THOMASVILLE, SEALY, ALPHA bedding, RIVERSIDE office furniture and more. What you don't see on the floor can be ordered from the catalogs. *CK, MC, V, AE, D*

★★★★★ Weir's Clearance Center — 972/445-6427

4510 Buena Vista — *Mon-Fri 10-5:30; Sat 10-6*
Dallas, TX 75205

If you like Weir's, visit the main store at 3219 Knox (214/528-0321) for inspiration. The prices there won't stagger you, but you might wonder Weir you can get it even cheaper. The answer is right across the street at their Clearance Center where you'll find the same great items for a lot less money. Here they have SPRING AIR mattresses, twin set, $218; full, $368; queen, $398; and king, $598; plus a $25 delivery charge within the Metroplex. They'll have you sleeping pretty in a flash for less cash. A large-scale, unique "Flintstones" coffee table with faux stone top and carved natural wood base, regular $1,637 was a paltry $199. A swivel rocker was $199. What a buy! Pretty antique cream metal headboard in queen or king size, queen was $78, king was $98, plus dining room, bedroom, leather and fabric, sofas, loveseats, chairs, armoires, desks, cocktail tables, lamps, art, rugs etc. Then it was off to a medium oak wall-unit with three shelves and two doors, regularly $878 for a pittance–$199. But the icing on the cake was a cherry-finished small-scale bench with padded fabric top regularly $249 for $49. So many deals, so little time to tell you all about them. See for yourself why we love Weir's. Even by Highland Park standards, there's nothing highbrow about their down-home, country-store atmosphere with special buys and close-outs sprinkled throughout their Knox Street store. From dinettes to four-poster beds (Cabot Lodge would have been impressed), savings were evident on such brands as BERKSHIRE, BRADINGTON YOUNG, HERITAGE and LANE. *CK, MC, V, D*

★★★★ Wholesale Furniture & Bedding — 972/247-8990

2470 Joe Field Rd. — *Mon-Fri 10-8; Sat-Sun 10–5*
Dallas, TX 75229

Budget-minded decorator types can't get enough of the wrought iron beds starting at $89; Italian leather sofa and loveseat sets as low as $795. Here's a store that believes in selling furniture like the big guys at Freed's, Haverty's or the Room Store–at about half of retail. Furniture for the living room, dining room, bedroom, den or family room at low prices is the battle cry of underground shoppers. Bedding names such as BEAUTYREST BY SIMMONS ("The Do-Not-Disturb Mattress"), alongside furniture labels like ASHLEY, BENCHCRAFT, CLAYBROOK, DIXON, FRISCO, HARDEN, SOUTHWEST and more are all here. From last year to this year, time has improved their presentation. Same-day delivery. Look for the huge sign in front of the more than 20,000-square-foot pebble and masonite building. Joe Field Road is one block south of Royal Lane, go west approximately three blocks. *CK, MC, V, AE, D*

★★ Wickes Furniture Clearance & Budget Center 817/640-7262

2400 Centennial Drive *Mon-Fri 10-9; Sat 10-6; Sun Noon-6*
Arlington, TX 76011

Where else but Wickes, say their commercials. Located in the back of their retail store, the clearance center looks more like a stockroom than a showroom. But, there is always hope that when they roll in the bargains, they will be priced to move out quick. The stock changes faster than I can wiggle my way to Arlington, but it's strictly an "odds 'n' ends" situation. Hit and miss, damaged and dirty, or dogs (what nobody wanted in the first place), are haphazardly strewn about with nary a thought to making a go of the clearance center phenomenon. Everything from lamps, rugs, paintings, beds, chairs, and sofas–what a way to go. Priced right. And off it goes. *CK, MC, V, AE, D*

★★★★★ Woodbine Furniture 817/514-0372

8705 Davis Blvd. *Tues-Sat 10-5:30; Thu 10-7; Sun Noon-5:30*
North Richland Hills, TX 76180

"Woodn't" it be lovely to Shaker-out, baby? No need to look elsewhere as this is the source for Amish-made furniture, from country armoires to five-piece cherry wall-units. Working in small individual woodshops, building one piece at a time, Amish furniture is crafted utilizing hand and medium-sized stationary tools. Can you believe, not mass-produced? Choose from many different styles: COUNTRY, MISSION, QUEEN ANNE and the sought-after SHAKER, or custom-made to your specifications. Many different options, such as lighted cabinets, beveled glass, glass shelving, mullion doors, claw feet, metal hardware and more are available. A full house–from dining room to toys, bedrooms to entertainment centers, children's furniture, wooden toys to ... well, there are more than 750 items available. Start collecting today's future antiques including Amish-made wrought-iron works, hardwood furniture and quilted linens and place mats. For a delicious country-gift, consider some of the Amish candies, jams and noodles, too. *CK, MC, V, D*

★★★ Wooden Swing Co./Children's Furniture — 972/386-6280

13617 Inwood Rd. — *Mon-Sat 10-6*
Dallas, TX 75244

The name says wooden swings, but there's more here than just for swingers. Located near Du Nouveau Hair Salon, you'll find market samples of children's furniture filling the room now, too. In fact, about half the store is children's furniture with most everything priced at retail though one California transplant found what she wanted for her daughter at $200 less than the bed she priced on the West Coast. We saw novelty beds, as well as one red and two white race car beds, which appealed to little Mario, while Andrea hopped aboard the bunk beds, starting at $399 and made of solid wood, plus hand-finished table and chair sets of kiddie proportions. Outdoor furniture and, of course, swings were hanging out. You'll also find plenty of wooden swing sets for little Tarzans or Janes, and lots of forts for anyone named Crockett. *CK, MC, V*

★★★★★ Your Furniture Connection — 940/382-0690

733 Fort Worth Drive — *Mon-Sat 9:30-6*
Denton, TX 76201 — *www.furniture-connection.com*

YFC is a true discount furniture outlet, specializing in market samples from the Dallas Market Center as well as closeouts, specials, overproductions and more, etc. With more than 45 years experience in all aspects of the industry, their clout allows them to also custom-order furniture at deeply discounted prices. Names that ring out loud and clear include ASHLEY, HAMMARRY, LA-Z-BOY, MILLINIUM, PULASKI, RIVERSIDE and others–just a few of the 38 manufacturers they represent. Savings of 20-80 percent are possible on just about any brand you want. Get comfortable in a recliner or on a motion sofa in their LA-Z-BOY "Comfort Center" and you'll never look back on paying retail again! *CK, MC, V, D, Financing, Layaway*

Gifts

♥♥♥♥♥ Basket Case, The

972/231-5100

700 University Village
Richardson, TX 75081
Mon-Sat 10-6

What I love about this job is that you can fall in love again and again. So, here I go again, in love with another little shop with a little bit of this, a little bit of that. AROMATIQUE potpourri, YANKEE candles, DREAMSICLES, Texas novelties, teapots, silk plants, framed prints, decorative home accessories, TY Beanie Babies, gift baskets–if it's cute, inexpensive and a great source of comfort, this is one quick shot at saving your sanity. Why be a real basket case when you can get your fill here? *CK, MC, V, AE, D*

★★★★★ Candle Outlet, The

972/446-7323

1818 N. Stemmons, Suite 100
Carrollton, TX 75006
Mon-Fri 10-6; Sat 10-5

As Jim Morrison said, "C'mon baby, light my fire." At The Candle Outlet, it's better to light just one little candle than to stumble in the dark. Or at least, we used to think so. Not any more, since this candle outlet's wick became our side trip on our way home from work. Just north of Belt Line on the service road, lots of shoppers are making regular detours because they, too, like to burn the candles at both ends. And why not? These are sold direct from the manufacturer, where you can easily save 30-60 percent on candles, candle holders, aromatherapy and candle-related gifts. They specialize in beeswax candles that last longer and smell stronger. Lots of double-scented votives, too. Choose from more than 40 scents, including those that can lull you to sleep or set the mood for love. Join their Votive Club and save even more. And for those who'd like to create their own candles, take a whiff of their scented oils and candle-making supplies. *CK, MC, V, AE, D*

★★★★ Creative Gift Baskets & Balloons 972/516-2940

1717 E. Spring Creek Pkwy. *Mon-Sat 10-9; Sun Noon-6*
Plano, TX 75074

Tired of saying it with flowers the same ole, same ole way? Then take respite from the ordinary and seek out the extraordinary. Since flowers are always a welcomed gift and baskets and balloons are sure to bring a smile, make sure you add a little oomph to the mundane by turning over a new leaf with Creative Gift Baskets & Balloons. Choose just the right occasion and send the very best. They have rose bouquets, romantic evening baskets, candlelight baskets, chocolate lover's basket, a boss's basket, gourmet treasures, wedding baskets and lots more. Prices were more than reasonable–from $35-$55. They also have TY Beanie Babies and Pokémon to throw abandon to the basket. *CK, MC, V, AE, D*

★★★★ Designs By Judy 972/312-9303

2432 Preston Rd., #300 *Mon-Sat 10-6*
Plano, TX 75093

Comfortably nestled into their far North Dallas/Plano location at the corner of Park and Preston, Designs by Judy is home to savings of at least 20 percent on everything. You don't have to go somewhere over the rainbow to find Judy and buy a garland or two. This home accessories/accents/furniture/plant store has blossomed from a silk-flower forest into a decorator's den of designing options. Expansion means it's now bigger and better. Now shop for those same silk plants and arrangements alongside framed prints, decorator lamps, porcelain bowls, silk trees, even furniture, custom drapery and bedding ensembles. Expect a designing woman to expect the very best. Ah, Judy, Judy, Judy. Just don't take her for Grant-ed! *CK, MC, V, AE, D*

♥♥♥♥♥ Foreign Objects 817/465-8319

3811 S. Cooper St. *Mon-Sat 10-9; Sun Noon-6*
Arlington, TX 76015

Furniture crafted with the Mexican flavor is anything but passé. The look is in and Foreign Objects has it all. Originals from Mexico, the handmade furniture kind, gifts and home accents that can transform a cookie-cutter, plain-vanilla abode into a home with a mission. Add the foreign touches that speak circles around the competition. Check directory for additional mall locations. Yes, there are bargains in them "thar" malls. Olé! *CK, MC, V*

Gifts

★★ Heirloom Candle Factory — 972/442-5288

Wylie, TX — *Mon-Sat 8-5*

A 1999 fire wiped out the Ballard store, but it hasn't extinguished the operations at Heirloom Candle Factory. Though the volume of production may have decreased, they are still producing beautiful special-order candles. In fact, they are all custom candles of any size, color and scent (they have 36 scents of votives alone.) They also can create novelty candles and specialize in wedding tapers. Prices range from $1-$30. Since they haven't yet rebuilt their store, all candles must be special ordered by phone. *CK*

★★ Hometown Threads — 972/242-4766

1231 E. Trinity Mills Rd. — *Mon-Sat 10-9; Sun Noon-5*
(Inside Wal-Mart)
Carrollton, TX 75006

Traditionally, embroidery has been the mark of quality, adorning the garments of the rich. But a certain Arkansas-based company's pricing sensibility has helped bring this beautiful technique to the masses at prices you won't believe. Designs are priced at $1.75 per 1,000 stitches. A design that looks good on a cap or a golf shirt should average 5,000 stitches, but a name or monogram will be closer to 2,000. They have a huge stock design catalog to select from, but if you want your company logo or own design immortalized in thread, they can do that, too. For custom orders, an extra $55 is added for digitizing (creating the computer file to run the design.) They have a limited selection of shirts, jackets, caps and bags, or bring your own (of course, I'm sure they wouldn't mind at all if you bought a sweatshirt from the big store they lease space from). Depending on how busy they are, you might have to wait a few days for your shirt; other times they are as quick as the one-hour photo shop in the next bay. The quality is adequate, particularly for the price, but can't compare to custom embroidery shops in the area. But of course, that's like comparing Wal-Mart and Macy's. There is a second Hometown Threads at the Farmers Branch Wal-Mart, 13307 Midway Rd. *CK, MC, V, AE, D*

♥♥♥♥♥ K-Double-K Promotional Products — 817/430-1674

Don't have time to shop? Have lots of employees, friends or family to buy for? Well, K-Double-K is your salvation. Just call them and tell them your needs and they will take it from there. You don't even have to leave your home or office. Their repertoire includes the fabulous tower of scrumptious treats wrapped in a luscious gold or charming holiday snowflake pattern tied with a red satin ribbon stamped (with your name or logo) in foil; or what about a fun cutting board with your name or logo branded right into the wood to serve your cheeses, mixed nuts, candies, etc., that come with it; or you can select from their wooden boxes which are cleverly branded with your name or logo so even after the nuts/candy are gone, there's still a reminder of you. The boxes stuffed with candy or nuts range from $12.50 to $22.90 per box. Not a big outlay, but what a great way to say "Thanks!" Great for business appreciation gifts and getting your name up there in thank-you notes. Call for their lists and let the fun begin. *CK, MC, V*

★★★★★ Liberty and Sons Designs — 214/748-3329

1506 Market Center Blvd. — *Tue-Sat 10-4*
Dallas, TX 75207

OK, we'll take it. At least 10 percent off competitors' prices are their mainstay, ensuring you liberty as well as death to high prices. This 10,000-square-foot showroom can be your ticket to the wonderful world of Trapp candles, "Pressed for Time" blank cards by Carol Wilwerth, antique garden items, "shabby chic" products, cottage décor, English chintz ware, painted faux finishes, appraisals and estate liquidations. Somehow or another, add it to your "must shop" list. *CK, MC, V, AE, D*

♥♥♥♥♥ O'Fiddlesticks — 903/892-4420

115 S. Travis — *Mon-Fri 10-5:30; Sat 10-5*
Sherman, TX 75090

Tucked away in a quaint shopping center is this small gourmet shop, packed to the rafters with kitchen and cookware. They offer travel mugs, cookie stamps, cookie cutters, backpack picnics, picnic baskets and more, including Neiman Marcus Sweet Shop chocolate fudge at prices below those at N-M. They also have a large selection of made-in-Texas products and O'Fiddlesticks if you can't make it to Kelly Square. *CK, MC, V, AE, D*

★★★★★ Obzeet Gifts and Home Décor — 972/867-6126

19020 Preston Rd. — *Tue-Sat 10-7; Sun 11:30-6*
Dallas, TX 75252

From around the globe to North Dallas, land on Obzeet Gifts and Home

Décor, for an out-of-the-world collection. Owners Zevy and Derval Kirshenbaum travel to Africa, Europe, India, the Philippines and other exotic locales twice a year to find those one-of-a-kind treasures to sell directly to the public. Along with collectibles and housewares, Obzeet also has a full restaurant and bar, featuring South African coffees, cuisine and desserts. Authenticity is paramount, as the Kirshenbaum family is from South Africa, and their imported hospitality is another reason to meet at Obzeet. Also look for them in Grapevine and on Lovers Lane. *CK, V, MC, AE, D*

♥♥♥♥♥ Rayvec Gallery — 972/490-5698

15757 Coit Rd., Suite 424
(Coit & Arapaho/Spanish Village)
Dallas, TX 75240
Mon-Fri 10-6; Sat 10-5

The name, as well as the selection, is a little different and more off the wall than anything you've probably ever seen before. Since moving from Prestonwood Mall to this 9,000-square-foot shop, the selection here has continued to grow and prosper. They have a diverse line of moderate- to high-end bronze, porcelain, crystal pieces, candelabras, paintings, centerpieces, tapestries, furniture and much more. Lamps and furniture imported from sources in Africa, Asia and Europe. Ask about their free bridal registry. Look for their second location, a 10,000-square-foot store in the upper-level, northeast corner of Valley View Mall. *CK, MC ,V, AE, D*

★★★★ Rock House — 214/381-7073

4721 Samuell Blvd.
Dallas, TX 75228
Wed-Fri 11-5

How would you like to be touched by an angel? This quaint little non-profit shop across from the Timberlawn Mental Health System Hospital and next door to the Dallas County Mental Health and Mental Retardation branch in East Dallas may be a God-send to your gift-giving quandary. Housed in a unique building of quartz, stone and petrified wood, they sell a collection of donated antiques, books, knickknacks and collectibles to benefit their neighbors in the mental health community. Whether it's from a chi-chi home in Highland Park or a garage sale reject, you can find it here. Buy it and treasure it. From a $5 framed photo of Julia Louis-Dreyfus (of "Seinfeld" fame) to a Tiffany-type lamp for $68 (worth $130 wholesale.) Those kind of deals are solid as a rock. *CK*

★★★★★ Rose Petal, The — 972/262-5253

515 E. Main — *Mon-Sat 10-5*
Grand Prairie, TX 75050

Located next door to Tommy Snodgrass, The Rose Petal offers a large selection of vintage and hard-to-find plants and furniture for your own secret garden. Swing into summer in a 1914 glider that will conjure up memories of days gone by. Geraniums that smell like mint, hard-to-find old-fashioned flowers your grandmother loved; there are flowers in abundance here. Gaze into Victorian gazing balls and find other unique and artistic accents for your home or garden. Handmade birdhouses, knickknacks and bric-a-brac, not mass-produced or run-of-the-mill. Barn-board potting benches, wicker chairs transformed into a planter, wind chimes, concrete benches, fountains, statues, birdbaths and other artistic touches at the best prices we've found. Some of the best finds in the Metroplex that add to your home's charm and drive-up appeal. *MC, V, AE, D*

♥♥♥♥♥ Stoney's Wine & Gifts — 214/953-3067

2701 Harry Hines Blvd. — *Mon-Fri 11-6; Sat Noon-6*
Dallas, TX 75201

Former *Underground Shopper* employee Diana Dill Savage and her husband, Stone, recently gave birth to another creative undertaking. With more than 115 selections of wines for under $12 to choose from, this former 1937 gas station, constructed of quarried stone, is the perfect site for their new venture. The aptly named Stoney's is a 300-square-foot shop brimming with inexpensive wine, candles, soaps and packaged pastas. L'chaim! *CK, MC, V, AE, D*

★★★ Technik Erde — 972/594-5113

Irving, TX 75038 — *Call for Evening Appt.*

Technik Erde is German for earth science. If you are interested in gems and minerals; look no further. They are a wholesaler of minerals, carved birds and animals cut from minerals. Todd Anderson has been importing minerals such as blue Andean opals, rhodochrosite and other tumbled stones along with small and large pyrite crystals from Peru for about two years and is ready to carve his niche in the world of gift-giving. The prices for the carved birds and animals ranged from $2 (about 3 cm in height) to $10 for 7 cm birds. The birds include owls, ducks, Chechens, cockatoos, parrots, sparrows, toucans and more. There are about 20 animals and birds available at any one time. The owner is a teacher by day so leave a message and he will get back to you. *CK*

★★★★★ Tuesday Morning 972/991-2996

14631 Inwood Rd. *Major Sales Throughout the Year*
Dallas, TX 75247 *www.tuesdaymorning.com*

Famous last words of Tuesday Morning, "Closed 'til August for restocking". That's the price you pay for being patient until their next major selling event. Though not a mail-order company, they do buy mail-order closeouts, so if there's one in your neighborhood, you might as well meet me Tuesday morning. You'll save 50-80 percent on name-brand gifts, housewares, linens, apparel, crystal and stemware, luggage and small leather goods, electronics and gadgetry, paper goods, toys, dolls, flowers, party decorations, furniture and accessories, jewelry, hair accessories, bed and bath, one-of-a-kind samples in categories all by themselves, area rugs, brass, games, cards, books–is there a close-out in the world they won't eventually get? Don't miss the sales around Christmas because you won't find a better selection of decorations anywhere. Did we forget anything? More than 300 stores nationwide where doors open during every major gift-buying season. Get on their mailing lists so you'll never miss out on a Tuesday Morning. *CK, MC, V, AE*

★ Welcome Home 254/582-9488

Hillsboro Outlet Center *Mon-Sat 10-8; Sun 11-6*
I-35 South (Exit 368)
Hillsboro, TX 76645

Keeping it warm and cozy is the secret of Welcome Home. Crystal and silver accent pieces lined all the shelves. BEARLY BEARS, MANN dolls, lace doilies, warm throws and more were just waiting to warm your home. Your dinner guests will feel welcome when your table is set in style with their placemats, napkins and coordinating napkin rings, candlesticks, afghans ... no, I save those for the chairs. Now that you're home, you really might like to stay put. This store's not that great, though, but if you must, you can also see them at the Denton Factory Stores and at the Gainesville Factory Shops. *CK, MC, V, AE, D*

★ Wishing Well Collectors Plates 817/244-0340

8652 Hwy. 80 W. *Tue-Thu 10:30-6; Fri-Sat 10:30-5*
Fort Worth, TX 76116

How many HUMMEL figurines can someone have? Well, collectors always wish for more. And here is where there were many lovely Hummel collector plates lining the walls. Also, if you're looking to obtain back issues of plates, WW makes it easy. Hummel figurines start at $40 and are discounted by up to 15 percent, but even so they're not for rough-housing. Enjoy browsing through the LILLIPUT LANE cottages, but prices were mostly retail. Well, we can always wish, can't we? *CK, MC, V, AE, Layaway*

Handbags & Luggage

★★★ Bag 'n Baggage Outlet — 214/349-1800

11067 Petal St. — *Mon-Fri 9-5:30; Sat 10-4*
Dallas, TX 75238 — *www.bagn-baggage.com*

Stop worrying if your luggage doesn't pass the grade after it runs through a few conveyor belts. If it gets broken or damaged, and the airline decides to fix it, it'll probably end up here–at the B 'n B service center. (No repairs though at the Grapevine Mills location.) But, if you want to replace it with new, consider this outlet for PULLMAN luggage and leather goods that have been cast aside with savings of 20-40 percent. It may even send you cross-country (since you prefer not to be saddled with full-price traveling companions). Being a frequent flier (and buyer) pays off in a smoother ride. Choose luggage, briefcases, wallets, portfolios, handbags and more from ANDIAMO, BOYT, DELSEY, HARTMANN, IMPULS, LARK, PEGASUS, SAMSONITE, SKYWAY, TUMI, VENTURA or ZERO HALLIBURTON. Can you handle one-of-a-kinds, discontinueds or irregulars when the prices are practically cargo-priced? TRAVEL-PRO was 50 percent off during our visit, but it's a madhouse. Pack your bags at their new outlet in Grapevine Mills or call 972/724-1049. *CK, MC, V, AE, D, CB*

★★★★ Cases Unlimited — 214/343-3494

10757 Mapleridge Dr. — *Mon-Fri 9-5:30; Sat 10-6; Sun Noon-5*
Dallas, TX 75238 — *www.casesunlimited.com*

Solving the mystery of what to buy and where to buy it is an open-and-shut case at Cases Unlimited. Two blocks south of LBJ and Plano Road, the missing case(s) are found waiting to be caught. Take a hands-on approach to saving money on eel-skin and leather briefcases, luggage, attaches and wallets. Have money left over to stash some cash away for a rainy day. This specialty/advertising company sells off their premium items at ridiculously cheap prices. Selection on the day of our discovery was plentiful (though at times has been sorely lacking). Never mind, there's always something. From a $15 vinyl portfolio to a $275 HALLIBURTON aluminum attaché, keep your paperwork in order and watch out. Speaking of watches, lots of them, from fashion-types to CITIZEN and SEIKO, are priced to ensure you'll never be ticked off. Then, before you head out, don't miss the hand-held electronics like calculators, cordless phones and other gadgets you can't live without. Case closed! *CK, MC, V, AE, D*

★★★★★ Dixie's Fashion Accessories Outlet — 817/649-1112

2500 E. Randol Mill Rd., #113 — *Mon-Fri 9-6; Sat 10-5*
Arlington, TX 76011 — *www.dixiesoutlet.com*

Life is go this side of the Mason-Dixie's line. Scoring a home run without having to have your wallet loaded, you'll whistle Dixie over their selection of jewelry at below wholesale prices. Did you hear what I said? Below wholesale prices on costume jewelry and sterling silver, displayed floor-to-ceiling. If you think you heard that woman jingling as she walked by you the other day, never fear. You aren't going crazy. Chances are she's been to Dixie's. Dozens of trays of sterling silver charms in all sorts of themes start here at just $3. At those prices, you can have a wistful of dangling charms and money left to jingle in your pocket. Thousand of ears in the Metroplex are pierced (or clipped) to perfection at 50-75 percent off, thanks to Dixie. Then pile it all in to your new look-alike BRIGHTON or COACH bag, priced $30-$40. The quality is so high, you'll feel guilty paying such low prices. Circling the bags and baubles are wallets, belts, hair accessories, even look-alike sunglasses at wholesale prices or less. We snapped up dozens of earrings for as low as $3 a pair (or even lower) that retail for $12 and up. From small and dainty to dramatic and eye-popping, entire sets of earrings and necklaces (just like the ones at Dillards) were half-off. (We never like to look a gift horse in the ears!) You'll also find handmade soap, yard flags and more, making this a true one-stop gift shopping nirvana that'll bring music to your ears and budget. During the holidays, call for additional hours. *CK, MC, V, AE, D*

★★★★★ Rynn's Luggage — 972/323-8520

1400 I-35, #108 — *Mon-Sat10-5:30; Wed 10-7*
Carrollton, TX 75008

Back up all those cares and woes, and here we go to Rynn's Luggage. Enter laughing ... all the way to the bank. The savings are 50 percent and more (don't bypass the clearance corner where closeouts and blemishes can be found for $15-$80). After all, one trip and there's always a few nicks and tucks anyway. Right? Rynn's the official airline repair center. Yes, if you fly, you can expect your bag to travel with the riff-rough. Need a good cosmetic surgeon to repair those dents and bruises? This is the most skillful place in town. But not only do they fix them, they sell new ones, too. Brands such as ATLANTIS, BRIGGS-RILEY, PRO-TRAVLER (those in the airline business use these) and SAMSONITE are just a few we'd like to carry on. Then, for the golfer who travels, don't forget, they need a bag, too. That's par for the course. Luggage accessories, totes, attaches, duffels, back packs–if it needs to be packed, rack up the savings here. *CK, MC, V, AE, D*

★★★★★ Sam Moon Luggage & Gifts — 972/488-1333

11429 Harry Hines (at Royal) — *Mon-Sat 9-6:30*
Dallas, TX 75229

Fly me to the moon and let me stay among the stars. But, don't forget to pack the sunscreen. One of the best places to land before you take off is at Sam Moon Luggage & Gifts for the widest selection of luggage, briefcases, totes, carry-ons, and gift items this side of the Mason-Dixon Line. To tow the line, though, you never want to pay retail. Do I have to tell you again, Sam, that here is the epitome of traveler-friendly items to carry on? Everything's discounted with names like AMERICAN TOURISTER, BRIGGS & RILEY, TRAVEL PRO, ALPHA, SAMSONITE, ATLANTIC, DELSEY, and LEXI, with boarding passes that provide you first-class service at tourist prices. Buckle up and return all trays to their full and upright position! TRAVELWELL rolling backpack with pull-up handle, organizer, front pocket, size 19 ½ x 12 ½ x 9, $49.50. EVEREST rolling backpack, $29.50. TRAVELWELL rolling duffle bag, $39.95. TRAVEL GEAR rolling duffle, $37.50. DELSEY rolling duffle, $119.50. *CK, MC, V, AE, D*

★★★★★ Tag Air — 817/226-2525

903 N. Collins, #101 — *Mon-Fri 1:30-6:30*
Arlington, TX — *www.tagintl.com*

At last, they've landed. Owned by a traveling stewardess and pilot, this is your ground-floor opportunity to save 50 percent on your flight necessities (70 percent if you fly professionally). Pack it all in–in AMERICAN TOURISTER, BRIGGS & RILEY, LARK, SAMSONITE, TRAVELPRO and others. No more bumpy flights. You know the plane always rides better at half price. One shopper needed luggage in two days, and it was sent to her by air the next day. Talk about coffee, tea and service! The highest quality suitcases, softsides, carry-ons and more. Plus sunglasses by KILLER LOOP, RAY-BAN, REVO and SERENGETI; travel apparel and accessories by ADVENTURE MEDICAL KITS, AUSTIN HOUSE, FRANZUS, LONDON FOG and VAN HEUSEN; gifts by KORCHMAN (crew only), RETRO 51 (pens) and STUFFED SHIRT; and backpacks and duffels by FIELDLINE and OUTDOOR PRODUCTS. Prices are quoted over the phone if you know exactly what you're looking for. Or visit their website at www.tagintl.com. The address above is their warehouse store; also visit their stores in Arlington (near the airport, natch!) at the Lexington Hotel, 700 E. Lamar Blvd. and at the Ball Park Inn, 903 N. Collins, Room #101. *CK, MC, V, AE, D*

★★★★★ Viking Luggage Warehouse & More — 972/690-3628

420 N. Dorothy Drive — *Mon-Fri 8-5; Sat 10-3*
Richardson, TX 75081

Known for braving dangerous travel situations, Viking Luggage has the largest selection of travel bags in the Metroplex. While they displayed more than 600 pieces in their air-conditioned showroom, if they don't carry what you're looking for, they'll search worldwide and find it for you, for less. Choose from top brand names at the best outlet prices in town. Set sail and conquer AMERICAN TOURISTER, BILL BLASS, BOYT, BRIGGS & RILEY, DELSEY, HERCULES, HORIZON, LEXI, LUCAS, MONARCH, PARAGON, PATHFINDER, SANSPORT, TRAVELER'S CHOICE and more. Not only do they have luggage for adults, they carry a nice selection of children's luggage, too. From sports/workout bags to a variety of totes, in all sizes and colors. They have the largest selection of duffel bags–with rolling wheels or without from XS-3XL. While you're there, plunder their gift section that changes with the wind. It might be holiday musical candles, wine racks, children's accessories, to anything goes. And the list goes on. Check out their "specials" and save even more. *CK, MC, V*

★★★★★ World Traveler — 972/724-1638

3000 Grapevine Mills Pkwy. — *Mon-Sat 10-9:30; Sun 11-8*
Grapevine Mills Mall
Grapevine, TX 76051 — *www.worldtraveler.com*

You can't be a world traveler until you pack it all up in one of these bags. At World Traveler, they sell luggage, leather goods, business and computer cases, sporting goods and travel accessories at the guaranteed lowest prices. (Unlike the airlines, who can't guarantee that your luggage will even arrive.) Choose from all of the famous brands such as ATLANTIC, BRIGGS & RILEY, DAKOTA, DELSEY, HARTMANN, JANSPORT, KENNETH COLE, RICARDO, SAMSONITE, TRAVELPRO and ZERO HALIBURTON. For starters, a JANSPORT Alpine Trek backpack, great for hiking in the mountains, was $119.00 (retail $150). A SAMSONITE Jumbo EZ Cart Suiter was $314.99 (retail $650). Or strike a deal on a Zero Halliburton attaché, made of aluminum and built by the same guys who designed cases to transport moon rocks, telecommunications equipment and other secret-agent type items. Did you know that this carrying case can withstand up to 50,000 pounds of pressure per square inch? We'd tell you how low the price is, but then this book would self-destruct. Forget to pack your money belt? Baggage straps? Voltage converter? Hanging cosmetics bag? Lock? It just doesn't get any easier to travel on a budget than here. Call or visit their website, too, at www.worldtraveler.com for out-of-this world prices and selection. Luggage can run from $62-$450. Everything's on sale, every day; then they run sales on sales. That's when they really soar! *CK, MC, V, AE, D*

Health, Medical & Fitness

★ A'Chen Relaxation Center — 972/490-8600

2040 Valley View Mall, #2092 — *Mon-Sat 10-9; Sun 11-6*
Dallas, TX 75240 — *www.achen-health.com*

If you have chronic pain (without being a chronic pain) and you need some relief, then A'Chen Relaxation Center is the place for you to visit. They have a wide variety of products that were created to help you relax. For tense backs or shoulders, stiff neck or a variety of aches and pains, they offer massaging chairs, specialty lotions and other massaging instruments that will end your pain. Besides, at A'Chen Relaxation Center, you won't even cringe over their prices. Pain-less, too. *CK, MC, V, AE, D*

✧✧✧✧ AmeriPlan USA — 972/671-9445

14180 Dallas Pkwy., Suite 504 — *Mon-Fri 8-5:30*
Dallas, TX 75240 — *www.ameriplanusa.com*

You can smile all the way to the bank if you're a member of this dental plan ($9 per month for individuals, $15 for the entire family and special rates for groups). You can save up to 80 percent on quality dental services. For example, if you need a silver filling, in Dallas-Fort Worth you'd pay around $60 on average; on the plan, you pay only $20 (a savings of 67 percent). The crowning glory, through, was crowns start at $195 ($545 elsewhere). Braces for kids and adults are also part of the deal, as is cosmetic dentistry. No waiting periods for eligibility, no deductibles, no claim forms and no limit on visits or dental services. And all (except for some instances of in-process orthodontics) pre-existing conditions are covered. There are even specialists on the plan. Under the prescription plan, you can save up to 50 percent on most generic prescription drugs (25 percent on brand names) with more than 50,000 participating pharmacies nationwide. You can also save up to 60 percent on vision care. The plan covers all prescription eyewear (with a 30-day unconditional guarantee) and includes special savings on contact lenses. The plan is accepted by more than 12,000 optical providers nationwide. Families (no limit on the number of family members) can be covered for $15 a month–imagine that, big mouth. *CK, MC, V, AE*

✧✧✧ Crazy Water Retirement Hotel — 940/325-4441

401 N. Oak Ave., Suite 100 — *By Appt. Only*
Mineral Wells, TX 76067

When the time comes to simplify your life and retire to living the good life, consider going home, but not alone, to the Crazy Water Retirement Hotel. A single costs $550 a month and includes three buffet-style meals daily, all utilities, maid/linen service, local phone service, satellite TV and all other amenities. There is a laundry on each floor, a game room, library, vending machines and planned activities. Want more luxury? The deluxe room goes for $600 and a suite upgrade, $750. Take in a roomie, and you only add $175 a month to the total bill. Compare that to other retirement living accommodations at $1,500-$2,500-plus a month and you'll see why folks have been flocking to this Mineral Wells retirement residence for more than 35 years. *CK*

★★★★★ Everything Uniform — 214/631-7283

1348 Inwood — *Mon-Sat 10-6*
Dallas, TX 75247

Formerly Uniform Outlet, this is the place to remedy the high cost of heath care. If you've got to stand on your feet all day, then at least don't run all over town looking for your uniform. This manufacturer's outlet offers you a healthy alternative to paying full price. Featuring more than 35 name-brand uniforms, shoes and accessories including ACTION LINE, BARCO, CHEROKEE, CREST, LANDAU, NURSEMATES, PEACHES, UNIVOGUE and more for both men and women, including plus sizes (up to size 5X), at last you can see a health plan that works to save you money. Doctors and nurses, take cover. The selection of scrubs was sensational and our family doctor was first in line for the BIRKENSTOCK "Super Birki" in blue and green for $48.95. Or slip into a pair of the hip CALZURO clogs for $64.99 or look the part in a pair of Nursemates white leather shoes for $48.99. IV pumping deals! Less than a mile from Parkland and St. Paul medical communities, why inflict any more pain? Take care. If your professional wardrobe calls for a uniform, at least look the part, fashionably. Formerly Uniform Outlet, this shop has narrowed its focus by phasing out everything but its healthcare selection, though you'll still find some chef and restaurant apparel, but the stock is limited. But you now will be able to pack your bags with hosiery, socks, stethoscopes, scissors and more. Easy access, no mall hassle. No pain. All gain. Additional locations in Waxahachie, Corsicana, Kaufman and Gun Barrel City. *CK, MC, V, AE, D*

★★★★★ Hearing Aid Express — 972/241-4620

11888 Marsh Lane, Suite 111 — *Mon-Fri 9-5*
Dallas, TX 75234

Celebrating almost a decade in the Metroplex, read my lips–Hearing Aid Express can save you money. We found specials on our visit for linear hearing aids at $395 for a custom in-the-ear style, $495 for canal-style (small as a dime), $595 for a micro-mini that fits in the ear canal and just $1,195 for a CIC (completely in the canal) style. Digital, programmable hearing aids start at $1,300 and go up to $2,500. You get a 30-day trial period, a one-year warranty, full FDA compliance, qualified repairs ($89-$119 any brand), batteries ($.50) and fast service (in some cases, same-day service) because they have their own on-site lab and full-time technicians on staff. Be sure to check out their new digital hearing aids with similarly low prices. They are the authorized dealer of the brand ReSound. Ever hear of it? Appointments are not required, but they are appreciated. *CK, MC, V, AE*

✧✧✧✧ Hearing Professional Center — 214/987-4114

5462 Glen Lakes Drive — *Mon-Fri 8:30-5*
Dallas, TX 75231

Bob, I wanted you to hear this one. Check it out. One block north of Central and Walnut Hill, on the south side of Glen Lakes Drive, look for the red brick building with parking and entry in the rear. See the world's first and smallest 100 percent digital, completely in-the-canal, hearing aid called "Senso." New from WIDEX, it's practically invisible. You have to try it to believe it. CD-quality sound processing in a discreet apparatus with no outward sign that you may be hard of hearing. Read my lips ... is just what the doctor ordered. The same technology that is used in CD players, with as much computing power as a desktop computer, still there are no buttons, no knobs, no manual adjusting because there's a built-in chip that makes 40 million calculations per second and pre-processes sounds up to 1 million times per second. It's so small, it can fit in the eye of a needle. Since 1983, located near Presbyterian Hospital, this place and its "hearing aid with a brain" could revolutionize sound. Bob, are you listening? *CK, MC, V*

★★★★ Herb Mart

972/270-6521

1515 Town East Blvd.
Market East Shopping Center
Mesquite, TX 75105

Mon-Sat 10-7

Looking for that Herb-an Cowboy? Well, mosey on down to the Herb Mart, Bart, and bargain your way, the natural way. Across from Town East Mall, expect to ingest savings of 50 percent off NATURE'S WAY–and be-bop all the way with the difference. Their everyday low prices also apply to some of the most popular requests in the healthy alternative lifestyles: ALMONDS, EMERGEN-C, GREEN MAGMA, METABOLIFE, PRO-GEST CREAM, RICE DREAM and more. Oh what price wellness, for goodness sake. *CK, MC, V, D*

Hill Top Research

214/265-1624

7515 Greenville, Suite 801
Dallas, TX

Call For Appt. Mon-Fri
www.hill-top.com

Hike up the hill, all you Jacks and Jills, to do some volunteer medical research. Ongoing research needs volunteers for swimmer's ear, irritable bowel syndrome, hormone replacement therapy and athlete's foot and that was just one week's call for health. Phew! Each study has individual requirements as to age and medical conditions but you can expect compensation for travel, along with FREE study-related medication and examination. If you are experiencing a medical condition, this might be a welcome relief to pay for a cure (then again, you may be getting a placebo and have what you came with). You're taking a chance as controlled studies are testing these new medications. Then again, you may get lucky.

★★★★ Homecare Medical

214/696-2525

11130 Petal St, Suite 600
Dallas, TX 75238

Mon-Fri 9-5; Sat by Appt.

When it comes to medical equipment, nothing but nothing beats the cost of zero. Often, Medicare or your secondary insurance coverage will provide you with access to lift chairs, for example, or an electric scooter. Hey, go, man, go. And it might cost you nada! Zilch! Get the message? Seventeen years in business ensures you that these folks are here to stay. They have the experience to advise you on all aspects of your home-medical purchases. They offer a full line of mobility and health aides. Where do you think I got my life-size medical scale that I stare at every day? (OK, I admit I sometimes use it as a coat rack.)

They supply lift chairs and recliners, home medical supplies and accessories. PRIDE Jazzy motorized wheelchair, MSRP $4,600, their price $3,895. QUICKIE P120 motorized wheelchair, MSRP $3,595, their price $3,195. Companion Wheelchair MSRP $525, their price $329. Talking digital thermometer $25, their price $20. Adjustable folding cane $21.95, their price $17.95. A & D Digital Blood Pressure kit, named the best digital kit in its class by *Consumer Reports*, MSRP $149.95, their price $129.95. Bathroom safety products, health-o-meters, and more, even those great chair seat lifts so you don't have to give up your favorite easy chair if you're having trouble easing out of it. They also offer free "test drives" on power wheelchairs and scooters by bringing the product to you for a free in-home evaluation. Get a life ... and get going. Financing available. *CK, MC, V, D, INSURANCE, MOC*

★★★★★ Medical Arts DME — 817/558-2971

604 N. Nolan River Rd. — *Mon-Fri 9-6*
Cleburne, TX 76031

Straighten up and act accordingly. Be a professional. It's easy once you know how to dress the part. Take Highway 67 right on Nolan River about a quarter mile between Henderson and Kilpatrick. This brand new 9,600-square-foot building is home to medically-related fashions. They were the only source locally for discounted mastectomy swimwear, bras and other lingerie necessities. Slip into a pair of CALZUROS for a shoe that's built for comfort. Add a uniform, at the lowest price in Johnson (and maybe even Tarrant) County. Everyday low prices, not sale prices, bring the doctors and nurses in by droves. In fact, they will match the competition plus give an additional 10 percent off. Bring in the entire operating room gang and another 2 percent gets whacked off. If time permits and you've worked up an appetite, enjoy the darling tea room called Taste of Time. They have been in the DME (durable medical equipment) business for over a decade and pride themselves on small-town prices on a full line of high-quality uniforms at 25-30 percent less than anyone around. *CK, MC, V, D*

★★★ Mixables — 214/341-5434

10201 Plano Rd., #112 — *Mon-Fri 10-6; Sat 10-5*
Dallas, TX 75238

Offering one of the biggest and best selections on health care apparel doesn't necessarily mean they also have the biggest prices. In this case, they just have the best prices. Scrub tops, pants and jackets and lab coats start at $10.

However, you have to buy at least six pieces to receive these wholesale pricing. These factory-direct uniforms are available in solids and prints in S-3XL. Nothing to add insult to injury. The reincarnation of the former A&E Apparel has hit upon a new wave of reinventing what used to be mixable 'n matchable sportswear. So be it. *CK, MC, V, AE, D*

✧✧✧✧✧ Natural Health Therapies — 214/341-0400

11615 Forest Central, Suite 105 — *By Appt. Only*
Dallas, TX 75243

Want the best massage in town? Want to pay less for it? And get twice the value? Well, here's the rubdown. Dr. James Snow is a licensed chiropractor, a diplomate in homeopathy and massage therapist. His wife, Carolyn Jo, is also a registered massage therapist. Together they offer individual or couples massages as well as various healing techniques that are like magic. The power of "laying on of the hands" must have had theirs in mind because when you leave their tables, you are in another world. Invigorated, renewed, stress-free and out only $45 for a full hour of massage. (Others charge $60-$100 in the Metroplex.) Life is good. So are they. Be sure to explore all the possible homeopathic remedies that have been used in Europe for centuries and are considered by Dr. Snow to be the natural way to healing. These natural medicines can treat many of your family's minor aches and pains, from the flu to diarrhea, insect bites to travel sickness. They even have a home medicine cabinet for sale, containing lots of different remedies that is a must for everyday maladies; and a personalized nutritional supplement program that is backed by science; and a natural weight-loss program. Remember, man does not always heal without a little help the natural way. *CK*

✧✧ Natural Silhouettes — 817/263-0014

5316 Trail Lake Drive — *Tue-Fri 10-5; Sat 11-3*
Wedgewood Shopping Center
Fort Worth, TX 76133

This Fort Worth service is a boon to women who are in need of the perfect-fitting breast prosthesis and bra. Besides having certified personnel on staff to aid in your recovery, they offer fashion consultation and support to women who have to deal with the devastation of hair loss. Sit back and relax. Let them suggest how to apply medical make-up, hats, and wigs and then take on the day! Donna's Wigs is located inside their shop if you are experiencing serious hair loss. Another shop, at 1600 Central, Suite 157 in Bedford, 817/858-0600, in the Respiratory Connection in the Oaks Shopping Center, is also available the natural way. *CK, MC, V, AE, D*

Health, Medical & Fitness

✧✧✧ Pat Walker's Body Therapy

972/353-3187

1372 W. Main St.
Lewisville, TX 75067
Mon-Fri 9-7:30

A "passive exercise" program for weight and inch loss sounds too good to be true. Well, you believe in magic, don't you? You just lie down on their five-position exercise unit and let it do the work for you. A most relaxing therapy for weight and inch loss, stiff joints, arthritis, lower back pain, high blood pressure, increased circulation, the relief of tension and stress ... and no exercise. Wow! They also counsel you on how to eat all the foods you love in moderation and in the right combination in order to lose weight. Everyone receives a full 30-minute complimentary treatment. With locations in Lewisville, 972/436-9266, and an associated shop in Denton, you have no excuse not to exercise. And, if you need a cattle prod to get you off the couch, I've found the miracle exercise program that is expected to realize the same cardiovascular benefits as if you had run or walked five miles. All this, without working up much of a sweat? Now we're talking. *CK, MC, V, AE, D*

✧✧✧ Reach Across America

972/4-DOCTOR

9 Medical Parkway, Suite 202
RHD Medical Center
Dallas, TX 75234
www.clinicaltrial.com

Does the cost of medical care make you sick? Well, why not turn the tables and let the medicine men pay you instead! Volunteers 14 years and older can check out being a test subject for a variety of medical conditions. During one period, they were seeking volunteers with allergies, sinus problems, bronchitis, high blood pressure and cold symptoms. Then, they asked about whether I'd be interested in the birth control study and that's when I called in sick. Study can include doctor visits, lab analysis, study medication and compensation for time and travel. One guinea pig signed up for the smoking cessation study, but threw in the towel half way though. Some work, some don't. You never know if you're getting the real stuff or the placebo.

♥♥♥♥♥ Relax the Back Store

972/277-BACK

624 Lincoln Square
Arlington, TX 76011
Mon-Fri 10-8; Sat 10-6; Sun 1-5
www.relaxtheback.com

Complaining about your achy-breaky back? Then this is the store for you. Dedicated to procuring products that will diminish, relax, or eliminate back pain, stop moaning and groaning and try the BackSaver Classic Recliner (starting at $995). It's probably the most comfortable chair I've ever sat in, cradling me from head to toe. I can fully recline with my legs comfortably raised and not feel like I'm trying out for the Olympics. It's a most compelling position to be in since it minimizes the pressure and stress on my spine. Kind of like my in-house chiropractor. Available in a variety of styles, this is the kind of item you should not turn your back on. Trust me. This is just the beginning of sitting pretty without the pity. You'll find a large selection of home, office, travel, sleep and health/fitness aides throughout the store. The supportive cervical pillows range from $80 for a small to $145 for an extra-thick queen. Exercise balls are a steal at $25-$40. For the outdoor lounger, there is a recliner for $200-$239. In addition to this location at I-30 and Cooper, look for stores in Dallas at 5425 W. Lovers Lane across from the Inwood Theatre, 214/357-3529; in Fort Worth at 6031 Camp Bowie, 817/732-6797; and two Plano locations, 8612 Preston Rd., Suite 107, 972/668-2225, and Texas Back Institute, 6300 W. Parker, Plano, 972/943-1814. *CK, MC, V, AE, D*

♥♥♥♥♥ Respond First Aid — 972/298-7152

915-A Gemini — *Mon-Fri 8-5*
Duncanville, TX 75137

Want to stand up and have it delivered? This company delivers emergency oxygen, respiratory and first aid kits to businesses, small and large. But what caught our eye was their back support systems that you see people wearing who need lots of back support when lifting heavy boxes and such. Since so many of us lift improperly, this might be the answer to back–squawk! They come in all different designs, from back boosters to vest designs. Both lightweight and durable, you'll receive full lower back support with triple lock closure on cinch straps in sizes S-3XL. Even strong bodies need extra support and this company does, too. *CK, MC, V*

♥♥♥♥♥ Sleep Medicine Associates — 214/750-7776

8140 Walnut Hill Lane, Suite 100 — *Mon-Fri 8-5 By Appt.*
Dallas, TX 75231 — *www.sleepmed.com*

With nearly 30 years of clinical experience to offer patients with sleep disorders, Sleep Medicine Associates of Texas, P.A. has the reputation and expertise to appropriately diagnose and treat all kinds of sleep disorders, from narcolepsy to sleep apnea. Their innovative solutions help patients improve their quality of life through better sleep. The services are usually covered under several managed health care plans so why not get a good night sleep, even if you have to change partners. (Sufferers of sleep apnea may have a C-PAP machine to bed down with every night.) What a difference it makes to those sufferers who complain they're always tired even after nine hours of sleep. This time, if you snooze, you might feel better.

★★★ SNS-Sports Nutrition Source — 214/361-1328

5500 Greenville Ave., #1105 — *Mon-Fri 10-7; Sat 10-5; Sun 1-5*
Dallas, TX 75206 — *www.snsonline.com*

Hey, sport, looking for the edge in your physical fitness regime? Join SNS-Sports Nutrition Source if you're needing to buff up. Here you'll find sports nutrition powders and supplements for less. Try it, you'll like it: FEM FIT, FAST FOOD, NORANDROGEN, ANDRO, BIG DADDY and more. Save 33 percent with your Frequent Feeder card off national and SNS brand products. If you have a GNC card, you can trade it in for a SNS card–for FREE. Check the directory for additional locations. *CK, MC, V, AE, D*

✧✧✧ Southwest Patient Care Solutions — 972/867-4613

3221 Independence — *Mon-Fri 9-6:30; Sat 10-2*
Plano, TX 75075

Need some assistance? Have special medical needs? Want a wheelchair? Cane? Walker? Take umbrage. This company may be your guardian angel. Working with several manufacturers, including GUARDIAN SUNRISE, INVACARE and LUMEX, they can even supply items that need to be custom built–such as baskets for wheel chairs. Yes, even wheelchairs. Another one of their specialties is in wound care products and diabetic needs. If they don't have it in the store, or if you can't get to the store, call their main number and they can help you by phone from in-stock or catalog items. Delivery, of course. Although they give a discount to people who pay at the time of purchase, there is an in-house insurance center that works with all the insurance companies and Medicare. Many catalogs to peruse, including those for infant pediatric and rehabilitation needs. Here you can forget your pains, and consider this source all gain. *CK, MC, V, D*

✧✧ Texas Dental Plans D/FW — 972/458-2020

12850 Hillcrest Rd., #200 — *Mon-Fri 8-5*
Dallas, TX 75230

Smile if you want to save money on your next trip to the dentist. Offering plans for companies, families, or individuals, this referral plan saves 30-80 percent on most dental fees, including preventive, restorative and cosmetic dentistry, oral surgery, prosthetics, orthodontics and periodontics. You'll pay a $15 enrollment fee and small monthly payments just to enjoy $4 bite-wing X-rays, $27 teeth cleanings, $29 silver fillings, $288 for a porcelain crown. Get it? A complete list of participating dentists will be furnished upon enrollment. Not just a few, but more than 120 dentists in the local area, including specialists. You can add the vision plan for only $1 a month more (though check out our Eyewear chapter before signing up). Another plan is offered that will cost $149 per year ($35 enrollment fee and $9.50 per month). If the $149 is not paid up front and you pay monthly, the monthly goes up to $10.50. With this plan, you get free vision and two free fillings. Not bad if you avoid seeing a dentist because of price. *CK, MC, V (By Application/Annual Fee)*

★★★★★ Vitamin World — 972/234-5030

607 S. Plano Rd. — *Mon-Sat 10-9; Sun Noon-6*
Richardson Square Mall
Richardson, TX 75081

It's a small world after all. And a visit to Vitamin World confirms it. Vitamin World, Nature's Bounty and Puritan's Pride are all owned by the same company, so if you like one, you'll like them all. (Puritan's Pride is the sibling mail-order business.) Just off the food court by Ross, lather up on soaps and shampoos. Basically, you're buying from the manufacturer–and hence killing off the middleman and coming up healthy and whole. This vitamin depot was established in 1976 and guarantees the lowest prices every day! Read, set, go. Save on top-quality vitamins, minerals, food supplements, herbs and more. Aisle after aisle, whether it's CO-Q 10 or Ginseng, the only brand you'll see is VITAMIN WORLD (who by the way makes NATURE'S BOUNTY and several others which Kroger and others carry). Of course, we couldn't dismiss checking out their selection of METABOLIFE and THERMOGENICS PLUS. It's always tempting to swallow the magic bullet for our diet makeover. Check directory for other stores in Grapevine Mills, Arlington and Irving. *CK, MC, V, AE, D*

★★★★★ Years to Your Health — 972/579-7042

503 E. Second St. — *Mon-Fri 10-6; Sat 10-5*
Irving, TX 75060

Add years to your health and dollars to your wealth by shopping here. If you know kola from COCA-COLA, you'll find more than 500 botanicals to choose from at prices 30-40 percent lower than most health-food stores. For the past

15 years, this husband-and-wife team has offered one of the largest selections in the country of bulk herbs, potpourris, spices, teas, candles, books, jewelry and vegetarian vitamins. They carry their own line of products, too, so isn't it time you discovered the exciting and wonderful world of herbs and healthy living? Powdered herbs and capsules, homeopathic aids, tinctures, essential oils and flower remedies, cosmetics and environmentally safe products are just part of their medicinal arsenal. Learn the history of spices and throw in some great spice recipes. Perhaps you'd like to consider an alliterative "root" to prescription drugs? A healing remedy? Quartz crystals and gemstones, tissue cleansing, massage oils, astrology, flower essences, vibrational medicine, mysticism and herbs for health and spiritual use? Tea blends included Root Beer Tonic for $2.75/ounce; Fruit Tea for $1.75/ounce; Night-Time Tea for $2.60/ounce. Try natural cocoa butter, 5 ounces for $4.15; Jojoba oil for $3.35 for a half-ounce; Garlic capsules, $4.40 for 50; or bee pollen for $5.35 for 50 caps. Think you know it all? Well, get a whiff of Native American raw tobacco twists, braided sweetgrass or sage; crystals and gemstones in clusters, points, wands, spheres, eggs, carved animals or other shapes. There's always a special 20 percent offer on more than 500 different botanicals in store as well as the usual bulk rates on herbs and such, where you can easily save 30-50 percent off the standard health food store prices. Soak in the charms of beautiful crystals (rumored to cure headaches). Drink up. From ALOE LIFE aloe vera juice (the concentrate of Orange-Papaya was recommended) or some authentic Aloe juice (fresh-squeezed, but quite bitter) plus oils, powders and homeopathic compounds are also brewed, ground and pureed to order. Make-your-own stash of potpourri, or sip gingerly on a bath of tea blends or spices. This company can charter your course to add Years to Your Life. Individual herbs, empty containers with glass droppers, clear glass, amber glass and white plastic, herbal formulas, natural oils, pure cosmetic ingredients, tea blends as well as gift certificates are available. *CK, MC, V, AE, D, B, PL*

Home Improvement

✧✧✧✧✧ 4 Seasons Design & Remodeling 817/589-8885

710 S. Main *Mon-Fri 8-5; Sat 8-1*
Fort Worth, TX 76104

Thinking about building a sunroom? Think in terms of value rather than savings. The folks at 4 Seasons decided this is where it's at and they don't look back. You, though, can look up or out your windows come rain or come shine if you let them build you a sunroom. If you've always wanted an addition but put it on the back burner because you thought rising energy costs would accompany it, think again. These sunrooms are double-pane insulated to let light in, not heat. Still not convinced? For more than a quarter of a century, 4 Seasons has been providing not only quality merchandise with a full 30-year warranty, but quality service as well. For any remodeling need, including a sunroom, consider 4 Seasons first. Brett was our guide and informed us they were no longer using the triple-pane glass. They now use double-pane (7/8-inch width) with an argon gas filler and a lifetime guarantee against the seal ever breaking or any construction leakage. Choose from either a glass or solid roof (solid is cheaper). A 20 x 20 foot sunroom with a solid roof and slab that has already been poured, will cost approximately $10,000-$15,000. Not bad considering you are adding a year-round room to your house. (Price a room addition and you'll see what I mean!) *CK, MC, V*

✧✧✧✧✧ AAA Quality Painting by Steve Holley 972/671-1765

By Appt. Only

Every few months we can recommend AAA Quality Painting by Steve Holley, then we have to keep our mouths shut because he gets so much business, he can't schedule any more! That's how good he is–one satisfied customer brings him so many referrals, he can't keep up. In business since 1979, he was listed by *D Magazine* as the "best painter" in town (guess who recommended him as the best). He provides an eight-page list of customer references. Registered with the BBB, AAA is A-OK. No smoking is allowed on the job; his crew is hand-picked, hand-trained-and no money changes hands until their hands leave the paint can and you are completely satisfied. Their "white-glove" approach to painting floors to ceilings includes cleaning up when they are finished. Others "pail" by comparison. *CK, MC, V*

★★★★ AAA-All Factory Vacuum Cleaners — 915/677-1311

3462 Catclaw — *Mon-Sat 9-6*
Abilene, TX 79601 — *Catalog Order*

Now cleaning up in their new location, vaccinate yourself against high-pressure salespeople selling high-price vacuums-the prices here are plain and simple. Less. They sell first-quality, brand-name dirtbusters like ELECTRA PURE, FILTER QUEEN, KIRBY, ORECK, PANASONIC, RICCAR, ROYAL, SANITAIRE, SANYO, SHARP, THERMAX and TRI-STAR. If you're looking for the RAINBOW, they've got those puppies discounted, too. But if you are smart, ask for a rebuilt one at an even lower price. Want to make a clean sweep of it and install a central cleaning system? Don't worry, be happy. They're here, too, along with bags, filters, accessories and attachments. If you need a repair, they even offer repair-by-mail (especially important if nobody can fix yours locally). Don't be a sucker. Vacuums are discounted up to 50-75 percent on some makes. AAA is one of the oldest and largest mail-order vacuum and floor care discount stores in the country. (Course they're in Texas, what did you expect?) Both home and commercial grades of cleaners, floor buffers and rug shampoos are stocked. Your satisfaction is 100 percent guaranteed or your money back. AAA issues their own product-protection guarantee for up to three years on "door-to-door" makes and provides factory-authorized warranties in your own locale for most other makes. Quality ceiling fans are another money-saving opportunity and a proven means of lowering energy bills both during the long hot summers and the cold wintry days. Your catalog fee is refundable when you mention The Underground Shopper. *CK, MC, V, D, C ($2)*

★★★ Acme Brick/American Tile — 214/348-4978

10550 Plano Rd. — *Mon-Fri 8-5; Sat 8-3*
Dallas, TX 75243

The first best thing to have around your house is Troy Aikman-but since he's already taken, call Acme Brick instead. Handy or not, this is the source for ACME, MANNINGTON and PAVESTONE tile and brick from $.50/square foot and up. Factory-direct pricing and plenty of able-bodied professionals to guide the do-it-yourselfer down the path of least resistance. Create an easy and affordable dramatic glass block window, wall, skylight-even a floor with the IBP glass block grid system. Since 1891, this company has been paving the way to many of the Metroplex's finest homes. *CK, MC, V*

✧✧✧✧✧ Advanced Foundation Repair — 214/333-0003

5601 W. Jefferson Blvd. — *Mon-Fri 8-5*
Dallas, TX 75211

Now in their new Dallas location (from Grand Prairie), when it comes to getting a lift, this is the company to trust. Don't be befuddled if you fall victim to a fast-talking salesman who suddenly disappears after you've paid for foundation repair. If they leave you high and not dry, or off the deep end, don't complain to me. But, if you want a company that has staying power, call Advanced Foundation Repair. They're the ones that back their claims and their work with a $400,000 cash trust account in the bank for your protection. Besides, they offer a lifetime transferable warranty, which means, when you go, it goes to the new occupants. They do it all: steel pilings to bedrock, pressed pilings, drilled piers, pier and beam, pressure grouting and drainage corrections. If all this sounds too technical, it's not. When you have a problem, these folks can make it right. You can count on them. *CK, MC, V*

✧✧✧✧ Affordable Handyman, The — 817/589-4232

By Appt. Only

Have a job that is too large for you to handle or a list of honey do's that just are not getting done? Then Steve Killen is the man you need to know. He's a whiz at installing doors, ceiling fans, doggy doors, attic power vents, dimmer switches, telephone outlets, cable outlets, shelving and light fixtures. And he'll do a bang-up job at repairing floor and shower tile, fences, gates, toilets, windows, French drains, minor brickwork, roof leaks and sheet rock. He's also willing to take on the nasty job of gutter cleaning. Bonded and insured and more than that, he's affordable. *CK*

✧✧✧✧✧ Affordable Inspections — 972/263-1007

DFW Metroplex, TX — *By Appt. Only*

When you need a house or termite inspection, look no further than this company that's been in business since 1985. When I recently moved, I called them to do the house inspection. You've got to be good to get me to say,"I was impressed." But seeing was believing. I was unduly impressed, to say the least.

This was an in-depth inspection that left me knowing everything I needed to know about my new home and everything I needed to do on the house I was selling (thank goodness that wasn't very much). They came out and spent more than two hours on their inspection on just one house. When they were through, they handed me a computer printout of everything they inspected and their findings. I know who I'll call if I ever have termites, or for anything else that might be "bugging" me. Remember, "old termites never die, they just go on living happily ever after." They even got their name right, too. They are "Affordable."

✧✧✧✧ Air Ducts America 972/416-DUCT

By Appt. Only

Remember, you can't put all your ducts in a row, but you can have them cleared out, for less. Do you know what evil lurks in your air ducts? Do you really want to know? Or do you just want to breath better? You can get all the dirt, dust and dander out of up to nine vents for $99 here. It also includes register cleaning and one return visit. That's sanitizing, and electrostatic air filters are also available. In Tarrant County, call 817/498-9777. Now put that in your vents and smoke it. *MC, V, AE*

★★★★★ Amazing Buildings 972/287-4842

Seagoville, TX *By Appt. Only*

How much is that doggie (house) in the window? If yours is priceless, then you're going to want to house them in the very best. Rodney Upchurch is the chief architect, builder, developer and construction foreman on site for any backyard addition. From custom doggie cottages to storage sheds, playhouses to forts, mother-in-law quarters to a teenager's retreat, he can build it. Storage sheds start as low as $200 with 10 years combined experience with the portable building industry and commercial buildings, Rodney takes pride in his craftsmanship, integrity and attention to detail. Don't expect assembly-line work, in spite of his less-than-retail prices. His mission is to create almost a work of art with every building he builds. Why settle for shoddy materials and slip-shod workmanship? He built the bridge to the workout facility at the Anatole Hotel, the locker room for the Mavericks, and room additions to Norm Sonju's house. Looking to cover up for the summer? How about an arbor patio cover for $180? Need to build a dog fence? What about an observatory for your telescope? An upstairs office? An artist's loft? Beating Morgan Buildings by as much as $2,000 on a bid, who says you can't beat the competition by a mile! Amazing Buildings is just that-a rare breed amongst builders. He actually cherishes his relationship with his clients to last as long as his buildings. Why not get your money's worth, even on a custom birdhouse, he reasons. What a wonderful breath of fresh air in a world filled with less-than-admirable contractors.

★★★★★ Amazing Siding 817/329-8830

Grapevine, TX *By Appt. Only*

Amazing Siding offers an amazing warranty on all of their work. So there. Would I dare defy the powers that be? Not me. When it comes to siding that is guaranteed against defects for a lifetime (and the guarantee is transferable to the next owner, too), you can bet this is a reliable covering to consider. If you want to save 30-50 percent, in most instances, over Sears' prices, consider Amazing Siding. No, the Amazing Kreskin is not their spokesperson, but if you consider replacing your home with premium vinyl siding, you'll never have to paint (or pay retail) again! Consider it to be your "vinyl resting place." They also do custom replacement windows and have a great relationship with the BBB (unlike many of their competitors). Although they are based in Grapevine, they serve the entire Metroplex and parts of the surrounding area. A ball park price on an average house, with no brick, was quoted at $7,500-$8,500 and believe it or not, that includes replacing the rotten wood. *CK, Financing*

✧✧✧✧ America's Handyman 972/247-2700

Mon-Sat 9-5:30

These small-project specialists are just what the doctor ordered. One repairman is all you get and he's supposed to be able to handle just about anything. For $56.50, which is their one-hour minimum fee, expect to pay extra for materials and additional costs surcharged at five-minute increments. Talk about pricing to the max. They assemble barbecue grills, bunkbeds, computer desks, retile your fireplace, replace a broken window, but if the job doesn't take as long as estimated, you pay only for the amount of time it does take. They may not clean windows, but they do caulking of baseboards, countertops, tubs, installation of appliances, attic stairs, basketball backboards, repair or replace bricks, cabinet drawers, fix chairs and furniture-that ill-fated list of things to do that is forever growing. Uniformed service technicians are radio-dispatched, licensed and insured to ensure a perfect project outcome. And most importantly, they come when called!

✧✧✧✧✧ America's Home Tenders 972/991-2927

15150 Preston Rd., Suite 300 *Mon-Fri 9-5*
Dallas, TX 75248

What a great idea! Got a house that's sitting vacant because you've already been transferred to L.A. but your house couldn't make the trip? Protect your assets by having someone move into it with their own furniture so the house will be "lived in." That kills two birds with one occupant. First, it's easier to sell a home with furniture and stuff. And second, vandals hate lived-in houses. If you're looking to be an occupant, the advantage is you get to play like you're rich (but you must have good-looking furniture) and live in a $100,000 plus house (some are even in the $500.000 to $1 million range) for as low as $500 a month plus utilities. There are some drawbacks, however, and you must meet their qualifications. Riffraff need not apply. You have to be willing to show the house to prospective buyers and move quickly in case the house sells. This business is owned by Bill and Linda Stall (and seen on The Oprah Show courtesy of you know who)! You pay a security deposit equal to one month's rent as well as maintain the lawn, pool and minor repairs. Pets are considered, but references are essential. However, unruly Akitas are not favored. Call 972/991-2927 or 214/803-0920. *CK*

✧✧✧✧✧ American Eagle Builders 817/588-2050

401 Crowley Rd. *Mon-Fri 9-5*
Arlington, TX 76012

Watch the sales price of your home soar with the help from American Eagle Builders of Arlington, Texas. With more than 14 years of building experience, and consistently ranked among the largest home remodelers in the nation, you don't have to have an eagle's eye to know you're in good hands. In September 1998, they were rated 40 out of 500 by *Qualified Remodeler* magazine. With an exclusive Homeowners Lifetime Workmanship Warranty, you can trust American Eagle Builders with your home remodeling needs: storm shelters, roofs, windows, carports, patio covers, gutters, soffit, fascia. The list is long, the reputation solid. They have been designated as premium distributors of Alside's Charter Oak vinyl siding, and are members of the Arlington Chamber of Commerce, and the Dallas Better Business Bureau. Check around before you take the plunge. Here's an eagle that won't be on the endangered species list anytime soon. *CK, MC, V, AE, D*

Home Improvement

✧✧✧✧✧ American Service Center 972/681-2222

15330 LBJ Freeway #210 *Daily 7-7*
Mesquite, TX 75150 *www.americanservicecenter.com*

This is an open and shut case. Call for the magic GENIE authorized dealer where you can get factory-direct, same-day service on your garage door. Free estimates–do you need the springs, glass, cables, or chains replaced? Uniformed techs are in radio-dispatched trucks and can somehow magically appear to rescue you coming or going into the garage. The entire Metroplex is served through their main office, but Fort Worth residents can call 817/436-3000, with North Dallas calling 972/335-5885. Whether it's garage doors and openers, residential or commercial installation, repair and replacement, this center can get you up and about in no time. AMARR 24-gauge steel garage doors started as low as $299 installed. They offer several different sizes and qualities alongside the Genie Pro Screw Drive garage door opener. This garage door offers a direct drive for maximum lifting force, a one-piece solid-steel screw for added strength and security, fewer moving parts for more years of reliability, a quieter operation and an automatic 120-watt lighting system for safer evening entries and exits. It also has a high-impact, heat-resistant polypropylene lens cover for easy bulb replacement. Both Genie Pro and LIFT-MASTER openers are sold. *CK, MC, V, AE, D*

American Video Equipment 281/443-2300

1617 E. Richey Rd. *www.americanvideoequipment.com*
Houston, TX 77073

American Video Equipment occupies a 45,000-square-foot facility in Houston where all design, production, sales, shipping and accounting functions are accomplished. They have been designing and manufacturing a wide range of closed circuit television equipment and accessories. Their products include cash register interfaces, mobile 12VDC VCR's, ATM interfaces, monitors, multiplexers, mini cameras, video switchers, time date generators, rear vision system, 12VDC accessories and more. At American Video Equipment you will find the surveillance equipment you are looking for. Their web site is an excellent information resource to help determine your needs, or call their sales staff.

✧✧✧ AMPC (Advanced Metro Pest Control) 817/265-4002

Arlington, TX *By Appt. Only*

Call out the pest control when you're in the thick of unwanted guests. They are insured, bonded, TPCL #10787, members of the Better Business Bureau,

Arlington Chamber of Commerce and they offer free quotes and written warranties. Giving you a lot of bang for your bugs, they are no newcomer to keeping pests under control. With more than 65 years experience serving the entire Metroplex, you can expect them to know the difference between a mite and a mongoose. Regular house control costs $69.95. *CK, MC, V, AE, D*

★★★ Anchor Paint Co. — 972/699-0151

715 N. Central Expwy. — *Mon-Fri 7-5; Sat 7-Noon*
Richardson, TX 75080

Hoist your anchor to those in the know. For professional quality paint, every stroke can make a difference. Rub elbows with painters and enjoy the same prices at Anchor. Flat latex paint (great for interiors) was $9.95/gallon in standard colors or $10.95 if you get a custom mix. Manufactured in Tulsa, OK, this high-quality grade of industrial paint is sold via their outlet for less. Ok, anchor your brushes alongside metal primers, architectural coatings, varnishes, sealers, high-temp coatings, zinc-rich coatings, lacquer stains, epoxies, solvents and vinyls. Painters' days start early, so get going, mate, to the west side of Central Expressway between Belt Line and Arapaho. *CK, MC, V, AE, D*

✧✧✧✧ Appliance Fixx — 972/466-0808

1311 E. Belt Line Rd., #3 — *Mon-Fri 9-5:30; Sat 10-4*
Carrollton, TX 75006

If it were up to me, I'd never stop at this shop, knowing full well I couldn't fix a thing. But, curiosity got the best of me and sure enough, I was wrong. The bulk of their business is appliance service and sales of refurbished units. And that's good. Every handyman I know, who claims to know it all, never does, so I'd put my money on hiring these guys. And if you're looking for a part, they've got plenty of parts on hand. If yours is broken, these folks can fix them. They service most makes and models and do so with a smile. After all, isn't that the neighborly thing to do? Between Josey and Old Denton Rd., this is appliance parts heaven for the do-it-yourselfer. *CK, MC, V, D*

✧✧✧✧✧ Around Town Movers — 214/350-3873

6700 Harry Hines — *By Appt. Only*
Dallas, TX 75235

When it comes to getting around town with your life's worth of home furnishings, this is the company to call. Since 1994, this husband and wife-owned company (the Greg Mitchell's) have commandeered a crew of 15-20 able-bodied men who lend their helping hands (and back) in helping you make the move. Whether up or down, across town or down to the Rio Grande, this company can be trusted. Expect their prices to be extremely competitive (having come in several times as the lowest bid). They can move you from one place to the next, across town or around the state with men who know the difference between an armoire and an armadillo. Whichever you treasure most, you want them carried in compassionate hands. They also move pianos, antiques, even computers whether yours is a commercial or residential move. Want to rent your own truck? Fine. They will unload and load them if you prefer to do the driving. Same day service on most jobs, but toward the end of the month, if you're moving a mansion, please try to give them a few weeks' notice. That's their busy time and they will schedule accordingly. *CK, MC, V*

Artistic Iron 303/791-6440

7241 W. Titan Rd. *Mon-Fri 9-5; Sat 9-3*
Littleton, CO *www.artisticironofcolorado.com*

Since 1978 Artistic Iron has been helping with exterior home improvement products. Artistic Iron offers the superior exterior home improvement products you would expect from a manufacturer. They eliminate the middle man. You are purchasing factory direct which keeps the prices low. Artistic Iron offers a wide variety of products for your home including replacement windows, steel security storm/screen doors, entry doors, patio covers, vinyl siding and seamless gutters. The patio covers are great for staying out of the sun or as a cover for your car, truck or RV. They have a great selection of entry doors with decorative glass. They were 25 percent off when we visited. Basement replacement windows were as low as $149 installed. The deals are waiting for you at Artistic Iron. *CK, MC, V, D*

✧✧✧✧ B & R Roofing & Remodeling 972/889-8981

809 Canyon Creek Square *Mon-Fri 8:30-5*
Richardson, TX 75080

From the ground up, this construction company does it all. Family-owned and operated, they've now added roofing by ELK, FIBERGLAS, GAF, TAMKO, TIMBERLINE to their game besides the usual room additions, kitchen and bath remodeling, patio enclosures, ceramic tile, exterior and interior painting, custom skylights, custom siding, concrete sidewalks and driveways–anything you want, they can get it done. This 19-year veteran of the hammer and nail business claims "No job too big or too small," and credits his builder-father with teaching him the ropes. Lots of references of homes in the area to verify their talented hands, plus 100 percent financing available, as well as home improvement loans. They provide their own in-house crews rather than looking to subcontractors. Too, that's good that they keep an eye on the job while they perform all facets of the work at hand. Make your tracks to B & R if you want it done right, the old-fashioned way. Now that they've finally moved out of the home-office, into an office-office, I'd say, welcome to the club. *CK, MC, V, Financing*

★★★★★ Bath-Tec — 972/646-5279

5142 Hwy. 34 W — *Mon-Fri 8-5*
Ennis, TX 75119 — *www.bathtec.com*

Take 45 south towards Houston, to Highway 251 (the Ennis/Kaufman exit). At the stop sign, turn right and go to the third red light. Then turn right at the four-way stoplight. Follow that road over the reservoir for not quite a mile to Bath-Tec. Fortunately, you won't have to swim back. Bath-Tec manufactures a complete line of luxury acrylic whirlpool bath tubs, soaking tubs and shower bases for residential construction and the lodging industry. They offer factory-direct pricing (my favorite words) plus quality and craftsmanship all rolled into one. Soak in an acrylic whirlpool bath or invite a friend into a two-person whirlpool. Or wash off in an acrylic shower manufactured from durable, easy-to-clean, high-gloss, cast acrylic that should keep you spic 'n span for years. The shower bases have a slip resistant surface, built-in flange, raised dam to prevent water leakage over the threshold and they're easy to install. (Famous last words!) The part I do understand is that they are available in a variety of sizes and colors with optional chrome or brass drains. Want a whirlpool faucet set in polished chrome, polished brass with lacquer coating or in 24K gold-plate in a waterfall or Roman-fountain style? Turn on here. If you are buying a multiple of tubs, the prices descend accordingly. *CK*

✧✧✧ Better Shelf Co., The — 972/578-1760

Plano, TX — *By Appt. Only*
www.bettershelf.com

Deep cabinets can hold a lot, but they can hide just as much. How many times have you moaned and groaned when looking for that omelet pan or that oregano? Roll-out shelves are the solution to your frustration of bending and groping in the dark. These retractable shelves slide out smoothly to give you access to the items. They also provide an additional level of storage space. Even if you could reach what you're looking for, you've probably broken a nail and blurted out a few expletives. Not any more. For future reference, roll-out shelving is the way to find things easily in your cupboards. Call for a free price quote and get your cabinets under control. Lee and Pat Pfoutz specialize in these shelves exclusively, keeping costs under the counter, and they are particularly good role models for their roll-out shelving. *CK, MC, V*

★★★★★ Binford Supply Co. 972/286-2881

2915 Hickory Tree Rd. *Mon-Fri 8-5; Sat 8-Noon*
Mesquite, TX 75180

This wholesale fence supplier invites the public to take the do-it-yourself challenge. Serving the Metroplex since 1950, this company can build you a fortress with a surround-sound fence in wood or chain link, ornamental iron or pickets, rails, posts and gates. If, however, you'd rather do-it-yourself, don't be shy and ask about the "contract-it-yourself" plan. They'll even help you. So go ahead, and "Do fence me in!" Besides, even Tim the Toolman uses Binford tools. *CK, MC, V, D*

★★★ Black & Decker/DeWalt Factory Service Center 972/620-8655

2257 Royal Lane *Mon-Fri 8-5; Sat 9-1*
Dallas, TX 75229

Of course, giving us a FREE carpenter's pencil was not the only reason we plugged into the B&D and DeWalt Service Center. After all, a refurbished single-speed jig saw for $19.99, a cordless drill for $39.99, VERSIPAK tool kits starting at $84.99 and a BLACK & DECKER Dustbuster rechargeable car vacuum for $14.99 were all other reasons we plugged into this store. With small appliances, drills, jig saws, mowers and hedgers all in stock at good prices, you can enjoy doing any improvement project. With a two-year home-use warranty, the only thing you could lose is ... a few fingers. But, careful shopping and careful use of these reconditioned and/or blemished tools gives you the epitome of a power buy. Located one and a half blocks west of I-35 E, they have another location in Garland at 718 W. Centerville Rd., 972/686-9302, Mon-Fri 8:30-5. *CK, MC, V, AE, D*

★★★★ Bosch Factory Service Center 972/241-5385

2457 Walnut Ridge St. *Mon-Fri 8-5*
Dallas, TX 75229

Get a grip on paying high prices–and consider the best that comes with one-year warranties. Join the Vice Squad and stop paying retail. If the names BOSCH or SKIL Power Tools mean anything to you, you'll be thrilled here. Cordless drills start as low as $20 and went up to $140. Who cares if it went through the drill before? Chances are, you can find what you're looking for sawed to the bare bones. Saws, too. A gentlemen's skill saw started at $41, rebuilt routers cost about $100, jig saws can cost between $30-$100. All of the tools are bargains because they have been reconditioned. They look like, they work like, they're practically like new. So new? What are you waiting for? Off Stemmons and Walnut Hill, go east on Walnut Hill and left at the second light, Abels. Turn left and it's at the corner of Abels and Walnut Ridge. *CK, MC, V, AE, D*

✧✧✧ Brennan Enterprises — 972/660-3106

608 Grand Ave. — *Mon-Fri 8-5*
Arlington, TX 76013

During the son's 20th anniversary sale, they offered CERTAINTEED vinyl windows at a buy one, get one free deal, then took another 20 percent off. Dad started the business more than 50 years ago, and they're still going strong in the home improvement industry. If putting blinds on a window is part of the job, they can get it done, but their expertise actually involves building the window, or doing exterior improvements to your home. They do siding by TECHWALL, roofing, patio covers and enclosures. Check out their new showroom and office at 608 Grand Avenue in Arlington, 817/251-0337. My, my, what a great addition you have, my dear! *CK*

✧✧✧✧ Brown's Construction/Awning Co. — 817/534-2192

6412 Crawford Lane East — *Mon-Fri 7:30-5:30*
Forrest Hill, TX

From firm foundation repair to awnings, Brown's will help your home look its best as well as save you some green. Brown's provides the "look of wood" with the reliability and durability of architectural aluminum. Lattice available in your choice of open lattice or solid roof design to complement your home's architectural style. Lattice systems are maintenance free and backed by a 10-year limited manufacturers' warranty. Family owned since 1970, 100 percent financing and free estimates available with payments as low as $75 a month. Foundation repair rage from $8,000-$10,000. They will work anywhere in Tarrant and Dallas counties. So, what do you want?

Home Improvement

★★★★★ Cabinet Depot, Inc. (CDI) — 214/637-5514

3004 Irving Blvd. — *Mon-Fri 9-5*
Dallas, TX 75247

Between Inwood and Mockingbird, in the heart of the Industrial District, you can knock on wood. CDI is home to the best factory-direct cabinets for your kitchen or bath including products from CARDELL CABINETRY and KITCHEN CRAFT. Close to 6,000 cabinets in stock with quality a notch above Home Depot's with prices a notch below. You can have it your way. Cash and carry or have their expert installers do it for you. Builders and remodelers have been shopping here for years. Now you, too, can experience factory-direct pricing on cabinets of the best products from the professionals. CDI even provides personalized computer designs to ensure the perfect fit. They're groovy and with more than 45,000 square feet of cabinet space, you can have everything at your fingertips. *CK, MC, V, D*

★★★ Casci — 214/421-3390

2615 S. Good Latimer — *Mon-Fri 8-4:30*
Dallas, TX 75215

A world of moldings and immense columns awaits your placement at Casci. Thinking about getting plastered? Why not go for ornamental plaster, medallions, brackets or cornices and at least be decorative? Go antebellum or complete your gothic scheme with ornate pieces from the Casci collection. All prices for molding and cornice based on orders of 50 feet or more. But who's counting when considering tapered, fluted or smooth Corinthian, Doric or Ionic columns? Doesn't everyone place one foot in front of the other? *CK*

★★★★★ Classy Closets — 972/355-7687

1565 W. Main St., #208-233 — *By Appt. Only*
Lewisville, TX 75067 — *www.classyclosets.com*

Setting up your home-office and want everything in its place? Call on the design pro here. They'll create a one-stop workshop that is not only a sight to behold but will hold everything you need to keep your home-office in tip-top shape. When it comes to closets, don't forget to ask for their free jewelry drawer (then ask me where to fill it up). Now, who can resist a secret stash of jewels? Don't overlook the potential organization that Classy Closets can bring to your home, bedroom, media room, garage, utility, or laundry room, any wall that needs a unit to display, hide, or keep your books, your trophies, your doll collection in place ... well, you get the picture. Why pay for extra storage units or stuff scrapbooks or pack away your porcelain dogs in the attic? Store them in a unit specifically designed for that use. Design ideas are only a phone call away. *CK, MC, V, AE, D*

★★★ Closet Care — 972/255-1889

By Appt. Only

If you care enough to have your closets organized, you might as well call on Karl. Family-owned and operated, with more than 10 years experience behind them, a standard closet, including free in-home design, may well start around $180, but it varies by job. It may be less, but with all the fun, extra doodads, expect it to cost more. However, even if you have a super-deluxe, mega-closet installed, you'll be paying at least 40 percent less than if you hired the competition. What woman in this city doesn't drool at the thought of having enough room to stuff a few more dresses into her already packed-to-the-gills closet? Do you really want to double your closet space to "Make Room For Daddy?" Do you think Marla had equal footing with the Donald? No siree! You need all the space you can get. Give these caring closeteers a call. There are no installation fees. Check special promotions, too. There's always something going on. Free estimates. *CK*

Closet Cents — 214/956-8833

Dallas, TX 75220 — *By Appt. Only*

Everybody needs a little space. Or a little more space. When your closet runneth over, it's time to call Closet Cents. They will remodel your closet to maximize the available space. Call for an appointment and they will come to your home to help design a new closet. You'll have a plan and cost estimate in about 30-45 minutes. When you OK the work, they remove all your existing shelves and rods, replacing them with industrial grade particle board in white laminate. Other colors are available, but about 90 percent of their work is done in white. They can give you more space in the closet, but organizing it is up to you. *CK*

★★★★ Closet Factory, The — 972/620-0606

3313 Garden Brook — *Mon-Fri 9-5 (By Appt. Only)*
Dallas, TX 75234 — *www.closetfactory.com*

This is an open and shut case. They are one of the few custom closet builders in the Metroplex that hasn't asked to redo mine–especially my shoe closet. Though you won't pay for installation, you will pay for custom workmanship (though affordable). They offer a free in-home planning session which lasts more than an hour. If you're opting for some organizational help, be prepared to eat a snack. Custom-built garage organizers and modular office spaces are also part of their repertoire. And if you think white is the only color choice, think almond or a variation on that theme. *CK, MC, V, D*

✧✧✧ Comfort Keepers 817/581-7131

By Appt. Only

He has a passing similarity to Mr. French, so what other line of work could Bill Harvey have gone into? Formerly called Butler Bill's, the company is now called Comfort Keepers, your one-stop call for personal services. Schedule him to visit once or twice a week or even bi-weekly and you'll be able to come home to a tidy house, made-up beds, clean laundry and a warm dinner, giving you more time to do more important things-like soaking in a hot tub or tuning in to "Who Wants to be a Millionaire?" He can also run errands, drive children to activities and much more. Fees start at $16 an hour. His key service area is Northeast Tarrant County, the Mid-Cities, Grapevine, Colleyville and Southlake; however, he is sometimes available for assignments outside that perimeter. After all, this man has his limits and can't be all things everywhere. *CK*

Custom Wallcoverings by Barbara 214/657-3032

By Appt. Only

Finding someone to trust your walls to is almost as tramatic as changing hair dressers! Never fear, Barbara's here! Barbara Davis has hung wallpaper in the DFW area for over 20 years. Fast, dependable, and most importantly, she keeps her seems straight and practically invisible. My kind of gal! Let her hang out at your place and see what a difference wallpaper can make.

✧✧ Dallas Plumbing & Air-Conditioning 214/340-6300

11055 Plano Rd. *Mon-Fri 8-5; Sat 9-Noon*
Dallas, TX 75238

What else can be said about a business that has been serving the Dallas area since 1903? Their track record speaks for itself. Over the last century, however, they have added a few new products and services to their line. With the dawn of A/C (central or otherwise), they rose to the occasion by becoming a CARRIER dealer. They offer 24-hour emergency service and the installation of CARRIER units, and will repair or replace whatever existing unit you have. But when visiting their glistening showroom, wear your shades indoors. The selection of kitchen and bath fixtures is blinding. Builders and professional plumbers have long availed themselves of their wide variety of name-brand plumbing supplies displayed invitingly in their showroom, but they also cater to the do-it-yourselfer. However, if you are among the mechanically-challenged, you can trust their years of experience to repair or replace your plumbing problems instead of asking you to insert your finger in the dike. Expect to save about 25 percent in their plumbing showroom; but service calls are pretty standard and not cheap. *CK, MC, V, AE, D*

✧✧✧✧✧ Dempsey Electrical Services 972/247-8995

11005 Indian Trail, #107 *24-Hour Emergency Service*
Dallas, TX 75229

Are you a hot wire? Then call on these fast and professional service technicians-be it residential, commercial, or industrial. This 40-year-old electrical company is au current. Zap! Licensed and insured for your protection, their prices will save you money. From fuse and breaker replacements to the installation of light fixtures, room additions, security lighting, aluminum wiring repaired and replaced, computer wiring, swimming pools, parking lot lighting, maintenance and new construction. If it's an electrical issue, don't get your wires crossed and shop anywhere else. City-wide service. *CK, MC, V, D*

✧✧✧✧✧ Devard's Heat, Air, Electric & Plumbing 972/422-1505

2710 S. Rigsbee, Suite A *Mon-Fri 8-5; Sat 8-2*
Plano, TX 75074

Whoopee! For both spring and fall tune-ups on air and heat, expect to pay a service charge of $69. Compared to the others we checked, not bad. Too, plumbing repair is not done hourly, but by the job with a price quote up front. Add that to routine check-ups, service on all TRANE heating and air-conditioning units and service contracts and you've got an A in our book. Can't sleep because you're wired (wrong)? Well, call on these service masters and let your electrical problems be their problems. (Like the hanging of ceiling fans.) They chuckled when I told them my "handyman" couldn't hang it because of all the wires! In fact, you can call this Johnny-on-the-spot for many of life's little problems. Why buy the instruction book when they have all the answers? Stop draining your budget, and let these guys keep you flush when the problem is your plumbing, too. (No, they are not GYN's!) They also do air conditioning and heating repairs. From French drains to creating an electrical circuit city in your home or office, this company's a live wire! *CK, MC, V, AE, D*

Home Improvement

♥♥♥♥♥ DFW Coating Concepts 972/488-2227

Dallas, TX *By Appt. Only*

Talk about being floored. If you suffer from oil- or dirt-stained garage floors, these folks are the surface doctors. DFW Coating Concepts offers more than 50 colors of floor coating to choose from and they all carry a 3 year warranty against stains, chipping or peeling. (Sounds like a good idea for warranteeing husbands, too.) They also do pressure washing, fence, pavestone and pool deck sealing. But it's their interior concrete acid staining that gets my vote for coating. A contemporary look with your budget and good taste in mind. What a concept!

✧✧✧✧✧ DFW Windows & Doors 972/378-0188

Plano, TX *By Appt. Only*
www.dfwwindows.com

If you don't call Dan Miller at DFW Windows & Doors, you will see what pane is all about. Great prices (no, the lowest prices) on custom windows and doors. And, if you buy a house full of windows, they'll even throw in a FREE top-of-the-line storm door. When real estate professionals comment about "drive-up appeal," this is what these make-over experts do for your windows and doors. Replace them with single- or double-pane windows–they offer a 10-year to lifetime warranty, and help reduce your energy bills by at least 25-35 percent and if you're in the Texas-New Mexico electric company area, you need all the help you can get! Let new storm windows, doors or solar screens do their part in lowering your energy use. Each comes with energy efficient glass that can be tinted gray or bronze and includes thermal break frames and a triple glaze. Be sure to ask about the Low-E modern glass, which has a low-"emissive" coating. This almost invisible metallic coating acts as a heat barrier to reflect warm inside air back into a house and reduces a window's heat loss by 35 percent. Same-day or next-day service. That's my man, Dan. And new this year, ask Dan about siding if you'd rather not have to ever paint your house again. Free price quotes and same or next day installation on windows and doors. *CK, MC, V, AE, D*

★★★★ Discount Countertops 214/951-0313

4735 Almond Ave. *Mon-Fri 8-Noon, 1-5*
Dallas, TX 75247

When it comes to countertops, if I've been asked once, I have been asked a million times, "Where can I get a deal?" Can you read my lips? Can you read the above store name? Once said, join the counter revolution and check it out. Between Mockingbird and Irving Boulevard, in the heart of the Industrial District, they are configuring away. From FORMICA to GILBRALTOR (¼-inch solid surface), you can bet they can cover counters in no time. Estimates and measuring done in-house (in your house or office) and free estimates are given, including additional remodeling finish-outs where required. A one-stop shop for discount countertops. Gee, that rhymes. Save 30 percent over Home Expo's prices, but expect to wait for an in-home estimate, they are booked solid. *CK, MC, V*

★★★★★ Discount Home Warehouse — 214/631-2755

1750 Empire Central — *Mon-Sat 9-5*
Dallas, TX 75235

Make Discount Home Warehouse your home away from home if you're in the market for home accents reclaimed from previous homes, offices, restaurants, banks, hotels-wherever. Spend a day dreaming from whence they came. If it's recycled, useable building materials or more interesting architectural salvage and unique pieces for the home, this is where the cow ate the cabbage. Easy to get to, off Stemmons and Harry Hines, dig in with both hands. The Hirosky family will make you feel right at home. Probably one of the many reasons why this place was chosen as a SHOPPER'S CHOICE AWARD WINNER for 1998. Why buy new when you can rummage through the remains of the day? This is the source that specializes in good, clean, recycled building materials at a fraction of the cost of new. Furthermore, they clearly mark their entire inventory with rock-bottom prices to avoid the normal haggling inherent in the business. Just a sampling of everyday items at 50-90 percent off includes doors, pedestal sinks, architectural relics, toilets, mantels, lumber, bath sinks, kitchen cabinets, glass door knobs, shutters, footed tubs, ceiling fans, HVAC, windows, oak flooring, crown molding, marble tubs ... all organized by subject matter. Remember, one man's salvage is another one's treasure. Have at it. *CK, MC, V, D*

♥♥♥♥♥ Elliott's Hardware — 214/634-9900

4901 Maple — *Mon-Fri 8-6; Sat 9-5*
Dallas, TX 75235

Who would have guessed that this hardware store would house such an impressive selection of Department 56 collectibles? But for more than 50 years Elliott's has been home to special gift ideas for everyone in the family, from gift items to housewares to, yes, hardware. This is the store that holds more hardware and home improvement gizmos, gadgets and goodies than a leopard's spots. Across the massive inventory, there are always across-the-board sales. Like one day, it might be accent lights, another day, it might be tools. Competing with Lowe's and Home Depot may be a tough road to haul, but if anybody can do it, Elliott's can-and does. Too, you can buy what you need and rent what you don't. Lots of rental options for periodic project needs is another plus for Elliott's Hardware. Tool around in Grapevine at 108 W. Northwest Hwy. at Main, 817/424-1424, too. *CK, MC, V*

♥♥♥♥♥ Fashion Glass & Mirror 972/223-8936

585 S. Beckley Ave. *Mon-Fri 9-5*
Desoto, TX 75115 *www.fashionglass.com*

Well, here's a source to put a lot of class into your next glass act. For more than 25 years, they have managed to stay clear of any sk-etchy projects and have remained clear with a top-notched reputation. Plus, they have the most innovative products and trained professionals in the industry. Look to them for mirror bi-passes, showers, leaded glass, etched glass, stained glass, mirrors and more. That's if your glass-conscious about having the best. *CK, MC, V, AE, D*

♥♥♥♥♥ Ferguson Bath & Kitchen Gallery 817/261-2561

2220 Duluth Dr. *Mon-Fri 8-5*
Arlington, TX 76013 *www.ferginc.com*

Wake up that kitchen and bath with the latest and greatest in fixtures. Turn on to Ferguson Bath & Kitchen Gallery, one of the largest distributors of bath and kitchen fixtures in the country. They have built a people-friendly, hard-working, and selling only the best products around reputation. With great brands like DELTA, JACUZZI, KOHLER and MOEN. Don't settle for anything less. Now it's time to "Skip to my loo," but call ahead for Missy to schedule an appointment. Check directory for locations nearest you. *CK, MC, V, AE, D*

★★★★★ Final Touch Interiors 972/385-7775

2015 Midway Rd., Suite 118 *Mon-Fri 11-5; Sat Noon-5*
Plano, TX 75093

Some may covet the Midas Touch. Smart shoppers prefer the Final Touch. With a showroom of more than 5,300 square feet, you're sure to find the perfect piece to add that final touch to your home decorating scheme. And with everyday prices at 40-60 percent off, you won't be adding a final nail in the coffin-it-up paying retail. Specializing in custom trees and arrangements, what you'll see is what you get after an on-site home or office consultation. Or, make it your final answer, and just whisk it away. They have a large selection of loose flowers, greenery, fruits, berries and more. The design center also offers the spectrum in builder discounts on carpeting, tile, marble, Formica, Corian, granite, cultured marble, cabinetry, wallpaper and wood blinds. In one-fell swoop with Final Touch Interiors. *CK, MC, V, AE, D*

★★★★★ Fireplace Factory Outlet 972/250-2006

4200 Westgrove *Mon-Sat 10-6*
Addison, TX 75001

Looking for a "Good Grill Hunting?" Then Fireplace Factory Outlet is ijust the factory-direct source to light your fire. They are the factory for all your fireplace needs. Incredible gas logs (you'll swear they're real!) This is it. Your golden opportunity to buy the highest quality fireplace accessories at the lowest prices-including the "Texas Bonfire" which sets the standard for beauty and realism in gas logs. No one can tell the difference, even me (except now I don't have to carry out the ashes and schlep the logs). Since 1970, this outlet has been providing fireplace items for area hearths, and my how time flies when you're curled up with a good book. This outlet is the Metroplex's #1 DUCANE grill dealer and they promise the lowest price. GOLDEN BLOUNT glass doors add elegance and protection to any cozy mantle and ROUND MOUNTAIN gas logs (manufactured in Dallas) are a must for winter fires. Discounts all year round keep the home fires burning for less. Family owned and operated, this manufacturer sells its own brand of gas logs, fireplaces, glass doors, folding screens and accessories to dealers and distributors nationwide. How lucky we are that they were born in Addison. Too hot for the fireplace, then heat up those gas grills and sear those steaks. It's barbecue time. Why get grilled at retail prices? The TEC Patio I Gas Grill offers unique advantages that are greatly appreciated, such as less cooking time (infra-red way of cooking meat at 1600 degrees instead of the normal grill's 400 degrees), more even broiling, and it also prevents meat from drying out due to long periods of low-intensity cooking. Plus, it's the kind used in your better steak houses. That alone could save you thousands over your lifetime of Del Frisco and Pappa's Steak House dinners. Anyway, it's time you stopped getting ribbed about being so cheap! *CK, MC, V*

Home Improvement

★★★★★ Fixtures of America

214/638-5990

2229 Valdina
Dallas, TX 75207
Mon-Fri 8:30-5; Sat by Appt.

While these people remain AA1 in our hearts, the name change fits. Need some extra shelving units for your garage? A kid's room? Your office? Then try saving up to 75 percent on a complete line of store fixtures (even if you're not a store). If you are one and don't know about this fixture resource, get with the program. You'll find them by taking the Wycliff exit off Stemmons and going west to Valdina. They buy and sell quality used fixtures, including a sizable selection of showcases. No one can outdo them on prices. Don't overlook items such as cube units, Étagére, glass gondolas, shelving, signs, showcases, double bars, bags, hat racks, slat and grid wall accessories, peg hooks, rounder and rolling racks, counters, two-, three-, four- and six-way clothes racks; they make great closet additions, garage organizers or accent pieces. *CK, MC, V, D*

♥♥♥♥♥ Fort Worth Marble and Granite

817/336-7474

117 Vacek
Fort Worth, TX 76107
Mon-Fri 8-5

Isn't it time you stopped taking marble for granite? Start Sharon the Stones at this recently relocated much larger showroom of more than 13,000 square feet of natural stone. Choose from marble, granite, stone, limestone, slate and more. They specialize in countertops, but will help you with any stone need (except headstones). Being both a retailer and wholesaler, their prices, selection and service are top-drawer. *CK*

✧✧✧✧✧ Free Construction Co.

972/613-4432

Garland, TX 75043
By Appt. Only

If any one can, the handyman can. Geary Free owns and operates this service but it's not free, though close. Reasonable prices for quality repairs is how his construction crew grew. For tile work, light electrical and plumbing, minor roof repairs, painting, fences, decks, sprinkler repairs; if it's broken, call and see if it's something for Free. Free estimates, for sure. Just don't call him to do any masonry work. That's where he draws the line. *CK*

★★★★★ G&S Sales

972/563-7821

4303 Hwy. 80 W
Terrell, TX 75160
Mon-Fri 8-5:30; Sat 8-5
www.building-materials.com

Selling everything you've ever needed for a home improvement project is how G&S Sales stays ahead of the game. There's a reason most smart shoppers go there to start or finish one off. Five acres of everything from carpet to shingles, portable buildings to cabinets, bathtubs to sinks, hardware to exterior shutters (painted, $2.99 a pair). Yikes! Is it any wonder folks come from hundreds of miles away to load up their pickup trucks, vans or semis? The few who come in cars, well, they had to make several trips. The prices are so good, the service so superb, the inventory so vast and diverse, it's a wonder they haven't been named to the *Guinness Book of World Records.* You'll walk a million miles for one of their dials, but it's a deal and worth the hundreds, if not thousands, of dollars you'll save. Saw some KOHLER $1,000 sinks for $199, brand new, in the box. Surplus, seconds, overruns, discontinued products or products that the home centers didn't sell-who cares? It's all here. Ceramic tile starts at $.79, with more than 30,000 square feet in stock. They have an equally large selection of carpeting, with prices starting at $3.99 for brands found elsewhere for $8.99. You'll also find lumber, windows, doors, JACUZZI and WHIRLPOOL, sheet metal, siding, materials for mobile home improvement and more. Bob Vila, eat your heart out! *CK, MC, V, AE, D*

Garage Door Brokers — 972/272-8733

3814 Miller Park Drive — *Mon-Fri 7-4:30; Sat 7-Noon*
Garland, TX 75042

Stuck in a rut? Motor is grinding to a halt? Garage door's about to collapse under the weight of 20 years of hard labor? Well, call on the guys who have put saving money on garage doors, openers and remotes on the map. Shop in their 15,000-square-foot showroom and buy what you need to buy–wholesale. Expect the brands to be the best–like MID-AMERICA and LIFTMASTER. Expect to see 300-400 garage doors in-stock at any one time. Expect remotes for new garage doors or your old ones that you've lost. Expect service and installation like you've never seen before. Bill and Don, at your service. And with a smile, no less. How can you go broke with these kinds of brokers. Go for it! Look for the 7,500-square-foot Fort Worth showroom at 1653 Hickory Drive, 817/222-3667. Now, the other half of the Metroplex gets to shop at the best garage-sale ever. After all, we do know an "open and shut" case when we see it. *CK, MC, V, AE, D*

♥♥♥♥♥ Garage Store Cabinets — 972/664-9943

Richardson, TX 75081 — *By Appt. Only*

Tired of garage clutter? Afraid if you park your car in the garage you may never find it? Consult these garage storage specialists (free estimate) and revamp. They offer a five-year limited warranty on storage systems that include cabinets, hanging systems, shelves, bins and drawers, pegboards, workbenches and more. The best part? Units are not permanent fixtures, so when you go, they can go, too. Just think what the neighbors will say! *CK, MC, V*

★★★★★ H2O Wholesale Plumbing 972/242-2289

2324 N. I-35 East *Mon-Fri 7-5; Sat 8-1*
Carrollton, TX 75006 *www.h2osupply.net*

Unfortunately, "Cats" on Broadway played to its final audiences this year. This Katz, however, is open for business on Stemmons and you can see purr-fectly discounted prices of 25-50 percent off retail. What's in a name? The symbol H2O is a clue to what's going down the drain here. The company doesn't advertise to the public, but sells every known plumbing fixture from top-of-the-line to imports. You'll find major name wholesale plumbing supplies, whirlpool tubs, faucets, water heaters, toilets, showerheads, shower doors, pipes, valves, fittings, fixtures and much more, because as they are quick to boast, "If we don't have it, we can get it for you wholesale." See, the apple doesn't fall far from the tree. They're still singing Katz's praises. *CK, MC, V*

★★★★★ Habitat for Humanity ReStore 214/827-9083

3020 Bryan St. *Mon-Sat 10-6*
Dallas, TX 75204 *www.dallas-habitat.org*

This is the place that has all Metroplex moochers making their way for the skinny. This philanthropic treasure is a virtual hotbed of bargains, two-fold. Not only do they sell stuff at ridiculously low prices, but the proceeds benefit a worthy cause–Habitat for Humanity, an organization providing low-income housing for the needy. Here you'll find new and used appliances, doors, windows, tile, tubs, sinks, plumbing supplies, flooring, hardware, fixtures, wiring and more for any home improvement project. New whirlpool tubs, for example, were $400 and CORIAN sinks were $30. All purchases are tax deductible and donations are always welcome. Shop and net a bargain and your purchase price is a double whammy. Fort Worth's ReStore sells surplus new and used building materials, too, at 50 to 90 percent below retail prices. New paint at $3 a gallon, exterior doors starting at $20, dishwashers $29 and up, even new kitchen sinks were a wash-out at $15 and up. When three 18-wheelers full of ceramic and floor tiles pulled up to their doors, there was pandemonium as they were priced $1 for smaller sizes up to $1.80 for 20 X 20 inches. Yes, even your purchases are tax deductible. Visit them at 3420 S. Grove St., Ft. Worth, 817/926-3585. *CK, MC, V*

★★★★★ Habitat for Humanity ReStore 817/926-3585

3420 S. Grove St. *Mon-Fri 9:30-5:30; Sat 8-4*
Fort Worth, TX 76110 *www.fwhabitat.org/restore/*

Fort Worth's philanthropic treasure is a virtual hotbed of bargains, two-fold. Not only do they sell stuff at ridiculously low prices, but the proceeds benefit a worthy cause–the Fort Worth Area Habitat for Humanity, low-income housing for the needy. The ReStore sells surplus new and used building materials at 50-90 percent below retail prices. All materials have been donated by local business and individuals. Here you'll find appliances, doors, windows, tile, tubs, sinks, plumbing supplies and more for any home improvement project. New paint at $3 a gallon, exterior doors starting at $20, dishwashers $29 and up, and even a new kitchen sink can be had for $15 and up. When three 18-wheelers full of ceramic and floor tiles pulled up to their doors, they were a steal at $1 for smaller sizes up to $1.80 for 20 x 20-inch tiles. All purchases are tax deductible and donations are always welcome. *CK, MC, V*

✧✧✧✧ Handyman Connection 214/357-2400

2351 W. Northwest Hwy., #2122 *By Appt. Only*
Dallas, TX 75220

Let's face it, when you need someone handy at fix-it jobs, you usually need it yesterday. Where to go? Connect to this Cincinnati-based franchise that brought the concept of saving 25 percent on small- to mid-range home repairs to the Metroplex, including painting, installing fans, hanging garage doors, carpentry, laying ceramic tile, minor plumbing and electrical jobs. These handymen have a list a half-mile long of what they won't do, such as structural work, but at least you'll have someone who'll show up. They bid by the job and try to keep their costs low by not driving fancy trucks or wearing monogrammed uniforms. There is no charge for a service call to evaluate a problem (18-plus servicemen are always on call) and they'll be ready to go to work immediately with your acceptance of the job. All of their repairmen have more than 10 years experience and they guarantee their work for one year. However, they insist you buy the materials so you avoid that markup. Labor is their contribution to your squeaky door or to laying that ceramic tile in the bath. Nothing that requires a building permit is done, such as roofing, concrete work, fences, siding, or highly competitive or complicated jobs. But what you do get is first-class service in repairs. They will not work on rental or commercial properties, either, or provide price quotes by phone. *CK, MC, V*

★★★★★ Harbor Freight Tools 972/231-1872

1704 E. Belt Line Rd. *Mon-Fri 8-6; Sat 8:30-5:30; Sun 10-4*
Richardson, TX 75081 *www.harborfreight.com*

Between Jupiter and Plano Roads, and next door to or east of the Richardson Square Mall, hang your tool belt on this company that guarantees if you can find it cheaper, they will match the price. Stop tooling around shopping elsewhere as it's all cheaper here, plus it all comes with a lifetime warranty. If you prefer to shop by mail, don't hesitate to ask for their catalog. They have tools you didn't even know you needed or that existed. They have shop equipment like wood lathes. Go figure. They have air tools and power tools. You name it! For everyone from the serious mechanic to the weekend warrior who'd rather do it himself, Harbor Freight Tools' catalog, and now outlet, features nothing but the best in tools and equipment. Bound not to harbor any ill will, they are known as a "category killer" (with store locations throughout California, Nevada and Kentucky). Now Texans can be the beneficiary of this 30-year business. They sell all major brands of tools and workshop equipment, including AEG, BLACK & DECKER, BOSCH, CAMPBELL HAUSFELD, CUMMINS, DELTA, DEWALT, HOMELITE, HONDA, MAKITA, MILWAUKEE, PITTSBURG, PORTER-CABLE, QUINCY, RYOBI, SENTRY, SKIL, STACK-ON, STANLEY and WEN at a savings of up to 80 percent. If you're serious about saving money, you ought to buy by the book. (It's free!) Everything from A to W ... automotive repair and maintenance equipment (engines, generators, heavy-duty jacks) to working tools. You won't have to shop around–it's somewhere in the pages of their catalog, or on their website. Lawn equipment like posthole diggers, home improvement must-haves like paint sprayers, power tools, metalworking and welding tools, wrench sets, MCCULLOCH chain saws, workbenches, air compressors and ladders. They even carry reconditioned equipment. Get the project and they will get you handled. Free shipping on orders over $50 in the continental U.S. via USPS. Lifetime guarantee on all hand tools. Half-price specials were enough to make even cynics take note. One handyman went bonkers over a CENTRAL MACHINERY Multipurpose Machine because it will mill/drill/lathe all in one, and all you have to do is go online to find the latest deals. *CK, MC, V, AE, D. MOC*

♥♥♥♥♥ HMi Architectural Antiques & Salvage 214/428-1888

200 Corinth, Suite 103 *Thu-Sat 10-5; Mon-Wed by Appt.*
Longhorn Ballroom Complex *www.hmiarch.com*
Dallas, TX 75207

Always adding new items of antique architectural elements, new furniture from rafted in the Ozarks, other interesting pieces from around-the-wo... t need to fly in the Concorde to get there. In the complex of the Long... room, step behind the bull and this is no bull, if splendor and nostalgia is where it's at for your home improvement project and you want to salvage "The Remains of the Day," then you've stepped into the right milieu. From huge ornate mantels, chandeliers, room dividers, brass fixtures, banisters and crystal doorknobs to antique doors, French doors, carved doors, old doors, shutters, vanities, toilets, sinks, tubs, marble slabs, columns, mahogany paneling–you name it, you will probably find it here! Miles of treasures, from art deco to distressed woods and one-of-a-kind items–home remodelers should shop here first before shelling out big bucks at the home improvement centers. New (and old) things arrive daily, as HMi also has a parent company (and a son who runs Orr Reed Wrecking Company–another boom to salvagers.) *CK, MC, V, AE*

★★★★ Home Depot 972/869-0330

6501 N.E. Loop 820 *24 Hours/7 Days*
North Richland Hills, TX 76180 *www.homedepot.com*

After any Texas weather disaster, is there anyone out there who hasn't become personally acquainted with their nearest Home Depot? Thousands of handyman and handymen-wannabees wander the aisles of Home Depots, dreaming of their next (or first) project. I know guys and gals who make several trips each weekend. From complete restoration to fixer-uppers, even a single crack can be measured, taped, wired, boarded, painted over, or completely redone by shopping here. The kitchen, bathroom, windows, walls, ceilings, floors, roof–every nook and cranny can be restored to a clean bill of health without wealth. Hobknobbing with other do-it-yourselfers can be an enlightening experience. One shopper even met her future husband in the hardware department. Now offering a bridal registry as part of their service, but being the big kahuna in town doesn't always mean you have the best prices or best service. (See Rug Mart for their Pergo prices, for example, or Lights Fantastic for lighting.) Nevertheless, it is all in one place under one gigantic roof, as is their specialty superstore called Home Expo on the Dallas North Tollway (but there, there's not a bargain in sight). Check the directory for additional Metroplex locations and hours. Not all Home Depots are open 24 hours. Check before you wander out for a O ring or a ratchet wrench at 2 in the morning. *CK, MC, V, AE, D, Home Depot*

★★★★★ Home Recycling Warehouse 214/631-3031

2950 Irving Blvd. *Mon-Sat 9-6*
Dallas, TX 75247-6211

Kings and queens love to cross over the moat to the kingdom of princely prices. In this instance, head for the 30,000-square-foot expanse by exiting Inwood southbound on I-35; go to Irving Blvd. and make a right. Whatever has been culled from a demolition site or a remodeling job can be reclaimed here at a close-out price. Also, there are new building supplies at outlet prices. Whether it's doors or windows, lumber, cabinets, wood flooring, HVAC, tubs, toilets or sinks; it was enjoyed before, enjoy it again. Don't be deterred if they don't answer their phones personally. They're probably helping someone rummage through the surplus, salvage and such. If you are looking to add something old to your new house, this can be a dead-heat for one of the best–especially if you are looking for old bricks (or bric-a-brac). Some new supplies, too, to add to their royal selection. *CK*

✧✧✧✧✧ Home Town Plumbing Co. 972/564-5151

Forney, TX *By Appt. Only*

Be glad you live in a town that has a few plumbing problems because you'll never go down the drain with Home Town Plumbing Co. They will keep you flush. For plumbing repairs and lifetime warranties on workmanship, call this hometown plumbing company, redundantly called Hometown Plumbing Co. Keep afloat, especially if you've priced repairs lately. Someone's gotta do it and it might as well be the one who guarantees your complete satisfaction. Seniors get a discount, too. Beeper is 972/585-6468. 24-hour service, 100-percent satisfaction. Specializing in new construction, repair and remodeling including faucets, plumbing fixtures, water heaters and, of course, certified plumbers. Not only Johnny-on-the-spot, but also as nice as nice can be. *CK*

★★★★★ IMC (International Marble Collection) 972/241-7796

11210 Zodiac Lane *Mon-Fri 7:30-5; Sat 9-Noon*
Dallas, TX 75229

Shop where the workmen shop, but don't take their pickings for granite. You, too, can get the low, low prices before they put their markups on this fabulous natural stone resource for granite and marble slabs. No, you won't scream for this Marble Slab Creamery, but you might consider them a top choice for a no-fat source for kitchen counters, fireplaces, islands and vanity tops. If your astrological chart calls for some major changes in your home life, you should make a path to this heavenly outlet. East of I-35 and south of Royal Lane, you can find top-quality stone tile in marble, granite, slate and limestone, marble fireplaces and contemporary granite fireplace surrounds. Extra phone number is 972/243-4234 in case you can't get through. And yes, delivery service is available. *CK, MC, V, AE*

✧✧✧ J & M Glass Co./Thermal Windows 214/630-5885

1201 Empire Central *Mon-Fri 8-5; Sat 9-1*
Dallas, TX 75247 *www.thermalwindowsdfw.com*

If your heating and air-conditioning bills are giving you a pane in the pocketbook, consider the cost savings factor of installing custom thermal replacement windows. Either residential or commercial, these folks are both the manufacturer AND the installer. Have it any which way you want–double hung, single hung, fixed windows, circle tops, rake heads, octagons, patio doors, casements, replacement or new construction. To make your job easier, windows come with tilt-in cleaning. Now, ask, do I do windows? A limited lifetime warranty with all jobs. Free estimates. For Fort Worth windows, visit that showroom at 4800 Camp Bowie, 817/731-8886. *CK, MC, V*

✧✧✧✧✧ J.J.'s Window Service 972/479-1302

705 N. Bowser, #102 *Mon-Fri 8-5*
Richardson, TX 75083

The J.J. I knew years ago was a monkey. But today, you can stop monkeying around when it comes time to lift the fog off those windows. Serving the Metroplex for more than 10 years has given J.J. an edge on the competition. They want you to see the world without thinking it's, "A foggy day in London town." Book a clear passage by calling J.J.'s Window Service. Cutting up in the back of their warehouse is nothing new as they replace glass, insulated glass, storm windows, install solar screens, utility screens and patio doors. Double and triple-plated glass only with a 10-year warranty. Don't even ask about front screen doors–they don't do them. But do ask their price as they will not be undersold. Free estimates. *CK, MC, V*

✧✧✧✧✧ Kelly's Air-Conditioning and Heating 972/436-4340

151 Ridgeway Circle *24 Hour Service*
Lewisville, TX 75067

Bigger is not always better. In fact, smaller service companies often are more reliable, less expensive (lower overhead) and more responsive. That's definitely the case with Todd Kelly, the owner, who runs his business with the highest level of integrity. They won't quit until the job is done and often it's something so minor, you feel stupid even asking. No extravagant charges just to keep your bill escalating. Reasonable rates and keeping their service area limited to Carrollton, Lewisville, Farmers Branch, The Colony, Coppell, Double Oak, Copper Canyon,

Flower Mound and surrounding areas keeps their response time almost immediate. If you're in their area, you're in good hands. *CK, MC, V*

✧✧✧ Kemiko Concrete Floor Stain 903/587-3708

PO Box 1109 *By Appt. Only*
Leonard, TX 75452

This coat has many colors (six to be exact). Pick your color and use one gallon of this concrete floor stain to cover a room of approximately 400 square feet (a 20 x 20 room). An interior or exterior transformation is easy, so try-it-yourself. When applied to a finished concrete floor, the stain gives the floor an opulent transparent color. A wax and a sealer follows to protect and enhance the depth of color. It can save you a lot of money over recovering your floors with tile or carpet. Remember, though, it takes two applications. Cost is $47.95 gallon. You can pick up the product, too, at Jackson's Pottery, 6950 Lemmon Avenue close to Love Field. Though they do not apply the product, they will recommend those who do. *CK, MC, V, D*

♥♥♥♥♥ Kitchen Distributors of America 214/827-9881

6322 Gaston *Mon-Fri 9-5; Sat 9-3*
Dallas, TX 75214

If you are looking for a one-stop design center for your kitchen or bath, this company could be a sink-in. But don't expect to get away cheap. Complete remodels range from $20,000-$40,000 but if you buy the cabinets from them, the design work is free. They use CRAFTMADE, CRYSTAL, DYNASTY, OMEGA and MERILLAT for cabinets with Merillat being the least expensive line. If you want them to supply the appliances, prices are comparable to other discount suppliers. Delivery and installation anywhere from one to six weeks depending on manufacturer with manufacturer guarantees applicable (usually five years on doors and drawer fronts and lifetime on drawers). Located at the intersection of LaVista and Gaston, Lakewood remodeling customers rave about their work. *CK, MC, V*

★★★★★ Kitchen Planners 817/831-1268

4708 McNutt St. *Mon-Fri 8-5; Every other Sat. 9-1*
Fort Worth, TX 76117

In a commercial/residential area close to Haltom and 121, Greg Carpenter has it written in the cards. With a name like Carpenter, he was destined to deliver the job. Do-it-yourself at this cabinet showroom (formerly Cabinet Sales) if you want to close the door to high prices. Since 1976, if you wood rather do-it-yourself, then this is the place "knot" to miss. Plan on spending a day hob-knobbing with the pros while you shop for factory-built cabinets, vanities and FORMICA counter tops. Do not pay retail. Do not pass up the FREE planning assistance. If you want to know where to buy the materials that the Handyman Connection can install, this is the place to add to your "to-do" list during the planning stages. Brands included ARISTOCRAFT (45 percent off), BROOKHAVEN (35 percent off), SHILOH (30 percent off) and WOOD-MODE (30 percent off) as well as countertops. Visit their showroom and if you need help, bring in your blueprints and they will help decipher. Take Highway 121 to Haltom Road Exit. Go past Haltom and follow to the right onto Parrish. Take a right on Oak Knoll and another right on McNutt. Call if you get lost! Call them, not me. *CK*

✧✧✧✧✧ Kitchen Store, The — 817/561-1200

4714 Little Rd. — *Mon-Fri 10-6; Sat 9-6; Sun Noon-5*
Arlington, TX 76017

Bob Johns is the man who knows more about kitchen remodeling than Julia Childs and The Galloping Gourmet combined. Rather than running all over the world and operating out of a TV studio kitchen, he's building kitchens right here in the Metroplex. But, when all is said and done, you can always expect a first class job, with money-saving every step of the way. Since improving your kitchen is sure to improve the resale of your home, as well as your cooking, turn the burners up full blast and get going. The finest cabinets are represented (WOODMODE) but there are always some ways to cut corners. Just let his professional crews guide you. *CK, MC, V, AE, D*

✧✧✧✧ Lone Star Locksmith — 972/724-7233

PO Box 270248 — *By Appt. Only*
Flower Mound, TX 75028

Looking to get in? Call on this Lone Star for the taming of the screws. Serving the entire Dallas/Fort Worth area, whether it's to open the door or keep the door locked, residential, commercial or automotive locks, call John Murphy for safe-keeping. If you want a custom decorative lock by BALDWIN, MEDECO or SCHLAGE, he can install these, too. This former security consultant knows his work inside and out and is Johnny on the spot, even in an emergency. *CK*

Home Improvement

★★★★★ Lowe's

940/320-1938

1255 S. Loop 288
Denton, TX 76205
Daily 6 A.M.-10 P.M.
www.lowes.com

Want low prices with high energy? Move over, Home Depot. Now that Wal-Mart has taken a financial position in Lowe's, maybe the playing field has leveled. Through thick and thin, "tooth and nail," how low does it go? First entering the Metroplex through the back door, first in Denton and now plastering the Metroplex, a weekend trip to the blue pyramid arches are commonplace. Just look for a Home Depot, and a Lowe's will not be far behind. Lots of free "how-to" clinics can keep you up to snuff with home improvement projects, such as installing a motion detector, an interior door, or how to make your home child-proof. Not to mention, of course, that all the tools of the trade, including the kitchen sink, can be found in one of the hundreds of nooks or aisleways. From major appliances to ceiling fans, closet organizers to storage buildings, cabinetry to gas logs, from home to hearth, from yard to garden, everything's discounted for your home-buying and budget-busting pleasure. Additional locations across the Metroplex. Check the directory for a location near you. *CK, MC, V, AE, D, Lowe's, Financing*

★★★★ Makita Factory Service Center

972/243-1150

12801 Stemmons
Farmers Branch, TX 75234
Mon-Fri 8-4:30

Make mine a MAKITA–one of the most respected names in the tool business. At their service center, on the service road off Valley View and just south of the Exxon Station, you can gas up, plug in or go cordless. Either way, you'll be saving money on the tools that come with a one-year parts and labor guarantee. What do you have to lose? Save up to 60 percent on rebuilt electrical equipment, a hodgepodge of sorts but fun to rummage through. Whether it's for the casual home user or a heavy-duty construction job, get your hands on circular saws, cordless drills, compressors, routers, rotary hammers, jig saws, reciprocating saws, grinders, miter saws and parts! Their service plan features a 24-48 hour repair turnaround (subject to parts availability), a seven-point safety certification, free estimates before repairs, 90-day warranty on all repairs. They also repair BLACK & DECKER, BOSCH, DEWALT, MILWAUKEE, PORTER CABLE, SKIL and other major brands. And if you'd rather let your fingers do all the work, request their catalog. *CK, MC, V, AE, D, MOC*

✧✧ Masco Metal Systems 817/477-2821

380 Cagle Crow Rd. *Mon-Sat 8-5*
Mansfield, TX 76063

Since 1965, this company has been putting a roof over your car, RV, patio, equipment and other structures that need protection from the elements. Tornadoes, unfortunately, are not covered in their assurances. But the real clincher was their do-it-yourself kits with easy-to-follow plans that were available for less than having a ready-made or custom-made cover. Don lives next door so it's easy to meet him at his home or office by taking I-20 west to the 157 exit. Go south to 287, then west again to Turner-Warnell and go south until you dead-end into a Baptist Church. Amen, brother. Then go right one block to the stop sign and take the right side of fork for one more block. Go left over railroad tracks and if just getting there hasn't deterred you, you're made of iron. However, these structures are all steel. Start with the kit but if you need a little help to get you over the top, Don will come out and pick up the pieces to complete the project. Since it shouldn't rain on your parade, duck for your new cover. *CK, MC, V*

✧✧✧✧✧ Master Cabinet Designs 972/221-7363

1310 N. Cowan, Suite G *Mon-Fri 8-6*
Lewisville, TX 75067

Every old kitchen deserves a new look, especially if you've decided to sell. (It's the only remodeling project that'll return 100 percent of your investment in the ultimate sales price.) New kitchen cabinets made by a master are the way to go. Call Jody Lee, of Master Cabinet Designs, and see what magic can be created today. From rewiring the lights, to building in a hutch or desk, this craftsman can work wonders with your remodeling budget. Not to be ignored, his artistry also works in other rooms like bathrooms, media rooms, studies, all rooms in the house for that matter. Bookcases and entertainment centers are his specialty and Lee takes pride in doing it right the first time around to ensure complete customer satisfaction. He is meticulous in his work because it reflects on his good name. Yea, the old school lives on! *CK*

✧✧✧ Merry Maids 972/516-8955

Dallas, TX *Mon-Fri 8-4:30; By Appt.*

Too busy to clean? Laundry's got you in hot water? As the story goes, eliminate the "Grime and Punishment" with one call to Merry Maids–they will tailor their services to meet your needs. They send out screened and trained teams that are both affordable and reliable. They provide their own supplies and equipment at no extra charge and guarantee their services. Get this: You can even earn frequent flyer mileage on their services if this is of interest. Free in-home estimates given while tailoring the job to fit only what you want done. No beating around the silk flowery bush. The above phone number is for north Dallas, Richardson, Plano, north Garland, Rockwall, Forney and the surrounding areas. All other areas have their own numbers: Park Cities and Dallas, 214/748-0686; Addison, Carrollton, Farmers Branch, Coppell, Lewisville and Flower Mound, 972/323-6243. *CK*

✧✧✧ Mini Maids 214/350-0330

Dallas, TX *Mon-Fri 8-5; By Appt.*

These Mini Maids offer maxi-service on homes from bachelor pads to high-falutin' mansions. The lean, green cleaning machines have been sweeping the Metroplex since 1973. As recipients of the "Best in Dallas" from *D Magazine* and the "Peoples Choice Award" from North Dallas People for serving North Dallas and all the northern suburbs, they are certainly not bashful. They willingly give free estimates over the phone and accept coupons worth $6 from the Yellow Pages, with Mondays, Tuesdays and Wednesdays designated as double coupon days. Mini Maids provides their own equipment and offer both occasional and regular services. They are known to be dependable and have the policy of guaranteed satisfaction. *CK, MC, V, AE, Gift Certificates*

✧✧✧✧ MirrorFlex Light 214/350-0305

3937 Vinecrest *By Appt. Only*
Dallas, TX 75229

Look, look, look to the rainbow of leaded stained glass lights that are diffused throughout this office/showroom. Skylines throughout the house that save dollars, the natural skylight way. Simple construction, with its own expandable reflective light channel, eliminates the need to build a light shaft from the roof to the ceiling. Therefore, it eliminates all the mess and expense of framing, sheet rocking, taping and floating, stippling and painting that is necessary when you install a conventional skylight. MirrorFlex is a thermal-glazed patented diffuser which casts an even, natural light over a broad area and is set into a handcrafted wood grain molding (which can then be stained or painted). The entire fixture is weather-stripped and, once installed, creates a closed system, thereby drastically reducing heat gain in summer and heat loss in winter.

This system also filters ultraviolet rays, which ultimately protects furniture, draperies, carpeting, and such from fading. It's also super-strong–able to withstand the impact of baseball-size hail, which we are all familiar with. Dah–do you live in the Metroplex? Now, they can match wallpaper designs, custom designs or custom colors. Call the number above or 214/543-3496 for an appointment and let the sun shine in. *Finance*

✧✧ Moisture Shield — 214/638-0502

2912 Barge Lane — *Mon-Fri 8-5*
Dallas, TX 75212

Moisture Shield strives on finding the solution for your water infiltration problems. Small words. Big problems. They do preventative and remedial waterproofing work of all sorts, you name it. And that's for starters. Add masonry restoration to stucco, concrete and brick, stone and wood, tuck pointing, power washing/cleaning. Not to be outdone, they also apply coatings, sealers/patching, paint striping/painting, dry wall, urethane, epoxy injections. Oh, did I forget? They work on sheet metal, too. Trained personnel are available to accommodate your busy schedule on the job site or in your office. Have problem, will travel to provide an on-sight analysis. *CK*

✧✧✧✧ Molly Maids — 972/235-6600

818 Firestone — *Mon-Fri 8-5:30*
Richardson, TX 75080

Jolly ole busy families have found the solution to dishing out the dirt. A call to Molly Maids, and you'll be cleaned to the bone. But only if you live in the Plano and North Richardson areas. Molly Maids is a bonded and insured house-cleaning service that provides supervised, dependable, uniformed, professional two-person teams, with their own transportation, cleaning supplies and equipment. Cleaning includes bathrooms, kitchen counters, appliance surfaces, floors and sinks, carpets and floors vacuuming, vinyl and tiled floors washed, dusting of baseboards, sills, décor and furnishings, spot cleaning to remove fingerprints and smudges. Other services are available, and they also offer gift certificates. Now that's a gift you'll have to keep giving and giving to enjoy the fruits of their labor. *CK, MC, V*

★★★★ Monarch Paint — 972/436-2001

701 S. Stemmons — *Mon-Fri 7-4:30; Sat 7:30-1*
Lewisville, TX 75067

Spread your wings and paint yourself from one end of the color spectrum to the other. No more dull finishes to dip your brush into. A flat latex wall paint was $11 gallon and straight from the manufacturer. Many of the area painters line-up early in the morn ready to paint the town ... well, if it's good enough for Pulte and Jim Miller Home Builders, it's good enough for my living room. Expect, of course, factory-direct prices with exceptional detail to custom colors. My eggplant-color bedroom and bath is the talk of the neighborhood. Monarch spreads its wings by making their own stains, varnishes, poly-coats, enamels and latex. How can you lose now that you're on such a winning streak! Check directory for the location nearest you. "I had trouble finding the shellac, though, because it had varnished!" *CK, MC, V, D*

★★★★★ Northern Tool & Equipment Co. 972/705-9545

110 W. Campbell Rd. *Mon-Fri 8-8; Sat 8-6; Sun Noon-5*
Richardson, TX 75080 *www.northern-online.com*

Positioned perfectly between a Home Depot concept and an Ace Hardware, you'd expect Southerners to find this Northern-er appealing. Based in Burnsville, Minn, they blanketed the Northern sites first, then went south to Florida, Georgia, the Carolinas and Tennessee, filled in with Iowa and then made their move to San Antonio and subsequently to Big D. Specializing in tools and equipment, you can expect them to be the lowest price on two-cycle lawn mowers, machine screws, marine accessories, water pumps, go-carts, hunting gear, storage units and equipment for trailers and RVs. Many popular brand names like CHANNEL LOCK, FULLER, HOMELITE, HONDA, STANLEY, VISE GRIP, YARDMAN and others. Their own brand is also a money-saver. Looking for a 20-ton vertical/horizontal hydraulic log splitter — that splits logs up to 24-inch long? Get one here for $829. Or how does a WOODSMAN 16-inch chain saw, 34cc engine, fully-assembled, factory-refurbished to perform like new for only $109 sound? Clean up that oil-slick driveway with a 2000 PSI pressure washer that blasts dirt at 3 GPM for $679. For outdoor enthusiasts, consider sleeping under the Northern lights in northern's heavy duty 5 x 7-foot tarp, water-resistant for only $99. Or go-go to a MANOO 3.5 HP Red Fox Pup go-kart with a 3.5 HP Tecumseh engine for $499. Keep it cut to the quick with a 5 HP walk-behind, chipper/shredder/vacuum with side rake-in and dump-in of materials for $379. Enough tooling around. We wound up with a HOMELIGHT gas-powered cordless blower, factory refurbished for $79 and called it a day. New this year was a complete line of pressure washers, generators, small engine parts, laser levels and HONDA lawn and garden equipment, (including being an authorized repair for Honda, Briggs & Stratton, Tecumseh engines.) Mow them down at Belt Line and I-30 in Garland or in San Antonio, 210/344-4294. *CK, MC, V, AE, D, Northern*

★★★★★ Old Home Supply 817/927-8004

1801 College Ave. *Mon-Fri 8:30-5; Sat 9-5; Sun 11-5*
Fort Worth, TX 76110

Wow! If you don't have an old home, you'll want to rush out and buy one after you see this "old home antique depository." Occupying four corners of the historic Fairmont District in downtown Fort Worth (including the old Tasty Bakery Building), Old Home Supply has found the perfect setting for a nostalgic paradise. Even if you have a new home, but long for the days of pedestal sinks and claw foot tubs, stained and beveled glass, antique cabinetry and hardware, glass doorknobs, solid wood doors, ornamental crown moldings–you can find it here in abundance! This repository is about one city block with each specialty housed in its own building (lighting, for example). Though their specialty is still architectural salvage, they are now carrying Mexican and wrought iron as well as antiques. This family owned and operated business has been booming for the past nine years. Contractors are known to come from out of state just to find objects from the past. The "tub yard" has more than 150 claw foot tubs in stock. One of their buildings includes a garden center. Most everything is restored to its original brilliance, or save even more money and restore it yourself! When you are ready to renovate to "retro upgrade," make a day of it. You can walk for hours and still not find all the treasures waiting to be unearthed. *CK, MC, V, AE*

★★★★★ Orr Reed Wrecking Co. 214/428-7429

1903 Rock Island *Mon-Sat 9-4*
Dallas, TX 75207

Take the mercy out of the demolition companies because whatever is salvaged can be a shopper's salvation. To start your journey in the down and dirty salvage business, start at this portal with over 28,000 doors waiting to be opened. All organized by size and function, if you like to hunt and peck, you've found the proper pecking order at this family haunt. Stay in the mood to love... and dig for some serious hardware, including lumber, paneling, cabinets, countertops, moldings and more. (Or else you'll miss one of the best places this side of the Rock Island line.) Their front showroom is an old-fashioned hardware store complete with nuts, bolts and screws. To ensure your item is in perfect shape when it leaves their doors, examine carefully. Truly a junker's paradise while remaining the "grand daddy of salvage yards." Sure provides a new-found respect in the many subdivisions around the Metroplex. *CK*

♥♥♥♥♥ Outdoor Lighting Perspectives 817/475-6112

By Appt. (Evening Only)
www.outdoorlights.com

Let Outdoor Lighting Perspectives take over where the sun and moon leave off. These trained lighting professionals will set up a free demonstration at your home to help you select the lighting scheme and style that highlights your garden path. Illuminates the exterior of your home for aesthetic and security purposes, then watch your neighbor's faces shine with envy. Turn on to Outldoor Lighting Perspectives for gardens, pools and fountains, too. Let there be light, just make sure it doesn't shine in the neighbors windows. *CK, MC*

♥♥♥♥♥ Outdoor Renovations 972/788-1712

13612 Midway Rd., #333-5 *Mon-Fri 9-5*
Dallas, TX 75244

In the olden days, homeowners had to survive outdoor plumbing. It'll be a cold day in August when we trudge out behind the barn to do our business again. Today's business is conducted in a totally different manner. This company has the outdoor business sewn up. Decks, arbors, gazebos, spas, patio covers, fences, color restoration and add-ons. Since we didn't ask about porta-potties, we can't confirm one way or the other if they have them, but we did confirm that they know what they're doing. A professional design staff provides free consultations. Everything else, however, costs! Beat the bushes to Tim Bush. He's known as a walking encyclopedia when the subject of wood arises. For customers in Fort Worth, visit their location at 1606 Jamestown; Ennis, 972/875-5500. *CK, MC, V (Credit, Add 3 Percent)*

★★★ Pest Shop, The 972/519-0355

2231-B W. 15th St. *Mon-Fri 12:15-6; Sat 11-3;*
Plano, TX 75075 *www.pestshop.com*

Just because Michael Bohdan appeared on "The Joan Rivers Show," "The Tonight Show" and "Donny and Marie" doesn't mean stardom has gone to his head. But with him, it's better dead than said. This is your one-stop emporium for products and information on pest control. Insecticides, fertilizers, sprayers, herbicides, rodenticides–to do it all yourself with Michael's professional guidance. In addition to the traditional products, they now have low impact and organic products to control pests. Bohdan can add author to his credit having had his first national book published. Entitled *What's Buggin' You?* It is a compilation of tips from his over 20 years of getting rid of pests effectively and a lot cheaper than calling on an exterminator. Saving 50-60 percent is possible if you do it his way. And while we're on the subject of pest annihilation and weaponry, don't forget to take a peek at the free in-store Cockroach Hall of Fame museum located at 15th Street and Custer in Plano, open during regular business hours. *CK, MC, V*

♥♥♥♥♥ Pony Express Gun Vaults — 972/272-9788

2645 Forest Lane — *Mon-Fri 10-5:30; Sat 10-3*
Garland, TX 75042

OY-ge-vault! All I ask is to never to leave a gun out where it doesn't belong. To ensure everybody's safety, why not keep yours locked up in a Pony Express safe unless, of course, if you are called into action. (Be sure to look in the gun section of the newspapers where classes on gun safety and usage are noted.) But that's not all that is protected under lock and key (less). Store important documents such as life insurance policies, will, stock certificates and jewelry that doesn't come from Diamontrigue. It's better to be safe than sorry. The Pony Express is a safe bet and a bargain in anybody's book. On Saturdays, Mike is away at gun shows but the showroom is still open for business. *CK, MC, V, AE, D*

★★★★ Premier Marble and Granite — 214/634-3777

740 Regal Row — *Mon-Fri 8-5*
Dallas, TX 75247

You can join the counter revolution and save money on close-outs on marble and granite tile, marble and granite slab remnants, marble and granite desktops and countertops. This is the premier source for granite, and since they are the fabricator and the installer of countertops, you can shave on the slab. Fortunately, there's nothing slacking on their service. *CK, MC, V*

✧✧✧✧✧ ProStar Security — 972/418-0600

3033 Kellway Drive, #128 — *By Appt. Only*
Carrollton, TX 75006

Call on a pro if you want the feeling of security. ProStar offers one of the best values in security today. How does a free basic system and installation of a state-of-the-art security system for home or business sound? No monthly equipment lease, you own the system outright. Or there's a free connection for new home or business customers who already have existing systems. Monitoring is by ADT Security. And, as the nation's largest authorized dealer, ProStar offers Protection One: rapid, reliable monitoring for about $1 a day with a 96 percent customer satisfaction rating in this area of more than 50,000 monitored customers. Expect a free lifetime service program for the length of your monitoring contract and for one year, you'll get a free SafetyNet guarantee which is unbelievable. They will reimburse your paid homeowner's insurance deductible up to $1,000 if you suffer a loss due to a monitored fire or burglary. See, some of the best things in life are still free. *CK, MC, V*

✧✧✧✧✧ Protection Network — 214/348-1501

10840 Switzer — *By Appt. Only;*
Dallas, TX 75238 — *www.protectionnetworks.com*

A company president who makes house calls? Sends customers a newsletter on security tips? Tells you how to avoid false alarm calls to the police department? And gives two months of free monitoring for referring a customer? These are just the extra benefits, besides superb service, offered by Protection Network. At the helm of this innovative company is president Christopher Geymuller, who prides himself on being able to separate himself from the rest of the pack. With state-of-the art monitoring and bend-over-backwards service, you are talking to a man who insists on taking the job of protecting your home and office seriously. Since there are a multitude of options (short of bringing home a killer dog), consider Protection Network for personal and family's protection. I did. (But I also have three killer dogs–they will lick you to death.) Security systems, door access controls, 24-hour monitoring, video surveillance, fire alarms, and sprinkler systems are all part of the package offered by this sales, service, consulting, and installation company. *CK, MC, V, AE, D*

✧ R.W. (Mannie) Sturkie — 972/221-2803

Lewisville, TX 75067 — *By Appt. Only*

This custom-craftsman will measure up to any of the competition. In fact, he will go to any lengths (by the inch or by the foot) to provide a custom-crafted work of art. On location, or you provide the measurements, he'll custom-build in his home/workshop most anything–an entertainment center, bookcase, desk-unit, etc–made at a fraction of the ready-made price. One shopper couldn't say enough nice things about his work or prices. In fact, the entertainment unit/bookcase that was custom-built for her family room was about $1,000 lower than any other estimate. Besides, his workmanship surpassed anything she had hoped for. Let me know what this Mannie makes for you as he never returned our calls. *CK*

✧✧✧ Re-Arrangements/Interiors 972/267-5200

By Appt. Only

Does your house need a ZAP job? Let Re-Arrangements/Interiors' designers perform their affordable magic in your home or office. If you've decided to throw in the towel and move, let them help prepare your house for sale with just a few rearrangements. Make your home appear more appealing to prospective buyers. Or if you just want to create a new look, they take that on with a vengeance. Working primarily with the furniture and accessories you already have, they will make suggestions on items that should stay, relocated, head to a consignment store–or be put out the door on the curb. Sometimes it's hard to let go, so let the professionals help with decisions that could turn your house into a home rather than a storage closet. *CK*

✧✧✧✧ Rent-A-Hubby 972/871-8696

Irving, TX *Mon-Fri 8-5; By Appt. Only*

Sorry girls, we aren't promoting an escort service. This is something much better if you're faced with a sticky door, a leaky faucet or a ceiling fan that needs hanging. For those without the time or know-how to do it themselves (or to save this project from becoming your own husband's latest Mr. Fix-it horror story), Rent-a-Hubby is a team of jacks-of-all-trades. The owners, James and Stephen Haley, have more than 30 years of service and construction experience tucked into their tool belts and are available in the Irving and Las Colinas areas for all types of "honey-do" projects. The service is always quick, courteous and affordable, and senior citizens receive a further discount. There is no service, repair or project that is too small or too large for them. They can handle doors, windows, locksmithing, repairs and seasonal cleaning to plumbing, electrical and air-conditioning systems, desk and fence work, exterior and interior upgrades, siding, roofing repairs, skylights, pavement, patios, summer rooms, landscape and irrigation systems, guttering, fans, carpet cleaning, underground pet barriers, drywall repair, light commercial construction and much more. Their standard work week is Mondays through Fridays 8-5, with weekend appointments scheduled and after-hour emergency availability. Hourly fees range from $38 to $60, with estimates given on fixed-price projects. Senior discounts are always available. The only hitch here is a definite woman-bias. Sorry guys, but if you call here looking for help, they will insist you put your wife, daughter, mother, girlfriend, grandmother, sister, aunt, niece or female friend on the line. As a service geared to help women, clients must be of the female persuasion. *CK, MC, V, AE, D*

★★★★★ Republic Industries, Kitchen & Bath Cabinet Outlet 972/484-8899

11074 N. Stemmons Fwy. *Mon-Fri 9-5; Sat 9-4*
Dallas, TX

When space is at a premium, think of getting an "all wood" cabinet from this cabinet outlet. Kiss all your storage problems away, as you get the cabinet of your choice from this storage store! Their helpful staff will assist you in choosing the cabinet of your dreams. They are an outlet for the REPUBLIC brand, with prices 40-50 percent below those of their competitors. With these great savings you can fully deck out your kitchen and bathroom without feeling guilty. Their showroom has a range of kitchen and bathroom cabinets, along with vanity cabinets. Prices start from $50-$80, for their plywood and laminate kinds that comes in all sizes, starting from the 9-inch up to the more roomier ones at 48 inches. (The sizes come in 3-inch increments.) If you want that "individual" look, you can get a counter top to go with your cabinet. Don't ask for CORIAN countertops; they aren't here, but they have others that are similar and cheaper. They can order WILSONART to be fitted to your cabinet. Located at Walnut Hill and Stemmons, this store is a one-stop emporium for all your cabinetry. *CK, MC, V*

Siding For Less, Inc 214/361-1636

By Appt. Only.

Sidings For Less offers some great deals if you keep your eyes open. The spring sale offered 50-percent off when you use their coupon in *The Dallas Morning News* for premium vinyl siding and vinyl replacement windows. For standard size, top-of-the-line windows, expect to pay around $400, which includes everything. Plus, ask about their security system installation, too. They offer 100-percent financing with no down payment for 90 days. *CK, MC, V, Financing*

♥♥♥♥♥ Skillful Improvements & Restoration 972/279-0119

2143 Gus Thomasson *Mon-Fri 8:30-4:30*
Mesquite, TX 75150 *www.gtesupersite.com/skillful*

A company that's serious about remodeling is an about-face compared to the thousands of make-shift contractors who promise the moon and deliver the craters. Ray Dettmer, owner, is a NARI-Certified Remodeler, and four of his lead carpenters are also certified. That means, they are no fly-by-nights. They continue refining and expanding their craftsmanship through educational seminars and workshops at night and are meticulous in their execution. Three of his employees are certified in restoration work. They have won all the top awards in the business–from Contractor of the Month to the Best Bath Award, Whole House Renovation to Best Exterior Facelift. Dettmer was even named the Regional Contractor of the Year. If you need restoration for an insurance claim, these are the folks that specialize in insurance repairs. They offer 24-hour emergency service to the greater Dallas area. Check out their website for some spectacular before-and-after pictures of their work. *CK, MC, V*

✧✧✧✧✧ Southwest Interior & Design 972/620-8091

12200 Stemmons, #301 *By Appt. Only*
Dallas, TX 75234

Let's make it easy. One call, that's all it takes to get your home or office up to snuff. Southwest Interior & Design's staff is the Picasso of paint, wallcovering, drywall, flooring and interior design. Since 1982, they've been recognized as the leader of the pack of painters, drywall repair, and resurfacing pros and the place to call for wallpaper and installation. Why call on anyone else when the experts here are committed to providing dependable and quality work and customer satisfaction? That's right. No leftover smudges and curling edges. No tell-tale seams and buckling rolls. No bubbles or blotches. Experienced and uniformed technicians provide the finishing touches, including custom finishes, to create a new look, a renewed look, a renowned look ... at a price that's pleasing to the total project. The owner himself or their in-house design staff comes to make a home visit to coordinate the colors and styles, works out a shopping list of options, reviews the most economical possibilities, and then even paints sample swatches on the walls to ensure you'll love the color. Since they are a full-service design studio, they can also help with furniture, flooring, window treatments and all types of accessories. They're not happy until you are. All work is guaranteed. *CK, MC, V*

♥♥♥♥♥ Stained Glass Overlay by Glass Solutions 972/570-4685

2814 N. O'Connor Blvd. *Mon-Fri 11-4; Sat By Appt.*
Irving, TX 75062

Want to add a custom work of art to your windows and doors? Need to have a clearer picture of your world through rose-colored glass windows? This company creates windows to look like stained glass with their patented process using mylar film and adhesive leading. A perfect addition to your doors, sidelight windows (or any window for that matter), skylights, ceiling panels, room dividers, cabinet door inserts, sliding glass doors, shower doors, or any other decorative piece. Choose from a variety of colors and privacy films and let your imagination soar. Glass etching and sandblasting are also available. Take in a picture from a magazine, your bedspread fabric, your wallpaper, your three cats, your love of flying, your logo, then have them translate it into a masterful work of art. It also adds a lot to your home's resale value. (Well, anyone want to buy my shower with the name Diva etched on the door?) *CK, MC, V, AE, D*

★★★★★ Staz-On Roofing — 214/357-0300

10889 Shady Trail, Suite 102 — *Mon-Fri 8-5*
Dallas, TX 75220 — *www.stazonroof.com*

Since 1981, this company has been fiddling on the roofs of the Metroplex. In fact, they are so good, they have NEVER had a complaint registered at the Better Business Bureau (isn't that something!). They offer the lowest prices on roofing and repair in the Metroplex. An estimate was faxed within 24 hours and the entire roofing job was completed in three days flat. How many months have you waited for a roofer to show up at your house? Or has it been years? Just getting them to call you back is worthy of consideration, you say? Wrong! Most any kind of roof–metal, clay, shingle and copper–is part of their repertoire. Metal, by the way, is stronger than traditional roofing materials and offers a wide variety of shapes and colors, allowing them to resemble different styles and materials such as cedar shakes, tile, slate and even asphalt shingles. The advantage of clay tiles is that they combine durability with a pleasant and lasting appearance. Clay tiles mellow with age and are resistant to exposure to the wind, rain, frost and sun. They offer the latest technology and a full six-year workmanship warranty along with up to a 50-year manufacturer's guarantee. Check them out for competitive pricing and a full range of options including custom sheet metal, waterproofing and repairs. They have done work west of Fort Worth, east of Dallas, as far north as McKinney and south to Waxahachie. A sure bet when it comes to covering the Metroplex. *CK, MC, V*

✧✧✧✧✧ Stephen W. Jones — 972/285-6415

Dallas, TX — *By Appt. Only*
www.connect.net/sjones

This man's so busy, he's never at home, but he'll return your call as fast as he can. An all-around, Steve specializes in small jobs that the big firms ignore. Decks, doors, painting, dog houses, fences, arbors, wood storage buildings, caulking, flooring, installing ceiling fans and building rocking chairs. In fact, he'll do most anything but plumbing and some electrical work. With over 500 references for your piece of mind, give Steve a call and get it all fixed-for-less.

♥♥♥♥♥ Stone-Tec 972/278-4477

2929 W. Kingsley *Mon-Fri 8-5; Sat 10:30-3*
Garland, TX 75041

Do you want to be part of the counter culture? Then think about replacing your shabby formica, tile or wooden kitchen countertops with beautiful imported (from India) granite in a variety of colors and textures. It doesn't stain, burn (hot pots no problem here) or warp, and takes very little maintenance. It's not half as expensive as you might expect, either. Since Stone-Tec is a direct importer, fabricator and installer, you eliminate any middleman charges. You can pick your slab of granite from the actual stock–and not just some little chip off the block to choose from. Add instant elegance to any room with countertops, accents or flooring. Mr. Shah (no, not that Shah) gave us the tour and some quick granite lessons. Another showroom opened this year at the Inwood Village Shopping Center, 5470 W. Lovers Lane, #333-A, Dallas, 214/654-9075; fax: 214/904-0633. *CK*

✧✧✧✧ Suburban Door 972/414-6900

10420 Plano Rd. *Mon-Fri 7:30-5*
Dallas, TX 75238 *www.suburbandoor.com*

After nearly 10 years, you can't slam them for offering great prices on garage doors, openers and repairs. They're the specialists to call if there's a glitch in any make or model. Be it a broken spring that needs replacing, a remote control fixed, or a brand new one installed (GENIE is sold here, but they can service all brands). The best part is there is no service charge, free estimates are given and the lowest price is guaranteed. If your garage door's a little tempermental, call on the Suburban Door doctor . All new makes and models come with a maintenance special of $39 (retail $59) that really saves the day. This complete door and opener service provided all the right moves so that your opener will last longer than your car. (Well, that depends on your wheels.) They'll tighten any loose nuts and bolts, lubricate the door and opener, adjust the track, etc. They even offered a new ½ HP Professional line of GENIE Garage Door openers installed from $229 with a $59 extra charge for that wireless keypad with purchase of opener. It comes with a lifetime motor and three-year parts/hardware warranty and an infrared safety light. Open sesame! And save some money. *CK, MC, V*

★★★★★ Sunbelt Fence Supply Co. 817/293-6972

10813 S. I-35 *Mon-Fri 8-5*
Fort Worth, TX 76028

Looking for "fenced" items? Well, don't shop here. But if it's a fence (wood, chain link, ornamental iron, custom gates, power gate openers, dog runs, pre-fab panels or back stops), this is the place to put your money where my mouth is. Corral these wholesale distributors and manufacturers who sell directly to the public. That way, you're sure not to get fenced in. They've been in this location for over 15 years and service the entire Metroplex. Displays are visible at both locations, though you wouldn't exactly call them showrooms. Close the latch on high prices also at 6504 Smithfield Rd., North Richland Hills, 817/498-0347. *CK, MC, V*

★★★★★ Sunshine Sunrooms 972/243-5390

2410 Glenda Lane *Mon-Fri 9-5*
Dallas, TX 75229

Sunshine, lollipops and room additions are all delicious coming from Sunshine Sunrooms. If you're looking for a room addition without paying for a contractor to build one from scratch, this is where it's at. This is where the sun and the moon set as far as I'm concerned. Their sunrooms, patio rooms, plant rooms, extra rooms–call it whatever you like, just buy the room and you'll be closer to heaven. If you can get to their showroom, you'll win a prize. Though you can see it from Stemmons, it's a small feat to walk through their showroom doors. But when you do, it's worth it. Exit Walnut Hill, turn east to the second light which is Ables; then left to Glenda. (It jogs around the sausage factory, but they don't offer snacks.) *CK, Financing*

★★★★★ Surplus Warehouse 972/287-5190

104 Simonds Rd. *Mon-Fri 8-5; Sat 8-1*
PO Box 876
Seagoville, TX 75159

If you stay firm to your convict-ions, this warehouse will meet your expect-ations. Exit Simonds off 175 and wind up across from the federal penitentiary. Escape from paying high prices. Start singing the Jailhouse Rock at this Surplus

Warehouse where a do-it-yourselfer can enjoy life ... laden with siding, paint, doors, hardware, cabinets, countertops, light fixtures, plumbing fixtures, shingles and more. Most are first-quality items, some are close-outs, some have been slightly damaged. Surplus Warehouse sells to builders and the public at the same price. It's practically highway robbery where savings can shave 50 percent off your sentence of paying retail. Watch the newspapers for blow-out events. You won't be punished if you stick to the rules of Never Paying Retail! Head east to Seagoville and wander through this warehouse in search of building supplies. Don't expect, though, to have someone holding your hand every step of the way–unless it's your last supper. Installers are not provided. *CK, MC, V, AE, D, Financing*

★★★★★ SW Canvas Products 817/624-9932

2418 Clinton Ave. *Mon-Fri 8-5; Sat By Appt. Only*
Fort Worth, TX 76016

For years, Fort Worth knew that Sam was the man to call if you're yawning for an awning. But Sam (Shorty to friends) retired this past year. Never fear, son Carlos has taken over day-to-day operations and has barely missed a beat. Talk about a decorator touch to your home or office building. This can separate you from the crowd. Stop canvassing the neighborhood looking for awnings. This company hangs the moon and the sun as well as specializing in all types of canvas products. SUNBRELLA brand materials are what they use for awnings, canopies, tarps, tents, truck and boat covers. If you want it made-for-the-shade, call SW ASAP Since 1956, they've been an covering the Metroplex and not hiding behind their canvas coverings. Expect an average window awning to run $200-$275 (average $225) installed with a steel-welded frame. And that's a steal! *CK, MC, V, D*

★★★★ Texas Tool Traders 972/278-0049

2414 S. Jupiter Rd. *Mon-Fri 7:30-5:30, Sat 8-Noon*
Garland, TX 75041

When it comes to OSHA-approval, this one wins ours. Besides, where else could a Texas carpenter find a cowboy hard hat for $29.99? Whether you're handy or not, this is the place to start hammering away. Great prices on tools and supplies for the professional or weekend fixer-upper. A HART straight claw, smooth-faced framing hammer was only $19.99. LIARS suspenders for fibbers, fishermen and truth-stretchers was a great gag gift for dad for only $8.99. A four-piece framers' belt for the Texas-sized household home improvement project was $39.99. For the builder handyman or woman, why not consider a PAT LODES Impulse gas framer nail gun that will drive 2-inch nails and up without the hassle of compressors and hoses for $399.99? But whatever the assignment, please wear safety glasses, $12.99. Check directory for four other area locations. *CK, MC, V, AE, D*

★★★★★ Tile & Marble Clearinghouse & Brokerage Firm 972/221-TILE

701 S. Stemmons, #112 *Mon-Fri 9-4; Sat 9-Noon*
Lewisville, TX 75067

Get a load at this Floor Show. All products are sold at manufacturers' or below contractor's price, including custom granite countertops. And that's just the beginning to this company's reservoir. Tile from $.85/square foot and marble from $2.50/square foot is a sure bet you won't be taking your tile for granite. This showroom is a good beginning to laying one on. Marble, granite, slate, ceramic, porcelain, Saltillo, cantera, limestone and more. If it was meant to be stepped on and remain beautiful just the same, you might as well save money in the process. If and when it comes time to lay out the red carpet, don't. Check here first for a free estimate. They are a little hard to find, but worth the effort. Head west off the I-35 Fox exit. Pull into the first drive that isn't connected to a conveinence store. They are directly behind the Black-Eyed Pea Restaurant. *CK, MC, V, AE, D*

★★★★ Tile America 817/595-7900

7337 Dogwood Park *Mon-Fri 8-5; Sat 9-2*
Fort Worth, TX 76118

Tired of all the "Tile and Error?" Give Fort Worth credit for having this terrific tile company. Don't side-step a huge selection of wall and floor tiles as low as $.89 a square foot. Like Ceramic Tile International, this resource has its own brand of all-glaze tile, from 8 x 8-foot squares all the way to 18-inchers. Though they don't install, they will give you the names of tile contractors that they do business with so you don't have to lay them yourself. When they offer their periodic close-outs, make a beeline to Dogwood Park. It's a honey. *CK, MC, V, AE, D*

★★★ Vintage Wood Works 903/356-2158

PO Box 39 *Mon-Fri 8-4:30*
Quinlan, TX 75474-0039 *www.vintagewoodworks.com*

If it's always been your fairytale dream to live in a gingerbread house, here's your chance! Vintage offers a selection of gingerbread trims to make your home a castle. Ah, a kingdom for some stairways, gables, newel posts and porch supports. Everything to charm your way through the Victorian era with accents at 30 percent less. The 224-page color catalog is specific about sizes, so you can find a princely fit for your needs. Their catalog is $3, but the cost is refunded with your first order, so be sure to ask. *CK, MC, V, D, C($3)*

★★★★★ Walnut Hill Paint Warehouse 972/484-5800

2720 Royal Lane Suite 172 *Mon-Fri 7-5:30; Sat 8:30-12:30*
Dallas, TX 75229

The sign says Walnut Hill, but you'll have to look on Royal Lane for famous brand-name paints like BENJAMIN MOORE, JONES-BLAIR, MARTIN SENOUR, MOBILE, PITTSBURGH, PRATT & LAMBERT and RALPH LAUREN for starters as low as $6.15 per gallon for flat paint. CABOT and OLYMPIC stains, too, to help seal your fate. Enjoy the variety of mixing and matching. Stand elbow-to-elbow with professional painters and handymen getting the goods for their jobs. Also mountains of great decorating tips to make your job seem like it's all downhill from Walnut Hill, but don't expect other wall coverings like wallpaper. This year, the concentration has returned to paint, and nothing but paint! Separate the real from the faux is now as easy as A-B-C. They've got all those faux finishes that are the rage these days. Now if only the walls could talk! *CK, MC, V, AE*

★★ Window & Storm Door Outlet 214/747-1717

3540 Irving Blvd. *Mon-Fri 8-4:30*
Dallas, TX 75247

Off Irving Boulevard, you're a stones throw away from window and storm doors direct from the manufacturer. Whether you're in the market for replacement windows or you're building anew, this manufacturer can deliver the goods the paneless way–for a whole lot less. ALL PRO solar screens, storm and insulated windows by ALCOA (vinyl) as well as aluminum windows that they also manufacture. Fiberglass windows, storm doors and insulated glass panes in all sizes and custom sizes fit an extensive selection of styles and shapes. And yes, energy efficiency is part of the package. *CK*

★★★★ Wrecking Barn 214/747-2777

1421 N. Industrial Blvd., Suite 102 *Mon-Fri 9-5; Sat 10-3*
Dallas, TX 75207-3905

Stop being a wreck when it comes to home dec. Let the pros do all the work. This Metroplex mainstay has been reincarnated behind the Anatole Hotel in what could be the start of a whole new area. Bits and pieces from businesses, churches and homes have been demolished and resurrected in this Industrial Street habitat specializing in architectural elements from all the no-longer places. If finding things for your home is your mission, whether it's Gingerbread or Mission, you'll find those things here. Medium-sized stained glass windows which range from $100-$300 and small wood panels which run for $40-$60 are catcher's catch cans. Chandeliers glistened from $40-$700 and pleasant surprise elements were everywhere. *CK, MC, V, AE, D*

Housewares

★★★ Ace Mart Restaurant Supply

214/351-5444

3128 Forest Lane
Dallas, TX 75234
Mon-Fri 8:30-5:30

This may be your Ace in the hole when it comes time to outfit your kitchen. Now relocated on Forest Lane from their original W Northwest Highway location. Shop where the chefs and restaurants' shop, but expect a discount only if you buy in dozens or in case lots. All new equipment that is priced the same for professionals as it is for peons. Who's going to know the difference? Go ahead, make it your way. From china to commercial gas stoves (not approved for home/residential use), what really turned us on were The Platters. (Now that dates us, doesn't it?) Cook up other restaurant supplies on Belt Line Rd. in Garland, which is open on Saturdays from 9-1, and in Haltom City at 5600 Denton Highway (817/498-5900). *CK, MC, V, AE, D*

★★★★ Active Rental Service, Inc.

214/630-7744

2939 Irving Blvd., Suite 301
Dallas, TX 75247
Mon-Fri 8-5

Whether you need an extra rollaway bed, or extra serving pieces at your wedding reception, Active Rental Services, Inc. is on the job. They carry a complete line of party equipment, chairs, tables, linens, dishes, silverware, even baby beds. Their rentals are top of the line brands such as LEGGETT & PLATT, MONROE, ONIEDA, PALMER, SAMSONITE, SNYDER, VINCO and more. Visit their 22,500-square-foot showroom. They stand committed to competitive prices and wonderful service. *CK, MC, V, D*

✧✧ American and European Clock Repair

214/460-2861

739 Woodlawn Ave.
Dallas, TX 75208
Mon-Sat 9-5; By Appt.Only

Losing minutes by the hour? If your clock's not ticking, take the time to run it by American and European Clock Repair. As an authorized Ridgeway technician with more than 20 years experience, all work is guaranteed, and they specialize in repairs on antique mechanical and electric clocks to case restoration. They'll also pick-up and deliver if you're completely out of time. They're currently building a new workshop in the back of this home-run business, so calling for an appointment isn't a timeless effort. *CK, MC, V*

★★ California Closets — 972/550-0409

4441 Lovers Lane — *Mon-Fri 8-5; Sat 8-8*
Dallas, TX 75225 — *www.calclosets.com*

Between MacArthur and Story, if you are between a rock and a messy place, California Closets may simply be your best storage solution. Head to the phones and call California. (But don't worry, it's a local call for a free in-home consultation.) Simplify your life as never before, be it the garage, your home office or your closets. Anything that needs a home can be custom-built to meet your needs. After all, doesn't everyone need a place to stuff their stuff when they've got no more room to stuff it? Since 1978 they've helped more than 2 million people turn wasted space into beautiful, productive, well-organized areas. *CK, MC, V*

★★★★ Case-Baldwin — 972/434-8197

890 N. Mill St., Suite 113 — *Mon-Fri 8-Noon, 1-5*
Lewisville, TX 75057

Yes, these folks take a serious one-hour lunch break and hang their "do-not-bother" sign on their front door from noon-1. But before then, or after, you can enjoy a clean sweep of their facilities. If you're looking for janitorial supplies and equipment, stop here; but even if you're not a professional, what household in the Metroplex wouldn't make good use of trash can liners, towels, tissues, disinfectants, a good industrial mop, and a bucket that won't tip over with a gallon of water? Add soaps and detergents, carpet-care products and floor waxes, and you will wax ecstatic over the selection. They even repair vacuum cleaners and decided a while back to open to the public. Although Lewisville is a clean-enough city, perhaps the surrounding areas need to take stock. *CK, MC, V, AE*

✧✧✧ Climate Works — 817/426-3366

101 E. Renfro St. — *Mon-Fri 8-5 By Appt. Only*
Burleson, TX 76097-0608

Climate Works carries a full line of products and accessories to help keep you in your compfort zone. Installing and maintaining your air conditioning and heating units, air purification, zoning systems, fireplaces and accessories is the climate they like best. They also sell you the best brands including FRIGIDAIRE, LENNOX and TRANE–and you know nothing can stop a Trane. They work on new projects as well as servicing both commercial and residential properties. Be sure to call ahead for an appointment. *CK, MC, V, AE, D*

★★★★ Clockery, The — 817/261-9335

2401 W. Pioneer Pkwy. — *Mon-Sat 10-6*
Arlington, TX 76013

From Highway 360, exit Pioneer Parkway and go west for 4 ¼ miles. Keep ticking. After you pass Fielder, it's only another quarter of a mile on the north side of the street. Choose from their 1,200+ different styles of clocks by all the major manufacturers to go hickory, dickory, clock, tick-tock, tick-tock. Nothing but the finest is sold here. Time flies when you're checking out the selection. We went cuckoo over their grandfather clocks alone. On a smaller scale, take a look at the LORICRON anniversary clocks between $50-$300, or their many exquisite wall and floor clocks. We found RIDGEWAY and SLIGH clocks in good supply. They have one of the largest clock selections in Texas. An AWI-certified clock-maker is on site and all floor clocks come with a one-year manufacturer's warranty. *CK, MC, V, AE, D, Layaway*

♥♥♥♥♥ Cookworks — 972/960-2665

5213 Alpha Rd. — *Mon-Sat 10-9; Sun Noon-6*
Dallas, TX

Based out of Santa Fe, Cookworks is cooking up a storm. Producing their own line of tableware, gourmet foods and top-of-the-line kitchen equipment to keep costs at bay, leaf through other brands like CIPRIANI, DERUTA, FAUCHON, PECK, PETROSSIAN and SIMON PEARCES. Monthly cooking classes in their state-of-the-art demonstration kitchen features renowned chefs–coming to Cookworks could be the start of your culinary course to greatness. Make life better with fondue and move over Julia! *CK, MC, V, AE, D*

★★★★★ Corning Revere Factory Store — 254/582-7326

104 NE I-35 — *Mon-Sat 10-8; Sun 11-6*
Hillsboro Prime Outlet Center
Hillsboro, TX 76645

Double the fun at the Hillsboro Prime Outlets, not only will you see their CORNING REVERE factory store but there's also a Corning Clearance Center at Suite 163 (same center, different phone number: 254/582-3957). Though you'd imagine their clearance center to be where the bottom of the barrel resides, the reality is they carry just about the same as their main line factory store with overstocks and discontinued items from across the U.S. Watch for their periodic weekend sales, when, during the first and last hour that they are open, you can take an additional 40 percent off their already discounted prices. Now, who says there's no such thing as a free lunch. Bake 'n' shake with CORNINGWARE direct from the factory for that meal-in-a-hurry. Individual pieces of CORELLE, CORNINGWARE, PYREX and VISIONS are sold directly to the public at 20-40 percent off. Save big $$$ by buying overstocks, seconds and discontinued stock. Cook up a group and drive to Hillsboro cause too many cooks won't spoil the bargains here. You'll also find them at Grapevine Mills (817/874-0920), the Inwood Trade Center (on Inwood two blocks west of Stemmons Frwy.) and in the Tanger Outlet Center in Terrell (972/551-9000). *CK, MC, V, D*

★★★★ Crate and Barrel Outlet Store — 214/634-2277

1317 Inwood Rd. — *Mon-Sat 10-5; Thu 10-7; Sun Noon-5*
Dallas, TX 75247

Crate and Barrel gets a standing ovation at their retail store. Imagine how our enthusiasm overflowed at their outlet! My plate runneth over; otherwise, I would have bought the 16-piece set of glass Radius dinnerware by ARCOROC for $9.95 (50 percent off). Instead, I admired a GIBSON 16 and 20-piece dinnerware set for $24.95-$59.95, ogled a 45-piece set of REED & BARTON flatware for $70 (which included eight-place settings and a hostess set) and drooled over barware as low as $.95 up to $4. Since 80 percent of their stock is discontinued, strike while the bargains are hot. Ordinarily, you'll save 20 percent and more across the butcher-block boards on terra-cotta dishes, glassware, vases, kids' stuff, table runners, rugs, herb wreaths, salt and pepper mills, neat desk accessories, clocks and more... for less. A great place for someone who's just starting out with their own apartment. We found a barrel full of bargains that for some reason didn't sell, were discontinued, or were flawed in flight. Prices haven't quite bottomed out of the barrel but they're certainly better than full price. The store is packed tightly on Saturdays with shoppers, so we prefer to take a quick look and then come back at a quieter time when it's dish fulfillment at its best. *CK, MC, V, AE, D, Crate & Barrel Card*

Decorator's Warehouse

972/964-0499

1441 Coit Rd., Suite # G
Plano, TX 75075

Mon-Sat 10-6

Quality silk plants at tremendous savings, silk arrangements, artificial trees, plants, vases, flowers, cabinet toppers, and other flora for the home. Always 40-70 percent off retail. The plants run anywhere from $15-$500 depending on the size and quality. This large nondescript store is right next door to Dickey's Barbecue and behind Cathy's Wok. They also have another location at 1535 S. Bowen in Arlington, 817/460-4488. *CK, MC, V, AE, D*

★ Dressler Table Pads by Superior

214/651-1400

Mon-Fri 8-5, By Appt. Only

This company has never tabled the issue of protecting your finest product. In fact, they've been covering up your table to protect your interests since 1937. The number above is actually a call center for the company, which is based in Houston. If you want to keep your table safe and mar-proofed, these table pads will do the job. Made the old-fashioned way with guaranteed warp-free, heat-proof insulation felt on the inside, a vinyl top with metal hinges for easy storage starts around $104.95. Leaf pieces start around $37. Plus, there are five different grades, each priced accordingly. Call for an in-house appointment for your table to get measured and then expect a not-so-speedy delivery. Product quality is fine, but the delivery time is dreadful. *CK, MC, V*

★★★★★ Executive Jungle

817/251-6606

567-B Commerce St.
Southlake, TX 76092

Mon-Fri 9-4; Sat 9-Noon

It's a jungle out there, but you'll still go ape over this place. At Executive Jungle, you'll find great deals on iron tables, accessories and pottery. Items they carry have been used to decorate restaurants such as El Chico, and since 1979, they've been THE place for pottery chimeneas and iron at wholesale prices. They also have interior and exterior plant designs and installation. Special orders are available. The regular business hours are limited, but they will schedule appointments from 9 - 4 Mondays through Fridays and 9 - Noon on Saturdays. *CK*

★★★★★ Forja y Arte

972/579-8077

1100 S. Wildwood, Suite 5
Irving, TX 75060

Mon-Thu 9-5

You don't have to speak Spanish to head for the bargains at this Irving store, but it sure helps. Armed with a Spanish dictionary, all you have to know is, *"Cuanto es?"* (How much is it?) Go east on Shady Grove off of Loop 12 for two blocks and stop when you see the white warehouse. Mexican hand-crafted home decorative accessories are at 50 percent off and more ensures your artistic integrity of never paying retail. In fact, many of the objects d'art were below wholesale prices. Choose from a myriad of candle holders, console tables, lamp tables, clay accessories and more. The variety of candle holders in all shapes and sizes ranged in price from $3-$50. Sure beats shopping at the border. *CK*

★★★ Fort Worth Shaver & Appliance 817/335-9970

1900 Montgomery St. *Mon-Fri 8:30-5:30; Sat 9-3*
Fort Worth, TX 76107

Shave a few bucks off reconditioned appliances with minor nicks or bruises. Perfect for outfitting your children's own first kitchen. Or, if you need your food processor repaired, this is the place for service and repair on most major small appliances, such as blenders and toasters. Let's cut to the quick. This is the perfect place to rejuvenate that juicer or to find an abandoned blender. They can fix just about any brand: BLACK & DECKER, BRAUN, KITCHENAIDE, KRUPP, NORELCO, OSTER, REGAL, SUNBEAM, WATER PIK, WESTBEND and more. Everything's in good working order if it's for sale. This service center for 35 different companies can whip up some delicious deals and blend in the bargains. Located on Montgomery near I-30, look for the big blue and white sign with their name and a Norelco shaver with eyes, arms and legs. If you've worked up an appetite by now, you're just down the street from Angelo's Barbecue. CK, MC, V, AE, D

★★★ Heritage House Clocks 972/934-3420

14450 Midway Rd. *Mon-Fri 10-6; Sat 10-5*
Dallas, TX 75244

When the big hand is at 12 and the little hand is at 10, Heritage House Clocks is open for shopping the world without leaving north Dallas. After 23 years in business, owners Val and Glenda Marchesoni have developed a reputation for having an outstanding selection of European, Canadian and American-made clocks, as well as many hand-made and special edition clocks you won't find anywhere else. Time doesn't stand still at this place. More than 50,000 clocks to choose from: ANSONIA, HARRINGTON HOUSE, HOWARD MILLER, NEW ENGLAND, SLIGH and others at savings from 15-50 percent. Factory-direct prices are the face-value here. Wall clocks, cuckoo clocks, mantle clocks, antique clocks–since 1974, this has been the grandfather of them all. Expert clock repair is also available and in-home service calls if your grandfather's too big for his britches. Clocks from around the world like Italy, France, Ireland, Germany, England and Holland as well as those made in the good ol' USA. If a ZIRO sleek, brushed aluminum clock is good enough for Tom Cruise, it's good enough for me. Make a date and don't be late. Other manufacturers include COMITTI OF LONDON, INTERCLOCK from Belgium, JAMES STEWART AND SON from Ireland, JEAN-CLAUDE ALONET from France and many more. A Comitti of London clock that retailed for $1,120 was $640; a LOUIS XVI Italian clock retailing for $2,145 was $1,199; and a fun, kinetic sculpture clock by GORDON BRADT retailing for $1,595 was $852. Some clocks have never been available in the U.S. before, so be the first on your block with these clocks. Over 20 different brands of Grandfather clocks alone–some with retail prices, boo hoo, but there's usually something on sale. Music boxes and porcelain pieces can be found here, too. *CK, MC, V, AE, D*

★★★ HomePlace — 972/732-6661

600 W. 15th St., Suite A — *Mon-Sat 9:30-9; Sun 10-6:30*
Plano, TX 75075

HomePlace is a dilly of a housewares emporium (and now even better since they've merged with Waccamaw pottery (a 43-store chain of home superstores, known for unique items, priced lower than department store sale prices). Wash those troubles down the drain with bed and bath ensembles, china and crystal, paper products and frames, dishes and silverware, pots and pans, pillows and pictures, cappuccino machines and oversized CANNON Royal 30 x 52-inch bath towels. Bright wall clocks for $7.99; gooseneck lamps for $9.99 were neck-and-neck with a three piece Rosette Bistro set in cast aluminum and iron for $129.99, and save some dough with an OSTER breadmaker for $59.99. Top it off with select window toppers for $8.99 and sink down in a percale bed-in-a-bag for $59.99. Hand-painted 16-piece dinnerware sets with service for four, were a shocking $29.99 and Mexican glassware sold for $4.99. Serve your coffee in a KRUPS coffeemaker and let the java flow. If it was meant for your kitchen, bath or bedroom, you'll find it here. Check the directory for the location nearest you. *CK, MC, V, AE, D, Optima, HomePlace Credit*

★★★★ Import Store Warehouse Outlet, The — 817/877-0150

1201 Henderson — *Mon-Sat 10-8; Sun 10-6*
Fort Worth, TX 76104

If you are Lost and Bound in downtown Fort Worth, you will find comfort at The Import Store Warehouse Outlet (housed in the old Mapsco Building). Finagle a front-end parking place and then plan on spending the day wandering the expanded rooms full of imported samples, overruns and one-of-a-kinds from Victorian Christmas decorations to Remington and Russell reproductions. The newest addition is imported pottery in their outside patio room. Appearing like antiquity, buy one (in the $49-$79) range and get the second one at half price. Don't expect some dainty planter-types. These were waist-high or bigger. Lots of frames, brass, dolls, birdhouses, candles, even sterling jewelry with the belly button jewels. Another room housed some wrought iron and wicker sets, and everything in the house was discounted around 30-50 percent. (Prices seemed higher this year.) Maybe their fame has caught up with them. *CK, MC, V*

★★★ Kitchen Collection — 254/582-2577

104 NE I-35, Suite 127 — *Mon-Sat 10-8; Sun 11-6*
Hillsboro Outlet Center — *www.kitcol.com*
Hillsboro, TX 76645

Ainsley Harriott is rumored to head to Hillsboro when he is in search for gourmet gadgets for his hit cooking show. Nice selection but prices have gone on a diet. Located in the south section in the back between Eddie Bauer and Bass, if you are mixed up, you can settle for ceramic mixing bowls with rims of blue, green and yellow for $19.97. Look for instant rebates on CIRCULON commercial cookware (the higher the price, the more the rebate). Pick up some pasta sets or a few skillets, along with some pots and pans..it's all part of this Kitchen Collection. Sample some discontinued and reconditioned items from ANCHOR-HOCKING, HAMILTON BEACH, PROCTOR-SILEX, WEAREVER for buys on appliances to utensils (even if you're not Ma or Pa Kettle). If you are looking for housewares, cast-iron sauce pans, knives, bowls–everything you need to stir up a scrumptious meal, you can find it here. But don't expect stupendous discounts. Those are reserved for their website. Now, we're cookin'! *CK, MC, V, AE, D*

♥♥♥♥♥ Kitchen Store, The — 817/561-1200

4714 Little Rd. — *Mon-Sat 10-6; Sun Noon-5*
Arlington, TX 76017

The Kitchen Store has everything for the kitchen except the cook. The Mid-cities can now have their cake and eat it, too. Look for cookware, baking equipment, cutlery, small electrics and gadgets. If you've just moved into a new place and need updated appliances, you will find what you're looking for without batting an eyelash. Toasters, can openers, juicers, and much more are available. A one-stop, everything you've always wanted for the kitchen (personal chefs don't count!) store. Also a small selection of cookbooks and hard-to-find gourmet items. The Kitchen Store also sells DENBY pottery from England, cheerio, and has a bridal registry. Area cooking maven, Carol Ritchie, teaches in the demo kitchen. Stop in for a class schedule and join in the Pot Luck! *MC, V, AE, D*

★★★★★ Kiva Pottery — 214/821-1700

1916 N. Haskell Ave. — *Tue-Sat 10-6*
Dallas, TX 75204

Just down from City Place is the wholesale-to-the public bonanza for Mexicana masterpieces. You're loco if you shop anywhere else for indoor and outdoor decorative planters, table tops and chimeneas, alongside south-of-the-border rustic wrought iron and pine furniture. The owner claims he has the best selection of chimaeras anywhere. A decorative urn, sold elsewhere for $155, was unearthed here for only $50. Their selection also includes 150 lines of clay pottery with an old-world Greek style. Pottery is a wonderful decorative accessory in any home, anywhere in the world. For out-of-this-world prices and selection, long live Kiva Pottery. *CK, MC, V, AE, D*

KnifeOutlet.com — 219/656-4127

66400 Oak Rd. — *www.knifeoutlet.com*
Lakeville, IN 46536

KnifeOutlet.com is your internet cutlery source. They have one of the best knife selections on the net. This on-line store makes it fast, convenient and secure for you to order products on the web. Their knives can be used in the kitchen or in the woods. For example, an EMERSON collector set include a partially serrated commander and a partially serrated CQC7B but in bead blasted finish instead of the usual black. Each set is serial numbered on the blade between 1-500 and both knives in the set have the same number. We found a Paul Chen Starship knife with blue anodized aluminum handle and three pearl inlays retails for $152 but sells here for only $99.95. The deals and selection are great at KnifeOutlet.com. *CK, MC, V, AE, D*

★★★★★ Liquidators Outlet 972/660-3206

2125 S. Great Southwest Pkwy. *Mon-Sat 10-6; Sun 1- 6*
Grand Prairie, TX 75051

Choose your outlet. There are two big ones here. Plan on spending some time, some money and having a whale of a time. Nothing fancy, mind you, just one warehouse that features furniture, art and lamps, home decorative items; the other has china, dolls, Christmas and bath accessories. Rumor has it that their merchandise comes from a variety of sources, but mostly from the World Trade Center. Oh me. Oh see. If you're looking for a wedding gift, look and see their collection of wedding frames and crystal pieces. One-of-a-kind items that have been used for photo shoots find their way to this outlet, too, where seeing is believing. In the front building-between china, LENOX crystal, china dolls, designer housewares from boutiques in Dallas, Egyptian cotton bedding and towels, high-end toiletries (including French), draperies (full set for $35/retail $200+); objects d'art, hand-painted bird houses, hand blown glass, sofa samples, hand-painted accent tables, plants, area rugs. Oh me, oh my. The list is exhaustive enough to tire Martha Stewart. And I'll meet you any morning, Monday through Saturday–but not to be confused with Tuesday Morning 'cause Liquidators Outlet is open every Tuesday, too. *CK, MC, V, AE, D*

★★★ Our Children's Store of Dallas 214/691-9411

437 NorthPark Center *Mon-Sat 10-9; Sun Noon-6*
Dallas, TX 75225

As a collaborative effort of the Dallas metropolitan business community, volunteer community and local non-profit organizations serving children in crisis, this store is designed to generate much-needed money for more than 50 local children's charities. Thanks to contributions from major sponsors of the project, 100 percent of the proceeds goes directly to the non-profit agencies that actually benefit the children. All operating costs and salaries are covered by those sponsors such as the Metromedia Restaurant Group (like TGIFridays), Channel 11, CBS, Delta Airlines, Lennox International, Dallas Morning News, Accubank Mortgage Corporation, Central & Southwest Corporation, Frito-Lay, Northpark Center, TLP and many others. Shoppers will find thousands of gift items that have been tagged with the name of the children's agency that will benefit from the purchase. Every time an item is sold, 100 percent of the proceeds is returned to that children's agency to help troubled and disadvantaged kids. The concept began in Portland, OR, in 1993, when the prototype opened as a holiday season shop where local children's charities could sell their holiday products and retain the profits from the sale. When you shop at Our Children's Store of Dallas you'll leave with a unique gift while leaving behind an equally important gift–it's truly a gift that gives twice. Linda, the store manager, will see to it that no one will leave empty- handed. Young, old, teenager, baby, man, woman, etc., from fun-stuff for Halloween to everything imaginable for the holidays. Thousands of gift items priced from pennies to $3,000, with most items falling in the $50 and less range. Holiday items, pet gifts, greeting cards, picture frames, leather goods, specialty baskets, aromatherapy items, pottery, home accessories, birdhouses and garden tools, children's gift items and more. Located in North/Park Center, upstairs next to Lord & Taylor. *CK, MC, V, D*

★★★★★ Pier 1 Clearance Store — 972/255-9811

2350 N. Belt Line Rd. — *Mon-Fri 10-9, Sat 9-9; Sun 9-6*
Irving, TX 75062

Don't plan on heading out to sea without hauling bargains from this Pier. But you don't have to stick with a nautical scheme for your home's décor. Nevertheless, schools of people swim in and out of this treasure chest for loot galore! Winner of a 1998 Shoppers' Choice Awards, you won't be lost at sea if you shop here. Now docked at their new larger Clearance Store in Irving across from the Irving Mall, shoppers sail in from surrounding states and line-up at the cash register to take the bait. (Well, the deals are hot, really hot!) Next to Target, see a jungle of wood carvings to posters, candles to canisters, art objects to gourmet food items, plates and platters, glassware and bar ware, brass and picture frames, wicker, rugs, placemats, napkins and napkin rings, furniture and fabric, and maybe a fish plate or two; you'll need a barge to float all your finds home. This is a one-stop port for billowing bargains. Everything in the store starts at 25 percent off and sails away at up to 90 percent off during their often-held blow-out sales. "Thar she blows!" The average discounts, though, are consistently in the 50-75 percent range. Laura, the captain of this ship, actually enjoys waiting on customers and never forgets to smile. You'll smile, too, over assorted napkins, $1.18 each; placemats $1.88; wooden birdhouse that retails for $17/$5.88; large stoneware plate retails for $35/ $12.18; glass pitcher retails for $35/$12.18, drinking glasses retail $5.50/$1.88. So get on board, hoist your sails and gig your jibs to Pier 1's Clearance Store. And for future reference, keep your eyes open for bargains on down the line on pieces from the new, expanded furniture collections. The company is increasing its offerings of loveseats, armchairs, ottomans, settees, magazine racks, coffee tables, end tables, entry tables, corner shelves, pedestals, screens, CD racks, etageres, papasans, headboards/footboards, nightstands, dressers, chests, mirrors, entertainment centers, armoires, trunks, wastebaskets, hampers, bed rails, dining tables/chairs, cabinets in a variety of materials. Cotton, rattan, pole, steel/pewter, mahogany, rubber wood, pine, bronze—even the Home and Garden Network would never run out of ideas. *CK, MC, V, AE, D, Pier 1*

★★ Pottery Barn — 214/528-2302

3220 Knox St. — *Mon-Sat 10-9; Sun Noon-6*
Dallas, TX 75205 — *www.potterybarn.com*

This 37-year-old home-furnishings chain has always been known for its classic and Shaker-looking salt and pepper shakers and a full spectrum of housewares. Now they are making waves on saying hello to good buys on furniture, wall and floor coverings and more. In store, there's a design studio where an 11-foot table awaits customers to doodle, smooze, sift through fabric swatches, browse through the sample books, or call upon the sales help for their design counsel. Simple. Chic. Affordable. Check out their other locations in Plano at 1900 Preston Rd. and in Fort Worth in the University Park Village. *CK, MC, V, AE*

★★★★ Promenade Clocks — 972/644-3979

1325 Promenade Center — *Mon-Fri 10-5:30; Sat 10-5*
Richardson, TX 75080

Take a walk down the Promenade for discontinued clock prices. "These are a few of hour favorite things!" Since 1962, Promenade Clocks has been ticking right on time. We like to Talk! Shop. The owner here likes to Talk! Clocks. What a swell fella is he. This full-service clock operation offers plenty of helping hands with the customers even while they're standing in line. Both the usual and the unusual to pick from with names on their faces that were plenty familiar: HOWARD MILLER, for example, was still running like clockwork and the inventory of grandfathers was priced from $600-$16,000. Other brands included RIDGEWAY, SEIKO, SETH THOMAS, SLIGH and THYTHUM. Time doesn't stand still here. There were over 1,000 clocks to choose from, plus other gift items, too. Cuckoo! Home service calls are available if your grandfather is too tall to tuck into the car. *CK, MC, V, D*

★★★ Protecto-Pak — 903/297-3985

PO Box 5096
1610 Willowview Street (75604)
Longview, TX 75608

Winding up a bag lady might be worth your while here. Zip it up in a

Protecto-Pak plastic bag and store the savings, as much as 35 percent below retail. Store just about anything that comes in sizes 2 x 2-inch to 13 x 15-inch. Or have Protecto-Pak print your company name on them and use them at work if your storage needs are great (minimum order for printing is 25,000). They have been known to carry some pretty expensive fish to restaurants, craft supplies to class, silverware to the party, baby food to the day care center and jewelry to the jeweler. Oh yes, they're great to promulgate seeds in, too. Price lists available, send a SASE (self-addressed stamped envelope) or by phone with a minimum order of $10. All products are guaranteed and delivery time is four-six weeks. *CK, PQ, C with samples ($2)*

✧✧✧✧✧ Rent-All Center — 972/495-8555

3221 Belt Line Rd.
(Belt Line at Jupiter)
Garland, TX 75044
Mon-Sat 7:30-6; Sun 10-4

Having a party? Don't know who to call? You can Rent-All here. Located between Shiloh and Jupiter on the northeast corner of Jupiter and Belt Line, rent anything you need for a party or wedding. Or, if you have a heavy-duty job around the house, they also rent contractor's equipment, exercise equipment, space walks, medical equipment, power and hand tools, floor and carpet care equipment, painting and plumbing equipment, camping and sporting equipment, automotive tools, equipment for your yard and garden, moving and towing supplies, video cameras, office equipment, stage/dance floors, machines to make cotton candy, snow cones, hot dog, popcorn and margaritas, $75/day plus delivery charge based on where you live. Don't even ask! What more could you ask? OK ... they also rent ice cream carts, a dunking booth, meeting equipment, tables and chairs. *CK, MC, V*

★★★★ Rio Imports — 817/277-9991

770 E. Road to Six Flags, #118
Arlington, TX 76011
Tue-Sat 10-6; Sun Noon-5
www.rioimports.com

No, there's not a taco or tortilla in sight. Nevertheless, this store is a genuine tamale. Wonderful imported furniture smack-dab in the middle of the road to Six Flags. They've hit the bull's eye and you will not have to kill the bull between the eyes. Their beautiful rustic furniture and accessories from the central part of Mexico makes shopping a novel cultural experience. Revel in the unusual sets of four clay pots for only $15.50. Talking about cracking up over these pots. Plus they have hand-carved tables and chairs for $300. And you did not have to pay duty. Bring home a slice of the Mexican heritage by shopping here without a green card. In Lincoln Square. Second light south of I-30 on Collins is Road to Six Flags. Turn right. Look for the landmark horse fountain, Rio is behind the fountain, next to Half-Price Books. *MC, V, AE, D*

★★★★★ Sincerely Yours

1316 Industrial **800/297-4860**
Mount Pleasant, TX 75455 *24 hours/7 days*

When you want to send a handmade gift and sign it, "Sincerely Yours," this may be a place to call for home delivery. But now, without visiting their outlet store in Mount Pleasant, you can shop closer to home in their new Plano location on East Plano Parkway. Discriminating catalog shoppers know a beautiful thing when they see it-and many beautiful items are created in this Texas-based studio. Direct from their designers to you, you can see an exclusive collection of custom furnishings and accessories plus great-looking silk floral arrangements, wreaths for your door, handpainted accent pieces, bedding, clothing and much more in their exquisite color catalog. If you want to get down to the wire, visit their outlet store for what's left from last season's catalog. No reason not to. *CK, MC, V, AE, D, C*

★★★★★ Tic Toc Clocks **214/321-9331**

8928 Garland Rd. *Mon-Fri 10-5; Sat 10-3*
Dallas, TX 75218

If there isn't enough time in the day to shop for clocks at 50 percent off, you're not in the same time zone as those of us in the Metroplex. Where does the time go when you're saving so much money? All grandfather, mantel and wall clocks, cuckoo clocks are selling for half price until they are going, going, gong. Tick, tock, tick, tock. Do you know what time it is? It's time to get the most for your money. Check out the selection of AMERICAN HERITAGE, ANSONIA, BALDWIN, BLACK FOREST, DOLD, HOWARD MILLER, LORICON, LINDEN, NEW ENGLAND, RIDGEWAY, SETH THOMAS, SLIGH and more. From battery-operated to key-wound, you will save money, hands down, on both new and antique clocks. ATMOS clocks and 400-day clocks were all present and accounted for. Expert clock repair (experienced since 1963) and restoration, cleaning, and oiling of any old clocks. Located eight blocks past Buckner Ave. and Garland Rd. *CK, MC, V, D*

Trademark Restaurant Equipment & Supply
972/276-6046

3690 Miller Park Drive — *Mon-Fri 8-5; Auctions Sat 10-3*
Garland, TX 75042

Going, going, gone to the hungriest chef. New and used restaurant and bar equipment goes on the block where you can buy by the piece or score a full restaurant. Huge auctions are held every three weeks and are open to the public, so call for dates. Specializing in auctions on furnishings/booths, chairs, tables and small wares, equipment like coolers, freezers, fryers, ice machines, mixes, ovens, stainless steel sinks and tables, stoves and Vent-A-Hoods. Makes for good home fodder, too, even if you'll never make it through the Cordon Blue. Sales are held every other week, with previews two - five days before the day of the auction on Saturday. *Certified CK, CK/Bank Letter/Guarantee*

Travis Mitchell Auctions
972/926-8888

3821 Dividend Drive — *Mon-Fri 8-5*
Garland, TX 75042 — *www.travismitchellauctions.com*

Last year, much to the delight of staff members and auction goers, Travis Mitchell moved from its Kingsley Road location to a new air-conditioned warehouse on Dividend Drive. Now when they claim to be the pinnacle of new and used restaurant and bar equipment via the auction block, they do so with a-plum! Items include anything and everything found in a restaurant or bar, including dishes, glassware, freezers, ice makers and more. Sales are held at the warehouse approximately every three weeks. Auctions start at 10 A.M. on select Saturdays, with previews from 1-6 P.M. on the preceding Friday. Items can be viewed during normal hours on any business day, but will not be tagged for auction until Fridays. A cash deposit of $100 is required to participate in the auctions. The deposit is refundable if you do not make a purchase; or applied toward your purchase if you do. A 10 percent buyers' premium is added to all purchases. *Certified CK, CK with Bank Letter of Guarantee*

UCC Total Home
972/952-0226

850 N. Dorothy Drive, Suite 502 — *By Appt. Only*
Richardson, TX 75081 — *www.ucctotalhome.com*

UCC Total Home is one of the largest private buyers organizations in the country. In business for nearly 30 years, UCC has grown to 90 locations in nearly 30 states and Canada. Membership has its privileges. Become a member here and you'll find just about anything you could imagine for your home including furniture, carpeting, wall coverings, window treatments, appliances, bedding, baby accessories and home decorator items from over 700 brand name manufacturers at up to 50 percent and more off of suggested retail prices. We found custom kitchen cabinets in a variety of styles at prices up to 70 percent off retail, as well as a bathroom suite with a whirlpool for about $1,350 (normally $2,300) and a brass faucet for about $70 (normally $180). Visit them online or call for a visitors pass to their facility, located near Arapaho Rd. and Greenville Ave. *CK, MC, V, AE*

★★★ United Rental — 972/492-0550

3749 N. Josey Lane — *Mon 7:30-5; Tue-Sat 8-5*
Carrollton, TX 75007 — *www.unitedrent-all.com*

Gotta dance? Gotta have a drink? Gotta have a party? Don't send out the invitations until you first call United Rent-All and Margaritas-R-Us. Drink up with different sizes of margaritas, bellinis (peach, raspberry, strawberry, Southwest), chaladas, pina-coladas, hurricanes, Mai-Tais, Long Island Iced Tea... just be sure you have a designated driver, just in case. Then, it's on to the serious party plans. Need a way to display your ice sculpture? Here's the place to rent (for $25) an ice carving display stand. Now it's hi-ho, Silver – your finest silver serving pieces, china, flatware, serving utensils, champagne fountains (up to $60), punchbowls and glassware, table cloths and other linens ... nobody will know you haven't brought them forth from your attic! Add chairs, wooden lattice screens, flower stands and call in the troops. For business meetings, rent office equipment that you only need occasionally like lecterns, easels, projectors, video cameras and players. For a garden wedding, what about a gazebo for $115? For your school's fund-raiser, what about party and carnival games that include at 15 x 15-foot spacewalk for $120, or a quarterback toss game for $60? Keep it all under the Big Top and rent a tent from a 10 x 10-foot for $95 to a 20 x 40-foot one for $425, or dance the night away under the stars with outdoor lighting and dance floors, concession and cooking equipment. You need it ... they got it. Delivery extra according to your zip code. *CK, MC, V, AE*

★★★ Weatherly's Clock — 817/294-1281

5041 Granbury Rd. — *Mon-Sat 10-6*
Fort Worth, TX 76133

This shop will make you coo coo for clocks. Don't expect a mouse to run up this clock as they don't have a website – yet, but if you're looking for a particular style of clock, this is the place for the dials. Even if they don't have a particular clock, they will order it for you. How can you go wrong? Their selection includes grandfather clocks, mantle clocks, cuckoo clocks and more. A new clock would look good hanging in your hallway. But a used clock would look just as good. That's right! They carry both new and antique clocks in their store. Drop by their store today but make sure not to be late because the clock is ticking. *CK, MC, V, AE, D*

★★★★ World Market

972/509-1843

1201 N. Central Expwy.
Plano, TX 75075
Mon-Sat 9-9; Sun 10-7

If all the world's your market place, then hop aboard their carts-for-less. Cost Plus, now known as World Market in some circles, is located between Plano Parkway and FM 544, just north of Collin Creek Mall. Going north on Central, exit 15th Street and make a U-turn. This California import's strong suit is gourmet foodstuff, imported candy, wine, domestic beers at competitive prices with 90 percent off its imports being glassware, ceramics, furniture and cool picture frames all under one roof. Whether it's a seasonal celebration, a festive family get-together, or just a quiet evening for two, their ever changing mix of over 20,000 products from 38 countries (many one-of-a-kind and exclusive to World Market) can make you delirious. Imagine shopping around the world without having to get airborne? Or a penne saved is a penne earned with Cost Plus Pastas. Whip up a 20 percent savings off the Panache Blender mixes, which are perfect for frozen Mocha Lattes! Also get frosty, creamy, low-fat espresso, wow! Wines from $4.99-$8.99. No backyard patio, outdoor picnic, or pool party should be celebrated empty-handed without a trip-in-the-sun to this basket full of goodies. Then, curl up around the fireplace and pop away. If it's foodstuff, you'll be stuffed after shopping here. Another location is in Grapevine at 1317 W. Highway 114 (817/416-1400), as well as at Lovers Lane and Greenville Ave. in Dallas. *CK, MC, V, D*

★★★ Your Place

972/386-5218

13510 Inwood Rd.
Dallas, TX 75244
Mon-Sat 10-6; Sun Noon-5

Your Place is the place to go when it comes to accessorizing the homestead. Bring your wallet and wandering eye and prepare to be dazzled. This is a site to behold. There are flowers and plants growing everywhere, on the floor, on the ledges, on the wrought-iron hedges, in the baskets, on the wall ... wherever you turn, you will see the phony philodendron and fake florid florescence. In other words, this is a place for silk flowers and plants, arranged or otherwise. Then add some Southwestern flair to your furniture and accent pieces, drape a woven rug over a loveseat, place a glowing candelabra for the perfect lighting, and position a Dhurri rug just so. Get the picture? No longer on Dragon St., this is the one and only Your Place. *CK, MC, V, AE, D*

Jewelry

★★★★ A Wink & A Smile Vintage

972/966-0092
Mon-Sat 10-7; Sat Noon-6
www.winksmile.com

Judi Scheele is a gemstone catering to area jewelry aficionados by specializing in antique and vintage jewelry and accessories at two Dallas area antique malls: Forestwood Antique Mall at 5333 Forest Lane (Inwood and Forest) and at the Lower Greenville Antique Mall, 2010 Greenville Ave. Just wink and you'll smile with an ever changing and exciting collection of vintage jewelry, the rage these days since the blockbuster "Titanic". The very best designs from bakelite and other plastics, to copper, silver, compacts and handbags, deco and period jewelry in the area that surely would suit every woman's style. A Trinity silk tapestry bag with ornate jeweled frame with glorious green cabochons in excellent condition was $85. A luscious brown alligator handbag from the days of CHANEL with double handles and leather interior was $115. An old TRIFARI deco pave bracelet–bright rhodium with even brighter stones was $110 and a Trifari retro-necklace, bolo-like design, with rose-gold gild-finished flat links and brilliant clear centers was $66. A Wink and A Smile has many new products coming in daily. A black carved bakelite with Buddha pin for only $155. Shop their easy-to-navigate website and smile! *CK, MC, V, AE, D*

★★ Accessory Corner

214/748-5421
1201 Main St.
Dallas, TX 75202
Mon-Fri 9-5

Find some hidden treasure just around the corner at Accessory Corner. Find the tunnel and you can scope out the sparkling earrings. Lots of gold chains, pins, brooches and matching sets. Expect to rope about 20 percent less than retail, and maybe more on those that look handcrafted. We found earrings at $3/pair and leather watch bands for $12.99. Clothes, too, in S-L, sizes 4-18. Denim dresses that retailed for around $70 were here for $39. Lots of accessories can be found here – so what else is new? How about tying one on with scarves or belts. Eelskin handbags squirmed out the door for $35-$65 squ"eel"ing – 30 percent off. Now it's time to shop or clam up. *CK, MC, V*

★★ Aurum Jewelry Co. 972/231-9638

753 S. Sherman St. *Mon-Fri 10-6; Thu 10-8*
Richardson, TX 75081

With 28 years in the same location, this jeweler is still sparkling. David Griffin certainly is a source for finding the golden goose. Low prices are golden here. How do they do it? By keeping the overhead low. This isn't your typical glittering, gleaming, spotless high-security jewelry store. In fact, if you're not looking for it, you'd drive right by. In fact, if you ARE looking for it, you still might drive right by. Custom jewelry, repairs, remounting, casting, fine diamonds and redesigns from your old jewelry is this Aurum's mainstay. Have a picture of a piece you'd like to own but wouldn't like to pay the price? Bring it in and have them re-create it, for less. *CK*

★★★ Beadworks 972/931-1899

7632 Campbell Rd., Suite 309 *Mon-Sat 10-6; Thu 10-7; Sun Noon-5*
Richardson, TX 75248 *www.beadworks-dallas.com*

If your beady little hands are groping for a beady little project, let Beadworks string you along. Classes are offered on everything for the beading enthusiast to create a masterpiece from A to Z. Gaze at their beautifully displayed beadery and see if you can make a crystal clear decision. Their forte is crystal, glass, bone, wooden, seed and one-of-a-kind beads, oh beady-eyes you. If you are not nimble with a thimble, they also have beautiful custom and ready-to-wear jewelry. If you want to learn the rudiments, classes are always in progress. Learn to make a lariat necklace or a flat peyote. Perhaps you need to shed some light on a new lamp shade. What about a beaded shade? On the southwest corner of Campbell and Coit, if you want a day of bargains and shopping, let Linda Hoffman be your mentor. *CK, MC, V, D*

★★★ Bermuda Gold Custom Jewelers Metro 817481-5115

404 S. Main St. *Mon-Fri 10-6; Sat 10-3*
Grapevine, TX 76051 *www.jewelrycreations.com*

Give or take a dozen years in business, the three jewelers on staff, utilizing computer designs, can translate high-technology into a work of art. Though they also carry CITIZEN watches, they specialize in custom-designed jewelry using 14-Karat and 18-Karat gold and platinum. Don't overlook their large selection of colored stones, either. They are located in historic downtown Grapevine. Capture the newest looks in diamond pendants just waiting to be strung around your neck. Strike pay dirt with in-house custom designs and watch repair including wedding sets, sterling silver, certified stones, estate jewelry and more. Now, this is one Gem Dandy! *CK, MC, V*

★★★★ Big Apple Diamonds & Fine Jewelry — 972/422-0899

1301 Custer Rd. Suite 482 — *Tue-Wed, Fri 10-6; Thu 10-7; Sat 10:30-4*
Plano, TX 75075

You don't have to go to the Big Apple to get fine custom jewelry at a discount from Big Apple Diamond. You can Sharon the Stone with this direct diamond importer who offers prices that are mined in authenticity. If the wedding is just around the corner, you might think it a wise decision to order the wedding invitations at the same time you are creating your rings–they're 30-50 percent off depending on which of the competition you're checking (and they can get them done in 24-hours if it's a quickie). You won't find any worms if you take a bite out of these jewels. Look for them under the Salon Unique sign on the southwest corner of 15th and Custer between Tuesday Morning and Coomers Crafts. There's a trio of designers and jewelers on site: Angela and Martin and owner David, who is a graduate GIA. *CK, MC, V, AE, D, Financing*

★★★ Billie B's — 972/669-0510

18 Spring Valley Village — *Tue-Sat 11-6*
Richardson, TX 75080

This Billie is rarely in these days so you might have to unearth her pearls of wisdom by utilizing the divining rod. Where or where has Billie gone? You can try to "B" yourself with accessories on the q.t. here. In previous lives, this buried treasure unearthed necklaces, earrings, wedding sets, rings, bracelets and gems of every dimension–with some cut to 75 percent off. Costume jewelry and custom jewelry, from modern classics to the very unusual was found without much "hoop-la". A good selection of lapis and patina jewelry, too, but finding her at Spring Valley and Central Expressway was easier said than done! *CK*

★★★★ Castle Gap — 214/361-1677

8300 Preston Rd., Suite 500 — *Mon-Sat 10-6*
Dallas, TX 75225

When Charlotte returns from the reservation, expect her tepees to be full of heavy metals. Helping close the gap on high prices, Castle Gap has been your sterling silver jewelry connection for more than 25 years. In fact, it's propably the only store that caters to silver jewelry – from the ordinary to the sublime. This is the fortress of contemporary choice for authentic silver jewelry at very reserved prices. From one reservation to the next, from Arizona to New Mexico, finding the latest designs and trends as well as tons of the latest in fashion jewelry from well-known designers is how this Charlotte weaves her web. Lots to choose from for very little wampum. Two other locations in town: Preston Town Crossing in Plano (972/612-1677) and in the Pepper Square Shopping Center at Preston and Belt Line (972/239-1677). *CK, MC, V, AE, D*

★★★★ Charles Cohen Manufacturing Jewelers 817/292-4367

4747 S. Hulen St., Suite 107 *Tue-Sat 10-6*
Fort Worth, TX 76132

Since 1947, Charles Cohen Jewelers has been providing a personal touch to generations of shoppers. This family owned jeweler offers jewelry repair to appraisals, custom designs to help in picking out the perfect stone or setting. It's like having a family jewel in your back pocket. They have withstood the strands of time and continue to provide value pricing on diamonds, colored gemstones and gold jewelry. On diamonds, for example, they offer a trade-up (to a larger diamond) policy where you'll receive the full current price back on any diamond purchased from them. That's right. And sometimes, bigger is better. In addition to their raw gemstones, such as inlaid malachite, lapis, precious opals, black onyx and a staff of graduate gemologists (GIA), they even offer a two-year, no-interest layaway plan. They sell gold wholesale by weight. (Not yours, silly!) If the occasion calls for putting on the nouveau ritz, and your budget is kaput, check out their specials throughout the year on gold and diamonds. Set your dial to a discounted ROLEX or the newest addition, the ROVEN DINO watch with a five-year warranty (comparable to TAG HEUER). Located between Pearle Vision and Bank of America in a small office complex at the back, diamonds are still a girl's best friend. *CK, MC, V, AE, D*

★★★ Claire's Boutique 972/524-6442

I-20, Exit 501 *Mon-Sat 10-9; Sun 11-6*
Tanger Factory Outlet Center *www.claires.com*
Terrell, TX 75160

Gotta little girl? Gotta go to the mall? Gotta get a pair of earrings? Gotcha! If you don't direct your little Miss Muffin to Claire's, then you don't know a good ring when you hear or see it. Gobs of goody-goodies to choose from at piggly, giggly low prices. Claire's is the store of choice for many mini-mavens on their mercy missions to buy – something. Anything! What fun, especially during their "Buy two, get the third one FREE!" Don't expect gem quality o–just plenty of trendy baubles and bows. Hide out in sunglasses, add a purse, and a ponytail clip in rhinestones and pearls. Go, girl! Buy a tote of charm for her to take to Sunday-go-to-meetin'. Everything here is 20 percent off their retail stores. With such low prices, no one will get mauled at the mall. *CK, MC, V, AE, D*

★★★★★ Dallas Gold & Silver Exchange — 972/484-3662

2817 Forest Lane — *Mon-Fri 10-6; Sat 10-4*
Dallas, TX 75234 — *www.dgse.com*

This little pearl from the Oyster fits the Bill when it comes to finding the best in gold and silver jewelry. Billy Oyster has spread his charms to become a force to reckon with; his jewelry emporiums are considered category killers and they are growing by Carat weight! Dallas Gold and Silver Exchange can offer great prices on diamonds, estate jewelry, watches and even gold jewelry (which is sold by weight). Not only do they have the largest inventory around, but they can also offer you the best prices for your estate or fine jewelry pieces and rare coins. Yes, a pre-owned ROLEX can be found ticking away here for substantially less than new, along with many of the finest brands of watches. Buy a pre-owned traditional men's "Presidential" ROLEX for $7,000, less than half the price of new. A ladies' DAVID YURMAN designer watch that lists for $2,550 was $950 with a two-year warranty; a BREITLING man's Chronograph watch that lists for $11,700 was $4,900; a ladies' PIAGET POLO 18-Karat dress watch, originally more than $18,000, was $3,900. A man's BAUME & MERCIER Riviera water-resistant watch that originally sold for $3,700 was only $1,295. And if you're "stocking" up on gold and silver, call for a quote on the latest prices on bullion. From LBJ go south on Josey to Forest and turn right. *CK, MC, V, AE, D*

★★★★ Dallas Watch & Jewelry Co. — 972/484-6700

12801 Midway Rd., Suite 505 — *Mon-Fri 10-6; Sat 10-3*
Dallas, TX 75244

Tired of playing phone tag when you're looking for a watch? We know how quite a few so-called watch dealers operate: you have to beep them or make an appointment to view the goods. Everything's so hush-hush. Not so at Dallas Watch and Jewelry. Since 1971, they've had a showroom to display exactly what you want, when you want it. Pre-owned ROLEXES were sitting around with time on their hands. Why pay such high prices for new when after you've worn it, it's pre-owned anyway? The reconditioned Rolexes come with a two-year warranty. A his and her stainless steel 18-Karat ROLEX with the new style sapphire crystal quick-set retailed for $5,330 (new); their price, like new in the box, was $2,999. Similar pricing for the ladies. The value of a ROLEX is the condition, not the year. Watch out! Some were scratched or beat up. Moving on, we did see good prices on BREITLING, CARTIER, EBEL, OMEGA, PIAGET and others. Got so many watches and not enough wrists? Then they would love for you to unload your extras and they're willing to offer top dollar for them (if they are in great condition). Or, they will repair your watch for a nominal fee. Family owned and operated, they offer 2-year warranties on used models, but you don't have to be a model to wear one. Knock three times and ask for Mel and Ernie. Tell 'em the Diva sent you. *CK, MC, V, 90-Day Layaway*

★★★★★ Diamond Broker, The 972/490-6060

11930 Preston Rd. *Mon-Sat 10-6; Thu 10-9*
Dallas, TX 75230

Call your broker! This broker can be your stock in trade when it comes to finding the stone of your dreams at wholesale or below prices. Buying direct is no longer a secret–it's a way of life for smart shoppers. We saw some beautiful rocks that were big as Gibraltar–larger stones are their specialty. A .52-Carat round HI SI was $875; .70-Carat heart was $1,350; 1.03-Carat round was $1,950; 1.03-Carat oval was $1,950; a 1-Carat emerald JK SI2 $2,900; 1.53-Carat Princess J SI1 $6,478; 1.54-Carat Marquis I VS1 certified was $8,776; 1.64-Carat Pear I Color was $3,750; 2.07-Carat Marquis FG SI $7,278; 2.58-Carat Pear H SI was $8,988; 3.04-Carat Pear IJ SI $11,936; 3.01-Carat Marquis EF Color was $15,093. Now we're talking big! Over 500 styles of platinum engagement rings from a 1-Carat round for $1,650 (H color, SI) to a stunning 2-Carat Marquis for $8,175 (SI). Zing went the ring of the cash register. Lots of mountings were displayed in cases to choose from, including platinum and invisible settings. So, when he's ready to put that ring around your finger, tell him to go for broke-r. *CK, MC, V, AE, D*

★★★★★ Diamond Cutters Jewelry Mfg. Wholesale Exchange 972/386-9088

14811 Inwood Rd. *Mon-Thu 9-6; Fri 9-3; Sun by Appt.*
Addison, TX 75001

Established in 1921, where have you been hiding? Knowing how I love Carats, there are plenty of loose diamonds, mounted jewelry with diamonds, watches with diamonds and estate jewelry with diamonds if you recognize that diamonds are still a girl's best friend. But there are those who'd prefer a pre-owned ROLEX (I won't tell) or a work of art, or an elaborate silver tea service. Whether you're buying or selling, or making a private loan on your jewelry, you will no doubt find something beautifully friendly. Between Spring Valley and Belt Line on Inwood. Look for a sign with jewelry and watches on it. Duh? *CK, MC, V, AE, D*

★★★★★ Diamontrique

972/934-1530

5100 Belt Line Rd.
Village on the Parkway
Dallas, TX 75240
Mon-Sat 10-5:30

Fee, fie, faux, fun–bet you can't tell the real from the unreal! Drop the insurance, honey, and be smart. Since 1978, Diamontrique has been out-foxing the best of them. Who would have thought that they'd be celebrating their 22nd year dedecking, bedazzling and bejeweling Texas's finest femmes fatale. But the secret behind these alternative stones...they only look expensive. Smart ladies go for the gold! Encircle your love in rings, bracelets, pendants and more–all resting in elegant nests. All 14- and 18-Karat or platinum gold, of course. If diamonds are not your best friend, try emeralds, rubies or sapphires. Simulated precious stones help round out your jewelry wardrobe–especially if you like to dress to impress. And if these hours don't work for you, they will make an appointment to suit your schedule. Before you take part in the best Happy Hour free buffet across the way at the Blue Mesa restaurant, stuff yourself with the jewels here. (After a taco/tortilla/fajita buffet, you always have room for more!) Show off an emerald ring that would cost $14,000 (if the real McCoy's were used) for only $1,400. Be treated like royalty in their salon approach with personalized service. Don't expect the great expanse of inventory to be on display–75 percent of it is not. Unique designs and luxury weight mountings at affordable prices. Join high-society and laugh all the way to the bank vault. As seen on the Ainsley Harriott Show, sure could have fooled Mother Nature! *CK, MC, V, AE*

★★★★★ Diva

214/361-1081

4412 Lovers Lane
Dallas, TX 75225
Mon-Sat 10-6; Thu 10-7; Sun 11-5

Been yearning for a YURMAN bracelet, but don't want to pay the price? Diva has one of Dallas' largest collections of look-alikes and we looked none too soon. Our big debut brought out all the stops including the sapphire and diamond engagement ring that Prince Charles placed on Diana's finger and the pearl and sapphire necklace she wore the night she danced with John Travolta. Who could resist? Being a princess, at any age, is what every girl wants. One of the largest collection of 14-Karat gold rings, bracelets, earrings and necklaces with simulated diamonds, emeralds, rubies and sapphires in the Metroplex. High-end sterling Yurman and LAGOS copies, gorgeous and flashy. A combination silver and gold-hinged bracelet from The Replica Collection was just waiting to encircle my wrist. New this year, a collection of 14-Carat jewels with Azurite, the highest quality diamond simulation on the market today. Only an expert gemologist can determine the difference and only after precise weight and heat probe tests. This stone is guaranteed against discoloring, clouding and breakage and can be manufactured in 14-, 18- or 24-Karat yellow or white gold or platinum and can be altered to most custom designs. Sterling silver lines by designers ALEJANDRO TOUSIER, CRISLU, JANICE GIRALDI, LENNI NAVARRO and LOIS HILL; replica collections from Italy; Victorian-inspired earrings and necklaces (bet you can't tell!). And for heavens sake, don't overlook all the earrings, necklaces and bracelets inspired by BULGARI, CARTIER, GUCCI and TIFFANY in gold or silver finish. They are the rage even if you're not the Diva. *CK, MC, V, D, Layaway*

★★★★★ Dixie's Fashion Accessories Outlet 817/649-1112

2500 E. Randol Mill Rd., Suite 113 *Mon-Fri 9-6; Sat 10-5*
Arlington, TX 76011 *www.dixiesoutlet.com*

Life is good this side of the Mason-Dixie's line. Scoring a home run without having to have your wallet loaded, you'll whistle Dixie over their selection of jewelry at below wholesale prices. Did you hear what I said? Below wholesale prices on costume jewelry and sterling silver, displayed floor to ceiling. If you think you heard that woman jingling as she walked by you the other day, never fear. You aren't going crazy. Chances are she's been to Dixie's. Dozens of trays of sterling silver charms in all sorts of themes start here at just $3. At those prices, you can have a wrist full of dangling charms and money left over. Thousand of ears in the Metroplex are pierced (or clipped) to perfection at 50-75 percent off, thanks to Dixie. Then pile it all in to your new look-alike BRIGHTON or COACH bags, priced $30-$40. Sure could have fooled me. The quality is so high, you'll feel guilty paying such low prices. Circling the bags and baubles are wallets, belts, hair accessories, even look-alike sunglasses at wholesale prices or less. We snapped up dozens of earrings for as low as $3 a pair (or even lower) that retail for $12 and up. From small and dainty to dramatic and eye-popping, entire sets of earrings and necklaces (just like the ones at Dillard's) were half off. (We never like to look a gift horse in the ears!) You'll also find handmade soap, yard flags and more, making this a true one-stop gift shopping nirvana that'll bring music to your ears and budget. During the holidays, call for additional hours. And if you become addicted to saving this kind of money on these kind of accessories, log on to dixiesoutlet.com and satisfy those urges 24-7. *CK, MC, V, AE, D*

★★★ Euless Gold & Silver

817/540-5242

1201 W. Airport Frwy., Suite 305 — *Mon-Sat 9:30-6*
Euless, TX 76040

If your favorite fairy tale is *The Three Bears*, here's your fairy godmother telling you where to cry wolf. The Bear family, Papa Bear (Cub) and his family of Bears, sells gold by weight, so there's no hanky-panky about comparing prices. (Fortunately, your own weight is not considered!) When you want to meet over lunch, make it full of Karats. Diamonds at 20 percent over cost is nothing to sneeze at. Their prices are really rock-bottom. Large assortment of ARTCARVED wedding and anniversary rings and one-carat diamond tennis bracelets from $225 and up. ROLEXES, refurbished to like-new, are sold with a one-year warranty. Buying and selling, either way you get a good deal–but don't ask for any porridge, please. At the intersection of Airport Freeway and F.M. 157 (near Burlington Coat Factory). *CK, MC, V, D*

★★ Family Jewels

972/424-8348

221 W. Parker Rd., Suite 431 — *Mon-Sat 10-6*
Plano, TX 75023

This small family owned jewelry store is rooted in helping you make a show-piece of your heirlooms. Trace your family tree to see if there are any gems in your genealogical heritage and bring them in for a little updating. Or melt down your own gold and allow them to transform it into something new–plus save $$$ in the process. Try creating something truly wonderful out of smaller items, or create little somethings from something big. Why hide them away in a jewelry box or in your vault? Bring them in and wear them all out. Everyone will think you've got a sugar daddy on the side with all the new jewelry you'll be sporting. You can even see the craftsmen at work at benches in the back. Most jewelry is custom-made. You can also expect this manufacturing jeweler to provide reasonable prices on custom work with an extensive selection of unmounted castings and SEIKO watches. *CK, MC, V, AE, D*

★★ Fashion with Pizzazz

972/387-9292

15201 Dallas Pkwy.
Addison, TX 75001

Mon-Sat 9-9; Sun 11-4

The Hotel Continental is the place to visit for a great selection of jewelry and accessories. The store inside is called Fashion With Pizzazz. They're the people you'll want to see. Pull out all the stops and enjoy this floor (practically to the ceiling!) show laden with earrings, necklaces, belts and more. Most items were priced less than you'd pay in the mall (some were downright cheap). We saw some designer copies of necklaces and some not-so-great plastic pieces for less, but nonetheless, it takes so little to dress up these days. They're a great source for accent pieces, sets, hair accessories and handbags, too. This northern boutique inside the InterContinental Hotel, formerly the Grand Kempinski, open Mon-Sat 9-9 and Sunday 11-4. Their Inwood Trade Center location is closed. *CK, MC, AE*

★★★ Faux Pas

972/691-2525

1900 Long Prairie Rd., Suite 136
Flower Mound, TX 75028

Mon-Fri 11-7; Sat 10-6

Fearful of making the ultimate faux pas? Not to worry. These Faux Pas are worn with pride. Wear them in your ears, around your neck, on your pinkie finger–any "wear" but not (especially when you're traveling.) Wear with ease jewelry that you don't have to watch your p's and q's with. Is it or isn't it? Maybe your best friend can tell. But if you're looking to buy jewelry that has the look without the price tag, this is it. Faux Pas takes 14-Karat gold and encases it with cubic zirconias. A neighborly selection of earrings, bracelets, rings, necklaces and more are all here. Hey big spender, they also carry sterling silver and costume jewelry at fair market value. They just look expensive while all the while being quite acceptable in the big city. *CK, MC, V, AE, D*

★★★★★ Fossil Outlet

254/582-7785

104 NE I-35, Exit 368
Prime Outlets of Hillsboro
Hillsboro, TX 76645

Mon-Sat 10-8; Sun 11-6

You don't have to be a relic to want to dig up some deals on these FOSSILS. Just watch out, though, you can get addicted. You can't stop at buying just one. And here, you can save 30-40 percent off retail prices, which is reason enough to own a Fossil-brand item. Watches, purses, leather belts and wallets for men and women, jewelry, alarm clocks, caps, T-shirts and sunglasses. We eyed sunglasses from $6.99-$20. Purses that cost $60-$80, were bagged at $39-$49. With these prehistoric prices, you can't go wrong digging around this stockpile. *CK, MC, V, AE, D*

★★★★★ Friendze 817/514-7700

654 Grapevine Hwy. *Mon-Sat 10-6*
Hurst, TX 76054 *www.friendze.com*

Make a friend of Friendze if you want to look rich without the frenzy of paying mall prices. What started as primarily a jewelry-finding store with components to make your own jewelry creations has evolved into a full line of adaptations like the LAGOS and YURMAN look-alikes. So, either way, have it your way if you want to look like you have arrived as a member in good standing of the Junior League. Say hello to your new best Friendze. Rows and rows and more rows of any motif: hearts and flowers, western, angels and cherubs, filigrees, crosses, Victorian luggage tags, frame corners or bar pins, drops, animals, novelty letters, religious, musical, school days, sports, stones, beads, kits–if you've got the gift of imagination and the desire to save money, making your own elegant designs is a gift from God–at a heavenly lower price. Meticulously detailed, Friendze's components are nearly indistinguishable from the originals from whence they came. Yes, there is a difference...and it's written on the price tag. Treat yourself to pure luxury, without the guilt of paying with this week's grocery money. *CK, MC, V, D, DC, MOC*

★★★★ Fuller's Jewelry 972/484-7581

15164 Marsh Lane *Mon-Sat 10-6; Thu 10-8*
Addison, TX 75244

Since 1949, Fuller's has been noted for selling and manufacturing jewelry at low prices. How do they do it? We've seen some pretty glaring examples featuring diamond-cluster earrings (retailing $1,000) selling for $250, and diamond ear studs (retailing $400) for $150. Read my lips: expect to shell out $2,610 for a .72-Carat pear-shaped I-SI1, $15,600 for a 3.01-Carat round brilliant K-SI2 certified diamond, $6,400 for a 1.01-Carat round brilliant D-VS2, or $6,925 for a 1.24-Carat pear-shaped I-VS1. That's buying power for you. Now consolidated into their one location, you can gaze at their beautiful presentation underneath lots of chrome and glass. Necklaces, rings and pearls are presented per piece by a salesperson and then calculated to determine the price after the discount. SEIKO watches are their loss-leaders and definitely a good buy in anybody's book. In fact, they're the best and Fuller's guarantees that they're the lowest price from any "authorized" Seiko dealer. Also, take note of their complete line of hard-to-find Tanzanite at prices much lower than those decked out on the cruise ships. Too, take advantage of their gold card financial plan–no payments or interest for 90 days and say, "Fuller up!" In a strip shopping center one block north of Belt Line on Marsh, they also buy diamonds and estate jewelry as well as sell, do insurance appraisals and expert watch and jewelry repair. *CK, MC, V, AE, D*

★★★ Greene's Gold & Diamonds — 972/233-1181

5519 Arapaho Rd. — *Mon-Fri 10-6; Sat 10-5*
Dallas, TX 75248

At Bobby Greene's, one man's fancy has turned to gold for customers. Greene is a former jeweler whose fame was in building one of the largest discount-chain jewelry stores in the Metroplex, and his expertise and wheeling-dealing has paid off. Stay in the Greene and fulfill your dreams of bridal sets and pre-owned ROLEXES. Oh, you were thinking of something a little bigger for that special someone? How about a diamond, any size, shape or clarity and plan on saving up to 50 percent. They have platinum mountings, of course. And if you've got a collection of cache that you wish to convert to cash, Greene's a buyer and seller of estate sets. Located behind Prestonwood Mall. *CK, MC, V, AE, Layaway*

★★★★★ Grissom's Fine Jewelry — 817/244-9754

9524 Spur 580 — *Tue-Sat 10:30-5*
Fort Worth, TX 76116

Grissom's Fine Jewelry has stood the strands of time. What's dreaming if you can't translate it into reality? Try on Grissom's for size. Celebrating over 30 years in business at the same location with the same traditions that have been handed down to the next generation. Since they are the manufacturers, you can save big bucks by buying direct. Having doubled in size from their original beginnings, walk through custom doors and have a seat. You'll will be treated like one of the family. Their diverse inventory runs the gamut in custom designs in platinum, gold and silver. They'll even give you an education if this is your first-time diamond experience. A Swiss watch repair center is on the premises with a watchmaker with years of experience in Switzerland. All types of repairs on watches at about 50 percent less than repairs elsewhere. BREITLING watches, sport watches and one-of-a-kind timepieces ... watch out! Too, the platinum and gold matching wedding bands caught our eye for $300 less than we saw in the bridal magazines.

Every stone over a half carat is sent to an independent lab for grading. Grissom's, if you'd like to know, certifies more diamonds than any single outlet operation in Tarrant County. Remember, according to Pat Grissom, "It's the cut that counts!" *CK, MC, V, AE, D*

★★ Harold's Jewelers — 972/221-8581

1288 W. Main St. — *Tue-Wed, Fri 9-6; Thu, Sat 9-4*
Lewisville, TX 75067

This mainstay on Main St. is Lewisville's Harold's Jewelers. Watch him if you're in the market for watches, watch repair or diamonds a cut above the rest. From his humble beginnings at Bachendorf's at Prestonwood Mall, he now does his own thing and you can ring in the benefits. No "ancient Gruens" here, but he does restore old pocket watches so you can keep the savings in your pocket for a change. Save 25-60 percent on SEIKO and BULOVA watches, gold chains, pendants, and rings. A watchmaker is on the premises, which means no matter what's wrong with your ticker, they can fix it quicker! *CK, MC, V, AE, Financing*

Herbert-Stehberg Jewelry — 214/631-3193

9160 King Arthur Drive — *Mon-Fri 8-4 (Nov. & Dec. only)*
Dallas, TX 75247

Browse through an entire warehouse of high-fashion accessories, jewelry and more at Herbert-Stehberg, located behind the Jerrell Company on Regal Row. Only open to the public the week before Thanksgiving and through the holidays. (Too bad. You never can get enough of a good thing.) Keeping the overhead low and selling wholesale during the busiest buying season makes for good bargain fellows. Nothing fancy, mind you, but you will have found a treasure trove of trinkets at wholesale prices. Thousands of earrings, necklaces, pins, pendants, even handbags (those little clutches are irresistible) are here for the choosing. Expect to pay 50 percent less than retail from this jewelry wholesaler who sells it all – from rhinestones to ethnic pieces during this short window of opportunity. Look for the wrought-iron bars on the door and open sesame – but only during the stocking-stuffer season. *CK, MC, V*

★★ Jelly Beans of Turtle Creek — 214/327-5649

Dallas, TX — *By Appt. Only*

Putting on the Rich is the way to fake it 'til you make it, Jelly Bean. Get your money's worth of Jelly Beans by picking your favorite colored stones (diamonds are a personal pick). And why not fool Mother Nature for a change. Rake in the fakes and forever hold your head up high. Call for your personal showing and preview hundreds of CZs for women (and a few thrown in for men). In some circles, they're called knock-offs; in others, they're called smart stones. Why pay high insurance premiums when you can have a 4-Carat look-alike for a fraction of the price of the real stuff? *CK*

★★★★★ Jewelry By Floyd — 214/821-9155

3300 Swiss Circle — *Mon-Sat 9-6*
Dallas, TX 75204 — *www.jewelrybyfloyd.com*

Live! Meet Floyd Bickel. Since 1981, his motto has been, "Why Pay Retail?" This little hideaway is tucked away in a not-ready-for-prime-time location with wholesale jewelry prices. They are gloating in the fact that they are one of the few small-time custom jewelers with big-time deals. They buy, sell or trade–whatever's your jewelry pleasure. Savings can be substantial due to the fact that some of the merchandise comes from repossessions, some from estate sales, and some, quite frankly, out of just plain desperation. Whether it's an engagement or wedding ring, loose diamonds or remounting your old ones, semi-precious stones, pearl restringing or a jewelry appraisal, trust Floyd's like Lloyd's of London. Cheerio. He also pays cash for diamonds and jewelry. *CK, MC, V, AE, D*

★★★★ Jewelry Connection — 972/247-1477

11427 Harry Hines Blvd. — *Mon-Fri 9:30-5:30; Sat 10-4:30*
Dallas, TX 75229

Costume Jewelry will do the trick! When you want to connect with a jewelry wholesaler, consider this your Jewelry Connection. High-fashion designer jewelry without the retailer's needless mark-ups. Buy direct from this wholesaler/importer of watches, earrings, necklaces, sterling silver rings, look-alike handbags, accessories and gift items at prices too cheap to reveal. Well, go ahead, twist my arm. Miniature decorative clocks were $4.99. Designer look-alike sunglasses were sun-blocked and bargain-priced. ANNE KLEIN and FOSSIL look-alike watches, YURMAN look-alike bracelets and earrings; LOUIS VITTON-like purses (unless you like the real ones for $785-$980) sitting majestically next to look-alike ANNE KLEIN, CHANEL, PALOMA PICASSO and others. Need I say more? *CK, MC, V, AE, D*

★★★★★ Jewelry Exchange, The

972/671-6700

318 S. Central Expwy. *Mon-Sat 10-6; Thu 10-8; Sun Noon-5*
Richardson, TX 75080

Claiming to be the highest volume jewelry outlet in the country, this gem has dangled many carats to area shoppers. Add to your jewelry war chest and just arm yourself with plenty of ammunition because they guarantee that their jewelry will appraise at twice the full purchase price. Then again, who charges full price these days? The Jewelry Exchange imports diamonds directly from Israel and India–where even the prime ministers don't know what jewels they're sitting on. They operate five other factories nationwide with the ability to price ready-made jewelry dirt cheap. Hit the mother lode without striking out. Choose 2-Carat tennis bracelets from $349, 1-Carat tennis bracelets from $199, 1-Carat stud earrings for $399, or a 1-Carat diamond solitaire from $599 is not exactly matzo balls soup. Remember, what your mother told you, "You don't have to shop around any more." All qualities of diamonds to satisfy anybody's budgetary constraints. Hundreds of styles and settings, sizes and shapes. Thousands of center diamonds are sold loose (the best way to buy them) and then mounted while you wait. Now, that's a real boon for your buck. *CK, MC, V, AE, D*

★★★★ Jewelry Factory, The

817/633-3333

2800 Forestwood Drive, Suite 114 *Mon-Fri 10-6; Sat 10-5*
Arlington, TX 76006

Has your watch lost its band width? Has your dial died? This factory can fix them both in no time. Besides watch repair, they also custom-make jewelry and sell CITIZEN watches at 25 percent off. They also carry a finely made, stainless steel watch called BEL AIRE. They continuously shop the competition to assess their strengths and weaknesses and have always risen to the occasion. You can shop direct and save up to 66 percent on repairs just one block west of 360 off of NE Green Oaks Blvd. in northeast Arlington from this husband and wife jewelry manufacturing team. Besides manufacturing, they import, wholesale and design 10-, 14-, 18- and 24-Karat gold jewelry chains, earrings, pendants, bracelets, rings, watches, silver and platinum jewelry, making this place a smorgasbord of savings. Expect to reap the benefits of paying the same price for quality stones that retail stores do. All services performed on site–in most cases, while you wait! Layaway, too, for those who can wait. *CK, MC, V, AE, D, Financing*

★★★★★ Jewelry Gallery, The

214/369-5361

5924 Royal Lane, Suite 170 *Mon-Fri 10-5*
Dallas, TX 75230

Consignment jewelry is a smart choice when it comes to buying or selling. Do you have more baubles than you have fingers or ears? Are they crowding the vault? How about that perfect wedding set from a not-quite-so-perfect marriage? Consignment pieces are priced at half of retail and by selling your jewels, the Jewelry Gallery receives a 17 percent commission (2 percent goes for insurance on your item). We found glittering rings, necklaces and bracelets at very low prices. An S-link tennis bracelet with a 14-Karat gold band and 2-Carat diamond was only $720 on consignment. Sales bring the prices down even more. Estate jewelry, bank-ordered liquidations and close-outs from other retail stores are all priced at least half off or more. We visited during their countdown sale and found additional savings of 60-75 percent off. Call for a rundown on the latest goodies in stock and stock up. After all, how can you go anywhere these days and not be decked out? *CK, MC, V, AE, D*

★★★ Jukajewels

817/488-8948

Grapevine, TX 76051 *By Appt. Only*

Call on the artistry of Jukajewels if you want unique neckpieces, earrings and bolos in quartz and other exotic stones. Specializing in one-of-a-kind works of jewel art, Judith Wills can be commissioned to create a look that would stop a clock. Make an appointment to see her pieces de resistance first-hand at this northeast Tarrant County location and let me know if you get this store's name right the first time out. The jewelry offered here is as far from being junky as you can possibly get, as you'll find nothing but jewelry masterpieces here. *CK*

★★★ Just Diamonds and Mounts Too

972/392-1990

Dallas, TX 75248 *By Appt. Only*

Sam Lipsie was a partner in a major jewelry store chain for the past dozen or so years. To keep his fingers in the pie, he and his wife Fran continue to offer jewelry store selection by appointment only. Keeping his overhead to the bare minimum, you can expect one-on-one personalized attention. After all, it's you, Sam, and the jewelry. Expect prices to be as low as they go. Comparing the size, quality and price is vital when comparison shopping. Most retailers do not identify the exact quality of a stone, making it hard for you to compare apples to carats. But Sam's your man to give you the lowdown. Selling any size diamond and certified stone that will cater to anyone's budget, expect to seeing the real thing, and nothing but. They also do bracelets, necklaces and earrings such as a .50-Carat round I color that sold for $1,050 retailed for $1,500); 3.02-Carat pear I color SI, for $14,500 (retailed for $22,500). Don't just ring the bell because an appointment is absolutely necessary. *CK, MC, V*

★★★★ Kazlow & Associates 214/373-3070

9400 N. Central Expwy., Suite 100 *Mon-Fri 9-5 or By Appt.*
Dallas, TX 75231 *www.kazlow.com*

This office tower is not only home to KVIL radio, but also to the showroom of Kazlow & Associates. Peek through their windows to hit a peak and chic. Add to your wish list. This downstairs jeweler can sell it to you cheaper because they're wholesalers with less overhead. No retail advertising. No mall security. And no watches. (If you want one, you'll have to order through their catalogs as none are stocked.) But if you're looking for an un-chained melody, tune in to any number of their gold chains, bracelets, mounted rings and loose stones in this salon-type venue. Shopping direct from the cutters helps chisel the costs to the core. Loose and luscious diamonds, all shapes and sizes, and you know what size fits the Diva! *CK, MC, V*

★★★★★ King Arthur Clock and Jewelry 972/423-2205

1201 N. Central Expwy. *Mon-Sat 10-6*
Plano, TX 75075 *www.kingarthurclock.com*

There's nothing plain about King Arthur. We have always courted the best for the least, and this grandfather is not only ticking 'round the clock but can save you up to 50 percent in the process. For more than 16 years, King Arthur Clock and Jewelry has carried one of the largest collections of Grandfather clocks in the Metroplex from $999 and up. HOWARD MILLER and SLIGH are just two manufacturers of the popular clocks to help you keep on the clock including wall, table and novelty models. A limited edition of Grandfather clocks, only 1,000 of which were made and fewer than 150 are left in the world, was standing tall amongst the hundreds of other Grandfather clocks and curio cabinets. Speaking of curio cabinets, do they have curio cabinets! They do make house calls for sick clocks in the Metroplex; and for a complete overhaul of your Grandfather (depending on its age and intricacy), expect to shell out around $300. Then, when they're through turning the clocks back, they'll sell you 14-Karat jewelry at $100 over wholesale. They're probably one of the best purveyors of gold jewelry and rope chains in the Metroplex, plus offering high-quality diamonds and an in-house repair service. Jim Forrest and his merry men are located at the southwest corner of 15th and Central, behind the Fina Station. *CK, MC, V, D, Layaway*

♥♥♥♥♥ Lapidary Arts

972/964-1090
3400 Preston Rd., Suite 250
Plano, TX 75093
Tue-Sat 10-6

Travel the world of opals and colored stones by landing at this showroom. Diamonds, sapphires, rubies, emeralds, rhodolites, topaz, Tanzanite and zircons are all here. But hold on to your pinkie, their specialty–opals that are bought direct from mines in Australia, Japan, Colombia, Africa and the Middle East. Prices range from $20-$20,000, but all pieces are a work of art. Rick Otte (aka, the "Opal Man") moved his store from Olla Podrida after 22 years and is now settled permanently in Plano at the intersection of Preston Rd. and Parker, next to Albertson's. He's ready when you are to put that perfect stone in (or on) your hands. Original designs that are anything but run-of-the-mill, these creations will have you shouting, "More! More! And A-More!" Deck out in the lapidary of life. *CK, MC, V, AE*

★★ Martin's Custom Jewelers

817/461-4300
412 Lincoln Sq., Suite 412
Arlington, TX `76011
Mon-Sat 10-6; Thu 10-8

Why run all over town for the Jewels Caesar. They may be in your own back yard. So, if you're looking for a jeweler that sells name-brand jewelry for less, try on Martin's Custom Jewelers on N. Collins St. just south of I-30 for a large selection of wedding bands, watches, pendants, bracelets, earrings and more. Circle your wrist with diamond tennis bracelets starting at $1,000 or wind up in a ROLEX, SCOTT KAY or TAG HEUER. Not bad company when you think about it. *MC, V, AE, D*

Medalias

214/526-1987
4901 Cole Ave.
Dallas, TX 75205
Tue-Fri 10-3

Sometimes yes, sometimes no, and sometimes their gorgeous antique-like silver jewelry can be donned by climbing to this second-floor showroom. Exit Monticello and you run smack dab into it. No signs. No address. Parking on first level. Upstairs, the showroom. It's worth the hunt for the silver bargains.

Save 50 percent and more off retail prices at their sample shop, if open. Maybe yes. Maybe no. Vintage jewelry with silver and pearls, stone and ethnic beads, gifts and belts. When Foree Hunsicker started this company 20 years ago, she had 21 luggage tags, three necklaces, one pair of earrings and a designer who doubled as a marketing and sales team. Today, she has thousands of pieces available globally in more than 1,500 specialty and department stores, including Nordstrom and Dillard's. Her Ruff Hewn Silver Collection features classic beaded and link chains matched with reproductions of antique medallions and sports' medals. Faux ivory and buffalo horn combined with sterling silver accents make up the line's Ivory Collection. The newest excitement is her Ruff Hewn Milagro Collection–small silver, bronze and copper "miracle" charms. Tiny prayer-aids, minute charms, bleeding hearts, trucks, brides, goats, donkeys, other animals, inspired by designs seen in Santa Fe's Folk Art Museum are all here, too. Hey, her designs are worn by Liz Taylor, Mary Ann Mobley, Candice Bergen and she was the winner of the Dallas Fashion Award, with another nomination this year. If and when it's open, wear Medalias proudly, for less. *C, MC, V*

★★★ Nature's Gallery — 972/446-1994

1106 South Elm St. — *Tue-Sat 10-5:30*
Carrollton, TX 75006

On the west side of the gazebo in old downtown Carrollton, look for Nature's Gallery if it's your nature to uncover the latest between a rock and a hard place. The best quality, variety and price of minerals, gems, custom lapidary, gifts and carvings in the Metroplex are available and unearthed by this Donald, the owner of the store, who is a geologist/chemist. Mosey on down to the OK Corral and see what he's unearthed. Though there are some ready-made earrings available, he prefers to custom make his own from the stones he has mined. I don't mind. Also, don't mind it if he makes them affordable. *CK, MC, V*

★★★★★ Oscar Utay Jewelry — 214/363-6591

8300 Douglas Ave., Suite 725 — *Mon-Fri 9:30-5; Sat/Evenings By Appt.*
Dallas, TX 75225 — *www.utay.com*

Carrying on the tradition established by his jeweler father, this Utay has pulled out all the treasures from the vaults his dad was hoarding from the '30s and '40s. Now, you can reap the benefits by buying these gemstones at yesteryear's prices. You may even opt for having them re-designed into a more contemporary setting. That's just one example of the kind of creativity this jeweler has to offer. A two-tone 14-Karat ROLEX that retailed for $5,300 was $1,600; a Jubilee band date model retailing for $2,600 was $1,350 with blue face and reconditioned with a 1 year warranty. A popular SUBMARINE GMT Masters in red or blue that retailed for $3,500 sped out the door at $1,950. Gold and sapphire cufflinks and a matching tie tack was $650/retail $1,200, and a money clip was $140/retail $225. Now, think of all the money you just saved. Isn't it time you called in the markers? *CK, MC, V, AE, D*

★★★★ Palazzo Diamond Importer — 972/239-3131

4532 Belt Line Rd. — *Mon-Sat 10-6; Thu 10-8*
Addison, TX 75244

Tennis anyone? Tennis bracelets, that is. Palazzo has 1- to 3-Carat diamond bracelets, with a 2-Carat model priced from $899. These delicious additions to an impressive circle of entrees whetted our appetite for more. (You know you can't stop with one chip!) Half-Carat diamond stud earrings started at $299, but what impressed us most was the courtesy and knowledge of the salesperson. He spent quite a lot of time educating us on the cut and color of the stones, and he even recommended a pair within our budget (over a more impressive and expensive but lower-quality possibility). First-class service with a smile was hardly secondary to the beckoning baguettes of emeralds egging us on or the fact that we were eyeing to scoop up several gold chains at 20 percent less than mall prices. Platinum work, jewelry repair and remounting was also available. Estate jewelry is sold and bought (usually on Saturdays when there's an estate buyer on location). Appraisals are $25 per item (which is a much better system than a percentage of the appraised value). All in all, a "Tower of Baubles." *CK, MC, V, AE, D, CB, DC, Layaway*

★★★★ Parkhill's — 817/921-4891

2751 Park Hill Drive — *Mon-Sat 10-5*
Fort Worth, TX 76109

Visit this little white house near TCU for lower prices on jewelry because it's really a manufacturer's outlet in disguise. Looking for something silver to serve up as a wedding or graduation gift? Expect 30 percent off sterling pieces as they make their own in Bangkok. Still manufacturing their own line called BARSE as well as designers such as BRIGHTON, MARY LOUISE, MEDALIAS and ROBERT CHIARELL alongside countless gift and decorator items. Gold chains to wrap around your neck and little items such as money clips, frames and small home-decor items that perfectly park in your home coffers. Park your car on Park Hill Drive, but have money left over to send your kids to Harvard's Yard. *CK, MC, V, AE, D*

★★★★★ Sam Moon Trading 972/484-3083

11429 Harry Hines Blvd. *Mon-Sat 9-6:30*
Dallas, TX 75229

To the moon, to the moon, fly yourself to Sam Moon's if you want an out-of-the-world collection of wholesale prices on handbags and jewelry. All the world loves this Moon and all the other little Moons running around helping the swarms of busy bargain beavers. Earrings and bracelets to circle the globe; enough crystals, gold, silver and rhinestones to line the runways of DFW Airport. The only problem besides the tight quarters and gargantuan crowds is having enough fingers and ears to do justice to their selection. This is the drawing card on Harry Hines that has bargain hunters pulling up from miles around, in Mercedes and pickups. Whatever your mode of transportation, this is the mother lode for loading down your handbags with jewelry and handbags. Next door, his luggage and gift outlet (Sam Moon Luggage & Gifts; see Handbags and Luggage) is also the reason he packs them in. You'll need a resale number to be tax exempt; otherwise, you pay the tax. Minimum ticket, $30. Of course, if you bought $500 worth of retail accessories for $200, giving Uncle Sam his fair share is but a pittance in return. This Sam may not be in government, but he's still the man. *CK, MC, V, AE, D, Financing*

★★★★★ Schandra 214/748-6819

2050 Stemmons Frwy. *Mon-Fri 10:30-5; Sat Call First*
Dallas, TX 75258

Though they have a showroom on the seventh floor of the World Trade Center, it seems they also want to sell wholesale to the public. Well, do they or don't they, that is the question. We headed to Market Center, across from the street from the Holiday Inn and down a bit from the Anatole, to see what we could see. Wow! Whoa! Hold that credit card! The free standing building with rocks on the side and a green canopy atop really can save you money. Lots of it. Buy fashion jewelry at wholesale or below prices. Own a piece of the rock and load up with sterling silver, watches and gifts, earrings, bracelets, bangles, necklaces and accessories. Thousands and thousands of items to choose–from handbags and scarves to SWAROVSKI crystal, from $1-$100 wholesale, this Schandra is a bombshell! *CK, MC, V, AE, D, DC, CB*

Silver Vault

214/357-7115

5655 W. Lovers Lane
Dallas, TX 75209
Mon-Sat 10-5:30

Discounts of 25-50 percent every day are found here on a huge selection of unique silver gifts, collectibles, silver jewelry, silver photo frames, baby gifts, cigar smoker accessories, barware, decanters and other wine items, as well as antique and estate silver at this shop on Lovers Lane just west of the Tollway. Custom engraving services and gift wrapping are also available. Look for extra savings (an additional 25 percent off prices) each January during the annual storewide clearance sale. *CK, MC, V*

★★★★★ Solitaires

972/517-1969

2070 W. Spring Creek Pkwy., Suite 306
Plano, TX 75023
Mon-Fri 10:45-5:30; Sat 10:45-5

The proof is in the prices. Winston Davis, a 28-year jeweler is a veteran of the jewelry business. He has been selling diamonds at up to 50 percent off at his store located next to Brookshire's at the corner of Spring Creek and Custer. This little gem of a showroom is dazzling the dames when engagement time nears. Grooms-to-be line up at Solitaires and commiserate with Winston at the intersection of Custer and Spring Creek. Why? Because Davis sells them for less. Period. Every facet of his business oozes with quality and creative juices. From engagement rings to fine Swiss watches, don't let time get away from you. Their watch brands include CALYPSO, CITIZEN, GENEVA, OMEGA, ROLEX, TAG HEUER and ZODIAC to name a few. He stocks 1-and 2-Carat diamonds (most jewelers must order them), so that alone tells you he's in it for the long haul. What a stash–for less cash! In ancient times, they used to believe that when the world was created, diamonds were solidified drops of divine essence embedded in the rocks. One of the earliest engagement rings was given to Princess Mary, daughter of Henry VII. It was the smallest ring ever given because the bride-to-be was only 2 years old. However, don't get any ideas. A girl's best friend isn't teeny, weenie. That much, I do know. *CK, MC, V, AE, D*

★★★ Southwest Precious Metals

972/644-1990

1425 E. Spring Valley Rd.
Richardson, TX 75081
Mon-Fri 10-5; Sat 10-3

Know your four C's before buying diamonds: Clarity, cut, color and ... well, these experts will help you out. Whether looking for rounds or fancies, you can stop looking for that diamond in the rough. Enough said. They sell loose diamonds as well as ready-made or custom-made jewelry. All that matters is that this family has been in the same location for almost 20 years and they sell quality, service and values. Repair and appraisal services available, and they carry colored gemstones and estate and antique jewelry. If what you C is not your cup of tea, then ask for another blend. *MC, V, D*

★★ Terry Costa 972/385-6100

12817 Preston Rd., Suite 136 *Mon-Thu 10-8; Fri-Sat 10-7; Sun Noon-6*
Dallas, TX 75230

Leave it to cleavage. This is Dallas' source for debutante jewelry and more. Located at Preston Valley at the corner of LBJ and Preston, this is the place to be seen at prom time when there's a phenomenal strapless, sequin and satin scene. When you want to tone it down for your own evening wardrobe, there's a vast repertoire of designer clothing in sizes 2-18 with accompanying accessories and jewelry. Our shoppers this year reported that only during sales are deals to be real. Still, TC is a wonderful merchant and they have joined the bridal business now in a big way. Their sportswear, too, fills in perfectly for those casual occasions where basic black just won't do. *CK, MC, V, AE, D, DC*

★★★★★ Travel Jewelry 214/369-4722

6123 Berkshire Lane *Mon-Sat 10-5*
Dallas, TX

Some folks travel far and wide to find the jewels of their dreams. In the Metroplex, all you have to do is visit Travel Jewelry. Leave the good stuff home and fool even the experts with what creative hands can craft. Wonderfully chic costume jewelry is this traveler's contribution to our mobile wardrobe at a fraction of the cost of the real thing. Why be a moving target for thieves? Impress them with more–not less! Only you and your jeweler will know. Is it or isn't it? *CK, MC, V, AE*

★★★★★ Ultra 972/724-2559

3000 Grapevine Mills Pkwy. *Mon-Sat 10-9:30; Sun 11-8:30*
Grapevine, TX 76051

Watch your gold mine discoveries become the envy of everyone's eye. This diamond and gold outlet covers the outlet mall locations by landing a gold mine in Gainesville Prime Outlets (940/668-2566), Hillsboro Prime Outlets (254/582-7070) and San Marcos Prime Outlets (512/392-2570). Quality diamonds, fine jewelry and name brand watches at guaranteed lowest prices of 20-75 percent off manufacturer's suggested retail prices every day. Then watch out. They also feature MOVADO and TAG HEUER watches, jewelry design and repair. *CK, MC, V, AE, D*

★★★★ Village Jewelers & Diamond Cutters 972/239-0323

13534 Preston Rd. *Mon-Sat 10-6; Thu 10-9*
Dallas, TX 75240 *www.villagejewelers.com*

A kiss on the hand may be quite continental, but diamonds are a girl's best friend. And at this Village, they are irresistible. Diamonds imported from South Africa and cut on a daily basis were priced at near wholesale. From marquis to baguettes, eternity bands to pave rings with rope edging, the possibilities for forging new friendships were endless. Ring mountings of 14-Karat, 18-Karat and platinum baguettes; invisible settings; channel settings all available. Custom work is done on the premises with lots of catalogs and magazines from which you can choose your design, or have them sketch out their thoughts. In-house, they perform watch and jewelry repairs, pearl restringing, appraisals, as well as purchase gold, diamonds and used ROLEX watches. They are also an authorized dealer for CITZEN, OMEGA, PHILIPPE CHARRIOL and TAG HEUER watches and jewelry. You needn't be a Village idiot. These guys know how to put the accent on the jewels, Caesar! Check the directory for the location nearest you, including their newest in Southlake. *CK, MC, V, AE, D*

★★ Zale's Outlet, The 214/689-0492

8701 John W. Carpenter Frwy., Suite 200 *Mon-Fri 10-6*
Dallas, TX 75247

Circling the globe, wonders never cease to amaze me. Zale's now have outlet stores. Rings, earrings, bracelets, pendants, watches, crystal and pens from Zale's stores (and other retailers around the country) at a savings. Well, if you mark it up high enough, then mark it down low enough, see how much savings you really get when all is said and done. Name recognition is one thing. Pristine glass-locked cases surround the perimeter of the store, including the traditional center island and at least five sales staff should would have fooled me. Watches branded with names like CITIZEN, ESQUIRE, MOVADO, SEIKO, SWISS ARMY and TAG HEUER were ticking away at less than retail prices. Check in to another location at the Prime Outlets

Center in Hillsboro, where there's much more gold jewelry, some precious and semi-precious stones and plenty of watches. *CK, MC, V, AE, D*

♥♥♥♥♥ Zozza Gallery 972/889-0440

2260 Promenade *Mon-Fri 10-6; Sat 10-5; Sun By Appt.*
Richardson, TX 75080 *www.zozza.com*

From A to Zozza, I'll give you the poop on how you can scoop up the best-looking jewelry and art class this side of the rainbow. Shop here. Plain and elegant. Yes, the prices are crystal clear and the selection will take your breath away. Our offices now look like a bull in a china shop. Glass works of art even have their own special lighting just to show it off. And, unless your name is Van Cleef or Arpel, you'll still want to shop here for a large selection of loose certified diamonds and extensive mountings in both contemporary and classic designs. And that's just the tip of the mine. Admire ... don't touch. These museum-like works of art sit gingerly side-by-side with fine jewelry, accessories and novelty watches. Each item is in a class by itself. From the whimsical to the avant-garde, this is the people's choice for conversational pieces de resistance. Assorted glass perfume bottles, sculpture (like the cat that swallowed the goldfish), candlesticks, wine buckets, vases, plates and center pieces plus gold and platinum jewelry, hand-pounded jewelry, diamonds, colored stones and freshwater pearls. Located between Belt Line and Arapaho on Coit Rd., see how the "Leisure Glass" lives. Feast your eyes on similar offerings in the Galleria at the south end of the first floor and three doors down from the Cheesecake Factory at Northwest Hwy. and Central Expwy., across from NorthPark Center in Dallas. *CK, MC, V, AE, D, Financing*

Legal & Financial

✧✧ AA USA Insurance Agency 972/644-7010

9241 LBJ Fwy., Suite 108 *Mon-Fri 8-6; Sat 9-4*
Dallas, TX 75243

Here's a refreshing revelation. A company that represents more than 30 different companies and specializes in seeking out the best price and value for your money. How's that for a change of pace? Get your insurance for less at this insurance agency and rest assured. Family owned and operated, each member of the ruling party gets in on the act making sure you get the best for less. No customer is refused, regardless of their past driving record. Seniors, young drivers under 25, first-time drivers, ticketed drivers, drivers with accidents, drivers with no prior insurance–no problem! Coverage is available for all 50 states and Canada. They even offer short-term policies (like one or two months) but they are no Rodney D. Young. If you prefer, they'll even split your down payment. If you're pleased with their service for car insurance, you'll be overjoyed with their other insurance coverage. *CK, MC, V*

✧✧✧✧ Anti-Shyster 972/418-8993

PO Box 540786 *Mon-Fri 9-5*
Dallas, TX 75254

Get a copy of this legal reform monthly for help in wading through the labyrinth of legal machinations. Get your thrills on courtroom kills. At least there is hope in that thar' legal system of injustice with a little help from Al Adask, et al. More than 10,000 copies monthly in print and now available at select newsstands in the Metroplex. If you are being strangled by the web of conspiracy between lawyers, judges and those chiefs whose cash resources seem bottomless, then start reading the news that's not fit to print elsewhere. Only available in this one-of-a-kind mood-altering alternative publication. (Do you think mainstream media would risk a lawsuit?) If you order a three-year subscription, the price drops to $20 per year. *Single Copy, $7.50; Annual, $30*

✧✧✧✧✧ Bud Hibbs, Credit & Financial Counseling 817/589-4284

PO Box 16522 *By Appt. Only*
Fort Worth, TX 76162 *www.budhibbs.com*

Once Bud becomes your om-buds-man, watch out TRW! When you're the first and foremost authority on consumer credit, you can bet your sweet credit report that life will never be the same. Author of best-selling books on the subject, *Stop It! A Consumer's Guide to Effectively Stopping Collection Agency Harassment* and *The American Credit System–Guilty Until Proven Innocent*, these are your guide books to getting back on your feet and back to answering your phone without palpitations. If you want Bud to see you privately, he works by appointment for an hourly fee; or he's available for seminars with your group or organization. This Bud's no lite (weight)! If you're desperate, drowning in credit card debt, remember, you don't have to file for bankruptcy! Meet your best friend in the credit-counseling business. Though he's not an attorney, he has done his homework and is the best at what he does. *CK*

✧✧✧✧✧ Bullock, Seger, Weaver & Co., L.L.C. 972/381-1272

17060 Dallas Pkwy., #215 *By Appt. Only*
Dallas, TX 75248

If you want savvy business advice when it comes time to crunch the numbers, this CPA firm is right up there with the best. Advising both individual and business accounts in tax planning, tax return preparation or, God-forbid, taxpayer representation, they are knowledgeable and articulate on the subject of saving you money. As much money as the law permits. This accounting service prepares financial statements, does audit reviews, helps in assessments for divorce proceedings to maximize your just rewards, complete business valuations, sales and purchases, even loan packaging. They're good. Very good.

✧✧✧ Consolidated Funding 972/644-4663

2301 Travis *By Appt. Only*
Plano, TX 75093

Get a real slugger on your side for a change and call Larry Dugger. Let him show you how to do a mortgage yourself. Whether you're purchasing or refinancing, wouldn't you like to know how to save a few hundred (maybe thousands) of bucks off that mortgage loan? Save time and trouble with a simple, one-page, loan application. Thanks to that (as well as low closing costs) you'll soon be able to join the ranks of the well-informed homeowners. *CK*

Legal & Financial

✧✧✧✧ Consumer Credit Counseling Service (CCCS) 214/638-2227

8737 King George Drive *Mon-Fri 8:30-2:50*
Dallas, TX 75235 *www.cccs.net*

Erasing your debts by filing bankruptcy is really not like wiping the slate clean. Bankruptcy does not give you that "easy start" that is promoted on TV. Rather, what the lawyers are selling you is Chapter 13 (or other bankruptcy filings). And after a bankruptcy, it is not easy getting credit for anything–a car, a home, a credit card, an education, sometimes even a job, so let your fingers do the dialing and call for an appointment with the CCCS. There are 32 offices throughout the Metroplex with counselors who will work with you and your creditors to take the pressure off. They do charge a percentage of what you owe as they whittle your debts down to a manageable amount. Expect to pay monthly, $5-$15 per month based on income, for no more than five years. To get to their main location, take I-35 to Regal Row, then east to King George and turn right. They're on the second floor of the second building on the right.

Credit Bureaus

To check your credit report once a year, you can call one of the three national credit bureaus:

TRW 800/392-1122
EQUIFAX 800/685-1111
TRANS UNION 800/916-8800

The reports are free, if you've been denied credit. TRW will send you a report yearly for free, upon request. Otherwise, the reports will cost about $8. If you find a mistake, holler! First file a dispute form and wait for a reply. The credit bureau must look into your problem and get back to you, usually within 30 days. (Be sure to clear up any errors with each of the three bureaus. If it's on one, it's probably on them all.) You can also sue the credit reporting bureaus if they do not correct the errors. But that's another story.

✧✧ Fathers for Equal Rights 214/741-4800

PO Box 50052 *Mon-Thu 8-4; Fri 8-3; Meetings Thu at 7 P.M.*
Dallas, TX 75250 *www.fathers.4kids.org*

Everything's big in Texas, and this Dallas chapter of Fathers for Equal Rights is no exception. One of the most effective support and lobbying groups in the country, this organization seeks to secure equitable treatment for fathers, mothers, children and grandparents struggling through the divorce courts. They hold weekly meetings, seminars and have legal research training available for members. With your yearly membership, you have access to a dozen simpatico attorneys and paralegals to help prepare court documents, though you will still have to pay for court costs. Join in the war stories–there is comfort in numbers. Meetings at 7 P.M. Thursdays. *$100/Annual Membership, V*

✧✧ FMI/First Mortgage Investors — 972/251-4212

1425 W. Pioneer, Suite 135 — *Mon-Fri 8-8*
Irving, TX 75061

Serving Texas since 1975, FMI claims the lowest rates and closing costs in town. Free automated loan approval (888/999-LEND), home equity loans, free credit check, confidential, individual service, first time buyer and Irving bond money are all part of their portfolio of services. Their appraisal fee was $325, credit report fee, was $55 and processing fee was $300; then, when the loan goes to an investor, there are additional fees regarding points, surveys, credit research, etc. *CK, MC, V, AE, D*

Glass, Stuart Evan (PC) — 214/363-7500

8300 Douglas Ave., Suite 730 — *By Appt. Only*
Dallas, TX 75225

Barristers and bargain are not words usually uttered in the same sentence. But there are exceptions, and Stuart Glass is one of them. He's both responsive and honest. No double dipping here. Services include litigation, contracts, business organization, commercial collections, personal injury, music and entertainment law, wills and probate, real estate, criminal matters and consumer deceptive trade litigation. This Rice University graduate in accounting and University of Texas School of Law graduate can cover the bases with basic common sense and practical application of the law. *CK*

Hill, Steven W. (CPA) — 972/242-8558

By Appt. Only

As a consulting expert with start-up businesses, Steven Hill will review your situation and advise you on doing business in a financially sound way. Number crunching and advisory munching are part of his package as are low set-up fees, one-week turnaround time, fully computerized reporting and a dedication to serving small businesses and keeping them on top of the latest tax and accounting rules. He provides a free consultation and reviews prior tax returns to make sure Uncle Sam has not received more than his rightful share. He also does turn-key bookkeeping services for small and medium-sized businesses, and is an expert in personal and corporate taxes, and business planning. As a former Big 6 accounting firm manager and community bank CFO, he provides high-fallutin' input at down-to-earth rates. This is one UTA graduate who scores with high marks.

✧✧ JobNet 972/503-5627(JOBS)

12890 Hillcrest, Suite K 109 *Mon, Wed-Fri 7:30-6; Tue 7:30 A.M.-9 P.M.*
Dallas, TX 75230

Out of work? Need a fast start? Or maybe you're looking for a temporary fix? JobNet may be the answer. This temporary, direct hire and online staffing company for administrative and office professionals is owned by Tamara Levy and is located at LBJ and Hillcrest on the southeast corner. Who says you don't receive benefits if you're a temp? After six months or the equivalency in hours, here you'll receive vacation and holiday pay. In fact, some temps are paid as much as $16 per hour. So, if you've got the skills, jump into the net. If you are looking for a permanent home, they do long-term placements as well.

✧✧✧✧ Keystone Financial Services 972/423-4170

1712 Alameda Court, Suite 100
Plano, TX 75074

Want to do-it-yourself? Then, this is the company to call if you want to sell your house "By Owner." Keystone will orchestrate the necessary promotional items like signs and flyers, as well as screen potential buyers. They'll take telephone inquiries from prospects and provide information about your house by phone or fax. They also qualify potential buyers to ensure they will qualify; therefore, no time is wasted if the candidate is not creditworthy. In return, they are able to talk up Keystone Mortgage lending opportunities. Neat idea since there are no fees involved to the seller. Keystone gets paid only if someone buying your house uses them for the mortgage. Eliminate all the hassle. This sound pretty promising. Also located in Houston.

✧✧ Paralegal Services Plus 214/637-4884

2777 N. Stemmons Frwy. *Mon-Fri 9-5*
Dallas, TX 75207

If paperwork is what you're after, rumor has it that these whiz-bangs can provide you an alternative route to routine legal matters. Specializing in will preparation, these paralegals can whip them out and set the record straight. Nothing complicated about it. It's cheaper, plain and simple. Also, these certified paralegals are notary publics and can notarize most anything as long as it's legal. All work is supervised by an attorney so there's no hanky-panky. You'll save money come hell or the Texas Probate Court. If you don't have a will, the state of Texas will be happy to provide one, but no promises that your mother-in-law won't get your favorite chair! *CK*

✧✧✧✧ Simple Law 940/575-2731

PO Box 8 *www.simplelaw.com*
Bridgeport, TX 76426

Simple Law offers online customers the opportunity to develop their own paper trail of paperwork regarding a court case. With their software, you can be sure that what you say is what you want and all details are completely accurate. By preparing your own documents with Simple Law Texas Software and Form Books, costs can be kept to a minimum. This service will save you a lot of money in the long haul. Preparing documents through a lawyer can be ... costly. They help you prepare documents for such cases as divorce, a name change, or a home equity loan. Visit them today at www.simplelaw.com. Case closed.

✧✧✧✧✧ Tinsley, Steven (Attorney) 214/221-0102

11551 Forest Central Drive, #309 *By Appt Only*
Dallas, TX 75243

If you're looking for a lawyer who sides with the good guys, this is your man. He believes legal entanglements should be avoided if at all possible, so his job is to educate his clients, keep them out of trouble and stay focused on productivity. If you've been ordered into mediation, or just want a guide through the maze of legalese, call on this consumer advocate before trouble sets in. It will pay off. He'll make you do some of the homework, like organizing the documents, or having a signed contract before you begin a relationshipto keep costs down. After you've done some of the preliminary work, he'll step in with the real "legal" eye. You can expect phone calls to be returned on the same day, filings filed on time, plus a sense of humor, compassion and integrity. Now, how many lawyers do YOU know who meet those requirements? *CK*

Legal & Financial

✧✧✧ Universal Passports and Visas

214/739-3400

7515 Greenville Ave., Suite 910
By Appt. Only
Dallas, TX 75231-3890

If you've waited until the last minute to get a passport (or to renew your existing expired one), these two veterans of the visa wars can help expedite matters. Cathy Stroud and Patrick Nicholson have over 20 years of experience getting folks off on the right foot as well as getting them in the air or on the high seas. For passports, if you aren't in any hurry, their fee is $45 for a seven-10 day processing. If you need one in a day, the cost is $125; two days, $95; and three days, $65. Visa fees depend on where you're going, but basically cost between $25 and $100. Give them a call if you need help crossing the border.
CK, MC, V, AE, D

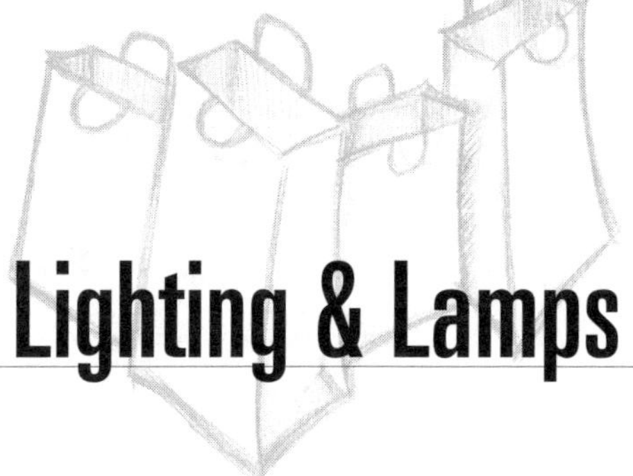

Lighting & Lamps

★★★ A to T Lamps — 972/219-9660

255A Huffines Plaza — *Mon-Fri 7-6:30; Sat 9-3*
Lewisville, TX 75057

Talk about a misnomer by any other name! This place sells light bulbs, but the light didn't go on long enough for them to get the name right. Ask about why they're missing six letters of the alphabet and maybe we'll all have a clue how this company thinks. But if you do need light bulbs, switch on. The carry fluorescents, floods, ballasts and specialty light bulbs including full spectrum and daylight fluorescents. Call for a lightning quick quote on any of your lighting needs and get out of the dark ages. *CK, MC, V, AE, D*

★★★ Arc Fan and Lighting — 817/268-2218

120 W. Bedford-Euless Rd. — *Mon-Fri 8:30-5:30; Sat 10-5*
Hurst, TX 76053

Want to be the Light of the Party? Shop for showroom lighting at its heavenly best at Arc Fan and Lighting. Be an ARC-angel, but first price it at Home Expo. Then, buy it here. Everything you've ever wanted for your home landscape, decorative, or utilitarian lighting needs is available. At least 50 different lighting manufacturers are represented, and if you don't see something you want, just let your fingers do the walking through their catalogs. Lots of them. Then, turn your attention to the ceiling fans, from CASABLANCA, CRAFTMADE, ELLINGTON, HUNTER and more, to keep your cool. Forget looking for the same old polished-brass lamps and consider the painted iron fixtures that are all the rage these days. Expect very competitive prices to rock bottom prices if you are buying a whole house full of lighting. *CK, MC, V, AE, D*

★★★★ Barrow Electrical & Lighting

817/834-2177

2820 E. Belknap St.
Fort Worth, TX 76111
Mon-Sat 7:30-5:30

For 32 years, Barrow Electrical and Lighting has been serving the Metroplex in keeping a light on the subject. If you are in the process of building a new home or have some problems with your old electrical hook-ups, then you'll want to turn to these guys first. And get this. They offer the unique service of repairing and rebuilding fixtures as well as selling you new ones. They provide electrical supplies and landscape lighting. Focus on those azaleas or that mulberry tree with a little lighting from Barrow. Also, there's a wonderful selection of brands that they sell wholesale or at direct-to-public prices. For instance, GENERAL ELECTRIC breakers, PHILLIPS lightbulbs or THOMAS LIGHTING at contractor prices. Now, you can see the light at the end of the tunnel. *CK, MC, V*

★★★★★ Benson Lighting

817/590-2266

2325 E. North Loop 820
Fort Worth, TX 76118
Mon-Fri 8-5; Sat 9-1
www.bensonlighting.com

Upscale lighting straight from the lighting markets is Benson's fame and fortune. The selection is like tripping the lights fantastic. This familyowned business wants to brighten your life and your home but not with just any old styles by any old manufacturer. Only the best will do–from contemporary to traditional, elegant to eclectic, this is your one-stop source for interior voltives. And don't keep the light just indoors. They sell flood lights, wall sconces, and path lighting, too. All the best ceiling fans help keep the lid on utility costs, too, sporting names like CASABLANCA, MONTE CARLO and REGENCY. Then, if you don't want to get up off your easy seat, log on to their online site where you can view their products before you move a muscle.

★★★★★ Classic Galleries Outlet Store

214/630-4074

7101 Carpenter Frwy.
Dallas, TX 75247
Tue-Sat 10-6; Sat 10-5

Shady ladies shop at Classic Galleries Outlet Store. Thousands of lamp shades and hundreds of finials (you know, those wonderful little toppings that every shade, not on a diet, deserves). Can't top that! Probably not. Theirs is probably the largest selection of lamp shades in the Southwest. But, I bet you didn't know they are also a source for frames, thousands of prints, framed art (from $10 up), accessories and more–but don't expect art to be discounted, unless marked on sale. If you're shopping for a frame, try-ons in the middle of the floor are welcome, and don't forget to choose from many unique and imaginative moldings for custom frames. Though they don't carry STIFFEL lamps, they do carry their lampshades. One last plug: they were full of ceiling fan pulls, too. Visit their other location in Arlington, 770 E. Road To Six Flags, Lincoln Square (they are behind the fountain) 817/795-8787, open Mon-Fri 10-6 and Sat 10-5. *CK, MC, V, AE*

♥♥♥♥♥ Cover Ups 972/496-3663

Garland, TX *By Appt. Only*

You spend hours of your time trying to get just the right lamps and lights to match your interior home design. So why not the covers on the switches that turn those lights on? Toland McKinney will design a Cover Up from an original artistic design. It can glow in the dark, match your fabric, colors, wallpaper, or sport your child's favorite team logo. Cover Ups start at $7 a switchplate, but are limitless when it comes to ideas. They will custom design wallpaper to match your furniture as well.

★★★★★ Dealers Lighting (Lighting Showcase) 972/509-0116

1400 Summit, Suite 3C *Mon-Fri 7:30-5; Sat 8-12*
Plano, TX 75074

Lighten Up! is their mission statement so expect to see one of the largest selection of first-quality discounted lighting in the Metroplex. Waiting to enlighten you, turn on to crystal, brass, iron-based lamps, be it for the table or the floor in brands such as GEORGIAN, LIGHTOLIER, KICHLER or QUOIZEL. Fan yourself with a CRAFTMADE fan or special order HUNTER ceiling fans as well as track or fluorescent lighting. If you're in the dark, choose from their wide selection of light bulbs, framed prints or decorative accessories. Whatever your plan, there's a staff lighting expert to help you. You know dealers will only shop at the low-price leader, that's why they're Dealers. So shop with the Dealers ... and spell it with all lower $ cases, please. It has been proven that if you lower your overhead, the shoppers will come. Being located in East Plano near the intersection of Plano Road/Plano Parkway has helped. Whether you're building a new home or simply adding a lamp, this electrical supply company will electrify you with their low prices. Light up your bath, kitchen or living areas for less. Such a deal(er)! *CK, MC, V*

★★★ Elect-A-Van/dba EVS Supply

972/231-5351
1350 E. Arapaho, Suite 126
Mon-Fri 8:30-5; Sat 10-3
Richardson, TX 75081
www.evssupply.com

Here's the source to reduce any assault and battery charges. Just like the Energizer Bunny, this little battery and lighting shop keeps going and going and going. Batteries and bulbs were available by check or charge in every conceivable shape and size, and they are especially noteworthy for vintage production and antique collectible lamps that won't work with the standard grocery store bulbs. There were batteries for everything portable, including custom-made models. Now that's a star performance. From incandescents to metal halogens, you can also select audio and video tapes (what?) at about 20 percent below retail. Go figure. *CK, MC, V, D*

★★★ Fan Factory Outlet

817/244-5888
7948 Hwy. 80 West
Mon-Sat 9-6
Fort Worth, TX 76116
www.fansales.com

Celebrating over a decade in business, this company has plenty of fans out there. Pay a visit and play, "Let's make a deal!" Fans, home lighting, bath bars, wall sconces and coach lights are part of the Walters' family inventory. He's got fans hanging around day and night with names such as AIRWIND, HUNTER, LIGHTOLIER, ROYAL PACIFIC and others. Shopping here for ceiling fans was a breeze. Lots of inexpensive fans to blow hot or cold were priced lower than the home centers and were in a multitude of colors and styles for under $39.95. Unless you want museum-quality or a fan that'll last a lifetime, these affordable fans (mostly made in Taiwan or by low-end USA manufacturers) can be found in all styles, some for as low as $25. Special orders are welcome. A 5-year warranty on motors should keep you revved up, at least for a while, with a smile. Think of them as a "quick fixture!" *CK, MC, V, AE, D*

★★★ Fans, Lights, Etc.

972/985-0096
2809 W. 15th St.
Mon-Fri 8-5; Sat 9-5
Plano, TX 75075

Talk about the glass ceiling that exists in some businesses today. Look to them to keep you suspended in fans and lights for a lifetime. Turn on to action, and scope out the joint. Low and behold, we found some pretty decent prices. They carry both the name-brand CASABLANCA as well as a lower-priced fan called CRAFTMADE, beginning as low as $54. Either can serve your purposes admirably. For a five-blade 52-inch fan, this was a sweet deal, though lights are extra. All your better lighting fixtures are available. Better quality than Home Depot and less expensive than Home Expo–well, that's good news. They have an admirable selection of decorative wall sconces, track lighting, dimmers, door bells and mirrors that came shining through this year, too. *CK, MC, V*

★★★★ Hughes-L & S Interiors — 214/750-4670

175 Preston Forest Village — *Mon-Fri 9-5; Sat 10-5:30*
Dallas, TX 75230

Hughes has been a source of shady deals since 1970. Not in the pejorative sense, mind you, but in being a recognized leader in selling lamp shades in every shape and size. James W. Kerr has offered thread-bare lampshades a way out of their darkened misery with more than 5,000 in stock. FREDERICK COOPER, STIFFEL and crystal WATERFORD lamps can always shed some light on the subject. With much of their inventory discounted to as much as half off, they don't stop there. Considered specialists in lamp repairs, $15.90 and up, they are also an authorized STIFFEL lamp repair service center. During our visit, all their chandeliers were 40 percent off–an illuminating experience! For custom reshading or restyling, you'll only be out $24.90 (sometimes more, depending on the intricacy of the job). Save 20-50 percent on floor lamp samples as well as custom draperies, mini-blinds, wood blinds, shutters and upholstery. Don't forget to rummage through the boxes of sample fabrics to save time as well as money. *CK, MC, V*

★★★★ Lakewood Lighting — 214/826-5980

341 Hillside Village — *Mon-Fri 9:30-5; Sat 10-4*
Dallas, TX 75214

Walk down the Abbey Road in the heart of legendary Lakewood, and lo and behold, you'll run into a plethora of prime-time lights. You can expect to find your usual fare of lamps and fixtures here along with ceiling fans, chandeliers and the like, but their real forte is in shades (starting under $10) and in making lamps out of unusual containers, such as your favorite vase, cowboy boot, or any treasure (antique or otherwise). At least, you won't have to keep your budget in the dark. Here, it can be kept in the shade. What really turned us on was the fantastic selection of market samples in table and floor lamps. Samples mean greater savings. The prices were electrifying! They can, of course, design one for you, too. Take your lamp in for some R & R (repair and restoration!)

as they are experienced craftsmen at the process of illumination. They are an authorized STIFFEL repair service, also. *CK, MC, V*

★★★★ Lamp House — 214/946-2372

923 Wynnewood Village — *Mon-Sat 10-5:30*
Dallas, TX 75224

The Lamp House has been burning bright in the same location for 30 years now, and it looks like it's going to remain a fixture on the Dallas scene. Turn on to lamps of all shapes and sizes–chandeliers, floor lamps, table lamps, Tiffany-styles, halogens, and wall scones with STIFFEL a stand-out name. Market samples at half-price were not a filament of our imagination, either. Head on down to the Lamp House and shed some light on the subject of saving money. If they don't have it in stock, they can order it at some of the best prices in town. This year they've expanded their selection to include French furniture and other brands like CELLINI, KIMBALL and UNION CITY. They are also an authorized STIFFEL lamp repair service and showcase for SCHONBEK chandeliers. *CK, MC, V, AE, Layaway*

★★★★★ Landscape Lighting Supply Co. — 972/480-9700

818 S. Central Expwy. — *Mon-Fri 8-5; Sat 10-2*
Richardson, TX 75080 — *www.landscapelight.com*

In the dark about a specialty lighting store? Let me illuminate you on the subject. They are the only folks in town to turn on to if you are looking for an extensive selection of outdoor landscape lighting. Expect prices to be wholesale. Did I say wholesale? They will refer you to an installer if you choose not to do-it-yourself. They are, in fact, a distributor for about 15 different manufacturers such as FOCUS, GREENLEE, KICHLER, LUMIERE and TECHLIGHT–all at wholesale prices. Did I say wholesale? "It is better to light just one little candle, than to stumble in the dark!" *CK, MC, V*

♥♥♥♥♥ Light Motif — 972/964-0630

3100 Independence Pkwy, Suite 304 — *Mon-Fri 10-6; Sat 10-5*
Plano, TX 75075

Put a light on any subject–literally. Not only does this store offer a wide selection of lamps and shades, they also provide a full compliment of interior design services. Unique custom lamps, window treatments, custom shades, lamp repairs and design suggestions for your home. What were you expecting. It's not a heavy motif. Watch for "buy one—get second at 50 percent off" sales; otherwise, you will be paying retail. *CK, MC, V, D*

★★★★★ Lighting Connection 972/964-1946

2001 Coit Rd., #164 *Mon-Fri 9-6; Sat 9-4*
Plano, TX 75075

Remember your mother telling you to not put your finger in the socket? Well, if you want to connect to savings (at least 20 percent across the filaments) on lights and ceiling fans, you'll have to turn on here. At Lighting Connection, you'll be in lights–more than 2,000 fixtures in stock. What a bolt of energy for war-torn budgets! In the bunkers, you can bank on indoor and outdoor lighting, wall sconces, foyer lamps in brands such as ART, FORECAST, GEORGIAN, MAXIM, THOMAS, SAVANT, WILSHIRE–both classic and design lighting can shade the glaring price of paying retail. When you care enough to light the very best, this is your connection. Turn on to another location in Irving, 3301 Royalty Row. So come on baby, light their lights. *CK, MC, V, AE, D*

★★★★★ Lights Fantastic 214/369-1101

4645 Greenville Ave. *Mon-Fri 9-6; Sat 9-5:30; Sun Noon-5*
Dallas, TX 75206

Light-en up! Brighten up! This is where you'll find one of the best selections, the best prices and the best names in the lighting business. That's why we are their biggest fans. And speaking of fans, do they have fans! They also have a stellar selection of lights, lamps and lighting fixtures, all the better quality brands, at store-wide savings of 20-80 percent off. They carry MOGUL BASE bulbs (you can't find them anywhere), CASABLANCA ceiling fans and the best in home decor lighting. Turn on to the GEORGE KOVACS collection of Halogen lamps and make tracks to LIGHTOLIER track lighting. Looking for QUOIZEL, the TIFFANY-endorsed replicas? Want a chandelier? Bathroom lighting? Outdoor lighting? Under-the-counter lighting? Also find plant lights, long-lasting bulbs and anything to do with fluorescent lighting. Plus, they have the largest selection and one-of-a-kind collection of contemporary lights in the Metroplex. My favorite? The ballet dancers strung across the ceiling. This is their only location in the Metroplex, so if you can't find it here, light a candle instead. *CK, MC, V, AE, D*

★★ Nathan Frankel Electric 817/336-5656

1109 Lamar *Mon-Fri 8-5; Sat 8-Noon*
Fort Worth, TX 76102

One Nathan was famous for hotdogs, this Nathan's into lights. So, let's shed a little light on the subject of lights, shall we? Nathan's is a small but bright Mom and Pop shop. By keeping a lower overhead, Frankel can provide lower prices. "Capiche?" You'll have plenty of choices in quality and styles just the same. We rang the NUTONE chimes, then breezed through the collection of QUOREM (formerly called DAVENPORT) brands of ceiling fans. Other notable brands included ADVANCE, PHILLIPS and PROGRESS for the full compendium of lighting complements, built-in vacuum systems, heat lights and range hoods. You just can't miss here. All lighting and electrical supplies are available, plus a down-home, "Can we help you" attitude. Now, that's a switch! *CK*

★★★★ Reese Interiors 817/292-9191

3861 S.W. Loop 820 *Mon-Fri 8-6; Thu 8-8; Sat 9-5*
Fort Worth, TX 76133

Exit Granbury Road, loop around to the south side of the service road, and you have made one of the best decisions your home will ever know. Under one roof, this is your one-source showroom for home decorating–for lighting, floors, rugs, drapery and wallpaper. The fun begins, starting at the bottom of the alphabet with carpeting, every kind of flooring is grounded on their low-price guarantee and includes installation over premium padding, moving of furniture and vacuuming. No hidden costs. We saw pecan flooring (the most durable in the woods) and knew we were nuts to ever pay retail again. Next, on to lighting–on DALE TIFFANY, the Tiffany-authorized reproductions, you not only get substantial discounts, you can be assured that they have the largest selection of Tiffany in Fort Worth (that means lamps, pendants, chandeliers and fixtures). Another winner is their FRANK LLOYD WRIGHT lighting interpretations...close to museum-quality, just not the real McCoys. They also feature professional lighting design and planning, and their lighting lab showcases energy-efficient fixtures that illuminate your home or office properly. Call for a free energy-audit for your home and let them shed some interesting light on the subject of saving you money. And lastly, custom draperies made in their own workroom ensure the perfect window treatment. Six months same as cash with no interest or payments with approved credit. And we didn't even make it to the 1,000s of rolls of wallpaper and borders. This is a go! *CK, MC, V, AE, D*

Lighting & Lamps

★★★★ A Shade Better 972/758-0926

4757 W. Park Blvd., # 104 *Mon-Sat 10-6; Sun 1-5*
Berkeley Square Shopping Center
Plano, TX 75093

Ah, shades of color, shades of mystery, shades for lamps. This store makes more than a shade of difference when it comes time to color in the lines. Color yourself smart with this lights-on addition to the Metroplex. More than 300 lamps, 200 finials and 2,000 lamp shades make the difference between a plain Jane and an electrifying showplace. Choose from colorful ceramics, wonderful wrought irons, pretty porcelains, classical crystals or beautiful brass styles. Located in the Berkeley Square Shopping Center in Plano, one block east of Preston Road, all lamps are priced 20-25 percent off suggested list price. Or, you can bring in your lamp and try on the many shades for the perfect fit. Even if your old lamp has seen too many hours, bring it on in as they don't discriminate against age. Repair service available. Their second location is in Lewisville at 500 E. FM 3040, #124, 972/315-6325. *CK, MC, V, D*

★★★★★ Texas Lamp Manufacturers 972/564-5267

505 E. Hwy. 80 *Mon-Sat 10-6*
Forney, TX 75126

Let there be lights! Head to Forney, folks, that's all there is to it. Exit Talty Road. Still one of the largest lamp manufacturing showrooms (7,000 square feet) in the Southwest, they moved last year from their Oak Cliff on E. Kiest in Forney where the action is. If you can't find a lamp to turn you on in their showroom, they'll custom-make one for you that will! Save 30-50 percent on hundreds, no, thousands (brass, crystal, and statue lamps) throughout their warehouse. They also have lamp repair, shades sold or recovered, custom shades, brass planters and accessories included in their inventory. Far from the maddening crowd, it's worth a drive to see where the King of Lamps has set up shop. The highlight of your trip will be that you can finally see the light. With the selection and the savings, your dim-witted days are over. *CK, MC, V*

Linens

★★★ Bed, Bath & Beyond

972/991-8674

5100 Belt Line Rd., #1000
Village on the Parkway
Dallas, TX 75240

Mon-Sat 9-9; Sun 11-7
www.bedbathandbeyond.com

Five locations in the Metroplex: Dallas, Addison, Plano, South Arlington, Grapevine; they guarantee that they will not be undersold. In fact, they even accept competitor's coupons. Their exclusive GLACIER stainless steel flatware 20-piece set is $49.99. LIBBEY 16-piece glassware set, $14.99. JOYCE CHEN four-piece wok set, $29.99. Sheet sets, $5.39-$119.99, including cotton, flannel, jersey and cotton/polyester. National computerized bridal and gift registry if you are stuck for a present. This is the place for value-conscious homeowners looking for a cheap sheet. They will match any competitor's prices, period, and they are always priced lower than department stores. More than 70,000 items are housed on two floors, with housewares and lifestyle accessories on the first floor and bed and bath items on the second. Their real strength, though, is in the numbers and in their supposed uncompromising service. (One out of two ain't bad!) Find BAY LINENS, CROSHILL, FARBERWARE waiting to be picked up. If it was made for the kitchen or bath, you'll probably find it here. On the weekends, the place is hopping with demonstrations. However, the discounts were a bit watered-down in our shopper's mind (which was also boggled by the time she left). Call 800/GO-BEYOND for the location nearest you. *CK, MC, V, AE, D*

★★★★★ Bedandbath.com

972/239-5336

www.bedandbath.com

At Bedandbath.com, when it comes time to say beddy (good) buys, you can say goodbye to retail prices. As its name suggests, you'll be online with good buys including ABUNDANCE, ACHIM, BEACON LOOMS,

BURLINGTON, CARNIVALE, CREATIVE BATH, CROSCILL, GALLIC ASSOCIATES, HOME SWEET HOME, JANIC, KIRSCH, MARTEX, NEWMARK, PEREGINA, PERFECT FIT and THE VINEYARD. You'll never leave your comfort suites with this pampering ensemble. When it's time to lay down to sleep at night, you will have the best prices on sheets, comforter sets, down and duvet covers, bedspreads, bed ruffles, mattress pads and accent pillows. Then, when the alarm goes off, it's off to the bath with towels, towel bars, bath rugs, hampers, shower curtains, wicker and personal care items. But don't let the neighbors peek. Cover up with window treatments, from toppers to kitchen curtains. At last, it's time to sit down for breakfast with your new table dressings complete with all the famous tabletop manufacturers; you'll find other home decor, too, like pillows, candles, lamps and storage systems. Lowest price guaranteed or they'll refund the difference, plus 5 percent. They pay for shipping for orders over $250 and they offer a 60-day return policy–no questions asked. Shop online at www.bedandbath.com for all of the great deals. *CK, MC, V, AE, D*

★★★★ C&E Custom Bedspreads — 817/485-4422

4209 Clay Ave. — *Mon-Fri 8-5*
Fort Worth, TX 76117

It's hard to believe, but there are still folks out there bedding down with retail-priced bedspreads, pillow shams, dust ruffles, custom headboards, pillows, and coordinating window treatments. What a sham! If you don't have a lot of dough-re-me, this is the place for your bedroom bounty. You supply the fabric, they do the rest (labor and batting). From twin size to king size, they can cover you head to toe from $174 (twin), $180 (full) and $215 (king), dust ruffles from $51-$73 and pillow shams ($31-$39.50). Cording, ruffles and extra stuff costs extra, of course. Allow three-four weeks for turnaround time; then it's time to go undercover. *CK*

★★★★ Home Elements — 214/637-0010

7900 Ambassador Row — *Mon-Fri 9-4*
Dallas, TX 75247

This outlet just can't make up its mind. Are they or aren't they in the outlet business? If they decide yes, you're in like Flint. If they're aren't, you are bereft! A place for linens and things like fabrics, pillows, table and bed linens made for some of the specialty and department stores like Bloomingdale's around the country can be found here. Between Mockingbird and Regal Row, you should be in thread-count heaven when you see the workmanship and upscale styles. Comforters, pillows, runners, place mats, napkins, and fabric, for example, neatly displayed adjacent to their manufacturing site. (Shar-pei on premises. Beware!) Beautiful $200-$300 green floral duvet covers in a multitude of sizes went out the door for $90. Not bad, considering the source! *CK, MC, V*

★★★★★ Linens 'n Things — 214/265-8651

10720 Preston Rd., Suite 1008 — *Mon-Sat 9-9; Sun 10-7*
Dallas, TX 75230 — *www.linensnthings.com*

Find a house full of items at this linen superstore to make your life more comfortable. Of the big- three linen superstores, shoppers liked this one best for prices as well as selection. They have aisles and aisles of CAMBRIDGE sheets, ROYAL VELVET pillows and comforters, small appliances, decorative accessories, and more. Save 25-50 percent throughout the domestics collection. FIELDCREST, WAVERLY, SPRINGMAID, WAMSUTTA, and CROSFEL are all names you can rest your head on easily. The competition has begun horning in on their territory, but as reported by area underground shoppers, this place still has the better prices for bedding, baths, and linens and things, but it's a good thing pillows don't talk! Check directory for location nearest you. *CK, MC, V, AE, D*

★★★ Luxury Linens @ Burlington Coat Factory — 972/613-1333

2021 Town East Blvd. — *Mon-Fri 10-9; Sat 11-9; Sun 10-6*
Mesquite, TX 75050 — *www.burlingtoncoatfactory.com*

There are more than just coats inside Burlington Coat Factory. Welcome to Luxury Linens, where you'll also find low, low prices on linens to help keep out the chill. With these sheets and comforters, you don't have to wear gloves! A full-size, hand-crafted Americana quilt was $39.88 compared with a retail price of $125. We also found cord and heart-shaped chintz throw pillows, floor pillows and bed rests at prices that kept us sitting up reading all night. They have great-looking framed posters and photo frames, all kinds of comforters and shams, plus a collection of Sheet Music that sang us to sleep. However, they don't have the depth of inventory as the other linen superstores. Nevertheless, they do tempt you to stay in bed all day. If you want to revolutionize your sleeping habits, start by cutting corners here. Check directory for other locations–all inside the Burlington Coat Factory stores. *CK, MC, V, AE, D, Layaway*

★★★★★ Peacock Alley Outlet Store

972/490-3998
13720 Midway Rd., #203
Mon-Sat 9:30-5:30
Dallas, TX 75244

Proud as a peacock, this Dallas-based manufacturer has a deal you can't refuse. Not if you love linens and lace and a trace of the Grace Kelly lifestyle. Seconds, samples and discontinued items as well as their complete line of first-quality merchandise (at regular price, though very competitive) are all stacked floor to ceiling. Duvet covers, pettiskirts, shams–what a shame you'll have to hide under their covers. Don't quack up, either. Their close-outs of down products, hand-woven blankets, throws, sleepwear and bath products are plumes in any linen closet. Too, if you like to lay out with a European flair, this is the alley to oop! Feather your nest or your next shower or wedding gift with something decadent for the bed or bath. Celebrations are held periodically and we snatched up half-price Egyptian cotton robes and 650 down-filled comforters; table linens for $35 and below; duvet sets from Portugal that included a pair of shams (embroidered white on white), queen-set retailed for $250, their price $99. Baby, baby, what a wonderful selection of baby items from bumper covers to duvets. Fabulous 100 percent cotton bath towels and bath sheets in white and ivory that were originally $60 were found for $25 and bath towels were soaked up from $30-$12. Now, all you have to do is not let the bed bugs bite! Located next to Cutting Corners between Alpha and Spring Valley. *CK, MC, V, AE*

★★★★★ WestPoint Pepperell Factory Outlet

940/380-0045
5800 North I-35, Suite 508
Mon-Sat 10-8; Sun 11-6
Denton Factory Stores
www.westpointstevens.com
Denton, TX 76201

You don't have to be a graduate of WestPoint to separate the wheat from the sheets. Why shop the department stores when you can get the same names at outlet prices from the factory? This one's a hum-dinger! It has the best prices on the most popular brands produced by WestPoint Pepperell in the Metroplex. Save by day as well as by night by shopping for designer linens at discounts of up to 70 percent off. Choose the lighter weighs of down comforters for year-round snuggling; the heavy-duty versions are best if you're moving to Minnesota. There are over 10,000 square feet of bed, bath and kitchen linens and things. Mattress covers, pillows, quilts, matching sets and individual items. Sleep on names like MARTEX, RALPH LAUREN and UTICA (STEVENS). Towels, bath sheets, duvet covers, comforters, pillow shams, shower curtains, bathroom accessories–I dare you to compare the selection anywhere else. Twin sheets for $2.99 is the best example of short-sheeting in the Metroplex. Frequent specials and huge bargain bins sweeten the pot-pourri! *CK, MC, V, AE, D*

Miscellaneous or Other

★★★★ Casket Store, The

214/696-3123

11111 N. Central Expwy. *By Appt. Only*
Dallas, TX 75243

If you suffer from claustrophobia, you'll probably feel boxed in here. It's really a dead-end issue, but if you want to save some money consider this direct-to-the-public casket store for caskets, markers and urns. Not sure if they still recommend the plain pine boxes, but they can save you thousands of dollars. Immediate delivery to any DFW funeral home. (Guess you don't want to wait too long.) And listen to this guarantee: "They promise the handles don't break off and the bottoms won't fall out." Sure glad to hear that. Located between Forest and Royal. Call 214/696-3443 for a recorded message. *CK, MC, V, D*

Coupon Explorer

Dallas, TX *24 Hours Online*
www.couponx.com

It's as easy as 1, 2, 3. First, select the city you want to search. Two, select a category. Three, select a company. OK, so there's a fourth and fifth step–print the coupon and head out to save money. You also have the option of doing a keyword search if you are more interested in a specific product than staying in your backyard to shop. By creating a profile, you can enroll in the personal coupon service and you will be notified when coupons matching your profile are added.

✧✧ Restland Funeral Home & Cemetery

972/238-7111

13005 Greenville Ave. *By Reservation/Appt. Only*
Dallas, TX 75382

It didn't take long for the big funeral homes to feel the squeeze from discounters. The movement afoot is nationwide to control costs on the last expenditure of your life. So, like other consumer categories in which you're dying to know where to get it for less, Restland has what they call their Caring Funeral Plan. A one-stop, all inclusive casket, service, transportation, and caring attention for a fee of $1,900. Of course, I haven't picked the fabric or the finish (of course, I would like a faux finish to simulate marble), but you can make these pre-arrangements for as little as $26/month. (Be sure, though, to inquire about the financing charges.) After the fact, it doesn't count. Burial plots can run from $2,650 each on up but there are often specials for quantity purchases. (Even funeral homes can offer "two-fers"!) Their standard package is a double (two plots) for $5,800, which includes a companion marker and two concrete boxes. Caskets are separate, as are burial services at the chapel or graveside. For the ultimate cheap, the lowest cost of a funeral, without casket, was $1,595. And, with good credit, some financing can be arranged. *CK, MC, V, AE, D*

Music & Books

★★★★★ 75% Off Books 972/423-8120

1717 E. Spring Creek Pkwy. *Mon-Sat 10-8; Sun Noon-6*
Plano, TX 75074 *www.75offbooks.com*

You won't have to read between the lines here. No "clause for suspicion!" This is it as far as books are considered. Aim your sites to the Plano Outlet Mall, between Garden Ridge and TJ Maxx, and discover what everybody's writing home about. Even if you're not a reader, you can still bookmark savings of 75 percent off. Like under $5, man. Like cheap, man. Art books, cookbooks, computer books, health and fitness books, maps, fiction, kids' books, coffee table editions, fiction, if it's in print, expect it to be sandwiched near a little café called Reza's for a little down-home cooking and you can even read through your lunch hour. All books are new! All are under $5! All are 75-90 percent off! For example, all Network Certification Books that were regularly priced at $49.99 were only $4.99. You don't even have to read the fine print. Am I impressed? You betcha. Turn the pages at another location at LBJ/Preston Road (on the northeast corner), 972/702-0414 and a huge new location at 5152 Rufe Snow Drive, Suite 2872 (Rufe Snow and Loop 820). *CK, MC, V*

♥♥♥♥♥ Bill's Records 972/234-1496

8136 Spring Valley *Mon-Thu 10:30-10; Fri-Sat 10:30-Midnight; Sun Noon-10*
Dallas, TX 75240 *www.billsrecords.com*

See no evil. Speak no evil. But hear everything else at Bill's Records. THE place to find anything recorded. Bill is a legend in his own time and in swing time, rock time, any old time. But if it's a hot time in the ole town tonight, he has it, too. If he doesn't, chances are you'll get no-Billed anywhere else. See what's spinnin' in the latest CDs and rockin' and rollin' to thc young "in" crowd and old "hip" too. Bill is definitely in tune with the younger generation and has amassed probably the largest collection of records, tapes and CDs in the Southwest. Don't groove on records? Try T-shirts, posters or the cool atmosphere instead. The hip staff can point you in the direction of your musical taste or suggest an interesting side-trip. Maybe you'd like someone to take you back to CHICAGO? Or does the FRANK SINATRA boxed set turn your brown eyes blue? The inventory here will make your head spin faster than a 78 rpm. Between the incredible selection and the knowledgeable staff, you'll find a trip to Bill's an experience that won't slow you down. *CK, MC, V, AE, D*

★★★★ Book Rack 214/221-0064

10233 E. Northwest Hwy., Suite 432 *Mon-Sat 11-7*
Dallas, TX 75238

Rack 'em up and pack 'em to go. If you're a bibliophile, this is heaven sent. What a novel idea! Trade two-for-one (or pay half price) paperback store. Now nestled into their new location on East Northwest Highway, you can begin thumbing through thousands of paperbacks that were read 'afore ya. Take half off the cover or leave the cover intact and trade two-for-one instead. They'll take paperbacks and magazines for in-store trade credits–but they don't seem to care much for hardbacks. Every book is alphabetized by author and category: mystery, biography, true crime, science fiction, fantasy, horror, suspense, women's issues, inspirational, young adult, children, classics and romance. You'll also find stationery, gifts like bookends, book covers and a myriad of different kinds of bookmarks, stickers, stencils, tattoos, T-shirts and other literary sidelines. They are also the place to come for assigned reading material for middle and high school students. Also check the Arlington store at 2304 W. Park Row, 817/274-1717, and the Rufe Snow location in North Richland Hills at 817/656-5565. *CK*

★★★ Book Swap 817/284-2513

6618 Grapevine Hwy. *Mon-Fri 10-6; Sat 9-5*
Richland Hills, TX 76180

Listen to your heart and read a "Word's Worth" of savings. Drop in and swap out. More than a million books (new and used paperbacks and hardbacks) are in stock every day at this incredible book source. Does that make your head spin? Never fear, if you lose your sense of direction, they've got maps, including Mapscos, here to get you back on track. Need to pass a final? Try cramming your head full of Cliff's Notes. Records, tapes, computer books, cassettes, and videos–join the readers in the '90s and recycle your reading matter. (In other words, a tit-le for a tat!) Watch for their legendary Christmas sale where everything in the store is half-off during the final Christmas shopping week. They ship books all over the world via their new website or in-town delivery. Read my lips. There's no excuse not to read a book. *CK, MC, V, AE*

♥♥♥♥♥ Booked Up 940/574-2511

216 S. Center St. *Mon-Sat 10-5*
Archer City, TX 76351

About 10 years ago, Larry McMurtry, author of *Lonesome Dove* and *Terms of Endearment*, opened a book shop/warehouse in the town used as the setting when they turned his novel *The Last Picture Show* into a picture show. You'll find Booked Up scattered over four large brick-and-stone store-fronts scattered around the town. (Just don't look for the actual "picture show" on the square. It burned down several years ago and hasn't been rebuilt.) Books range from $5 for new to $5,000 for rare collector editions. McMurtry has been building the business as a way to heal both the dying small town as well as himself. Don't be surprised if you find the famed author himself hauling books around or if you are heartily greeted by Book Kitty (the stores' official feline). Even more likely is this small town becoming a book mecca. *CK, MC, V, AE, D*

★★★★★ Budget CDs & Records 972/278-4333

2918 S. Jupiter *Tue-Fri 11-7; Sat-Sun 10-7*
Garland, TX 75041

Talk about a Title Wave! These folks are all the rave. But turn on your caveat emptor meter when shopping here, for although CDs were touted as being indestructible when first introduced, we've learned otherwise now that they're reaching old age. Hold it up to the light and look for deep scratches and you'll be fine. You'll find more than 6,000 new and used CDs in stock, more than 5,000 new and used cassettes and almost 10,000 new and used LPs. Plus they have a huge selection of new and used movies. Whew! The selection is indeed hard to beat. Get out those headsets and turn on to everything from Pink Floyd to Van Halen, Pearl Jam to the Beatles, Hanson to Manson. On the west side of Vikon Village, just north of Kingsley. Bring your walking shoes and expect large crowds on the weekends. *CK, MC, V, AE, D,*

★★★★★ CD Source 214/890-7614

5500 Greenville Ave., Suite 201 *Mon-Thu 10-10; Fri-Sat 10-10:30;*
Dallas, TX 75206 *Sun Noon -10*

Add CD Source to your Chopin Liszt but not for Chopin or Liszt. Why pay more when you can turn the tables and head to this source located in Old Town Shopping Center? Boogie on down to find hot new and old music at cool prices. Find new and used compact discs (more than 70,000 in stock) at the lowest prices in Dallas. Hear the harmonious commingling of their gigantic selection of imports, hard-to-find items as well as thousands of new titles for $7.99 or less. These wonder-discs come with a 30-day guarantee (but only with receipt), so abused sounds need not be a concern here. CD Source buys more and pays more for your CDs ($4.50 and more on trades just can't be beat!) *CK, MC, V, AE, D*

★★★ CD Universe 972/307-3337

4043 Trinity Mills *Mon-Wed 11-9; Thu-Sat 11-10; Sun Noon-6*
Carrollton, TX 75287

Around the world with the Sounds of Music makes perfectly good sense when you shop CD Universe. They are a wonderful source for saving money on the more than 4,000 pre-owned, gently heard compact discs in stock. If you want to buy, sell or trade CDs, this is a good starting place, whether you are in Carrollton or Valley Ranch (their second location is now open at MacArthur and Belt Line). Look for sale CDs–you never know what you'll find of interest in the "we haven't been able to sell it yet so we're marking it down" stack. Bring a stack of your outcasts with you and leave with plenty of new to add to your racks. *CK, MC, V, AE*

★★★★★ CD Warehouse 817/469-1048

1114 N. Collins St. *Mon-Sat 10-10; Sun Noon-8*
Arlington, TX 76011 *www.cdwarehouse.com*

Can you Handel it? This chain of melodies lingers on throughout the Metroplex and although they don't look very warehousey, they hold enough CDs to merit the name. Gently used CDs could be heard from 30-50 percent off new, priced at $5.99 and $9.99. The selection is substantial–every CD we ever wanted (or didn't know even existed) was in stock. Brand-new titles could be had for $10.99-$12.99. They buy, they sell, they trade and we win. Slow sellers of major artists are bought for $2. Hear the sound of music on more than 20,000 titles! Lay down $20 for imports and gold discs, and you're hearing a winner. This title wave is sweeping the Metroplex. Check directory for other area locations. Examine all merchandise carefully to make sure everything's in harmony so that the melody will linger on. *CK, MC, V*

Music & Books

★★★ CD World

214/826-1885

5706 E. Mockingbird, Suite 170
Dallas, TX 75206
Mon-Sat 10-10; Sun Noon-8

Around the world in 80 minutes should be their motto here. Since the world has shifted to a CD mode, if you want 80 minutes or 80 days of music, tune in here. You can duet! If you're still running at 33 rpm, you need to consider getting with the program before it's too late and DVD takes over the CD world. Prices here were right in line with the giant music superstores. Used CDs at rock bottom prices ($4.91-$8.91) and even new ones were discounted–average price somewhere between $10 and $13. Also carrying a limited number of videos and T-shirts. Located near the intersection of Upper and Lower Greenville, you'll find lots of eclectic titles mixed in with a world-wide selection at CD World. *CK, MC, V, AE, D*

★★★ CD/Game Exchange

214/739-6331

5409 Greenville Ave.
Dallas, TX 75206
Mon-Fri 11- 8:30; Sat 11-7; Sun Noon-6

Out to lunch? Be Bach at one. Well, maybe not Bach but certainly something else, out of the ordinary. You don't have to be a practicing pagan to enter, so with a shot of courage and a friend's good luck charm, we went, we saw, we played. The sight of so many nose rings almost made us turn back, but the sounds of what may have been a Gregorian Monk chant enticed us to investigate further. It turned into a new wave tune before long, so who are we to judge a record from its cover? From eclectic to just plain weird, the selection was vast (how about more than 70,000 titles in stock?) and varied. The new CDs were on sale for $9.99 each or less. And thousands of CDs at $2.50 and $5. A heavy emphasis is now being placed on their game selection, with hundreds of new and used PLAYSTATION, DREAMSCAPE and even original NINTENDO cartridges. Prices for used games range from $5 - $35. *CK, MC, V, D*

★★★ Collector's Records

214/327-3313

10616 Garland Rd.
Dallas, TX 75218
Mon-Fri 11-7; Sun Noon-4

Want to meet the Avant bard of music? Then, let me introduce you to Bud Buschardt, the Metroplex's leading musicologist. But if you want a collection that would rival his, let me introduce you to Collector's Records. You'll find virtually every oldie but goodie in 45 form, plus thousands of

LPs and 78s. Prices vary considerably based on rarity, condition and age. If they don't have it, chances are you'll never find it anywhere. Call to inquire about your favorite lost tune, or better yet, go in and dig through the stacks yourself–you may find that there are dozens of acceptable muses to satisfy your nostalgic cravings. Hear ye! Hear ye to the sounds of yesteryear. *CK, MC, V, AE*

★★★ Earful of Books 972/239-4028

11810 Preston Rd. *Mon-Fri 8 A.M.-9 P.M.; Sat 9-9; Sun 11-6*
Dallas, TX 75252 *www.earful.com*

Can you read, steer, talk, drive, put on your makeup (or shave), comb your hair and sing all at the same time? Well, you can at least eliminate reading while you attempt to do the others. With an average commute time of 25 minutes each way in the Metroplex, here's a way to squeeze an extra hour or so of productivity out of your day. Instead of listening to the radio and getting brain-burn, rent an audio book and educate yourself. Everything from self-help to sci-fi, literature to cookbooks, it's all here–more than 7,000 titles to choose from. Get an Earful of their $2.99 rentals (you can't even buy a book for that!) and dig through the gently heard rack for titles to take home and keep. Rental period varies–keep it for a day, three days, seven days, up to a month. If you get busy and can't listen to your selection, a quick phone call will renew it for another three days. There's an initial $10 membership fee, but it drops to $5 in subsequent years. Pick up a catalog or even order on the web at www.earful.com. *CK, MC, V, AE, D*

★★★★ Emusic.com 336/274-4448

1991 Broadway, Second Floor
Redwood City, CA 94063 *www.emusic.com*

When you hear "Burn, Baby, Burn!" coming from the kids room, you'll know they're downloading fromthis musical site. At Emusic.com they sell their music through an MP3 system. If you are not familiar with MP3 then listen up because it will save you a bundle on music. When you buy music through the MP3 system, albums are downloaded onto your harddrive. Once you have downloaded an album, you are then able to play the music over your computer. If you want your music on CD then all you need is a CD burner. A CD burner burns the music into a CD for you. Voila! Your own CD and you never left home. Emusic.com sells you their music through direct relationships with leading artists and exclusive licensing agreements with more than 600 independent record labels. Individual tracks sell for 99 cents each or entire downloadable albums for just $8.99. This is one of those things that sounds too good, but is true.

Friends of the Dallas Public Library

214/670-1458

603 Munger Ave. at Market
Dallas, TX 75202
Mon-Fri 9-2:30

Trying to stay "calm, cool and collected" is much easier these days thanks to the Friends of the Dallas Public Library periodic sale. Usually held in August or September, just in time to get back to school, when you get word of the annual book sale at WestEnd Marketplace, expect to turn the pages of time. Remember "The Golden Rule" and "Never Pay Retail!" Plan on spending the day turning the pages of thousands and thousands of books for sale that benefit the library–hardcovers, $1, paperbacks and children's books, $.50. They also sell first editions and rare books. Be a friend, buy a book. Book donations, though, accepted at any time of the year and at any Dallas library location.

★★★ Half Price Book Barn

817/335-3902

1001 Hemphill
Fort Worth, TX 76104
Mon, Thu-Fri 10:30-5:30

They don't keep what I would consider farmer's hours and technically they aren't even part-timers. But when you have more than 100,000 used books to round up, I guess you have to close four days a week to give you time to rein-in the inventory. It's a little tough, though, for us to get by to see them during their office hours...but it's worth the extra effort. It's a great store for senior readers with plenty of time for leisure activities. Listen up! They also buy, sell and trade records and tapes. What are you waiting on? Get moo-ving! *CK*

★★★★★ Half Price Books

214/363-8374

5915 E. Northwest Hwy.
Dallas, TX 75231
Mon-Sun 9:30-11
www.halfpricebooks.com

No need to get writer's cramp. Somewhere in this 53,000 square feet of books, you will get inspiration. Their flagship store on East Northwest Highway has always been a perennial favorite, however they are no longer in the same location we have all grown to know and love. But don't fret, just look across the street and you'll find them. The new store is much larger and features the "Half Pint Books" children's area (which includes a walk-in playhouse built by Habitat for Humanity and a dinosaur display from the Museum of Natural

History), a community room for events, a coffee shop/bistro and even a post office substation. But even with all that going on, don't worry that they've lost track of what brought them to the dance. Half Price Books continues to be one of the leaders of the previously read pack. Already a formidable resource for the reading public, they are quickly becoming a vast reservoir for other items such as software, videos, LPs, cassettes, CDs and even reading glasses. And, best of all, almost everything is half price or less. Whether it's new or used books, they'll help you find your way. After all, they are the ones that gave birth to the concept. In addition to the used books, they occasionally get publisher overruns and the past year's editions. You can find 45s at $.10 each, cassettes for four bits, albums and CDs at similar savings. Paperbacks run from a dime to half the original cover price. Clean off your bookshelves and traipse on over to the nearest location for an in-store credit. But don't expect to get much for your trouble–we took a trunk full of old books with cover prices totaling more than $300 and got a whopping $5 to use toward our purchase of other books. Also look for stores in Irving, Lewisville, Mesquite, North Dallas, Plano and Richardson, as well as Arlington, Bedford and Fort Worth. *CK, MC, V, AE, D*

★★★★★ Movie Trading Co., The 214/361-8287

6109 Greenville Ave. Sun-Thu 10A.M.-11P.M; Fri-Sat 11A.M-Midnight
Dallas, TX 75206

The Mark Cuban of the used CDs and now used videos is expanding across the Metroplex. CD Warehouse was first on the drawing block and now, it's the movie video market. In less than a year he went from one store to four, with more planned. More than 20,000 copies of 15,000 titles are stocked at each store, with prices on Bruce Willis in "*Die Hard*", $5.99, "*Happy Gilmore*", $8.99 and "*Barney's 1-2-3-4*", $8.99. Called a trend-setting entrepreneur, the this Mark is Mark Kane and his The Movie Trading Co. is worth watching with a box of popcorn. Is the website far behind? Until then, look for additional locations in Dallas, Plano and Arlington. *CK, MC, V, AE*

★★ Paperback Trader 972/219-8400

1112 W. Main Mon-Wed, Fri 10-6; Thu 10-8; Sat 10-5; Sun Noon-4
Lewisville, TX 75067

"*The Last Picture Show*" could wind up at Paperback Trader, all things being equal. Why not thumb through the pages of these previously worn, but not torn, books. Thousands of used paperback, hardbacks and audio tapes are available at this neighborhood shop complete with bell, book and cat. All paperback titles are at least half the cover price (and even cheaper for most hardbacks) if you want to buy them outright. But for even better savings, bring in books to trade. For each trade-in title, you'll receive a credit of 25 percent of the publisher's price. Use that credit to buy another title and you'll end up saving at least 75 percent off the cover price. Look through the funny pages of comedies and cry over the spilled milk. What a tragedy! If your books are lost and bound, bring them here for a new home away from home. It's not bad once they've settled in. Besides, reading them is lovelier the second time around. *CK, MC, V, D*

✧✧ Personal Profiles — 214/351-0800

16200 Dallas Pkwy., Suite 225 — *By Appt. Only*
Dallas, TX 75220 — *www.personalprofiles.org*

You may never go down in history as the author of "*Profiles in Courage*", but you can leave a legacy of your life in print. If you've always thought you oughta be in pictures, call Milli Brown Whitworth, the conduit to preserving family memories in book form. Your family's story can be passed down from generation to generation. Milli and her staff interview members of a family and expand upon a personal history of grandparents and their parents, through your birth and beyond. Possibly the only such service in the country, they write and publish the memoirs into a very personal life story. As your father probably told you, "get it in writing!" This is the place to do it. You can get published for as little as $1,000, but the taller the tale to tell, the steeper the price to pay. Milli also sells a do-it-yourself kit with a leather three-ring binder titled "The Memories and Reflections of My Life," a case, dedication page and pages to be filled in with all the pertinent information. At $59.95, it's a cheaper way to go down in history. For tips on collecting your family history, there's the book "*How to Interview a Sleeping Man*" for $14.95. Now there's no excuse for letting your family's story slip through the cracks of time. *CK*

★★★★★ Recycled Books, Records & CDs — 940/566-5688

200 N. Locust — *Mon-Sun 9-9*
Denton, TX 76201 — *www.recycledbooks.com*

Don't want to Title Tattle, but this is Denton county's finest book source. Join the plethora of Pavarotti fans who sing the praises of this Denton discounter—now the color purple. Indulge in three floors of a book lover's nirvana. Seek and ye shall find books, records and CDs for 50 percent off the cover price.

Period. No additional sales, no further hassles. Nothing overpriced. Lots to choose from. Float your boat without sinking a small fortune into expanding your music and literary library. Located next to the Denton courthouse, you will want to keep one eye on the speedometer, as Denton is not known for its kindly legal system. You might wind up with more time to read than you bargained for! *CK, MC, V, D*

★★★ Top Ten Records 214/942-7595

338 W. Jefferson *Mon-Sat 10-6; Sun 1-5*
Dallas, TX 75208

Keeping up with the Joneses is how this Top Ten Records keeps going and going. Like the Energizer Bunny, it's still the hip-hop place for cool cats of all kinds to hang out. Back in the '50s and '60s, it was because records were the rage; today it's CDs and Top Ten jumped into the fray and is still going strong. Oak Cliff has changed, too, but this oldie but goodie will always be a throwback to the good old days when rock 'n' roll was king. About 80 percent of their music is Latin (meaning they realize it doesn't begin with Ricky Martin and end with Marc Anthony) but they do carry R&B and rock titles as well. Check here when you can't find your tunes anywhere else. They are just a hip-hop, skip and jump off I-35 at the 12th Street exit. *CK, MC, V*

Musical Instruments

★★★★ Brook Mays Music Co. 972/570-1600

2521 W. Airport Frwy. *Mon-Fri 10-8; Sat 10-6; Sun 1-5*
Irving, TX 75062 *www.brookmays.com*

No, it doesn't babble or have any relationship to the King of the May. It's Brook Mays and is your source for – what exactly? Glad you asked. Most people think it's simply keyboards, but that's just the start of the symphony of savings. They not only sell pianos, they throw in the entire orchestra. We found guitars on sale–FENDER, IBANEZ and YAMAHA for 50 percent off – and a TAMA five-piece drum kit for $729 (regularly $1,199). Plenty of musical accessories, from guitar stands ($13.95) to a tune-up kit for $79. Look for the red tag sale on discontinued and floor model instruments and save even more. They also will match their competitor's prices (that is, if you find any that are lower.) Join the Performer's Club for special prices all year 'round. Visit their Keyboard Superstores at many Metroplex locations for deals on synthesizers, digital pianos and multimedia supplies, not to mention one month of free lessons with each keyboard purchase. And the band played on. *CK, MC, V, AE, D*

✧✧✧✧✧ Carroll's Piano Service 972/221-3806

By Appt. Only

If there's any "dischord" in your life, you'll want to hear what Carroll does. Want to play by ear? Or would you rather play piano with your hands? Listen up. A piano should be tuned every six months for the first year or two, then at least once a year AND every time it's moved. (If that's the case, maybe I should stay put!) When it comes to singing the praises of a piano tuner, Carroll's is no looney tuner, but rather one who is crazy about tuning your piano. Major or minor repairs, as well as rebuilding your entire sounding board, sounds good at any performance level. If it were left to Beaver, he'd surely sing this Carroll's praises. He had at least 88 key references on hand. *CK, MC, V*

★★★ Clearance Keyboard Outlet — 972/490-5397

14235 Inwood — *Thu-Sat 10-6*
Dallas, TX 75244

We were reduced to tears when we heard they had reduced their store hours. So, if you are a frustrated musician of any kind (professional, frustrated, wannabe or rank amateur), then hunker down on these keyboards and play a little tune or two. Nothing is more depressing than a new or used keyboard sitting silent in warehouse, waiting for a new owner to help them sing again. So this outlet prices their inventory to help move them back into a more melodious environment as quickly as possible. These pianos are in exceptional condition and are available through either consignment or because they have had the misfortune of being repossessed. Either way, they are priced well below even wholesale. KORG, ROLAND, SONIC and YAMAHA are just a few of the names on the inventory roster that changes daily. If you don't find what you're looking for the first time, check back–frequently. Bring in your old keyboard and let them sell it at the price you want (plus a few points for themselves). Who was that masked man I saw in there last night? Could it have been the Tone Arranger? Hit the 88s on a BALDWIN, KAWAI, SAMICK, SUZUKI or YAMAHA, for example, strum a FENDER, GIBSON, ROLAND or MARTIN–all your popular guitars. Get on the band wagon and save on the tune-makers without going loony. Nationwide financing and layaway available. *CK, MC, V, AE, Keyboard Credit, Financing*

★★★★ Dallas Piano Warehouse & Showroom — 972/231-4607

9292 LBJ Frwy. — *Mon-Thu 10-8; Fri-Sat 9-6; Sun 1-6*
Dallas, TX 75243

Who hasn't notice that red (or whatever the color of the day might be) Liberace-style piano in the window? If you're anybody who has driven down 635, you can't miss it once you come upon the Abrams exit. At Dallas Piano–it's better to be seen and heard, so listen to some of the top 10 brands of pianos in the country and see some of the best prices in town. Now add to that their fine selection of quality used pianos (with warranties) and it's music to our ears. Tickle the ivories of BOSENDORFER, KAWAI, ROLAND, SCHIMMEL, STEINWAY, TECHNICS, YOUNG CHANG and more in pianos and keyboards. What really pounded us were the player pianos. Though we were a bit out of practice, we might be able to sound like Billy Joel one of these days. Dallas Piano continues to win awards for selling more YOUNG CHANG pianos than anyone else around. Their best piano is the BOSENDORFER. You might need to mortgage your house to afford one, but they carry them and it's still my dream. Layaway and financing available. *CK, MC, V, AE*

✧✧✧ Dallas School of Music, The — 972/380-8050

2650 Midway Rd., Suite 204 — *Mon-Thu 10-9; Sat 9-4*
Carrollton, TX 75006

What kind of instrument are you ready to play? How about the piano? How about the flute? You can receive instruction for almost any instrument at this school. This is the only professional family music education facility in the area, so if you don't learn it here, you won't learn it anywhere. They have been offering musical education to people of all ages and abilities throughout the area for years now. Bringing together a team of educators throughout the country, they have created an environment where toddlers, school-aged children, professional adults and seasoned citizens can access a wide variety of musical venues–making it quite a symphonic symposium. They offer individual instruction, ensemble performances, concerts as well as courses. Rates are based on length of contract and number of lessons but being the one and only, well, you gotta pay if you wanna play. *CK, MC, V*

★★★★ Guitar Center — 972/960-0011

14080 Dallas Pkwy. — *Mon-Fri 10-9; Sat 10-7; Sun Noon-6*
Dallas, TX 75240 — *www.guitarcenter.com*

Heads up to the big daddy of the stringed instruments. Drum on your drum, but strum on your new guitar. And if it's one of these stringed beauties you're looking to get your fingers on, be happy – the Guitar Center guarantees the lowest price, so you won't have to fret over your fretboard. Now, that has a nice ring to it. With 44 locations nationwide, their buying power ensures your gear will be finely tuned to the penny. For home-recording professional tips, tune into their workshops at all locations (721 Ryan Plaza Drive, Arlington, 817/277-3510, and 7814 N. Central Expwy., Dallas, 214/692-9999.) From pro mikes and headphones to digital wireless systems, work stations to amps, spotlights to keyboards, you can strum to the tune of a different drummer. You can't buy guitars or other accessories online but you can get further information at www.guitarcenter.com. *CK, MC, V, AE, D*

★★★★★ Jack Whitby Piano 214/381-9571

8326 Scyene Rd. *Mon-Thu 10:30-7; Fri-Sat 10:30-5; Sun 3-6*
Dallas, TX 75227 *www.jackwhitbypiano.com*

Well, I'm tickled pink over the green I saved at Jack Whitby Piano. In fact, the one I wound up buying is the same brand (SAMICK) that is only sold through STEINWAY. So, I figure I'm getting closer and closer to the top. Located in the Mesquite area, even if I can't pronounce their street name, I do know to pronounce them the best buys for pianos. Specializing in pre-owned KAWAI and YAMAHA pianos, restored to better-than-new at prices of used, I am now singing the praises of their pricing. Most sizes of vertical pianos available including consoles and professional upright models U-1, U-2 and U-3. Most grand sizes and series, too, in YAMAHA C and G series and KAWAI KG, GS and CA. Their KAWAI pianos start from at $5,500. No doubt, you'll hear more pre-owned Japanese pianos in Texas than anywhere in the state. Sure would have fooled me – they could easily pass for new. Expect to be tickled ivory since the prices will be about half the cost of a comparable new piano. Also pre-owned favorites such as an occasional BALDWIN, CHICKERING, KNABE, MASON-HAMLIN, the Chinese-made PEARL RIVER, STEINWAY and others show up in their facility. All pianos are thoroughly serviced and checked out by their technical crew who can also install the Q.R.S. Player Piano system with MIDI-Orchestration, if you want the full shebang! No one would guess their pianos are not new. Sure sounds the same to me. *CK, MC, V, AE, D*

✧✧✧✧✧ Karl's Piano Tuning 214/381-7390

Dallas, TX *By Appt. Only*

Need a tune-up? Is your pedal not hitting the medal? Are your crescendos sounding like diminuendos? Goes F sharp sound flat? It's not just the dogs that have great ears! This man can hear a keyboard that's out of sync anywhere in the Dallas metro area. Make this note: His tune-ups are major. Since most of us don't have perfect pitch, you might as well call Karl for his. Basic rate is $75, but additional repairs, additional money. Believe me, he can make sure your key sounds are in tune with Middle C. *CK*

★★★★★ Keyboard Exchange 817/784-9600

4101 S. Cooper, Suite 111 *Mon-Sat 10-7; Sun Noon-5*
Arlington, TX 76015

If you want to measure up to the pros, let the staff at Keyboard Exchange get you in tune. Satisfy your craving for ivory without endangering an elephant.

(Tusk! Tusk!) New and used pianos, digital pianos, player pianos, keyboards and organs from most of the major players: KAWAI, LOWERY, ROLAND, TECHNICS, WURLITZER and YOUNG CHANG. Prices were minor on several floor models, up to 50 percent off, and that's music to our ears. Since 1926, this company has been playing our song and welcomes trade-ins. Located at I-20 and next to Toys R Us, financing is available and 90 days same as cash. *CK, MC, V, AE, D*

★★★★★ Lone Star Percussion — 214/340-0835

10611 Control Place Drive — *Tue-Fri 9:30-5:30*
Dallas, TX 75238 — *www.lonestarpercussion.com*

If you can't beat 'em, try Lone Star Percussion instead. They beat the competition on the price of all kinds of drums, brushes, books, mallets, sticks, effects and books around 40 percent–some more, some less. After 20 years, you'd think they'd stop beating around the brushes. Their "Discount Price List" (online or by mail) is an extensive 48-page price list of more than 6,000 items in stock with a convenient table of contents to direct you to the drumming accessories of choice. You can't beat 'em. Online specials indicating list price and their price is staggering. For example a five-piece LUDWIG junior drum set lists for $350, but sells here for only $209.95; a 15-inch LUDWIG snare bottom lists for $21, but is found here for $10.45; a 10-inch single-beryllium copper tambourine lists for $95 but sells here for $74.05. For the Latin bands, a set of five dry Agogo bells are $127 retail/$76.15 at Lone Star, with a salsa sergio deep-pitch cowbell for $26.95 that is $45 elsewhere. Duck, quail, crow, nightingale and other specialty calls range from $5.55 to $24.10. Professional wire ZILDJIAN brushes found elsewhere for $25.95 are just $15.55 here, American snare drum sticks are $6.95 ($9 elsewhere), corpsmaster marching sticks are a steal at $7.30 to $17.20 and ALEX ACUNA bombo/leguero Argentine model sticks are $14.35 ($24 retail.) So, the next time someone asks you to pass the drum sticks, just call Lone Star Percussion instead. Then again, at these prices, there's no reason not to snare. (Rim shot, please!) *CK, MC, V, PL, C*

★★★★ Mars Superstore — 214/361-8155

8081 Walnut Hill Lane — *Mon-Fri 11-9; Sat 10-7; Sun Noon-6*
Dallas, TX 75231 — *www.marsmusic.com*

Neither celestial or candy-coated, nevertheless, this Mars is out of this world. In addition to the more than 16,000 name-brand products available at discounted prices, this 38,000-square-foot store has some unique features that are music to any serious shopper's ears (and blow the competition out of the water). There is a demo room, for example, for musicians to jam in, a state-of-the-art recording studio and a permanent stage for in-store performances and clinics. There's also music equipment, recording and lighting equipment, microphones, sheet music and more. DJs can save up to 40 percent on cartridges, slip mats, single-sided headphones, gooseneck lights, LP and CD cases. Add classes, first-rate teachers, turntables, mixers and CD players and you start to get a feel for the depth of music-related services they offer. While all this might come with a premium price at some stores, at Mars that is never a concern. Mars will beat any advertised price, plus refund double the difference, up to $50 if you see a lower price advertised within 30 days of your purchase. How can you not join in? Look for additional locations in Arlington, 817/465-1444, and Plano, 972/633-1250. *CK, MC, V, AE, D*

✧✧✧✧✧ Piano Restoration by Bill Powell — 972/285-9755

1320 Hwy. 80 E — *Mon-Sat 8-6*
Mesquite, TX 75149

Bill Powell is the man to turn to when you need your 88-key investment restored to its former self. Is your once magnificent piece of musical machinery in a state of depression? Out of tune or out of sorts, when I needed my decades' old BALDWIN grand refinished and entire keyboard rebuilt, I entrusted Bill to work his restoration magic. There are some decisions you wish you could take back, but this is one where nary a regret ever entered my mind. Thanks to his good hands (and $375-a-foot refinishing), it is now in shape to be played again and again. (And valued at five times the investment made.) Whether it is restoring, refinishing or rebuilding (or all three) a piano, pump organ or player piano, a restorer with any other name would be nothing but din and discord. Bill Powell doesn't come cheap, but he can take a reject and transform it into a work of art. *CK*

★★ Rhythm Band, The — 817/335-2561

PO Box 126 — *Mon-Fri 8-5*
1212 E. Lancaster — *www.rhythmband.com*
Fort Worth, TX 76101-0126

Have you got the rhythm down pat? Then play pattycakes and jam with this company. Although they sell primarily to elementary schools, they sell to individuals at the same reduced rates, with no minimum order required. Prices are about 15 percent less if you order through their catalog which displays rhythm instruments like bells, bongos, castanets, cymbals, drums, glockenspiels, kazoos, maracas, rhythm sticks, ukuleles and xylophones. Popular items include the RB 1545 15-chord Chromaharp, which retails for $375, is sold here for $189; or AULOS AlO3N recorders, retail $11, discounted to $6.50. Now, isn't it about time to get on the Rhythm Band method of saving money? We found it hard to resist the Boomwhackers (a set of toned tubes); Belleplates; Charlie Horse Music Pizzaô Rhythm Band 10-Piece set; Kidsplay six-piece rhythm kit; RBI Egg Shaker: Handle Castanets; Jingle Tap; Automatic Hand Castanets; Wrist Bells; Rhythm Sticks; Finger Cymbals; Quiro Tone Block; Tick Tock Block: Sand blocks; triangles; guitars; ukuleles or anything else in their extensive inventory. What about you? *CK, MC, V, D, C*

✧✧✧✧✧ Richard's Band Instrument Repair — 972/446-4081

1311-B E. Belt Line Rd. — *By Appt.*
Carrollton, TX 75006

Strike up the band here with Richard's finely tuned ear. You might be more inclined to call this "Professor Harold Hill's" Band Instrument Repair after meeting owner, Richard Thomas. His musical resume reads as if he were the Music Man himself. Aspiring musicians (and their parents) unable to afford the services of the big name, mainstream companies have turned to Richard's for years to keep their instruments from wailing the blues. They know a swing by here will get them back up to speed, blowin' and goin' before they hit the retirement community. But he's more than just a Johnny one-note. He's got much more to offer than new pads for the sax and an unjammed valve for the trumpet. He's taught band for years (all instruments except the guitar and drums) and is a saxophone virtuoso himself and available to play at parties. He also sells used band instruments at prices so low, they are guaranteed to be back to making sweet music in no time at all.

★★★★ Speir Music/Roomscapes — 972/272-1700

510 S. Garland Rd. — *Mon-Fri 10-8; Sat 10-7; Sun 1-6*
Garland, TX 75040 — *www.speirmusic.com*

This Speir slices through the competition and high prices, bringing you guitars, keyboards, percussion and more at half-off. That's music to anyone's ears. They stock AUDIO TECHNICA, BOSS, CUSTOM AUDIO ELECTRONICS, GIBSON, JBL, MARTIN, OVATION, TAKAMINE, TAMA and more in their exhaustive inventory. Where else will you find lessons, repairs and 90-days-same-as-cash offered alongside more than 1,000 guitars? After nearly 40 years in business, Speir knows how to harpoon prices. Start with a FENDER ProTone Straticaster electric guitar, list $699/their price $399, TAKAMINE acoustic/electric guitar, list $699/their price $425. ALESIS QS-7 keyboard, list price $1,599/ their price $1,225. Guitar stands, $15.99 each. Books are 1/3 off list price. All sales people are factory trained, certified and happy to help. Their specialty is great customer service. No place else provides such a selection, such prices and such service. Financing and layaway possible. *CK, MC, V, AE, D*

★★★★★ Sword's Music Co. 817/536-8742

4300 E. Lancaster Ave. *Mon-Sat 10:30-7*
Fort Worth, TX 76103

Since 1969, Sword's has been helping you slash through the high prices some other companies charge to find a beautiful band or orchestral instrument. Stars such as FENDER, GIBSON, IBANEX or MARTIN guitars; CRATE, FENDER, MARSHALL or ROLAND amps; CB-700, LUDWIG, PEARL, TAMA drums; KORG or ROLAND keyboards; as well as P.A. systems, trumpets, saxophones, clarinets, oboes, French horns, violas are all priced at up to 40 percent off, making it easy to jump on the band wagon. They also gladly price-match so don't be shy. Occasionally they have older/vintage instruments (such as an original small 1930s HAMMOND organ) for sale. Not necessarily priced at a C note, but still to scale. Play it every way–sales, rentals, repairs and lessons, too. They'll never string you along. Mention you saw the information in *The Underground Shopper* and you might even hear a different tune. Financing available. Strike up the band here as easily as you can strike a deal. Sounds good to me. *CK, MC, V, AE, D*

Office

A-Box Connection — 214/357-2088

2671 Manana
Dallas, TX 75220
Mon-Fri 8:30-5; Sat 9-1

Looking for a few good boxes? This small office/store can send you packing. A good selection of new and recycled moving boxes on display along with bubble wrap, tape, foam and markers. Lots of overruns and misprints are on hand to save you money. The price list included small recycled packing boxes to heavy-duty boxes for dishes and glasses. Prices started as low as $.50 cents for a 16- x 12- x 12- model or $.80 for a 24- x 18- x 27- box. A wardrobe box with metal bar included was just $8. A heavy-duty dishpack box was $3.25. Honeycomb packing started at $4. They have new, used, misprints and overrun boxes and the always needed peanuts. Now, pack up the kids, pack up the car and pack it all in. *CK, MC, V*

★★ Aaron Rents & Sells Office Furniture — 972/385-9472

14105 Inwood
Dallas, TX 75243
Mon-Fri 9-6; Sat 9-5
www.aaronrentsfurniture.com

This Aaron's a carin' kind of warehouse store when what you see is what they rent. The clearance items, though, are not far behind and that is where the buys are. Some items in mint condition, others have been around the block a few times, but will still serve your purpose. A four-drawer vertical file was $129 (new) and a two-drawer lateral file was $199 (used) ... go figure! A basic, plain desk new was $399–a price too steep for our deep-discount mindset, but others that were used were much better buys (from $244-$279). For rental furniture, they offer a 12- and 24-month lease/purchase plan as well as short-term rental opportunities. (Could this be for fly-by night companies?) An executive mid-back chair was perfect for any CEO at $169-$179 (used). Who would know if some other boss sat there before? Other chairs by GLOBAL and LA-Z-BOY start as low as $49. Expect delivery to be $50, plus tax. *CK, MC, V, AE, D*

★★★★ Acquisition Specialists Inc. (ASI) — 972/888-1500

15160 Marsh Lane — *Mon-Fri 8-5*
Dallas, TX 75001

Are you in the acquisition mode? If so, copy this. Next door to Fullers, in the old CompUSA Building, is another gem in the ocean of office equipment sources. Sell him your old copier (or give it to them as a grant of good will), trade-in, trade-up, anyway you want – just get yourself one that works (such as a rebuilt copier with a 3-year warranty or a new one with a 5-year warranty). Now, at last, you can duplicate yourself without really trying. Brands such as RICOH, CANON, SAVIN or XEROX are rebuilt, refurbished and ready to roll. They also carry GESTETNER and OKIDATA machines. Instead of paying for a new copier, a rebuilt one will set you back considerably less but will still do the job, thank you very much. Low lease rates, current models, equipment warranties, service contracts, supplies and toner–how can you buy just one? A full service department supports your every acquisition. *CK, MC, V, AE, Leasing*

★★★ Administrative Purchasing, Inc. — 972/620-1500

2755 Valley View Lane, Suite 101 — *Mon-Fri 8:30-5:30*
Dallas, TX 75234 — *www.apibuys.com*

Score one for the little guys! API serves as a go-between, an ombudsman (that's our word, not theirs) for small businesses and various vendors and suppliers. They negotiate pricing contracts with office equipment suppliers, furniture manufacturers, computer companies and more. What this means is the small business owner can receive the same favorable pricing that was previously available only to high-volume consumers. They even help reduce ordering hassles with their SNAP order system. So if you run a small business (and API defines "small" as anything less than a Fortune 500 company), you need to see how API can help level the playing field. *CK, MC, V, AE, Financing*

★★★★★ Advantage Copier Equipment (ACE) — 214/350-4532

2636 Walnut Hill Lane, #325 — *Mon-Fri 9-5*
Dallas, TX 75229 — *www.acelaser.com*

Advantage, Budget. When it comes to copiers, faxes and laser printers, the Advantage here is perfectly clear. If you adhere to the strictest of budgetary guidelines, there's nobody better to call than Greg Budde (sounds like booty) to keep costs under control. Copier, fax and laser printer sales, service and supplies, he's your ACE in the hole. Laser jet printers from HEWLETT-PACKARD are $49.95 and $79.95, while one from CANON is $59.95. Fax machines start at $49.95. A toner cartridge from SHARP is $49.95, while one from XEROX is $79.95. Spend more than $100, and there's free delivery in the Metroplex. Orders of less than $100 dollars carry a $10 delivery fee. You shouldn't be ranting and raving about the copier being down, again. Keep your office running smoothly without duplicating efforts. Remanufactured laser cartridges start around $39.95. Office workers unite! Looking for remanufactured cartridges for your laser printer, plain paper fax, or copier? Call ACE. These guys are the top card in this playing field. Also carry new commercial grade products starting around $2,000. *CK, MC, V, AE, D*

★★★★★ American Contract Furnishings — 214/747-6791

1202 Industrial Blvd. — *Mon-Fri 8:30-5; Sat 10-2*
Dallas, TX 75207

When it comes time to getting down to business, this could be the beginning of the next Industrial Revolution. Located half-way between Oak Lawn and Continental, look for the American Contract Furnishings sign atop the building. Upon entering, to the left of the front door, you'll see a painting of a desk and chair–kinda giving you a hint of things to come. Save up to 50-70 percent whether you buy, rent or trade from this Dallas old-timer. Desks start at $50 and range up into the $1,000s, depending on the style and size. Two-drawer files are $25-$35, and there is a good selection of chairs in the $25-$100 range, complete with arms and castors. ACF has also moved into the manufacturing and upholstery business. You can get custom desks, chairs, couches and drawers here, or get your own reupholstered. Their 24,000-square-foot selection is mind-boggling–from high-end traditional to budget pre-owned antique office furnishings (some of the area's finest business establishments ... like from your ex-attorney's office!). *CK, MC, V, D*

★★★★★ American Discount Office Furniture — 817/640-0179

2251-A E. Division — *Mon-Fri 8:30-5:30*
Arlington, TX 76011

Can we talk ... business? If so, then this "business interiors company" (as they call themselves) is where to sit and talk about saving 20-40 percent on office furnishings. Do you need approval from your parent company? If so, get it. Whatever your office needs–executive chairs, computer tables, printer stands, the works—can be bought or leased. Chairs with arms start at $139 and come in a variety of fabrics. A two-drawer file is just $89, with locks available for an additional $9.75. If it's not on the floor, you can order it through the Quikship Catalog. Order DMI, HON, LA-Z-BOY, NATIONAL, PAOLI, RIVERSIDE or STEELCASE, for example, from contemporary Scandinavian computer furniture to bookcases, lateral files to stackable chairs–this could be your one-stop office furniture depot. *CK, MC, V, AE, MOC, 90 Days Same as Cash*

★★★ Art Hoera

817/332-2109

600 S. Main
Fort Worth, TX 76104
Mon-Fri 9-5

Since 1962, they have been defining the "Art of the Deal!" Art has been making deals on quality used office furniture for nearly 40 years, then passing those savings on. We found four-drawer file cabinets for $60 and several like-new chairs for less than $100 ($300-$500 retail). Ever wonder who will fix your steel swivel chair when the back comes off? For $15, he'll pick up broken chairs and deliver them back to you good as new. Additional charges depend on what needs to be done to fix your chair. If you're tired of seeing your profits eaten up by the high cost of office furniture, this is the man who'll swivel into action. Art also does expert doctoring on many other kinds of office chairs–frankly, he's a repair man of all kinds. Call for details. Remodeling or updating your style? Trade in. Buy up. Sell out. Art Hoera also buys used furniture when you decide to call it quits. Located on South Main and Pennsylvania, he doesn't carry new chairs, but it's a great place to get your old ones redone. *CK*

★★★ Benefit Store, The

972/470-0700

235-B N. Central Expwy.
Richardson, TX 75080
Mon-Fri 9-5:30; Sat 10-2

The move to far North Dallas, actually Richardson to be exact, has its benefits. Between Belt Line and Arapaho, area shoppers can now give more and save more. Just ask the Colonel (Col. James P. Caston, that is), whose devotion to this worthy endeavor has all area offices wanting to either be a beneficiary or a benefactor. Whether donating or buying, a good cause is a good cause. This colonel offers finger-lickin' good office furniture that has been donated for sale, and the proceeds benefit the Children's Medical Center. Desks start as low as $80 and go as high as a few thousand dollars. Chairs go from $25-400. Not only are you (the purchaser) the recipient of good deals at the office, but the children are the benefactors of the colonel and his merry platoon. For more than 10 years, this group has raised millions of dollars for Children's Medical Center, and now when you buy that desk or file cabinet, there should be less pain all the way around. Donations arrive daily–so shop often. *CK, MC, V, D*

★★★★ Bob Carney Office Furniture — 214/827-2537

3901 Main
(Main at Washington)
Dallas, TX 75226
By Appt. Only

Talk about banker's hours. Bob (no relation to Art) Carney is in the office from 3 to 5 during the week and on Saturdays, from 8:30-5. If you can squeeze into those parameters, than you've got Bob's full attention. With more than 40 years in the office supply and furniture business, he deserves a break today. But, the honeymoon's not over 'til it's over. This is how Bob defines retirement and the reason he won't give up the ship is simple. There are still folks flocking to his doors because of the discounts in store. With more than 350 items in stock, there's a reason for his longevity and his mini-work load. Take a memo, please. "Find good-quality used office furniture" and sell it cheap. So what if it has "concealed damages" (dents and scratches) or it's a manufacturers' return? It's the bottom line that counts. For example, where else can you buy a four-drawer legal file for only $75? We found a teacher's desk for $100. Similar models can be had for $45 if you don't mind refinishing them. Look for the two-story red brick building and follow the yellow brick road to the side door. Traditional, conventional and contemporary pieces and matching office ensembles are priced to sell faster and furious. If no one answers, they may be on a delivery call, so your patience is appreciated. Call ahead to be safe rather than sorry. Go five blocks south of Baylor, Doc. Delivery available. (Sorry, no babies.) *CK*

★★★★★ Business Environments — 214/637-6336

8900 Chancellor Row
Dallas, TX 75247
Mon-Fri 8-5; After-hours by Appt.

Talk about a royal appointment. Formerly Corporate Interiors/Wholesale Office Furniture, make a date with Business Environments. In the heart of the industrial district, Michael is your guide to saving on the best that office budgets can buy. PAOLI is the name that puts your office on the worldwide map. Jump aboard and surf at 50 percent off. Then, if you select one that has been returned (for some reason), you can slash another 20 percent off. You can shop the above address when Michael's available and see what's lying around or make an appointment to see the entire PAOLI line at the showroom during regular office hours of 8-5 Mon-Fri. PAOLI comes with a 10-year warranty and a promise that nothing will mar your relationship with it (not even nail polish!). Delivery/installation is extra. If you're a big spender and order an office full, they'll deliver it, uncart it, level the guides, make sure everything is in tip-top shape—even hang the Pendaflex file bars and then haul off the trash. If PAOLI's not your pleasure, you can also buy COUNCIL-CRAFTSMAN, EFI, HAHN, HERMAN MILLER, LA-Z-BOY and others at half price. Now sit down. They also carry SUPERIOR and UNITED CHAIRS. What a contribution to your official domicile. Whether it's new or used, this merchandise is only for corner offices with panoramic views. *CK, MC, V, AE*

✧✧✧✧✧ Business Furniture Services — 214/637-2371

2777 Irving Blvd., Suite 208 — *Mon-Fri 8-5; By Appt.*
Dallas, TX 75207

Talk about a suite deal. This is the place for refinishing office furniture, even if they have members of AARP. Yes, they even do millwork on wooden items, if need be. They will paint, touch up, reupholster and repair desks, chairs and files. They can re-key locks, move, reconfigure and do complete new installations as well. They'll even warehouse your furniture until you are ready for the move. If you are wanting to make some changes around your office and want to keep your people doing what they do best, these are the people to call. Their construction/remodeling services include sheetrock repair, tape and bedding, painting and minor millwork. With their cleaning services, they offer construction site cleanup, post-move cleanup, weekly contracts and even just carpet cleaning. They are fully insured. Dallas is their home base, but they have branches in Houston, Austin, San Antonio, Oklahoma City and Tulsa. They regularly send crews to New Orleans, Baton Rouge, Shreveport, Lake Charles and Monroe, Louisiana. Hourly rates are based on normal business hours and vary from $20 up to $40. If you need them on the weekend or at night, expect a night owl premium of 50 percent. (No guarantees that they're a hoot!) *CK, MC, V, AE, D*

★★★★ CFSI (Commercial Furniture Service, Inc) — 214/233-5500

14289 Welch Rd. — *Mon-Fri 8-5*
Dallas, TX 75244

What a commercial for new and used office furniture. Find the best. Sell it for less. ERGON, GLOBAL, HERMAN MILLER, HON, NATIONAL and about 150 other brands congregate in their 7,500 square feet of new and used. One of the specialty services they offer is to take ERGON and HERMAN MILLER chairs, for example, that sell for $800 new, refurbish them when worn out by replacing almost everything but the frame, then reselling it for $195. What a cushion. A fine line of solid traditional executive office furniture was 40 percent off list at CFSI. Keeping up with the Joneses is made easier here, so pay attention to those words of wisdom. Though selling new, too, used is always easier on the bottom (line). Plus, there are times you may have difficulty finding used sets that match). Recycle to the max, is our motto here. *CK, MC, V, AE*

★★★★ Dallas Desk — 972/788-1802

15207 Midway Rd. — *Mon-Fri 8:30-5:30; Sat 10-5*
Dallas, TX 75001 — *www.dallasdesk.com*

Even if you office in Timbuktu, you can buy your office furniture from Dallas Desk. These folks are Top Drawer. Don't file this away under Deep Six. They sell some of the very best in brand-name office furnishings from such stellar performers as COUNCIL, DMI, HOOKER, HAMMARY, HECKMAN, LA-Z-BOY, LEATHERCRAFT, PAOLI and STANLEY to name a few. Mahogany veneers in classic styling were available in a number of designs from traditional to contemporary. President Dennis Stein presides over a 45,000-square-foot showroom/warehouse catering to any official furniture statement, from home to the boardroom. From $69 office chairs to small computer desks from BUSH in that same price range (in fact, two in the bush is better than one at full price), they try to appeal to any budget and any taste level. And yes, they still sell ugly old used furniture–cheap! A five-drawer file is $339 used, $389 new. GLOBAL chairs start at $389 new. A five-roller, hi-back gray/black cloth chair was $169 while a leather version was under $300. A 36- x 72-inch executive conference desk was $1,275 and a matching bookcase credenza was $1,049. Though not always the lowest prices in town, they are usually right up there with the stiffest competitors. The selection is ripe for the pickings. Whether in-stock or special order, you can rewrite your new "Office and a Gentleman." *CK, MC, V, AE, D, Financing*

★★★★★ Dallas Midwest — 972/866-0101

4100 Alpha Rd., Suite 111 — *Mon-Fri 7:30-7; Sat 9-1*
Dallas, TX 75244

If you're tired of sitting in the same old pew every Sunday, talk to your minister about getting new ones from Dallas Midwest. This 40-year-old company specializes in institutional furniture for schools, churches, day care centers and libraries. Park yourself on a park bench or at a picnic table; they've got bike racks, lecterns, storage units, bulletin and magnetic boards for use with markers and magnets, indoor and outdoor signs and all at 30-60 percent off list price. Besides pews for the church, they also have pulpits, choir risers, office furniture and other items. For schools, they have new desks (with no names carved into them), chairs and lockers. Call for their free 90+ page color catalog or a price quote. All products carry a 15-year product warranty. *CK, MC, V, AE, D, PQ, C*

★★★★★ Desk & Chair Outlet, The — 972/661-2508

15301 Midway (retail store) — *Mon-Fri 9-6; Sat 10-5*
15307 Midway (outlet store) — *www.thedeskandchair.com*
Addison, TX 75001

Several doors down from their mainline store on Midway off Belt Line, expect to find incredible deals on new furniture for your home, office, or even home office. The Desk and Chair Outlet deals primarily in factory overruns, close-outs and showroom samples, passing the savings on to you. Get new name-brand furniture such as BODYBUILT, CHROMECRAFT, GLOBAL, GUNLOCKE, HARDEN, HON, KAUFMAN at 55-70 percent off retail. What an asset. Any way you slice it, you will be able to get a handle on your office expenses. From traditional executive U-shape desks, credenzas, lateral files, bridge and stack-on hutches, check the outlet before you buy and save up for a well-deserved vacation instead. Their inventory changes often, so check in often. *CK, MC, V, AE, D*

★ Emory Booty Co. — 972/401-1099

1901 Royal Lane, Suite 110 — *Mon-Fri 7:30-5*
Dallas, TX 75229 — *www.emorybooty.com*

The booty is bountiful in the office department at Emory now that they have settled into new digs on Royal Lane. Specializing in office machines like copiers and faxes, Emory Booty has been delivering copiers since 1942. Keeping up with the demand of office work, they also deliver fax machines–TOSHIBA faxes in particular. A Toshiba copier, such as the 1360/70, copies 13 copies a minute (it does reductions and enlargements, too, a big feature) and a Toshiba 2060 that copies on both sides, produces 20 copies a minute and collates up to 10 copies. There goes somebody's job. Plain paper faxes were also in abundance. One heavy-duty machine that caught our eye was a Toshiba TF 6316/71. This fast machine can transmit one page every three seconds. *CK, AE*

★★★★★ Executive Privilege — 214/352-1588

2615 W. Mockingbird — *Mon-Fri 9-4*
Dallas, TX 75235

Join the members of the privileged class. This is an tough act to follow. First, though, you have to call and ask for Joe. Sounds like my kind of place. If you're looking for an office environment with class, you might not want to pass this by. So what if you don't warrant an office with the best view, the least you can do is look like you belong. This furniture repository houses pre-owned office furniture at 70-90 percent off retail prices. One such example was a DMI computer desk, credenza, and hutch in cherry wood for $2,000; whereas a pre-owned 36- x 72-inch executive desk was $250 and a KIMBALL desk and credenza (with a few water stains) was outstanding at $350. D'URSO, HERMAN MILLER, KEIL-HAUER, KNOLL, MAITLAND, NOVIKOFF, SMITH and STEELCASE–names that you won't see often in your competitor's office–were available alongside desks, chairs, conference tables, computer desks and all the office accessories to accompany your promotion. Interior design services also available. One-half block west of Love Field. *CK, V, MC, AE*

★★ Fax Plus — 972/484-5522

12801 Midway Rd., #111 — *Mon-Fri 10-5; Sat 10-1*
Dallas, TX 75244

Just the fax, ma'am and nothing but. Just south of LBJ, this company has stuck it out by focusing on one category and one category only–faxes. Plain paper faxes. Plain-paper MURATA fax machines (no flimsy paper to struggle with) started as low as $299 (if new, would be more than $500). Higher-end machines such as OKIDATA and RICOH are also here. This niche in the office equipment business is often overlooked. But not here. Refurbished thermal fax machines were as low as $189 (though most were around $300). BROADCAST faxes, too, with 90-day warranties on all refurbished models. They had a RICOH 4800L for $3,095, a RICOH1700L for $1,249, an OKI 5300 for $999 and a MURATEC F-95 for $1,249. A good way to get the fax and once you're addicted, you can always trade up. Second location at 3105 Carpenter Freeway, Irving, but that store is mostly fax parts and pick-up. *CK, MC, V, AE, D*

★★ Faxfix

972/241-1111

11311 Stemmons, Suite 12
Dallas, TX 75229
Mon-Fri 8-5

If you can affix your name to a fax, you can call on Faxfix. They will even tell you if it's worth fixing at all. Though they're not the only game in town, they are a player. Since 1984, they have been repairing all makes and models of faxes, as well as selling reconditioned and new fax machines. (They only sell new plain-paper fax machines.) Faxes from $65-$995 can get you online, sending messages across the miles. However, with the new thermal-plus paper that is thicker and now has an anti-curl ingredient, you might forgo the plain paper fax and get old curly fax paper instead. Save money on a new machine and receive on site or in-house service. That's also part of their fast fix. If they can't fix it, nobody can. Besides, they will save you 50-90 percent if you buy a refurbished model or keep yours running hand-over-fax. Trade-ins welcome. *CK, MC, V, AE, D*

★★★ Freedom Office Furniture

972/385-7368

13810 Welch
Dallas, TX 75244
Mon-Sat 10-7
www.freedomfurniture.com

Escape the tyranny of full prices just one block north of Alpha. Watch prices descend to the basement level when the subject of buying office furniture surfaces. New and pre-leased office furniture can capture the moment by reducing your debt load. Desks from $299 and up, chairs from $29, two-drawer lateral files were $99 and up, and the brand names spotted included CHROMCRAFT, DMI, GLOBAL, HON, MILLER and NATIONAL. Not bad company to be in if you've got to work in an office, wouldn't you say? Freedom also has a retail store on Welch Road as well, featuring brands such as BROYHILL and CUSTOM CRAFT. Don't expect, even with such illustrious names, to have solid wood furniture to kick around anymore. These are bargains free from the strife of full price. *CK, MC, V, AE, Financing*

★★★★★ Front Desk Office Furniture Outlet

214/904-9045

10401 Harry Hines Blvd.
Dallas, TX 75220
Mon-Fri 9-5
www.frontdeskdallas.com

Attention all office furniture buyers: Front and center. Whether you've been assigned the task of finding the best prices on name-brand office furniture, or you want the best and didn't know who to ask, welcome to Front Desk–The

Underground Shopper's official office furniture outlet. When it comes time to make the move, you're in good hands. When we moved our offices (and expanded to more than 100 employees), Jay and John Criswell saw to it that all our offices came complete with desks, computer hutches, chairs, conference tables–everything needed to continue business as usual. Besides, when you open your doors to opportunity, Dr. Spencer Johnson (*The One Minute Manager* and *Who Moved my Cheese*) says you must look the part. Find desks and office furniture to suit any official business needs. From receptionist desks to executive board meetings, you won't want to write the desks off here. Shop for LA-Z-BOY and THOMASVILLE office furniture priced at wholesale or below. That's right, kill the competition with kindness. Used furniture with names such as HERMAN MILLER, KNOLL and STEELCASE line the warehouse floor (30,000 square feet of used and 5,000 square feet of new) with a front-carpeted showroom displaying some of the finest remains from the good old boom days of the '80s. Don't miss the selection of two-drawer, four-drawer and specialty store units that fit each project to a T. Entire conference rooms, reception areas, cubicles or just a piece here and there can be found for a lot less than your premiums for workman's comp. You could also cushion the blow with fine executive office chairs that were half price. The pros here even provide space planning (with your budget in mind) if you need help with remodeling or expanding your company's work area. And don't forget the lunchroom or break area. After all, men and women do not live by work alone. Ask for their recommendations on delivery if your two-seater can't handle the load. Shop online at www.frontdeskdallas.com. *Company CK, MC, V, AE, D*

♥♥♥♥♥ Home Office Solutions 972/407-1400

14540 Midway *Mon-Sat 10-6*
Farmers Branch, TX 75244

Home offices never looked so good! This showroom is packed with hard-to-find, high-quality, reasonably priced executive suites to computer tables that will add to, not distract from, your home's décor. Leather chairs start at $499, while computer task chairs were $195. Desks can range anywhere from $199-$4,000, depending on style and size, but $500 will get you a very nice solid piece of furniture. Styles ranged from contemporary to traditional, with items in pine, cherry, oak, mahogany, maple and more. Then be wowed by the heirloom-quality custom or completed wall units, corner units, executive desks, armoires, wood file cabinets, writing desks, bookcases and even wall beds (however, they maintain a "Don't ask, don't tell" policy on this subject). They also offer accessories and accent pieces including wine racks, compasses, sextants, antique-style telescopes, magnifying glasses, chests, picture frames, coasters, rosewood boxes, letter openers and more. *CK, MC, V, AE, D*

★★★★ Joe Wallis Co. — 817/335-1295

401 Bryan Ave. — *Mon-Fri 8-4:30*
Fort Worth, TX 76104

Find a niche and stick to it. Get a grip on recycling and consider redoing your kid's room (or a disheveled garage) with used lockers. Since Joe Wallis Company supplies them to schools, imagine the selection on overruns or used lockers that can be relocated to another much-needed storage facility ... your home or office. Expect to pay about $40 apiece. I'd run, if I were you. Shopping here makes great organizational sense and with the emphasis on simplicity, these units can now be considered contemporary accessories for almost any room. Great for toys. Great for office supplies. Great for doggie treats. Just about anything. They also carry metal storage cabinets, 72 x 36 x 18, for $166, along with metal shelving. *CK, MC. V*

★★★★★ New Again by Contract Network — 214/340-6400

10390 Brockwood — *Mon-Fri 8-5*
Dallas, TX 75238 — *www.newagain.com*

If you are considering an office romance, start by falling in love with these custom-made, remanufactured work environments at 60-80 percent off retail. What's old is new again in the warehouse setting of this big office furniture company that remanufactures major brands like HERMAN MILLER and STEELCASE. That means, if you've got cubicles in your office, this is a good source to save some serious bucks. Even in today's office climate, you can still fall in love with something at the office. (Serious romances, notwithstanding.) They even buy back used furniture when and if your love-connection wanes. See more than 500 choices in laminate colors for modular office environments and watch your money tree grow. Design staff available. Located near Plano and Miller Roads. *CK, MC, V (Add 2 percent for credit), C*

★★★★★ OFCO Office Furniture — 817/429-3553

200 W. Rosedale — *Mon-Fri 8:30-5:30; Sat 8:30-5*
Fort Worth, TX 76104

I hate to table the issue when the subject of saving money is concerned. So, let's get real. If you could buy office furniture and save a lot of money, would you look this gift horse in the mouth? Doubt it. Buyers at OFCO only buy direct from the manufacturer or distributor, and pass the savings along to you. You'll notice price tags are always displayed with the retail price and the OFCO price. Hang on to your executive chairs: 60-90 percent off if used (depending on condition) and 40-60 percent off on new. Some new items that are part of the "scratch and dent" department sell for even less. Who cares? Secretary chairs for $29 (if new, $249), or $49 for breakroom tables (new $245). Only new will do? So, new? How about a two-drawer mahogany lateral file cabinet for $149 (up to $935/new) or an executive walnut desk for $399 instead of $699? I'd say they're on to something. They offer desks, credenzas, file cabinets, hutches, computer desks, and more. Displays in every nook and corner of their 30,000-square-foot showroom with everything from acceptable to the best. No commission sales personnel, another plus. They also office out of 740 W. Pipeline in Hurst, 817/268-0981 and at 4433 River Oaks Blvd. in Fort Worth, 817/625-1880. Fort Worth's finest office furniture aficionado got our attention. *CK, MC, V, AE, D*

★★★★ Office Depot — 972/438-9177

1000 W. Airport Blvd. — *Mon-Fri 7 A.M.-9 P.M.; Sat 9-9; Sun 10-6*
Irving, TX 75061 — *www.officedepot.com*

It should be obvious to most that Office Depot is the power player in office equipment and supplies. Such "pen-ache!' They've got it all: telephones, fax machines, computers, office furniture, plus supplies for all of the above. One-stop shopping if time is uppermost in your Daytimer and prices are a consideration. Bulk buys seem to have the biggest discounts, but the fact that they offer free delivery in a local area on purchases more than $50 draws rave reviews from many shoppers from one end of town to the other. Shopping online is a breeze and we're not blowin' smoke, folks. So many locations, we've lost count. *CK, MC, V, AE, D, Office Depot*

★★★★★ Office Furniture Source — 972/613-9092

12620 E. Northwest Hwy. — *Mon-Fri 8:30-5:30; Sat 10-4*
Dallas, TX 75228 — *www.furnituresource.com*

OK, so I sit behind a gorgeous art deco bleached-wood desk that joins a wraparound, drop-down computer desk, that's the focal point to a matching credenza, that flows into my r-r-really big entertainment center which houses the TV and VCR ... what's it to ya? I'm not stingy with my shopping secrets or seating arrangement, for that matter. Where did we get it for a song? OFS, that's where. All the better brands can be bought, sold or leased–you can do it your way. New and used office furniture are filed accordingly in their gigantic warehouse/showroom. From files to furnishings, new to refurbished (that looks brand new), an entire office can be dressed for a lot less. Dress for business success for less with CAMPBELL, DMI, LA-Z-BOY, PAOLI and others. A JEFFERSON COLLECTION traditional desk and credenza was available at more than 50 percent off. A used five-drawer STEELCASE lateral file in mint condition was an open-and-shut case. The DMI transitional collection, available in cherry or mahogany finishes, list price, $2,472 is 60 percent at OFC. (Desk, computer credenza, four full-suspension file drawers, writing slides included). Full service, or do-your-own thing–either way, have it for less. *CK, MC, V, AE, D*

★★★★ Office in My Home — 214/348-4741

10101 Royal Lane — *Mon-Sat 8:30-5:30; Sun Noon-5*
Dallas, TX 75238

Welcome to the 21st century when going home may be extinct. You may already be home, at your home office. Going east on LBJ, exit Royal and Miller Road, watch for the big sign facing LBJ. If you're going west on LBJ, exit Plano; either way, you wind up in a industrial area for artifacts to make your in-home office workable. Start with a 30- x 60-inch steel laminate desk. Debit your account just $149, then add it to your balance sheet. Check out their reconditioned, refurbished and new furniture, too, for your home office or your office away from home. Name brands, volume discounts, custom computer armoires, color matching any existing pieces and a complete reupholstery department makes it official. One-stop shopping without leaving home. *CK, MC, V, D*

★★ Office Liquidation Center — 972/438-4499

3215 E. Carpenter Frwy. — *Mon-Fri 8:30-5*
Irving, TX 75062

Liquidating both new and used close-out office furniture next to Lone Star Boot Outlet, these professionals have a huge stock to choose from, with a selection you're sure to get a kick out of. From full office sets, credenzas, work stations, secretarial desks, computer desks, lateral files, bookcases, and chairs, if you need something for your office that is not part and parcel of the paper chase, this is the place to begin your hunt. STEELECASE four-drawer lateral files were $299, and the two-drawer lateral was $149. Pretty good for filing around. Desks started at $129, including a secretarial extension. Also pretty good. Only problem, nobody claims to be a secretary around here. Don't expect junk or the "put two-screws together and you have yourself a computer desk" selection. These are solid hunks from defunct law offices and other top brass from around the country as well as new office furniture. *CK, MC, V, AE, D $60 Delivery Fee*

★★★★ Office Max — 972/613-4099

1515 Town East Blvd. — *Mon-Fri 8-9; Sat 9-9; Sun Noon-6*
Mesquite, TX 75182 — *www.officemax.com*

Looking for the perfect office mate? Aye, aye, mate. If your budget's maxxed out, explore this office superstore online, by phone or in person. Taking office supplies to the max, save 40-60 percent on more than 7,000 name-brand office products. From pens and paper, fax machines to copiers, computers and software, secretarial desks to staplers, you can find it here–with a little help from the Max. Specials seem to change daily, so check before jumping in with both feet. Look for specials in their mailers and newspaper ads. Check directory for location nearest you; certain stores have different hours. Check directory for 13 area locations. *CK, MC, V, AE, D, OfficeMax*

★★ Paper Plus — 214/748-7587

2025 Irving Blvd. — *Mon-Fri 7:30-5:30*
Dallas, TX 75207 — *www.paperplus.com*

Create a paper tiger with this division of Monarch Paper (if I'm lion, I'm dying!). Save a bundle on bulk buys of paper goods, especially if you're an ad agency or a printer. You're probably already a fan but it doesn't hurt to advertise. For little guys, continuous feed computer paper was $19.99-$26.26 a case and plain bond paper, 5,000 sheets to a carton, $23.75. That's a lot of pen pals. Pick up your paper, graphic and office supplies all in one place. That's a plus. Check out the paper trail also at 2101 Midway Rd. in North Dallas, 972/490-8809. *CK, MC, V, AE, D*

★★★★★ PS Business Interiors — 214/688-1925

3131 Commonwealth — *Mon-Fri 8:30-5*
Dallas, TX 75247

With offices in Dallas, Atlanta, Baltimore, Philadelphia and San Diego, PS loves you (espccially if you need office furniture and modular workstations). A friendship that began on the golf course between Robert Paul (the P) and Jack Schure (the S), now boasts a multi-million dollar partnership selling quality used office furniture. Since 1984, this duo has been buying office furniture that is 3-7 years old and in acceptable, if not superb, condition, bringing everything up to snuff, recycling what others outgrew or out-loved. Isn't love supposed to be lovelier the second time around? STEELCASE designs in wood go for around $1,200. Expect to save between 70-80 percent off retail. Desks, credenzas, secretarial chairs, lateral and vertical filing cabinets, conference tables and chairs, storage cabinets–whatever it takes to run your office is the closing note here. Cubicle systems are always available here, in new, used and refurbished varieties. Is it any wonder their lines are ringing off the wall? As an added service, they are now selling new furniture, too. Check out their other location at the northeast corner of Miller and LBJ, 214/343-1925. Ask for Manuel–the guy with a hands-on approach to helping you solve your business interiors. A second location just off LBJ Fwy., 10220 Miller Rd., Dallas, 214/343-1925. *CK, MC, V, AE*

★★ Sav-on Office Supplies — 817/926-7071

2508 W. Berry St. — *Mon-Fri 8-7; Sat 10-5*
Fort Worth, TX 76109 — *www.sav-onofficesupplies.com*

Sav-on. Sav-on. Sav-on is the battle cry of this Fort Worth institution. Lucky, too, those in Big D and Arlington can enjoy the big D(iscounts) on office supplies. With locations at 11333 Northwest Hwy. and 310 Hillside Village, it looks as though they've got East Dallas covered. Competing with the big boys in business isn't easy, but Sav-on makes it easier said AND done. Price-wise, they're comparable on most products. Comparing apples to apples in name-brand office supplies and equipment will net you around 20 percent savings, which helps anyone's bottom line. Mostly name-brand computer and office supplies, but they are pretty neighborly, too, offering a public fax and copier. Helping hands and knowledgeable sales personnel, a nice change of pace. Hang out also at 2407 S. Copper in Arlington. *CK, MC, V, AE*

★★★★★ Signs Manufacturing & Maintenance Corp. — 214/339-2227

4550 Mint Way — *Mon-Fri 8-5*
Dallas, TX 75236 — *www.signsmanufacturing.com*

Want you name up in lights? Want to as-sign someone to price shop the sign market? Well, consider the signage here. You can travel to their South Dallas manufacturing site or call them for an on-site estimate. Lighted or unlighted, large or small signs and letters are priced wholesale to the public from this radio-dispatched sign company. No cost for an estimate. If you're looking for an identity, they have all the licenses for you to turn on the lights and are insured and bonded for your protection (they are a UL-approved manufacturer). Some examples include an individually lighted "channel" sign complete with faces and neon, 18-inch for $76 and 24-inch was $99. Other type faces and styles available. This company has been lighting the Metroplex and the world since 1979 and have been featured in national magazines, as well as newspapers, movies and commercials. To their credit, they made and installed all the signage and neon for the world's largest movie theater. Once you've signed on, your signage and logo graphics are stored in permanent memory in their graphics computers for quick availability (especially important for precision duplication at a later date). Moving around and keeping your own identity can be costly if you don't shop around. Like mother always said ... *CK, MC, V, AE*

★★★★ SuppliesOnline

11111 Zodiac Lane — *24 Hours/7 Days*
Dallas, TX 75229 — *www.suppliesonline.com*

Why pay for the overhead, warehouse personnel, store-front real estate and a hefty advertising campaign? Shop online right from your desktop for all your computer supplies at the lowest possible prices. SuppliesOnline is a member of the BBB Online Registered Sites and offers free delivery the next business day via FedEx on orders placed by 4 P.M. Everyday low prices and no minimum order required on more than 10,000 products available on the site. Office supplies, too, like pens, paper, pencils–the entire office supply cabinet can be replenished. Your 100 percent satisfaction, money-back guarantee with customer service that is second to none. *CK, MC, V, AE, D*

★★★★ Tarrant Business Systems — 817/927-8893

3221 Cleburne Rd. — *Mon-Fri 8-5*
Fort Worth, TX 76110

If you're in Tarrant County, pay attention to this memo. Near the TCU campus, this learned company has been keeping many an office going at full speed. In business for more than 10 years, with fewer than 20 employees, they have outfitted more companies than they have reams of invoices in their files. Dedicated to service and quality at the best price, this is no idle gossip around the water cooler. They're legit ... selling both new and refurbished copiers, faxes, shredders, folders and much more. If you're just getting started as a classic entrepreneur operating on the proverbial shoestring, you can even get equipped with a long- or short-term rental or lease. Check out the newest top-name copier, the COPY STAR. TBS is an equal-opportunity merchant servicing copy machinery as far east as Mesquite. (Probably because they love the rodeo, don't you reckon?) Also visit their second location in Granbury. *CK, MC, V, Financing*

★★★ TCS Corporate Services — 972/238-9123

1571 N. Glenville Drive — *M-F 7:30-5*
Richardson, TX 75081 — *www.tcstoner.com*

Formerly Toner Cartridge Services, this company is a Prints Charming. If your laser printer is down and dirty, let these folks clean up your act. No on-site trip charges anywhere in the metro area, free phone estimates and in-house parts inventory makes them one of the top choices for dependable and professional same-day, on-site service on laser printers. Why stay down when TCS can get you running on all full cartridges? Names like HEWLETT PACKARD, LEXMARK, TECHTRONICS are well-acquainted here. Pick-up and delivery of toners, too, with 90-day parts and labor warranty. *CK, V, MC, AE*

★★★★★ Tiger Paw of Dallas — 214/358-2332

2636 Walnut Hill Lane, Suite 309 — *Mon-Fri 8:30-5*
Dallas, TX 75229

Do you roar every time you have to buy a toner cartridge for any of your office equipment? Join the environmentally correct revolution and consider buying your replacement cartridges the Tiger Paw way (no relation to Tiger Woods). This company remanufactures toner cartridges for LASER printers, PC copiers, plain paper FAX and ink-jet printers. Their price includes pick-up and delivery and minor preventative maintenance. Put a tiger in your tank and rest easy because they guarantee your 100 percent satisfaction with a "no-questions-asked" unconditional warranty. In addition to selling cartridges, they service personal computers and printers and sell computer, printer, FAX and copier supplies. Prices are quoted on request. They buy empty cartridges and install long-life Tiger Paw image drums, which provide superior print definition and the ability to be reused up to five times. By the way, preventive maintenance and cleaning are free. One-on-one instruction on printer care is offered at no charge. Tiger Paw offers special toners, too, to include colors, MICR and graphics. Expect your office bottom line to improve with their savings of 20-50 percent per cartridge plus a 20-25 percent increase in page output over the original manufacturer's laser cartridge. Next day delivery free in the Metroplex. Nothing but the fax, ma'am. *CK, MC, V, AE*

★★★ Xerox Service 214/503-5600

10490 Vista Park Rd. *Mon-Fri 8-5*
Dallas, TX 75238 *www.xerox.com*

Supply is limited, but when they have refurbished copiers, they also have great deals. Do I need to duplicate this message? Save more than 70 percent on refurbished copiers that come with a 90-day parts and labor warranty. Not bad for a name that means copiers. For example, a XEROX 5240 copier that retailed for $1,295 was $299, toner extra or a Xerox 5260 for $459. A 25-pound personal copier, #5222 was as low as $195, or a Xerox 5280 for $429. Why not make eight copies per minute? Reduce and enlarge? Copy onto 8 ½- x 11-inch or 8 ½- x 14-inch size paper? Stop chasing all over town and go where the action is for a whole lot less. *CK, MC, V, AE*

♥♥♥♥♥ XPEDX Paper and Graphics 214/651-0331

501 N. Stemmons, Suite 300 *Mon-Fri 7:30-5:30; Sat 8-Noon*
Dallas, TX 75207 *www.xpedx.com*

This company has literally gone from A to X. Avery Paper's new name and new location six blocks from its original could be the start of something great. After merging with Palmer Paper, they have been updated by expressing themselves with a new paper chase. Paper, paper and more paper and not a drop of ink. (Just kidding–taking poetic license, that's all.) Their image of being a leader in office supplies is still going strong, with paper, laser paper products, printer's supplies, stationery and more. Anything else not in stock can be ordered and delivered in 24 hours. Visit also at 15408 Midway Rd. in Addison and 2158 Jupiter Rd. in Garland. *CK, MC, V, AE*

Outlet Centers

Allen Premium Outlet Center

Allen, TX

Look who's coming to North Texas! I hear it will open in October, hopefully sooner than later. Don't make a move until you hear about who's coming 'round the (Willow) Bend. The fanciest, schmanciest upscale outlet development in the country. Woodbury Commons in Central Valley, NY, the largest outlet center in the world is building a sister site just north of the Metroplex. (Houston will open before Dallas, boo hoo.) Don't know for sure the tenant mix but if it's like their others, you can expect outlets such as BARNEYS, BETSEY JOHNSON, BIG DOG, BROOKS BROTHERS, BURBERRYS, CHRISTIAN DIOR, COACH, COLE HAAN, DONNEY & BURKE, ESCADA, FOSSIL, HARTMANN LUGGAGE, JOAN & DAVID, JONES NY, JUDITH LEIBER, KASPER, LOUIS FERAUD, POLO, PRADA, ROYAL DOULTON, ST. JOHN KNITS, TOMMY HILFIGER, VERSACE, VILLEROY & BOCH, WATERFORD WEDGWOOD ... their outlets, clearance stores ... but nothing's set in stone yet, so continue to watch this space. Need I say more? Other locations besides the Woodbury Commons site include centers outside Boston, Los Angeles, San Francisco, Sacramento, Portland, Cleveland, Washington DC (Leesburg, VA), the Napa Valley, Palm Springs, the Monterey Peninsula and Hawaii ... just in case you're a jet shopper. *Credit Vaires with Merchant*

★★★ Denton Factory Stores — 940/565-5040

I-35 at Loop 288
5800 N. I-35
Denton, TX 76207

Mon-Sat 10-8; Sun 11-6
www.dentonfactorystores.com

Who says you have to drive a million miles for one of styles you see in *Fashion! Dallas.* Just a little north of the Metroplex, not even a day-trip away, you can harvest the bargains at one of Denton's best shopping mecca's. It's easy to find. Just go north past Denton on I-35 and exit 470. Park your car and head for the shops. The line-up is anything but defensive. Be on the offense and walk down the aisle with BRIDAL CO. OUTLETS, Suite 505, 940/484-2660 for a bridal gown as low as $99; DRESS BARN's another good companion piece in Suite 200B, 940/565-6638. Need comfortable shoes? Try FAMOUS FOOTWEAR OUTLET, Suite 306, 940/565-6559. Need a wedding gift? LENOX FACTORY OUTLET, Suite 501, 940/891-6011 is not too shabby. Stay out of the glare of the crowd by pairing with SUNGLASS HUT, Suite 309, 940/891-1380. Guys are not forsaken, either. VAN HEUSEN, Suite 305, 940/382-3970 will give you the shirt off their backs. Spend the night on a bedroom ensemble from WEST POINT PEPPERELL, Suite 508, 940/380-0045 and don't miss US FACTORY OUTLETS, Suite 201, 940/384-0124 for everything else. Start early to avoid the gold rush, but when it comes time for a lunch break, enjoy the meal deals at GOOD EATS. *Credit Varies with Merchant*

★★★★ Factory Stores of America — 903/439-0118

Exit 124 off Hwy I-30, Exit 124 — *Mon-Thu 9-7; Fri-Sat 9-9; Sun Noon-6*
Sulphur Springs, TX 75482

Drive a hard bargain and don't miss Exit 124. Factory Stores of American is down-right patriotic in the savings. Uncle Sam wants you to reap the benefits of shopping these stars: BASS SHOES, BON WORTH, DRESS BARN, EASY SPIRIT, FIELDCREST/CANNON, FACTORY BRAND SHOES, FACTORY CONNECTION, KITCHEN COLLECTION, L'EGGS/HANES/BALI, MORGAN ASHLEY, PAPER FACTORY, RUE 21,VAN HEUSEN and VANITY FAIR. Oh dear, you can win the American Cup race at Vanity Fair. It's smooth sailing all the way to the bank with the savings. Put on your walking shoes, or buy a pair when you get there. Shop 'til you drop and then grab some great Mexican food at TAMOLLY's. *CK, MC, V, AE, D*

★ Festival Marketplace — 817/213-1000

2900 E. Pioneer Pkwy. — *Wed-Sat 10-8; Sun Noon-6*
Arlington, TX 76010

Even with the addition of Iron Works, the Festival is still not the drawing card it could be. With 750,000 square feet of possibilities, you can walk and walk and walk and nary a deliverance. Except for Dilliard's Clearance Store, most of the vendors are of the typical flea market ilk and frankly, not much to write home about. Some of the so-called deals were discovered to be not such a deal after all. Counterfeit goods were confiscated by the Arlington police. Originally conceived as a wholesale-type value mall, flea "marketeers" wound up opening shop because the rent was cheap. (Those were their words, not ours!) Some merchandise was appealing–most was not. If you've got the stamina to walk a million miles down one of their aisles, you may find something that could make me a believer. Go ahead, make my day! *Credit Varies with Merchant*

★★★★ Fort Worth Outlet Square 817/415-3720

3rd & Throckmorton *Mon-Thu 10-7; Fri-Sat 10-9; Sun Noon-6*
Tandy Center *www.fwoutlet.com*
Fort Worth, TX 76102

With the tornado ripping through downtown Fort Worth, it's a wonder the multi-story Tandy Center is still standing. The outside took a beating, but inside, God was looking out over Fort Worth Outlet Square, the closest in-city outlet shopping experience. It still is, thank goodness, the downtown home to more than 45 stores including BUGLE BOY, CARTER'S, CLAIRE'S, DRESS BARN PETITE, DRESS BARN WOMAN, EVELYN'S FLOWERS, FACTORY BRAND SHOES, FORT WORTH STORE, GOLDSMITH SHOP, GOURMET BASKET, HAGGAR CLOTHING CO., KEENA STYLING, L'EGGS/ HANES/BALI/PLAYTEX, LORIANNA, MIKASA, NINE WEST OUTLET, PERFUMANIA, PRETZLEMANIA, PRIMECO, PUBLISHER'S WAREHOUSE, RADIOSHACK OUTLET, RECORD TOWN OUTLET, REMINGTON FACTORY OUTLET, ROCKY MOUNTAIN CHOCOLATE FACTORY, SAMSONITE COMPANY STORE, SPIEGEL, S&K MENSWEAR, SUNSHINE HALLMARK SHOPPE, SWEET EXPRESS ICE CREAM & CANDY, TANDY STORE, TOTES, SUNGLASS WORLD and VITAMIN WORLD, to name a few. But the real twist on the old outlet mall package was a SAMSONITE COMPANY STORE, carrying AMERICAN TOURISTER luggage. Since shoppers who love to shop do not live by luggage alone, there was even an American Express Travel Agency inside this outlet store. Make sure you get the lowest priced fare, however. (Remember the vow?) Another interesting sidebar is the Fort Worth Store, which offers (at retail–did I say that?–prices) goods related to some Fort Worth attractions, including the zoo and Texas Christian University. Rent a pair of skates and give the ice rink a piece of your behind. Since they are part of the entire downtown revival of the city's core, Sundance Square is hopping with activity. Make sure you get your parking ticket validated at Taylor and 2nd, Taylor and Belknap or Weatherford and Cherry, otherwise it will cost. However, parking is free after 6 p.m. and on weekends. Free parking is also available at the Fort Worth Outlet Square subway lot, located off Henderson Street. *Credit Varies with Merchant*

★★★★★ Grapevine Mills Mall 972/724-4900

3000 Grapevine Mills Pkwy.
Highway 121, Exit Bass Pro Drive
Grapevine, TX 76051
Mon-Sat 10-9:30; Sun 11-8
www.millscorp.com/grapevine

Gotta go even if you don't wanna. Why? Because everybody else does. D/FW's hybrid enter-shopping mall is a cross between shopping, outlet shopping and show business. No doubt, it will give you and your pockets a workout. The place is huge in size, depth and breadth–but not always brimming with bargains. Tourists love it. Shoppers have to be discriminating if they intend to save money. Don't get carried away with the facade and buying frenzy. Probably 300 tenants line the runways, including an AMC 30-screen stadium-seating complex. Kids go crazy at GAMEWORKS or at POLAR ICE while Mom and Dad can take a breather at DICK CLARK'S AMERICAN BANDSTAND GRILL (by the way, the food AND the ambience are first class!) Plus Dick and I are friends now, and I recommend my buds. Anchor stores include AMERICAN OUTPOST, BED BATH & BEYOND, BOOKS A MILLION, BURLINGTON COAT FACTORY, GROUP USA-THE CLOTHING COMPANY, JCPENNEY CATALOG OUTLET, MARSHALLS, OFF 5TH THE SAKS FIFTH AVENUE OUTLET, OFF RODEO DRIVE, OLD NAVY, VIRGIN MEGASTORE and outlets like ANN TAYLOR LOFT, BANISTER SHOE STUDIO, BIBLE FACTORY OUTLET, BIG DOG, BROOKS BROTHERS, BUGLE BOY,CASUAL MALE BIG & TALL, CORNING REVERE, FLORSHEIM, GAP, KIRKLAND'S, PERFUMANIA PLUS, SUNBEAM/OSTER and WORLD TRAVELER OUTLET–mostly outstanding outlets in our book. Some favorites that you should be on your shopping agenda include the JCPenney Catalog, Kirkland's, Perfumania and World Traveler (see their individual write-ups and see why) while others are run of the "mills!" *Credit Varies with Merchant*

★★★★★ Inwood Trade Center 214/521-4777

1311 Inwood Rd.
Dallas, TX 75247
Hours Vary with Merchants

Want the in's and out's of outlet shopping? Then head to this in-town shopping complex that is easy to access. Pull up to the front doors of every merchant at the Inwood Trade Center (though on the weekends, arrive early to get a parking place) and you're practically inside. Take I-35 and go two blocks (south or right depending on direction) after exiting Inwood. If you're a plus size, there is no other place to shop but Seventh Ave. Plus Sizes. The largest (pardon the expression) plus size outlet in the Metroplex (11,000 square feet). Whoever said bigger is better probably just shopped this outlet. Others will be equally impressed. For frugal fashions to decorative discounts, shop the CLOTHES OUT CLOSET, CRATE AND BARREL OUTLET, MATERNITY DESIGNERS OUTLET, OAKLAWN ANTIQUES & CONSIGNMENTS, INTERIOR ALTERNATIVE, PAPER USA, ROYAL OPTICAL, SHOE FAIR, SUZANNE'S, DISCOUNT DRESSES, ONCOR FLORAL, EVERYTHING UNIFORM and more. (See individual write-ups.) If you're part of the "in" crowd, don't miss "out-let." *Credit Varies with Merchant*

★★★★★ Plano Outlet Mall — 972/578-1591

1717 E. Spring Creek Pkwy.
Plano, TX 75074

Mon-Sat 10-9; Sun 10-6
(Garden Ridge is open 9-9)

Nothing plain-old about the Plano Outlet Mall. There are a million and one reasons to shop in this fair city. And one of them is 75% Off Books. Read all about it. You can buy coffee table, $60 books for $4.99. Load up on books ... all kinds of books. Nothing higher than $4.99. Then you're off and running. Start at NOSTALGIA CRAFT MALL with antique and craft vendors leading the way, then curl up in your easy chair on an area rug from FACTORY OUTLET RUGS, then bag it up in a BRUCE ALLAN BAG. There's something for everyone. Shop them all and save up to 75 percent, every day. Garden Ridge is a big draw, no doubt about it. But so is T.J. MAXX and L'EGGS HANES BALI PLATEX Outlet. At least I give them my support! CREATIVE GIFT BASKETS and BALLOONS for last-minute gift ideas, BUGLE BOY for the little guys, DALTEK COMPUTERS for the big boys and DRESS BARN, DRESSWARE, FAMOUS FOOTWEAR, FINISH LINE, GOLD UNLIMITED/INTERNATIONAL JEWELRY & GIFTS, HIT OR MISS and LADYBUG ACCESSORIES are just fine for the females. Oh, did I forget to mention METROCALL PAGING, RUE 21, RUSTIC FURNITURE OUTLET, SPORTS PLUS, SUNNY COMFORT and THE VIDIOT VIDEOS, CDs and DVDS? Some good, some better and a few of the best. It's definitely an easy rider to Plano and worth every gallon of gas. (Even at these prices!) Grab a bite in Reza's Café and life after shopping is good. Very, very good. Located on Spring Creek Parkway, just east of Central Expressway. *Credit Varies with Merchant*

★★★★ Prime Outlets at Hillsboro 254/582-9205

I-35 South, Exit 368A *Mon-Sat 10-8; Sun 11-6*
Hillsboro, TX 76645 *www.primeoutlets.com*

A great shopping experience (if you know your retail prices first) offering discount coupons and shopping bags for group tours awaits you south on I-35 and that now famous 368 exit. Check into some of the names that have shoppers driving for miles: AMERICAN OUTPOST, ASHWORTH, BANISTER SHOE STUDIO, BASS, BIG DOG, BOMBAY, BUGLE BOY, CAROLE LITTLE, CARTERS, CASUAL CORNER, CASUAL WOMAN, CHICAGO CUTLERY, CHRISTMAS CLUTTER, CLAIRE'S, CORNING REVERE, COUUNTRY CLUTTER, CZECH AMERICAN, DESIGNER BRANDS, DRESS BARN, DUCKHEAD, EDDIE BAUER, ELISABETH, ETIENNE AIGNER, FACTORY BRAND SHOES, FAMOUS BRAND ELECTRONICS, FAMOUS BRAND HOUSEWARES, FARBERWARE, FILA, FLORSHEIM, FOSSIL, THE GAP, GUESS?, HAGGAR, HARRY & DAVID, HAROLDS, HOOVER, IZOD, JOCKEY, JONES NY, KASPER, KITCHEN COLLECTION, KORET, J. CREW, LAS VEGAS GOLF, LEATHER LOFT, LEVI'S, LIZ CLAIBORNE, MAIDENFORM, MATERNITY WORKS, MIKASA, NATURALIZER, NIKE, NINE WEST, OLGA WARNERS, ONEIDA, OSHKOSH B'GOSH, PAPER FACTORY, PAUL HARRIS, PERFUMANIA, PEPPERIDGE FARM, PETITE SOPHISTICATE, POMEROY, PRESTIGE WAREHOUSE, REEBOK, ROCKY MOUNTAIN CHOCOLATE, RUE 21, SAS, SAMSONITE, S & K MENSWEAR, SOCKS GALORE, SPRINGMAID, SUNGLASS OUTLET, STARTER, TOTES, TOYS UNLIMITED, VAN HEUSEN ... whew! With more than 92 stores, there's surely a bargain a twixt and between. Plenty of parking, an ATM machine, and a marvelous food court for snacking and giving your tootsies a rest. *Credit Varies with Merchant*

★★★★★ Prime Outlets of Gainesville 940/668-1888

I-35, Exit 501 *Mon-Sat 10-9; Sun 11-6*
Gainesville, TX 76240 *www.primeoutlets.com*

This is prime meet-ing for a perfect rest stop for the dressless shopper. Just three miles south of the Red River and chock full of outlet stores, this is a great layover on the road to Oklahoma. It only means a few hours (or a few days) out of you way to make your day. Lots of goodies in store but shop with a critical eye as the discounts are not always substantial. But what fun. With more than 86 stores that line the highway turnoff, turn into A LITTLE

BEHIND, AMERICAN OUTPOST, ANN TAYLOR LOFT, BABY B'GOSH, B C BAGGIES, BIBLE FACTORY OUTLET, BOMBAY, BON WORTH, BROOKS BROTHERS, BUGLE BOY, CARTER'S, CASUAL CORNER, CHICAGO CUTLERY, CLAIRE'S, CORNING CLEARANCE CENTER, CORNING REVERE, DANSK, DANSKIN, DESIGNER BRAND ACCESSORIES, DRESS BARN, EASY SPIRIT, ETIENNE AIGNER, FAMOUS BRAND SHOES, FAMOUS BRANDS HOUSEWARES, FAMOUS FASHIONS, FABERWARE, FLORSHEIM, GIFTS GALORE, GUESS?, IZOD, JOCKEY, JONES NEW YORK, K B TOYS, KASPER, KITCHEN COLLECTION, KORET, LEATHER LOFT, L'EGGS/HANES/BALI/PLAYTEX, LEVI'S, LONDON FOG, LORIANNA, MATERNITY WORKS, MIKASA, NATURALIZER, NIKE, NINE WEST, NOCONA BOOT CO, OLGA/WARNER (CALVIN KLEIN), OSHKOSH B'GOSH, PARKHILL'S JEWELRY, PAUL HARRIS DIRECT, PEFUMANIA, PETITE SOPHISTICATE, PUBLISHER'S WAREHOUSE, REEBOK, ROCKY MOUNTAIN CHOCOLATE, RUE 21, S & K MENSWEAR, SAMSONITE, SAS, SAVANE/FARAH, SPRINGMAID/WAMSUTTA, VAN HEUSEN and more. Then saddle up to the Burger Grill or China Court or hunker down a corny dog, and hot dog, you've got a budget shopper's delight. (Actually, the nicest part about eating in these fast-food joints is seeing all the "stuffed shirts" who wouldn't be caught dead in them!)
Varies by with Merchant

★★★★ Tanger Factory Outlet Center — 972/524-6034

I-20, Exit 501 — *Mon-Sat 10-9; Sun 11-6*
Terrell, TX 75160 — *www.tangeroutlet.com*

Take I-20, and stop when you sense savings. You'll be in Terrell, the home of 44 authentic brand-name manufacturers' and designers' outlet stores such as BASS (a favorite of one shopper who claims a savings of $15-$20 off shoes and $10-$15 off shirts, while another boasts she found three polo shirts that were $65 for $20 and khaki shorts for $25/retail $55), BIG DOG, BON WORTH, CASUAL CORNER OUTLET, CHRISTIAN BOOKSTORE, CLAIRE'S ACCESSORIES, CORNING REVERE, DRESS BARN, FAMOUS BRAND SHOES, FAMOUS BRANDS HOUSEWARES, FARAH, FLORSHEIM, GEOFFREY BEENE, IZOD, JOCKEY STORE, KITCHEN COLLECTION, HANES/BALI/PLAYTEX, LEVI'S OUTLET, LIZ CLAIBORNE, NINE WEST, OSHKOSH B'GOSH, PAPER FACTORY, PERFUMANIA, PUBLISHERS WAREHOUSE, REEBOK FACTORY DIRECT, ROCKPORT FACTORY DIRECT, ROCKY MOUNTAIN CHOCOLATE FACTORY, RUE 21, S&K

MENSWEAR, SAMSONITE COMPANY STORE, SAS FACTORY SHOE STORE, TOTES/SUNGLASS WORLD, VAN HEUSEN, VITAMIN WORLD and WELCOME HOME. Thank heavens they had an ATM machine. Save an average of 40 percent off retail. It's a great stop over to and from East Texas. So why feel guilty? You're saving money, aren't you? *Credit Varies with Merchant*

★★★★★ Vanity Fair Factory Outlet

903/885-0015

I-30, Exit 124
Mon-Fri 9-8; Sat 9-9; Sun Noon-6
Factory Stores of America
Sulphur Springs, TX 75482

Not much else to brag about except savings of 50 percent on the following: HEALTHTEX, JANSPORT, JANTZEN, LEE, VANITY FAIR and WRANGLER. Need I say more? All under one roof, why not trip out? Located in the Sulphur Springs Factory Stores of America, find selection and price without missing a beat. Definitely worth the drive. *CK, MC, V, AE, D*

Warner Bros. Studio Outlet

972/874-0280

3000 Grapevine Mills Pkwy.
Mall Hours
Grapevine Mills Mall
www.wbstore.com
Grapevine, TX 76051

Say hello to Tweety, Bugs and Scooby-Doo! Then expect to save up to 75 percent off Warner closeout products that could be anything from backpacks and accessories to a head-to-toe outfit. Children's raincoats and galoshes were truly cute and cheap. Don't overlook this source of fun and functional represented with some of Americas best-known faces.

Party & Paper

★★★★ ½ Price Cards 972/315-2591

2325 S. Stemmons, #304 *Mon-Sat 9:30-7; Sun Noon-5*
Lewisville, TX 75067

What a card! If you care enough to send the very best, why not send it for 50 percent less? Too proud to save money? Then, why don't you buy twice as many instead? They have a vast selection of cards as well as unique gifts, decorative plates, party favors, balloon bouquets and anything else you might need to make your get-together a success–for less. In addition to the "off-the-rack" selections, this store adds to their variety by offering imprinting on most of their paper products for about 20 percent less than retail. So if bridal or wedding invitations loom on the horizon, stay on the sunny side of the street. Their physical store is really on FM 3040 (near Schlotsky's), so don't panic if they're not visible from Stemmons. *CK, MC, V*

★★★ Active Advertising/Promotion Sales 214/821-1561

1912 Summit *Mon-Fri 9:30-5*
Dallas, TX 75206

If you're a pro-Active kind of shopper, than start advertising. Spread the word about your company, your favorite team or your best friend's birthday. Call Neil Liebrum at Active Advertising for the best deals in promotional items. He's been in business for 38 years, and the quality shows it. Check out the dozens of novelty publicity items available here to help your customers (future, past or present) remember that you cared enough to send the very best (of course, at the very least) – calendars, balloons, wooden nickels, pens, pencils, bumper stickers, key chains–there are more than 10,000 ideas here. We loved the toothpick holders (rumored to have been made for the governor), but I forgot to ask which one! In the Lower Greenville area near Whole Foods, you'll find the healthiest business booster in town. *CK*

★★★★ Brass Register, The

972/231-1386

610 James Drive
Richardson, TX 75080

Mon-Sat 9-5:30

Party planners (professionals and otherwise) know this source for jukeboxes and slot machines. Well, you've hit the jackpot here. Between Spring Valley and Belt Line off Central Expressway, whether you're a fan of hip hop or golden oldies, they have the (Miami) Sound Machines for the next dance. Both new and antique boxes sit side by side with barber chairs and Poles (Czechs welcome here, too). Slot machines were hands-down winners and the video poker machines got a hands-up on the competition. In fact, their prices are peanuts by comparison. When the sale is made on any one of their antique cash registers, you'll be saving 30 percent and more off retail. So why not "Kunkel" down at discount prices and join the Top Brass. Old WURLITZER juke boxes can be rented for the perfect entertainment center for your next party. More than 300 records to play, to sing and sway with Sammy Kaye. And, if you have a juke box that goes on the fritz, they restore them to working order. If you're looking for a new to way to arrive at a party, The Brass Register now carries GOPEDS motorized scooters. *CK, V, MC*

★★★★★ Card & Party Factory

817/274-8044

2215 S. Cooper
Arlington, TX 76013

Mon-Sat 9-8

Party, party, parties everywhere! So what's a girl suppose to do? Turn to this Card & Party Factory chain where there's cards, gifts, Mylar balloons, party favors, children's activity books ... the stuff that traditional card and gift shops are made of, except without the hefty prices. Party packs make it easy to plan your party in one fell swoop. A real blow-out is available with any one of their fabulous balloon bouquets or some nifty party favors to go with the matching paper and plates, that match the napkins, that match the centerpiece. Bouquets of 12-inch party balloons went up, up and away: 10 for $4.88. Cards are 50 percent off retail, and giftwrap rolls out for $2-$3 per roll, or four rolls for $10. You think the party's over by calling it a wrap, but no, here comes the bride. Wedding decorations, seasonal ornaments, specialty items for any occasion sport savings from floor to ceiling. Table top trees to make your season bright were another way to save the day. Roll on over and save. With 23 Texas locations, check for the store nearest you. *CK, MC, V, D*

Party & Paper

★★★★ Cardsmart

972/496-5222

6850 N. Shiloh Rd.
Garland, TX 75044
Mon-Fri 10-7; Sat 10-6; Sun Noon-5
www.cardsmart.com

Smart shoppers pass the test by buying what they need for the party at half the price. No need to flunk the course. Cardsmart 101 is the first step in getting your Ph.D. Shop smart for cards, wrapping paper, gift ideas and collectibles. Sign your name on the inside of national greeting card brands and wrap up the gift with paper at half the price. That's why customers flock to their doors. Discounts. Quality products. Excellent customer service and it spells loyalty. Shoppers return to a Cardsmart an average of 3.5 times per month. Double your pleasure at another Cardsmart at the southeast corner of Parker and Custer in Plano, 972/964-8778. *CK, MC, V, AE, D*

✔ Christmas Warehouse

214/638-7867

1331 Regal Row
Dallas, TX 75247
Mon-Sat 10-6; Sun Noon-5

At Christmas time, shoppers "flock" to this warehouse wonderland. This seasonal power player can have you in the green at a fraction of retail with trees, wreaths, garlands, ornaments, ribbons, boxed cards and so much more. Start with the artificial trees and work your way to the top. Once there, add a crowning glory and call it a wrap. (Gift wrap was as low as $1 for a 26-square-foot roll!) Send a few thousand cards (half off retail) and don't overlook some of the neat-o gift-o items that would be a perfect fit under the tree. And the tree are also offered at half-off retail! Usually opens the first week of September and closes mid-January. Seek and ye shall find another location in Arlington at 2215 S. Cooper, 817/274-8044, but the sun doesn't shine after the holiday season. Fort Worth location: 6216 Hulen Blvd. (behind Denny's), 817/361-5631. *CK, MC, V, D*

★★★★★ Discount Paper Warehouse (Blue Sky)

972/552-5295

207 E. Hwy. 80
Forney, TX 75126
Thu-Sat 10-5:30
www.discountpaperwarehouse.com

Blue Sky shining above, nothing but Blue Skies all day long. But only on Thursday, Friday and Saturday can you do serious damage and buy your party supplies at serious discounts. Across from Clements Antiques, you will see gift wrap and greeting cards so low, just be glad their hours are limited. Prices are so low that retailers buy from them–that's why they're known as The Gift

Packaging Source. Expect prices up to 70 percent off at this three-day a week party store. If you faint every time you walk into the (can't say the name) card store and spend a fortune on cards, here's where you can buy thousands of greeting cards priced at two for $.99 (regularly $1.75-$3.95), gift wrap by the foot (just like what the department stores do), gift totes, bags at giveaway prices. Tissue paper, 70 sheets for $1.99. Complete selection of gift basket supplies, ribbons and bows, boxes and much more at wholesale prices. They just added a selection of candy for your sweet tooth at 60 percent off mall candy store prices. Gift wrap sells three for $.99. Go ahead, what are you waiting for? And if you're interested in organizing a group shopping spree for a fund-raising event, your cause will receive 20-25 percent off the sales generated by your group's expenditures. Call the number above and ask for Carolyn Walker, ext. 139, for more information on fund-raising. Or ask about their catalog and let your fingers to the shopping. *CK, MC, V, D*

✧✧✧✧✧ Entertainment Alliance — 972/495-3768

2001 Lancecrest Drive — *Mon-Fri 9-6*
Garland, TX 75044 — *hometown.aol.com/mwmagic/page/index.htm*

Enter into this peace treaty when the time comes to call for a truce. For all the fun, and none of the fuss, call Entertainment Alliance to put the life back into your party. Not only will they do the planning, they will also arrange the catering, buy the supplies, decorations, and book the entertainment. From Marty the Magician, to sketch artists, to just about anything to ensure your party's a roaring success. Sit back, relax, have a real good time by putting the party in their capable hands. *CK*

★★★★★ Holiday Market — 972/285-4113

2414 Hwy. 80 E, Suite 402 — *Tue-Sat 10-6 (Jan.-Sept.); 7 days 10-6 (Oct.-Dec.)*
Mesquite, TX 75149

When the season dictates, discounts rule. As their name implies, the Holiday Market merchandise reflects the current season's "must-haves" with prices from 30-75 percent off retail. During the spring, find florals, decorative accessories and gift items for Easter and Mother's Day. In the fall, you'll fall for fall bouquets, items for Halloween and Thanksgiving, plus a million-and-one Christmas decorations. They have the largest selection of gift wrap in the Dallas area, with about 4,000 rolls. One of their favorite items is an intense indoor/outdoor light called rice lights. Selection changes constantly, so come in often for unique items at low prices. *CK, MC, V, AE*

Party & Paper

✧✧✧✧✧ Marty the Magician — 972/495-3768

Garland, TX 75044 — *Mon-Fri 9-6*

Abbra Gadabra is Marty Westerman's magical slight-of-hand specialty. First you see it, then you don't. What a swell party it is. Dressed as Charlie Chaplin, he's stone-faced and doesn't move a muscle when working his magic on the audience. Folks were glazed-over in amazement. Though they try to figure it out ... they can't! You be the judge. He's a wonderful addition to any party-planner's book of tricks, whether it's for child's play or grown-up fun, he's the one to call. (See also Entertainment Alliance.) *CK*

★★ Palmer Sales — 972/288-1026

3510 E. Hwy. 80 — *Mon-Fri 9-6; Sat 10-4*
Mesquite, TX 75149

Since 1948, this business has been the life of the party. Celebrate your next happy occasion with discounted party supplies, fund-raising products, carnival supplies, religious items, balloons, toys and holiday decorations by shopping through the book. At Palmer Sales, they sell tons of party accoutrements at both wholesale and retail prices. To take advantage of the good prices, (savings up to 30 percent), you'll need to stock up. Party supplies, novelties, plush animals, trinkets, charms, holiday decorations, confetti, plastic dinnerware, piñatas, party favors, and just about anything else you might need to party, smarty. Believe me, there's nothing worse than a dull party–it's actually a féte worse than death. Escape from the looney bin and enjoy savings on LOONEY TUNES plush animals. On all returns (30-day return policy), there is a 10 percent restocking charge. Most orders are shipped the same day they are received. Make a date and order their free 55-page color catalog; it makes for good reading. *CK, MC, V, AE, PQ, C*

★ Paper USA — 214/630-4999

1220 Conveyor — *Mon-Fri 8-5:30*
Inwood Trade Center — *www.paperusa.com*
Dallas, TX 75247

Two blocks west of Stemmons, head for the chase, the paper chase, if you need to paper the town green with savings. If it was made to print on a computer or printer, expect Paper USA to be a source for it, for less. Although they usually sell graphic supplies and paper to printers, they have a small retail area open to the public. Don't expect them to be open on the weekends, though. Mid-week, make your move. Start making plans for the weekend by creating your own invitations with matching stationery and envelopes. (Though one of the pleasures of giving a party is having it over!) *CK, MC, V, AE*

✧✧✧✧ Parties Portable — 817/467-3087

PO Box 150001 — *By Appt. Only, 24-Hour service*
Arlington, TX 76015 — *www.parties-portable.com*

If you need to add life to the party, consider Parties Portable. Weddings, bar mitzvahs, showers, parties, Lico Reyes can provide the much-needed entertainment: Experienced professional DJs, professional sound systems, spectacular light shows, music from the '40s to the '90s, karaoke, magicians, dancers, comedians, clowns, bands and emcees, celebrity lookalikes or a carnival dunk tank. They may even have been the first mobile DJ in the country, having started in 1970. Packages start at $90 per hour with a three-hour minimum. This is such a deal, especially considering that Lico has not raised his prices since 1980. Services can be conducted in English, Spanish or Vietnamese. They will go anywhere you need them; previous parties have even taken them to the Bahamas and Mexico. *CK (Prefer company checks), MO*

★★★ Party City — 972/985-9853

2412 Preston Rd. — *Mon-Sat 9:30-9; Sun 10:30-6*
Plano, TX 75093 — *www.partycity.com*

Unlock this party chain and swing from the rafters. This city inspires more than just a par-a-dice. They've got other games sure to spice up the party as well as the supplies to have a blast. PC has all the licensed paper products to make your kiddo's next party one they rave about. Costumes for every party known to man–some worth the wig. Though they have balloon bouquets, I never can fit them in my car. What does fit are the WILTON cake supplies, but I've given up baking. Instead, I wait for Halloween and go all out. Plenty of helium balloons rise to the occasion but buying them was trying on our souls. The wait didn't abate and we hated to be late for our date. At other times, though busy, balloon buying was a breeze. Holiday party givers will find this place "A Sale for All Cities." With 11 other franchised locations throughout the Metroplex, this City is exploding at the seams. *CK, MC, V, AE, D*

★★★ Party Universe — 972/446-3084

2540 Old Denton Rd., #167 — *Mon-Fri 9:30-8; Sat 9-6; Sun 11-5*
Carrollton, TX 75006 — *www.partycelebration.com*

Planet Hollywood is for people-watching; Party Universe, with its more than 7,000 products on hand, is for party-shopping. Specializing in balloons, paper and plastic plates, cups, table covers, food service items, trays, cutlery, place mats, candles, custom imprinting, napkins, gift wrapping, greeting cards, decorations and more, you can entertain your options at the guaranteed lowest prices. Not only do they sell all greeting cards at $.99 every day, but they also sell one dozen helium balloons for $3.99. Up, up and away with those beautiful balloons. Even the 18-inch Mylar balloons were only $1. Assorted plastic bowls and trays were $.50-$3.50, watermelon designer bowls were $.90-$3.90 (a fruit-shaped party tray was no lemon either at $1.99). They have the latest theme-party items to help your small ones be the talk of the town with "Pokéman", "Toy Story 2" and other hot licenses leading the pack. You can get every type of paper product if you have the stamina to endure the hunt through the balloons. This is the place for the competitive hostess who likes to boast that she's the mostest who bought it for the leastest. At the southeast corner of Trinity Mills and Old Denton Rd. (next to TJ Maxx) in Carrollton and in Dallas at 1152 N. Buckner, #105. *CK, MC, V, D*

★★★★★ Print Team — 214/496-0505

Dallas, TX — *By Appt. Only*

When we were in desperate need of a printer, we called Scott Moore and he did the job at more than 50 percent less than the closest bid. Turnaround time was so fast it made our heads spin. Service was wonderful, printing was great. What more do you want? How about pick-up and delivery because that's the only way he does business. Say "good-buys" to printing every step of the way. After all, how many frogs do you have to kiss to end up with a printer who's a Prince? *CK*

★★★ Republic Industries — 214/361-7123

11440 N. Central Expwy. — *Mon-Fri 8:30-5, Sat 9-Noon*
Dallas, TX 75243

Not to be confused with the Republic Industries that manufactures kitchen and bath cabinets, this Republic Industries sells Pachinko machines and the Pachislo Skill Stop slot machines that are imported from Japan. For example, a Pachislo Skill Stop slot machine retails for $695; their price, $399. A Pachinko machine that was regularly $399 was a drop in the bucket at $189. These models are the original commercial machines that were used in Pachinko parlors but have been completely reconditioned to like-new condition. In this classic game of skill, when you score, the jackpot cycles are hit, lights flash and music plays, leaving you on Cloud Nine. Don't think, though, that this is a gambling device. It plugs into any household outlet and it's strictly a game that goes whiz, bang, thank you ma'am, 'cause no money is accepted. *CK*

✧✧✧✧ Texas Queen 972/771-0039

PO Box 335 *Mon-Fri 10-5*
Rockwall, TX 75087 *www.texas-on-line.com/graphic/txqueen.ht*

Anchors away, my friend. When you're looking for a new wave kind of place, head east to Rockwall for the boat that launches a thousand laughs. For an entertaining, and delicious, change of scenery, hop aboard the good ship Texas Queen and leave the steering to the captain. No need for a passport, just an occasion. A romantic night on the lake, a celebration of The Shoppers Choice Awards, a wedding ceremony–it has only just begun. Ernie will take care of all the details; All you have to do is sit down, sit down, 'cause you're rockin' the boat. Bon voyage! Reservations required. *CK, MC, V, AE, D*

✧✧✧ Trax City USA 972/252-7827

321 W. Airport Frwy. *Mon-Sat 11-7*
Irving, TX 75062 *www.traxcityusa.com*

Liven up your next party with a song and a dance. This is the rhythm method for jive and hip hop to mambo and cha-cha-cha. Hear the tunes of different drummers and rent a karaoke machine, plus all the cassettes and CDs of your favorite tunes. If you'd rather not do it yourself, hire one of their DJs to do it for you. Music from the '50s to the present, including golden oldies, rap, rock, folk, country, blues, big band, children's, Broadway tunes and more to tap 'til you're ready to drop. Rock around the clock with these folks who are your audio and karaoke professionals. Home party systems start at about $75 for a 24-hour rental, longer if you rent it on Saturday. So, it's your party and I'll come if you invite me. *CK, MC, V, D, AE*

★★ Trophy Arts 817/336-4532

519 Pennsylvania *Mon-Fri 9-5:30*
Fort Worth, TX 76104

Whatever the award, don't leave home without the trophy. Present and accounted for, sir. Even if you don't win an Oscar, you don't want to lose the Oscars. But if you do, you can still honor your award winners with a trophy or plaque by Trophy Arts. High-quality awards are statuesque and waiting for the envelope, please. Wooden plaques, custom trophies, medals, ribbons–even custom engraving. Let them design an eye-popping trophy for your corporate function when recognition is called for. Consider calling on this winner when you want to reward a winner. Trophy Arts is also an authorized ASI dealer, so if your team or company needs advertising or promotional specialties, give them a call. Most orders are delivered within three working days. Call for details. *CK, MC, V, D*

★★★★★ Under Wraps 972/669-9120

13590 Floyd Circle, Suite 100 *Mon-Sat 10-5*
Dallas, TX 75243

These guys have real staying power and roll with the punches. You can't keep a good store under wraps for long. Here, you can save 80 percent on designer wrap at either one of their two locations open year-round. Accent your gifts with bangles and bows, tie-ons and ribbons, and roll around in the savings. During the Christmas season, they also have additional stores at numerous malls in the Dallas and Fort Worth areas. You'll find 25 feet of gift wrap foil for $5.50-$6 per roll. Curses, foiled again! Here, 25 feet of regular paper ranges from $2-$4. When Christmas season descends upon you, that's when they open their warehouse doors and offer blow-out prices on gift wrap sure to blow you to kingdom come. More than 100 patterns and designs to choose from, so, you can, "Call it a wrap!" *CK, MC, V*

Pets & Vets

★★★★ ABT Tropical Aquarium 972/644-3474

1002 N. Central Expwy., Suite 699 *Mon-Fri 10-8; Sat 10-7; Sun Noon-6*
Richardson, TX 75080 *www.abttropical.com*

Put the tropics in your living room with the best-stocked fish tale around. When the subject turns to fresh- and saltwater tanks and water gardens, here's where to dive. More than 500 tanks are in the store stocked with fish, snakes and turtles ready to sock-eyed to you. ABT Tropical Aquarium has everything from new finned friends to Flipper's food. You can trust them to have what you are looking for in stock, along with the most exotic offerings in aquarium pets. Add accessories, such as live plants for aquariums and water gardens. (After all, this isn't government housing.) FLUVAL, HAGEN, OCEANIC and TETRA were just some of the fishy brand names we encountered. Jeepers creepers! *CK, MC, V, D*

★★★★★ Aquarium Warehouse 972/480-9779

1401-A TI Blvd. *Mon-Thu 10-6; Sat 10-7; Sun Noon-5*
Richardson, TX 75081 *www.aquariumwarehouse.com*

Swim on over to Aquarium Warehouse for the "cream of the crappies" (or the star of the school) when it comes to accessories for your tank. Their custom cabinets and tanks are the featured attraction here, as well as filtration systems, coral and anything else you need to make an interesting aquatic statement. They have more than 300 tanks up-and-running and filled to the brim with exotic and hard-to-find fish. Treat your new-found friends to gourmet food, gravel and cleaning supplies, from lines such as AQUAMARINE (agents and strips), ICE CAP, FISHSTUFF, LITTLE GIANT, MARINE ENTERPRISES, RIO PRODUCTS and so much more. Fish are displayed in more than 30,000 gallons of water in a 10,000-square-foot area. The sales personnel were friendly and information-driven. For either "a-fish-ionados" or beginners, one stop and you'll be hooked by this home for Big "D" ichthyologists. *CK, MC, V*

★★★★★ Backtalk Bird Center 972/960-BIRD

6959 Arapaho Rd., Suite 513 *Mon-Tue, Sat 10-6; Wed-Fri 10-7; Sun Noon-6*

Dallas, TX 75248

This is the only place Backtalk is acceptable. And while we're at it, I don't want any squawking about their prices ... many were below dealer's price. Cheap, cheap went those charming cockatoos and the prices on cages were the lowest around. For birds, there is none other. That's right, they are the only all-bird shop in town. Since we're all into nesting and birds of a feather flock together, why not get one? Though they do make for noisy bedfellows, you can always consider a dove, the bird of peace. Flock to see the conures, macaws, African birds, Amazon parrots, or any of the other species of aviary splendor. They might even like to spread their wings and fly home with you. (These friends, though, don't fly free.) Zebra finches were the lowest-priced birds on the totem pole, selling for around $12/pair. They carry lots of birds from finches to big macaws, but expect prices to soar with the more exotic and rare species such as the ledbeatter (Major Mitchell) which is $3,499 when in stock. Then again, the red-belly parrot was only $349, and boy was he a spectacular sight for sore ears. African grays are one of the most popular buys at Backtalk, going for $799. The hyacinth macaw, priced at $7,000, would have to reside in the vault for safe-keeping because I know five cats who would have a field day. *CK, MC, V, AE, D*

★★★★ Boutique Pet Shop & Aquarium 214/321-1219

9035 Garland Rd. *Mon-Fri 8-7; Sat 8:30-6, Sun Noon-5*

Dallas, TX 75218

Since 1968, your pet has been in good hands. Whether yours swims or walks, this is the only place where oil and water mix. This water specialty shop near White Rock Lake is one of the largest and best fish stores in the Metroplex, but the fish tale doesn't stop there. It's also a salon for your dog. On the one hand, see 55-gallon aquarium combos for $99.98 (though you'd have to spend $50 to pay this low price), plus aquarium plants and tropical and marine fish. This house doesn't just sell fish. Other pets can be fed and fashioned here as well) though I think the grooming of fish is a fish tale). You can get supplies for your dogs and grooming charges range from $20-$50 depending on size and condition of your dog. Same day grooming is possible unless Max has to be de-toxed and de-tangled. Throw in your line and see why they were named the Best Fish Store in '97 by *The Dallas Observer. CK, MC, V, AE, D*

★★★★ Canine Commissary 214/324-3900

11504 Garland Rd. Mon-Wed, Fri 9-7:30; Thu 9-9; Sat 9-6; Sun Noon-6
Garland, TX 75218

Take the bite out of barking up the wrong tree and shop at Canine Commissary. Whether it's for your canines or felines–I don't want to appear catty, but you, too, can enjoy discount pricing on dog and cat supplies, kennels, dog runs, show supplies, grooming supplies, doggie fashions, doggie life-jackets and car seats, carriers, toys, bowls, bones, cards and even a library with an A to Z inventory of "how-to" books for dog and cat fanciers. No breed is discriminated against here. They are an equal opportunity supplier. Like the PX, it's your RX for after-surgery supplies, halters, harnesses, beds and all brands of premium as well as economy-brand food. (Problem is, my Persian only eats Fancy Feast on a bone-china plates.) Three other locations should satisfy your animal instincts. Other locations: 3614 Greenville Ave., Dallas, 214/821-7700 and 1301 Custer Rd., Plano, 972/985-3900. *CK, MC, V, AE, D*

✧✧✧✧ Carrollton Animal Hospital 972/242-7606

1903 N. Josey Mon-Thu 7:30-7; Sat 8-3
Carrollton, TX 75006

Although he no longer has his mobile clinic, Dr. Kent Daniels, D.V.M., is still head honcho at the Carrollton Animal Hospital. If you're looking for low-cost vaccinations, come in Saturdays from 10-2. Lab tests, heartworm and flea prevention medications, etc., can be prescribed, as well as other medical treatment and surgery. His services are first-class, his prices are dog-gone cheaper than the competition and his bedside manner is doggedly delightful. *CK, MC, V, AE, D*

✧✧ Coit Valley Animal Hospital 972/234-5035

14055 Waterfall Way Mon-Fri 7:30-7; Sat 8-3
Dallas, TX 75240

Boarding the pooch for a family vacation can certainly take a chunk out of your mad-money, but it doesn't have to add to your worries. Board them at this full-service veterinary clinic and boarding facility and relax. Coit Valley is very large and offers everything from routine maintenance care to a complete hospital complex. You can bring your pets to this place and feel very comfortable knowing that they are in capable and loving hands. Boarding costs are $12.97/day for pooches under 20 pounds and $12.97/day for kitties (even if they weigh more than 20 pounds). Bring proof of all shots and vet checks from the last six months and be sure to call ahead for reservations and details. *CK, MC, V, AE*

✧✧✧✧✧ Dallas Cat Clinic/Dr. Steve Wilson — 972/907-CATS (2287)

PO Box 550932
Dallas, TX 75355
Mon-Fri 8-8

Just the cats, ma'am, and nothing but. Dr. Wilson is board-certified in feline medicine. For more than eight years Dallas Cat Clinic is an in-your-home feline-only practice offering full service veterinary care for cats. This completely equipped mobile veterinary van provides the same professional services as a stationary vet clinic. The difference is the convenience. You don't have to crate, dislodge, and traumatize your pussy cat while taking him or her there. (Don't they just love it!) Besides, there's no additional charge for the drive-by. The clinic comes to you. If you have a menagerie of more than one cat, this is the only way to call off the dogs. This driving force in the Metroplex is a pussycat himself, willingly driving from downtown Dallas to Allen, and as far west as I-35 and as far east as Rockwall. In-between appointments, he's driving again to the next "kitty-kat," who at this very moment is curled up on the window sill waiting for the Doc to pull into the driveway. *CK, MC, V, AE, D*

★★★★★ Diamond Pet Center — 972/442-7500

4412 Dillehay Rd. (F.M. 2551)
Parker, TX 75002
Mon-Fri 10-7; Sat 8-6; Sun 1-5

This store is for the birds–particularly exotic birds. At the beak of their careers, Diamond Pet Center specializes in domestic hand-fed exotica. Being a working bird ranch helps keep them pure and tweet-tweet. While its location, east of Plano off F.M. 2551, may not be the most readily accessible, it is a bird's paradise. Watch their wing spans soar and see parrots, cockatoos, cockatiels and several varieties of macaws, including green wings, harlequins and camelots. Flutter at the thought of buying elsewhere. Diamond Pet Center boasts one of the most extensive and best-priced lines of bird products and accessories in the Metroplex. Is it a bird? Is it a plaine? Is it a plain bird? Not at Diamond Pet Center. *CK, MC, V, AE, D*

✧✧✧ Find-A-Pet — 214/827-4357(HELP)

6301 Gaston Ave., Suite 600
Dallas, TX 75214
Mon-Fri 8:30-5:30
www.petdata.com

No charge service to help find your lost pet. Call and follow instructions for information and description on your pet. Through "Petdata.com," their goal is to enhance animal registration programs, educate communities, increase registration rates to help solve animal control problems and at the very least, help find Fido.

✧✧ Guardian Pet Sitters 972/625-5272

PO Box 560501 *Mon-Fri 10-5 (office); 24 hours/7 days (phones)*
The Colony, TX 75056

Does Rover seem to pine away in a boarding kennel? Move over Red Rover, and let GPS come over. Don't leave your doggie whining in the window. Instead, get professional sitting but expect to pay the price. Neighbors may do in a pinch, but it's a cinch these folks are the pros who are bonded and insured for your protection. Costs vary depending on the number of animals and the type of care required. References are available upon request. Allow your snooze machines to snooze in their own beds, eat from their own bowls, and lounge around during the day in their familiar territory. Since 1992, sitters serve from downtown Dallas north to McKinney, east to Rowlett and west to Flower Mound and everything in between. Owned by Sharon Jones, this company also provides transportation to vets and groomers, plus daily puppy care. They even change the cat box every day. One of the oldest in-home pet care services, Guardian Pet Sitters has a list of credentials a mile long, including membership in the National Association of Professional Pet Sitters and Pet Sitters International. Credit cards should be accepted by press time and a website is in the works. *CK*

✧✧✧✧✧ Homeward Bound Animal Rescue 817/792-5122

Weekends

Homeward Bound is where homeless pets can head to with a little help from their new best friends–you! Make a match that will provide a haven to a lost soul who in turn, will help you make it into heaven. It's the perfect relationship. They never complain that dinner's not on the table; then again, they never mind that dinner's on the table. It is a fact that a pet is the perfect companion for longer health and happiness. Homeward Bound is a non-profit organization that rescues and adopts animals and ultimately places them in loving homes, rather than route them to the death chambers. They always welcome donations, cages, kennels, cat and dog food, cat-boxes and litter, shampoo, flea dips or sprays, animal toys, and, of course, your loving arms. They can be found at the PETsMART at 4005 W. Airport Frwy. in Irving on the first and third Sunday of each month and on the fourth Saturday of each month. Find them at the PETsMART at the northwest corner of I-20 and Hulen St. in Fort Worth on the second and fourth

Sunday and the second and third Saturday of each month. Check PETsMART for pet adoptions throughout the Metroplex. *Non-profit; Donations Accepted*

✧✧✧✧✧ I-20 Animal Medical Center 817/478-9238

5820 W. I-20 *24 hours/7 days*
Arlington, TX 76017

One of the only area pet hospitals to be featured regularly on the local news (and national Pet Cable Station) for innovations in pet treatment. Either they have a terrific public relations department or a terrific clinic. I'd say they have both. Emergency or not, this clinic does it all, except haircuts. (Unless, of course, you consider neutering a Pro Cut!) Appointment hours are Monday-Friday 8-7 and Saturday 9-1, but emergency care is 'round the clock. With 15 veterinarians on staff, 26 technicians, a board-certified critical-care specialist (one of only 57 in the country), and an approved residency program (one of three in the country), you can feel confident that your pet will get the medical attention and state-of-the-art treatment needed. Diagnostics, baths, dips, nails, EKG's, ultra-sounds and boarding in this 15,000-square-foot hospital that is probably the most impressive in the state. Nothing's too good for mine. What about yours? However, expect to pay the price. *CK, MC, V, AE, D*

♥♥♥♥♥ Invisible Fencing Pet Containment 972/434-4544

1320 W. Main St. *Mon-Fri 8:30-5:30; Sat 8:30-2*
Lewisville, TX 75067

Some you see and some you don't. These are the ones you don't. Plus, with Invisible Fencing Pet Containment, you can forget ever painting, restoring, refinishing, or replacing your fence again. If those four-legged rascals love to give you a run for your money, contain them on your front lawn with an invisible fence. Professional installation and veterinarian approved, it's an investment worth considering. An underground wire with radio emissions keeps your pooch in place. How many dogs have you lost? How many have wreaked havoc in the neighborhood? How many flower beds have been trampled? There's a 1-year pet containment guarantee and financing, so take your barker and keep him out of harm's way. *CK, MC, V, AE, D, Financing*

✧✧✧✧ Man's Best Friend 972/988-0991

1290 W. Pioneer Pkwy. *Mon-Thu 9-8; Fri-Sun 9-5*
Grand Prairie, TX 75051 *www.mansbf.com*

It's woman's best friend, too, make no bones about it. One of the few dog training centers that provides both group support as well as individually prescribed programs. All breeds and all ages are welcome to take the course.

(Course, they haven't finished with my brood yet; I'll keep you posted on the pee-pee problem.) If it works, you can bet your "sweet bippy" I'll be singing their praises loud and clear. That'll be one more feather in their cap. This state-licensed facility offers obedience training, family-protection training, and behavioral problem-solving, such as housebreaking and incessant barking. They also have inside boarding with air-conditioned kennels and, if you're looking for a dog that has already graduated, they will sell you one that has at least graduated with honors. Also at 3201 Skylane Drive in Carrollton (972/407-1704) and 5615 Rufe Snow Drive in North Richland Hills (817/788-9688). *CK, MC, V, AE, D*

♥♥♥♥♥ Metroplex Veterinary Centre and Pet Lodge — 972/438-7113

700 W. Airport Frwy. — *24 Hours/7 Days*
Irving, TX 75061

There's nowhere short of the Mayo Clinic that would do for MY pets when the chips are down. So, consider this clinic the place to go when there's a canine or feline crisis. Even if your cat needs a cat scan, consider the Metroplex Veterinary Centre and Pet Lodge. Services ranging from boarding and grooming to critical and intensive surgery and care, Metroplex features advanced diagnostic equipment, such as MRIs, ultrasounds and endoscopies. All the vets are certified specialists and will work with your regular vet in the case of emergency situations or referrals. *CK, V, MC, AE, D*

Mobile Veterinary Services

Various Locations — *24 Hours/7 Days*
DFW, TX

A complete mobile veterinary clinic, Dr. Hawk or one of his associates sets up the clinic in Denton, Lewisville and Grapevine on alternating days to see be accessible with no appointments necessary. You will find him ready to help you and your pet on Mondays and Thursdays from 4-7 in Grapevine at Master Feed, 702 S. Main St.; Tuesdays from 4-7 and Saturdays from 9-Noon in Denton in the Kmart parking lot, 2300 W. University Drive; and on Wednesdays from 4-7 and Sundays from 2-5 in Lewisville in the Kmart parking lot, 1019 Fox Ave. For other times, call Metro 817/925-0339. *CK, MC, V*

♥♥♥♥♥ Nature Labs — 940/691-8881

6232 Southwest Pkwy., Suite 106 — *Mon-Fri 9-5*
Wichita Falls, TX 76310

One whiff and you'll be hooked. This company was founded by a chemist who was bored with the same ole, same ole olfactory options available for dogs and cats. So, he created a line of satirical pet fragrances that will having you singing "Happy Tails To You." Choose from K-9, Timmy Holedigger and Pucci. Believe me, they're "scent-sational." The packaging and fragrances alone are enough to make your pup runneth over. Each fragrance resembles and hinges around their human-product counterparts (some buyers even use them on themselves) which makes them even more appealing. Sure does smell like the real stuff. Pumps and aluminum packaging are first class. Sold in pet mail order catalogs and in pet stores, Underground Shoppers can save 20 percent on gift packs. Sniff! Sniff! *CK, MC, V, AE, D, C*

✧✧✧✧ North Texas Emergency Pet Clinic 972/323-1310

1445 MacArthur Dr., Suite 246 Mon-Thu 6 P.M.-8 A.M.; Fri-Sun 24 Hours
Carrollton, TX 75007 www.ntepc.com

Bark if there's an emergency. Since emergencies only happen when it's inconvenient (that means the doctor's on the golf course), where can you go for help? If your pet has declared a state-of-emergency when its doctor is approaching the 10th hole, call on these vets who handle the medical crisis after-hours and on the weekends. Almost 30 vets have joined forces in this 2,200-square-foot, full-surgical facility to handle minor, as well as major, catastrophes. Leave the cattle and horses at home, but hamsters, birds, dogs and cats are welcome, even if they only have diaper rash. They don't do routine vaccinations or spay or neutering. Expect to pay a $60 fee for small animals and $75 for exotic ones. They're even open during holidays. *CK, MC, V, AE, D*

✧✧✧✧✧ Operation Kindness 972/418-7297

3201 Earhart Drive Mon-Wed, Fri-Sat 11-4:30; Thu 11-8; Sun 1-4:30
Carrollton, TX 75006

Nestled into their new and improved expanded location one mile north of Belt Line, one street south of Keller Springs, two blocks west of Midway in Carrollton, Operation Kindness is all purrs and kisses. This is the greatest little pick-up joint in town. Pick a pet and adopt a friend for life. You "petcha!" You'll live longer. And happier. This no-kill animal shelter is the perfect place to pick-a-pet for life. Give the gift of love and enjoy the creature comforts of owning and loving them. Where else do you receive unconditional love–even at those times you're not so loveable. Besides, spoiling them means just more licks and kisses. Cats cost $60 and dogs, $70 (includes spaying and neutering, as well as the first round of shots). Looking for the perfect pet gift? How about the state-of-the-art litter boxes or crates, bandannas, sweaters, the fashion wardrobe befitting the North Dallas socialite. Cookbooks, T-shirts, umbrellas, some jewelry and photo frames, too. Johnny's on the spot as their fearless leader to one of my favorite charities. Donations welcomed. All proceeds benefit the 2,500 homeless animals they care for each year. Jazz, our Operation Kindness dobie-shepherd mix has been the leader of our rat pack for several years and is the best behaved of the motley crew. *CK, MC, V, D*

✧✧✧ Pet Salon, The — 972/221-0360

1565 W. Main St., Suite 105 — *Mon-Fri 7:30-6:30; Sat 7:30-7*
Lewisville, TX 75067

There's nothing that brings a smile to a bad hair day better than a trip to the Pet Salon. And this is no clip joint. Rather it's a full-service salon that dips and blowdries for less. They also have discounted supplies for dogs and cats. Grab a few rawhide chews every time Poochie or Gucci gets a good report card from the groomers. Pick up an argyle sweater to keep out the chill on cold winter days. Mutts, mongrels and world champions are all treated like kings by these stylish clippers. Doggie bones, shampoos, leashes, pet food–you can get the works. They also offer boarding–making this Lewisville salon your one-stop shop for the pampered pet set. The staff is knowledgeable and friendly. Call ahead for appointments, as this is a very popular "must do" salon. *CK, MC, V, AE, D*

★★★★ Petco — 972/221-8816

201 N. Summit Dr. — *Mon-Sat 9-9; Sun 9-7*
Lewisville, TX 75067 — *www.petco.com*

Getting down to pet business without getting the brush-off is why so many folks sing Petco's praises. In fact, you can twist and shout at this pet-lover's paradise. Don't be shocked to see the store personnel's personal pets or customers' four-legged friends hanging around at the checkout counter getting a treat or two. One-stop shopping for your entire brood (dogs, cats, birds, rabbits, reptiles, rodents and fish) will keep you out of the doghouse. Then again, you can buy another doghouse, grooming supplies, litter boxes, kennels, toys and more with one sweep around the superstore. Some locations have a complete selection of aquarium supplies and fish, too. All manufacturers' coupons are accepted. Look for their full-color mailers in your mailbox. Check directory to find one of the more than 20 locations in the Metroplex. After all, it's still a dog's life. *CK, MC, V, AE, D*

★★★★★ PETsMART 972/407-0101

6204 W. Park Blvd. *Mon-Sat 9-9; Sun 9-7*
Plano, TX 75093 *www.petsmart.com*

Get smart, shop PETsMART–or PetSmart. Whichever way you spell it, it still means savings in your pocket. Do your part for the hundreds of thousands of dogs and cats in Texas that wind up in area animal shelters. All it takes is one dog or cat to bring love into your life while you save a life in the process. During special promotions called Luv-A-Pet, this discount superstore allows humane organizations to adopt their animals. Save money. Save a pet. This warehouse-style merchandiser distinguishes itself from the competition with a line of gourmet goodies from Three Dog Bakery. Also look for a chuck wagon full of rawhide treats, beef ears, pig ears, tail chips and ham bones. Cat treats include Gym Pets, TOPINI white cheese or trout-flavored and mouse-shaped treats. Sounds pretty good, huh? Shop at PETsMART (including the vet and prescription pet foods) for everything that will keep your new pet set for life–dog houses, leashes, food, toys–all at discounted prices. Then again, what price can you put on love? Check directory for the location nearest you. *CK, MC, V, D*

♥♥♥♥♥ Puppy Love Mobile Dog Grooming 972/243-8331

Dallas, TX *Mon-Sat By Appt.*

No ifs, angoras or beagles. They do them all. And we all love Puppy Love. Since 1977, this van has been parked in more driveways than your morning newspaper. In 1999, by popular demand, they extended their service area to include the mid-cities and Arlington. Personalized service comes complete with door-to-door grooming in one of their 21 completely equipped vans manned by professional groomers. No cages, no tranquilizers, no going to and "fro"–just a gorgeous new "fro" for the poodle down the street and a new "do" at the Diva's Doggie Estate and Kitty Kondo. Yes, they do lion cuts on cats, too. Expect to pay the price for quality and convenience but it's worth every last hair ball. Charges of $36 for the first 10 inches in height and $1 for each additional inch, plus a $2.50 trip charge. This service includes bathing, grooming, clipping, cleaning ears, draining anal glands and a spritz of after-shave cologne. Now they've gone computer, and you'll never have to give them all the details again; just say "Like last time," and that's what you'll get. Too bad Our Miss Priss doesn't shave. She's much too young. Besides, she's heard about laser hair removal and is purring to try it. *CK, MC, V, AE, D*

Riding Unlimited, Inc

940/479-2016

9168 T. N. Skiles Rd.
Ponder, TX 76259
Tue-Sat: Call for times
www.ridingunlimited.org

Ride 'em cowboy. This is the place to ride it out. Saddle up at Riding Unlimited, a center that uses horse-back riding as therapy for both children and adults. 10-week sessions in the spring and fall and a six-week session in the summer are available. Tuition's $250 for the 10-week sessions. They are always looking for volunteers to help with their programs; so if you're a people person who also loves horses, this is the place to call. The center has 12 therapeutic riding horses for children and adults with physical or mental disabilities. Call Marietta Sterling for training times and information and see what a difference a horse makes. *CK*

✧✧✧✧✧ SNAP (Spay-Neuter Assistance Program)

214/372-9999

4830 Village Fair Dr.
Dallas, TX 75224
Tue-Sat By Appt. Only
www.snaptx.org

You can't cut it much closer than $25 to spay or $15 to neuter your cat. For dogs, it's $30 to spay and $25 to neuter. A small price to pay for protection against an unwanted affair. Located in a former Red Lobster restaurant, at least their claws don't pinch your budget. Even if you've discovered a wild cat on the loose, these folks will sterilize it for free (ask for details). You must have an appointment for surgery. SNAP has opened a new wellness and vaccination clinic at their Village Fair Drive location. Help control the animal population and love your pet by bringing it here. Only licensed veterinarians are in residence. Located six miles south of downtown Dallas near I-35 E and Ledbetter Drive (Loop 12). *CK, MC, V*

★★★★★ Southland Farm Store

214/350-7881

5855 Maple Ave.
Dallas, TX 75235
Mon-Fri 8-6; Sat 8-5

Even if you're not the teacher's pet, you'll find what you need for your pet at Southland Farm Store. More than 5,000 square feet of air-conditioned pet shopping and an additional 30,000 square feet of warehouse space should cover all the bases when it comes to your pet. The warehouse has been moved to Irving and ultimately will be used for wholesale only leaving the Maple Ave. location the source to fill your pet's pantry. Not only are all the major vet-recommended brands available, but so are many unusual and unique items fit for a hearty, healthy and happy hound (as well as for hamsters, hares, horses, or other hairy friends, too). Since they are distributors of premium foods, Southland offers daily specials and a guaranteed low price on all products such as IAMS, KAL-KAN, KEN-L-RATION, NUTRO, PRO PLAN, SCIENCE DIET, SENSIBLE CHOICE, WAYNE and more. But that's not all. Southland carries a complete lawn and garden section, a do-it-yourself pest control department and probably the largest selection of wild birdhouses, feeders and supplies in the Metroplex. Also look for them at 400 Cascade Drive in Irving. *CK, MC, V*

Plants & Gardens

♥♥♥♥♥ Backyard Birds & Garden Accents 972/671-7664

1373 W. Campbell Rd. *Mon-Sat 10-6; Sun Noon-4*
Pavillion One Center
Richardson, TX 75080

Perch at this Backyard if you're looking for gifts for the garden and patio, oh birdbrain. You won't fly off the handle when you see such gifts as clocks, stained-glass window hangings, hand-painted welcome slates, sun catchers, ornaments, puzzles, jewelry, mugs and mouse pads. All guaranteed to get you fluttering. Write a note on bird stationery; there's birdy wrap it up with gift wrap and greeting cards, bird and gardening journals, T-shirts, totes and note cards. For the garden and patio, choose marble and resin statuary, cherubs, angels, children, animals, St. Francis statues, pedestal and wall-mounted fountains, garden homes for butterflies, lady bugs and toads ... well, how many neighbor's backyards do you have to be green with envy? Add doormats, flags, bench pillows, wind chimes, outdoor clocks and thermometers, rain gauges and seeds to attract most any kind of bird and you've got a glimpse of what's possible from this backyard. And if it's birdhouses, it's one-in-a-million chance they don't have what you'd want. Every conceivable shape, size and style birdhouse, from ranch-styles to contemporary, split level to town homes, some under $20. But if you're a member of the nouveau riche, try putting a copper-roofed, hand-painted one over their heads. Those will set you back around $100. Not wild about birds? Then there's plenty of gardening tools and items to choose. Owners seem very friendly and shop was bustling on the day of our visit, especially for a weekday. Hm-m. They had hummingbird feeders, too. *CK, MC, V, D*

★★★ Beyond the Border 817/465-4707

3406 Cooper St., Suite 100 *By Appt. Only*
Arlington, TX 76015

Love the tacos at On the Border? Then you'll love shopping here. Head to

Beyond the Border if you want to corner the market on Mexican imports and pottery. Shop where this Jackie (Cambora) shops for plant pots, stands, decanters, chimeneas and more from south of the border. In Texas, that might not be the incentive to get your off your duff, but there're enough unique items to make it worth your while. The combination of quality and price equals a round of "Olés!" in the bullring. Trucks pull up regularly, so make sure your passport's up to date. The latest, the greatest in Mexican pottery, Talavera planters and wrought-iron stands in a variety of styles and finishes. The decanters are lead free, the colors are vibrant, and there's no doubt about it, this is not your run-of-the-mill Mexican pot shop. Look for Jackie at the Dallas Farmer's Market in Shed 2 on Sat/Sun 10-4 during the spring or fall, or call for appointment and tour the warehouse for mucho grandé deals. *CK, MC, V*

★★★★★ Bright Flowers — 972/247-8818

11363 Denton Dr., #104 — *Mon-Sat 9:30-5:30*
Dallas, TX 75229

Want to milk the silk flower market? Want to extricate every last penny out of the prices of silk plants and flowers? Then, this could be the root to solving the problem. Everything dirt cheap here with one exception. You don't need dirt to enjoy these flowers. In fact, you don't even have to water or fertilize them. Do nothing ... just relax and smell the flowers. A little dusting now and then is all that's required and the perfect addition to home decorative accents. Located in the International Plaza complex, save 50-80 percent on thousands of stem flowers and greenery, seasonal arrangements and Christmas trees (7- and 9-foot models were $95 each–that's 70 percent off). They carry silk flowers only–no live or cut. Many of them have been created for them exclusively so let's arrange a few and see what materializes. Don't overlook the other bright side: beautiful dolls, doll furniture and collectibles. *CK, MC, V, AE, D*

★★★★ Bruce Miller Nursery — 972/238-0204

1000 E. Belt Line Rd. — *Mon-Sat 8-6; Sun 10-5*
Richardson, TX 75081 — *www.brucemillernursery.com*

Want a blizzard of bargains? Located in a former Dairy Queen, Bruce Miller Nursery is your fast-plant operation that delivers the greenery to the scenery. This home-grown nursery has strong roots in Richardson but it's not just your plain vanilla varieties. Just look at the bedding plants out front, and you'll know how much creative green thumbs had their hands in the planning and producing of these flowers, shrubs, trees and ornamental plants. Most are shipped in from

Miller's own farm outside Canton so you're really get direct-from-grower quality and prices. Prices are shades below gardening superstores. We found 5-gallon crepe myrtles for $16.99 and lots of herbs for about $2 each, including 4-inch pots. They also have a large selection of garden tools, fertilizer and top soil treatments. A nod from his dog Cody warns you "Not to bark up the wrong tree." Seasonal promotions net the deepest discounts. *CK, MC, V, AE, D*

★★ Calloway's — 972/994-0134

8152 Spring Valley Rd. — *Mon-Sun 9-6*
Dallas, TX 75240 — *www.calloways.com*

Beautiful ads do not a nursery make. Sometimes, beautiful plants don't either. The old adage, "People who live in glass houses shouldn't sell flowers" may hold true here. In spite of the convenient locations, abundant choices and holding their own in the Metroplex, the prices at Calloway's are no runaways. Branching out with their awesome greenhouse facades and every line of fertilizer, plant food, seed and tool to get you "mow-tivated," prices are par for the course. Sales, though, are another story. Waiting with baited breath, by the time the prices descend, the planting season for them is often over. C'est la rose! Large and small shrubs, bedding plants, flowering plants, indoor plants, grab a wheelbarrel and roll out the barrel. Knowledgeable albeit hurried staff help choose appropriate plants when the spirit moves them. Check directory for the location nearest you (17 in Dallas area). *CK, MC, V, AE, D*

✧✧✧✧✧ Coker & Coker Landscape — 972/446-8733

Carrollton, TX 75006 — *By Appt. Only (Phone answered Mon-Fri 7-5)*

Mow, mow, mow the lawn, cheaper than you think. This company wins hands on. Coker & Coker Landscape contractors are not lawyers to clip you but great landscapers and their crews to nip your lawns and gardens. Very few stray blades of grass are left blowing in the wind. Service with a smile at prices that are beguiling. Front and backyard service on a middle-sized home costs around $30 a week. This includes mowing, edging, weeding and blowing. They also do custom landscaping with water features. If you are looking to spruce it up, and don't want to do-it-yourself, give them a call. *CK*

★★★★★ Cox's Plant Farm — Metro 817/467-2431

2405 W. Harris Rd. — *Mon-Fri 8-4:30; Sat 8-4:30*
Arlington, TX 76001

Add flowers to your rock garden–just make sure they're from Cox's Plant

Farm. Plant yourself down and don't dig another hole without this wholesaler of bedding plants. Finally, this grower has opened his farm to the public. In business more than 20 years, Kenny Gill's in charge of production and oversees the 108 greenhouses and more than 250,000 square feet of growing area that ultimately winds its way into your front or backyard. Head south of I-20 about three-quarters of a mile off Cooper Street to get your hands on bedding plants, shrubs, roses and equally lush and lower-priced indoor tropicals. Remember, the cheap shall inherit the earth! *CK, MC, V*

CyberSeeds.com

P.O. Box 171102 *www.cyberseeds.com*
San Antonio, TX 78217

For some of us having a garden and planting our own seeds is a spiritual and uplifting experience. Nurturing a plant from its early beginning into a full fledged tree or plant is truly astonishing. If you have a green thumb and are looking for a great place to buy plant seeds or grow your own herbs then visit CyberSeeds.com. They have a great selection of seeds including cactus, herb, house plants, medicinal plants, alter native grasses, trees, oak, ornamental grasses, palm tree, potpourri, roses, stir fry, veggies, vines, bonsai, fruit, lilac and tropical plant seeds available. You can get 1,000 cactus seeds for only $9.95. How about 20 seeds of roses for only $2.50? Not bad huh? Start your own garden today with the help of CyberSeeds.com. *CK, MC, V, AE, D*

Deco-Curb 972/554-8482

1205 Mayleaf Dr. *By Appt. Only*
Irving, TX 75060

Get those gardens under control and put an end to unruly roots. Get an edge up on the competition with Deco-Curb. Decorative landscape curbing around the perimeter of your garden helps separate the garden materials from the rest of the lawn. Not only does this form of edging look very elegant and precise, it also saves you the wear and tear of edging and trimming weekly. Being concrete, it is very durable and will withstand weathering. Set your garden apart from the rest with Deco-Curb and never look back. *CK*

★★ Diana's Silk Plantation 817/788-0222

1009 Cheek Sparger Rd., #108 *Mon-Sat 10-6*
Colleyville, TX 76034

Why shop at the farm when a Plantation will do in a pinch? Forget flowers that wilt the night away, deader than a doorknob after a few days? Diana's flowers are eternally fresh, never need watering, and do wonders with an occasional brush-off. The flowers from Diana's Silk Plantation may not smell as sweet as nature's but that is curable with a few spritzes of perfume. When other flowers start to sag, Diana's will still be fresh as daisies. Best of all, they are ready and available the next time you need to say, "I'm sorry." Silk flowers are an inexpensive addition without looking like the same old garden variety. Lots of knick-knacks and accessories including candlesticks, picture frames and other cheeky things. *CK, MC, V, AE*

✧✧✧ Do-It-Yourself Pest & Weed Control — 972/867-7649

2109 W. Parker Rd., Suite 108 — *Mon-Sat 9-6*
Plano, TX 75023

Get rid of those nasty pests that seem to appear just when your in-laws are coming for the weekend. Though you won't go to jail, you can kill 'em legally here. (No, not your mother-in-law, silly). You'll even be able to save money on your weapons of choice. This do-it-yourself pest and weed control outfit offers at-home service technicians for a basic charge of $69, plus tax, to come on-site and rid your home or office of general infestations. Or, you can pay retail price for the products and do it yourself. Remember, either way, they can't offer anything harmful to the environment. Everything they sell, if used properly, is OK (unless you're a fan of the Dirt Doctor). Then again, since they also carry lots of organic products and have people on staff that can train you in their proper usage, even Howard Garrett would approve. *CK, MC, V, AE, D*

Duncanville Landscape (Plant Depot) — 972/296-8070

4503 W. Redbird Lane — *Mon-Fri 8-4*
Dallas, TX 75236

Formerly Plant Depot, nothing comes between them and their jeans. Landscaping jobs including installation are their forte. Open in August for fall plantings and then in the spring for seasonal color additions, just don't expect them to say it with flowers during the summer. Ten minutes from downtown, here's a depot that's on the right side of the tracks. Though they no longer sell plants or flowers through a retail site, if you want the look without any of the effort, these folks are dirt cheap when it comes to landscaping. Choose your plants and away they'll go. If you are a sufferer of begonia breath after a hard day at the office, they are life savers. *CK, MC, V, AE, D*

★★★★★ East Side

214/340-0855

10228 E. Northwest Hwy. *Mon-Fri 9-6; Sat 9-5*
Dallas, TX 75238

Formerly Floral Group, these are the folks to make your day. Whether it's a party, wedding, or a celebration of any old kind, say it with fresh flowers. And while you're at it, why not buy them from the same place that grocers and florists do? At the East Side, fresh flowers are sold to area florists and flower shops. This wholesale flower warehouse wouldn't be caught dead with artificial or potted flowers, though. Only fresh-cut will do. One-dozen long stem red roses cost $19.99, with vase $35. To keep from offending their customers, they do no advertising to the public, but if you are planning a shindig with flowers, why not buy in bulk here and save a bundle? Call for the lowest prices around on daisies, roses, or whatever's in season or in stock, as well as floral design supplies, wedding arrangements, wedding bouquets, corsages, altar arrangements, design classes and delivery. Plenty of brides we know wouldn't take the walk without them. But what if the florist is getting married? Who does his flowers? Just checking. *CK, MC, V, D*

★★ Fannin Tree Farm

972/335-4880

8420 Preston Rd. *Mon-Sat 8-5; Sun 1-5*
Plano, TX 75024

This farm is a legacy in its own time. Just 1.5 miles north of Legacy, a hop, skip and a trunkload of trees await you from this grower and tree contractor. (Just don't bark up the wrong tree!) If you don't like a good oak, where else wood you get your laughs? Fannin has live oaks and red oaks, even Chinese pistachios and Aristocrat pears to prune. Large native trees are sold from 3-inches to 12 inches with 1- to 2-year guarantees. Competitively priced, depending on the season, you'll pay on average of $100 per caliper inch. A 3-inch tree (round), for example, would cost around $330 delivered, planted and guaranteed, while a 4-inch beauty could be yours for around $490. Enjoy a lunch or dinner at The Backyard Grill overlooking this lush landscaped setting and spend some time Fannin away the hours. *CK, MC, V, D*

★★★★★ Flower Market

214/521-8886

5315 N. Central Expwy. *Mon-Fri 9-6; Sat 9-5*
Dallas, TX 75205

To market, to market, this little lady went to the Flower Market. Whether you want yours by the stem or an arrangement, be it for a funeral, a wedding, a reception, a party–the choice is yours and, boy, do you have choices! A virtual reality of glorious blooms on any given day. How about 40 different varieties, a choice of more than 100 colors, and priced, well, cheap for Highland Park chic. Tulips by the stem, 10-count with just a bow wrap are reasonably priced, though prices vary with the type of tulip. They also have good deals on a dozen pink rhapsody roses with Queen Anne lace in the vase or a dozen of the same roses loose with wrap (unless it's Valentine's Day and then it's what the market will bear). You can access the Flower Market on the southbound service road of Central Expressway, just south of Mockingbird near McCommas and adjacent to the Steinway Hall Piano. You can tickle the ivories first, then tickle your fancy and come out smelling like a rose. Best prices in town. And we're not talking teeny-weenie little buds, either. This bud's for you. *CK, MC, V, AE, D*

Flower Ranch — 817/431-3830

901 Pearson Ln. — *Mon-Sat 8-6; Sun 10-5*
Keller, TX 76248

You won't be singing, "Don't Fence Me In," at this Flower Ranch. Flowers, flowers everywhere and mostly sold by the flat. Up to 22,000 flats were sitting there as we rounded the bend. Expect a flat to be flat-out priced at $13. (Not bad, considering they're so sharp.) This commercial grower opens to the public periodically, closing out their overstocks of blooms and selling them off by the flats. Alyssum, petunias, celosia, hibiscus, bougainvillea, impatiens, moss rose, begonias, Joseph's coat, ferns, marigolds, salvia, coleus ... what did you expect, a blank landscape? *CK*

★★★ Green Mama's Organic Garden Market — 817/514-7336

5324 Davis Blvd. — *Mon-Sat 9-6; Sun 11-4*
North Richland Hills, TX 76180 — *www.greenmamas.com*

Introducing Big Mama to Green Mama. It's all a matter of the environment. Purists know how to pave the way to politically-correct gardens. And here's the place to go au natural. Head to Green Mama's to save some green. Off 820, exit Highway 26/Grapevine, go north to the light and then turn left. Nursery plants, water gardens, wildlife supplies, gifts–if you buy whole flats of bedding plants, shave another 10 percent off. Bed down with lots of organic gardening books, but don't expect the yard art, wind chimes and such to be organic. So be it. A trip here is a real education. It includes a wildlife feeding center (anything you would need to feed the wildlife), a verdant pond department where you can get everything it would take to build your own as well as instruction on plant placement. Right next to Hudiburg Chevrolet, see the USA and save the planet. *CK, MC, V, D*

★★★★★ Hartwell's Landscaping Nursery 972/436-3612

1570 N. Stemmons *Mon-Fri 8:30-5:30; Sat 8:30-5*
Lewisville, TX 75067

A tree may grow in Brooklyn, but here in the Metroplex, we buy ours at Hartwell's. And why not, they plant them, free. Now that has a nice ring to it! This home-grown source for greenery is located smack-dab in the middle of a mixed bag of boat dealerships, RV outlets, sporting-goods warehouses, funeral homes, and barbecue joints, yet Hartwell's has kept its roots planted firmly on the ground. While the surrounding area blossoms with other kinds of business and seasonal activities, this nursery near the shores of Lake Lewisville, has plants and trees plus a landscape architect on staff. Colorful crepe myrtles out front catch your eye when in season, but also lots of smaller trees–fruit, pecan, Chinese pistachio and Bradford pear. Plant them yourself or have them installed by their crew. One-gallon shrubs and Hibiscus were well below retail, and 2-gallon wax myrtles were well cut, too. They specialize in trees, 5-gallon sizes for $9.88. See cedar elms, silver maples, live oaks, loblolly pines, globes and weeping willows–all guaranteed for one year. We thought our friend was breaking for turtles when she veered off the highway at FM 407 heading north on I-35, but we soon found out otherwise. A nice detour to satiate your green thumb. A good place for organic supplies too, like: green sand, lava sand, pine mulch, humate and "Garrett Juice" to keep your intentions honorable. *CK, MC, V, AE, D*

★★ Herb Market 972/446-9503

1002 4th St. *Mon-Sat 10:30-5:30*
Carrollton, TX 75006

The spice of life is nice when it's a simple as shopping at the Herb Market. Lana Jones, a devoted cook and gardener, grew her own herbs until her cup ran over; then she decided to open shop and share her secrets. You can buy bulk herbs and save money over grocery-store prices. For example, garlic will cost you around $3 in the store or $1.25 for one ounce of organic garlic here, pure and simple. More than 100 different dried herbs are available alongside 60-90 (depending on the season) fresh herbs rooted in healthy living. This little house is beckoning just over the railroad tracks in old downtown Carrollton. Essential oils (essential for aromatherapy), herbal soaps, teas, books on the subject, gift items and dried herbal wreath arrangements are also part of their market availability. Be sure to ask about their candle-making and soap-making classes. *CK, MC, V*

♥♥♥♥♥ I Love Flowers

214/357-9577

4347 W. Northwest Hwy.
Dallas, TX 75220

Mon-Fri 8-6:30; Sat 8-6

For tip-toeing through the tulips, to waltzing through the wisteria, everyone loves flowers. In the springtime. In the fall. Really, anytime at all, I Love Flowers. So when you're feeling flush and not thinking twice about the price, give I Love Flowers a call. Their bouquets are heaven-sent. They'll literally take your breath away. The variety is voluminous. Quality is hand-picked. But arrangements are market price. Not to worry. Get to the root and you'll save some money. Cash and carry prices will whittle the prices down somewhat. Don't expect, though, the ordinary Lazy Susan's. There's mostly the unusual and the sublime ready to be swooped up–like an orchid arrangement or tipped roses. I envy the gals who get orchids. Me? I get forget-me-nots. Delivery charges range from $5-$10. *CK, MC, V, AE, D*

★★★★★ Joy Silk Flower Outlet

972/241-1466

11252 Harry Hines Blvd., #201
Dallas, TX 75229

Mon-Sat 9-6.30

You've heard of the Joy Luck Club, maybe I could interest you in the Joy Silk Flower Outlet. If not, you'll be out of luck. Silk flowers of every description for every season is available for the picking. What a wonderful array of floral displays, wreaths and bouquets ready for delivery; or, have a custom arrangement made to your specifications. Wedding and other special occasion flowers can be created with flowers beginning as low as $1 a stem. Though the more exotic blooms can shoot your wad at $10-$12 a stem, have you priced them elsewhere? Now that's a thorn in my budget's side. *CK, MC, V, D*

★★★★ Lake June Garden Center

214/391-4005

8634 Lake June Rd.
Dallas, TX 75217

Mon-Sat 9-5:30; Sun 10-3

Though not near a lake, or a spring, this garden center delivered watered down prices on plants, plants and more plants. Reap and ye shall see plenty of plants at this full–service nursery, but they are still not mow-tivated to selling lawn mowers. They are one of the sponsors of the Xeriscape Contest held each year through the Dallas Water Utilities Department. Competing participants set out displays of native plants requiring little watering which is dear to Lake June's heart. Lake June specializes in native and naturalized plants specific to Texas and dry climates. Too, they offer several unusual plants alongside a healthy variety of mainstays. Most plants are discounted about 20 percent–more during specials. Selling star brand roses for the past several years appears to be a stellar performer. Construction of additional fencing has increased their shade and fruit trees making this orchard an "plantiful" opportunity. If you need help with design, call on their landscape services, complete with a computerized plan or an individual consultation. *CK, MC, V*

★★★ Leonard's Farm and Ranch — 817/332-2283

501 E. Belknap — *Mon-Fri 8-6; Sat 8-4*
Fort Worth, TX 76102

Down at the farm and ranch, we saw quite a few weekend warriors cutting up at Leonard's–but alas, no Leonard. We did, however, see what makes Leonard's run–lots of mowers, small tractors, sprinklers, flower bed equipment and the whole nine yards (or acres) ... including CUB CADET, LAWN BOY, SNAPPER, TORO, TROY BILT and others riding high. For added value, don't overlook their selection of commercial-quality, lesser-known brands usually favored in performance by serious farm-to-marketers. We snagged a MCALLEN lawn edger for $300 and then cut out. Down-home folks with down-home prices, a nice change of pace. *CK, MC, V, AE, D*

★★★★★ Little House on Pearl, The — 214/748-1443

514 S. Pearl — *Wed-Sun 9-5*
Dallas, TX 75201

There's a good reason Farmer's Market attracts millions of shoppers each year. If you want to mingle with the masters, the faster you corral a dried flower from here the better the bargain. A plant for all seasons is another good reason to shop this little house. Put together a lunch bunch of bittersweet and you'll be basking in the sunflowers forever. Add some pepper or tallow berries, poke around the artichokes and, for spice, add some cinnamon sticks. Want to assemble a Tex-Mex mix? Well, ogle the okra pods and chile peppers, add some pine or star cones, sprinkle the raffia, and tuck in the birch twigs–it's all yours for a fraction of the cost of the ready-made varieties. This house in the prairie called Farmer's Market has the best selection of dried flowers and plants anywhere this side of the Oklahoma border. They also carries candles and other tabletop accessories. *CK, MC, V, AE*

★★★★ Luckman Silks 214/739-9298

11661 Preston Rd. *Mon-Sat 10-6; Sun Noon-5*
Dallas, TX 75230

Now planted into a new North Dallas location, Luckman Silks may just be your winning ticket. Go green with dozens of silk plants and flower arrangements that never need tending (maybe dusting). Luckman offers high-quality silks at discounted prices and sitting in the garden of splendor (in the grass). Ficus tress, ferns, ivy–almost anything green will compete for every last decorating dollar. Browse through their lush forest for the cream of the crop. We found a 6-foot ficus (regular and red) plus we picked up some lush ivy to place on the fireplace mantel. Open seven days a week, you can't seem to go out the door empty-handed. They sun also shines at the location in Colleyville at 4209 B. Colleyville Blvd. *CK, MC, V, AE, D*

✧✧✧✧✧ Metro Irrigation 817/877-5052

1622 Rogers Rd. *Mon-Fri 8-5*
Fort Worth, TX 76107

Looking for a lawn doctor to keep the grass greener on your side, for a change? Off I-30, exit University and go south toward the Fort Worth Zoo if you don't want to get soaked. Just before you get to the zoo, there's an Owen's restaurant on University and Collingsworth, turn right on Collingsworth and it will dead-end into Rogers. Look to your right for the large free-standing white building. Keep up with the Jones's lawn and have an in-ground sprinkler system installed. If you buy the whole system, they will save you 35 percent off list price. Do-it-yourself, and you'll save even more. Where to buy the parts? Stay put. They sell pipes, sprinkler heads or just about anything you would need for your own irrigation system. (You might even think of them like a urologist for your lawn.) *CK, MC, V, D*

★★★★★ Mr. Russell's Flower Market 817/337-4003

1540 E. Price St., Suite 140 *Mon-Fri 8-7; Sat 9-6*
Keller, TX 76248

The difference between a flower shop and a flower market is the variety and quality of the flowers, plants and services. At Mr. Russell's Flower Market you get the best of all possible blooms. They carry plants and planters, will arrange fresh flowers or silks, consult for weddings, and will come to your home to help you decide just what you might need to add color and fragrance to your home life. Talk about flower power. Their selection is as phenomenal as it is unique as evidenced by their FTD Award of Excellence. They are members of Teleflora and inspect all arrangements before they leave the shop. Quality, quantity and care are the products that make this florist a stand-out in any market, and when you add extremely reasonable prices, they get our stamp of approval, too. Before you enter the world of fresh larkspur, lilies, stargazers, tropicals, gladiolas, Gerber daisies, freesias, snap dragons, roses (even purple ones), iris, tulips, sunflowers–grab a few extra bouquets outside for $3 and see what glorious blooms you can take home for dinner. *CK, MC, V, AE, D, House Accounts*

★★★★★ Oncor Factory Outlet — 214/689-8833

1325 Inwood Rd. — *Mon-Fri 9-5*
Inwood Trade Center
Dallas, TX 75247

When you demand a command performance, give this outlet a round of applause. (Just don't fault them for not knowing how to spell.) But if you want to save money and not have to chop down the tree yourself, this is a large manufacturer's outlet for artificial plants and flowers. Tiptoe through the tulips throughout this 7,000-square-foot forest of greenery. See bushes and blossoms and green-colored Christmas trees at prices that generate rave reviews. For $.50, you can take home seven heads of flowering bushes; $2 for 14 heads; a 6-foot ficus tree, including basket, $20. Unless you have entry to the Garden of Eden, this is the second location. China is home to their manufacturing site and their distribution center is in Oklahoma City, so they located their outlet in Dallas. Natch! Plant all of their floral and greenery in a multiple of blooms without fear of dying. At last, I can promise you a rose garden at a bargain! *CK, MC, V, D*

★★★★★ P&E Plants — 214/741-9209

1204 S. Central — *Mon-Sun 6 A.M.-6 P.M.*
Dallas, TX 75201

In 7th grade, I avoided P.E. like the plague. Today, P&E is one of my favorite subjects. Millions of shoppers make the trek to Farmer's Market for good reason. Right in the thick of it all is P&E Plants and Mr. Eddie Comer. Nursery and flowering shop–but no cut flowers. Bring colorful drama to them "thar" hills. Three-gallon shrubs were $5.50 (like red tip photinia, buford holly, azalea, boxwood and yaupon holly). Then it was the Impatiens. Frankly, my dear, we were star-struck with all 20,000 of them in every color of the rainbow. An outlay of $12 a flat for pansies or $10 for 5-gallon red tip photinias was relatively painless. Lush and green peered around every corner. We then wanted to add some oomph to the patio so we bought a few hanging baskets–but don't worry, we left about 10,000 still hanging out. When it comes to selection and price, these bloomin' idiots sell it so cheap, it's practically a free-for-all! *CK, MC, V, AE, D*

★★★★ Plant Market, The — 972/867-1105

500 Spring Creek Village
Belt Line and Coit
Dallas, TX 75248
Mon-Sun 9-5:30

How green is your pasture? If it's not, then take your little pinkies to the Plant Market to Belt Line and Coit bordering Richardson. Though nurseries make strange bedding-fellows, this is a shoe-in for a perfect fit. Spring and summer, expect their hours to extend and another location at 3200 Thunderbird in Plano to be blooming at the roots. This location is next door to Thunderbird Skating Rink and is their organic gardening headquarters. Their main plant quarters at Belt Line and Coit (across from C & S Hardware) is home to plants that are grown in their greenhouses in McKinney. Indeed, when they say, "Direct from Grower," they should know from whence they sow. Better plants, better pots, better selection–this nursery is open to the public seven days a week. Asking price for pansies was $12.88/flat. They carry landscaping plants, seasonal flowers, some trees, Christmas trees, clay pots and other seasonal items. They also carry a complete line of organic products for the yard including BRADFIELDS, GARDEN FILL, HOWARD GARRETT, MASTER GROW and more. *CK, MC, V, AE, D*

✧✧✧ Plant People Landscaping, The — 817/237-4439

3017 Caddo Trail
Fort Worth, TX 76135
Mon-Fri 8-4:30
www.theplantpeopletx.com

We the people hold these truths to be self-evident. The Plant People start at the top and work them way down. Weeds, watch out. All jobs are entered into the computer so it's easy keeping up with the Joneses. First they work with you to determine what is the best use for the area without losing sight of the ultimate look you are trying to achieve. Talk about realizing some real "curb appeal." They can swap things around and show you what the effect will be for each season before the first shovel of dirt is ever turned. All eventualities can be explored in seconds, instead of a long period of trial and error, saving you, your hard earned money and lots of backaches. Unfortunately, they stick pretty close to home, with 90 percent of their work done in west Fort Worth, so Plano's definitely out of the ballpark. *CK, MC, V*

★★ Plant Shed

817/540-3792

1501 A West Airport Fwy. *Mon-Fri 9-5; Sat 8-5; Sun 10-5*
Euless, TX 76040

Snakes may shed their skins, but the Plant Shed can help you if you're a skinflint. So, if you're looking to shed some light on the subject of saving money, head to the Shed. Two Plant Sheds remain standing on terra firma. Though once they had spread their roots like monkey grass, they are now focused on two locations where plants and all their glorious supplies are waiting to be uprooted. The prices are pretty and good. Jasmine was a mere $1.29 per four-inch pot, one-gallon Azaleas were $3 and a 40-pound sack of potting soil was $1.88. Lots of colorful choices were surrounded by green and more green. Another location in Fort Worth, but 'tis best to look for specials because prices appeared to descend dramatically only during special sales. *CK, MC, V*

★★★★ Plants and Planters

972/699-1281

1050 N. Greenville *Mon-Sat 9-6; Sun 10-6*
Richardson, TX 75081

If you're like an elephant and remember everything I say, you could buy elephant ear bulbs for $3.99 (in season) and they were of the jumbo variety. Bedding plants were $12.88 for 36-count and ground covers in four-inch pots were $.88. I'd say we're on to something. North Dallas greenery at Plants and Planters was lush and plentiful. You'll find an assortment of flowers, shrubs, pots, by the flat, by the bush, all waiting to go to your house and grow old gracefully. Our helpful salesperson was a bit taken aback with our request for pansies in the middle of summer, but recovered enough to suggest that perhaps we wanted begonias or marigolds for the hot weather? We did, and they were $12.88/flat. If our digs were a mansion and our fantasies would materialize, maybe next year, a live-in gardener would also be nice. Move over, Martha. Second location at Northwest Highway and Plano Rd., 214/340-1020. *CK, MC, V*

★★★★★ Ruibal's Plants of Texas

214/744-9100

601 S. Pearl Expwy. *Mon-Sun 8-6*
Dallas, TX 75201

When it comes time to show and tell on Channel 11, we did–from Ruibal's

Plants of Texas. We left with half of what we came with, though, as the crew decided they couldn't live without those begonias. Next weekend, may I suggest a pit stop at Farmer's Market where these two sheds deliver some of the best 10-inch baskets of begonias, petunias and impatiens this side of heaven. Pansies were $15/flat in 4-inch pots. No doubt about it–you'll wind up a basket case when you see over 5,000 baskets towering overhead. Tons of greenery–for window planters, plants for your patios, pools or sunrooms ... from bedding plants, ground cover, perennials and tropicals, you can pick your pleasure. Why not try your hand at a topiary with bedding plants and herbs? Though creating topiaries has never been high on my "to-do" list, now that I've done one, I've decided to go all out. All you need is a topiary basket, a pole and a grid and you're in business. From simple and straight-forward to elaborate and eye-catching, you can create a bountiful garden of greenery with bedding plants, tropicals, hanging baskets and herbs; or plant in the ground for year-round color. *CK, MC, V, AE, D*

★★★★★ Season Flower Intl. — 972/488-3073

11398 Harry Hines Blvd., Suite 101 — *Mon-Sat 9:30-6*
Dallas, TX 75229

Fruity-tuitty, these flowers are a plum of a find. In this case, though, seasonal flowers refers to artificial flowers, which has no season. For all good reasons, eliminate those cares and woes, and consider those made from this maker. They have a large selection of silk and latex flowers (from delicate roses to large magnolias) and bushes. Prices range from $.50 for individual flowers to $7 for potted "bushes." A nice silk rose arrangement was only $6. Yes, there are flowers, flowers everywhere, but not a fruit to bite. To look at and enjoy, yes, but not to tast. See their artificial fruits–from grapes to apples to greenery, with an average price of $1–that are the rage displayed in bowls on coffee tables in homes across the country. Groupings for all seasons eliminate the worry of watering and cleaning up falling petals and leaves, and an occasional dusting should ensure they retain their vibrant colors. *CK, MC, V, AE, D*

★★★ Shades of Green — 972/335-9095

8801 Coit Rd. — *Mon-Sat 8-5:30; Sun 10-5*
Frisco, TX 75035

This is no Irish folly or a new-fangled window covering, but rather an oasis carved out in Frisco that is surely a watering hole for yard lovers. Located on Lebanon Road and Preston (Highway 289), 1.7 miles north of Highway 121, look for the building with a big yellow barn in the front yard. You can't miss it. Shop for all your landscaping needs, herbs, trees, shrubs, perennials, seasonal color, mulch, fertilizer, organics, groundcovers, concrete urns, benches, birdbaths–everything under the sun is available at Shades of Green. Collin County sure is growing and green is the color of distinction behind everything they sell here. While there, grab lunch at Gulf Coast Seafood next door–a snail's price less than dining in North Dallas. Then, load up the Jeep with 18-count flats of flowers or trees by the gallon or inch. Not bad if you like to dig holes. *CK, MC, V, AE, D*

✧✧✧✧✧ Stonebriar Landscape Services

972/306-4462
By Appt. Only

They say the apple doesn't fall far from the tree. In this case, the owners of Fifth Avenue Dinette gave birth to a son with basically good roots who has established them to the core. Talk about taking a bite out of the landscaping business. Good service harvested by knowledgeable and talented groomsmen can be delivered with aplomb. Call for an estimate for your yard and garden landscape needs, and enjoy the fruits of Richard's labor. *CK*

★★★★ Sunshine Miniature Trees

214/691-0127
7118 Greenville — *Mon-Sun 9-6*
Dallas, TX 75231 — *www.sunshinebonsai.com*

Sunshine, lollipops and bonsai trees are this family's claim to fame. Since 1964, the Sunshine's have been serving the needs of discriminating plant enthusiasts at their family owned and operated nursery. Their motto: "Excellence at the most reasonable price." They import some of their plants from Asia, but many plants are started from seed, tissue cultures and cuttings and grown with care right in the heart of Texas. They are well-known for their finished bonsai's, but they also offer unfinished and rough plants, so you can create your own work of art. Looking for hard-to-find plants like Texas Ebony and miniature orange trees? Here's the sunshine you've been dreaming of. Let a smile be your umbrella by letting a bonsai into your life. A little touch of the Orient, for indoors or outdoors, adds mystery to history while this delicate and intricate tree (that's as small as a houseplant) graces an entry table. They will deliver or ship anywhere. One monthly special on the web was a finished bonsai juniper with humidity tray and care sheet for $26.95. Most prices are 20-40 percent less than you'd find elsewhere. Shipping is free for UPS ground service; second-day air is available for an additional charge. You'll most likely receive your order in about five business days. *CK, MC, V, AE, D*

★★★ Willhite Seed

817/599-8656

PO Box 23
Poolville, TX 76487-0023
Mon-Fri 8-Noon, 1-5
www.willhiteseed.com

Will you seed it and save this year? If so, you can plant your garden while the sun is up in July and enjoy he fruits of your labor come fall. Willhite Seed, Inc. is one of the largest mail-order seed companies in the U.S. What did you expect? It's Texas-born and bred. Located between Weatherford and Bridgeport, they even have a store if you'd rather "see-d" it yourself. Whether you plant seed directly into the ground or start seeding ahead for planting after the last frost, it's certainly a fun as well as economical way to sow your oats. From lettuce to beans, radishes to rhubarb, you can buy a bag of radishes for $1.49 or more, or you can have a whole garden full for only $.85. And no pesticides, no finding a parking space, and no twisted wheels on a shopping cart. *CK, MC, V, C*

★★★ Your Place

972/386-5218

13510 Inwood
Dallas, TX 75244
Mon-Sat 10-6; Sun Noon-5

When push comes to shove, it's better to be at Your Place than mine. And Your Place is the place to go when it comes to accessorizing your home. Bring your wallet and wandering eye and prepare to be dazzled. This is a site to behold. There are flowers and plants growing everywhere, on the floor, on the ledges, on the wrought-iron hedges, in the baskets, on the wall ... wherever you turn, you will see the phony philodendron and fake florid florescence. In other words, this is a place for silk flowers and plants, arranged or otherwise. Then add some Southwestern flair to your furniture and accent pieces, drape a woven rug over a loveseat, place a glowing candelabra for the perfect lighting, and position a Dhurri rug just so. Get the picture? No longer on Dragon St., this is the one and only Your Place. *CK, MC, V, AE, D*

Pools & Yards

★★ Aqua USA

972/329-7627

841 Dalworth Drive
Mesquite, TX 75149
Mon-Sun 10-4
www.aquausa.com

Looking for (under?) the kitchen sink? Or on top, countertop, under-the-counter? If you hate the taste of your tap water, take a long, cool drink by using this water filtration system. Wholesale to the public, countertop and under-the-counter systems sell for mere drops in the bucket. The same system that is used by public water systems, school buildings and commercial buildings can be ordered for home use. Enjoy worry-free water by filtration. No, they don't sell water, just the filtration systems. On the day of our visit, they were offering some countertop systems at 25 percent off; and under-the-counter filters, regularly $900, were $500. Filters can be attached at a faucet or to your main water line. Just don't ask for any bottled water, please. For Perrier, you're on your own, too. Look for another location in Trinidad if you are headed that way. *CK, MC, V, AE, D*

♥♥♥♥♥ Aquatic Landscapes

214/327-POND

9132 Sweetwater Drive
Dallas, TX 75228
By Appt. Only
www.aquaticlandscapes.com

Henry David Thoreau would have loved sitting by a golden pond from Aquatic Landscapes. This company is all wet as they create lush and willowy water gardens for your yard. They also offer lake and waterway control services, building of Japanese Koi ponds, theme park water features, movie and trade show displays, even zoological and museum exhibits. If you want the best, consider none other. They have a 16-acre research and development center in East Texas where they even grow their own fish, including Koi as well as aquatic plants. Don't expect these to come cheap, though. The smallest Japanese Koi pond started at $3,000. Then again, you can build one yourself and drown in the process. (Four or five trips to Home Depot can mount up, you know.) Call for your personal appointment for tours. Their Fairview location is home to Celebrations in the Country, if you are needing a place to host a garden wedding or company picnic and want it catered to the hilt. Call Pat Stixrood at 214/562-8119 to arrange the particulars. Or go online to view more than 20 different gardens they've designed. Plus, see their displays at Southwestern Baptist Theological Seminary in Fort Worth and at Strong's Nursery. They'll also show up at the Dallas and Fort Worth lawn and garden shows each spring. *CK, MC, V*

★★★ Aries Spa Manufacturer 972/771-6286

4176 I-30 *Mon-Fri 8-5; Sat 9-3; Sun 10-4*
Rockwall, TX 75087 *www.ariesspas.com*

If your sign is Aries, you know you need to cool off. But even if you aren't a ram, we are in an age where everyone's jumping in and soaking their troubles away. You don't have to get soaked, however, if you shop factory-direct at this manufacturer's outlet. Best time to buy? Right after the home shows. Then you can really net a whopper. A six-person beauty that will actually seat up to eight people can cost $3,000-$4,500, which includes delivery, installation, preparation and cover. Keeping your head above water is not for the faint-hearted. They also sell hot tub/spa supplies. Located on the eastern edge of Rockwall near I-30 and F.M. 549 (Exit 70), these are some of the best-price spas in town. Why spend a fortune when you'll end up all wet anyway? *CK, MC, V, D*

★★★★★ Artforms Fountain Outlet 972/494-6787

3828 Cavalier Drive *Mon-Fri 8-4; Sat 10-5; Sun 1-5*
Garland, TX 75042

How's your form? Or function? If both are lacking and you want your fountain to floweth over, it's time to consider an Artform Fountain. These works of art are made in Garland, Texas, not Florence, Italy. What you'll see are copper fountains, whimsical garden sculptures, garden and gift accessories all priced at wholesale-plus. If that doesn't make your interest bubble over, you need to have your head (faucet) examined. *CK, MC, V, AE, D*

✧✧✧✧ B & B Lawn and Tree Care Co. 972/475-9813

Rowlett, TX 75088 *By Appt. Only*

Looking for a way to cut costs? This blade-runner specializes in tree and shrub care serving all of the Metroplex. Offering complete lawn services is a way to cut to the quick. Weekly yard service for an average yard (hills, acreage, extra services cost more) runs $25-$30. They also offer fertilizing, planting, sod installation, pruning and shaping of trees, which is at the root of their basic talents. Free estimates by owner Bill Blundell himself. Seniors even get an additional cut. Serving the Garland and Rowlett areas for regular maintenance, but for big jobs, they'll go anywhere. *CK*

★★★★ Barbecues Galore 817/468-3939

4605 S. Cooper St. *Mon-Fri 10-7; Sat-Sun 10-6*
Arlington, TX 76017 *www.bbqgalore.com*

Ready for a grilling? Then, stake out at America's largest chain of barbecue stores (five area locations that guarantee they'll beat any advertised price. Have a hot time in the old town tonight. Remember, where there's smoke, there's a guy with an apron firing away. Smokers and grills are their specialty. BROIL-MATE'S gas grill, tank and cart was $239; a MECO Water Smoker was $28.95; a FIESTA gas grill, tank and cart was $99; and a portable gas table grill was tabled at $17.99. Do you find yourself wondering if your steak is ready? If you do, then try their thermometer fork for only $14.99. One block south of I-20, we found the WEBER Bar-B-Kettle for $49.70 and the CAPT'N COOK three-burner with porcelain cast-iron cooking grids for $639 (a $10 increase over last year) Other brands seen were BRINKMAN'S, CAJUN COOKIN', GREEN DIAMONDS and NEW BRAUNFELS. A nice touch ... all FARBERWARE was discounted 20 percent. Isn't it interesting that backyard cookouts became popular AFTER the kitchen became modernized. Check directory for nearest location. *CK, MC, V, AE, D*

✧✧✧ Blue Haven Pools and Spas 972/644-0494

13349 N. Central Expressway *Mon-Sat 9-5; Sat 10-5*
Dallas, TX 75243 *www.bluehaven.com*

Enjoy a lifetime of outdoor fun, courtesy of Blue Haven Pools and Spas. Blue Haven has been building custom gunite (concrete) pools since 1954. Having been around for nearly a half century, Blue Haven is capable of providing excellent prices on parts and construction without sacrificing quality. Don't know which pool or spa is right for you? Blue Haven has hundreds of standard models to choose from, or a consultant will design one for you for free. Since pools are so much easier to enjoy when you don't have to worry about maintenance, Blue Haven has developed the SmartPac Pool System. SmartPac includes a water purification system, which almost eliminates the need for chlorine, the largest filter available, an automated vacuum and more. We understand each location is a franchise, so differences exist. Get local references in your area to ensure those digging the hole are the same that satisfied customers from your neighborhood. Check the directory for additional locations. *CK, MC, V*

★★★ Brandon Industries 972/542-3000

1601 Wilmeth Rd. *Mon-Fri 8:30-5*
McKinney, TX 75069 *www.brandonmail.com*

Making a bee-line to the front door can be dangerous in the dark. Not any more. Builders, developers and property owners (home or office) can now see their way clear with the lighting from here. For safety or security sake, light your way with wholesale and below prices on lighting. Aluminum lighting and mailboxes were available at prices from the Dark Ages. A painted (white or black enameled) 44-inch mailbox was around $160; if you want organic green, it's $10 more. Shipping was $15, but you can save money by picking them up yourself. Over 40 styles of mailboxes ranging in price from $100-$800 were seen; or stay home and shop online if you want to keep the light on. There's no reason to miss your mail. One exit north of U.S. 380 on U.S. 75 in McKinney. *CK, MC, V, C*

★★★ Breez-Lite Awning Co. 214/321-2626

8940 Garland Rd. *Mon-Fri 9-4; Sat 9-1*
Dallas, TX 75223

Need a breeze during those long hot Texas summers? Here's one way to help ease the way as well as reduce your electric bill. Consider shading your windows or covering up that patio with an awning. Up to 40 percent less expensive than the competition, these baked-enamel aluminum awnings come in hundreds of colors, and they never have to be replaced. Stay cooler in summer, warmer in winter, and aesthetically pleasing and physically secure all year round. Though the initial investment may be $1,000 or so, it was definitely 30 percent less than others' prices. Breez-Lite also builds carports and patio covers with similar construction and savings. No canvas products can be found here, however. Most of their items come with a 10-year warranty on the paint and a 1-year warranty on the workmanship. See their awnings on full display if you need convincing. *CK, MC, V, AE, D*

♥♥♥♥♥ Care Free Plastic Fence & Design 214/339-1396

4307 Shilling Way *Mon-Fri 8-5*
Dallas, TX 75237

Want to be environmentally correct? Then go carefree and save a tree. That's the motto at this polyethylene privacy fencing company for either residential or commercial use. With a 20-year warranty, you can throw away the paint brushes and never replace that fence again. Besides, it's the only way to give your nosy neighbors the brush-off. Recycled high-density polyethylene is the way to go if you're in the know. *CK*

★ Casual Living 972/245-7789

3400 N. I-35E *Mon, Thu 9:30-8; Tue, Wed, Fri 9:30-7; Sat 9:30-6*
Carrollton, TX 75007

The casual lifestyle has propelled this retailer to move into larger digs and none too soon. Their moving sale prompted me to shop, but to say the savings were meager was an understatement. Maybe 20 percent because they wanted to not move it–was their moniker for months and months. In spring and summer, when thoughts turn to dining al fresco, their collection of patio and outdoor furniture is a way to start but do not think substantial discounts. Then when you start to feel The Big Chill, turn to their collection of fireplace equipment, all at competitive prices but nothing to jump over the moon for. Save a little on an extensive superstore selection with names like ARLINGTON HOUSE, MALLIN, SUN COAST, WINSTON and WOODARD, plus awnings, gas grills, fountains and children's CHILDPLAY systems (they are the exclusive dealers). For warmth and coziness during the winter, snuggle up to the fireplace and experience why gas logs are an easy way out. At least you can keep the home fires burning. Another 12,000-square-foot location in Plano at 8700 Preston Rd., Suite 103 (972/668-6040) obviously hasn't deterred their expansion plans. *CK, MC, V, AE, D*

✧✧✧✧ Chair Care 214/638-6416

8804 Sovereign Row *Mon-Fri 8-4*
Dallas, TX 75247

Are your chairs in need of repair? Then don't worry, be happy. Chair Care is the fairest in the land. And you don't have to be in strapping shape to take advantage of the straps at Chair Care. Every strap is replaced and, if need be, your frames are restored to like-new condition. They specialize in your better patio brands, such as BROWN JORDAN, TROPITONE and WOODARD in either wrought iron or aluminum. If, for example, you had a BROWN JORDAN set that you wanted re-strapped and repainted, the arm chairs would cost you $130 per chair. A standard 36-inch table would cost $120. So, for less than $900 (table and six chairs), you could be living in the lap of luxury with what looks like a brand new set. Have you priced your better brands of patio furniture these days? It's definitely cheaper to repair with care than to buy a whole new set. *CK*

★★★★★ Comfort Cushion — 214/748-2242

1717 Levee St. — *Mon-Fri 7-3*
Dallas, TX 75207

They're up and open at the crack of dawn, but if you're an early bird, you'll definitely get the goods at Comfort Cushion. This manufacturer and wholesaler is a cut above the rest. Need new cushions for your patio set? This is the source for repair and replacement, but you'd better know your sizes–not all cushions are created equal. Both ready-made and custom, standard sizes can be anywhere from 18- x 18-inch up to 23- x 72-inch. They can get you covered, no matter, from PVC furniture slings to umbrellas. At least they won't let it rain on your parade. Only open Saturdays during the summer months. *CK*

✧✧✧✧✧ Crack Doctor, The — 972/420-6442

1702 S. Hwy. 121, Suite 303 — *Mon-Fri 8-5 (By Appt. Only)*
Lewisville, TX 75067

A good joke is not the only thing to crack up over! But those cracks in your pool are no laughing matter. Call these underwater repair specialists who can repair any crack in your pool regardless of its origin. Cracks, grout, tile, mastic repair, stain removal and leak detection are just part of their pool tools. They perform underwater inspections, acid washes, and year-round underwater service. With FREE estimates and a warranty, what do you have to lose? (Except high water bills and serious potential pool damage.) *CK, MC, V*

♥♥♥♥♥ Creative Water Gardens — 972/271-1411

2125 W. Kingsley Rd. — *Tues-Sat 10-5*
Garland, TX 75041

Frogs love to sit by a gorgeous pond and so do I. If you do, too, aim your sights to the corner of Garland Road and Kingsley and swim *without* the sharks for a change. Here, the concentration is on your water garden, plain and simple. From water lilies, lotus, Koi and goldfish, you can now sit back and reflect on your perfect pond without the headache of drowning in debt. They do ponds, water plants, display ponds, waterfalls (both installations and set-ups), as well as carry some statures, lawn ornaments and fish. (But by no means can you deep fry these!) *CK, MC, V, AE, D*

★★ Dallas Custom Swings
214/341-3727

11660 Plano Rd. *Mon-Sat 10-5*

Dallas, TX 75243

Swing high, price low. Dallas Custom Swings is strictly for swingers. As the leading source for backyard activities, they'll even seal the swings so the kids won't get splinters. Ouch! This year, you could buy the Lunar Explorer Kit for serious do-it-yourselfers who have the patience and skill to put it together for $1,146 (delivered unassembled to your yard). Me, I'd rather let them put-it-together for $1,504 installed and sealed. For the ultimate gym workout and playing field for kids, consider the ever-popular jungle gym bars, swings, slides and a mini-tree house. What a perfect playhouse for lunar launches! Second location at 17435 Preston Rd. in Dallas (972/818-3727). *CK, MC, V*

★★★★ Decksource
972/539-6948

1000 Spinks Drive *Mon-Fri 8-5*

Flower Mound, TX 75028

This is the source for deck material but not the deckhands to hammer in the last nail. Though most of their business is to contractors, we got a whiff of what they were up to and decided to take a chance on love. It was love at first sight. They said they would not only help us design a deck, but they would also sell us the ingredients at 10 percent less than the competition. Expect pressure-treated cedar, CHOICE DEK, pine, redwood, TREX, and if you want the lumber to be delivered to your backyard for a do-it-yourself project, there's no charge (unless, of course, you want to build a lanai in Maui). They also will refer you to some reliable deck hands if you are not handy with a hammer and nails 'cause they only sell supplies and are not the ones to lend a hand. *CK, MC, V, AE*

✧✧ Dickson Brothers
972/288-7537

204 N. Galloway Ave. *Mon-Fri 8-5:30; Sat 8-5*

Mesquite, TX 75149

This family-owned business used to be a favorite for installing spas, but now they just fix them. You won't find a nicer, more honorable group. When your spa, pool or fish pond goes on the blink, these are the people to call. Want a wonderful water garden? They can fix you up fast. They don't build them; rather, they just sell the equipment and then you can hook up with those who can. Broken pool filters, no-bubble JACUZZI, clogged-up pipes on your frog pond? Give them a holler. And best of all, you don't have to hold your nose. They sell water garden and pool supplies, too. *CK, MC, V, D*

Du-Good Services

817/572-3170
3604 Fort Hunt Drive
Arlington, TX 76016
By Appt. Only

When your honey-do list has grown to two pages, why not consider hiring this honey, Ron Hicks, to mow, trim and edge your lawn. He does mulching, too, but you "gotta" bag it yourself. That helps the environment, he says. When you are too busy to think about getting your lawn back in shape, then take advantage of this the perfect service for you. He charges anywhere from a minimum of $25-$35. A great deal for all of the leisure time you'll have left to enjoy. Leave the weekend chores to someone else and give yourself a break. *CK*

★★ Elliott's Spas, Pools & Service

972/562-7902
1505-B W. University Drive
McKinney, TX 75070
Mon-Fri 10-7

Got a spa with a leak? Or a pool with a problem? With more than 15 years in the business, Malcolm and Marianne Elliott are not only leaders in the pool business, but they also service spas, sell spa covers, and have expert pool service, too. Sunbelt Spa Manufacturing Company has designated them the authorized dealer of spas in their area, and Elliott's can make you a deal! We priced them to be around 20 percent lower than California Pools or Morgan Spas (one of the most expensive pool/spa dealers in town) and more important, you can trust that they'll be around if you need service. *CK*

✧✧✧✧✧ Fairview Landscape

972/317-9113
By Appt. Only

Want a fair price for quality service? Just keep up with the Joneses by calling the Johnson's. Alan Johnson runs one of the most professional lawn and landscape crews in the Metroplex. They show up, perform and leave without any major water pipes bursting or other nightmarish disasters. The Johnson's are so sophisticated that they have the entire city on specialized computer software so they can bid your job accurately–to the square inch. For a standard lot, expect to pay $30 for mowing, edging, weed eating and blowing. Why wait until the perfect 70-degree day for your neighbor's kid to decide if or when he'll cut your lawn? These guys do their job without whining and making you feel guilty. Professional landscape design, licensed sprinkler system installation, custom decks and stone work are also part of their repertoire. But if you live in The Colony, forget it. They don't do windows or cut up in that area. *CK, MC, V*

★★★★ Four Seasons Design & Remodeling, Inc — 817/334-0367

710 S. Main St. *Mon-Fri 8-5; Sat 8-1*
Fort. Worth, TX 76104

Looking for a sunroom to add that much needed space? Or maybe, you just want to add some more light in your life and sunshine in your heart. Either way, this company can be called on all year long for their specialty–designing and installing glass sunrooms with double-paned, argon gas-filled windows or choose wood or aluminum. Usually, they'll install a heat pump for heating and cooling, but if necessary, duct work can be included. Stop moaning about not having your own private space. This could be the place. *CK, MC, V*

★★★★ Hobert Pools — 972/690-8118

300 S. Central Expwy. *Mon-Fri 8-5; Sat 8-4; Sun 1-5*
Richardson, TX 75080 *www.hobertpools.com*

Nothing Ho-drum about a Hobert pool. Hobert Murphree has a reputation for dependability. After 25 years in the business, his company has built more than 5,000 swimming pools. His reputation is the result of the hands-on expertise of his staff, individually and collectively. Their goal is simple: to build a pool in a way that will save you time and money. To do that, Hobert Pools recognizes the three most critical factors in ensuring a successful pool project. One, competitive cost; two, quality construction; and three, a timely completion. If you want to get a feel for various looks, call for a personal tour of their five on-display pools. All pools come with a lifetime guarantee and 100 percent financing is available. On Central Expressway, one block south of Belt Line Rd. in Richardson; Lewisville, 1297 F.M. 407, Suite 306 (Justin exit off I-35 E. 972/317-4121); and in Frisco at 9741 Preston Rd., 972/377-6444. *CK, Financing*

★★★ Hot Springs Spa/Coleman — 817/572-0004

4820 SE Loop 820 *Mon-Sat 10-6; Sun 1-5*
Fort Worth, TX 76140

Whatever you call it, it still means a good time in the hot tub tonight. Known as Hot Springs Spa, though the name on the door is "Coleman, Bright Ideas For Your Home", you can still jump in with both feet–the water's fine. For your next spa, gunite pool, patio furniture or sunroom, dive in off of I-20 next to Cowtown Polaris. Look for sales and bonuses on top-of-the-line products.

Patio furniture brands include BROWN JORDAN, TELESCOPE and TROPITONE–all aluminum and stylish with 15-year guarantees. After 40 years in business, they haven't drowned yet, but look for their year-end clearance sale when savings can eddy-out at 50 percent off. *CK, MC, V, AE, D*

★★★ Inside Out Patio and Fireplace 972/931-0626

17390 Preston Rd. *Mon-Fri 10-8; Sat-Sun 10-6*
Dallas, TX 75252 *www.insideoutshop.com*

When the folks here opted to move on to Casual Living, the manager supposedly bought the Inside Out location and life continues to be good. DFW area shoppers can continue to relax in style with casual and cast aluminum, wicker and wood furniture for the patio and all their fireplace needs. For the patio, stretch out in names like BROWN JORDAN, HOME CREST, JENSON JARRAH, KINGSLEY BATE, MALLIN, O.W. LEE, SAMSONITE, WINSTON, WOODARD and WROUGHT IRON. And for the fireplace: BECKWOOD, GOLDEN BLOUNT, HARGROVE, HEATALOR, MAJASTIC, PETERSEN, PILGRIM, RASMUSSEN, SUMMER CLASSICS and UNIFLAME. With each log kit purchased, you will receive a free ($49 value) snap crackle and pop kit. Go north, shoppers, north of Campbell and save 40-45 percent off. Load up on umbrellas and cushions without blowing the whole home-furnishings budget. Huff and puff throughout their 3,000-square-foot outlet store next door for additional savings. And lastly, visit online for additional money-saving coupons. *CK, MC, V*

★★★ Jamar's Koi Farm 972/771-4143

3502 Parker Rd. *Mon-Fri 9-5; Sat 9-2*
Rousseau Shopping Center
Plano, TX 75023

If you've gone to Rockwall or Wylie lately looking for Jamar's you might think something fishy's going on. Well, those stores went under and the only tall tail to report is swimming in Plano. For pond supplies, quality fish and wholesale prices, Jamar's is where it's at. All breeds of Japanese koi, from $2-$3,500 and everything beautiful moving through the water in between. Prefer to build your own pond? Want them to do it for you? Need some help? What about supplies? Love water lilies? Lacking just a water pump? Been looking for a bio filter? Swim with the fishies at Parker and Central Expressway (the northwest corner in the Rousseau Shopping Center across from Target). *CK, MC, V*

Pools & Yards

✧✧✧ James Hendriksen 972/412-4015

By Appt. Only

All decks on hand. Want to add a deck to your house? Then don't scrimp on workmanship. Call on this captain of craftsmanship with 16 years of deck-building experience. This veteran deck-maker will cut you a deal, saving you at least $100 off a custom deck–and every notch helps. On average, expect to pay $7.50-$8 per square foot and most decks run 300-400 square feet. Then again, you can do-it-yourself and sweat it. *CK, MC, V*

★★★★ Lawn and Garden Warehouse, The 817/921-2458

3762 McCart Ave. *Mon-Sat 8-5:30; Sun 11-4*
Fort Worth, TX 76110

The "mow" the merrier. Selection here is way past the cutting edge. Wow! Have you priced riding lawnmowers lately? We recommend this warehouse because of the selection of money-saving reconditioned machines. Seems like it's the only way to go to mow down high prices. A TORO 4.5 HP, 21-inch mower was right up our alley at $250. Try your luck with DICKSON (the one with a zero-degree turn radius), HONDA, SNAPPER, STIHL or TORO plus other brand-name tools. All were standing tall waiting to be "Snapper-ed" up. There also carry a full line of garden supplies, but remember to stay on the cutting edge and never pay retail. *CK, MC, V, AE, D*

★★★ Leslie's Swimming Pool Supply 972/231-3793

1260 W. Spring Valley Rd. *Mon-Sat 10-6; Sun Noon-5*
Richardson, TX 75080 *www.lesliespoolsupplies.com*

With new locations popping up everywhere (Dallas, Duncanville, Irving, Carrollton, Coppell and North Plano) in addition to their existing nine locations, means the pool business is booming. With more than 30 years in the business, this veteran of swimming pool supplies and service will keep you in the swim of things. Dependable and well-priced, Leslie's is an AQUA QUEEN, ARNELSON, KREEPY KRAULY and POLARIS pool-sweep dealer but they also carry solar covers, pumps, heaters, motors and lights. Expert repair service and leak detection, too. (And you won't have to float a note to keep from getting way over your head!) What a shock to your budget! Some of the best buys, though, are their private-labeled goods, such as their superfloats for $59.99 (paid $99 elsewhere for another brand). One of the best features in the house is their free water tests. They'll show you everything you need to know about maintaining your pool. And your complete satisfaction is guaranteed. Check the directory for the location nearest you. *CK, MC, V, D, Leslie's, D, PQ*

★★★★★ Lockhardt Pools 972/467-0859

By Appt. Only

Lock in satisfaction with a Lockhardt Pool. Former Dallas Cowboys linebacker Eugene Lockhardt is now playing the field, underwater. He decided it was sink or swim and that's exactly what he did. Build the best pool for the least amount of money and make sure he would be able to stand behind every last one. His good name and reputation were important elements of his business profile and he intends to keep it that way. Each Lockhardt Pool is custom-designed to fit aesthetically into your backyard. Waterfalls, beach entries, slides, diving boards, volleyball pools-your ideas can materialize in one fell splash. To see their artistry, take a look at the mosaic artwork at the Dallas Art Museum's pool. No pools on display to show you but they will bring you pictures of pools that they've built alongside references. Mention *The Underground Shopper* and receive a free waterfall or landscaping package with each pool ordered. *CK, Financing*

✧✧✧ Marjorie's Lawn & Garden/Custom Fence & Repair 214/350-4238

3044 Webb Chapel Extension *Mon-Sat 8-5; or By Appt.*
Dallas, TX 75220

Old-fashioned service at a reasonable price, Marjorie's Lawn and Garden helps "fight poverty by working!" Offering ten-year guarantees on new fences and five-year guarantees on fence repairs, this company also provides yard work, sprinklers and drainage services. Tree trimming and planting, too; plus, they're not drips. Looking for some regularity? Prunes are one thing and pruning your trees is another. These folks do regular mowing and clean-up and bill monthly although for a one-time service, you pay as you go. Sprinkler installation and sprinkler repair, another specialty. Expect the mowing of an average yard on a weekly basis to be from $45 minimum to $90–but they show up, do the job and leave without leaving you a mess. Clean up prices depend on the job and not an hourly rate. Plumbing, air conditioning and handyman services are all offered, too. *CK, MC, V, D*

★★★★★ McGrath-Barnes, Custom Pools 972/768-5650

By Appt. Only

Get in the swim of things with a custom-built pool–just don't get in over your head. Here they recommend first to get three bids at your location, and not over the phone. If they don't want to see your yard, they're not a serious pool builder. The bid we got was $14,495 and that included a 380-square-foot pool (30- x 14-foot with an 80-foot perimeter, 3- x 6-inch to 5 feet deep), 300 square feet of aggregate decking, cantilever form, water line tile, shallow end steps, cartridge filter, time clock, 1.5 HP pump, a 500-watt pool light, maintenance tools, 100 feet of electrical, steel, gunite, white plaster, 5 feet of plumbing to the equipment, skimmer and three returns, love seat, start up instructions, complete chemical balance, and if that weren't enough, lots of TLC. Whew! They know their stuff. For example, some cities require a backwash line ($400) and/or a P-trap ($300). These folks were right on the mark with all the latest city ordinances. There's even an architect on staff. Expect to be swimming (not in debt) but in your pool in 23 days. The above phone number is a voice mail to leave a message. They guarantee the hull of the pool for a lifetime. Too bad the Titanic wasn't as water-worthy. *CK, Financing*

★★★★ Mobile Mini — 214/333-2222

3550 Duncanville Rd. — *Mon-Fri 8-5; Sat 8-Noon*
Dallas, TX 75236 — *www.mobilemini.com*

Make your yard socially acceptable with these containers. Low-cost, ground-level, portable mini-storage containers are custom-built from 5, up to 40 square feet and delivered to your location direct from the manufacturer. Store unsightly lawn mowers or pool equipment (in my case, it's shoes and research notes) where they'll be there tomorrow without cluttering up the garage or front-door entry. Buy them new or used; either way, these storage units have a patented locking system with doors on one or both ends. You can rent or buy, as your need dictates, for home or for business. They finance, too, with approved credit. *CK, MC, V, AE, Financing*

✧✧ Moonshadow Hot Tub Rental — 972/625-6909

By Reservation Only

Why buy a hot tub if you only like to get down-under occasionally? Rent one instead. Jenny Cranfill Miller has a better idea. Her company rents portable hot tubs. They rent deluxe, portable models that are delivered and set up, inside or outside, 6 feet round and capable of seating four adults comfortably. Hot tubs are delivered empty and sanitized, filled with crystal clean water and plugged into a standard 110V outlet. No special wiring or plumbing needed. Gift certificates, too. Excellent for hydro-therapy, can be a tax deduction for professional athletes, and many insurance companies will cover the cost of the rental. Perfect for Valentines Day or other romantic occasions in front of the fireplace or for a pool party, graduation, wedding or anniversary celebration. *CK, MC, V*

★★★ Morgan Whirlpool/Spas

972/247-3986

2377 Walnut Hill Lane
Dallas, TX 75229
Mon-Fri 8-6; Sat 9-6; Sun 11-6

OH2Oh-h-h! There's nothing better than a gazebo spa in your own backyard for dipping and relaxing. A couple of years back, the Morgan salesman told us they were the most expensive spa outlet in town and prices were quoted from $3,500 - $10,000. Quite a soaking! This year, we found spas priced from $2,495 (still not cheap for a three-person spa) and $4,400-$6,000 (six-person), delivered, set-up and leveled with chemicals added. During one special, a $300 spa cover was free with purchase. At least you know that their 34 years in the business brings plenty of experience and a history of dependability. Too, for above-ground pools, you can jump feet first into a one-foot round model for as low as $895. Be sure to start your shopping at their clearance center location above, as this is the one that displays their factory seconds (the ones with blemishes or scratches, showroom demos, etc.). *CK, MC, V, AE, D*

✧ Mower Medic

972/466-9093

2540 Dickerson Pkwy.
Carrollton, TX 75006
Mon-Fri 8:30-5; Sat 8:30-2
www.mowermedic.com

Call in the Mower Medic for your sick mower. The fix-it paramedics for your lawnmowers here are the remedy for any brand, including HONDA, MONTGOMERY WARD and SEARS. They are also an authorized service center for BRIGGS & STRATTON, HUSQVARNA, MTD, MURRAY and TECUMSEH. Figure on spending anywhere from $20-$500 on repairs, depending on the size and severity of the problem. Bring your mower to the parking lot as that's where they do their diagnosis. To get a mower ready for a spring tune-up, it'll cost around $49.95 plus parts (usually around $25) and tax. You can see their sign from I-35 E and Trinity Mills, but they still need "mower" cordial phone instruction. *CK, MC, V, D*

★★★★★ Mower World

972/298-7554

435 E. Danieldale Rd.
Duncanville, TX 75137
Mon-Fri 9-6; Sat 8-5

If you want to cut a rug, don't dance here. But, if you want to cut a lawn, there's no better place to go. Mower World is the largest lawn, garden, and outdoor equipment place in the world. Plus they save you green. Chosen as the MASSEY FERGUSON dealer to showcase the limited edition of the Dallas Cowboys special tractor (and there were only 50 made), if you snoozed, you missed it. Of course, the price of $3,399 might have deterred you to begin with. If it's mowers you want, they have every brand, every size, and every price range. Bet you didn't know there are special lawn mowers just for women? (I can just see me now.) The same holds true for garden and lawn tools. This is the place for all those great gadgets you see in gardening magazines but never can find–like that bulb planter that looks like a hole digger, or barbecue grills, wood swings and more. Top-of-the-line mowers at prices that are cut to perfection. HONDA Harmony II push lawnmower, $289.99; HONDA Harmony Mini-Tiller, with 2-year warranty, $299; and a STIHL grass trimmer, $129.95. If it's for the yard, they've got it. During special sales, prices can be cut to as much as 60 percent off. Besides, did you know that they also have the biggest selection and best prices on Christmas trees (starting in October)? In fact, there's over 20,000 square feet of trees, ornaments and trimmings glowing to go. *CK, MC, V, AE, D, Financing*

✧✧✧✧✧ Mustang Contracting Services of Dallas — 214/369-3353

Mon-Sat 9-5 (office)
gtesupersite.com/mustang

Is it a car? Is it an animal? Is it a sprinkler repair and installation company? What is your final answer? You don't have to be a millionaire to enjoy what hundreds of others have given a "thumbs-up" to since 1990. All over the Metroplex, yard owners have called this Mustang for their sprinkler repairs and installation. They offer a 24-hour emergency and same-day service. Licensed in of Texas (state license #6224) and a member of the Dallas Irrigation Association and the Texas Turf Irrigation Association, their credentials are impeccable and their prices in-line. *CK, MC, V, AE*

★★★ My Own Backyard — 972/818-PLAY

17390 Preston Rd. — *Mon-Fri-10-6; Sat 9:30-5:30*
Dallas, TX 75252 — *www.myownbackyard.com*

What fun! Shop this new kid on the block who can help create a kid's backyard entertainment center. Outdoor living is finally a breeze and certainly nothing to sneeze at. Order your children's backyard summer fun with outdoor play equipment from here. Now with two locations to play with (the other's in

Lewisville at 2455 E. Hwy. 121; 972/939-5050), look to them for a child's dream tree house, fort, log cabin, playhouse–if it's outdoor real estate for months of living outdoors, these play-centers provide the necessary abode. (And when you sell your house, chances are you won't have to list your backyard house with multiple listing.) Also, look over their wooden play centers, Prairie House playhouse, basketball goals, trampolines and "quadro" (multi-function) modular play-structures. Sets can include an open-air, two-story tree house complete with jungle gyms, swings and ladders, or an enclosed cabin-in-the-woods with verandah and windows. Let them enjoy the good life in their own Andironack chairs and leave the serious stuff indoors. Whether it's indoors or out, choose from lots of different options. *CK, MC, V, D*

✧✧✧✧ Nik Tree, Irrigation & Landscape — 972/380-6666

17710 Davenport Rd. — *By Appt. Only*
Dallas, TX 75252

Pipes and dreams are this company's rule of thumb. Not only is it the best place to call for a sprinkler system (and only the best brands will do), but we got one of the lowest bids from them on both the system as well as professional installation. Always confirm, if you're all thumbs, that you're not being taken in by an all-thumbs "dirt-dogger rope" so that you'd drown in his handiwork. Nik has since sold his business to Alan Elkon, so you can have him or his crew plant or prune a tree in his honor. They will do it and they will not put a thorn in your budget in the process. *CK, MC, V, AE, D*

★★★★★ Patio One/Fullrich Industries — 972/633-5522

1501 Summit Ave., Suite 4 — *Mon-Fri 9-5; Sat 10-6*
Plano, TX 75074

Step right up ladies and gentlemen. Tell you what I'm gonna do. Direct you to this factory-direct outlet if you're in the market for imported teak and NAY-TOH patio furniture from Indonesia. A knock-out look for your pool or patio, elegant enough for sunrooms, too. Savvy shoppers get lost in their thoughts as they wander through the 3,000 square feet of heavenly deals in tables, chairs, benches, sun umbrellas, lounges and more. Umbrellas start at $50-$90 for a 9-foot beauty. Choose from a rainbow of colors and designs. Save up to 50 percent on their already low prices. Located across from Collin Creek Mall, take the Plano Parkway exit off of Central Expressway. We gave this store a thumb's up! Number one in our book. *MC, V, AE, D*

Pools & Yards

★★★★★ Pool & Patio Landscaping

972/263-6606

2026 SE 14th St.
Grand Prairie, TX 75051
Mon-Fri 8-6; Sat 8-4; Sun Noon-5
www.pool-and-patio.com

Nineteen years ago, Nancy and Bill Sexton had a better idea. To build a great pool company the old-fashioned way, one pool at a time. With a foundation of integrity, quality and workmanship, Nancy particularly was aghast at the shoddy work of many pool builders who promised to dig a hole in the ground in record time but somehow deposited your check before the hole-digger even arrived on the scene. Greed and speed sometimes go hand-in-hand. Another bone of contention was the maintenance performed on a pool. Why hire a pool service when today's pools can be built virtually maintenance free? Since there are not many female pool builders in the business, you can be sure this one intends to stay with her reputation intact. From the basic package (where the homeowner can do some of the work himself) to the elite Champagne Edition, you can have your pool and drool, too. Pools, glorious pools. Sun decks, sunshine, sunflowers ... the only thing that's missing is the pool. Jump into one of theirs for less than a one-time luxury vacation. At least this time, the good times will keep going, and going, and going. During the winter months, they do not stay open on Sundays. Weather permitting, you'll have a pool in 14 days. On the winter day we checked, the website wasn't open either, but hopefully it'll thaw with the spring sunshine, just in time to help you make a splash. *CK, MC, V, Financing*

★★★ Pool Environments

972/985-1576

5304 Sandy Trail Court
Plano, TX 75023
Mon-Fri 8-5

Try them, you like them. Pool Environments will custom build you the pool of a lifetime. Imagine salvation from the brutal Texas sun. Jump in, the water's fine. Come on in. Two foot, four foot, eight foot; well, maybe. Dip into a custom water environment that comes with a lifetime warranty on the shell of your pool. You new in-ground pool will be constructed of gunite while the name brand parts including the pumps and pool cleaners come with a standard 1-year warranty. Pool Environments offers extremely competitive prices depending on the size and design of the pool but expect them to be here today and not gone tomorrow. *CK, MC, V, Financing*

★★ Recreational Factory Warehouse

972/509-9707

700 Alma Rd., Suite 116 — *Mon-Fri 10-8; Sat 10-6; Sun Noon-5*
Plano, TX 75075

Located at the northeast corner of Plano Parkway and Alma, if you've got time on your hands, this is where to hang out. They guarantee the lowest prices on all LEISURE BAY products (after all, they're the maker), but then again, since you can't find it anywhere else, where can you compare? A WINDJAMMER BAY six-person spa with seating for up to six along with an ARISTECH acrylic spa shell complete with fully adjustable therapy jets were both priced at $1,399. A HOUSTON VII slate pool table was another good buy at $1,399. On top of that, they'll throw in a $350 bonus package with deluxe playing accessories and professional delivery. Sounds too good to be true? Well, somewhat. One shopper thought shopping at Recreational was like the worse-case scenario at a used-car lot. She referred to it as, "Haggle City". She claimed they're not definite about any of their prices. We would agree and discovered, after closer scrutiny, it's not as pure as pure could be. Tanning beds and supplies can be found here, too. See for yourself at two other locations in the Metroplex, 6801 NE Loop in 820 North Richland Hills, 817/498-4811 and in Garland at I-30 and Belt Line Rd., 972/203-2220. *CK, MC, V, AE, D*

★★★ Robertson Pools and Spas

972/304-0208

569 Coppell Rd. — *Mon-Sat 9-6*
Coppell, TX 75019 — *www.robertsonpools.com*

Being a member of the National Spa and Pool Institute and the Better Business Bureau gives some credibility to Robertson's cool pools. Founded in 1981, like a fish takes to water, their pools and spas take to your backyard. With approved credit, you can be swimming in your new pool for as low as $124 a month if all the other considerations, like local building codes, utilities and ground conditions are favorable. They even offer a three-week completion guarantee. Be sure to sink your teeth into their General Store for custom patio furniture, pool supplies and chemicals, toys, pool games and accessories, but don't expect to hold your breath at bargain prices. Still, you can live in the lap of luxury and enjoy a Robertson pool. Also look for them at 1639 W. Northwest Hwy. in Grapevine (817/481-7351); 2250 Morriss Rd. in Flower Mound (972/355-0450); and 105 Butler Rd. in Allen (972/396-8044). Open afternoons on Sundays during the summer. *CK, MC, V*

Pools & Yards

★★★★ Spas Unlimited

972/317-4164

2999 N. Stemmons Frwy.
Lewisville, TX 75067

Mon-Sat 10-6; Sun Noon-6
www.spas-unlimited.com

Hot zippity dog! Sink your teeth into one delicious Texas-based contractor who not only gets you into the swim of things, but will surround you with a solid mahogany deck, too. For more than ten years, Spas Unlimited has been carrying CALIFORNIA SPAS and CATALINA spas as well as providing their own in-house service. A six-person spa costs anywhere from $3,200 to $8,000. You'll get a 1-year warranty on the pack, pump and labor, a 5-year guarantee on acrylic, and a 10-year warranty on wood. Consider their landscape, woodwork and rock work, too. Then if it's an above-ground or below-ground pool, you can also dive into their handiwork without springing a leak. Their above-ground pools are made of polyester and vinyl on the outside but are steel-bar reinforced from the inside. They cost between $1,800-$3,000 and that includes the startup, chemicals, water analysis, hoses, pumps, filters and brushes. Want a gazebo to gaze in? They can hook one up to the spa or build around it–even enclose it in glass ... and the glass used is warranted for up to 15 years against hail damage. All prices include delivery, cover, steps and chemicals—just not the set-up. Their website was under construction when we checked, but might be above ground by the time you check. *CK, MC, V, D, Financing*

★★★★ Splash Pools & Spas

817/590-0333

827 Airport Frwy.
Hurst, TX 76053

Mon-Fri 10-6; Sat 9:30-5:30; Sun 1-5

When you want to talk pool parties, this is where to save some cash. Splash into this emporium where economy is brought down to scale. Over 500 patio sets in stock, wrought iron, aluminum, resin – pick your potion. Their low prices are guaranteed, and since they've been in business since 1951, chances are they haven't had to call in the chips very often. They carry only top-of-the-line products, like HOMECREST, RANDAL and WINSTON. Because they deal directly with the manufacturer, they can cut you a great deal – especially during clearance sales. They are also the exclusive DOUGHBOY dealership and offer 30-year warranties on their above-ground pools (no in-ground pools). Financing is available and seasonal sales are the best times to save. For spas, they carry the Majestic line of ARTESIAN. (Hint: The best time to shop for pools, spas and patio furniture, believe it or not, is Christmas. Even as early as September, they offer 50 percent off all patio furniture in stock and rebates on all their pools in stock.) Spas range in price from $2,995-$9,000 carrying anywhere from 2-8 persons. Their spas also have 8-51 jets depending on which one you like. Splash has a reputation for quality, service and reliability and we found their sales staff to be knowledgeable, courteous and attentive. Spoil yourself and take a Splash - for less cash! *CK, MC, V, AE, D, (Financing Available)*

♥♥♥♥♥ Splendor in the Grass — 214/328-5011

8626 Garland Rd. — *Tues-Sat 10-5:30; Sun Noon-5*
Dallas, TX 75218

A little birdie told me about the two little white houses across from the Dallas Arboretum with fountains, planters, wind chimes and bird feeders. But that's not all they nest. A little of this, a lot of that is the compilation of yard and gift items at Splendor in the Grass. If you've given any thoughts to the great outdoors, think about something from their large selection of concrete fountains and feeders. Get through your garden chores with a little help from their gardening tools. Snip away. Add some stain glass artwork to your garden area then deck out indoors with something around your fingers or ears. Jewelry came as a complete surprise. All part of Splendor in the Grass. *CK, MC, V*

★★★★★ Sun Time Pool, Spa & Patio — 817/548-8100

1001 NE Green Oaks Blvd., Suite 131 — *Mon-Fri 10-7; Sat 10-6;*
Arlington, TX 76006 — *Sun Noon-5*

It's hard to believe the Metroplex needs another patio store, but when it's good, it's very, very good. In fact, you might hear us suggest, "Y'all come here real soon!" As the distributor of SUN CHEMICALS for swimming pools, they'll keep you swimming in clear, cool water. Known for their concentrated quality, they'll last longer which means you'll invest less money. For comfort and a clean sweep, extend your budget and save at least 20 percent on patio furniture. Brands include AQUA-RITE, HAMAMINT, HAYWARD, JACCUZI, LETRO, PAC FAB, POLARIS, SARATOGA SPAS, SUN COAST, TELEDYNE and more. Expect the best for less, none of those rickety-types accepted. All patio furniture is made of heavy gauge aluminum or slings and last from season to season. Stay in the shade with an impressive array of umbrellas, and don't forget they also offer pool and spa supplies, equipment, water toys, as well as servicing and remodeling of all pools. Remodeling extends beyond pools to include decorative resurfacing of decks. Is there any other relief in the sun that these folks don't cover? *CK, MC, V, AE, D*

Pools & Yards

★★★★★ Texas Greenhouse Co., Inc.

817/335-5447

2524 White Settlement Rd.
Fort Worth, TX 76107
Mon-Fri 8-5; Sat 10-2
www.texasgreenhouse.com

Red-faced over greenhouse prices? There is no reason to be hotheaded over hothouses with Texas Greenhouse kits. (When you build your own greenhouse, only your plants will get steamed.) Since 1948, this company has manufactured their own greenhouses and accessories so their prices are factory-direct. About 15-20 brands are carried, including MODINE heaters and CHAMPION coolers. Choose from free standing, lean-to and bay view window models with a complete line of accessories and installation packages, such as climate control, misting and watering systems, timers, controls, benches and shelves to enhance your gardening experience. Prices are very competitive. Most orders are delivered within six to eight weeks with a one-year guarantee. A 15 percent restocking charge is assessed on returned merchandise. You'll have to put a 50 percent deposit down with your order, and the balance is due on delivery. Call, write or go online for their catalog. *CK, MC, V, AE, D*

★★★★★ Texas Patio

817/831-2266

5742 Airport Frwy.
Haltom City, TX 76117
Mon-Fri 10-7; Sat 9-6; Sun Noon-5
www.texaspatios.com

This patio purveyor is Texas-size and priced-wise. With fountains and bird baths and everything in between, there's nothing left to discuss if the topic is outfitting your pool or patio. Let one of their guides lead you though the "ins and outs" of building your own fish pond. Choose the shape and away you go. Buy it by the foot and do it your way, for less. Located near the Carson Street exit on the south side of Airport Freeway (S.H. 121), you can reach the pinnacle of yard and garden luxury at Texas Patio. See shadows of the downtown Fort Worth skyline and bathe in the bargains at this 30,000-square-foot landmark. If it was meant to house furniture near the water or to cushion your outdoor lifestyle, you can count on it being at Texas Patio. Water fountains, waterfalls, black fiberglass pools to line your own kidney-shaped fish or lily pond, bird baths, pumps and, of course, patio and porch furniture–be it wrought iron, teak, steel or cast aluminum. If you care enough to sit on the very best, you might as well buy it here for less. Exclusive lines such as BROWN JORDAN, TROPITONE and others made us ready for some R&R. They also have a second location at 6080 S. Hulen St. in Fort Worth, one mile south of Hulen Mall, 817/292-7599. *CK, MC, V, AE*

Tontine

214/363-1271

11661 Preston Rd., Suite 280
Dallas, TX 75230
Mon-Sat 9-5

HEATMASTER gas logs starting at $35 warmed me up right away. Add tool sets, screens, wood holders, andirons, fireplace doors ... well go see their eight burning displays and fall in love. Located at the southwest corner of Preston and Forest in North Dallas, check out one of the oldest businesses in the area. They've been dealing in gas logs and other merchandise since 1941. *CK, MC, V, AE, D*

★★★★★ Venture Pools

972/416-1324

2550 Trinity Mills Rd.
Carrollton, TX 75006
Mon-Sat 8-5; Sun 11-4

Having a locally owned company install your pool is a must in case you spring a leak, and Venture Pools is no risky traveler when it comes to taking risks. They offer a 3-year, bumper-to-bumper guarantee on equipment and labor at no cost to the homeowner, plus a lifetime structural warranty. They are members of the National Spa and Pool Institute and the Dallas Better Business Bureau. The brands they offer include LAARS, POLARIS, TANDY, TELEDYNE and their HAYWARD equipment comes with a 10-year warranty. They have plenty of referrals and *happy letters* on in-ground swimming pools and spas–just ask and you shall see. Then get ready for a summer (and winter if you choose to add a heater) of splashing. It's the next best thing to taking a dive in Hawaii. *Financing*

★ Vita Spa Factory Outlet

817/226-7727(D/214)

2542-C E. Abram St.
Arlington, TX 76010
Mon-Sat 10-6; Sun Noon-5

Ever talk to a smacked mackerel? This company needs an attitude adjustment. Otherwise, sorry, Charlie, maybe you need a booster shot? Though there were more than 100 spas we could have warmed up to in their showroom (located at S.H. 360 and Abram, next to Cowboys), they gave us the cold shoulder. No, it was more like an icy reception. Their VITA spas run anywhere from $1,000-$6,000, and their 7- to 8-foot slate pool tables by AMERICAN HERITAGE and KASSON were priced $1,000-$2,700. Frankly, we put them behind the eight ball until further notice. They also carry gazebos. Though they are one of the largest spa showrooms in the Metroplex, unless they take a course from Dale Carnegie, we suggest you jump in elsewhere. They claim to offer 25-50 percent off retail with 100 percent financing. So be it. *CK, MC, V, D, Financing*

Pools & Yards

Warehouse Pool Supply

281/556-5442

2412 Highway 6
Houston, TX 77077
Mon-Sat 9-9; Sun 10-6
www.warehousepools.com

Since 1989 Warehouse Pool Supply has provided the largest selection and best value of pool and spa supplies for their customers. All of their products are the highest quality available. For example, the chlorine that they use for their customer's pools is stabilized so it lasts four times longer than regular chlorine. Get a 15-pound bucket of chlorine for $50.48 or a 25-pound bucket for $61.48. They also have carry Pristine Blue Water Treatment System. This is an alternative to chlorine that is better for the environment and will not irritate your eyes or skin. All of their chemical products have child-proof lids for added security and safety. Warehouse Pool Supply also carries a full range of pumps, filters, automatic time clocks and other supplies to keep your pool clean and pristine. Once your pool is ready for swimming, enjoy their line of floating chairs, toys, goggles, masks and other fun accessories. They have 12 locations around Houston, Austin and San Antonio to best serve you with more on the way. Warehouse Pool Supply has now made it possible for the public to shop at their web site, so that everyone can benefit from their great selection and prices, however many items can not be shipped out of Texas. *CK, MC, V, AE, D*

★★★★★ Yard Ideas

817/379-5644

136 N. Main St.
Keller, TX 76248
Mon-Sat 10:30-5:30

One reader says, "After driving to Keller to see what Yard Ideas was all about ... I'm a believer in *The Underground Shopper* more than ever before". Yard Ideas on U.S. 377 is outrageously wonderful! Great garden fountains for $225; they make their own and prices start at $95. This is unheard of low pricing. "Even when I was in the nursery business, I could not find fountains this large at these kinds of prices," exclaims another happy camper. Shoppers are united in their praise of Yard Ideas. They also carry benches, tables, decorative animals, bird houses, children's tables and white and terra-cotta pottery. An appreciated 20-40 percent off retail prices on statuary, bird baths, fountains and concrete patio sets are displayed throughout their garden. Small statuary went for $25 and angel statues for $20. Small three-tier fountains with a pump and a 3-foot tall pedestal were watered down to $175. Prices are good in every way, though they're not carved in stone. *CK, MC, V, AE, D*

Shoes

★★★★★ Banister

972/724-0749

3000 Grapevine Mills Pkwy., Suite 240
Grapevine Mills Mall
Grapevine, TX 76051

Mon-Sat 10-9:30; Sun 11-8

Just a footnote. Hold on to this Banister, especially when taking a walk. This shoe store typically brings hordes of shoe-hungry shoppers to its doors on a Saturday morning. We found a stellar selection of brands: BANDOLINO, CAPEZIO, EASY SPIRIT, FREEMAN, FRENCH SHRINER, JOYCE, LESLIE FAY, LIZ CLAIBORNE, 9 WEST, PAPPAGALLO, REEBOK, SELBY, SPERRY and others. Practically any foot can get covered, sizes 4-11 women's and 7-14 in men's. No longer carrying children's shoes, but overall, you'll save 20-60 percent on more than 40 name brands under the famed Banister banner. Remember to never buy shoes at a shop where the only comfortable ones are worn by the salesmen. Visit also at Prime Outlets in Hillsboro. *CK, MC, V, AE, D*

★★ Burlington Shoes & Bags

817/571-2666

1201 Airport Frwy.
Euless, TX 76039

Mon-Sat 10-9; Sun 11-6

No, you won't find any coats at this Burlington store–this is shoe country. We saw plenty of familiar names, though: CALICO, CANDIES, DEXTERS, REEBOK and others with lesser name recognition. Expect to shell out around $29.99 which seems to be the popular price choice, along with $19.99 and lower during sales. Bag a few name brands like ANNE KLEIN and a few VALENTINO'S but mostly KAREN LEE, ROBERTA ROMA and TAUROS. Best values during sales and clearances, so shop often and wisely. Check the directory for other locations in the Metroplex. *CK, MC, V, D, AE*

♥♥♥♥♥ Cartan's

817/923-7463

1201 W. Magnolia Ave.
Fort Worth, TX 76104
Mon-Sat 9-5:30

Pack up your kids, then pack up the carts and head to Cartan's, a bastion in footwear for years. What price are you willing to pay just to have a pair of shoes that fit? Right? Left? Either foot, if it's hard to fit, Cartan's is your cushion. But don't expect discounted prices right off the bat. They are retail, so shop during sales to save a few bucks. Never mind, you'd even pay retail or more, wouldn't you, just to find a pair of size 4s in A-EEE widths? What about a 12? Even a few 2 EE. OK, we don't mean you're Big Foot or anything, just that with hard-to-fit feet, you have a problem. Slender, quads and wide are part of Cartan's football-size selection of CLARK sandals, EASY SPIRIT, NATURALIZER (in sandals), SELBY, SOFT SPOT, TROTTERS and more. During their sales, especially their two-for-one's, run, baby, run. Ask for Delores. She's a doll. Just don't live like the old woman who lived in a shoe–and have to squeeze into a pair that was several sizes too small. Head to the intersection of Henderson and Magnolia in Fort Worth to fit your feet. *CK, MC, V, AE*

★★ Converse Factory Store

972/488-9252

3844 Belt Line Rd.
Addison, TX 75234
Mon-Fri Noon-8; Sat 10-6; Sun Noon-6
www.converse.com

Remember your first pair of CONVERSE brand shoes? Walk down memory lane or get the latest and greatest in athletic shoes at the Converse Factory Store. They have cross-trainers, canvas shoes and running shoes. Your break into a sweat while running into the store; once inside, relax–the prices will cool you off. Nothing over $40. This clearance center scores a bulls-eye as they're right on target. *MC, V, AE, D*

★★★★★ Crown Shoe Warehouse

972/424-0158

900 W. Parker Rd.
Plano, TX 75075
Mon-Sat 10-9; Sun Noon-6

No more thorns in this Crown's customer service department. What an improvement. For those of us who are well-heeled, this warehouse paves the way for shoe savings. Expect to serve yourself and not be catered to as you walk the aisles. In fact, you may even feel ignored–until of course, check out time. But that's the norm for shoe stores these days. Keep it clean. Keep it quiet. Keep it low-keyed. Keep prices low. Names such as ADIDAS, JONES-WEAR, MADELINE STEWARD at prices up to $49, or children's can slip out for an average price of $9.

NATURALIZER pumps were $16 in your choice of colors. Be the walk of the town in women's sizes 5-12 in narrow and wides, another plus. Men's shoes by NUNN BUSH and STACY ADAMS, for example, in sizes 6-14 were seen at prices from years' past. Don't pass this Crown without checking out their athletic shoes. NEW BALANCE is one of the best brands available and they have them here for $29-$49. This location is the bargain basement to their sister store, DSW/Designer Shoe Warehouse, so it's as low as it goes. *CK, MC, V, AE, D*

★★★★★ DSW (Designer Shoe Warehouse) 972/233-9931

13548 Preston Rd. *Mon-Sat 10-9; Sun Noon-6*
Dallas, TX 75240 *www.dswshoe.com*

DSW is A-OK in DFW, that's for sure. The only thing bigger than the savings is the selection. Shoes, shoes and more shoes–more than 36,000 pairs in 900 different styles brimming with designer and name-brand shoes for men and women. It's a shoe-in with prices 20-50 percent less than department stores. Guys can pair off with BALLY, FLORSHEIM, NUNN BUSH, STANLEY BLACKER and more in sizes 7-15; women's sizes 5-12 had designer names everywhere. NEW BALANCE running shoes, usually selling for $80+ were as low as $29. But it was the DOC MARTENS that sent our hearts a-flutter. Chestnut oxfords, retailing for $115 were $89.50. Also choose AIGNER, AMERICAN EAGLE, ANNE KLEIN, BASS, COLE HAAN, DEXTER, ENZO, EVAN PICONE, HUSH PUPPIES, LIZ CLAIBORNE, NINE WEST, SELBY, VIA SPIGA, ZODIAC and more. They have a "Reward Your Style" frequent shoppers program which gives you $25 off for every $250 spent. Also save on handbags, evening bags, backpack-like totes, and a small selection of hosiery. Every dollar counts in their gigantic, no-frills warehouse. Visit also in Fort Worth at Bellaire and Hulen, and in Lewisville at Vista Ridge Plaza (the southwest corner of Round Grove and MacArthur). *CK, MC, V, AE, D*

♥♥♥♥♥ E J Geller/ Mephisto 214/373-8066

8411 Preston Rd., Suite 116 *Mon-Sat 10-6*
Dallas, TX 75225

Located in Preston Center, if you are a MEPHISTO fan, you know how to cover your feet. These shoes are handmade one at a time of vegetable-dyed, full-grain leather with a superb cushioned shock-absorbing heel, and are quickly gaining momentum as the walking shoes of choice. Their only Texas store is in Dallas, lucky for us and they gladly accept phone orders. Ask for their FREE catalog if you prefer to let your fingers do your feet a favor. Both men's and women's shoes are available in narrow and medium widths with other European-sounding names, but don't expect to walk out for less. They swear they never have sales, so the price you see is the price you pay. Brands include BEAUTIFEEL, ECCO, MEPHISTO, NAOT, PAUL GREEN, PORTANIC, RICHTER, THERISIC and WOLKY with prices ranging from $75-$350. No discounts or sales, but they do have great service. People who walk in their shoes, whether casual or dress, claim to be able to walk a million miles. There's a 10-day return policy, but no worn shoes are acceptable. Mailing charges are $10 for first pair, $2 for each additional pair. *CK, MC, V, AE, D, C*

★★★★ Famous Footwear — 817/732-8491

4656 W. I-20
Overton Park Shopping Center
Fort Worth, TX 76109
Mon-Sat 10-9; Sun Noon-6
www.famousfootwear.com

Looking for your sole mate? Then consider this famous addition to the shoe business. Athletic shoes, dress shoes, casuals and boots, they really have a foothold in the marketplace. They're everywhere–from the outlet malls to strip centers with prices at 20-40 percent off. The brand names are–famous ones such as ADIDAS, ASICS, CONNIE, DEXTER, KEDS, NIKE, NUNN BUSH, REEBOK, ROCKPORT, SKECHERS–we're practically on a first name basis. During a back-to-school clearance, if you bought two pairs, the second pair was half price. (Haven't I read that somewhere before?) Huge selection, good size range, plentiful locations and pleasant personnel. And as my grandmother used to say, "Never judge a woman's feet by the shape of her shoes." Check directory for the location nearest you. *CK, MC, V, D*

★★★★ Fashion Shoe Liquidators — 214/678-9967

2222 Vantage St.
Dallas, TX 75207
Mon-Sat 9:45-6; Sun Noon-6

This reincarnation is the epitome of eternal optimism. While going bust in one company (Vantage Shoe Warehouse), just open up another. Another name. Another stab at keeping a step ahead of the crowd. Close-out prices on men's and women's shoes in brands like EASY SPIRIT, ENZIO, NINE WEST and lots of other Spanish and Italian imports. Take ad-vantage of shoes priced from $3-$48–even boots. Not many tennis shoes, but a few, especially for men. This could be the start of something big. Love is lovelier, the second time around. Also shop their second location at 11255 Garland Rd. in Dallas (972/328-3603). *CK, MC, V AE, D*

Shoes

★★★★★ Fossee's 214/368-1534

5925 Forest Lane, Suite 600 *Mon-Wed, Fri-Sat 10-6; Thu 10-8; Sun 1-5*
Dallas, TX 75225

Contemporary Cinderella's converge at the northeast corner of Preston and Forest Lane if they want to dance the night away. Slip into a pair in sizes 4 through 12 and you'll be two-stepping in no time. Fossee's has created the perfect Broadway hit starring AEROSOLES, AMALFI, ANDRE ASSOUS, ANNE KLEIN, ARCHE, BANDOLINO, CALVIN KLEIN, CHARLES JOURDAN, COLE HAAN, DONALD PLINER, EVAN PICONE, FERRAGAMO, I. MILLER, J. RENEE, LIZ CLAIBORNE, MR. SEYMOUR, PREVATA, SESTO MEUCCI, RANGONI, STUART WEITZMAN, UNISA, VANELI, VIA SPIGA, YSL – the list is exhaustive enough to tire even the chorus girls. Shoes selling in fancy salons for up to $250 can be bought here for 30-60 percent less – including hundreds of shoes for under $100 and none higher than $150. While not exactly cheap, these shoes deserve a round of applause for how they can be choreographed with your designer outfits. Encores welcomed. Also shop their newest store at 19009 Preston Rd. in North Dallas (972/380-0992). *CK, MC, V, AE*

★★ Just for Feet 214/363-3668

9390 N. Central Expwy. *Mon-Fri 9:30-9:30; Sat 9:30-10; Sun 11-7:30*
Dallas, TX 75231 *www.feet.com*

Open and shut boxes make this company a coming-and-going concern. And the shopping experience is a real blast – you'll need a set of ear phones to carry on an intelligent conversation. (Come to think of it, you may find it difficult to find someone who talks your language.) Famous for their "Buy 12 and the 13th pair is free," it's a place for kids to be seen and heard (mostly heard!). A pair of NEW BALANCE infants' running shoes (regularly $32.99) was $10, men's and women's running and cross-training models were reduced from $10-$40. Names like ETONIC, NIKE, REEBOK and SAUCONY were seen running around the bins. All shoes, though, are fit to be tried (though not always noticeably discounted). Slip into a pair of men's sizes 8AA- 16EEEE and women's sizes 6AA-10EE and check the directory (I'd check before every visit.) for other locations. The last we knew, they were still in Arlington, Lewisville, Mesquite and Plano. *CK, MC, V, AE*

★ Larry's Shoes

214/691-2688

9665 N. Central Expwy. *Mon-Sat 10-9; Sat Noon-6*
Dallas, TX 75231

It's entertainment, folks. Larry's has finally gone "Entertainment Tonight" with prices creeping closer and closer to retail. Someone has got to be paying for the cappuccino machines, "Soho" art signage, and large screen TVs. Guess who's really footing the bill? So, in spite of their selection of men's shoes, including ALLEN-EDMONDS, BALLY, BOSTONIAN, DEXTER, FLORSHEIM, FREEMAN, NUNN-BUSH, TIMBERLAND plus a full array of athletic colleagues, Larry is nary a big player on the discount scene. Sizes 7-16 including narrow and wide widths with knowledgeable sales personnel counts for something, but savings of only 10-15 percent is where we lower the boom. Check the directory for location nearest you. *CK, MC, V, AE*

♥♥♥♥♥ Mehl's Shoeland

817/924-9681

2900 S. Hulen St. *Mon-Sat 10-5:30*
Fort Worth, TX 76109

OK, shake those booties if you're having trouble finding shoes that fit those tootsies! At last, a store for ladies and kids with not only sizes 4-12, but a substantial selection in real narrow and super-wide widths (Ds and Es), too. They also prepare corrective shoes if you bring in the doctor's prescription (if not already in stock). Since 1950, this has been the place to go if you're singing the Taco Bueno song, "I think I need a bigger, better box!" Then, too, why is it that women with little feet have to pay a bigger shoe bill? What's not available? No high heels. The shoes here are all in the comfort zone: loafers, pumps and sandals with names like HUSH PUPPIES, MONRU and NEW BALANCE. *CK, MC, V, D*

★★★★★ National Shoes

972/387-8329

102 Preston Valley Shopping Center *Mon-Fri 10-8; Sat-Sun 10-6*
Dallas, TX 75230 *www.national-shoes.com*

Congratulations to one of the sole survivors of shoe discounting. National has weathered the storm and can keep Dad shod in brand-name shoes. Best of all, they will be discounted. Got your attention, eh? National Shoes is ever-alert to protecting men's financial interests. Since 1929, they've been selling first quality, name-brand shoes like NUNN-BUSH, ROCKPORT, TIMBERLAND and more–saving $10-$55 on every pair. Sizes 6-15 and in AAAA-EEE widths is something to brag about. They also sell comfy leather house slippers from EVANS–a no-brainer gift for Father's Day. Kick full retail prices goodbye at the intersection of Preston and LBJ. Though not as theatrical as Larry's Shoes, the prices are more nationalized. *CK, MC, V, D*

★★★ Off Price Shoes — 214/327-1150

410 Big Town Mall — *Mon-Sat 10-7; Sun Noon-5:30*
Mesquite, TX 75149

From Off-Broadway to Off and Running, this plain vanilla store is racked with shoes, glorious shoes in sizes to 11 in sandals, canvas slip-ons, boots, dressy and casual – if it's meant to be worn on your feet, forget sole-searching any further. Just don't ask too many questions – conversation is practically a mute point. With other locations in Dallas at Wynnwood Village (Illinois at Zang), LBJ at Preston (next to Denny's), and the newest at Six Flags Mall in Arlington, they must be doing something right. *MC, V*

★★★★★ Rack Room Shoes — 214/327-3663

Casa Linda Plaza, Suite 294 — *Mon-Sat 10-9; Sun Noon-6*
Dallas, TX 75218

Rack up the savings and walk proud in these shoes. More than 17,000 pairs line the runways with names like ADIDAS, AIRWALK, BONGO, CANDIES, CAPEZIO, CHILIS, DEXTER, EASTLAND, ESPRIT, FLORSHEIM, GAROLINI, GBX, MIA, MOOTSIES TOOTSIES, MUSHROOMS, NEW BALANCE, NICHOLE, 9 & CO., OSHKOSH B'GOSH, ROCKPORT, SKECHERS, TIMBERLAND, WEEBOK, WHITE MOUNTAIN and more. Rack after rack, don't get your back up against the wall, these shoes were made for walking, running, climbing, dancing – they even look good with your feet up on the couch. TIMBERLAND for the entire family were also part of the Rack, Jack. We saved $10-$30 on Kid's EUROHIKERS at this northeast Dallas store. Additional locations include Grapevine Mills (972/539-2818); Cameron Crossing in McKinney (972/542-7155); 2823 Market Center Blvd. in Rockwall (972/722-3747); LBJ at MacArthur in Irving; and also in Hurst. *CK, MC, V, AE, D*

★★ SAS Factory Shoe Store — 972/296-6185

3643 W. Camp Wisdom Rd. — *Mon-Sat 10-6*
Dallas, TX 75237

Who would have thunk that SAS stands for San Antonio Shoes? All these years, and I thought they were made in Timbuktu. That means they might have strolled down the River Walk before making their moves to Dallas. These shoes were made for comfort – especially crucial for those who stand on their feet all day. Perfect for doctors and nurses, beauticians, lab-techs, young mothers – but to see these shoes is to hate them. They are lovingly referred to as the ugliest shoes in the world. But what price comfort? It's all in the feet of the beholder. These shoes are made to walk in, work in, stand in but why do the most comfortable styles have to be the least attractive? Well, maybe it's a good omen that the next generation of women shoppers won't have bunions. Women's shoes ranged in size 4-12, prices averaged $40-$50. Men's shoes (6-15) are now available. But women's sandals, loafers, oxford-style and walking shoes are still their foot forte. Check directory for other locations. Unfortunately, the only place where they're *really* discounted is at their outlet store in San Antonio. So be it. *CK, MC, V, D*

★★★★★ Shoe Cents — 972/964-5900

2432 Preston Rd. — *Mon-Sat 9:30-9; Sun Noon-6*
Plano, TX 75093

You don't even have to be in the mood for "cents-ible" shoes to take advantage of Shoe Cents (a stepchild of Famous Brand Shoes out of St. Louis and part of a 34-store chain nationwide). At the northeast corner of Preston Road and Park Blvd. (next to Ulta), park your car and do an about-face. The brands are the same found in most department stores: AIGNER, BASS, CALICO, CLARKS, ESPRIT, HUSH PUPPIES, IMPO, KEDS, LIFESTRIDE, MUSHROOM, NATURALIZER, NICOLE, NINE WEST, RED CROSS, REEBOK, SAM & LIBBY, SRO, WESTIES and more – nothing far-out, nothing exotic, your basic best shoes and all priced right on the money. Dress shoes, evening shoes, casual shoes, work shoes, play shoes – all with savings from 20-40 percent off. More than 14,000 pairs of women's shoes stand ready for action – most priced under $25. Sizes this year have expanded to include extra small and extra large (including size 11) pumps, loafers and casual leather shoes that were originally priced up to $50. No wonder I had to add a shoe closet that wraps around my entire garage. Also try on for size their Dallas location at 11411 E. Northwest Hwy. (at Jupiter Rd.; 214/503-8998). *CK, MC, V, D*

★ Shoe World — 214/948-5505

318 Jefferson Davis Center — *Mon-Sat 10-7; Sun Noon-5*
Dallas, TX 75237

For kicks, try shopping Shoe World. It's a shoe-in for family footwear. Shoes for kids (infants to size 8), women (sizes 5-12) and men (sizes 6-13) are available in famous names for your feet like JORDACHE, L.A. GEAR and REEBOK, among others. Casual, dress, pumps, sandals, canvas, leather – a worldly representation of every type of shoes was available about 10-20 percent under retail. Check directory for other locations. *CK, MC, V, AE, D*

Sporting Goods

★★ "Tut" Bartzen Tennis Shop 817/257-7960

3609 Bellaire Drive N. *Mon-Fri 9-9; Sat-Sun 9-7:30*
Fort Worth, TX 76109

Don't let the name scare you off. Named after the long-time TCU men's tennis coach, this place has netted some pretty good deals over the years for the wannabe tennis pro. In the middle of the TCU campus, it has won more matches for Horned Froggies than for those who have kissed princes elsewhere and lost. Play by their rules and never pay retail in their fully stocked pro shop. You don't even have to be a student to ace the same good deals on tennis equipment, as it's open to the public year 'round. Racquets, shoes, balls, clothing and sundries, as well as racquet restringing can all be found here. They re-string your racket so that it feels like an extension of your hand, plus they also offer private and group lessons and clinics for adults and juniors. Just down the street from the wonderful Fort Worth Zoo, you'll enjoy the student-size prices and the captive service. *CK, MC, V, AE*

★★★★★ Academy Sports and Outdoors 817/346-6622

6101 W. I-20 *Mon-Sat 9-9; Sun 10-7*
Fort Worth, TX 76132 *www.academy.com*

The only drawback in being a good sport is that you have to lose to prove it. In this case, you can win and lose paying full price. Enroll at this Academy of sports equipment whether you're into golfing, camping, fishing, biking, swimming, basketball, football or soccer. Save your green before you hit the green. They've got everything for the sports enthusiast. Check out the TIMBER CREEK Renegade 7 x 7 foot tent that sleeps three, $40; COLEMAN Northstar electric lantern, $30; COLEMAN two-burner gas stove, $45; IGLOO 5 beverage cooler, $20. They also have coffee mugs, coffee pots, cups, insect repellent, cookware, DIAMOND BACK or ROADMASTER bikes for a great ride in the hills (Argyle and Oak Cliff are particularly good, challenging hilly sites). Slip into a pair of ADIDAS, CONVERSE, NIKE, REEBOK or SPALDING shoes and you'll be playing to win at any aerobic event. Check the directory for other area locations, including 7441 NE Loop 820 in North Richland Hills (817/428-1618); 8050 Forest Lane in Dallas (214/221-2284); 3305 Dallas Pkwy. in Plano (972/781-2970); and in Arlington at 1100 W. Arbrook Blvd. (817/472-9700). *CK, MC, V, AE, D*

★★ Alpine Range Supply Co. — 817/572-1242

5482 Shelby Rd. — *Daily 8-6*
Fort Worth, TX 76140

Looking to case the joint? Then shoot straight from the hip and save a few shells. This company supplies hunting-related reloading equipment, primers, casings, presses for pistols, books and more that will save you about 10 percent (more during sales). They carry all the top brands in rifles such as BROWNING, REMINGTON and WINCHESTER and in pistols, COLT and MAGNUM. In fact, if they don't have it and it's legal, they can get it. Rifle through their inventory by phone for a quote, or when you're in the DFW area, practice on any one of their four pistol ranges, a rifle range, three skeet fields, a trap field, five-stand sporting clays as well as an archery. *CK, MC, V, D, AE, PQ*

★★ American T-shirts — 972/289-8262

1228 Scyene Rd. — *Mon-Fri 9-5; Sat 10-3*
Mesquite, TX 75149

Down to one location and a catalog, this T-shirt warehouse features every color of the rainbow in every imaginable size. But you'll have to cross your T's and buy in bulk to outfit those young baseball players to get the rock-bottom prices. Or you can settle for single units at well-below average prices. Three-button children's baseball shirts were $6.15 apiece; coaches will have to ante up $7.85 each. Plain T-shirts went for $3.54 each. If you're an aspiring rock star, why not outfit your fan club for less? Remember, though, it's cheaper "buy" the dozen. Play ball! *CK, MC, V, AE, D, MO, C*

★★ Army Store, The — 817/531-1641

2466 E. Lancaster Ave. — *Mon-Sat 9-6*
Fort Worth, TX 76013

Call out the F-troops when you're ready to hit the bunkers. Enlist the aid of this sporting goods relative 'cause Uncle Sam is not the only source that pays commissions. It pays to commission The Army Store for outdoor/camping/

hiking/fishing gear guaranteed to keep you armed and ready to engage in the sporting life. You'll find all kinds of camping equipment in the traditional Kelly greens or Gulf drab. They've got backpacks for roughin' it and utensils for cookin' it (though no big pots) plus cots, tents, sleeping bags, wool blankets, and just about anything else you might want for an authentic bivouac. Lots of jackets and fatigues for the entire family, too. If you're ready to scout out the area beyond the city life, here's a place to salute. *CK, MC, V*

★★★ Athletic Wearhouse — 972/219-0073

1780 N. Stemmons Frwy. — *Mon-Fri 10-7; Sat 9-6*
Lewisville, TX 75067 — *www.athleticwearhouse.com*

Shoot when you see the color of this athletic supply store on I-35 E near Lake Lewisville. Come in for shoes and accessories for many major sporting events. Play ball and suit up. Ball gloves by LOUISVILLE SLUGGER, MIZUNO and WILSON; baseball-related T-shirts, jackets and jerseys by all of the above plus NIKE and RAWLINGS. If it's padding, bats, balls or any other necessity, this is the place. Mostly children and youth sizes are available. Older boys and dads are not in their game plan. However, if your little one is needing a uniform that they don't stock, they are happy to order it. You'll score a home run at this "wear-house" site if landing in the dugout is where you wind up. Hopefully, they can stick with a promise of a two-week turnaround on uniform orders. Remember my Uncle Charlie's favorite musing, "Every athletic team has a coach and Charley horses to pull it." Shop online, too, for a winning team. *CK, MC, V, AE, D, C*

★★★★★ Ball Billiards Ltd. — 972/424-4533

1305 Summit Ave, Suite 10 — *Mon-Fri 6-4:30; Sat 9-3:30*
Plano, TX 75074

Get out from behind the 8-ball. Here, shop for custom pool tables crafted by this dad, lad and friend. Cue up and make it big with custom pool tables starting at $2,195. Their lowest-priced 8-foot table includes a slate top, oak or mahogany wood, personal choice of felt and pocket colors, four cue sticks, Belgium Arimus balls, chalk, cue rack and installation. Even an exotic African mahogany table with six legs is within the realm of possibility. Have you priced ready-mades lately? For more than 10 years, they have devoted themselves to tabling any other projects. No big sign on the front door; exit Plano Parkway off Central, go east to Avenue K, turn left and take the first right, which is Summit. Turnaround time for orders is usually two weeks except during Christmas when they can't keep up with demand. Your best bet, even if your name's Minnesota

Fats, is to order before Thanksgiving to be guaranteed delivery at Christmas-time. All tables come with a lifetime guarantee and are totally handmade. They shoot straight; at least here you can pocket the savings. *CK, MC, V, AE, D*

★★★★ Bass Pro Shops Outdoor World 972/724-2018

2501 Bass Pro Drive *Mon-Sat 9 A.M.-10 P.M.; Sun 10-7*
Grapevine, TX 76051 *www.basspro.com*

You'll fall for Bass Pro Shops hook, line and sinker. What's not to love about the Bass Pro Shops, one of the country's leading sports retailers with savings up to 50 percent across the moat? Stop fishing for compliments. This is where the "big one" lands. Whether it's for fishing for the halibut or the shooting arcade, save on everything. What an arsenal for the hunter and the fisherman – from securing the necessary licenses to the best selection for outdoor game sports. Departments include fishing, the White River fly shop, boating, golf pro-shop, camping, hunting, clothing and more. Saving money at Bass Pro Shops is no laughing matter. Shoot straight from the hip, from archery or hunting equipment and gear. They've gathered everything imaginable for the fisherman, except the fish. (Holy mackerel, that's your job!) Shop online and subscribe to Uncle Buck's Newsletter for additional savings. Specials change often, so if you don't reel them in when you see them, you might wind up empty-handed. *CK, MC, V, AE, D*

★★★★★ Bicycle Exchange 972/270-9269

11716 Ferguson Rd. *Mon-Fri 9-7; Sat 9-5*
Dallas, TX 75228

If ever there was a wheeler-dealer in town, this is it. If you thought they couldn't do anything to improve on your old two-wheeler with handle-bar brakes, jump into the 21st century. Now they have electric motor bikes that comes completely assembled and the $729 price includes the recharger. The future is here, and it looks promising. Of course they haven't forgotten their roots. Shop for all-terrain, freestyle and BMX bikes for the amateur to the professional, they've written the book on Easy Riders. Bikes in all sizes – from children's models to adult mountain bikes; even custom-made wheelchairs and special-needs cycles (as well as repair or modification). Brands are stellar: CANNONDALE, DIAMOND BACK, GT, LOWRIDER, MONGOOSE, ROLAND, SHIMANO, TREK, YAKIMA and more. Used bikes are the easiest rider on your budget. In-store technicians don't discriminate between used or new. Even though they can't guarantee their turnaround time on repairs, they do guarantee their service. Their claim to sell more bicycles than anyone else in the Metroplex hasn't been questioned – yet. They've been at this location for 24 years and don't give discounts – just good deals. Ride over to their Carrollton location in Old Town at 1305 S. Broadway (972/245-5510) for another go-around. *CK, MC, V, D, AE*

★★★★ Billiards & Barstools

817/355-1355

1803 W. Airport Frwy.
Euless, TX 76040
Mon-Fri 10-7; Sat 10-5

Always on the lookout for a fast game of pool? Minnesota Fats recommended we check out Billiards & Barstools. Since merging with its much smaller sister store in Arlington, this store now carries more than 50 pool tables and 240 barstools. Bigger means you don't have look behind the 8-ball for what you need. If you are looking to furnish your game room, you can rack up the savings here. Too, they specialize in the home entertainment business and provide in-home service. Custom two-piece cues, cue cases, foosball tables, shuffleboard, ping-pong tops, bar stools, cue racks, poker tables, juke boxes and billiard lights are all available from AMF, BRUNSWICK, GANDY, PETER VITALIE, PLAYMASTER, POLHAUSEN, RENAISSANCE and STERLING. Check out their other locations in Richardson at 2080 N. Collins Blvd. (972/445-5485) and in Dallas at 4004 Ross Ave. (214/821-5744). *CK, MC, V, D*

★★★★★ Boditek Fitness

972/867-0200

18484 Preston Rd., Suite 108
Dallas, TX 75252
Mon-Thu 11-8; Fri-Sat 10-6; Sun Noon-5
www.boditek.com

Tech out your body and get in shape with new and gently used better brands of athletic equipment. Stay home and work out like the pros. Most used equipment comes with a 90-day warranty; three-five years for new. Step right up, ladies and gentlemen. A used PRECOR treadmill can be had for about one-fourth the price of a new one. A pacemaster (as opposed to a pacemaker) was also about 75 percent off the new list price. Their in-store brands are BODY GUARD, KEYS, TREADMILL, TRIMLINE, and they also carry 18 different brands of treadmills. Plus, they do repairs on location so you don't have to lug the machine into their shop. Then again, you might like to reconsider. It could do wonders for your biceps and abs. Shop online for their full line of products. *CK, MC, V, D, Financing*

★★★ Brass Register, The

972/231-1386

610 James Drive
Richardson, TX 75080
Mon-Sat 9-5:30; Sat 11-3
www.goped.com

For a fun way to get around the neighborhood, hop aboard a Goped. These small motorized scooters were invented in 1985 and have dramatically increased in popularity since then. Built to not exceed 20 miles per hour, they are fun for all ages (with the proper safety gear, of course). For the more experienced thrill seekers, there are speed-increase packages available. Gopeds are remarkably durable and have set records for being able to carry 20 times their empty weight. If you want a leisurely ride through the park or some X-Games-kind of fun, these Gopeds are ready when you are. *CK, V, MC, AE*

★★★★ BSN Sports

PO Box 7726 *Mon-Fri 7:30-6*
Dallas, TX 75209 *www.bsnsports.com*

Here's a place to soccer-to-them! Call for your free catalog, get your online ordering password and then jump for joy at the deals. Sports equipment for all sports is the name of the game here – from gymnastics and archery to weight training. Score big on the MVP (most value pricing) products, 'cause that's where the buys are. AMF, ATEC, BULLDOG II, EASTON, EVERLAST, GAMECRAFT, IGLOO, MACGREGOR, MITRE, MIZUNO, NORTH AMERICAN RECREATION, PORT-A-PIT, PRO DOWN, REEBOK, ROL DRI, SPALDING, TACHIKARA, VOIT and WILSON are some of the name brands you'll find here. Participate in the sporting life: basketball, scoreboards, volleyball, baseball, soccer, football, fitness, track and field, coaches' supplies, clothing, tennis racquets, boxing, wrestling, archery, camping, golf and game tables. If it's part of physical education, you'll go to the head of the class. Ace their tennis nets, kick a soccer goal, field their field markers for football or field hockey, or choose from their "8-Color Pack" which includes eight footballs, soccer balls, volleyballs and basketballs in eight different colors for $345. Schools and YMCA-type organizations probably know about them, but if you're a team leader, you might not know that if you order $250 or more, you get two free pizzas from Pizza Hut. Shipping and handling charges, though, are a stiff 12 percent of your total order. Credit terms are net 30 days for public institutions or non-public companies. For individuals, they take only checks or credit cards. *CK, MC, V, AE, D, C*

★★★★ Buddy's Sporting Goods Athletics 214/941-5506

123 W. Jefferson Blvd. *Mon-Fri 9:30-6; Sat 9-5*
Dallas, TX 75208

Buddy's my buddy when it comes to outfitting the playing field. Join in the game and look the part. They've got all kinds of shoes, jerseys, mitts and pads. Get baseball gloves by RAWLINGS, WILSON and others. Their specialty line is HIGH FIVE but it takes no time or trouble to order any brand you want including ADIDAS, CONVERSE, NIKE, REEBOK – whatever's your pleasure. Keeping your score low and your budget in shape is what Buddy's is all about. This mainstay is practically an institution in Oak Cliff. Teams aren't out for the count, either. If your child's starting soccer, complete uniforms start at $4.99 for socks, $9 for shorts and $5 for the team shirt. Plus, add $1.25 for a number and 35¢ for each letter. Uniforms are usually available within 10 days from ordering, though there's no assurance your team will win. Play ball at their second store in Duncanville at 749 W. Wheatland Rd. (972/780-8177). *CK, MC, V, D, AE*

★★ Busybody Home Fitness — 972/960-7573

5403 Arapaho Rd., Suite 103 — *Mon-Fri 10-9; Sat 10-6; Sun Noon-5*
Dallas, TX 75248 — *www.busybody-fitness.com*

In the dictionary a *busybody* is a person who meddles into the affairs of others. When I want to know what's going on in the fitness arena, I just ask Mickey, our "quickie" tour guide and he tells all. Busybody Home Fitness is "America's fitness equipment headquarters." Boasting one of the largest fitness equipment showrooms in the Metroplex, this place offers all kinds of exercise equipment for those with good intentions. Busybody offers high dollar, never-used equipment at reasonable prices. They even claim they sell it for the lowest price, guaranteed. Problem is, though, they are supposed to have certain lines on an exclusive basis, so nobody else would be selling it anyway. Then, of course, they can sell it for whatever price they wish. Can't fault them for bragging, though. They have treadmills, stationary bikes, recumbent bikes, weights, and just about anything else you might need for a home gym. In addition to accepting all major credit cards, this company makes buying easier by offering no interest financing through a third-party credit company (HRS) for any purchase over $599. They even guarantee a credit response within 5-10 minutes. If you can avoid the Schlotzky's in the parking lot, you'll find a fitness paradise here or at any of their multiple locations throughout the Metroplex. *CK, MC, V, AE, D, Financing*

★★★★ Cheaper Than Dirt — 817/625-7171

2522 NE Loop 820 — *Mon-Fri 7-8; Sat 9-3*
Fort Worth, TX 76105 — *www.cheaperthandirt.com*

New owners bring out the survival instincts in us all. Even the fittest needs a little help from their friends. While out there in the wild, you'll need to outlast the mosquitoes. So, don't drop your pants until you buy the bug spray here in survivalist quantities. Stock up on MRE's, guns, bullets, radios, knives and then take your newly purchased camping equipment (just about anything you might need or imagine) and sit back and wait for the world to end. It's OK because you're prepared – even with a samurai sword. Military buffs, survival aficionados and everyday Joe Cool's can find plenty of stuff at the Cheaper Than Dirt store, or order from their free catalog. Cheaperthandirt.com was the darling of the media as we entered the new millennium and the world did not come to an end. They carry a selection of over 3,500 products – all at discounted prices to turn to if there's a major power failure (though they have electric products, too). An INVICTA triple-sensor watch with altimeter, barometer, thermometer, 100-meter water resistance, shock resistant, electro-backlight, calendar, date, and alarm sells for only $79.97. A SANGEAN AM/FM short wave radio was only $49.97. Whether to counter any millennium bug or to put an end to the seven-year itch of the mosquitoes, Cheaper Than Dirt is ready to get the job done. *CK, MC, V, AE, D*

✔ Cheerleader Outlet — 214/350-TEAM (8326)

3701 W. Northwest Hwy., Suite 140 — *Mon-Thu Noon-6:30; Fri-Sat 10-3*
Dallas, TX 75220

Rah! Rah! Rah! The big deals to cheer about are only during their periodic warehouse sales. But, if you've got to root for the home team, this place is a winner. Friendly service and great sales makes for a winning combination if you're a cheerleader or the mother of a cheerleader. All of their cheerleading outfits are NCA brands. Girls' outfits run $24.95 for skirts and $15.95 for tops as an everyday sale price. Watch or call for frequent sale dates and locations. Fall's a good time to cash in on a variety of Sis-Boom-Bah savings and selection. GO, TEAM, GO! Just don't go without calling first to see that they're open. *CK, MC, V, AE, D*

★★★★★ Consignment Sports & Fitness — 972/437-1222

300 N. Coit Rd. — *Mon-Fri 10-7; Sat 10-6; Sun Noon-5*
Richardson, TX 75080

No sweat! Run all the way to get in on the good deals at this consignment sports store. If you like to skate, play hockey, ride a bike, ski, box, play racquetball or tennis, you can get equipped for less at Consignment Sports and Fitness. You can buy, sell, trade, or rent equipment at some of the lowest prices in town. A staff of fitness experts directs you to the appropriate treadmill for 50 percent less. (Even if you consider them the greatest plant stand.) Trade your tired, old equipment in for cash, or receive a discount off your next purchase. If you want to implement your fitness regime into a family affair, get a WEE JOGGER and help keep it off – together. Also, there's usually a huge selection of well-priced and hard-to-resist treadmills and BODY SOLID weight equipment. Three other locations besides their Richardson store: 5419 W. Lovers Lane in Dallas (214/350-4448); 3340 Garden Brook Drive in Addison (972/488-3222); and 3401 W. Airport Frwy. in Irving (972/255-1222). We're still waiting for the new locations to open in Plano and Grapevine. In the meantime, check out their warehouse in Carrollton for even more bargains. Watch newspapers for ads. *CK, MC, V, D*

★★★★★ Cycle Spectrum — 972/480-9588

1310 W. Campbell Rd. — *Mon-Sat 10-6; Sun Noon-5*
Richardson, TX 75080 — *www.cyclespectrum.com*

Almost as old as *The Underground Shopper*, this cycle shop has been doing wheelies around the competition since 1970. With locations all over the Metroplex, and 33 stores nationwide, you can't ride anywhere these days without bumping into a cyclist who hasn't bought his/her bike from Cycle Spectrum (and bragging about what a good deal they got). The name brands are top notch: BELL, BLACKBURN, DYNO, FREE AGENT, FREE AGENT, FUJI, GT, KRYPTONITE, LOOK, MOTOBECANE, PEUGEOT, PRIMAL, PURE SHIMANO, POWERLITE, RALEIGH, RHODE GEAR, ROCK SHOK, SRAM, TEKTRO, UNIVEGA and VISTALITE – at some of the best prices we circled. Lifetime service warranty on all bikes will keep you riding worry-free. Routine maintenance, gratis. And for the kiddos, don't forget to helmet up. Here, they carry the BELL helmets. Check the directory for location nearest you. *CK, MC, V, D*

★★ Dallas Golf — 972/270-0989

4600 Broadway Square — *Mon-Fri 9-7; Sat 9-6; Sun Noon-5*
Mesquite, TX 75150 — *www.dallasgolf.com*

You might find the lights are bright on Broadway (Square), but so is the selection of brand-name golf equipment. Set your tee times swinging with PING, PRO-LINE, TITLEST, WILSON and others similarly inclined. The discounts, though, are not that steep, but noticeable. But with a knowledgeable sales staff, you might want to overlook it and go for the know. Visit their Irving location at Story Rd. and 183 (they also handle repairs onsite). Three additional locations: 429 N. Central Expwy. in Richardson (972/231-9399); 3963 Belt Line Rd. in Addison (972/866-0007); and 2326 W. Airport Frwy. in Irving (972/255-3639). *CK, MC, V, AE, D*

✔ Dive West

214/750-6900

5500 Greenville Ave. *Mon-Fri 10-6; Thu 10-8; Sat 10-5; Sun Noon-5*
Old Town Shopping Center *www.dive-west.com*
Dallas, TX 75206

To the depths of the deep, blue seas, Dive West for the best selection of diving equipment in the Metroplex. Usually in March, there is a Super Saver warehouse sale. Dive in with both feet and defeat the cost of paying full price. Other times, you'll have to hold your breath. Either way, though, with an indoor heated pool to immerse yourself in, you'll enjoy shopping this location even during non-warehouse sale days. They not only sell you the equipment, they also teach you the ropes, the lines, the tanks. (It's still hard for me to understand Henry David Thoreau living beside a pond, but never owning a pair of water skis or a snorkel.) If your youngster is interested in learning to dive, lessons begin at age 12. Expect to shell out $268 for a two-weekend (Friday night, Saturday and Sunday) course. Classes on Monday and Wednesday cost $238. Textbooks are included in that price but masks, fins and personal accessories are not (they do offer 10 percent discounts on equipment if you're enrolled in class). They are pros in the know with the cutting edge on scuba-diving equipment. For fun and practice, they take monthly dive trips to Cozumel and offer other dive packages for just about anywhere you might want to head feet-first. Dive into three other locations in north Dallas, Irving and Plano. You can't go wrong with Dive West. *CK, MC, V, AE, D*

★★★★★ Doug & Lynda's Ski Shop

972/542-0214

227 E. Louisiana St. *Mon-Sat 10-6; Sun 1-5*
McKinney, TX 75069 *www.winterwearhouse.com*

Sleigh bells ring, are you listening? Ski buffs know what I'm talking about. If schussing down the slopes is your winter fun, this is definitely a place to visit. See an Olympic-sized selection of ski clothes and equipment at 20-70 percent off in champion names like AIRWALK, ATOMIC, BLACK BEAR, CB SPORTS, COLUMBIA, DESCENTE, DYNASTAR, FILA, HEAD, K2, MORROW, NORDICA, OAKLEY, OBERMEYER, RAICHLE, ROFFE, ROSSIGNAL, SALOMON, SIMS, SNUGGLER, SPYDER, TECNICA, VOLANT, VOLKYL, WHITE STAG and more. Then ogle over the goggles, gloves, headbands and fanny packs. During an end-of-the-season markdown, savings descended to 75 percent off snowboards and skis with bindings. Their full-service repair shop keeps skis and snowboards ready to head downhill. It's worth the drive to McKinney if you want to spend your money on lift tickets instead of retail price tickets on ski apparel and equipment. *CK, MC, V, D, Layaway*

♥♥♥♥♥ Empowered Women's Golf — 972/233-8807

5344 Belt Line Rd. — *Mon-Sat 10-6*
Dallas, TX 75240

Ladies hate playing with men's golf clubs. So now, they have a place they can call their very own. You don't have to be Nancy Lopez to command a set all to yourself. Empowered Women's Golf is for women what a toupee is for men – hopefully, a perfect fit. They've got all the makings service, selection and style. Find first-rate clubs and equipment from CALLOWAY, CLEVELAND, COBRA, PING, PROLINE, TAYLOR MADE and TITLEIST, for example. Since golfers have a unique, shall we say, sense of style, and you can find golf apparel by ASTRA, BAHAMAS, COMO, CUTTER & BUCK, MARSHA, TOMMY and others. Keep your feet fashion forward while making your way to the 19th hole in shoes by FOOT JOY and LADY FAIRWAY. Now, birdie the hole! *CK, MC, V, AE*

★★ Finish Line — 972/881-1213

1717 E. Spring Creek Pkwy. — *Mon-Sat 10-9; Sun Noon-6*
Plano Outlet Mall — *www.finishline.com*
Plano, TX 75074

The end result at the Finish Line? End-of-the-season clearance stuff and generally a sale. Always a sale. Good foot covers in evidence like ADIDAS, ETONIC, NIKE, PUMA, REEBOK – you know, the stars. Just don't expect the latest look. If it's an athletic shoe and you don't care what year, what model, what color as long as it has a right and left foot, Finish Line could be your first line of defense. Other locations: Collin Creek Mall (972/424-7197); Richardson Square Mall (972/783-4877); Irving Mall (972/594-1039); Vista Ridge Mall (972/315-3602); The Parks of Arlington Mall (817/465-2170); North East Mall (817/595-0763); and Hulen Mall (817/370-0441). End of discussion. *CK, MC, V, D, AE*

★★★★★ Fitness Headquarters — 972/980-7788 or 93

11930 Preston Rd. — *Mon-Thu 10-8; Fri-Sat 10-7; Sun Noon-5*
Dallas, TX 75230 — *www.fitnessheadquarters.com*

So, now you know. I broke down and bought a recumbent bike and it's the best investment I've ever made (except for my education, of course.) You, too, can put the pedal to the medal and get with the program. Ride in a more relaxed position, turn the music up, and away you go. Like the Pointer Sisters, "I've got a new attitude!" Head to these quarters and choose a personal plan of action that's right for you. LAND ICE, SPORTS ART or TANURI treadmills start from $500. Add a reading rack, a pulse monitor and all kinds of extra gadgets to ensure a perfect fitness workout. They are the exclusive southwest distributor for STAIR MASTER so expect to see factory-direct prices. Since they are also the designated shopping site for the Cooper Clinic, you can bet they run circles around the competition. Pricing is the most aggressive in town. At least 20 percent off legitimate MSP, plus there's a well-equipped department for consignment equipment. They buy, sell and trade with the personal touch. Service separates them from the glut of mass-market fitness options. Delivery, set-up and installation another plus. If it's good enough for the Maple Leafs and the Mavericks, it's good enough for the me and the Metroplex. Another location is in Plano at 1805 Preston Rd. (972/267-6665). Work out online, too. *CK, MC, V, AE, D, Financing*

♥♥♥♥♥ Flatlander Ski and Sport — 972/690-4579

1750 Alma Rd., Suite 122 — *Mon-Sat 10-6;*
Richardson, TX 75081

The mold out of which good skiers are cast is usually plaster of Paris. But at least at this place, you have a choice. During the winter months, shop for all of your snow-skiing fashions. If there is lots of white snow (and Blue Cross), it could make shopping for downhill skiing a safe bet. Schuss down in an outfit from BOULDER GEAR, COLUMBIA, FERA, NORDICA, NORTH FACE and more. Prices ranged from bunny slope to double diamond, so ski carefully. During the Spring, the emphasis changes to wind and sand. Shop here when you're ready to hit the beaches of Waikiki with appropriate ocean gear. Then, too, on the boardwalk, their inline skates may do the trick and keep you on dry land. Be a sport, though, and shop them when their sales are on. Otherwise, you'll be hit with those dreaded retail prices. *CK, MC, V, D, AE*

★ Foot Locker Outlet — 817/451-4602

5116 E. Lancaster Ave. — *Mon-Sat 10-8; Sun Noon-5*
Fort Worth, TX 76112

Although their service department needs to put their running shoes on, put your foot in the door of this outlet for family athletic footwear. For a reasonable deal on ADIDAS, CONVERSE, NIKE, REEBOK and more, jog to the Foot Locker Outlet. Go for the prices not for the friendly service 'cause you'll be in for a rude awakening! Hey folks, just because this place is labeled an outlet store doesn't mean they have to be weak with the cheek. A smile goes a long way. Visit with patience, though, as your best deals are found at end-of-season. Choose also boots, coats, caps, even shoe laces for a foothold into containing your expenditures. Lock up a great deal at this outlet store and beat the price in the mall by 20-50 percent. Prices are great until they run out of the closeouts, then they can jump to regular prices unless they're having a sale. Forget shopping at the beginning of the school year. It's a mad house. *CK, MC, V, AE, D*

★★ Gaston Billiards

972/412-6309

3001 Century Drive
Rowlett, TX 75088

Mon-Fri 8:30-4; Sat By Appt.

Being located down the street from the police station might be what prevents this store from racking-up the prices on slate pool tables. We found prices starting from $699 for a 7-foot table. For a full-size table expect to pay a bit more. A MAVERICK, made in your choice of oak or maple with leather pockets, can be in your home for $1,499. (This includes cues, balls, chalk, a rule book, delivery and installation.) Other models can range up to $2,500. On the lower end of things, you can find a wood laminate table for a very reasonable $995. It doesn't hurt to lay your cards on the table and dream for the best. *CK, MC, V, AE*

★★★ Golf Place

940/891-0933

2436 S. I-35 E, Suite 346
Denton, TX 76205

Mon-Fri 10-6; Sat 9-5

For great prices on golf clubs, tees, balls, hats, putters, gloves, shirts, and any other golf-size accessories, putter up to this place. With a second location in Lewisville near Vista Ridge Mall (972/315-3090), they haven't teed-off any golfers yet. This place meets all the needs of the accomplished or aspiring golfer. We were entertained by the practice putting ranges and impressed with the patience of the staff when confronted with "silly putting" golf questions. To check out the Denton store, drive north on 35 and look for Luby's. As they say at the Golf Place, "If you can find Luby's, you can find us." The only difference between the two locations that we can tell is that one doesn't smell of baked fish and pecan pie. *CK, MC, V, AE, D*

★★★★★ GolfEssentials.com

972/633-9934

24 hours / 7 days
www.golfessentials.com

Slice off 50-75 percent and you'll see why we scored a hole-in-one at this online golf source. Custom-fit golf equipment: irons, woods, putters, wedges, left/right, men/women's/juniors and accessories by DYNACRAFT, PEERLESS and ZERO TOLERANCE; bags and covers by HARVEY PENICK and ZERO TOLERANCE, as well as golf balls. In other words, everything you would ever need to play a round or two. Tee off with custom-built "trend design" golf clubs at prices 50-75 percent less than name brand equipment. If the already low prices weren't enough, click the link at the bottom of the left column for monthly specials on different brands and equipment. Your clubs will be built using only the finest golf components from names such as: ALDILA, BOB TROSKI, DYNACRAFT, GOLF PRICE, GOLFSMITH, GRAFFOLLY, HARRISON, HARVEY PENICK, KZG, PEERLESS, SNAKE EYES, TRUE TEMPER, UST, WALTER HAGEN and ZERO TOLERANCE by professional club builders who are full-time employees of Golfessentials.com. They are not "knockoffs", which are often substandard. All clubs have an unconditional 30-day warranty. *CK with prior approval, MC, V, AE, MO*

★★★★★ Golfsmith Pro Shop — 972/991-9255

4141 LBJ Frwy. — *Mon-Sat 10-7; Sun Noon-6*
Dallas, TX 75052 — *www.golfsmith.com*

From their humble beginnings in the basement of Carl's Plainfield, N.J., house in 1969 and a few hundred dollars, Carl and his brother Frank Paul began a business in Austin that is going gangbusters today. Mail order and their own line of golf equipment was their initial offering. Now that it is flourishing, they've opened outlet stores and gone online. Their huge storefronts (20,000 square feet plus) are the epitome of how popular the sport of golf is today. There's just about everything a golf enthusiast would need except a full-scale driving range. (They do have a net available for taking a few practice swings, however.) A tremendous selection of clubs (CALLAWAY, COBRA and TAYLOR MADE), accessories, components, shoes, balls, golf-flavored gifts – just about everything you might expect from a golfing giant with the name GOLFSMITH. (They also own the HARVEY PENICK line.) The wall of TVs, the computerized swing analyzer and more means hours of shopping and having a swinging good time. "Find a man who has his feet firmly on the ground, and I bet he's about to make a putt!" If you are in Austin, visit and play out at their corporate headquarters and golf course at 11000 N I-35 (512/837-3878). Or shop closer to home in Arlington at 1001 W. I-20 (between Matlock and Cooper; 817/557-5077) or in Plano at 900 Central Expwy. (972/424-4823). *CK, MC, V, AE, D*

Sporting Goods

★★★ Innovation Skate Shop 817/417-5283

1201 W. Arbrook Blvd., Suite 101 *Mon-Fri Noon-7; Sat 11-6; Sun 1-5*
Arlington, TX 76015

Get out of your rut. Es-skate from the hum-drum of your life. Give Innovation Skate Shop a whirl. Dealing primarily in skateboards with some gear for in-line skaters, it's the only store in the Metroplex catering exclusively to skateboarders. Prices are extremely competitive so if you're a skateboard aficionado, you'll flip. The deck is stacked with pricing between $34.99 to $54.99, so the sport is relatively inexpensive compared to football, golf or baseball. But for complete sets, expect to skim the edge from $69.99 to $129.99. Innovation carries helmets and pads (this helps assure repeat business) along with gift items such as key chains, videos and T-shirts. They are located near The Parks of Arlington Mall. *CK, MC, V, AE, D*

★★★★★ Ladylike Ski Shop/The Ski Loft 972/442-5842

1000 N. Hwy. 78 *Tues-Fri 10-6; Thu 10-8; Sat Noon-6*
Wylie, TX 75098

After the original location on Ballard St. was destroyed by fire, the Ladylike Ski Shop/The Ski Loft has been resurrected in a new location at 1000 N. Hwy. 78 in Wylie. Brand new store, same great deals. Since the first Underground Shopper in 1972, they have helped skiers climb a million mountains and schuss down a zillion slopes. After all, skiing is a wonderful sport, from beginning to – end! (That's where I usually end up.) But, whether you're a lady of the night-time skier or a daytime cross-country buff, you'll still want to dress the part. Get a HEAD start on your skiing wardrobe and head to Wylie – a hop, skip and a ski-jump from Plano. If it's apparel for the slopes, they have it all – from toddlers, women's, up to 5XL in men's at half-price and less. Get bibs, pants, jackets, jumpsuits, gloves and goggles, but don't come looking for skis or any Aspen movie stars (though those traveling to Aspen can look like movie stars). With brands like COLUMBIA, HEAD, INSIDE EDGE, OBERMEYER and RAEDACKS leading the pack, you only have to make Wylie your one-stop shop for all your family's skiing or wintry apparel. Don't let the name fool you, even men and children can get a lucky break and dress the part from this Wylie institution. *CK, MC, V, AE, D*

★★ Las Vegas Golf & Tennis 972/668-5090

8612 Preston Rd. *Mon-Sat 9-6; Sun Noon-5*
Plano, TX 75024 *www.lvgolf.com*

You don't have to roll the dice in Las Vegas to take a gamble on the game of golf. When you have Las Vegas Discount Golf, you can hit the jackpot. This tiny shop carries a tremendous inventory of golf clubs, balls and accessories. Check out their whole line of top name brand products from CALLAWAY, CLEVELAND, COBRA, NIKE, PING, TAYLOR MADE, TOMMY ARMOUR, TOP FLITE and WILSON, as well as their very own VISION GOLF brand. They sure do pack a lot into this high rent district store. Between Preston and the Tollway, if you're into golf, this could be a birdie in your cap. If you're taking a trip south, stop in at the discount store at Hillsboro Prime Outlets at 104 NE I-35, Suite 162 (254-582-1022). *CK, MC, V, AE*

★★★★ North Texas Golf World — 817/457-9345

1100 E. I-820 S. — *Mon-Fri 8-5; Sat 9-2*
Fort Worth, TX 76112

If you're a swinger who doesn't enjoy the long trek around the golf course, maybe a new or used golf cart is in order. North Texas Golf World offers new and used BOMBARDIER, E-Z-GO and YAMAHA golf carts which have been high on many a pro's "gotta-have" list. Prices range from a $750 used three-wheeler to $1,200-$1,800 for a 3-5-year-old model. Like-new, rebuilt cars range from $2,850-$3,400. New cars start at $4,000. Too, North Texas Golf World features new, used and custom-made clubs. *MC, V, AE, D*

★★★ Oshman's SuperSports USA — 817/467-0090

4620 Cooper & I-20 — *Mon-Fri 10-9; Sat 9-9; Sun 11-6*
Arlington, TX 76017 — *www.oshmans.com*

Oshman's SuperSports has taken a strangle hold in the marketplace. With 12 superstores in the Metroplex, bigger in this case is better, or so the story goes. Naturally, at the helm, is a woman whose name was once Oshman, and she is directing the course for the future. We found spectacular savings during sales (25-70 percent off retail) on exercise equipment, athletic apparel and footwear, in-line skates, aerobic wear, licensed apparel, warm-ups, backpacks, hiking and camping gear, hunting and fishing equipment, golf, tennis, team and water sports. Shoot some hoops, take a few swings in the batting cage or at the punching bag, try for a hole-in-one (yes, in-store demo areas let you try before you buy) and it should give you an overview of fitness and fun for everyone. Names from their Olympic line-up at 30 percent off included SPEEDO swimwear, ADIDAS, ASICS, NIKE, REEBOK and YUKON shoes plus HEAD, PRINCE and WILSON tennis rackets and golf gear, ROLLERBLADE and BAUER in-line skates and equipment for under $100 ... ready, set, go. Check directory for other locations or call the

800/PLAY-OSH for the one nearest you. Don't stop 'til you feel the burn. *CK, MC, V, AE, D, DC*

✧ Paintball Games of Dallas — 972/554-1937

3305 E. John Carpenter Frwy.
Irving, TX 75062
Call for hours and times
www.paintballgames.com

Join the battalion of paintballers who fight 'til they see the whites of their eyes and the red, blue, green or brown all over their opponents' faces, arms and legs. Pistol-type or rifle-type, choose your weapons. The guns use CO2 as a propellant, so it's not just a kids' night out. They shoot marble-sized balls that ooze with lifelike red paint (or other colors). Hundreds of accessories are available for purchase at this, the largest paintball-exclusive store you'll find anywhere, including paintball-correct clothes, masks and holders. For $20 a person, you'll get a gun, mask and 100 rounds of ammo for a two-hour indoor or four-hour outdoor session – what a blast! I dare say if they ever go on strike, it could be a paintbath if they don't get their way. *CK, MC, V, D*

★★★★★ Play It Again Sports — 972/720-9666

14902 Preston Rd., Suite 506
Dallas, TX 75240
Mon-Fri 10-8; Sat 10-6; Sun Noon-5
www.playitagainsports.com

Frankly, the most interesting sport to watch is the contest between an irresistible blonde and an immovable bachelor. But, for those interested in other contact sports, when it comes time to trade up, or trade off, you can – at Play it Again Sports. Trade your gently used sports equipment for new equipment or credit. This sport and fitness resale franchise also secures close-outs and overstocks from major sporting goods manufacturers and retailers but most often capitalizes on your short attention span with already-bought equipment. Sports covered include hockey, skiing (from cross-country to water), football and baseball, golf, roller and figure skating, fishing and camping, soccer, tennis, biking, scuba diving, and of course, exercise equipment. One day you may find a goalie shirt, another day, a full gym set-up. Check around for the brands and gear you are looking for. Get rid of equipment not being used, and trade for something new. Just no junk, please. Well-organized and neat displays make the game of shopping easier on the eye as well as the pocketbook. One drawback, though, there is no computerized inventory between their multiple stores. Check directory for multiple locations in the Metroplex. *CK, MC, V, AE, D*

★★★★★ Ray's Sporting Goods

214/747-7916

730 Singleton
Dallas, TX 75212

Tue-Sat 9-6
www.rayssportinggoods.com

Everything for the killer instinct is found at this big game hunter. For the past 50 years, Ray's has been known as the "firearm specialist" and the target for anything you might need in the way of guns, ammo, knives and, yes, targets. (Personally, I headed for the earplug selection.) Find hand guns by COLT, CIMARRON, MAGNUM and more. Shotguns are from WINCHESTER, ACCUMARK and SKB. Considered the best find when the subject turns to bang, bang. Since it's your constitutional right, you might as well dress the part, too. Camouflage clothes for the hungry hunter can be purchased here while even the NRA can't help you out in that department. (Talk about dressed-to-kill.) Ray's is not the place to find black powder supplies, but if you're a hunter, you'll love to hole up here. If you're an animal lover, you'll probably run and "hide." When we checked, the website was missing in action, but they promised to send out the dogs to track it down. *CK, MC, V, D, AE*

★★★ REI Recreational Equipment

972/490-5989

4515 LBJ Frwy.
Dallas, TX 75244

Mon-Sat 10-9; Sun 11-6
www.rei.com

The one disadvantage of an outdoor life is that it cannot be enjoyed indoors. But if you join the physically fit crowd at REI, you won't care. This sporting goods legend has one of the best catalogs as well as well-stocked, state-of-the-art mountain gear for living the good life – outdoors. Clothing and equipment for climbing on the wild side or camping on the mountain side. Or perhaps you'd like to slide into a pair of cross-country skis, ride the tide in bicycle gear in most any fashion sportswear. That's just what Jim Whittaker did when he became one of the first Americans to climb Mt. Everest. He was REI's former company president and I'm sure did not settle for anything but a peak performance. Prices, though, are somewhat downhill from full retail but the brands are ahead of the pack; JANSPORT, KELTY, SIERRA DESIGNS and WALRUS to name a few. Although they no longer carry MOSS, their own REI brand (about 90 percent of the stock) offers comparable quality to big-name brands and helps keep prices under control. REI has millions of members nationwide and if you join their club, you can share in the company's profits at year's end as well as receive a rebate of what usually amounts to about 10 percent of the cost of your year's purchases; hence, they consider themselves a consumer co-op. Lucky for us, Dallas is one of only 11 stores that has "The Attic." It is a clearance area, so look around and see what great finds you can uncover. Online shoppers can check out Rei-outlet.com for more bargains. *CK, MC, V, D, MO, C*

★★★ Richardson Bike Mart — 972/231-3993

1451 W. Campbell Rd. — *Mon-Fri 10-8; Sat 9-6: Sun Noon-5*
Richardson, TX 75080 — *www.bikemart.com*

'Round and 'round you spin your wheels looking for the best bikes in the Metroplex. Then, if you're smart, you come to a full stop at Richardson Bike Mart. They also have a location by White Rock Lake at 9040 Garland Rd., 214/321-0705, but it's technically in the Richardson boundaries. Call on them if you're into a SCHWINN bike because that is their specialty. But don't worry, be happy. They also carry TREK, YETTI and many more. If you are riding through the park or riding over the mountains (or the hills that pass as mountains around here), the staff will make sure you get the right bike at the right price. They can outfit your toddler or custom-make a state-of-the-art mountain bike just for you. If you can't find it here, you can't find it anywhere, so say their many repeat customers. *CK, MC, V, AE, D*

★★★★★ St. Bernard Sports Outlet — 214/352-1200

2707 W. Mockingbird — *Tue-Sat 10-6*
Dallas, TX 75235 — *www.stbernardsports.com*

On the northside of Mockingbird, just west of Denton Drive, look for the "world headquarters" of St. Bernard Sports. (Their retail store is in Inwood Village, Lovers Lane and Inwood). But for outdoor enthusiasts wanting to get "in" at their "outlet," head to their warehouse where savings made a downhill descent of up to 50 percent off. There, in their 3,500-square-foot warehouse, you can start at the top and work your way down the hill. Close-outs and last-season's models from COLD AS ICE to FILA, PATAGONIA to WESTBEACH; if it's skis or snowboard equipment, accessories, ski-wear, in-line skates, including a huge selection of kids' ski and snowboard wear, the St. Bernard Outlet is a lifesaver. Their rather melted-down website featured some "net specials" on readily recognized equipment, but the best prices were found at the outlet store. Now open year-round, stick with the outlet for the best buys. *CK, MC, V, AE, D*

★★★ Sun & Ski Sports Outlet

817/284-0052

7410 Grapevine Hwy.
North Richland Hills, TX 76118
Mon-Sat 10-9; Sun Noon-6
www.sunandski.com

This place pulls double duty for both summer and winter sports at up to 40 percent less. What's in a name? Well, everything. Whether the weather's running hot or cold, you can be active for less. Rollerblade or ice skate, it's all in a day's work ... out. ROLLERBLADE LIGHTNING and ROLLERBLADE FUSION in-line skates were well below retail, much to our delight. If you like strapping a couple of sticks to your feet, no matter what the weather, then daring Mother Nature to knock you down is right up your alley. Do it all at this chain of (active) events. They carry all kinds of ski equipment to take you to the top – gloves, goggles, hats, stretch pants, not to mention skis, bindings and poles. If it's sunnier dispositions you see in your horizon, try water-skiing in names like H O SPORTS and CONNELLY. Actually, they have it all – except the boat. Sales are held on a regular basis depending on inventory and season. Their retail stores are located at 3032 Alta Mere in Fort Worth (just south of I-30 on Hwy. 183) and in Dallas at 5500 Greenville Ave. at Lovers Lane. But the outlet above is where we land upright. *CK, MC, V, AE, D*

★★★★★ T-Shirt Outlet

972/241-7030

14015 N. Stemmons
Farmers Branch, TX 75234
Mon-Sat 10-8

Get with the program. With a minimum of 36 shirts (100 percent cotton or 50-50 percent cotton/polyester), they will screenprint your team's name or logo right on the spot. Besides, their T-shirt prices are so cheap, you might have enough left over to take the team out to the ball game. Baseball is, after all, the only place in life where a sacrifice is really appreciated. You, on the other hand, will appreciate the children's T's at five for $10; S-M-L-XL. Adults, too, can now get the same five shirts for $10. Oversized shirts (2XL, 3XL) are a bit pricier at three for $10, but that's still a deal. Then Mr. T could afford a few more gold necklaces if he shopped here often enough! *CK, MC, V*

★★★★★ Tour Line Golf

817/560-4700

7616 Hwy. 80 W.
Fort Worth, TX 76116
Mon-Fri 10-6; Sat 9-5
www.tourlinegolf.com

OK, sport fans. If you are looking to play WITH pros, you might as well play LIKE the pros. Country Club pros across the country send Tour Line Golf the equipment they take in trade. In fact, they are America's largest clearinghouse for used tour line equipment. They, in turn, sell this equipment at a fraction of the cost of new, and you are the benefactor. Major name-brand clubs only (CALLAWAY, CLEVELAND, KING COBRA, PING, TAYLOR MADE, TITLEIST). No clones or copies, just the originals, sir. What a selection! What prices! Move over Fred Couples, this store stands alone. Quality used irons, woods, putters and drivers alongside new apparel and accessories. It's also the best price on golf balls in town. Swing over to their Dallas store, 5500 Greenville Ave, 214/692-9411. Todd's the swinger who will putt a deal together in used pro-line golf clubs. Ninety percent of their inventory is coming from all over the country. ODESSY putters, for example, have won more major tournaments than any other on the PGA circuit. They don't do consignment, but rather buy your clubs outright. So, whether you're buying or selling, this is the place to score. Another location is at 5500 Greenville, Suite 502 at Lovers Lane (NE corner) in Dallas, 214/692-9411. Store hours are Mon-Thu 10-7; Fri 10-6; Sat 9-5. Ask for Todd. *CK, MC, V, D*

★★ Two Wheel World — 817/261-0012

1922 Pioneer Pkwy. — *Mon-Fri 9-7; Sat 9-6*
Arlington, TX 76013

Don't fly on a wing and a prayer. Visit Two Wheel World if yours has quit pedaling. But don't make any mistakes about thinking this shop is for motorcycles. They do carry an occasional bike on-consignment, but their specialty is fixing them and selling parts and accessories. This shop is filled with the biker crowd. If you want to cushion the blows of paying top-dollar, it's possible to rev your motors up here for less. They repair and sell the parts to most brands besides HARLEYS, such as HONDA, KAWASAKI and YAMAHA. And if you've been wondering where you can swat some MOSQUITO'S, this is the place. Mosquito's is the name of the maker for the motorized skateboards with handles you see kids wheeling around on. Not legal on the street if you're under 18, check your local city laws before purchasing. Yet if Junior has to have one, expect to pay $500. Helmet over to their Garland location at Garland and Miller Road, too, or call 972/864-0190. *CK, MC, V, AE, D*

★★★★★ Wally's Discount Golf Shop — 817/261-9301

900 E. Copeland Rd. — *Mon-Fri 9:30-6:30; Sat 9-6*
Arlington, TX 76011

Don't expect a Sunday visit to Wally's 'cause they hang a "Gone Golfin'" sign in the window. But Monday through Saturday, they're right on course saving you money. They even offer a custom-fit program for those who want a bigger, better Bertha. If you want any major name-brand golf equipment or apparel to turn heads at the club, such as PING, TITLEIST or many others, Wally has it at a discount. True to form, they boast having the largest selection in the Metroplex. Swingers who want to score a hole-in-one head to their outlet store at 9090 N. Stemmons at Regal Row. That way, they have enough money left over to attend the Byron Nelson Classic. Better yet, play Pebble Beach. A little birdie told us about a line of unique "golfing gifts" for last-minute gift ideas. Fore. Enjoy the driving range and the putting green inside the Stemmons outlet as well as keeping your score low with prices even lower. It's par for the course in Dallas, Mesquite, Plano and Richardson but no longer in Addison. There's also a warehouse in Garland, but it's not open to the public. *CK, MC, V, AE, D, Layaway*

★★★ Wheels & Fitness In Motion 972/644-2221

2550 Promenade Shopping Center *Mon-Sat 10-8; Sun Noon-6*
Richardson, TX 75080

We love to shop in cycles at Wheels in Motion 'cause they try to keep us perpetually in motion. Nominated as one of the top 100 dealers in the country for many years, if you want to wheel and deal, here's where to put the pedal to the concrete. They're no slouch in other fitness arenas either. Expect competitive pricing on bikes such as CANNONDALE, DIAMOND BACK and RALEIGH. Round the bend with new in-line skates; start the new year with a treadmill or STAIR STEPPER. Frankly, if you want to sweat, this is the place where the action is. They are located in the middle of everything in Richardson and extend their hours for daylight savings time. A VISION R2000 exercise bike with a five-function display that shows RPMs, time, speed, calories burned and distance with a two-year warranty on parts and electronics caught our eye; a TRUE treadmill, comparable to PRECOR was available but it didn't fold up and out of the way. (I hate constant reminders of what I should do looking me square in the eye.) Other brands included GIANT, K2, LIFE CYCLE, TRUE, LIFE FITNESS and VISION. Six months interest-free financing on both new and demo models. Check the directory for additional locations. *CK, MC, V, AE, D*

Surplus, Salvage & Pawn

★★ Bargain Depot/Christian Community Action 972/219-4319

128 S. Mill *Mon-Fri 9-8; Sat 9-6 (Donation Area Closes at 5)*
Lewisville, TX 75057

When it comes time for a little spring cleaning and you're ready to rid yourself of clutter just to create a little more closet space, give this charity a call to pick up the pieces. They're more than willing to haul it off to a worthy cause (except for paint, waterbeds and water heaters). Even non-working appliances are welcome. Discounts are divided between good and great; merchandise is equally divided between good and heaven only knows. They aren't the most stylish in the clothing departments or the housewares are not always high-tech, but the hunt is still half the fun. We found a great pair of ROCKIES for $5 and some brand-new skirts for $3.50. Then we wrapped ourselves around a JUSTIN belt for $4 (retail over $20) that looked like it had never been worn. Toys, furniture, knickknacks and household items make this depot a crowded spot even during the week. The selection is always changing so don't miss out. While you're in the neighborhood, why not pay a visit to their sister spot, Pay-less ReSale at 201 South Mill, Suite 101, which is open Tuesday-Saturday or call 972/219-4319. *CK*

★★★★★ Builder's Surplus 817/831-3600

6016 E. Belknap *Tue-Fri 9-6; Sat 9-4*
Haltom City, TX 76117

The importance of being furnished with some of the best names in the building supply business is obvious here. If you're in the market for the next best thing to a full-service hardware store (except the full service prices) is Builder's Surplus's claim to fame. They'll have your home fixed up in no time. No second-class merchandise, "no siree," just surplus and factory seconds of the names you're familiar with already. Only it's more than the retail hardware store could handle. The taming of the screw at Builder's Surplus is a fait accompli. Save plenty of money on such names as ATRIUM windows and doors, H & R WINDOWS, STANLEY, WILSONART and more. They have wonderful prices on ceramic tile and vinyl flooring, too. Need new cabinets? Want to spend less for them than at Home Depot? Then lock hands with name-brand cabinets, doors, counter tops, tools, locks and the list goes on. After all, the more the merrier. You never can get enough of a good thing.

★★★★★ Depot 42 — 940/648-3344

1429 West FM 407 — *Mon-Sat 9-6*
Justin, TX 76247

Formerly Justin Outlet, this 25,000-square-foot closeout carnivore is home to a great selection of food and housewares. But the best part? Everything was half price or less. Kitchen gadgets galore by RUBBERMAID, coffee makers by MELITO, cookware, dishes, serving pieces, stainless steel (tons), storage containers, school supplies, stereos, luggage, purses, knives, tools, get the picture? Then it's time to wrap yourself in a GRUEN or SEIKO watch, a sport watch, even kids' watches were eyed at wholesale prices or below. We wound up wandering around in a daze and tip-toed through the pottery, vases, glassware, handbags, T-shirts, jackets, but only wound up buying a toaster. So what? We didn't get burned, did we? They also have a location in Fort Worth at 4405 River Oaks Blvd., 817/624-4240. *CK, MC, V, AE, D*

★★ Disabled American Veterans — 972/790-2185

2310 Rock Island — *Mon-Sat 9-5:45*
Irving, TX 75061

A couple of times a year, I bag up my outcasts (or "outgrowns") and head over to drop them off at Disabled American Veterans. The merchandise is then fixed or cleaned and made ready for resale in one of their retail outlets. You never know what you're going to get, that's for sure. Clothing ranges from 1970s rejects to last year's GUESS? jeans on any given day. We've found EVAN PICONE and Kmart clothes at prices consistent with all thrift stores – from pennies up to a few bucks. Some furniture out back in the warehouse, some toys in the room next door, but nothing for the toy-polloi. Unattended deposit boxes were also scattered around town for your convenience. They've discontinued their pick-up service for economic reasons. *C*

★★★★ Freight Outlet, The — 972/289/7499

11903 Lake June — *Tue-Fri 10-7, Sat 10-6*
Balch Springs, TX 75180

Little red semi, chug, chug, chug, driving down the highway bringing buys,

buys, buys. OK, if "it's shipped by truck, they have it, had it, or will have it." All legal, except maybe the prices, and they're killers. The Freight Outlet gets new merchandise and old. It's a big treasure hunt where you never know what will turn up. Expect to see much of the standard fare like sundries, beauty supplies, canned goods – typically grocery and drug store items, but some perishables, too, like bacon for 99¢ a pound and corny dogs. Take the bite out of paying full price and save pennies, dollars, sometimes lots of dollars. Plus, the personnel are the nicest in town. (Must be a Balch Springs trait.) Take 635 E to Lake June Road and go west. Two blocks west of Wal-Mart. Land at their second location called Freight Outlet Plus in St. Joseph, TX. Call 940/995-2776 for directions. *CK*

★★★★★ Genesis Thrift Store — 214/520-6644

2918 Oak Lawn — *Mon-Fri 10-5; Sat 10-4:30*
Dallas, TX 75219

Meet me at this Bargain of Eden if you want to take a bite out of extravagant spending. Make an Exodus to the corner of Oak Lawn and Cedar Springs and unearth a genuine find. This upscale thrift store is like no other. In 7,000 square feet, you'll see goods organized and well-displayed, by sizes and by categories. They have clothing from some of the finest closets in town for both men, women and children. Toys, furniture, household goods ... the world is their oyster (and maybe your pearl). All proceeds from the thrift store benefit the Genesis Shelter, a full-service care facility helping battered women and recipient of this year's Shoppers' Choice Awards' charity-of-choice. Their care facility houses 14 rooms, they can accommodate women and their children into a six-eight-week rehabilitation program that includes help in finding housing, jobs and providing 24-hour counseling (especially in the area of self-esteem). ALCOVE, a Jewish Women's Council, offers this child-care assistance facility free giving women a real second chance at re-establishing a healthier lifestyle (one without the batterer). All women are screened prior to entering the program for drugs (they're the only shelter that does so). There are times when you cannot get help, but there is never a time when you cannot give it. Visit their second location for upscale resale at 5417 Lovers Lane. *CK, MC, V*

★★★★ Goodwill Industries — 214/638-2800

2800 N. Hampton Rd. — *Mon-Sat 9:30-6; Sun Noon-6*
Dallas, TX 75212

There is no shame in shopping at the Goodwill Store. Goodwill = Good Deals, plus you'll be benefiting a very worthy cause. We have always gotten lucky at the Goodwill stores. All kinds of odds and ends, small appliances, dishware, glassware, family clothing and toys. No pick-up service, though, since there are drop-off donation centers around town. Goodwill provides jobs for those who may not otherwise be able to work. Check directory for the closest location and lend a helping hand. Every little bit helps. Remember, generosity begins at home. *CK, MC, V*

★★★★ Home Recycling Warehouse

214/631-3031

2950 Irving Blvd.
Dallas, TX 75247
Mon-Sat 9-5

Salvage kings and queens love to cross over the moat to the kingdom of princely prices. In this instance, head for the 30,000-square-foot expanse by exiting Inwood southbound on I-35; go to Irving Blvd. and make a right. Whatever has been culled from a demolition site or a remodeling job can be reclaimed here at a close-out price. Also, there are new building supplies at outlet prices. Whether it's doors or windows, lumber, cabinets, wood flooring, HVAC, tubs, toilets or sinks, if it was enjoyed before, enjoy it again. Don't be deterred if they don't answer their phones personally. They're probably helping someone rummage through the remains. If you are looking to add something old to your new house, this can be a dead-heat for one of the best – especially if you are looking for old bricks (or bric-a-brac). Some new supplies, too, to add to their royal selection. *CK*

★★★★ Ladies of Charity Thrift Store

214/821-5775

2710 Samuell Blvd.
Dallas, TX 75223
Mon-Fri 9:30-3:30; Sat 9:30-1

Ah, such Sweet Charity. These folks provide low prices on donated items for sale to which all monies received, less expenses, provide help for the needy (from approved donors). Such items as their rent, utilities, transportation, clothing, food or prescriptions are covered by the proceeds collected. Other items always welcome by donors include non-perishable food items, household supplies, clothing, toys, medical appliances, baby furniture and layette items. Here's a worthy note: Donate items in memory of a loved one and the family will be notified with an appropriate card. Volunteers in the thrift store are always needed, too. And remember, all items donated are tax deductible. 'Tis better to give than to receive. As my mother once said, "Go to friends for advice, to women for sympathy, to strangers for charity, and to relatives for nothing." *CK*

Surplus, Salvage & Pawn

★★★★★ Orr Reed Wrecking Co. 214/428-7429

1903 Rock Island *Mon-Sat 9-4*
Dallas, TX 75207

Knock on wood, this is your doorway to seeing stars. When the subject of salvage is discussed, it begins with Orr Reed, period. And if you want to rock, head to see their version of The Doors. Over 28,000 of them await your key, all organized by size and function. If you're in the mood to dig and hunt, just take a look into some serious hardware, including lumber, paneling, cabinets, countertops, moldings and more. (Orr else you'll miss one of the best places this side of the Rock Island line.) Their front showroom is an old-fashioned hardware store complete with nuts, bolts and screws – ensuring your item will be in perfect shape when it leaves their domain. Truly a "junker's" paradise where being the "granddaddy of salvage yards" means respect in the nouveau subdivisions around the Metroplex. To get there, go almost to the end of Industrial, turn right before you get to Corinth. *CK, MC, V*

★★★★★ ReStore (Habit for Humanity) 214/827-9083

3020 Bryan *Mon-Sat 10-6*
Dallas, TX 75204 *www.dallas-habitat.org*

This is the place that has all Metroplex moochers making their way for the skinny. This philanthropic treasure is a virtual hotbed of bargains, two-fold. Not only do they sell stuff at ridiculously low prices, but the proceeds benefit a worthy cause – Habitat for Humanity's low-income housing for the needy. Here you'll find new and used appliances, doors, windows, tile, tubs, sinks, plumbing supplies, flooring, hardware, fixtures, wiring and more for any home improvement project. New WHIRLPOOL tubs, for example, were $400 and CORIAN sinks were $30. All purchases are tax deductible and donations are always welcome. Shop and net a bargain and your purchase price is a double whammy. Look for their one-story warehouse three blocks east of Central Expressway or call for directions. *CK, MC, V*

★★★ Salvation Army 214/630-5611

5554 Harry Hines *Mon-Sat 10-6*
Dallas, TX 75235

Whatever happened to Pavlov's dog? It was donated to the Salivation Army. Anything else is fair game here. Attention! Fall into formation and advance to the Salvation Army. You won't find Army surplus here, but there is plenty of garage sale-type items from more homes than could ever be organized for a rummage sale. Rummaging is the key here. Dig through the furniture, clothing, antiques, bric-a-brac, baskets, jars, and other collectibles and accessories ... some to fix up, others to impress your neighbors. We found brand name clothing such as GAP, RALPH LAUREN and TOMMY HILFIGER. It all depends on your ability to find these items on their racks. We found a great polo shirt by RALPH LAUREN for only $1.50. Those shirts retail for around $60-$70. One time through the washing machine and it's ready to wear. Prices range from pennies to 1/3 of retail. Remember the ringing bells at holiday times – it all goes to worthy causes. Currently looking for boat, car and motorcycle donations, too. Check directory for one of the seven Salvation Army locations in the Metroplex. *CK, MC, V*

★★★★★ Seconds & Surplus — 972/263-2661

909 Regal Row — *Mon-Thu 8-7; Fri-Sat 8-5; Sun 10-3*
Dallas, TX 75247

Seconds & Surplus just keeps growing and growing and just when we thought there was no room for improvement, it got even better. New owners assumed the helm of this 13-year-old staple in the home improvement industry. Their Regal Row location encompasses 52,000 square feet of crawl space, so with that much warehouse expanse, you can bet they fill it with all things that are low priced but high quality. There are doors, lots of doors, that close the door on high prices saving you 50-70 percent. Both new and used doors. Exterior, interior, louvered, bi-fold, leaded, patio – it's an open and shut case as to what they carry. Plus cabinets, skylights, moldings, trims, hinges, stair parts, windows and ARMSTRONG vinyl. How about a great selection of vanity mirrors and sinks for your bathroom? Seconds & Surplus is one of the best bets when it comes time to haul home improvement hardware. Check them out before building or remodeling. And if you're looking for flooring, don't back out without checking out their sister stores, they'll all part of the family: Ceramic Tile and Marble Outlet (marble and tile) and the Carpet Outlet (for every kind of floor covering). *CK, MC, V, AE, D*

★ T-Mart Bazaar — 817/534-7709

3137 E. Seminary — *Mon-Thu 10-8:30; Fri-Sat 9:30-9*
Fort Worth, TX 76119

T-Mart looked a lot like an old Kmart in selection. I'm sure the bargains were there, but you really had to look hard to find them. Mostly, we saw leftovers and low-quality lines. The furniture, we should say, was the four-piece simulated maple varieties at cheap prices that should cause you, even in your most desperate state, to consider other alternatives (buying used, or sleeping on the floor came to mind). They carry a good selection of clothes, shoes, and jewelry as well. In the other categories, you might score a home run. Beeper prices were pretty low. In fact, they were some of the lowest in town. Beepers started at only $17.99, and include the activation and the first month's air time fee; then it would be $8.99 per month to stay in touch. For me, it's more important to get a good night's sleep. *CK, MC, V, AE, D*

★★ Thrift Town — 817/625-2864

2444 Jacksboro Hwy. — *Mon-Fri 9-8; Sat 11-7; Sun 11-6*
Fort Worth, TX 76114

Any thrift store that comes with a dressing room is a bargain in our book. Air-conditioning is another plus (most thrift stores keep it so hot you don't want to stay long, much less try anything on). Clothing, furniture, and more can be found here at reasonable prices. Be prepared to go elbow-to-elbow with other bargain hunters, and on Saturdays, it often looks like family night at the Demolition Derby. They carry furniture, clothes, shoes, toys, housewares, bedding, books, and jewelry. There is a lot of selection here. The furniture section yielded some great buys but they were few and far between. Most items, as in most thrift stores, are eye-balled, sorted, and the good stuff grabbed within minutes of their arrival. Visit their other locations on Westmoreland in Dallas, North Richland Hills and Arlington. *CK, MC, V, D*

★ Thrift Village — 972/278-1026

1829 S. Garland Ave. Garland Shopping Center — *Mon-Sat 9-8; Sun Noon-5*
Garland, TX 75042

This village is a mixed bag. While some clothes here were right on the money and style, others seemed as though they belonged in the Village People's wardrobe. The selection is mainly clothing from infants to women's and men's, but we did see some housewares, furniture, sporting goods including tennis rackets and golf clubs. They also have a selection of books, toys, shoes and other knickknacks looking for a new home. Prepare to dig for some bargains and dig and dig until you've hit the bottom of the heap. Although some items seemed practically new, others had definitely seen better days. Pillage at the Village and you'll be the winner. *CK*

★★★★★ Top Line Warehouse Store

972/262-5326

433 E. Church St.
Grand Prairie, TX 75050
Mon-Sat 9:30-6

Top-of-the-line merchandise sits proudly on these shelves waiting to be picked. But if you don't grab it, you might miss it. Inventory fluctuates daily, but they do have cat and dog food from brands like HILLS and SCIENCE DIET that freight carriers have mis-loaded, mis-handled or returned on a regular basis. What you see, is what they sell – for a whole lot less. The majority of the items, though considered freight damaged, is not. In fact, about 90 percent is simply mis-marked, mis-loaded or mis-routed. If it's been handled and shipped by motor carrier, it might wind up here. Their 25,000-square-foot warehouse is neatly stocked and well-organized, with surprises at every turn. Across the street, is this sibling rivalry, Top Line Select at 208 N.E. 5th St. That location specializes in clothing, fabrics, toys and books, open Tue-Sat 10-5. Bud Bobbitt founded this company in 1975 and likens his business to Sam's – without the membership fee. So, if you're looking for relief from high prices, you'll find lots here at wholesale or less. Everything from furniture to groceries including perishables. They are officially licensed in the sales of pharmaceuticals. Located at the corner of Church and 5th Street, this is your top-of-the-line. *CK, MC, V*

★★★★ Trading Post

972/263-7117

818 W. Main St.
Grand Prairie, TX 75050
Mon-Sat 9:30-6; Sun 9:30-5

If your budget needs a good shot in the arm, take your prescription here. Buying, selling and trading is this post's practice for acquiring tools, TVs, VCRs, appliances, furniture – whatever, Find new and used items, ranging from AVON to TUPPERWARE. They even sell washer and dryers but since they used, expect the prices to be excused from top dollar. Brand names include GE, KENMORE and WHIRLPOOL. They ranged in price from $139/each and up. The selection depends on what they get in stock. Both new and old find comfort in the remedy for suturing the wound without paying blood-sucker's prices. TY Beanie Babies, both new and retired were hanging out alongside new and used tools. How's that for a juxtaposition! This is an all-day excursion into bargain shopping at its best. Dress accordingly, otherwise they might think you don't need to save money. And, of course, wear your walking shoes. *CK, MC, V, AE, D*

Surplus, Salvage & Pawn

★★★★★ Unclaimed Freight & Liquidation Sales — 817/577-1817

4850 N.E. Loop 820 — *Mon-Sat 10-8; Sun Noon-6*
Haltom City, TX 76117

Singing the Unclaimed Melody, lay your claim to someone else's missed opportunities. Somewhere in this 35,000-square-foot furniture warehouse you will unearth savings from 30-70 percent off unclaimed shipments, dealer cancellations and other factory overstocks. Some market samples direct from the World Trade Center were also seen at unheard of prices. Mattresses were being featured and piled floor to ceiling. A gorgeous eight-piece dining set by BASSETT for 50 percent off sat alongside plenty of bedroom and living room ensembles with recognizable names. Unlock that retail stranglehold that has kept you from outfitting your home in name brand furniture – dining room sets, sofas, love seats, sectionals, entertainment centers, everything for the home, works! Visit also in Arlington at 1841 W. Division, 817/265-1591 or 817/277-8441 and in Fort Worth, 9320 S. Freeway, 817/568-0495. Their second Arlington location at 7003 S. Cooper St., three miles south of I-30 is off and running. If you thought their pint-size siblings were good, you should see them now. *CK, MC, V, D, Financing, Layaway*

Telephones

★★★ Cellular Warehouse

972/436-3326

701 S. Stemmons Frwy.
Lewisville, TX 75067
Mon-Fri 9-6:30; Sat 9-6

Who'd believe we could run out of phone numbers and have to split the city with new area codes, not once, not twice, well, progress is progress, right? Cellular Warehouse is here to help you join the communications ratrace. Check them out for pagers, glass tinting–and yes, cellular phones. An authorized AT&T WIRELESS SERVICES agent, specials are frequently advertised, so check the newspaper for the latest dial-a-deal spiel. And don't be afraid to ask questions. Trying to figure out which plan is right for you, you've got to be a rocket scientist. Will you only be calling locally? When you travel, will you be making tons of long distance calls? Are you long-winded? Is roaming cheaper? Fortunately, the sales staff is very patient at explaining, and deals could be had. At the time we shopped, we could buy 900 minutes, including roam if we traveled, and pay $49.99 per month–not including the price of the phone. But they offered a deal on an ERICSSON LX 6377 for $49.99 with a $30 rebate and $19 discount (so basically the phone was free if you signed up for service). Check out their "safety plans" for a low-cost monthly fee. Several AT&T digital one-rate plans were available. All 50 states, one low price; no long-distance charges; no roaming charges. Every call is like a local call. Check directory for other locations. *CK, MC, V, AE, D*

★★ Cellular World

972/418-2233

3504 Belt Line Rd., Suite 104
Farmers Branch, TX 75234-2422
Mon-Fri 9-7; Sat 9-5

The Cellular World war is still underway with more and more outlets entering the fray. It's practically impossible to tell the good from the bad or the ugly. The founder of this company moved on to found another (Communication Expo) which also moved on (to the ultimate underground). But if you want to give them the No-Bell prize, you can. They only deal in Southwestern Bell services. They carry ERICSSON, MOTOROLA and NOKIA telephones. Just west of Marsh Lane, they offered the latest in wireless digital services. Get hooked up for $19.95 per month, with 20 minutes on weekdays and 500 minutes on weekends, not including the phone. You could buy an Ericsson KF788 with a $20 donation to the Ronald McDonald House, add the $35 one-time activation fee, and you're all set. Now, it's up to you to compare. *CK, MC, V, AE, D*

★★★★★ InterCell+ — 972/492-7807

3030 N. Josey Lane
Carrollton, TX 75007
Mon-Fri 9-6; Sat 10-2
www.intersell.com

Breathing new life into your old batteries is this company's energy flow. Whether it's the battery for your cell phone, video camera, laptop, cordless tools or lead acid batteries, this is the company you can say, "Charge it!" to. Bought your kid a radio-controlled toy and it's already run out of juice. Want more bang for your battery? Compared with the $70 cost of buying a new battery for your cell phone, InterCell+ can revitalize your old one for $9.95. Most cell phone batteries will hold up to 350 charges, but are quick to de-juice once they hit 150. Think of it as a 150 charge tune-up for your phone! Look for accessories, too, like digital battery analyzers, hands-free units and PULSETECH batteries, which boost battery life by years. Our U.S. military tanks and rocket launchers wouldn't leave home without them. And even though most people leave analog phone users high and dry, InterCell + comes through again. And let us not forget to mention that everything here is priced way below what you'll find anywhere else. Over and out. *CK, MC, V, AE, D*

★★★★ Pagenet.com — 972/985-2552

www.pagenet.com

With more than 10 million customers, PageNet is the supplier of choice for nearly one-quarter of all Americans who use pagers. Impressed? Then you also need to know they are leading the wireless messaging industry in winning new customers, and they're also dedicated to keeping their business, with very impressive customer satisfaction figures. Once you cut through all the impressive statements and posturing, the bottom line is this is a good place to go to get a reliable pager. Their basic plan, on sale, costs $99 per year. This includes the pager, service plan for 12 months, and necessary options. You can add numeric retrieval for another $2 per month. Prices and options go up from there.

Telephones

★★★★ PrimeCo Personal Communications

972/337-3000

5221 N. O'Connor Blvd., Suite 1000
Las Colinas, TX 75039

24 hours/7 days
www.primeco.com

It really doesn't take pink aliens from outer space to emphasize that PrimeCo is helping you save green. The move is on to bring this service to everyone across the United States, watch for them in your area–even Hawaii. When it comes to wireless, this company is tireless. The leader in digital wireless personal communications, digital wireless is to talkers what the microwave or fax was to shoppers when they first came out. First, a novelty. Then a luxury. And now, who can live without them? Aligning themselves with strategic partners like AIRTOUCH COMMUNICATIONS and BELL ATLANTIC; wireless phone suppliers such as PHILIPS, QUALCOMM and SONY and technology by LUCENT–how can they lose? And you're the winner. For example, 100 "Anytime Minutes" cost $24.99/month; 300 "Anytime Minutes" cost $39.99. And best of all, these minutes are priced to use anytime, travel with you to any PrimeCo digital service area, gets you free Voice Mail and Caller ID ... and is virtually crystal-clear. No more snap, crackle and pop! One of the best parts, no activation fees and no long-term contracts. Check directory for multiple Metroplex locations. *CK, MC, V, AE, D,*

★★★ ProCom Wireless

972/401-2594

1801 Royal Lane, #700
Dallas, TX 75229

Mon-Fri 8-5:30; Sat 11-5
www.procomwireless.com

Keeping up with changes is a plus for any business. ProCom is staying in the game and now carries ERICCSON, MITSUBISHI, MOTOROLA and NOKIA wireless phones, as well as providing AT&T advantage programs. Pagers were priced below wholesale, though there is a programming fee and annual billing required. Nationwide, you can talk 'til you're blue in the face. But if you want to stay in the field and stay connected to your home or office, this is a force to reckon with. For more than 30 years, ProCom has consistently provided customers with state-of-the art wireless products and services. They offer only top brand names, backed by their modern, in-house repair facility. Telephone services started as low as $24.95 for 290 minutes per month on special, and escalated to $149.99 for 1,400 minutes, plus added costs for services like digital secretary. ProCom Wireless now has six locations in the Metroplex, so check directory assistance for the nearest location in Lewisville, Carrollton, North

Richland Hills, Mesquite and in west Fort Worth at Ridgemar Mall. In the meantime, watch out for those other roaming charges! *CK, MC, V, AE, D*

★★ Telephone Warehouse

972/241-8400
Mon-Fri 9-7; Sat 10-6

2905 Forest Lane (LBJ & Josey)
Josey Village Shopping Center
Dallas, TX 75229

Calling all cheapskates. Dial into the many good deals at Telephone Warehouse. They offer AT&T WIRELESS, NEXTEL AND PRIMECO service plans beginning at $19.99 month, not including the phone. If you need a phone, they carry brand names such as ERICSSON, MOTOROLA and NOKIA. Ericcson's start at $49, but with a mail-in rebate for $30, final cost was only $19 on the LX677 model. The Nokia 5160 is $90, but they also carry refurbished Nokia 6160 phones, retail priced $200, now $99. Located at the corner of Forest and Josey, check your area directory for one of the many locations to plug into. *CK, MC, V, AE, D, DN*

Toys

★★★ Bobby Hall's Hobby House 214/821-2550

4822 Bryan St. *Mon-Fri 9-6; Sat 9-4:30*
Dallas, TX 75204

Visiting this Hall brings out the kid in all of us. Unfortunately, it's not really a kids' store because most of the items are geared for adults. For model toys, airplanes, cars and trains, these folks kick the caboose out of the competition. They've been in business for more than 50 years, and they're still going strong with radio-controlled airplanes and cars and remote-launch rockets. You can still get rubber-band airplane kits, rockets and plastic models appropriate for younger children, but the majority of kits have engines, and the smart flier needs to carry insurance. Expect to share the 2,000-square-foot space with lots of other model lovers (mostly guys), especially on a Saturday when all of North Dallas comes to play. A serious hobby-fanatic's heaven, this is really not a place for the idle hobbyist. For a real radio-controlled model airplane, expect to pay $400. It's not often, but they do get used planes in and they are considerably cheaper. They boast all kinds of trains, in brass and plastic, plus airplanes, rockets, plastic kits of all kinds, books, magazines and lots of small parts for emergency landings. An area dealer for HALLMARK model trains, try their website for more information then head here to buy, www.hallmarkmodels.com. So climb on board and enjoy this ride. *CK, MC, V, AE, D*

★★★★ Constructive Playthings/U.S. Toy Company 972/418-1860

1927 E. Belt Line *Mon-Fri 9-6; Thu 9-8; Sat 9-5; Sun 1-5*
Carrollton, TX 75006 *www.ustoyco.com/*

Be the leader of the parade after buying your supplies here. This company is the source for wholesale prices on carnival and party supplies, seasonal decorations, novelty toys, stuffed animals, balloons ... for as low as a penny for each thought. They consist of two basic divisions, one is for educators; the other for consumers. Both are award-winning suppliers of the finest early childhood educational toys, equipment, books, records, tapes, videos, art supplies and teaching aids around. Then, in another division, Toy Magic, watch your boredom disappear–abracadabra. Stage magic supplies, tricks, ideas and magic books along with a complete clown section with costumes, professional make-up and videos. If you're in Leawood, KS, a suburb of Kansas City, don't disappear without stepping foot into their store, the home of the world's largest magic show (room). The U.S. Toy Company's catalog is free for the asking and is a plethora of masks, costumes, streamers and decorations, penny candy, hats and party favors for every imaginable festive occasion with savings up to 70 percent. Lucky for area shoppers, one of their stores is located in Carrollton. *CK, MC, V, C*

★★★★★ Discount Model Trains — 972/931-8135

4641 Ratliff Lane
Addison, TX 75248
Mon-Fri 11-6; Sat 10-5

Clang, clang, clang went the trolley. Chug, chug, chug went the train. Hop aboard the area's largest supplier of model trains and supplies. Over 45,000 different items in stock discounted by 20 percent across the track. Model trains in sizes HO (the most popular size in the industry), N and G hit the tracks with brand names ARISTOCRAFT, ATLAS and CATO. Located just around the corner from the Wilson Building on the right, pull into their parking lot and follow the signs around the corner. Then, track your savings while you chew the breeze with this lovely couple (the Petersons) doing what they do best. Not only do they offer the largest selection of model railroad equipment in the Metroplex, they also have the scenery and glue to put your railroad depot on the map. Expect to hop aboard with a starter set starting around $80 all the way up to $8,000. This includes the engine, some cars, a power supply and oval track. Newly remodeled and enlarged this year, be sure to get on their newsletter list for quarterly updates. *CK, MC, V, D*

★★★ Doll Collection, The — 972/458-7823

15757 Coit Rd., Suite 332
Dallas, TX 75248
Mon-Fri 10-5:30; Sat 10-5

Oh, you beautiful doll! It's almost a fine art to collect dolls, and there are some collectors who are offended that we even include dolls in the "toy" category. Well! At this shop in Dallas, if you are a collector, you can collect right to the top (though their specialty is contemporary artists' dolls). Featuring all the newest and most famous doll artists (like MADAME ALEXANDER) at 20 percent off, this Doll Collection also sells accessories for your collection such as furniture, clothing and doll stands. If variety is the spice of life, this is a pantry for party dolls. Look for their 50 percent off table for the really dolled-up savings. They offered a selection of Barbie's, but her accessories have gone buy-buy. Be sure to browse their selection of clothes to fit dolls from the AMERICAN GIRL collection (but they don't carry the dolls). Located on the northwest corner of Coit and Arapaho, be sure to stop in for a bite to eat at Mexi-Go–a delicious meal deal for real live dolls. *CK, MC, V, AE, D*

★★★★★ Doll Village — 817/329-1333

1110 E. Northwest Hwy. — *Tue-Sat 10-5*
Grapevine, TX 76001

If it takes a village to sell these beautiful dolls, then I'm all for it. Located on the corner of Dallas Road and Hwy. 114 business exit, Doll Village contains a mixture of collectibles and wooden dolls, porcelains and hand-crafted dolls, high-class dolls like GOETZ, LUNA BABIES and ZWERGNASE to name drop a few. The Zwergnase are German dolls by artist Nicole Marshcholland that look like real children ranging in price from $500–$1,500. Only 250 are made per series. Owner Nancy Csolk has been a collector herself for the past 25 years, so you're not buying from a novice. She is considered a doll connoisseur with hundreds waiting to be adopted. Dolls from the '50s, '60s and '70s, collectible dolls, past and present, include ANNETTE HIMSTEDT, DADDY'S LONG LEGS, EFFANBEE, MADAME ALEXANDER, MATTEL, MIDDLETON, RAIKES BEARS, ROLANDA HEIMER, XAVIER ROBERTS plus certified one-of-a-kinds, porcelains, antique, artist dolls, doll clothing, furniture, collector doll and bear books. Oh yes, Barbie's, too. After all, when summer comes, we never forget to have a Barbie Q! *CK, MC, V*

♥♥♥♥♥ Dolls of Yesterday & Today — 972/242-8281

1014 S. Broadway, # 108 — *Wed-Sat 10:30-4:30*
Carrollton, TX 75006

When my momma told me that she would buy me another dolly, I immediately said "Hello!" But whether you're looking for a MADAME ALEXANDER or an antique beauty, a doll from today or yesterday, this store has the doll to fit your bill, just not for a song. Dolls, dolls and more dolls, from cute and cuddly to almost "too-beautiful-to-touch" porcelain, you can find the doll of your dreams without batting an eyelash. Don't expect discounted prices since most of these cuties are collector's items. All of their new dolls relate to the past, and their old dolls are part of the past, comprendez-vous? Look for Barbie,

Madame Alexander and all other beautiful babes in Toyland, including rare German bisque dolls. *MC, V, AE*

★★★ Game Exchange — 972/420-4263

1118 W. Main
Lewisville, TX 75067
Mon-Fri 11-8; Sat 11-6; Sun Noon-5

Day-by-day opportunities change at this game store. Buying, selling or trading is the name of their game. Gameboy from $25, ATARI Jaguar systems, $49.90, computer CDs for a low, low starting price of $3 and none higher than $18, SEGA Geneses from $40, even Virtual Boy with case and game was $55. Thirty-day warranties on all systems. Next to Eckerd, the least you can do to relieve the pain of paying high prices for electronic games–any electronic game but not the kind with LCD screens. How do they do it? Well, the prices will go up and down depending on the popularity and the scarcity of the game. When we checked, they were out of Gameboy, NINTENDO 64 systems, SEGA and SONY, but what we saw, is what we got (several computer games). No big deal. *CK, MC, V*

★★ Hammett's Learning World — 972/270-3155

63 Driftwood Village
Driftwood Village
Mesquite, TX 75150
Mon-Fri 9-8; Sat 9-6; Sun Noon-5

Class isn't over until you learn about this education resource. Formerly called The Teacher's Store, Hammett's Learning World is still teaching us a better way of delivering school tools at bearable prices. Still, "An apple a day won't make the teacher's troubles go away." They're still overworked and underpaid. Gather a few ideas here for children in grades K-6. You don't have to be a teacher, though, to check out the selection of paints, crayons, scissors, stickers, pens, pencils, flash cards, letters, poster board and classroom clutter to keep students' minds aflutter. What isn't in the store can be ordered through their huge catalog. If you want the catalog, it costs $5 and is sold at any of their locations: Carrollton at Frankford and Josey, Arlington in the Lincoln Square Shopping Center and in Plano at Independence Parkway. *CK, MC, V, AE, D*

★★ Iron Horse Hobbies — 972/317-7062

1400 Moccasin Trail, #5
Lewisville, TX 75067
Tue-Fri 11-6; Sat 10-5

Ride 'em, Iron Horse. Get on the track to savings. This is one of the area's full service train shops and one of the best, including the friendly conductor (owner). If you're choo-choo-choosy about whether to buy brass or plastic models, this hobby source is where to begin your journey. They carry all popular scales and gauges of model railway equipment, or can special order most others. Their prices are at least 10 percent off retail and often more. For train enthusiasts, they carry N, HO, O, G and S as well as a nice selection of "how-to" books and magazines to make your hobby manageable. Stock increases greatly around October in anticipation of the holiday rush. *CK, MC, V, AE*

★★★★★ KB Toys Outlet Store 254/582-1052

Southwest Outlet *Mon-Sat 10-8; Sun 11-6*
104 I-35 NE *www.kbtoys.com*
Hillsboro, TX 76645

If play's the thing, then this is the finale–a KB Toys Outlet Store. Yippee! No more, "where the toys are," questions. The answer is perfectly clear. Hop, skip and jump for joy while you save. Need video games? Find a NINTENDO 64, PLAYSTATION or a DREAMSCAPE. They also have videos and DVDs, as well as related merchandise featuring popular DISNEY characters, like Tarzan. Shopping online couldn't be easier. Shop by age, by brand or by category. For an added bonus, KB Toys website has links to great bargains, ranging from under $5, $5-10, $10-20 and over $20. There are many locations in the Metroplex, call 877-522-8697 for the nearest store, or better yet, head to the outlet for EZ KB savings. *CK, MC, V, AE, D, DC*

★★★★★ Mattel Toy Club, The 817/354-2360

15200 Trinity Blvd. *Tue-Sat 10-5*
Fort Worth, TX 76155

This club has written The Toy Story, both the chapter and verse. Well-versed in the toys that your children love to play, day in and day out, The Mattel Toy Club is the source for undivided attention. Save 20-50 percent and more, with the name FISHER-PRICE or MATTEL. Could life get any better? This warehouse is brimming with the biggies. Some damaged, unclaimed, overstocked, or undersold, who cares! What a lifesaver at birthday party time. Load up when the price is right. Have you noticed how educational most toys are these days? (They teach us how little we can get for our money!) Not here. There were lots of Barbies (even collector Barbies–even *Barbie Bazaar* magazines), HOT WHEELS, MATCHBOX and more discounted up to 70 percent. Weekly specials result in an ever-changing inventory, so call before you shop. Be mesmerized by the Disney spell-big names such as Sesame Street, Disney, Winnie The Pooh and, of course, Blues Clues, a perennial favorite. Located just five miles south of DFW Airport off 360, exit Trinity Blvd. Head to the last driveway before the street ends. This is your last chance to beat the other parents and grandparents who line up. Be sure to check prices carefully as some appeared retail. Strike only when the deals are hot! Mail order available. *CK, MC, V, MO*

★★★ Merrill Discount Trampolines

972/424-2285

1909 Hillcrest
Plano, TX 75074
Mon-Sat 9-5

Up and down we go, where we land, nobody knows. But if you want to jump upon a deal on trampolines, this was the only place to do it. Choose round or rectangle, in various price ranges and, if they're out of the model you want, theirs are manufactured locally for faster delivery. For example, a 14-inch round was $280, a 6- x 12-inch rectangle was $470 or a 7- x 14-inch rectangle was $600. Now featuring a 14-inch round springless safety trampoline with ultra flex for only $300. It comes with a weather cover and stronger frame with concealed stitching. Coming out later this season is a model where the pads won't blow off the springs. They also have the mesh cage that runs about $200 and, if you want to jump high, they do carry JUMP KING. Just be sure not to leave the kids unattended as too many jumpers can spoil the fun. Delivery and setup, extra. But one way or another, they are sure they can save you money on your trampoline purchase. *CK, MC, V*

★★★★★ Not Just Dolls

214/321-0412

2447 Gus Thomasson
Dallas, TX 75228
Tue-Sat 10-5

Imagine dolls so precious, they're actually family. That's what the name Not Just Dolls means to the owner of this doll house. Collectors know about this little shop where MADAME ALEXANDER and Barbie are soul mates and share the spotlight. One of the largest selections of antique and new dolls in the Metroplex. Antique porcelains to baby dolls, it was hard to keep focused. However, our attraction was riveted to the star dolls. See the violet eyes of Liz Taylor dressed in fashions from "Father of the Bride" or "National Velvet." For every girl's fantasy or for collectors, this is a treasure-trove. Other collectibles and most-admired stars included EFFANBEE, GINNY, GOTZ, JERRI, LEE MIDDLETON and MUFFY dolls, too. Did I mention their prices? They were good. Real good. But, the doll cases, trunks and stands are retail prices. A single stroller sold for $49.99 and a double was $69.99. There's also a nice selection of collectible teddy bears from V.I.P, ANNETTE FUNICELLO, and MARIE OSMOND. *CK, MC, V*

★★★ Toyco **972/539-0433**

3000 Grapevine Mills Pkwy. *Mon-Sat 10-9:30; Sun 11-8*
Grapevine Mills Mall
Grapevine, TX 76051

After weathering the frantic days of the Beanie Baby frenzy, Toyco has turned out to be a sweet, but not always cheap, deal. They are not a discount or outlet store, but lots of items were marked for clearance. All the popular toys and collectibles, DIGIMON, FISHER-PRICE, HOT WHEELS, LEGO, L'IL TYKES, MATCHBOX, NINTENDO, PLAYSKOOL and POKEMON were available when last checked. Pokeman collectible cards, in the Fossil and Jungle packs, were buy two, get one free and the flex packs were $6.99. Lego was on sale for 20 percent off and die-cast collectible model cars were 25 percent off. Sweet deals, but remember, they change frequently, so when they're "board silly," this could keep Beth and Billy entertained for days. *CK, MC, V, D*

★★★★★ Toys From the Attic **972/671-0770**

2159 Buckingham Rd. *Mon-Fri 10-6; Sat 10-8; Sun Noon-5*
Richardson, TX 75081

This is the ultimate Playhouse of the August Moon. Come birthday time, (or any other occasion that reeks of a toy,) and head to this attic. The selection is better than lofty. Brimming with quality used toys, find move than 2,000 square feet of collectibles, hard-to-find, current and popular toys to delight young and old. They also carry cribs, baby swings, car seats, toddler beds, high chairs, strollers and other baby needs. Don't forget to look for outdoor toys like sandboxes, cozy coupe cars, and maybe even a FISHER-PRICE "Grow With Me" picnic table. Selection changes daily, but it's like a walk in the park. Located at the northwest corner of Buckingham and Jupiter, next to Albertson's. *CK, MC, V, AE, D*

★★★★★ Toys R Us **972/385-8541**

5505 Arapaho *Mon-Sat 9:30-9:30; Sun 11-7*
Dallas, TX 75248 *www.toysrus.com*

"R" you ready, Freddy? Or are you too pooped to pop the weasel after a morning of shopping this toy and kids' superstore? Aisles and aisles (cunningly arranged for maximum profits) of games, electronics, strollers, rocking horses, dolls, stuffed animals, and more. From the smallest matchbox car to the largest swing set, it can be found here. Just try to cruise down the NINTENDO/SEGA aisle on any give Saturday–you'll see what prosperity means. Dodge first-time parents ogling the FISHER-PRICE section and wind your way through sky blue swarms of BLUE'S CLUES to the cash register. Prices are good on an everyday basis and drop to fantastic during sales, but be prepared to jostle for position at every turn. Check directory for the nearest location. *CK, MC, V, AE, D*

★★★ Twice Loved Toys 214/823-5799

5810 Live Oak *Mon-Sat 10:30-6*
Dallas, TX 75214

Love is lovelier, the second time around. So are some toys. Such favorites are so great they deserve to be loved over and over again. That's the concept behind Twice Loved Toys. Now located in Then & Now in the heart of the Lakewood area, if your children have outgrown Tinker Toys or GI Joe, perhaps you need to trade them in and pick out some others. (After all, it'll be new to them.) Discounted a tad from retail, we saw a few sample dolls and a few sample toys, it's the resale toys that'll net you the biggest return. From infants through toddlers, to whatever age they stop playing with toys (some never do), you will see lots of LEGO and BRIO (especially the wooden trains and tracks); Barbies (but no Ken to keep her company), books, puzzles, games and some decorative items for their rooms. *CK*

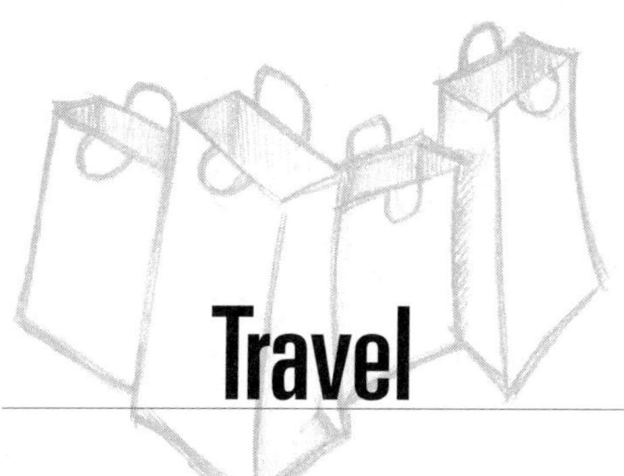

Travel

♥♥♥♥♥ Abercromby Suites/Painted Valley Ranch — 940/627-7005

PO Box 21 — *members.aol.com/txbby/home.htm*
Decatur, TX 76234

Romantic weekends are just a few miles away when you stay at one of these two bed and breakfast getaways. Sounds good, doesn't it? At the Abercromby Suites, you'll stay just off Main in Decatur close to a variety of activities. Three suites of accommodations of the pampering kind. Go shopping, come for a massage or maybe tie the knot–again! They offer complete wedding packages that are performed on the premises. How about an exciting murder mystery? Not many of us have experienced that sort of entertainment on a weekend getaway. Or head to the Painted Valley Ranch. Peace and quiet, for a change of pace. Exchange the ordinary and experience the extraordinary at these comfy retreats. Pamper yourself, and be sure to mention this ad for an additional 25 percent off. *MC, V*

★★ Air King — 214/638-4357

9090 N. Stemmons — *Mon-Fri 9:30-5:30; Sat 9-1*
Dallas, TX 75247

You can be a pauper and still grab this King's attention. Flying isn't just for the rich and famous. But you can travel to places that will give you the illusion. Air King will take you to faraway palaces on a wing and a prayer, or almost. Hawaii, from Monday to Monday was $698 and Boston was a bargain at $289. San Francisco was on the money for $225, but Cleveland was no deal at $289–have you ever been to Cleveland? Try these folks if you have to be somewhere fast–they have plenty of "no advance fare" bargains. Accents, on occasion, were hard to understand, but keep trying. As always, prices are subject to change. All prices change periodically throughout the year depending on the season and where you are going. If you get stranded, e-mail them and they'll fly it right to you. (Some folks like to travel the world; I myself prefer to remain in-continent!) *CK, (Credit Cards Vary Per Airline, plus 5 percent)*

♥♥♥♥♥ America's Hometenders 972/991-2927

15150 Preston Rd., Suite 300
Dallas, TX 75248

Realtors suggest a house that's "lived-in" sells faster. If you qualify (got nice furniture, good credit report, no animals, no smokers and don't mind showing the house to a prospective buyer,) do they have a deal for you. Bill Stoll and his company are looking for you. If you would love to house-sit in a mansion for a fraction of the cost, this is where to reside. Preferred areas of empty houses include Addison, Carrollton, North Dallas, Plano and Richardson. One lucky couple is living in a $1.5 million home for $800 a month. Then again; remember you're responsible for the utility costs and the monthly pool service. If you pass their stringent requirements and don't mind moving often, give them a call.

★★★ Best Fares Discount Travel Magazine 817/261-6114

PO Box 170129 *www.bestfares.com*
Arlington, TX 76003

Up, up and away ... the magazine for the travelin' man. *Best Fares* keeps track of travel promotions that the public doesn't hear about. Promotions, they say, that "sound too good to be true ... but ARE TRUE." All offers are investigated and must be legitimate to be included in the magazine. Discounts also include up to 50 percent off at over 10,000 hotels, up to 30 percent off the lowest fares to Europe, the South Pacific and more. How would you like to save $100 on air fare by buying a romance novel? Or travel to Australia for $1,000, getting a few hundred dollars knocked off the price of your next flight, to boot? Samples of the magazine aren't available, but they do offer a pro-rated refund if you decide your subscription wasn't worth it. Subscriptions are $59.90 per year for 12 issues. Prices on trips could vary depending on when you go and for how long. *MC, V, AE, D*

✧✧✧✧✧ Carlson Wagonlit Travel/Freeport Travel Service, Inc. 972/929-8510

8445 Freeport Pkwy., Suite 220 *Mon-Fri 8:30-5*
Irving, TX 75063

Traveling professionals and families on vacation have learned to understand the term, "Don't leave home without us." Before you go, get in the know. This travel service will book your flight, arrange your car rental, hotel, get tickets to Disney World or put you on board a cruise. You name it, they'll get it for you for the best prices around. Like some, they don't take their job lightly by opting for the first available source; they'll work it until they first get your travel needs met and be sure it's priced for less. Located off Highway 114 and the Freeport Parkway exit, they're in the Bank of America Building. Consider their primary concerns to be two-fold: superb customer service and their willingness to shop for the best travel deals. Anchors Away, my friend. *CK, MC, V, AE, D*

★★ Cruise Masters

972/458-1000

13101 Preston Rd., Suite 300
Dallas, TX 75240

Mon-Fri 10-6; Sat 11-3; Sun Noon-5

Sale away with the award-winning cruise specialists at Cruise Masters. Consistently, they offer special discounted prices on thousands of sailings worldwide. All major cruise lines in the world are represented and accommodations range from cramped (but still with cruise amenities) to palatial. Every cruise is discounted every day. Open seven days a week, these folks know their cruises–most are CLIA accredited or are master-cruise counselors. We set sail for a three-day Bahamas cruise for as low as $294, then returned later in the year for a seven-day Caribbean cruise (on the Royal Caribbean) for $699 while we were price-shopping. Cruises can be a broadening experience, especially if you eat at every one of their 11 daily food calls. Located at the corner of Preston and LBJ in the Chase Bank building. As every traveler knows you have to jump on prices because they change in the blink of an eye. *CK, MC, V, AE, D, CB, DC*

★★ CruiseOne

972/727-2460

www.cruiseone.com

Ahoy there mateys! Set your sights on savings up to 50 percent off brochure rack rates by calling one of these independently owned cruise specialists under the banner of CruiseOne. Hop aboard and walk the plank for less. Around the World in 80 Days or a short three days in the Caribbean, their buying power on land and sea commands attention when the ship comes in. This website is very user friendly for beginners as well as well-traveled veterans. They give you reviews on several different cruises. There are over 192 offices nationwide so you can sail away at a discount. (Often fathoms from the competition.) *CK, MC, V, AE*

★ D-FW Tours

972/980-4540

7616 LBJ Frwy., Suite 524
Dallas, TX 75251

24 Hours
www.dfwtours.com

Don't let the hometown name fool you. D-FW Tours is a unique travel service that offers you both wholesale air and tour packages to hundreds of destinations around the globe. One of their big attractions is their user-friendly website. Just point and click and you'll be on your way. But be careful, when we checked the website, we didn't find all the security locks to help protect you from online thieves. In this instance, getting a quote, making a reservation, and paying online might be riskier than actually getting to your destination. *CK, MC, V, AE, D*

★ Discount Travel — 817/261-6114

5024 Trail Lake Drive — *Mon-Fri 9-6*
Fort Worth, TX 76133

If you can make it through the web of phone lines, good for you. We gave up. It might take the patience of Job to wait for what seemed like "From Here to Eternity." Make it through, and you can luck out with a plane taking off to Boston for $313, Phoenix, $183, New York, $293, Los Angeles, $283 and Washington, D.C., $213. Because they utilize all the possible special discounts, they suggest you call the airlines directly to get their best fare first and schedule of departures. Then call Discount Travel to make sure they can beat it. They have no time to do your shopping for the best fares for you. So, you'll have to straighten up–to fly right! *CK*

♥♥♥♥♥ English Manor, The — 903/586-9821

540 El Paso St. — *By Reservation Only*
Jacksonville, TX 75766 — *www.engmanor.com*

The charm of this 1932 English Manor makes it a must-stay retreat in East Texas. Located in the heart of the Piney Woods, somewhere south of Tyler, the test of time has proven they're still one of the best in Texas. From the small-town antique shops to the best buys on bedding plants (90 percent of the bedding plants are grown in and around neighboring New Summerfield), there are lots of reasons to retreat to this three-diamond AAA-rated treat. The Holleys are your guide to where to shop during your stay at their elegant countryside manor. Linda Holley might even tell you about The Basket Factory and where to buy plants at $3 a flat. Opulent rooms and outstanding breakfasts ... what more could you ask? Looking for some outdoor fun nearby? State parks, hiking and mountain bike trails are practically in their backyard. And since they are the only B&B accommodation in the U.S. with a AAA rating from the Mobil Guide, I'd say you're in good hands. *CK, MC, V, D*

★★★★★ Hartmann Travel

972/392-9797

7616 LBJ Frwy., Suite 421 — *Mon-Fri 8:30-6*
Dallas, TX 75251 — *www.hartmanntravel.com*

The operative word here is saver, whether it's a super saver, a cable saver, or a diva saver. Fly round-trip to Memphis, for example, to see the ducks at the Peabody Hotel for $99. Or, would you rather grab a double-decker corned-beef sandwich at the Carnegie Deli after a concert in NYC? Fly there round-trip for $179. Don't expect these prices to be constant. Just that at Hartmann, they really go for the jugular on your budget's behalf. Ski trips to Steamboat Springs, including air and hotel, were $299.75. Kids under 12 were able to fly free with an adult on Vanguard Airlines. Why gamble with your money? Vegas was a steal for $285 and that included air and hotel. But it was the Greek Island cruise that really whet our chops – OOPS – shops. An 11-day tour and cruise for $1,999 was worth every drachma. From Lewisville to London, their bendover backwards service (besides their lowest prices) are garnering rave reviews from critics who used to walk everywhere. Remember, travel is a pleasure ... but space travel could be ... out of this world! Stay tuned. Mars may be next on your itinerary. *CK, MC, V, AE, PQ*

♥♥♥♥♥ Heritage Inn

940/565-6414

815 Locust — *By Reservation Only*
Denton, TX 76201 — *www.firsttravelchoice.com*

Head to Denton Factory Stores and shop. Then kick back and relax at the Heritage Inn. One exit down from the outlet mall, check into this complex arrangement of a great place to stay. What used to be the Red Bud Inn and the Heritage have combined. How sweet it is! Each has it's own unique features. Enjoy a private room with its own bathroom (Americans are spoiled, you know) decorated with turn of the century furniture at yesteryear's prices. Rooms and suites were $56-$76 during the week and $75-$90 Friday and Saturday. If rooms are available, drop-ins are welcome. After the sun sets, take a five minute walk into town, walk the square, then grab a bite at the Locust Street Grill, a popular local diner with the best handmade potato chips in the world. (A real chip off the old block!) Other popular websites to check out for quaint inns include bedandbreakfast.com, placestostay.com and bandbonline.com. If you're looking for something quaint, log on. *CK, MC, V, AE, D*

★★★★★ Hotel Reservations Network 214/361-7311

8140 Walnut Hill Lane, Suite 203 *Mon-Fri 8-6*
Dallas, TX 75231 *www.hoteldiscount.com*

Their IPO made them very, very rich. Their discounted prices will make you very, very happy. Tired of paying New York prices for a hotel room in The Big Apple? Paris? London? Orlando? Vancouver? Lots of major U.S. cities are represented on HRN's menus of room accommodations–your connection to saving big bucks on big rooms in big cities in a lot of big countries. Chicago, Chicago, a toddling town. We waddled into the magnificent Drake Hotel in Chicago for only $99 a night. Same held true for the Sir Francis Drake on Union Square in San Francisco. (I don't mind leaving my heart there, but at least I can return with my wallet intact!) You can even book rooms for most major city events even when every hotel in the city is sold out! But when there's a sell-out, all you care about is getting a room, period! Then expect to pay regular rates. (Beats sleeping on a park bench.) Call their special sold-out number at 800/715-ROOM (7666). As always the prices can change frequently. *CK, MC, V, AE, D*

♥♥♥♥♥ Mansion on Main 903/792-1835

802 Main *www.bbonline.com/TX/mansion*
Texarkana, TX 75501

Rhett would have returned to Tara if it offered as much as this Mansion. Stress is "Gone With The Wind" and good times await in a six-room bed and breakfast offering a sensational stay away from home. Cost is $60-$109 a night unless you can hit one of their discounts which could be as much as a third less. Don't drive. Instead, hop aboard an Amtrak train for $54-$98 round-trip and roll into the train station owned by a local doctor. The earlier you call Amtrak (800/872-7245) the better as they only have so many $54 tickets available; then the price goes to $66, and up to $98. The Mansion on Main, built in 1895, takes you back to a time where strolling the 2,500-square-foot verandah was a wonderful night's activity. Just seeing 14 columns extending up 22 feet makes you want to go home, again. The chef once owned a cajun cooking school, so expect her to be able to cook up a storm (literally and figuratively). This upscale inn may be sitting in an urban setting, but it's Texas to the very core. Plenty to see including paying a visit to the Perot Theatre. The Ross family has restored the theater to a point that puts the Majestic to shame. Visit Ross Perot's boyhood home and, if history interests you further, head to Hope, AR (about 30 miles) and visit Bill Clinton's boyhood home. Visit Old Washington, known as "the last town in the U.S." by Davy Crockett and where Jim Bowie and Sam Houston sat head-to-head planning the independence of Texas. And get this–it is the town that saw the invention of the Bowie knife. The Little Tavern still serves up great old-fashioned soul food and Old Washington is still the only place in the country where "blacksmithing" is offered at the college level. *CK, MC, V, AE*

♥♥♥♥♥ McKay House — 903/665-7322

306 East Delta — *Mon-Fri 9-5*
Jefferson, TX 75657

Who says you have to go to the other ends of the earth to get a little peace and quiet? A safe, tranquil bet would be the McKay House in Jefferson (known as the Bed & Breakfast capital of Texas) and the "Williamsburg of the Southwest." Cost of $99-$135 per night with, on occasion, the third night free, offers additional ways to save the day. They also offer nice discounts on an availability basis. If you really want to get away from it all, travel by Amtrak (www.amtrak.com) and rent a car when you get there. Again, call for tickets well in advance. Once in Jefferson, the McKay House is a high-class, New Orleans-style Greek revival house built in 1851. It contains seven units, six of which have fireplaces. The largest unit is a two-room suite with the two rooms separated by a bathroom–making comfy but roomy accommodations for four. You will enjoy your breakfast in a glass-walled conservatory overlooking the gardens. They provide an old-fashioned Victorian gown or sleep shirt when you retire and your choice from their hat selection to don for breakfast. Hats off, when you dine on a 16-foot table from an old mercantile store nestled by the fireplace. Your bathroom may even have twin "his and hers" antique bathtubs. The house has a large front porch and balcony off the wide foyer needed for circulation in those good ole days. Sleep where Fabio, Ladybird Johnson or the late Alex Haley slept. Eat breakfast where George Bush's staff did. This house has been recognized as one of the top 10 most-romantic inns in the USA by *Vacation Magazine* and for good reason. While there, take an old-fashioned buggy or trolley ride, a boat ride down the Cypress River which meanders through town, or a miniature steamboat (it will hold up to 30 people) ride on Caddo Lake, Texas' only natural lake–complete with narration. And did I forget to mention that Jefferson is also a great spot for antique shopping? *CK, MC, V, AE*

♥♥♥♥♥ Miss Molly's 817/626-1522

109 ½ W. Exchange *By Reservation Only*
Fort Worth, TX 76106 *www.missmollys.com*

Good Golly Miss Molly! Since it's within walking distance of The Stockyards and Fort Worth Outlet Square, make your reservations here on your "to do" list. Kick up your heels, then take them off and stay awhile. Once a prim and proper boarding house, and later a bordello, this historic hotel is one of the grandest in the land, featuring eight luxurious rooms furnished in a variety of ornate styles. What's your pleasure, ma'am? One room is home to carved oak furniture and a very unique private bath named in honor of the madam of the house back in the '40s. Another is a turn-of-the-century room, meticulously restored with a white iron double bed, lace curtains and detailed hand-worked linens. For those travelers who like the flavor of the Old West, bed down in the room with pictures of both famous and infamous gunslingers. Then two-step around to Billy Bob's, enjoy a mouth-watering steak at the historic Cattleman's Restaurant, and top it all off with a nightcap at the White Elephant Saloon. There's no place better for you or your Yankee visitors to get a taste of how the West was really won. Rates run from $75-$170. Located over the Star Restaurant. *CK, MC, V, AE, D*

Optimum Travel Services 800/575-1030

First class and business class travelers, only, can save up to 50 percent on air travel to Europe, Australia and Asia by using this service. All major airlines offered with no restrictions. Also check on deals to save up to 40 percent on four-star and five-star hotels.

★★★★★ Snowballers Tours 817/335-SNOW

1500 W. Fifth St., Suite 5A
Fort Worth, TX 76102

Here's a Dallas tradition that charges down slippery slopes. And you can too. How? Easy. Join the club ... the Snowballers Ski Club to be exact. They take ski trips to new heights. No membership fees required, but you must put down a deposit when you sign up for one of the five trips this group arranges per year. Ski outings and other options available, too. Trips are planned for November, December, January, February and April. Prices run $239-$349 per person. Travel varies from sleeper bus to a 727 charter jet. Destinations include Crested Butte, Squaw Valley, Mount Rose and Taos. And since all trips sold out last year, you better hop on the bunny trail quick. Can't beat it. Established in 1972, this club has withstood the test of time for continuing good fun. (If only I could graduate from the tow bar.)

♥♥♥♥♥ St. Botolph Inn Bed & Breakfast — 817/594-1455

808 S. Lamar St. — *By Reservation Only*
Weatherford, TX 76086 — *www.bnbfinder.com*

If you're looking for history, this family has it. Return to *The Age of Innocence*, where the simple pleasures were enjoyed amidst Victorian splendor. At this 100-year-old historic mansion resting majestically atop five hilltop manicured acres, don't stop 'til you see the tower through the treetops. Fifteen rooms are nestled comfortably in this peaceful residential neighborhood, eight blocks from the famed Weatherford courthouse. The downstairs bedroom with 12-foot ceilings and 8-foot windows, comes complete with a queen-size antique bed and full bath. But upstairs is where most of the action is. There's a gorgeous domed ballroom (perfect for 75-125 guests for the dance party or wedding) and three other grand bedrooms. The perfect wedding suite comes with a four-claw-foot bathtub and wicker canopy queen-size bed. They've added two more cottages with Jacuzzis and remodeled all their other rooms. The grounds offer a picturesque setting for a wedding ceremony, and then the bridal party can go right to bed. Talk about location, location, location! Sip Victorian tea in the late, lazy afternoon on the verandah, take a quick dip in the pool, and in the morning, pick out your breakfast pleasures from their 15-item menu. If you come on a First Monday weekend, check out the First Monday Market in Weatherford that runs Friday through Sunday. Less than three miles from I-20 and an easy 30-minute commute from Fort Worth, or an hour from Dallas, Weatherford is the birthplace of Mary Martin and the setting of Larry McMurtry's novel "Lonesome Dove". Rooms rent from $80-$165. Owned by the Botolph family, who came to this country in 1653, they've filled their home with antiques just for your viewing and using pleasure. *CK, MC, V*

♥♥♥♥♥ Thee Hubbell House — 903/342-5629

307 West Elm — *By Reservation Only*
Winnsboro, TX 75494 — *www.bluebonnet.net/hubhouse*

Take thee to Thee Hubbell House in Winnsboro, just 90 miles east of Dallas in the Heart of Lake Country. For holiday getaways, put this information under the tree and save for future reference, as Winnsboro is also the Christmas Tree Capital of Texas. For a grand Bed & Breakfast bonanza, hit it big at Thee Hubbell House, home to a mansion, a carriage house, and a cottage all on the same two acres of lush landscaped lawns. Plan your wedding, business retreat, or family reunion in a setting to be remembered. Individual rooms start at $90 and go up depending on different options selected. Each room is accompanied by a private bathroom and common areas of casual formality complete with fireplace and piano in the main room, a dining room for breakfast (Yummy!), spacious verandahs, an upstairs gallery, a garden room and a patio. For romantics, don't overlook the candlelight dinners (by reservation only) or a soak in the hot tub to end the perfect day. For those who can't sleep unless they shop right 'till they drop, they even have their own antique shop on the premises. A signed Elvis teddy bear that sang or the actual bronzed hands of Abe Lincoln are just some of the many splendid things for sale. All-in-all, there are 12 bedrooms all with private baths priced from $85-$175 and worth every penny. Be sure to check out special discounts. *CK, MC, V, AE, D*

♥♥♥♥♥ Victorian House (The Angel House) 817/599-9600

PO Box 1571 — *By Reservation Only*
1105 Palo Pinto St.
Weatherford, TX 76086

Weatherford is fast becoming Heaven when it comes to bed and breakfasts. The Angel House (aka, Victorian House) is a 1896 restored, three-story 10,000-square-foot Victorian mansion with 10 huge bedrooms (all around 18 x 22 feet) each with private baths and resplendent with custom bedspreads, draperies, 25-inch cable-TV, armories and antiques. (No, this is not what we call "roughin' it!") One half-canopied bed alone cost $25,000. Rock the night away on the wrap-around porch and savor the 3½ landscaped acres that are green year-round. A three-course breakfast is served in grand style, but the site is also perfect for a wedding-the bridal walk down the staircase alone is guaranteed to produce an avalanche of tears. They can accommodate 300 guests for outside weddings or 100 guests inside. Caterers in the area are recommended, or you hire your own. This is also a perfect site for private dinner parties, receptions, or any special occasion besides the weekend getaway for rest and revival. Rooms cost $99-$199. With the website under construction, you'll have to call the 800-687-1660 for information. *CK, MC, V, D*

♥♥♥♥♥ Woldert-Spence Manor 903/533-9057

611 W. Woldert St. — *By Reservation Only*
Tyler, TX 75702 — *www.tyler.net/woldert_spence*

If peace and quiet aren't enough and you yearn for the calm beauty of yesteryear, then breakfast is served at the Woldert-Spence Manor in Tyler. For under $120 (room prices run $75-$115 and all include a private bath), you get a full breakfast in the formal dining room after you spend the night in one of their six luxurious rooms. Soak in the tub. Then after you come clean, you can shop the nearby antique stores and enjoy a small respite from the stresses of city life. The first floor of the building was built in 1859 and the second floor was added in 1910. Even the original floors are still intact and the attention to period details is extraordinary. Patricia isn't only your hostess, she adds the "mostest" with her recommendations on what to do and where to go while spending time in Tyler. And on the way up (or back), don't forget a bargain-shopping layover at Tanger Factory Stores in Terrell. Check out their website at www.tyler.net/woldert_spence for lovely color photos of the building and grounds. *CK, MC, V, AE, D, DC, CB*

Windows & Walls

★★ 3-Day Blinds — 817/784-9200

3810 S. Cooper St., #144 — *Mon-Fri 10-6; Sat 10-5*
Arbrook Oaks Shopping Center
Arlington, TX 76015

In a hurry? Then call 800/800-3-DAY for the area's closest 3-Day Blinds window covering store. Either way, they can get you covered. Their Essentials Mini Blind (based on 23- x 21- inch, 1-inch aluminum blind) was a glaring $5 each, but it was not available through their Shop-at-Home Service (800/590-SHOP). As their name implies, you'll be blind-sided with names like HUNTER-DOUGLAS, LEVOLOR and KIRSCH. Expect delivery, as their name implies, in three days. (At least they're supposed to be made and shipped in three days.) Other window treatments to consider are vinyl verticals, wood blinds and horizontal blinds. Locations besides Arlington include Denton, Fort Worth, Irving, Mesquite and Plano. Save anywhere from 12-53 percent, which is about par for your windows. *CK, MC, V, AE, D*

★★★★★ American Plantation Shutters — 972/960-6691

4140 Billy Mitchell Dr. — *Mon-Fri 8-5; Sat 10-2*
Addison, TX 75244

Can we talk, shutters? I'm talking handmade in their own factory, custom-crafted one at a time, shutters. What was once considered useful as a security precaution, are now the window treatment of choice for anyone living outside the "Planet of the Drapes!" Yes, they do screen out harmful direct sunlight. Yes, plantation shutters are the best insulators of those windows, helping to decrease both heating and cooling costs. (Especially if your home has lots of windows.) And if it's top-of-the-line window dressing you want, then knock on wood, these are the best. For those who not only want the best quality but the most unique, consider those with leaded-glass sunbursts and waterfalls. Ask any Realtor what addition to a house generates the most curb appeal, and the answer is often plantation shutters. Also at American, they now carry wooden, handmade children's toys and accessories: toy boxes, puzzles desks and much more in bright colors and affordable prices. *CK, MC, V, AE, D, PQ*

★★★★★ Blind Alley 972/404-1944

7211 Authon Dr. *Mon-Sun 8-9*
Dallas, TX 75248 *www.blindalley.net*

Forget shopping in a back alley. Instead, see clearly the savings of up to 80 percent off. Make an in-house appointment, or travel to their North Dallas showroom for a personal tour; these two guys work magic with your window panes. Choose shutters, 2-inch wood blinds, pleated and double-cell shades, miniblinds, verticals, arches ... What's your window's pleasure? Fabrics by IRVIN ALAN, KASMIR, ROBERT ALLEN, this is one-stop shopping for your drapery, carpet and upholstery needs, too. Their designers will assist with all of your interior requirements from start to finish and you won't fight when you see the whites of their eyes. They will match any name brand product's price plus an additional 5 percent off if you find it for less elsewhere. Open wide and say, "Ah-h-h!" Watch for new website at blindsavers.com. *CK, MC, V, AE, D, DC*

★★★ Blind Ambition 972/539-4457

Mon-Fri 8-5; Sat 10-2

Custom window fashions at up to 77 percent off is the driving force behind Blind Ambition. Does anybody pay retail for window fashions today? Does the name HUNTER-DOUGLAS impress you? Then consider their discount program called HUNTER-DOUGLAS "Value Express" Window Fashions. Save up to 77 percent on custom window treatments, such as honey-comb or pleated shades, fabric, or PVC verticals, 1- and 2-inch wood blinds, or aluminum mini-blinds. Custom-made and ready within a week is nothing to sneeze at plus 90 days same as cash. Colors galore and in-home estimates are another plus so as to not pull the shades over your eyes. An added incentive for purchasing here besides the discounts is the fact that you'll earn AAdvantage miles. How's that for a buy-and-fly program? Free no obligation in-home estimate. *CK, MC, V, AE, D, Financing*

★★★★★ Blind Place, The 972/881-0201

601 W. Parker, Suite 105 *Mon-Fri 10-6; Sat 10-4*
Plano, TX 75074

When you're ready to place your money where your window is, here's the place to do it. See clearly the savings of up to 80 percent off. Create the perfect solution to your bland and boring windows. If your current window treatments are thread-worn and not "shabby chic," then the Blind Place is your seeing-eye guide. From crystal-pleated shades, wood blinds (1-inch and 2-inch slats in a wide variety of stains and paint colors) and a rainbow of choices in verticals, you can correct your visionary decorating scheme by placing your faith here. All the brands that are fit to hang out with and all the windows of opportunities to choose-blinds, shutters, draperies, swags, cascades because they all can't be topped. There's also a 90-day, no-interest financing plan. *CK, MC, V, D, PQ*

★★★★★ Blinds Plus — 972/216-9222

1765 Town East Blvd., Suite 143 — *Mon-Fri 10-6; Sat 10-4*
Mesquite, TX 75150

The pluses are endless at Blinds Plus. Direct from the manufacturer, choose vertical blinds, two-inch wood and PVC blinds, pleated shades, vinyl and aluminum blinds-all at a savings of up to 82 percent. Brands included GRABER, HERITAGE, HUNTER-DOUGLAS, LEVELOR, MARK, METROPOLITAN and PACIFIC. They specialize in those exterior solar screens (that block 70 percent of the heat) to keep the Texas sun at bay. We found double cellular shades (24- x 72-inch) for $57 and 2-inch wood blinds (24- x 72-inch) for $63 (about $20 less than last year's price). Other options included in-house professional installation, delivery within three-five working days, and a "90 days same-as-cash" policy with approved credit. Now you can see why they're one of the highest volume dealers in town. It doesn't get much better. *CK, MC, V*

★★★ Casa Linda Draperies — 214/388-4721

4111 Elva Ave. — *Mon-Fri 8-5*
Dallas, TX 75227

Check out this full-service window treatment company if what ails you is to air your dirty windows in public. Not only will they custom-make your draperies, they'll clean them, too! Offering free in-home estimates, and free (I love that word!) labor on pinch-pleated lined drapes made with their fabrics, this company also promises quality workmanship. Operating full-steam ahead since 1971, take advantage of the beauty, quality and value offered. Around the corner from the Jim Miller and Military Parkway intersection, why not make it a clean sweep for your swags? *CK, MC, V*

★★★★★ Charles Curtain Co. 214/630-7967

1352 Crampton *Mon-Fri 8-3:30; Sat 9:30-Noon*
Dallas, TX 75207

Visit the prince (Charles!) of draperies at his "faux"-actory outlet-a source for saying "curtains" to paying full price since the '50s. Not necessarily housed in a castle, this outlet is just 1,000 square feet, but the resident (who sells to JC Penney and other large department stores) sells overstocks and samples of bedspreads and matching draperies direct to the public at a savings of 50 percent and more. Pick a pair or two and plan on sleeping cheap. Drapery and bedspread fabric available, too. Shop early, as the prince turns into a pumpkin at 3:30! Curtains could run from $6-$300 for a triple panel. Tailored panels, blouson valances, jabot and filler valances, pole top drapes, pinch-pleated drapes, scarf valances, bedspreads, shams, dust ruffles are in abundance in prints and solids both. Expect to pay $2-$10/yard. Exit Irving Boulevard between Wycliff and Motor Streets. *CK*

♥♥♥♥♥ Cornelius Draperies 817/731-8469

3526 W. Vickery *Mon-Fri 10-5*
(Vickery @ Montgomery)
Fort Worth, TX 76107

Do you value a new valance? Desire new drapes? Call on Cornelius for custom-made draperies that are sewn in their own workroom. The specialty of the house is stitch-for-stitch quality sewing so don't expect a lightning-turnaround time. Labor charges vary, from inexpensive to high-dollar and prices depend on the fabric. Very few fabrics in stock, though, but virtually anything can be ordered. Choose from their many sample books. Matching bedspreads also done in the same outstanding meticulous way, one stitch at a time. This is a working workroom with sewers stitching away. It was easy, however, to see the quality in their workmanship. *CK*

★★★★ Custom Coordinates 817/498-7353

4709 Colleyville Blvd., #500 *Mon-Fri 10-6, Sat 10-5*
Colleyville, TX 76034

Coordinating color and custom work is the name of the game here. Choose your coordinates: wallpaper, fabrics, draperies, bedspreads, furniture, blinds or shades. Wave good-buys on WAVERLY, the main name here, with 50 percent off all in-stock patterns (and there were over 100 to choose from), 20 percent off custom orders. Blinds were discounted up to 70 percent off. Free in-home estimates and in-house decorators offer a way to get two birds with one check. If you would like to do your own in-home matching and mixing, you can even borrow their sample books for a $25 deposit (but they don't expect to send overdue notices). Books are due back the next day. *CK, MC, V, AE, D*

★★★★★ Dallas Drapery Outlet — 214/654-0177

2970 Blystone — *Mon-Fri 9-5; Sat 9-2*
Dallas, TX 75220

Around the corner from their factory is this showroom where you can reward your windows and walls by saving up to 70 percent on custom-made window treatments. During one special sale, fabric was discounted up to 90 percent. Almost from the inception of the first *Underground Shopper*, this decorating dynasty has been custom-making draperies, top treatments, swags, cornices, valances, bedspreads, pillows and more. Having their own in-house workroom keeps costs to a bare minimum. But don't stop there-they also sell GRABER mini-blinds, verticals, duettes, Roman and balloon shades and shutters as well as perform custom surgery if you need it (reupholstery). A combination workroom/showroom, they boast custom drapes as their in-house specialty as they can usually roast the competition (especially when they're providing free labor on draperies). Lots of in-house fabric to choose from. Got a ready-made spread that you need cut down? They can do that, too. Visit their second showroom in Plano, 972/881-0233. *CK, MC, V, AE, D*

★★★★★ Decorette, The — 972/964-3580

1909 W. Parker Rd., #145 — *Tue-Fri 10-6; Sat 10-4*
Plano, TX 75023

Since 1979, The Decorette has been singing the Merry Window in enough homes to be heard around the world. Offering some of the lowest prices in town (up to 85 percent off mini-blinds), they give you a lot for your money, honey. Custom window and wall treatments are their specialty. From custom draperies to shutters, there isn't a window that will go naked in the big city if they have something to say about it. Cover them with verticals, balloon shades, or louver drapes-talk about window shopping! Add custom bedding (as low as $195) and a fabric headboard that matches the fabric duvet cover that matches the shams that match the vanity bench. It's all in a day's work. Custom draperies, valances, valances, save on them all. What about the 2¼-inch or 3¼-inch louvers, poly-resin vinyl with a permanent finish that resists dents and scratches, patented locking tilt bar, two-part hinges for easy removal of panels that will help reduce your energy costs. (Plus they're easy to clean and maintain.) In-stock fabrics by KASMIR, ROBERT ALLEN, KASMIR and SCHUMACHER/WAVERLY were $6.95/yard retailing to $28/yard. Even special order fabrics were 20 percent off. *CK, MC, V, MO*

★★★★★ Design Resource & Remodeling 214/742-1996

1308 Dragon St. *Mon-Fri 9-5; Sat Appt. Only*
Dallas, TX 75207

This is the dragon that slew the full-price design studios. Everything you need done for a face-lift to your house can be done here in-house (thereby eliminating the middleman). Casey will take you by the hand and help you work your way through any project, including interior design, layout, construction, draperies and interior finish out. They can help you with everything except the roofer, plumber and electrician, who are sub-contracted. Wholesale to the public in the Dallas Design District is no big deal, you say? Well, try going into a retail showroom at the Design Center and see what the going rate is. This particular resource is a cut above the rest, offering discounts on dry wall and painting, draperies, both fabric and labor of 30 percent plus 65 percent off wood blinds and 20 percent off interior design, carpentry and remodeling. Since they specialize in interior and architectural design, can heaven wait for anything more? Come see their 6,000-square-foot workshop, where they build furniture and make the draperies. Browse through the sample books. Regardless of your taste requirements, this is one-stop shopping from contemporary to neo-classic with talented artisans waiting at every turn. *CK, MC, V, AE, D*

★★★★★ Designer Draperies Floors & Furniture 817/451-6890

5324 Brentwood Stair Rd. *Mon-Fri 9-5:30; Sat By Appt. Only*
Fort. Worth, TX 76112

Designer Draperies is the perfect closure to neighborhood gossip. Keep out "shady characters" and keep them talking. Besides custom draperies and window coverings, this Fort Worth resource was a winner of the best carpet and floors store at the "Street of Dreams." You, too, can be a winner. A couple that designs together, stays together. Max and Beverly are a design-duo bringing hundreds of designer fabrics under one roof for you to choose. Roof! Roof! Furniture, too, from chairs to loveseats, sofas to recliners, sleepers to ottomans. Keep your chin up as well as your feet and expect lines like ESTATE HOUSE, FLEXSTEL and RIVERSIDE at 30-50 percent off to keep you glued to your seat. You pick the material and they get it done. The best in Tarrant County for one-stop decorating. *CK, MC, V, AE, D*

✧✧✧✧✧ DFW Windows & Doors

972/378-0188

Plano, TX

By Appt. Only

www.dfwwindows.com

If you don't call Dan Miller at DFW Windows & Doors, you will see what pane is all about. Great prices (no, the lowest prices) on custom windows and doors. And, if you buy a house full of windows, they'll even throw in a FREE top-of-the-line storm door. When real estate professionals comment about "drive-up appeal," this is what these make-over experts do for your windows and doors. Replace them with single- or double-pane windows–they offer a 10-year to lifetime warranty and help reduce your energy bills by at least 25-35 percent–and if you're in the Texas-New Mexico electric company area, you need all the help you can get! Let new storm windows, doors or solar screens do their part in lowering your energy use. Each comes with energy efficient glass that can be tinted gray or bronze and includes thermal break frames and a triple glaze. Be sure to ask about the Low-E modern glass, which has a low-"emissive" coating. This almost invisible metallic coating acts as a heat barrier to reflect warm inside air back into a house and reduces a window's heat loss by 35 percent. Same-day or next-day service. That's my man, Dan. And new this year, ask Dan about siding if you'd rather not have to ever paint your house again. Free price quotes. *CK, MC, V, AE, D*

★★★★★ Draperies & More

972/353-2672

1565 W. Main St., Suite 220
Lewisville, TX 75067

Mon-Fri 10-6; Sat 10-4:30

Window, window, oh so bare, who's still paying retail, I shouldn't care. But I do. And you should know better. At this Lewisville hideaway, this designer fabric shop is sewing up a storm, offering one-stop shopping for all your window's woes. At the corner of Garden Ridge and Main, you'll see horizontal and vertical blinds, shutters, carpet, custom furniture, reupholstery, custom draperies and shades. Hang out with brand names from CAROLE, GRAEBER, HUNTER-DOUGLAS, KASHMIR, RALPH LAUREN, ROBERT ALLEN and WESCO. Deck the walls with grand names such as IMPERIAL and YORK. Discounts soar to 70-80 percent off list price on wood blinds, PVC blinds, mini-blinds, vertical blinds, pleated shades; up to 30 percent off fabric/lining on valances and window treatments; 10 percent off comforter sets; 30 percent off carpet and wallpaper. Shop for the fabric selection alone, or go for the big pay-off in beautiful custom bedspreads and window treatments. Another store is located at 3733 Josey Lane., Carrollton, 972/394-4893. Either way, you've got it made in the shade! *CK, MC, V, D*

★★★★★ Dungan's Floors, Blinds & More — 972/562-9444

1434 N. Central Expwy. — *Tue-Fri 8:30-5:30; Sat 10-4*
McKinney, TX 75070

Founded by Linnie and Lou Jenkins 18 years ago., Dungan specializes in custom window treatments, custom bedding, wall coverings, flooring of all kinds and much more at everyday low prices. They offer everything you'll find at the manufacturers' showrooms, plus they can usually beat the do-it-yourselfer discount stores on price. Judy Crosson, Dungan's in-house designer, is available to assist with everything from a simple window covering to coordinating an entire home with custom draperies, swags, sheers, or hard window coverings such as wood blinds and shades of all kinds. Mrs. Crosson is also adept at creating custom bedding. Mrs. Crosson's husband, Dean, also works for the company and oversees the fabrication and installation of all Dungan's custom window coverings. "Shoppers often comment on how much time and money they save shopping with us because they avoid costly mistakes," Mr. Jenkins says. Everyday discounts of 30 percent on all first-quality SCHUMACHER/WAVERLY wallpaper and upholstery fabrics. They don't sell paint, but they always keep samples available to make it easier for clients to coordinate everything with one-stop shopping. *CK, MC, V, AE, D*

★★★ Elite Blinds — 972/418-1380

2145 N. Josey — *Mon-Fri 10-4:30; Sat 10-5*
Carrollton, TX 75007-2992

Want to be a part of the elite and famous? Then let me introduce you to designer vertical blinds, pleated shades and arches at 70 percent off; 75 percent off honeycomb shades and two-inch PVC wood look-alikes. Sing the praises of their SYMPHONY shades and a full orchestration of window coverings including HUNTER-DOUGLAS at blind-siding prices. Have your measurements ready! (Waist measurements don't count!) Order in custom draperies plus accompanying or matching bedspreads, cornice headboards, everything for do-it-yourself projects to full design services, it's your call. Free installation on some services a big plus. Go past the high school and look to land at the Subway. They're next door. *CK, MC, V, AE, D, DC*

Windows & Walls

♥♥♥♥♥ Fine Art Finishes 817/992-9230

Fort Worth, TX *By Appt. Only*

http://web2.airmail.net/all2real

Looking for that Trompe Card? Then consider bringing ancient England and Italy into your living room. On call to Fine Art Finishes and it's a done deal. Artist Rodney Ray uses glosses and glazes to simulate ancient concrete, stucco and marble walls. He can even add layers over murals to create the illusion of a newly discovered piece of antiquity. Actual wood columns on the marble simulations give a positively Athenian atmosphere, and vines on the wall create the look of "ye olde" English garden. It's all part of his Fine Art Finishes. *PQ*

★★★★★ JMS Interiors 972/818-7008

3301 Wells Dr.
Plano, TX 75093

If you're experiencing Window Panes, here's the prescription for relief. For shutters, blinds, cellular shades, draperies and more, JMS is your saving grace. With more than 25 years in the business, they are experts at creating window treatments fit for a queen. And the designer draperies are offered at wholesale prices. They represent AMERICAN DREW, ASHLEY, BASSETT, BENCHCRAFT, CHROMCRAFT, HIGHLAND HOUSE, HENRY LINK WICKER, HOOKER, KINCAID, LANE, LEXINGTON, MILLENNIUM, MORGANTON CHAIR, SAM MOORE CHAIR, SEABROOK, SPRINGAIR, STANLEY, STEIN WORLDS, SUNCOAST OUTDOOR, TROPITONE, UNIVERSAL, WAVERLY and more. *CK, MC, V*

★★★★ Leland Interiors 817/226-7890

2021 S. Copper *Mon-Fri 9-6: Sat 10-5; Sun Noon-5*
Arlington, TX 76010 *www.lelandswallpaper.com*

Arlington's own Gary Leland has been doing home decor for years. If it was meant to go indoors, it is part of his repertoire. Expect 45 percent off in-store wallpapers and all special-order books are discounted 30 percent and more. Choose from hundreds of books representing thousands of options. When Gary's on a roll, he'll buy out another store's stock and move it to the Bargain Corner where rolls roll out as low as $5.99. This one-stop shop also serves up mini-blinds, Duette shades, wood blinds, custom shutters, verticals, floor coverings, matching bedspreads and more. Names you trust adorn the walls and are discounted every day: DAVID & DASH, FABRICUT, GRABER, GRAMERY,

HUNTER-DOUGLAS, IMPERIAL, KASMIR, M & B, ROBERT ALLEN, WARNER, WAVERLY/SCHUMACHER, WESTGATE and others are either in stock or can be ordered in a matter of days. *CK, MC, V*

★★★★ Lone Star Blinds — 214/766-0330

Dallas, TX 75230 — *By Appt. Only*

www.lonestarblinds.com

How much are those treatments on the window? You know, the ones with the roaming shades? Welcome to the world of Ram. Give him a call and he'll come a-callin' decked out with samples in tow. Keeping his overhead low, he's had more than 16 years of experience selling window treatments with low prices and brand names. GRABER, HUNTER-DOUGLAS and TIMBER brands are his preference. He carries an extensive and varied list of window treatments: shades (pleated, cellular, silhouette, Duettes, luminettes), Roller and Roman shades, louvers, one- and two-inch blinds, aluminum, vinyl, polywood and verticals, woven woods and shutters. In short, a professional, convenient, dependable and inexpensive source for window coverings. For example, 2-inch woods 23 x 72, $61; 35 x 84, $94; 47 x 72, $104. Take those blinders off. Nobody pays retail in the Lone Star state. *CK,MC, V*

★★★★★ Michael's Window Treatments — 817/496-4520

By Appt. Only

www.michaelsblinds.com

This Michael may not row the boat ashore, but he can certainly deck out your windows and floors. Staying afloat for more than 26 years, this Michael has staying power. Featuring GRABER and TIMBER products for window treatments in Silhouettes, mini-blinds, vertical shutters and cellular shades up to 80 percent off retail means he holds the window to your soul. No more soul-searching for floor coverings. Call for full house quotes or in-home consultations. Either way, he'll get you covered. *CK, MC, V*

★★★★ Mini Blind Warehouse — 817/277-1014

2707 S. Cooper, #105 — *Mon 10-5; Tue-Sat 10-6*

Arlington, TX 76015

Manufacturing their own blinds for 14 years, this must be the place to play hide and seek. Chic window coverings are lying in wait behind the Ace Hardware store in an unobstrusive shopping center. Since their prices are so low, they won't quote by phone, so seeing is believing. We went undercover and decided to cover our windows that we couldn't close during winter, or open in summer. Choose from one or two-inch aluminum blinds, two-inch wood blinds, vertical blinds or pleated shades for your home, office, boat, airplane; if you must, custom-made to your specifications. They can have your custom-made window coverings complete in about two weeks. Wood blinds for a 35- x 72-inch window cost around $119, while their aluminum KIRSCH counterpart cost $36. All blinds are manufactured on site and take a maximum of four days for completion. Call Carol to book your appointment in advance, as they are often booked solid for days at a time. *CK, MC, V, D*

★★★★ PR Designer Shutters — 972/867-4467

3247 Independence Pkwy. — *Mon-Fri 9-5*
Plano, TX 75075 — *www.prdesignershutters.com*

Come to PR Designer Shutters because, as they like to say, you can't hang a Rolex in your window. Before you take a hammer, a nail and an $18,000 watch and try to prove them wrong, please note that their slogan simply refers to getting the finest quality for a good price. Since 1983, PR Designer Shutters has been providing its customers with superior customer service and professionalism. High-quality engineering help reduce the problems of warping and sagging, so your shutters will look as good as new for years to come. You don't have to be in the PR business to recognize an open-and-shut case when you see it. *CK, MC, V, AE, D*

★★★★★ Rainbow Blind and Shade — 972/222-0037

Dallas, TX 75181 — *By Appt. Only*

Somewhere whether over or under the rainbow, there are bluebirds singing the praises of Rainbow Blind and Shade. Surely, had Dorothy not left Kansas, she would have installed custom hardwood shutters before her arrival in Oz. Anybody with half a brain would know by now that if you want plantation shutters, and you buy 10 of them or more, sizes 36- x 72-inch, the price at Rainbow is $280 per shutter (about a $75/per shutter savings). They even install custom molding at no additional cost. Free installation and estimates given. They guarantee finished and installed in seven to 10 weeks so expect patience to be a built-in perquisite. Wood blinds, pleated shades, too. They will meet or beat any competitor's prices, so chances are, if you've bought elsewhere, you've paid too much. Next time, "Look, look, look to the rainbow." *CK, MC, V, D*

♥♥♥♥♥ Rushman Magnolia Shutters 214/638-6032

2929 Irving Blvd. *Mon-Fri 10-6; Sat 9:30-5:30*
Dallas, TX 75247

This long-time staple (since 1970) has been creating window treatments with the reputation of being the best in quality and customer service. Get that wonderful custom look of wooden shutters in 2-, 3- and 4-inch louvers and they will custom paint or stain-match to your specifications. Sunburst and arch-top shutters are also available for those hard-to-fit window shapes. Especially noteworthy, their new "one-touch adjustment" for arches and shutters-the perfect fingertip touch control that aligns your louvers or other treatments perfectly. Same way with their plantation shutters. For those who want to be really spoiled, ask about their remote-controlled shutters and arches. Now that's living! Don't settle for an inserted boxed frame shutter! These are the most uniquely engineered in the business and all custom-made. Increase visibility up to 40 percent. No unsightly stick divider in the middle to block the view. Hand-finished. Flush mounted so no need for framing. Magnolia Shutters are available in many different sizes including a full radius sunburst arch and those designed to cover French, Dutch and Atrium doors. Call for more details but don't be in a Rush, man. They take their time getting it right the first time. Call metro 214/263-9914 for price quotes by phone if you live outside the immediate area, or you can also visit their showroom at 3600 Preston Rd., Suite 106, Dallas, 972/668-2600. They sell factory direct, but they aren't cheap! Basic price is $22.50 per square foot. A 36- x 72-inch was quoted at $405 per shutter. Free installation, free estimates and a lifetime warranty makes it all worthwhile. All wood, custom colors and custom paints also available. *CK, MC, V, AE, D*

♥♥♥♥♥ SGO-Designer Glass 972/245-5454

1014 S. Broadway, #102 *Mon-Fri 10:30-3:30; or By Appt.*
Carrollton, TX 75006

SGO-Designer Glass has all the class that any glass needs. SGO-Designer Glass is located in Old Downtown Carrollton and their product is a process of coating glass with color until you have a new work of art. Pick a design, pick a color, custom match your favorite material-it doesn't matter. Use on windows, bath shower doors, front entry doors, as a room divider-your imagination is your only limit. Consider turning your entire home into a rose-colored garden with tinted glass at truly affordable prices. *CK, MC, V, AE, D*

Windows & Walls

★★★★★ Shutter Craft Mfg.

972/424-3855

5401 E. 14th St.
Plano, TX 75094

Mon-Fri 8-4:30; Sat 8-Noon

Since their shutters are made of a basswood material and carry a lifetime warranty, would you shop anywhere else? Pay attention. Take Central/75 to the East Plano exit and go east past Plano Road, Jupiter and Shiloh. The road will curve north over the railroad tracks. Turn right at the Diamond Shamrock station where you should be able to see a communication tower. You will be heading toward the tower as it sits in front of the Shutter Craft factory. You will be going east and pass a golf course on left hand side. Take an immediate second left. At the gravel road entrance, turn right. You have arrived! This little white house with gray trim is your door opener to the factory that manufactures shutters on-site. Their 36 x 72 inch shutter runs $350 with free installation, free estimates and custom color. Additional discounts for five or more shutters. In business since 1974, consider their movable louver-shutter a great insulator, versatile as well as durable. Now, if I haven't lost you yet, you're a better shop-finder than I. *CK, MC, V*

★★★★ Smart Looks

972/699-7160

101 S. Greenville Ave.
Richardson, TX 75080

Mon-Fri 9-5:30: Sat 9:30-5; Thu 9-7

Smart shoppers are the norm at Smart Looks. Service is above and beyond the call of duty. With one location to concentrate all their attention, you're going to get the best in window treatments, walls, custom blinds, verticals, plantation shutters, balloon shades, pleated shades, silhouette shades, rolling shutters, woven woods, and custom draperies. Looking for exterior shutters? They were the originators. Professionals help you sort through the decorating decisions especially helpful to keep the coordinates coordinated. Bedspreads and matching pillows, table drapes, headboards, drapery treatments, the works. Save up to 75 percent off 2-inch wood blinds and about 30 percent on custom draperies with fabrics by KASMIR and FABRICUT. And shutter at the thought of ever paying retail for shutters again. Since they took over the SHUTTER-CRAFT factory, you can expect factory-direct prices. Whether it be commercial or residential windows, bay-bow or arched, no problem. Color matching and special finishes are a specialty. Free estimates and all custom prices include installation. *CK, MC, V, D*

★ Southwest Interior Design, Inc. 972/422-0003

3209 Premier Dr., Suite 109A *Mon-Fri 9-3*
Plano, TX 75075

If you insist on HUNTER-DOUGLAS, then Southwest Interior Design Inc. is the place to hunt down. They discount up to 65 percent on selected products and offer low prices on others. Not everything here is discounted, though, so buyer beware. Luminette privacy sheers, Vignette and silhouette window shadings were glaringly retail. Still, digging around can net a bargain or two plus they offer the convenience of shop-at-home service. The ease of payment here is also a plus. They offer 90 days same-as-cash financing and accept all major credit cards. They even said they would accept postage stamps, as long as you have enough of them. If you can't fight 'em, lick 'em! *CK, MC, V, AE, D, Financing*

♥♥♥♥♥ Stained Glass Overlay by Glass Solutions 972/570-4685

2814 N. O'Connor Rd. *Mon-Fri 11-4; Sat by Appt.*
Irving, TX 75062

I think that I shall never see a stained-glass shower door as lovely as thee. Their patented technique of making stained glass overlays brings great beauty to your home's dÈcor. One look and you're hooked. Well, what is it? It's actually a work of art that is created for your doors or windows. Or you can add it to a skylight, a ceiling panel, a room divider, a cabinet door insert, a sliding glass door, a shower door-the list is endless, but don't expect masterpieces to come cheap. Do you think anyone had the nerve to negotiate with Michaelangelo while he was hanging from the ceiling? Since it's a secret how they do it, the only way you can enjoy it is to buy it. Seeing is believing. Drop by their studio to behold a work of art. The studio is at O'Connor and Rochelle, which can be confusing to some first-time visitors. The two streets intersect twice. Glass Solutions is two lights north of 183 on O'Connor, not in the Las Colinas area where O'Connor and Rochelle again intersect. Karen is almost a one-woman show at the shop, so when a customer calls, she hits the road. Unfortunately, that means you'll sometimes find a closed sign on the door during normal business hours, so appointments are encouraged. *CK, MC, V, AE, D*

★★★★★ Sunburst Shutters 214/343-2601

10990 Petal St., #100 *Mon-Fri 8:30-5*
Dallas, TX 75238 *www.sunburstshutters.com*

Star bright, star light, first star I see tonight. Hopefully, it's a Sunburst Shutter.

You, too, can hob-knob with the stars by shopping for quality shutters without busting your budget. Shutter at the thought of buying them elsewhere. Here, they are custom-built, measured, manufactured and finished by the craftsmen themselves! Over 300,000 shutters have graced fine windows in Phoenix, Houston, Tampa, Orlando, Las Vegas and of course, Dallas. Bursting (but not at the seams) from the manufacturer at direct-to-you prices, a new POLY-WOOD synthetic shutter (bet you can't tell the difference) is an interesting twist on the wooden shutter craze. Since it's not the real thing, it insulates three times better than wood, is water-resistant, non-flammable and warp-proof. Available in white or off-white, they are also less expensive. Did you read that? Custom wood shutters are also available in custom colors direct from this mover and maker. *CK, MC, V*

✧✧✧ Twin Designs — 972/712-8946

7151 Preston Rd., #101A — *By Appt. Only*
Frisco, TX 75034

The sister act at Twin Designs won't sing you a song, but they can dance their way into some new window treatments. Whether you need blinds, shutters or drapes, Twin Designs has it at a reasonable price. One sister acts as the handler of accessories. Her name is Julie. She charges $45 to make a house call, but if you spend $500 or more, it is credited to your purchase. Her sister does the free consultation for the windows and assists with placing furniture, wall hangings and other decorations to help create an entire room. Don't expect to find them waiting behind a desk for you to call. They are usually out on appointments and it is definitely recommended that you make an appointment before showing up at their front doors. *CK, MC, V, AE, D*

★★★ Wall & Window Gallery — 972/396-1001

206 N. Greenville, Suite 300 — *Mon-Sat 10-6*
Allen, TX 75002

Here's a gallery that's got your windows and wall in mind. (Their Lewisville shop concentrates on wallpapers and is called appropriately, Wallpaper Gallery, 102 Lakeland Plaza, Hwy. 121 and I-35, 972/436-9255, and includes a complete WAVERLY home fashion vignette with matching wallpaper, table mats, window toppers and more.) If you order by the book, you can expect a 30 percent savings (though a few books were discounted only 20 percent). In-stock wallcoverings, however, can save you around 50 percent, but won't include any Waverly (yet Tom claims most customers prefer to custom order and pay the price)?

Small town ambiance with big city savings is the reason to shop the north reaches of the Metroplex. Personalize service on custom window treatment in blinds, plantation shutters, draperies, another good reason. *CK, MC, V, AE, D*

★★★★ Wallpaper For Less — 972/329-3414

2110 N. Galloway Ave., Suite #104 — *Mon-Fri 10-6; Sat 10-5*
Mesquite, TX 75150

Want to wallpaper the town for less? Then, roll into a Wallpaper For Less store and put your money on the table. There were plenty of rolls to give you a continuous look. Some discontinued designs could be snatched up for $5-$9 per double roll but shoppers who prefer the current selections can expect to pay $15-$21.99 per double roll. Top-of-the-line WAVERLY could be hanging around for $19.98 (remember, that is the double roll.) But what if you have a fabric fetish? Does IMPERIAL fabric for $9.99/yard appeal to your obsession? How about WAVERLY for $10.99/yard? If you don't mind saving 50 percent off retail, then here's another secret. This chain has the town wallpapered with locations in Arlington, Mesquite, Lewisville and Rowlett. So what will it take to get you to the nearest wallpaper of opportunity? *CK, MC, V, D*

★★★★★ Wallpaper Source & More — 214/987-2369

612 Preston Forest Shopping Center — *Mon-Thu 10-7; Fri-Sat 10-6; Sun 1-5*
Dallas, TX 75230 — *www.wallpapersource.com*

Window shopping is easy when you consider the source. This source, in particular. When it comes to adding wallpaper with coordinating pillows, window treatments, chair pads, rugs, art, ceiling moldings, accessories, custom floral and shutters, head to the source, Wallpaper Source. Save 30-75 percent off in-stock patterns (over a thousand books and 450 patterns in-stock alone) and 20-50 percent off special orders. With these kinds of savings, you won't have to roll over and play possum. Choose from such manufacturers as IMPERIAL, RALPH LAUREN, SEABROOK, STROHEIN & ROMAN, SUNWALL, WAVERLY, YORK and more–there isn't anything they won't try to find. Then mix in the interior design staff who will help sort through the maze of paisley and polka dots, moirés and grass cloths. If wooden blinds are part of the picture, expect to close the windows on high prices because here they're up to 75 percent off. Hang-it-yourself or call in some of their helping hands. Window treatments from blinds to silhouettes, Duettes and shutters with prices up to 70 percent off. Mailing charges determined by the pound. Returns accepted within 30 days on in-stock rolls only with your receipt. However, no returns accepted on special orders. Watch for expansion coming soon. *CK, MC, V, D*

★★★★ Wallpapers Galore for Less 972/381-7664

17194 Preston Rd. *Mon-Fri 10-6; Sat 10-5; Thu 10-7*
Dallas, TX 75248

Hundreds of rolls of first-quality wallpaper at great prices with good service, too, is just what the doctor ordered. Choose from more than 300 patterns in stock, hundreds of borders, too. Wallpaper books representing just about every major manufacturer at 50 percent off in stock items and 30 percent off items from books including ANTONIA VELLA, GRAMMERCY, LAURA ASHLEY, KATZENBACH & WARREN, MOTIF, RALPH LAUREN, RONALD REDDING, SEABROOK, STERLING PRINTS, VILLAGE, WAVERLY, WESTMONT and YORK to name drop a few. Shoppers are welcome to sit down and take as much time as they need to make selections. Staff is available to assist in creating a new look for home or office. They also offer KASMIR, LADY ANNE and NORBAL fabrics and custom blinds. *CK, MC, V, D*

★★★★ Wallpapers To Go 972/503-8616

14560 Midway Rd. *Mon-Sat 9-7; Sat 10-6; Sun Noon-5*
Dallas, TX 75244-3109

Rollin', rollin', rollin', keeps those rolls a rollin'. Nothing raw about these deals. You can even hide behind dirty walls if you learn the paste and glue method of covering up. But, if you'd rather have someone else do your dirty work, consider shopping at Wallpapers To Go. Area designers and decorators have been pleased with the new look and new owners. Everything's coming up roses, or daffodils, or herringbone, or star bursts. Over 1,000 patterns await your approval, including brands like SUNWALL, WARNER and WAVERLY. Save 20-60 percent off retail on a container load of in-stock wallpapers and custom window fashions. Expert decorating advice is available, as well as free "how-to-hang" clinics. One bargain table of close-outs (a few rolls here and there) for $.99 should get you rockin' and rollin' (but you probably wouldn't look the same). Open seven days a week. Professional installation service can be arranged. Check directory for other locations. *CK, MC, V, AE, D*

★★★★★ Window Fashion Center 817/261-5009

2590 Pioneer Pkwy. *Call for Appt.*
Arlington, TX 76013

If you've got any window sense at all, this Window Fashion Center makes sense.

Designer elegance at discounted prices always rings loud and clear in my book. Custom draperies, shutters, reupholster, mini-blinds and verticals, pleated shades, wood blinds, area rugs and carpet, bedspreads and furniture—all for less. Up to 75 percent off HUNTER-DOUGLAS wood blinds and up to 40 percent off wallpaper are just a few examples in this fashion city. Ninety-days, no interest, same as cash, a pioneering concept whose time has come. *CK, 90 days no interest*

Merchant Index

A

Merchant Index

B

Merchant Index

C

Merchant Index

Merchant Index

D

Merchant Index

Merchant Index

E

F

Merchant Index

G

Merchant Index

H

Merchant Index

K

Merchant Index

L

M

Merchant Index

P

Merchant Index

R

Merchant Index

S

Merchant Index

Merchant Index

T

T

U

Merchant Index

V

W

W

X

Y

Z

Brand-Name Index

A

B

Brand-Name Index

B

C

Brand-Name Index

D

Brand-Name Index

E

F

Brand-Name Index

G

H

Brand-Name Index

I

J

K

L

M

Brand-Name Index

N

Brand-Name Index

Brand-Name Index

Q

R

R

Brand-Name Index

S

S

Brand-Name Index

T

U

V

Brand-Name Index

W

Waterford . . . 255, 519, 571

W

X

Y

Z

Notes

1331 Regal Row. 9-6. m - Sat. / 12-6 Sund

left on Regal Row under (183) for 1 1/2 bk.

left on King Arthur (back towards 183)

60-70 yds. around. (back door)

Notes

Notes

Notes

Notes

Notes